Herald INTERNA'

Guide to Business Travel EUROPE

Alan Tillier
Roger Beardwood

PASSPORT BOOKS
a division of *NTC Publishing Group*

Published by Passport Books, a division of NTC Publishing Group.
© 1990 by NTC Publishing Group, 4255 West Touhy Avenue,
Lincolnwood (Chicago), Illinois 60646-1975 U.S.A.
Library of Congress Catalog Card Number: 89-63689
Manufactured in the United States of America.

9 0 RA 9 8 7 6 5 4 3 2 1

CONTENTS

ACKNOWLEDGMENTS

Many people and organizations helped us with the research for this guide—more than we have space to list. All shared with us unstintingly their intimate, detailed knowledge of the cities and countries covered. Without their assistance, this guide would not be as complete as it is.

Our special thanks go to: Amsterdam, Odette Taminiau; Athens, Francis Cassavetti; Barcelona, Jane Walker; Belfast, Eddie O'Gorman; Brussels, Elisabeth Puttaert; Copenhagen, Hilary Barnes; Dublin, James Farrelly; Düsseldorf, Renata Bartlett; Edinburgh, James Filbin; Frankfurt, Ferdinand Protzmann; Geneva, Marie-Laure Bonard; Helsinki, Olli Virtanen; Istanbul, Thomas Goltz; Lisbon, Peter Collis; London, Diane Chanteau; Luxembourg, Carlo Rock; Madrid, Bill Bond; Milan, Godfrey Deeny; Moscow, Felicity Baranger; Munich, Bob Tilley; Oslo, Nina Krohn; Paris, Françoise Catelain; Rome, Chris Matthews; Stockholm, Sara Webb; Vienna, Traudl Lessing; Zurich, Ulrich Schneider.

Most vital statistics came from the Organization for Economic Cooperation and Development, and we have to thank Peter Gaskell, of the OECD's information service, for opening doors to this rich storehouse of knowledge in Paris.

FOREWORD

In publishing this guide for business travelers, the *International Herald Tribune* reaffirms its century-old bond with the international business community.

Founded in Paris in 1887, the IHT circulates today from eleven international printing centers to nearly half a million readers each day in 164 countries. No longer are most of these readers Americans. Many of them are international business leaders. Over a third are traveling at the time they see the IHT. Virtually all of them are at least occasional international travelers.

But our daily newspaper is not the only way in which the IHT is linked to this global business community. We also seek to address its needs through an expanding conference program and a variety of other products and services. This book is one leading example.

In its pages, two distinguished international journalists, Alan Tillier and Roger Beardwood, offer their special insights into 27 European cities. In doing so, they draw not only on their own long experience as roving correspondents but also on intensive new research by a corps of experienced journalists. From the start, their objective has been a guide that is comprehensive in scope while also remaining compact and concise, a factual, practical business tool that is also highly readable—"user-friendly," to use the currently popular adjective.

We are especially pleased that the editors—following their own good sense of where the news is leading us—have included an informative chapter on the development of the Common Market as well as a new look at doing business in Moscow.

A brief word may be in order on what this book is not. It is not, above all, a tourist guide. Tourists are on vacation—with very different needs from those who carry the responsibilities of work with them from country to country. Nor is the book some sort of definitive encyclopedia. It is, rather, a collection of what we think are unusually well-informed perspectives and impressions. And we expect that part of the enjoyment readers will take from this book is the pleasure of uncovering an occasional oversight, or challenging an occasional finding.

All in all then, we hope this volume will be one that both entertains and instructs, one that helps its readers open new doors even as it helps them avoid embarrassment. Ideally it will be a tool not only for saving time and reducing stress but also for deepening the sense of exploration, satisfaction, and accomplishment which should be the ultimate reward of an enlightened business traveler.

Lee W. Huebner
Publisher
International Herald Tribune

INTRODUCTION

Business trips are seldom fun, but an enjoyable visit is more likely to be successful than a dismal one. We have designed this guide for the business traveler who is determined to arrive in a foreign city briefed with vital information. Among the essentials are how to avoid such problems as noisy, uncomfortable hotels that fail to pass on messages; crowded, overpriced restaurants; schedules that can't be kept; and inadvertent social blunders that threaten business relationships. Above all, the business traveler must avoid the tiresome attitude that "if this is Tuesday, it must be Brussels."

An important theme: Know the culture of the city and country you are visiting. By culture, we don't mean mainly that which is commemorated and sometimes mummified in museums and art galleries—though that is vital to an understanding of a society's roots. Rather, we mean the living culture—and, in particular, that of a society's business, banking, bureaucratic, and political systems.

We ourselves have learned these the hard way. We have, between us, been bouncing around Europe for more than 50 person-years. We have lived and worked (separately) in Barcelona, Bonn, Brussels, Lisbon, London, Paris, and Vienna. We have visited often (and continue to visit) all the other cities listed. Quite early on, we found that there's no reason to be an innocent abroad—if one does the research.

We soon discovered that most guides written for tourists are of little help to the busy business executive. Tourists and businesspeople visit the same cities, but they don't see the same things because they have very different purposes and needs. The tourist is there to gaze at places, the business traveler to see people. The tourist is filling time; the executive is rationing it. If the tourist doesn't know the local customs, the stiffest penalty he or she is likely to pay is a padded bill. The executive who blunders may, in contrast, endanger future business relations.

This guide contains the quintessence of our garnerings. Some things we discovered for ourselves by making mistakes and learning from them. Other lessons we learned from our congenial mentors, colleagues who became friends over the years. With patience, good humor, and example, they showed us how to get the best out of the cities in which they live and work.

The guide's format is simple and practical. We start by running the tape measure over countries in which listed cities are located. The table in this introduction lists comparative statistics for 18 of the 20 countries in which the 27 cities are located. The exceptions are Liechtenstein, where living standards are similar to those in Switzerland, and the Soviet Union. Western economists and statisticians have long been wary of Soviet figures. In the era of *glasnost,* the Soviet authorities have admitted that there's either more or less (usually less) in their figures than meets the eye. Because we don't want to compare real oranges with imaginary bananas, we haven't even tried to reconcile official statistics for the Soviet economy with estimates from Western sources.

Our main focus is on Western Europe, particularly the Common Market, or European Community (EC). With a population of some 323 million, the 12 EC countries are potentially the world's largest trading bloc. By the end of 1992, all internal barriers to the free movement of goods, services, capital, and labor are due to crash to the ground in a cloud of faded red tape. Perhaps that will happen, perhaps it won't. We have included an executive briefing on the subject in the following section, titled "Europe: Realities, Rumors, Myths."

We move then to the guide's core: detailed entries for each city. We have organized these in the way we think is most helpful. We start with the city's vital statistics, and turn then to what we call **Background Briefing**—a summary of the city's (and country's) key characteristics. Each entry continues with these sections:

Arriving. Our emphasis is on airports and ways of getting to and from the city center. But Europe also has trains, some of them superb, so we provide a guide to railroad terminals as well as to airports. Where it is appropriate—Stockholm and Helsinki are examples—we look also at ferries.

Money. As all seasoned travelers know, some of them from costly experience, there are exchange rates and exchange rates. The situation may improve with the alignment of European currencies.

Language. English is the *lingua franca* of European business, but that doesn't mean everyone in the city speaks English. What is the local language? (There may be more than one.) What should one know about it (or them), apart from speaking it?

Communications. Not so long ago, a wry joke said much about France's—and Europe's—telephone systems: "Half the country is waiting for the dial tone. The other half is waiting for a telephone." Western Europe today is a world leader in telecommunications. Even so, a few gaps remain.

Getting to know the city. A city's center may or may not be the business district as well. We explain the topography and try to give the reader a feel for the city as a living organism.

Moving around. The business traveler wants to get around quickly and efficiently but also has an eye on expenses. Is a taxi faster than a bus? How good is the subway (often called a "metro" in Europe)—and how safe? Are there special discounts for visitors?

Hotels. What are the criteria by which a hotel should be judged? Some are obvious: its location, the size and comfort of rooms, and the competence and friendliness of the staff. Others are more subtle, going under the rubric of ambience or atmosphere. Then there are such vital matters as secretarial and interpreting services. Our selected hotels offer these services—or know where to find them. How good and helpful is the concierge? A really skilled one is the traveler's strong right arm: the man (there are few female concierges) who can obtain the unobtainable theater ticket, reserve a seat on an overbooked flight, and make a multiplicity of difficult services seem easy. We've selected hotels that meet our high and possibly idiosyncratic criteria.

Restaurants. There is, thank heavens, no such thing as "European" cuisine. There is, instead, a rich ragout of national and regional dishes, and in this section we guide you to restaurants serving the best of them. But should one eat only French food in Paris, German in Frankfurt, Spanish in Madrid? Of course not.

Tipping. In most cities, but not all, restaurants and bars automatically add a standard service charge to the bill. Should the satisfied customer add something extra? Where a tip isn't included, how much should it be?

Doing business gets down to specifics: where it's done, how and when it's done, and the role of government—a concise guide within a guide to the most important facets of deal-making.

Europe in Figures

	Total area 1000 sq. km	Population × 000s 1987	Population × 000s 1980	Population growth rate 1987/1986	Total labor force 000s 1987	Change since 1980	Government employment as % of total	Government social expenditures as % of total GDP
Austria	83.9	7,586	7,549	0.1	7,775	2.2	20.5[a]	28.8[a]
Belgium	30.5	9,834	9,847	0.1	4,217	1.5	20.2[b]	34.9[a]
Denmark	43.1	5,127	5,125	0.2	2,799	5.1	29.4	33.9[a]
Finland	337.0	4,932	4,780	0.3	2,583	4.4	21.3	23.8[a]
France	547.0	55,630	53,880	0.4	24,073	3.0	23.1	34.2[a]
Germany	248.6	61,199	61,566	0.2	28,216	3.7	16.1	25.2
Greece	132.0	9,994	9,642	0.3	3,884	12.5	—	19.5[a]
Ireland	70.3	3,543	3,401	0.0	1,319	5.8	16.0[a]	26.1
Italy	301.2	57,331	56,416	0.2	24,031	6.6	15.2	26.4
Luxembourg	2.6	372	365	0.5	173	8.8	12.0[a]	—
Netherlands	37.3	14,665	14,150	0.7	5,933	9.8	15.7	30.7[a]
Norway	324.2	4,187	4,087	0.4	2,171	11.9	23.3[b]	24.8
Portugal	92.1	10,270	9,819	0.5	4,522	3.7	10.3[c]	17.3[c]
Spain	504.8	38,832	37,386	0.4	14,676	9.1	14.6[b]	17.0[a]
Sweden	450.0	8,398	8,311	0.3	4,421	2.3	33.0[b]	32.0[a]
Switzerland	41.3	6,619	6,385	0.7	3,297	3.8	11.2[b]	20.5[b]
Turkey	780.6	52,893	44,737	2.2	19,304	9.9	—	—
United Kingdom	244.8	56,930	56,314	0.3	28,211	5.1	21.6	20.6

	Gross domestic product (at market prices)		Per capita at current prices		Gross fixed capital formation		Net national savings ratio % of GDP
	At current prices and exchange rates billion $ 1988 – provisional	Average annual volume change % 1987–88	Using current exchange rates $	Using PPPs (1)	Total at current prices % of GDP	Machinery and equipment at current prices % of GDP	
Austria	126.7	3.4	15,470	11,664	22.6	9.7	11.7
Belgium	147.5	3.3	14,071	11,802	19.1	8.1	8.3
Denmark	107.2	-0.3	19,730	13,241	23.5	9.7	6.6
Finland	104.6	4.6	18,151	12,838	19.4	8.3	7.8
France	941.9	3.2	15,818	12,803	19.4	8.4	7.0
Germany	1,204.6	3.4	18,280	13,323	17.4	7.1	11.4
Greece	53.0	3.3	4,719	6,363	17.4	9.2	5.5
Ireland	31.3	1.7	8,297	7,541			8.9
Italy	826.0	4.0	13,244	12,254	19.9	10.0	10.0
Luxembourg	6.3	2.9	16,138	14,705	22.6	9.0[d]	44.7
Netherlands	227.2	3.1	14,530	12,252	20.3	10.0	11.5
Norway	90.8	1.0	19,756	15,405	28.0	7.9[b]	8.8
Portugal	41.9	4.5	3,761	6,297	25.3	14.7	23.2
Spain	339.3	4.9	7,449	8,681	20.7	7.8	10.9
Sweden	179.4	2.8	18,876	13,771	19.0	8.5[b]	6.5
Switzerland	184.8	3.0	25,848	15,838	25.2	8.2	21.6
Turkey	74.1	5.9	1,296	4,247	24.5	8.6[c]	18.6
United Kingdom	805.6	4.2	11,765	12,340	17.3	8.1[b]	5.4

Source: Organization for Economic Cooperation and Development, Paris

Notes: All figures are for 1987 unless otherwise indicated.

1. Purchasing power parities (PPPs) are the rates of currency conversion that eliminate the differences in price levels between countries. This means that a given sum of money, when converted into different currencies at these rates, will buy the same basket of goods and services in all countries. PPPs are given in national currency units per U.S. dollar.

a. 1985.   b. 1984.   c. 1986.   d. 1982

Useful phone numbers are just that—the phone numbers of airlines, consulates and embassies, and sources of business information. Of course, we also include the numbers of emergency services. We list government ministries and agencies in many countries; in others we don't. The reason for this ostensible inconsistency is that in some countries such institutions are helpful, while in others they are not, displaying signs of bureaucratic *rigor mortis*. The usefulness of chambers of commerce also varies greatly. In some cities, they play a pivotal part in business life. In others, they are little more than social clubs. Even so, they can be helpful, if only because they can provide the visiting business executive with valuable introductions.

As with chambers of commerce, so there is variation among consulates and embassies. We have found that some are superb, able to brief us expertly and open doors. Others are staffed by bureaucratic time-servers who think that their main function is to file information rather than distribute it. Generalizations are dangerous, but we'll venture one: Small countries' diplomats are usually more vigorous than are large countries'.

Shopping is what the folks back home expect you to do—and if you're not careful, you can end up by paying more for a gift than you would have paid in your own city. There are few bargains in Western Europe, but there are some, and you won't usually find them in the airport duty-free shops or just around the corner from your hotel. We guide you to the places where you will find distinctive goods at value-for-money prices. We also explain tax-free deals.

After hours. Business dinners tend to go on, and on, and on—and on to a nightspot. The tired traveler, perhaps suffering from jetlag, might be yearning for a cool shower and a spacious bed, but hostly tradition dictates that he or she must take the guests out for a nightcap. Where? In major cities, our task was to sift the best from the abundance available; in minor ones, to find any nightlife worthy of the name.

Sights and sounds describes the places that make a city memorable, from such unavoidable landmarks as the Eiffel Tower in Paris (its attractions include an excellent restaurant) to Barcelona's Sunday-morning perambulations up and down the Ramblas, where the grayheads gossip while the young folk flirt. What do these sights and sounds have to do with business? Quite a lot. Business is not an activity divorced from the surrounding culture. It is, rather, a component part, its nature and character determined by political and social history.

Out of town. Time off, if you have any, should be used for a refreshing break that recharges depleted mental and physical batteries. We've chosen places that offer both tranquility and stimulation—an uncommon combination, but one that can be found close to most big cities.

Spotlight features alert readers to everything from the unavoidability of sauna baths in Finland to the quirks of Scottish dialect in Edinburgh, through street crime in London to fishing in Oslo and *tapas* bars in Spain. Those and other Spotlights are vivid reminders of a fact often overlooked or discounted. Europe is the smallest continent after Australia, but it almost certainly packs more social, ethnic, linguistic, topographical, and climatic variety into its confines than any of the others, square mile for square mile (or square kilometer).

Some practitioners of futurology argue that the balance of geopolitical and economic power is moving away from Europe and the United States to Asia, from the so-called mature industrial "Atlantic" societies to such blossoming Pacific Rim states as South Korea, Taiwan, Malaysia, Singapore, and Hong Kong—the newly industrialized countries, or NICs. Japan led the way, so the argument runs; and the rest are following in its trail. Indeed, some Asian NICs are competing so fiercely in world markets that Japan itself is worried. An American ambassador, a friend of ours, reported after a recent swing through the Pacific Rim area: "I've seen the future, and it's there. But that doesn't mean we should write off the U.S. and Europe—or not just yet." Our own swings through Europe confirm that view.

In *relative* terms, Europe may indeed be declining. In *absolute* terms, however, this small continent is still an economic and industrial powerhouse. No forecasting wizards ourselves, we describe what we see *now,* not what the next 10, 15, or 20 years may hold. What we see is a continent girding itself for the future, with the European Community as a centripetal force, tearing down old barriers, taming ancient antagonisms, and creating a single market that will be second only to the United States in personal purchasing power and capital investment.

Ours has been an exciting assignment. It has taken us from Europe's southernmost countries to the northernmost; from mature, stable democracies to one nation where the democratic ideal is still fragile—Turkey—and to another, the Soviet Union, where an astonishing new frankness presages—what? The Soviet Union is the wild card in the European pack. President Mikhail Gorbachev is a westernizing reformer in the tradition of Peter the Great. However, throughout its long history, Russia has swung many times between emulation of Western models and suspicious retreat into its Slav heritage. We describe rather than prescribe but believe strongly that the glaciers of European differences are thawing into a common stream of purpose: belief in the efficacy of market economics and its political concomitant, democracy.

If that stream becomes a flood, it may sweep away the rocks of misunderstanding and mutual suspicion against which East and West have dashed and damaged themselves for some 70 years. We are not naïve, though. The best we can hope for is a new mutual tolerance practiced by proponents of competing systems.

Alan Tillier
Roger Beardwood
Paris, 1989

EUROPE
Realities, Rumors, Myths

We are publishing this business traveler's guide at one of the most exciting and pivotal periods in recent European history. All 12 members of the Common Market, or European Community (EC), have pledged themselves to demolish the remaining barriers that hobble trade among them in goods and services and the free movement of capital and labor. The economic and social implications are enormous and the subject of much debate.

The EC's sales slogan is "Europe without frontiers." Simple and clear: everyone can understand it. A bonfire of bureaucratic controls is long overdue. Grand are both the vision and the design. If all's right on the night—and the EC's self-imposed deadline is midnight December 31, 1992—the last of the red tape will be consumed in the fire of political will. The result: a free market of some 323 million people. Questions remain, though:

- Will the EC be able to keep to its own schedule?
- Will the benefits be as great as 1992's supporters contend?
- What will a frontier-free EC mean for countries left on the outside looking in?

For the United States, Japan, the newly industrializing countries, and European states that are not EC members, the last question is the first in importance. Many people fear a "Fortress Europe"—an EC that raises both tariff and nontariff barriers against imports from the rest of the world. Major corporations are already moving to ensure their future within the EC. Some are doing so by merging with or acquiring EC companies; others by building manufacturing plants within the EC; some by doing both. But what *is* a "European" product? Many members of the EC cannot agree upon a common definition, their particular targets be-

▶1

ing plants that they categorize as "screwdriver assembly points"—those heavily reliant upon components imported from outside the EC.

The definition of Europe, in the EC sense, is also the subject of intense and sometimes fierce contention. Will the EC remain a Club of Twelve, or will it soon embrace other European states? The Council of Europe— not to be confused with the EC—has 22 members. Add some ministates and the countries of Eastern Europe, as well as the Baltic nations that seem determined to gain autonomy from the Soviet Union, and the count is more than 30.

Already, Turkey has applied for EC membership. Norway, which rejected membership in a 1970s referendum, is having second thoughts. Austria, Cyprus, and Malta are waiting in the wings. These members of "the other Europe" see a cloudy future from 1993 onward unless they can come to some kind of arrangement with the EC.

Within the EC there are also worries. Is 1992 a hope or a hype, a promise or a threat? Nobody knows. The EC Commission, its executive body, has publicized some enormous gains—between 1.5 and 5 million new jobs, for example. Many business executives take a more somber view. In a study done for international management consultants Booz-Allen and Hamilton, European chief executives were pessimistic: only 5 percent of respondents agreed "strongly" with the commission's job-creation forecasts; 21 percent agreed "a little;" and an overwhelming 69 percent disagreed with them "a little" or "strongly."

The same study found that 75 percent of respondents believed 1992 and all it stands for would move power toward the EC bureaucracy in Brussels, and 47 percent felt that national identity would be reduced. A buzz phrase around Brussels and in the European Parliament is the "democratic deficit," a term that means national legislatures, democratically elected, will more and more become rubber stamps for EC directives.

Symbolizing the arguments over the EC's future are three highly contentious issues that are both practical and political:

- Harmonization of value-added taxes
- Creation of a common European currency
- Establishment of a European central bank

Value-added taxes (VAT) are the most pressing issue. VAT is, essentially, a sales tax, though a highly complicated one, since it is levied at each stage of adding value to a product or service. However, the company that, for example, has paid VAT on a semifinished product can claw the money back from the fiscal authorities. Only the ultimate consumer pays, and the rates range from a high of 38 percent in Italy on some luxury goods to a low of no tax in Britain on food, children's clothing, books, magazines, and newspapers.

In theory, the EC ended customs duties on intra-European trade years ago; in practice, differing VAT rates mean that trade is hampered by paperwork at national frontiers. Paolo Cecchini, who runs a noted Brussels research team, estimates that the cost of such work and delays is about $245 billion a year. But that huge cost—and it's really a guesstimate—won't be cut substantially, and frontier-free Europe won't work unless the EC members can agree on common VAT rates, or at the very least narrow the differences between them.

At present, EC members hold very different views on what should be taxed and at what rates. Denmark charges more than fifteen times as much as Italy on a bottle of Scotch. Britain rakes in twice as much proportionately as Belgium on tobacco. One EC Commission proposal calls for only two VAT bands. The first, "normal," would be between 14 and 20 percent. The second, "reduced," would vary from 4 to 9 percent. Such variations would be small enough, or so the argument runs, to eliminate the need for border controls and end the temptation to smuggle goods across frontiers. The temptation today is strong. One estimate is that if you could ship a container-load of cigarettes from Greece to Ireland, bypassing all customs barriers, you would make an 800 percent profit on your investment.

If VAT rates are not harmonized—and agreement is far from guaranteed—the whole idea of a unified Europe could be undermined. Americans look at this bickering with amazement. Sales taxes certainly differ from state to state; but the United States is a single market. So why can't the Europeans get their act together?

The answer is that they are trying, but they do not share a common set of laws, traditions, and fiscal policies. Southern members of the EC depend heavily upon VAT because evasion of income tax is a national sport; understandably, they're reluctant to cut the rates.

Furthermore, Europe doesn't have a common currency, apart from the embryonic European Currency Unit, or ECU. Look at the practicalities: An importer in Lille, France, has to pay an exporter just across the border in Mons in Belgian francs. Exchange rates fluctuate; banks charge commissions, take a "turn" on the rates, and also charge VAT. In contrast, a California company buying from a supplier in New York pays in dollars, which are just as good on the East Coast as they are on the West Coast.

A strong case for a single currency? Undoubtedly. But the argument takes the circular route back to the whole question of sovereignty. If a country finds that its currency is overvalued—that its exports are being priced out of markets—it can always devalue. To be sure, the rules of such organizations as the International Monetary Fund forbid what are known as competitive devaluations, but forget the rules and look at the practice. Devaluations are common, whether official or determined by the foreign-exchange markets. If there were a single European currency, however, a country would be no more able to devalue than, say, the state of Iowa is today. Such inflexibility has little appeal for countries that have used devaluation as a competitive crutch in the past and suspect that they might need to use it in the future. A single currency would also remove another economic weapon from national governments—the use of interest rates to increase or reduce demand.

If there isn't a single currency there is a poor case for a European central bank, the equivalent of the U.S. Federal Reserve Board. Even if there were a single currency—the ECU, for example—who would run such a board? Who would control it politically? How would power be shared?

Europe 1992—or 1993—is a grand idea. If all goes well, and it may, abolition of border controls and bureaucratic barriers against free trade will make the EC more competitive and cut costs. What we've tried to avoid in this guide are the extremes of either Europhoria or Europessimism.

The business opportunities are large. Seldom have the Europeans been more open to new ideas, more keen to exploit them, and more confident of their ability to take on the rest of the world and win. That confidence is vital. In the 1970s and early 1980s Europessimism was widespread. The two oil-price shocks, severe competition from Japan and the newly industrialized countries (NICs), and rising unemployment strained both the fabric of society and the economic system itself.

Many of the challenges remain. Chief among them are unemployment, excess productive capacity, and lack of innovation. We believe those challenges can be met. Slowly, perhaps too slowly, virtually all EC members are shaping their policies so as to unleash the dynamic force of business enterprise and relax the bureaucratic stranglehold that in the past stifled—and in some states still stifles—the entrepreneurial spirit.

If 1992 achieves nothing else, it will alert politicians, business executives and the voters to Europe's potential and make most of them impatient to realize it.

AMSTERDAM

City of Diamonds, Rough and Otherwise

Population: 688,100 (1980). Commercial capital of the Netherlands (population: 14.6 million). *Location*: province of North Holland, at junction of Amstel and IJ (or Y) rivers; connected with North Sea and Rhine River by ship canal. *Economy*: shipping, chemicals, foodstuffs, textiles, diamond cutting, metalworking, banking and financial services, education, and tourism. The Netherlands is a member of the European Community (EC) and the Organization for Economic Cooperation and Development (OECD) and a signatory to the General Agreement on Tariffs and Trade (GATT).

▷ Background Briefing

A funny thing happened to Amsterdam on its way to the twenty-first century: It became a playground for tourists and a city where almost anything went. Then the burghers had a change of heart. Among the things that went were drug-zonked dropouts from all over the world, many drug dealers, and a live-and-let-live municipal policy that had forced thousands of middle-class city dwellers into suburban exile.

Amsterdam today is a cleaned-up city, but still one that offers the raunchy life to those who seek it. They don't have to seek far. Given the city's history and its centuries-old role as a major international port, it's not surprising that red lights twinkle and girls (and boys) wink. What the good burghers have insisted is that the twinkling and winking be confined to their traditional neighborhoods.

But even in the 1960s and late 1970s, when Amsterdam was a haven for the hapless, the hopeless, and the harpies, it continued to be a great commercial and financial center run by notably shrewd and businesslike people. Stolid? Perhaps, but mainly in the view of those who don't know the city or the Dutch. Look at the Old Masters' paintings in the Rijksmuseum: the rubicund faces and ample figures are those of people who enjoy the good things of life.

Nobody knows who first called Amsterdam the Venice of the North. The appellation is simultaneously apt and inept. Like Venice, Amsterdam is intersected by canals, is rich in art and architecture, and was a pioneer of banking and international trade. It's hard, though, to carry comparisons further. Only by torturing parallels into artificially straight lines could one contend that Venice and Amsterdam today are cities to be measured by their resemblances rather than differences. Unlike Venice, Amsterdam is a great entrepôt and banking center; those brisk North Sea winds, bitter in winter, keep hard Dutch heads clear of cobwebs. And though Amsterdam welcomes tourists, its real business is just that—business.

Starting in the mid-1980s, Amsterdam redoubled its efforts to be known as the "Gateway to Europe." Other cities claim that title, but Amsterdammers cite their long history of trading worldwide. With typical Dutch vigor, they are developing the port area near the main station and building Teleport, an island of offices and homes northwest of the city.

Typically again, the Amsterdammers are open to ideas from abroad. They have sought the advice of planners of London's Docklands and have borrowed from the United States the so-called "PPP system," private-public partnership. The city's planners are determined, too, not to repeat mistakes made elsewhere. Inner Amsterdam remains essentially a seventeenth-century city; the new developments are of the twenty-first rather than late twentieth century.

▷ *Spotlight* ◁

The typical Amsterdammer is strongly independent. One symbol of that independence: Unlike virtually all other Europeans, citizens refuse to carry an identity card. Though the Dutch are not great churchgoers, reli- gious affiliations remain strong. Sports clubs are organized along religious lines, the Red Cross has three denominations, and there is even a Roman Catholic goat-breeders' association just outside the city.

▷ Arriving

By Air

Schiphol is a department store with runways. Often voted Europe's best airport for business travelers, and sometimes the world's best, Schiphol is

15 kilometers (9.5 miles) from Amsterdam. Duty-free shops offer real bargains: You can buy everything from cheeses, through diamonds, to cars. More important for the business traveler, the airport is fast and very efficient.

Efficiency isn't surprising, but speed is. Recently, Schiphol has been taking about 13 million passengers a year, and management is planning for 25 million in the 1990s. Buses and trains to Amsterdam leave every 15 minutes or so and cost a quarter of the taxi fare. Particularly during rush hours, public transport is often faster than private. However, at the other end you will have to find a taxi to take you from the Central Station drop-off point to your hotel, and that isn't always easy. Taxis don't queue up as neatly in Amsterdam as they do in London.

By Rail

Fast and frequent trains connect Amsterdam with other cities in the Netherlands and other European cities. The Trans-European and Inter-City expresses, which cross frontiers, offer deep-armchair comfort and, usually, good food. Customs and immigration formalities are done while the train is rocketing along. Door-to-door—for example, from Amsterdam to Paris—the total journey time is not much more than that by air, if one counts the trip to and from airports, checkin waiting, baggage delays, and all the other hiatuses.

▷ Money

The guilder or florin is the basic unit of currency. International code: NLG. Colorful bank notes include a set of slightly raised dots that allow the blind to distinguish the dominations. Of course, they are also printed with numbers. The guilder is fully convertible, and there is no check on how much you can take into the country or leave with, though a customs officer might ask some pointed questions about a full briefcase of cash. As in the rest of Europe (and, indeed, the world), try to change your own currency into the local one at a bank rather than a hotel: almost invariably the rate is better.

▷ Language

Dutch. But the Dutch are among the world's most accomplished linguists. Many educated people speak three or four languages as well as their own. One reason is, of course, that Dutch is spoken by relatively few people in Europe: the Dutch themselves and their Flemish neighbors in the northern provinces of Belguim, a total of only about 22 million people. Another reason is that Dutch is closely related to German and English, which makes those languages fairly easy for native Dutch speakers to learn. Undoubtedly, though, the main reason that so many people in Amsterdam speak English is that Dutch educators take languages seriously. So it probably isn't worth your time trying to pronounce a hotel name properly in Dutch when the cabbie is very likely to reply in near-perfect English.

▷ Communications

Excellent. Country code: 31. City code: 20. The telecommunications system is one of the best in Europe. So is the post office. Several hundred publications use the Netherlands as their central distribution point, and the national airline, KLM, specializes in mail and freight-forwarding services. Maastricht, a "hub-and-spoke" cargo airport, is the operations center for several international air-freight companies.

▷ Getting To Know the City

Amsterdam's street plan is dictated by the canals. Many of these are lined by buildings several hundred years old: tall, narrow-fronted, elegant. With their brick façades, some of them bulging with age, the buildings of old Amsterdam offer little grandeur. What they do offer is the comfortable proximity of venerable neighbors, and the white lace curtains in the windows are a homey touch. There are no grand avenues, no spectacular perspectives, in the style of Paris. Amsterdam is a bourgeois city rather than a noble one.

Until a few years ago, much of it was shabby. Then the municipal council and real estate developers started to clean up the Central Station area and the streets leading from the Dam square. Amsterdam today has recovered some of its charm without trying to find its salvation in skyscrapers (which would probably sink, anyway).

▷ Moving Around

Huge streetcars—jointed in the middle, air-conditioned, and equipped with loudspeakers—trundle along the streets and around sharp corners. They are among the best ways of traveling. There are buses, too, many of them able to bend around curves, and except when it's raining (rather often) there are plenty of taxis. Most drivers of streetcars, buses, and taxis speak English, or at least understand it. You can buy books of discount-rate mass-transit tickets at the central tourist office (marked with the initials VVV) near the Central Station and the Dam, or you can ask your hotel concierge for help.

▷ *Spotlight* ◁

Barges. Amsterdam is a watery city, traversed by canals upon which barges ply. They give the visitor an unusual view of the city, passing both the fronts and backs of houses and offices. And when street traffic is at its peak, barges may be faster than taxis. The hotel front desk can advise.

▷ **Hotels**

In the past few years, Amsterdam has added some 3,000 hotel beds to its stock, taking the total to 23,000. Half of these are in the top categories, but hotels range from that level down to those with quiet, clean rooms but no elevators. Many new hotels are in the Central Station area; all of them emphasize services for the business traveler. These include meeting rooms, sauna baths, and fitness centers. A sampler:

American, 97 Leidsekade. Tel.: 245322. Telex: 12545. Fax: 253236. Rooms/suites: 180. A historic, renovated hostelry, close to the opera and concert halls and to nightspots. Probably the best coffeehouse/reading room in the city.

Amstel, Professor Tulpplein. Tel.: 226060. Telex: 11004. Fax: 225808. Rooms/suites: 111. This notably elegant establishment has occupied a position of honor on the banks of the Amstel River since 1867 and is now part of the Inter-Continental group. Superb personal service. The hotel blends skillfully a romantic ambience with high efficiency.

Amsterdam Hilton, 138 Apollolaan. Tel.: 780780. Telex: 11025. Fax: 626688. Rooms/suites: 274. A comfortable—and comforting—favorite in a quiet, safe, and convenient location, close to both airport and city. Highly predictable decor, food, and service—that is, like Hiltons almost everywhere, this one has high standards. There is a casino (tel.: 664-9911).

Apollo, 2 Apollolaan. Tel.: 735922. Telex: 14084. Fax: 739771. Rooms/suites: 228. Top Trusthouse Forte hotel at the confluence of five canals. Large, modern; goes out of its way to attract and help business executives. Good bars and restaurants.

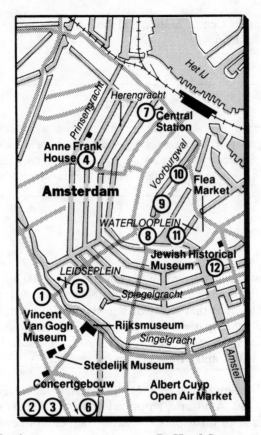

1. **Hotel Marriott**
2. **Hotel Hilton**
3. **Hotel Apollo**
4. **Hotel Pulitzer**
5. **Hotel American**
6. **RAI Congress Hall, World Trade Center**
7. **Hotel Sonesta**
8. **Hotel Europe**
9. **Hotel Pullman**
10. **Grand Hotel Krasnapolsky**
11. **New City Hall**
12. **Hotel Amstel**

Grand Hotel Krasnapolsky, 9 Dam. Tel.: 5549111. Telex: 12262. Fax: 228607. Rooms/suites: 300. Mata Hari slept here; she had good taste in hotels, if not in men and politics. The Krasnapolsky is in a world of its own, more than living up to the "Grand" tag. Its new conference center opens in 1990.

Hilton International Schiphol, Schiphol Centrum. Tel.: 5115911. Telex: 15186. Fax: 178437. Rooms/suites: 281. This Hilton specializes in caring for the needs of business travelers. Executive floor with private lounge; pool and sauna. Shuttle bus or three-minute walk from airport terminal and railroad station.

Hotel de l'Europe, 2-4 Nieuwe Doelenstraat. Tel.: 234836. Telex: 12081. Fax: 242962. Rooms/suites: 114. Straight out of *la Belle Epoque,* with strong emphasis on service and food, some of which arrives overnight from Paris. The hotel's *Excelsior* restaurant is one of the two or three best in Amsterdam. Sauna and pool; golf by arrangement. Overlooks Amstel River and the famous Mint Tower.

Marriott, 19-21 Stadhouderskade. Tel.: 835151. Telex: 15087. Fax: 833834. Rooms/suites: 395. Close to everything, including the Rembrandts and Van Goghs and the World Trade Center. Marriott does its usual competent job with food and service.

Okura, 333 Ferdinand Bolstraat. Tel.: 787111. Telex: 16182. Fax: 712344. Rooms/suites: 373. East meets West in this skyscraper (by Amsterdam standards), with its Japanese garden, two Japanese restaurants, and rooms designed by Britain's David Hicks. Best views of the city. Close to airport and World Trade Center.

Pulitzer, 315-331 Prinsengracht. Tel.: 228333. Telex: 16508. Fax: 276753. Rooms/suites: 200. Nearly always full, the Pulitzer is housed in 24 historic buildings on the banks of the famous canal. A hotel of great personality and charm.

Pullman Hotel Capitool, 67 NZ Voorburgwal. Tel.: 275900. Telex: 14494. Fax: 238932. Rooms/suites: 148. A new resting place close to the Central Station, the Royal Palace, and the diamond district; the Capitool is designed and located for the business executive. Sauna and solarium.

Sonesta, 1 Kattengat. Tel.: 212223. Telex: 17149. Fax: 275245. Rooms/suites: 425. Some suites have roof gardens. Recently refurbished and completely air-conditioned, the Sonesta offers a distinctive blend of the international and Dutch styles. The *Koepel Cafe* is a Dutch pub within the hotel, and if too much beer threatens the guest's waistline, there is also a fitness center. Good location, close to Central Station, Singel Canal, and the historic Koepel Kwartier.

Recommended three-star hotels, all comfortable and specializing in business travelers' needs: *Ambassade,* 341 Herrengracht. Tel.: 262333. *Arthur Frommer,* 46 Noorderstraat. Tel.: 220328. *Borgmann,* 48 Koningslaan. Tel.: 735252. *Roemer Visscher,* 10 Roemer Vischerstraat. Tel.: 12551. *Zandbergen,* 205 Willemsparkweg. Tel: 769321.

▷ **Restaurants**

The Netherlands has long suffered from a reputation for dullish cuisine. As in any country, of course, you can find heavy, unimaginative food without really trying. With a little effort, you can also find restaurants that match or strive to reach the highest standards. Most of these offer Dutch, French, or Indonesian cuisine, and some offer all three. Indonesian is popular because of Holland's former role as an imperial power in the Far East. The selective list below is of restaurants with distinctive Dutch ambience and a clientele in which businesspeople are prominent. Reservations are essential.

Bali, 95 Leidsestraat. Tel.: 227878. Long-established and famous for its Indonesian dishes, particularly *rijsttafel* (literally, "rice table") a sumptuous meal featuring over a dozen small samples of exotic foods. A real dining adventure.

Beddington, 6-8 Roelof Hartstraat. Tel.: 765201. The formal atmosphere can be intimidating. But as French actress Arletty said, "Make your own atmosphere." Meanwhile, the chef makes some of the best dishes in town.

Bordewijk, 7 Noordermarkt. Tel.: 243899. Rather trendy, but the food and service are excellent.

Dynasty, 30 Reguliersdwarsstraat. Tel.: 268400. Behind the Singel Canal flower market and in a neighborhood with more than its share of gay bars and cabarets. Chinese and Thai dishes.

Kersentuin (Cherry Garden), 7 Dijsselhofplantsoen. Tel.: 642121. Good, if super-yuppie. In the Garden Hotel, opposite the Hilton.

Le Pecheur, 32 Reguliersdwarsstraat. Tel.: 243121. Designed to make an impression, with its food as much as its decor. Specialty: fish.

Raden-Mas, Stadhouderskade 6. Tel.: 854041. A new, excellent Indonesian restaurant (a well-known name already in The Hague and Rotterdam). The mayor pops in, along with gourmets from far afield. You can even arrive late and eat steadily for four hours.

Silveren Spiegel (Silver Mirror), 4 Kattengat. Tel.: 246589. Quaint, excellent, and a favorite with the business set. Opposite the Sonesta.

Speciaal, 142 Nwe Leliestraat. Tel.: 249706. Probably the best Indonesian and Chinese food in town. The Duke of Edinburgh has certainly eaten here; rumor has it that the local head of the KGB has also dined.

't Swarte Schaep (the Black Sheep), 24 Leidsedwarsstraat. Tel.: 223021. Set in all the liveliness of the Leidseplein nightclub area. Very highly recommended.

▷ Spotlight ◁

Pubs. Amsterdam is famous for its pubs. Some, of course, are dives, but many others are snug hostelries where businesspeople gather at lunchtime and after hours. A sampler:

Amstel Hotel Bar, 1 Professor Tulpplein. The best of the hotel pubs, with a stunning view of the river. Piano at cocktail time; food.

De Drie Fleschjes, 18 Gravenstraat. More elegant than most, this tavern dates from 1650 and attracts stockbrokers, lawyers, and journalists. Closes at 8:30 p.m.

Frascati, 59 Nes. Directly behind the European Options Exchange on Rokin, Frascati is favored by bankers. Food.

Hoppe, 20 Spui. The most famous of the "brown cafés," so called for their lavish use of wood. Hoppe claims to sell more beer than any other pub in Holland. A constantly changing crowd from 7:00 a.m. to 1:00 a.m.

L'Entree, 42 Reguliersdwarsstraat. Probably the trendiest bar in the city. Interior resembles an old ocean liner. Lots of yuppies in the late evening.

Papeneiland, 2 Prinsengracht. The prettiest of the brown cafés, this once housed a clandestine Catholic church in the cellars; these are now a students' club.

Pieper, 424 Prinsengracht. A brown café that attracts lawyers and students. Busiest in the early evening.

Pilsener Club, 4 Begijnensteeg. No bellying up to the bar here: tables only. A timeless place where many of the customers seem timeless as well. Snacks.

Wijnand Fockink, 31 Pijlsteeg. A tavern where the tasting of Bols gins is taken seriously, and has been since the seventeenth century.

▷ Tipping

Taxes and tips are included in restaurant checks and in taxis, only taxes in bars. It's good manners to leave the small change, particularly if you want to be welcomed back for a second visit. Leave at least one guilder, more for checks approaching 20 guilders.

▷ Doing Business

The export-oriented economy of the Netherlands is dominated by big multinationals and companies aspiring to that label and size. Among the leading players: Royal Dutch/Shell Group; DSM and Akzo, both in chemicals; Philips, in a wide range of electronics and electrical goods; Fokker, in short- and medium-range aircraft; DAF in trucks; and Unilever in consumer goods such as margarine, soap, frozen foods, soft drinks, toothpaste, detergents, toiletries, and much, much more.

Many of the multinationals are headquartered outside Amsterdam, but that doesn't mean they are far away, for Holland is a small country. Fast express trains and multilane highways link Amsterdam with The Hague and Rotterdam. All three can be visited comfortably within a day.

The Big Two banks, ABN and Amro, both headquartered in Amsterdam, are truly international. Both recently have been building up fee-related services, such as mergers and acquisitions, securities trading, investment advice, and asset management. ABN is particularly strong in the Middle East; its twice-monthly *Economic Review* is required reading. Rabobank, a specialist in agribusiness, has its headquarters in Utrecht— again, not a day's march from Amsterdam.

The Netherlands has by far the highest population density in Europe: 388 persons per square kilometer, compared with second-ranking Belgium's 323 and sparse Finland's 15. Land is consequently expensive, and the authorities encourage investment in light and service industries that score low on the land-use and pollution scales.

▷ *Spotlight* ◁

Amsterdam's Central Station itself is bright, clean, and efficient. But though the police are out in force, the station and its neighborhood are still afflicted by petty thieves and pickpockets. Do not leave luggage unattended or your car on the street overnight.

As in most other European countries, privatization is sweeping the Netherlands—that is, the sale of state-owned industries to private and institutional investors. Among the privatized is the Dutch phone system. Already one of the most efficient and enterprising telecommunications corporations in Europe, the Dutch system prides itself on excellence and tries to sell both its management techniques and its technologies to the rest of the world.

Privatization is among the factors that have made the Amsterdam securities markets more lively. The stock exchange has introduced far-reaching automation but kept the trading floor. Chicago's Midwest Stock Exchange has advised. The Interprofessional Market System (AIM) has done away with fixed commissions and is a dealer's system along London lines. The European Options Exchange, used mainly by private investors, has more than 35 different kinds of contracts in stocks, bonds, currencies, precious metals, and market indexes.

Teleports are seen as a way of attracting national and international investment. Traditionally, foreigners have preferred the charms of a once-stately home on the canals. The Dutch would like newcomers—big companies such as Nissan and Alcatel who are establishing European headquarters because of the favorable NV company status—to go to the office parks. Many firms have moved from the city center to the World Trade Center. The teleport, just to the west of the city, will be one of the largest in Europe with its 125 acres of offices with digital business telephone exchanges, housing, and hotels. It's been designed to fit into the road and rail system. Dutch banks were the first to go west.

▷ Useful Phone Numbers

Emergencies

Car repairs	268251
Doctor/dentist	6642111/791821
First aid	5669111
Lost/found	
Public transport	5514911
Trains	5578544
Police	222222

Local Information

Airport	
Arrivals, departures	5110432
Shopping	5172497
Bicycle rental	276296
Canal trips	227788
Car repairs	268251
Train schedules	202266
City tourist office	266444
City guides	736512
Communications	
Phone, telex, fax	743654
Taxis	777777
Water taxis	750909

Trade and Commercial Information

Chambers of Commerce	
American	(070) 659808
British	277359
French	269691
Italian	442351
Japanese	6621457
City Hall	552911
City promotion (AMPRO)	5753026
European Community	(070) 469326
Stock Exchange	239711
Teleport	606500
Trade information center	5753140
World Trade Center	5753046

Consulates

Australia	(070) 630983
Austria	268033
Belgium	0429763
Brazil	16624085

►15

Canada	(070) 614111	Alitalia	5576333
Denmark	234145	Austrian Airlines	234980
Finland	249090	British Airways	852211
France	1-248346	El Al Israel Airlines	220191
Germany (West)	736245	Finnair	244799
Greece	43671	Gulf Air	271081
Italy	240043	Iberia (Spain)	5891582
Japan	243581	Japan Air Lines/JAL	2604011
Luxembourg	6649111	KLM Royal Dutch Airlines	747747
Mexico	730230	LOT Polish Airlines	264867
Morocco	736215	Lufthansa German Airlines	263511
Norway	242331		
Philippines	261944	Northwest Airlines	0220022
Surinam	426717	Olympic Airways	233614
Sweden	242699	Pakistan International Airlines	264715
Switzerland	6644231	Pan Am World Airways	262021
Thailand	220078	Qantas Airways (Australia)	838081
United Kingdom	764343		
United States	6645661	Sabena Belgian World Airlines	262966
Uruquay	799182	SAS Scandinavian Airlines	763015
Venezuela	228301	Singapore Airlines	464546

Airlines

Aeroflot Soviet Airlines	245715	South African Airways	164444
Aerolineas Argentinas	268881	Swissair	6626526
Aer Lingus (Ireland)	239589	TAP Air Portugal	246268
Air France	5731585	Transavio (Italy)	5187518
Air India	227657	TWA	262277
Air UK	747747	UTA (France)	268665
Alia Royal Jordanian	226566	Varig (Brazil)	227671

▷ **Shopping**

Antiques, furniture, clocks, chinaware—all are in the area around Nieuwe
Spiegelstraat. Stores arrange for specialized cargo agents to ship by air or

sea purchases too large or heavy for you to carry yourself. That won't be a problem, of course, with diamonds, one of Amsterdam's specialties.

Aronson, 39 Nieuwe Spiegelstraat. Tel.: 233103. Exquisite plaques, vases with Chinese decoration, figurines. All rare stuff, and at rare prices.

De Porcelynen Fles, 170 Prinsengracht. Tel.: 227509. Old and new Delftware from the Royal Factory.

Frank Govers, 500 Keizersgracht. This interesting designer's mission is to introduce more bravura into Amsterdam life and, of course, into that of the visitor's hometown.

Department stores are a Dutch specialty, and the best sell everything you can think of, and some things of which you probably never dreamed. Among the best: *De Bijenkorf,* 90a Damrak. *Vroom and Dreesman,* 201 Kalverstraat 201 and 162 Rokin.

▷ Spotlight ◁

Diamonds. On February 10, 1908, Joseph Asscher fainted. The first time he tried that day to cut the Cullinan diamond—at 3,106 carats, the largest ever found—his blade broke. The second time the blade didn't break, but he did—with relief. From that South African diamond, he eventually cut the 530-carat Cullinan I, which adorns the English crown, as well as nine large and 105 smaller stones. The Asscher family is still in business, at the *Amsterdam Diamond Center,* 1 Rokin. Tel.: 245787. Paul Asscher talks of strong demand for stones between 0.50 and 1.50 carats.

But are diamonds forever—in the investment sense? In 1983, a top-grade one-carat stone could fetch $45,000. Then the price fell to $8,000 before rebounding to $15,000. Diamonds are forever fascinating, though, as witnessed by the almost 1 million people who tour the Amsterdam Diamond Exchange each year.

Among the top cutters and dealers: *Coster Diamonds,* 2-4 Paul Potterstraat. Tel.: 762222. *Gassan Diamond House,* 17-23 Nieuwe Achtergracht. Tel.: 225333. *Bab Hendriksen Diamonds,* 89 Weteringschans. Tel.: 262798. *Holshuysen-Stoeltie,* 13-17 Wagenstraat. Tel.: 237601. *Van Moppes Diamonds,* 2-6 Albert Cuypstraat. Tel.: 761242. *A.S. Bonebakker & Zoon,* 86-90 Rokin. Tel.: 232294.

Gerard Pijper and his brother and sister are among leading cutter-designers who have moved to center stage in recent years. They are to diamonds what *nouvelle cuisine* chefs are to food. A ring of modern design can cost as little as $100. You can find the Pijpers at *Goldart,* 4 Spiegelgracht. Tel.: 252172.

▷ After Hours

A long time ago (we shan't disclose how long), one of the authors of this book visited Amsterdam for the first time. Wandering along a narrow street in the old part of the city, he saw a superb Victorian oil lamp in a window and was just about to dash in to ask the price when he also noticed in the window a rather scantily clad woman. He made a U-turn on the sidewalk and ever since has wondered what would have happened if he had asked, "How much is that oil lamp in the window?" Older, but obviously no wiser, that same author two or three years afterward traipsed into a late-night bar, goggled at the pretty ladies, and was warned by the doorman that they were all transvestites. Our intrepid investigator made an excuse and left, as the saying goes.

All this is by way of introducing a rather delicate and touchy subject, Amsterdam's famous—or infamous—"red-light" neighborhoods, most of which are in narrow and picturesque streets radiating from the Dam square and Central Station areas. You'll know you've found them when you see the marquees that spell out the offerings in no uncertain terms. Though tourists are advised to stroll in small groups rather than alone, the streets generally are safer at night. After all, the flesh peddlers don't want muggers to empty visitors' wallets. But the red-light areas are also tawdry, and both the touts and the girls have become more aggressive since the AIDS epidemic began to cut their takings.

Amsterdam's after-hours life tends toward the raucous. The late-night places we've listed are the pick of a not-very-appetizing crop.

Bimhuis, 73-77 Oude Schans. One of the city's most famous jazz venues.

Bios, Leidsplein. Flashy, loud, even tasteless, yet very popular.

Cafe de Nol, 109 Westerstraat. A traditional Dutch nightclub and disco in the Jordaan "artistic" district. Red paint, lace, rather schmaltzy.

De Kroeg, 163 Lijnbaansgracht. Small, dark, smoky; jazz and salsa.

Escape, Rembrandtplein. Claims to be Europe's most modern and highest-tech disco, with room for 2,000.

Mazzo, 114 Rozengracht. Haunt of the media crowd. Videos, big floor, pretty barmaids; trendy.

Richter, 36 Reguliersdwarsstraat. Some of the most beautiful of younger Amsterdammers congregate here.

Roxy, 465 Singel. Mix of art deco and other styles; three floors with widely varied musical entertainment. Probably the city's best late-night place.

The String, 98 Nes. Open seven nights a week with a menu of top folk music including country and western, blues, flamenco, and Latin American music.

▷ Sights and Sounds

There's a sight, if not a sound, whenever one turns a corner in old Amsterdam: a pretty house of mellow pink brick, a mirror-calm canal, a barge with potted flowers in the wheelhouse, a small square with a curio shop and a pub. The sights are endless, and the best way to see them is on foot or bicycle. A word of caution about the latter: Cyclists in Amsterdam take their biking seriously, and there are a lot of them. Try to stay out of their way.

Rembrandt, Van Gogh, and Anne Frank are the three "stars" of the city, each with his or her own museum. In all, there are 40 museums of note, and the VVV (tourist) office can make many tour suggestions. These include Maritime Amsterdam, Amsterdam Sculpture, and Amsterdam Architecture. The VVV will also point the way around Jordaan, built in the 1600s for workers but now an area for artists, musicians, and students.

A sampler of museums—check days of opening and times, which vary with the seasons:

Rijksmuseum [national gallery], Stadhouderskade. Collections include Dutch Masters, with Rembrandt's *Nightwatch* probably the most famous painting; Delftware, Meissen and other porcelain; and Asiatic art, with its famous dancing Shiva of the twelfth century.

Rembrandt's House, 4-6 Jodenbrestraat. The great man lived and worked here for 20 years.

Rijksmuseum Van Gogh, 7 Paulus Potterstraat 7. A short walk from the other Rijksmuseum. No need to pay $20 million for a Van Gogh: His other "Sunflowers" can be seen here, along with 200 other paintings and 500 drawings, the world's largest collection of the tragic artist's work.

Anne Frank House, 263 Prinsengracht. The young Jewish girl and her family hid here for two years before betrayal and death in a Nazi concentration camp. A visit is a very emotional experience, even for people who have not read Anne Frank's diary.

Peter Stuyvesant Foundation, 21 Drenthenstraat. A museum of the kind of modern art favored by banks and companies for their walls. Here are many of the 600 paintings and 100 sculptures that the tobacco company circulates around its offices and factories.

▷ *Spotlight* ◁

Aalsmeer. The Dutch sell almost two-thirds of the world's exports of cut flowers, with West Germany taking half of them. Aalsmeer, near Amsterdam, is a 22-hectare (54-acre) complex where more than 3 billion roses, car-nations, frisias, lilacs, and other flowers are auctioned each year. Roses alone are a $250-million annual market. Open to visitors from 8:00 a.m. to 12 noon Monday through Saturday.

Amsterdam offers some of the best musical sounds to be heard anywhere. The main concert hall, the Concertgebouw, has noon and evening concerts. The Oude Kerk (old church), which dates from 1724, and the Nieuwe Kerk (new church), which paradoxically dates from 1665, have organ recitals on summer evenings. The new Muziektheater is home of the Dutch National Ballet, the Dutch National Opera, and the Netherlands Dance Theatre.

▷ Out of Town

The Netherlands' high population density doesn't mean that the country has been concreted over or that its topography and architecture conform to a gray norm. Within easy reach of Amsterdam there is much to see and to savor.

Haarlem (yes, that section of Manhattan was named for the old Dutch city) has a notable museum housing the works of a former citizen, one Frans Hals. *Edam* is known as the cheese town, for its eponymous product, and offers as well the sight of ancient houses and cobbled streets. *Marken* and *Volendam* fishing villages are a glimpse of life as it was lived centuries ago. The 33-kilometer (20-mile) drive along the enclosing dam of the Zuider Zee, now a freshwater lake, shows how the Dutch have tamed the North Sea. *Zandvoort* is a lively beach resort on that sea.

Den Haag (The Hague) is the Netherlands' political capital, has a population of half a million, and is home to most ministries and embassies, not to mention Queen Beatrix. She lives part of the time at the Huis Ten Bosch Palace and has another palace for state occasions, Noordeinde. Near to The Hague is the bustling, popular coastal resort of *Scheveningen*. (It's said that if you can pronounce this name, you're halfway to speaking Dutch. Unfortunately, nobody has yet devised a way of expressing it phonetically on paper, so we shan't even try.) Telephone area code for The Hague: 070.

Hotels in The Hague

Hotel des Indes, 54-56 Lange Voorhout. Tel.: 469553. Telex: 31196. Fax: 31196. Rooms/suites: 77. *The* grand hotel, frequented by diplomats, CEOs, and foreign correspondents pursuing them. The *Copper Kettle* restaurant is superb. Ghost of Mata Hari, too.

Park Hotel, 53 Molenstraat, Tel.: 624371. Telex: 33005. Fax: 614525. Rooms/suites: 114. A rambling, medium-priced hotel in the heart of the old city that has attracted a faithful clientele.

Promenade, 1 Van Stolkweg. Tel.: 525161. Telex: 31162. Fax: 541046. Rooms/suites: 101. Modern hotel within walking distance of the Netherlands Congress Building. All rooms have views of woodlands. Bar and bistro open until 1:00 a.m.

Pullman Hotel Central, 180 Spui. Tel.: 614921. Telex: 32000. Fax: 639398. Rooms/suites: 159. Central's the word: close to government ministries and embassies.

Restaurants

There are no fewer than 82 Indonesian restaurants in The Hague and Scheveningen. Many connoisseurs believe the best of them all is the *Bali,* 1 Badhuisweg, Scheveningen. Tel.: 502434. Well worth the brief taxi ride from the city center.

Sports

Golf. *Amsterdamse Golfclub.* Tel.: 943650. *Golfclub Olympus.* Tel.: 651863. *Netherlands Golf Federation.* Tel.: (035) 830565. For further information: *Golfline,* Tel.: (020) 645453.

Tennis. *Wildenhorst Tennis Center,* Sloterweg 301, Badhoevedorp (near Schiphol airport) rents rackets and finds partners. Tel.: (02968) 7307.

Sailing. VVV, the Amsterdam tourist office, provides specialized brochures describing the many possibilities.

ATHENS

The Glory That Was—And Is To Come?

Population: 885,136 (1981). Metropolitan area: 3.2 million. Capital of Greece. Republic (population: 9.9 million). *Location*: east-central Greece. *Economy*: banking and financial services, commercial and transportation center, chemicals, textiles, food processing, oil refining, printing and publishing, tourism. Greece is a member of the European Community (EC) and the Organization for Economic Cooperation and Development (OECD) and is a signatory to the General Agreement on Tariffs and Trade (GATT).

▷ Background Briefing

The Acropolis, the Parthenon that tops it, the glory that was...One doesn't have to be a classical scholar to know that Athens (and Rome) helped to shape the Western world, its languages, and its philosophies. But consider Athens today. Is it a monument to ancient glory, or merely a grubby, twentieth-century metropolis? The answer: a little of both.

The city sits in a basin, surrounded by mountains on three sides. Industry, sited mainly to the southwest, towards the port of Piraeus, generates a dust-laden smog that clogs throats, especially in the high season. This smog is worsened by the low-quality diesel fuel used to heat most buildings and burned by the city's buses and 15,000 taxis.

Some relief is provided, in theory at least, by a recent regulation supposed to halve the number of vehicles in the city center on a given day. Cars with plates ending in odd numbers are allowed in only on odd-numbered dates; those with even-numbered plates on even-numbered dates. Better relief comes when a northeast wind blows the smog out to sea.

But don't confuse Athens with Greece. Just as London isn't England, Paris isn't France, and New York isn't the United States, Athens is an exception to the Greek rule. Most of the mainland and 2,000-odd islands remain beautiful and unspoiled. History is around many corners. Early civilizations date from at least 1500 B.C. The Greek invaders from northwest of the Balkan mountains soon formed many small, independent city-kingdoms. Between 750 and 550 B.C., the city-states founded colonies in the northern Aegean, on the shores of the Black Sea, in southern Asia Minor and Cyprus, along the Nile delta and near Cyrene, on the northern shores of the western Mediterranean.

Greek and Roman civilizations and history are deeply intertwined; but ancient Greece never achieved political unity, as Rome did, and over the centuries that weakness made its peoples prey to many invaders. That enriched Greek culture, but to this day central government remains relatively ineffective. In the 1400s, the Ottoman Turks conquered Greece, and not until after the war of 1821–29 did the country achieve independence.

Turkey is Greece's hereditary hostile neighbor. The tides of war and conquest have left both peoples deeply suspicious of each other. Closer to our own times, Mussolini's legions attempted to repeat the feat of arms performed by their Roman forebears, failed, and were rescued by Nazi Germany. At war's end, the conquering Allies restored the Greek monarchy—ironically, held by a family of German origin. Even that did not end the strife. A fierce civil war between the communists and a diverse alliance of democratic forces racked the country between 1946 and 1949.

Democracy was a feeble plant. In 1967 a group of colonels overthrew the civilian government of King Constantine II and established one of the world's nastier military dictatorships. After failing to pull off a counter *coup d'état,* Constantine went into exile, and the colonels later abolished the monarchy. In the following year the military turned over power to civilians, in part because the country was becoming ungovernable and its social and economic problems baffled simple soldiers and sailors. A new constitution adopted in 1975 made Greece a republic, with a president as head of state and a prime minister as head of government.

Greece's political travails were far from over, however. The Socialist government of prime minister Andreas Papandreou, which came to power in 1981, lurched from crisis to crisis and scandal to scandal in the late 1980s, and in 1989 lost its parliamentary majority in a general election. Democracy now seems firmly entrenched, but political instability means that government has not been able to tackle vigorously Greece's linked economic and social weaknesses.

▷ Arriving

You can reach Athens by road, rail, sea, or air. To do so by road, you need patience, stamina, and plenty of time. The same qualities help if you travel from northern Europe by train, as the journey takes 40 to 50 hours. There are boats from Italy—Ancona, Brindisi, and Venice—to the ports of Athens and Patras.

The two-terminal Athens airport is busy, reasonably efficient, and just as confusing as any other international airport. One's flight seems always to arrive at or depart from the farthest point from the terminal. (Who are those lucky people who have merely to stroll a few yards or meters?) The bus or taxi ride to the city center will take about half an hour, more during rush hour.

▷ *Spotlight* ◁

Terrorism. Is Greece a playground for terrorists? The government says not— but it would, wouldn't it? In one recent horror, terrorists opened fire with automatic weapons and threw grenades among passengers in a sightseeing boat. Nine people died, and about 40 were injured. But how far can any democratic country go to protect people if security itself is not to become oppressive? It's as though tourists boarding a Circle Line boat in New York or a *bateau mouche* cruise on the Seine in Paris had to be searched as rigorously as passengers boarding an aircraft. At one time lax, security at Athens airport is now strict, and is certainly up to international standards. The unavoidable fact is that every time the authorities anywhere close one security loophole, determined terrorists find another.

▷ Money

The basic unit of currency is the drachma. International code: GRD. All the main banks—and you almost trip over them in the city center— change money at about the same rate. Hotel exchange rates vary greatly and are always less favorable than the banks'. If you cash a foreign check with the aid of a bank card, beware of the heavy commission charged, the same absolute sum whatever the amount you are changing.

▷ Language

Greek, spoken and written. Most Athens businesspeople speak workable English and/or French. Of course, they appreciate a visitor's having even a smattering of Greek and trying to use it. *Compendium Bookshop,* 15 Nikis Street, about 200 meters or yards from Constitution Square, has an excellent selection of pocket-sized dictionaries and phrasebooks.

The Greeks use a lot of body language. Often, the words *nay* (yes) and *ochi* (no) are not spoken. "Yes" may take the form of a swift nodding of the head forwards and slightly sideways; "no" is a swift jerk of the chin up and a bit backwards. The range and precision of Greek gestures are probably unique, and any foreigner who understands them all qualifies for a job in cryptology. Do not signal the number five by extending your fingers: that's the sign for a curse or the evil eye.

▷ Communications

Country code: 30. City code: 1. The standard is highest in Europe, but phones, faxes, and telexes often work reli; in all other cities, check your hotel's markup for phone calls: it high. So if you're planning a long-distance (and long) phone ition, you'll save money by having your office call you back.

▷ Getting To Know the City

The hub of Athens life is wedged between the Acropolis to the southwest and the little conical mountain to the northeast, Lycabettus. Roughly equidistant between them is Syntagma (Constitution) Square, with its sidewalk cafés facing the old royal palace, now the Parliament Building. Between Syntagma and the other main square, Omonoia (Concord), is the Plaka, a cluster of winding, cobblestoned streets that comprise the heart of the old market district. The smaller Monastiraki Square is near the Plaka, which is nestled beneath the Acropolis. Where as Syntagma is modern and emphatically touristy, Omonoia has more local flavor and is teeming with Greeks haggling and debating on the sidewalks. Clearly, they don't pay the first price asked.

▷ Moving Around

On a first or even second visit to Athens, you will do better to take taxis than risk the hazards of overcrowded buses bearing destination boards in the Greek alphabet. All taxis have meters so make sure the one in yours is switched on before the journey starts. Most drivers speak English of a kind, or at least understand it, but some become surprisingly tongue-tied if you try to negotiate a fare instead of relying on the metered price.

▷ Hotels

The business visitor to any city needs a base, a hotel that will take care of every need. Our criteria for Athens, as for other cities, are basic but essential: comfort if not luxury, prompt and intelligent service, good telecommunications, and concierges who know both their city and their jobs. Only when you have settled into a hotel can you get down to business. Take with a large pinch of skepticism the official hotel ratings. In our experience, these can be decidedly misleading. Here is a selection of the best and the better hotels:

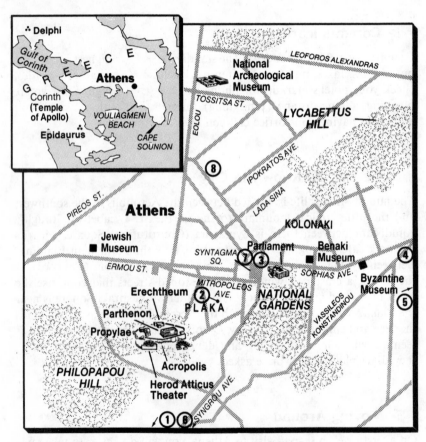

1. **Athenaeum Inter-Continental**
2. **Electra**
3. **Grande Bretagne**
4. **Hilton**
5. **Holiday Inn**
6. **Ledra Marriott**
7. **Meridien**
8. **Titania**

Athenaeum Inter-Continental, 89-93 Syngrou Avenue. Tel.: 902-3666. Telex: 221554. Fax: 921-7653. Rooms/suites: 559. In the heart of the business district, with spectacular view of the Parthenon. Gourmet and informal restaurants plus Greek taverna. Health club; seven meeting rooms.

Athens Gate, 10 Leoforos Singrou. Tel.: 923-8302.. Telex: 219660. Fax: 325-2952. Rooms/suites: 202. Two minutes by taxi and 10 minutes on foot to Syntagma (Consitution) Square.

Electra, 5 Ermou. Tel.: 322-3222. Telex: 216896. Fax: 322-0310. Beds: 180. Just off Syntagma (Constitution) Square; medium-priced.

Electra Palace, 18 Nokodimou. Tel.: 324-1401. Telex: 216896. Fax: 324-1875. Beds: 196. In the Plaka artists' quarter. Medium-priced.

Grande Bretagne, Syntagma (Constitution) Square. Tel.: 323-0251. Telex: 219615. Fax: 322-8036. Rooms/suites: 409. A favorite with diplomats, businesspeople, and journalists since 1862. Facing Parliament and the national gardens. Popular late-night rendezvous spot for Athenian society. Newly refurbished rooms have news-at-a-glance videotex service.

Hilton, 46 Vassilissis Sofias Avenue. Tel.: 722-0201. Telex: 215808. Fax: 721-3110. Rooms/suites: 492. Faces Acropolis, within walking distance of business district. Four restaurants, eight meeting rooms, outdoor pool.

Holiday Inn, 50 Michalacopoulou Street. Tel.: 724-8322. Telex: 218870. Fax: 724-8187. Rooms/suites: 189. About 1 kilometer ($2/3$ mile) from city center, 13 kilometers (8 miles) from airport. Satellite TV, outdoor rooftop pool, bowling. Greek restaurant. Room service around-the-clock.

Ledra Marriott, 115 Syngrou Avenue. Tel.: 934-7711. Telex: 221833. Fax: 935-8603. Rooms: 242. Suites: 16. Five minutes by taxi to Syntagma (Constitution) Square, 15 minutes to the airport, 10 minutes to the port of Piraeus. Spacious, light, and airy rooms; color TV, in-house movies; direct-dial phones; refrigerator. A selection of restaurants and bars. Rooftop pool; golf 10 minutes away.

Méridien, Syntagma (Constitution) Square. Tel.: 325-5301. Telex: 210568. Fax: 323-5856. Rooms/suites: 173. France in Athens: Brasserie des Arts restaurant features both Greek specialties and French *nouvelle cuisine*. Rooms are soundproofed as well as air-conditioned.

Titania, 52 Panepistimiou. Tel.: 360-9611. Telex: 214673. Fax: 363-0497. Rooms/suites: 370. Large, comfortable, middle-priced; handy for Syntagma (Constitution) Square.

▷ Restaurants

Athens being a cosmopolitan city, you find almost any kind of cuisine you want, including French and what is described, vaguely, as "international" in some of the major hotels. Not to be missed, though, is authentic Greek food. At its best, it is spicy, delicious, and varied.

Well-recommended formal restaurants include:

Abreuvoir, 51 Xenokratous. Tel.: 722-9106. In the elegant Kolonaki district, not far from Constitution Square and the foot of the Lycabettus hill. French cuisine; top of the chic list.

Antonopoulos, 1 Frederikis, Glyfada. Tel.: 894-5636. In a resort area just outside the city; noted for fish and other seafood.

Gerofinikas, 10 Pindarou. Tel.: 362-2719. Situated in fashionable Kolonaki. Greek cuisine with shrimp specialties and roast veal *en papillote.*

Iridanos, 7 Iidanou. Tel.: 722-4154. Part of the Hilton; one of the best Greek restaurants in town.

Kublai Khan, 89-93 Syngrou Avenue. Tel.: 902-3666. Part of the Inter-Continental Hotel; probably the best Chinese cuisine in Athens.

Sympossio, 46 Erechtiou Street. Tel.: 922-5321. Famous for trout with almonds, various filets, and cheeses.

Among top restaurants specializing in business lunches:

Atheneum Bistrot, 8 R. Amerikis. Tel.: 363-1125. International cuisine.

Da Walter, 7 R. Anapiron Polemou et Evzonon, Kolonaki. Tel.: 724-8726. Italian.

Kendriko, 3 R. Kolokotroni. Tel.: 323-2482. Greek.

For many business travelers, sated with dishes that vary little from country to country (that, perhaps, is the true meaning of "international"), simple Greek *tavernas* make a welcome change. For people on a *per diem* meal allowance, they make another kind of change—money in their pockets. Tavernas are cheap.

The heaviest concentration of tavernas is around Omonoia and between Syntagma and the Acropolis. In many of them you are invited to inspect the food in the kitchen and point to what you want. If you like or take to *retsina,* the pine-flavored Greek wine, always order "retsina chima"—from the barrel. It's usually better and always cheaper than any bottled version.

Recommended tavernas:

Corfu, 6 Kriezotou Street. Good selection of traditional Greek dishes, comfortable, cheerful.

GB Corner, ground floor of Grande Bretagne Hotel. Honest food; half international, half Greek. Good for business lunches or dinners.

Gierofinikas, 10 Pindarou Street. Old taverna, plenty of atmosphere, wide selection of Greek dishes; a place to relax.

Philippou, corner of Xenocratou and Plutarchou streets. Another typical taverna with excellent food and friendly service.

Zonar, Panepistimiou Street, just off Syntagma Square. A large café-brasserie that's easy to find and pronounce, making it a good place to meet.

▷ *Spotlight* ◁

Eating habits. The traditional Greek businessman is very wary of accepting a lunch or dinner invitation from a visiting foreigner; that is not his style. An invitation may not scupper a deal but is unlikely to help. Older Greeks still like to do the inviting themselves in their own city and country. Younger Greeks are more relaxed about foreigners' invitations, but a good hint is to issue them casually, giving your potential guest a chance to refuse without seeming impolite.

▷ Tipping

A service charge is included in hotel and restaurant bills, but it is customary to leave an extra 5 percent on large bills and 10 percent on smaller ones. Round off the check with small change in cafés. However, it is not customary to tip taxi drivers.

▷ Doing Business

The Greeks' reputation as shrewd traders is no Greek myth; old or young, they bargain hard and intelligently. Dealing with the older, traditional type of businessman was and sometimes still is a tortuous affair, calling for an oblique approach to counter a suspicious, devious, and Byzantine mentality. Younger men and women, educated better than their elders and usually widely traveled, have more self-assurance and seem less afraid of being bamboozled by a high-powered foreign executive.

Bargaining has become open and direct, but it can still be hard to obtain a clear-cut decision quickly. That is not always the business executive's fault, because Greece has a powerful, slow-moving government bureaucracy with fingers in most economic pies.

Try to concentrate your business appointments into mornings. By lunchtime, most offices—and very definitely government ones—are deserted, possibly for the day, certainly until four or five in the afternoon. *Siesta* may be a Spanish word, but it's also a Greek institution.

▷ Spotlight ◁

Getting the facts. Before going to Greece, or to any other country he or she does not know well, the business traveler would be wise to bone up on essential facts and figures. Embassy commercial counselors can be helpful; so can chambers of commerce. Less known, and independent of government, is ICAP, a firm of financial and marketing consultants. The ICAP *Financial Directory of Greek Companies* lists the 200 largest, ranking them by both assets and revenues. The work also provides vital economic statistics and is published in English as well as Greek. ICAP Hellas SA, 64 Vas. Sophias Avenue, 115 28 Athens. Tel.: 724-7884. Telex: 215736.

Greece is the European Community's least industrialized country, with some 28 percent of its labor force in agriculture, fisheries, and forestry. That could change though, and change rapidly, if the promise of the 1992 European Single Market is kept. Geography, trade barriers, and a small, impoverished home market have so far prevented Greece from becoming an advanced industrialized country, but increased access to the rest of the EC may well boost its attractions as a low-cost producer and exporter.

As the EC's poorest nation, after Portugal, Greece qualifies for substantial regional aid, so it's worth talking to the country's commercial counselor at an embassy or consulate before leaving home. Financial, tax, and other incentives can be generous and usually justify the time it takes to negotiate a package. You'll find government ministries helpful, too, but don't expect fast decisions.

▷ Useful Phone Numbers

Emergencies

Ambulance	104
Fire	199
Antipoison	779-3777
Pharmacy (all night)	107
Police	100
Tourist police	171

Local Information

Airport	
(domestic)	9892604
(international)	9892631
Buses	142
Ferries	143
Trains	145

Government Ministries

Agriculture	524-3539
Commerce	361-6241
Defense	644-2918
Economics	324-7742
Finance	322-4071
Foreign Affairs	361-1257
Education	323-5730
Environment, Town Planning, Public Works	643-1461
Industry, Energy, and Technology	770-8615
Justice	522-5930
Labor	523-0385
Merchant Marine	411-3340
President of the Republic	723831
Prime Minister	323-8710/360-2119

Transport and Communications	325-1211

Chambers of Commerce and Trade Groups

Association of Commercial Agents	323-2622
Chambers of Commerce	
Athens	360-4815
American-Hellenic	363-6407
British-Hellenic	362-0168
International (ICC)	361-0879
Export Promotion	322-6871
Fine Arts	323-1230
Handicrafts	363-0253
Hotels	323-6641
Shipping	411-8811

Embassies and Consulates

Algeria	751-3560
Argentina	722-4753
Australia	775-7650
Austria	821-1036
Belgium	361-7886
Bolivia	801-6970
Brazil	721-3039
Bulgaria	360-8411
Cameroon	672-4415
Canada	723-9511
China (People's Republic)	672-3382
Colombia	647-4457
Costa Rica	360-1377
Cyprus	723-7883

Czechoslovakia	671-0675	Sweden	729-0421
Denmark	724-9315	Switzerland	723-0364
Egypt	361-8812	Syria	671-1604
Finland	751-9795	Thailand	671-7969
France	361-1163	Turkey	724-5915
Germany (East)	672-5160	United Kingdom	723-6211
Germany (West)	36941	United States	360-2635
Hong Kong	682-9701	Venezuela	770-9962
Hungary	671-4889	Yugoslavia	777-4344
Iceland	672-6154	Zaire	701-6171
India	721-6227		
Indonesia	881-4082		
Ireland	723-2771		
Israel	671-9350		
Italy	361-1723		
Japan	775-8101		
Korea (South)	701-2122		
Kuwait	647-3593		
Lebanon	778-8158		
Luxembourg	721-7948		
Malaysia	991-6523		
Mexico	723-0754		
Morocco	647-4209		
Netherlands	723-9701		
New Zealand	641-0311		
Norway	724-6173		
Pakistan	729-0214		
Panama	363-1847		
Poland	671-6917		
Portugal	729-0096		
Romania	671-0820		
Saudi Arabia	671-1691		
Senegal	4526-2364		
South Africa	692-2125		
Soviet Union	672-5235		
Spain	721-4885		

International Organizations

European Community	724-3982
European Parliament	722-3422
United Nations	322-9624
UN Environment Program	723-6586

Airlines

Aer Lingus (Ireland)	961-6161
Aeroflot Soviet Airlines	322-0986
Aerolineas Argentinas	324-0233
Air Afrique	323-0501
Air Algerie	326-0504
Air Canada	323-5143
Air France	323-0501
Air India	360-2457
Air Lanka	324-9098
Alitalia	322-9414
American Airlines	323-0791
Austrian Airlines	323-0844
Balkan-Bulgarian Airlines	322-6684
British Airways	325-0601

Cathay Pacific Airways	324-0233	Nigeria Airways	324-9074
Continental Airlines	324-1116	Olympic Airways	961-8161
Cyprus Airways	322-2641	Philippine Airlines	324-1116
Czechoslovak		Pan Am World	
Airlines/CSA	323-0174	Airways	323-5242
Eastern Airlines	324-1116	Pakistan International	
Egyptair	323-8907	Airlines	323-1931
El Al Israel Airlines	323-0116	Qantas Airways	325-0521
Ethiopian Airlines	323-4275	Royal Air Maroc	324-4202
Finnair	325-5234	Sabena Belgian	
Gulf Air	322-6684	World Airlines	323-6821
Iberia (Spain)	323-4523	SAS Scandinavian	
Iran Air	363-6650	Airlines	363-4444
Iraqi Airways	922-9573	Saudi Arabian	
Japan Air		Airlines	322-8211
Lines/JAL	324-8211	Singapore Airlines	323-9111
Kenya Airways	324-7000	South African	
KLM Royal Dutch		Airways	324-7108
Airlines	325-1311	Swissair	323-7581
Korean Air	324-7511	TAP Air Portugal	322-1888
Kuwait Airways	323-4506	Tarom (Romania)	362-4807
LOT Polish Airlines	322-1121	Thai Airways	324-3241
Lufthansa German		TWA	322-6451
Airlines	329-4411	Turk Hava Yollari	322-1035
Luxair	363-2572	United Airlines	922-9186
Malev Hungarian		Varig (Brazil)	322-674
Airlines	324-1116	Yugoslav Airlines/JAT	323-6429
Middle East Airlines/			
Air Liban	322-6911		

▷ Shopping

Bargaining is as much part of Greek life as sunshine, history, and olive oil. But note two key differences. You cannot haggle over the price of a tube of toothpaste, a razor, or a screwdriver; the stated price is the real price. You can haggle—and should—over the price of tourist-type goods: leather belts and handbags, brass- and copperware, icons, carpets, jewelry, and—for those with bulging billfolds—gold and furs.

Like most of their counterparts in southern Europe, Greek store-owners and clerks enjoy haggling. Indeed, if you pay the first price asked, they feel they should have asked more. If you bargain the price downward, they respect you for your skills. The process is neatly triadic: the store asks Price X, you offer Price Z, and the owner or clerk compromises on Price Y. Is the store trying to cheat you? Sometimes yes, sometimes no, and "cheat" may be the wrong word. A better explanation is that stores try to charge what the market will bear—and since you, the customer, are the market of the moment, the price varies according to your willingness and ability to pay.

The process is akin, of course, to that of the haggling of a buyer and supplier of components and subassemblies anywhere in the world. The supplier doesn't expect the buyer to pay the first price demanded, and the buyer's representative or agent wants to be able to tell the boss, "Gee, did I drive a hard bargain! Those guys at International Widgets must have been out of their skulls when they asked two bucks fifty a unit. So I said; 'You want the business, or don't you? You want it, we'll pay a buck seventy-five.' So they compromised on a buck ninety." Whether in Athens, Georgia, or Athens, Greece, both sides feel good.

The Kolonaki area is known for shoes, handbags, and clothes with international labels. Near Syntagma is the busiest commercial artery, Ermou Street, with a range of shops selling jewelry, clothes, and shoes. Stadiou Street also is good for jewelry. To the north is the commercial center of Kifissia, noted for arts and crafts. The Monastiraki section near the Plaka has the flea markets. Unusual shops include *Kato,* corner of Skoufa and Traklitou Streets, for gold and silver jewelry; *Kourtidis Antiques,* 6 Kanari and Polyplanos 16 Lycabetou, for arts and crafts; and *Acrobat,* 56 Ermou, for clothes with a Greek accent.

Greece's recent alignment with "normal" European hours means that shops are open from 9:30 a.m. until 6:30 p.m. They close on Monday mornings and Saturday afternoons.

▷ After Hours

Two or three decades ago, the visitor could share the spontaneous and uninhibited life of ordinary Athenians in tavernas where the *bouzouki* music throbbed into the wee hours, waiters and everyone else threw flowers and joined the dance, and in that dawn it was good to be alive. No longer. With few exceptions, the music is artificial, so is the atmosphere, and the prices are punitive. Among those exceptions:

Lycabetos, just off Kolonaki Square. Relaxed, almost rustic; moderate prices.

O Platanos, 4 Diogenous Street. In the Plaka area. Good, inexpensive food, traditional music.

Rodia, 44 Aristipou Street, corner of Kolonaki Square. Old traditions maintained; friendly service, pleasant atmosphere.

Theophilos, corner of Vakchou and Vironos Streets. More old traditions burnished and cherished.

Most of the major hotels have roof or terrace bars, some with a good view of the Parthenon. These include the Ledra Marriott, the Inter-Continental, the Athens Gate, and Titania. At street level is **Seventeen,** 17 Voukourestiou Street, an agreeable, civilized watering hole. It is particularly good for visiting women executives, since the barmen ensure that ladies are not propositioned (unless they want to be) by the kind of men known in Greek as *kamaki*—literally, "harpoons." The city's most famous and elegant disco is probably **Nine Plus Nine,** 5 Agras, at Platia Stadiou (Tel.: 722-2258). This is where the jet-setters go. Dress accordingly, and make sure your credit-card rating is good.

▷ Sights and Sounds

Although Athens has a glorious history that spans over two millenia, it is not notably rich in museums, art galleries, and other celebrations of the nation's cultural heritage. One reason may be that military and other marauders have plundered Athens of much physical evidence of its illustrious past. For example, Greece is still trying to recover from Britain the sculptures known as the Elgin Marbles. Originally part of the Acropolis, they were bought by a British nobleman named Elgin in the 1800s and today reside in the British Museum in London. Another reason is that modern times have not been kind to ancient Athens. Indeed, a nice point of argument is whether barbarians and colonial plunderers of the past did more than contemporary real estate developers have done to turn Athens into the city it is today—which is certainly one that lacks charm, even if some corners of it have escaped the developers' bulldozers, cranes, and breakfast-cereal-box architecture.

Not to be missed:

Acropolis. The remains of the building; also the small museum, which helps to explain why the Acropolis was built.

Benaki Museum, 1 Columbia Street. Wide range of exhibits, most of privotal historical interest, many on loan from private collections.

National Archeological Museum, 44 Patission Street. An unforgettable storehouse of classical sculpture and much else.

▷ Out of Town

You don't need a free weekend to see some of the glories of Greece. Beautiful places are reachable on a day trip and repay well in memories the time spent. On the mainland are such classical sites as Mycenae, Epidaurus, Tyrins, and Sparta. Delphi is also within a day's reach, but it's worth spending a night there to see it at sunrise. At the southernmost tip of Attica, a drive of one to one-and-a-half hours from Athens, is Cape Sounion and its Temple of Poseidon, where the English poet Lord Byron scratched his name in the stone. In the winter, there is good skiing on Mount Parnassus, close to Delphi.

The Saronic Gulf islands are a quick and comfortable voyage away by hydrofoils, known colloquially as flying dolphins. Among the most picturesque Gulf islands: Poros, Aegina, Hydra, and Spetsi.

And everywhere there are beaches, so don't forget a swimsuit and the suntan lotion.

BARCELONA
Going for the Gold

Population: 1.75 million (1981). Metropolitan area (estimated): 4 million. Administrative, political, and commercial capital of the Spanish autonomous region of Catalonia, which includes the provinces of Barcelona, Lerida, Gerona, and Tarragona (estimated population: 5.9 million). *Location*: Mediterranean shore of Spain, 526 kilometers (327 miles) east-northeast of Madrid. *Economy*: banking and finance; chemical products; electronics; engineering; food processing; maritime services, including shipbuilding and ship-repairing; oil refining; paper, printing, and publishing; textiles; tourism; transportation equipment. Spain is a member of the European Community (EC) and the Organization for Economic Cooperation and Development (OECD) and is a signatory to the General Agreement on Tariffs and Trade (GATT).

▷ Background Briefing

Caταláns are fiercely proud of their ethnic, linguistic, and cultural identity—an identity that, they claim, sets them apart from other peoples known to the outside world as Spanish. The Caταláns date their capital city from the 200s B.C. Their culture is a rich mix of the peoples who have ruled before and since. These have included Phoenicians, Greeks, Carthaginians, Romans, Visigoths, and Franks, a Germanic tribe that through a complex web of wars, treaties, and strategic marriages became a powerful force in the welding together of the elements that make modern France. Perhaps because of that northern element in their history, the Caταláns are sometimes called the Germans of Spain, and, certainly, they are a hard-working, methodical people.

Over the centuries the Cataláns have tried many times to become either independent or autonomous within the Spanish state—and sometimes have succeeded. In this century alone, Catalonia was autonomous in 1932–34 and again in 1936; lost its limited independence in 1939, when the forces of Generalissimo Francisco Franco Bahamonde triumphed; and only in 1980 won autonomy once more, this time from the democratic, post-Franco government. During the Franco years, teaching of the Catalán language and culture was forbidden. Yet that culture flourished, if only underground; and, practical people that they are, the Cataláns seldom ceased to strengthen their economy. A key indicator: With only 16 percent of Spain's population, Catalonia accounts for no less than 20 percent of the country's gross national product.

Success breeds success. Catalonia today is attracting a rising tide of foreign investment, and in 1992, Barcelona will become more than a name on a map to hundreds of millions of people around the world.

After bidding for the 1924, 1936, and 1972 Olympic Games, the city has at last been chosen as host for the 1992 Summer Olympics. Whoever wins the events, Barcelona has already won what it craves: international recognition as a great city. One result of winning the Olympic bid is a huge construction program, much of it financed privately, and a cleanup that will rejuvenate an already attractive city.

And 1992 is also the 500th anniversary of Christopher Columbus' landing in America, an expedition financed by the Spanish crown. Columbus didn't sail from Barcelona but did make port there upon his return.

As if that were not enough, 1992 is the year in which remaining barriers to trade within the European Community are scheduled to tumble. Barcelona, long an important seaport and international trading center, is gearing up for that event.

Barcelona has much to celebrate and is celebrating in the way it knows best—by going for the gold.

▷ Arriving

By Air

Barcelona's Prat Airport is about 14 kilometers (8.75 miles) from the city. There's nothing wrong with this airport that a slump in tourism wouldn't cure. As it is, about 30 percent of Spain's airborne vacation crop passes through Barcelona. Particularly in the summer, the business traveler has to put up with multiple delays: landing (and taking off), arrival of luggage, and at customs and immigration barriers. Travelers must also grin and bear it when charter-flight passengers arrive bombed out of their minds and already wearing (if that's the word) scanty garments more suitable for the beach than for the Boeing. If airline and airport officials look tense and harried, that's because they are. And who can blame them? Counting on more passengers rather than fewer, the airport authorities are building a new terminal and improving the existing one. That won't cut airborne delays, but it should make getting in and out of the airport faster—or at least less unpleasant.

Buses and trains leave for the city every 20 minutes. There are plenty of taxis, and airport-to-city-center time is less than a half-hour.

By Rail

Fast and frequent trains link Barcelona with the rest of Spain and with European cities. Barcelona has two main railroad stations, Sants, terminus for most national and international trains, and Estación de Francia. In the early 1990s, if all goes according to plan, Barcelona will be linked with the rest of Europe by a new, high-speed rail network based on the highly successful French TGV system.

▷ Money

Currency: peseta. International code: ESP. For other details, see Money section of Madrid entry.

▷ Language

All Barcelonans speak Castilian Spanish. About three-quarters of the people are fluent speakers of their *llengua mare* (mother tongue), Catalán, but fewer write it. Catalán is closer to the French dialect spoken in Provence than it is to Spanish. Since 1983, all schools have been required by law to teach Catalán, some of them as a first language. Even university professors are forced to give some of their lectures in the local language. Many of them feel that Catalonia would be doing more for its future if children were required to learn English or French rather than a language spoken only in that province and a few other areas such as Valencia and Alicante, the Balearic islands, the city of Alghero in Sardinia, and Andorra. Most businesspeople speak English and/or French.

▷ Communications

Country code: 34. City code: 3. See Madrid entry for additional information on Spanish telecommunications.

▷ Getting To Know the City

Central Barcelona is laid out with mathematical precision into magnificently wide avenues. The longest, Avenida Diagonál, runs across the city for 10 kilometers (6.25 miles). Other main thoroughfares are the Gran Via de les Cortes Catalanes, the Paseo de Grácia, and the lively Ramblas, which run from the Plaza Catalunya right down to the port. The Plaza is the hub of city life, with a clock and beds of flowers in the center and main offices of major banks and shipping companies and large department stores on the periphery.

The Ramblas is a tree-lined boulevard with a wide strip in the center for strolling (the *paseo*), meeting friends, and buying flowers or birds from the colorful stalls. On either side of the Ramblas are two of Barcelona's less geometrical areas: the Barrio Chino, the red-light district; and the Barrio Gothico, site of the Generálitat (legislative assembly) and city hall, which face each other across the wide and open Placa San Jaume. Leading from the square is a maze of narrow streets, some dating from the 1200s and 1300s. Particularly in the Barrio Chino, don't carry much money and guard carefully what you do.

▷ Spotlight ◁

Architect Antonio Gaudí i Cornet (1852–1926) created startling new forms that paralleled the stylistic development of *art nouveau*. Many of his buildings resemble sculptures, among them blocks of apartments, stores, and offices and—above all—his Expiatory Church of the Holy Family, the Sagrada Familia. Technologically adventurous as well as aesthetically audacious, Gaudí is in the Cataláns' cultural pantheon. He died after being hit by a streetcar, and though he left no plans, work on the church continues in the architectural tradition he bequeathed.

▷ Moving Around

Barcelona provides good, fast transportation by bus, subway, and taxi. Taxis are cheap by western European standards and can be hailed in the street, found at cab stands, or ordered by radio. Cabs show a green light when they're seeking passengers.

▷ Hotels

Barcelona regularly plays host to trade fairs and conferences and is gearing up for the 1992 Summer Olympics. Little wonder, then, that it has

14,000 hotel rooms and is building more. Many hotels go for the tourist trade; we've chosen those that make life as easy and efficient as possible for business travelers.

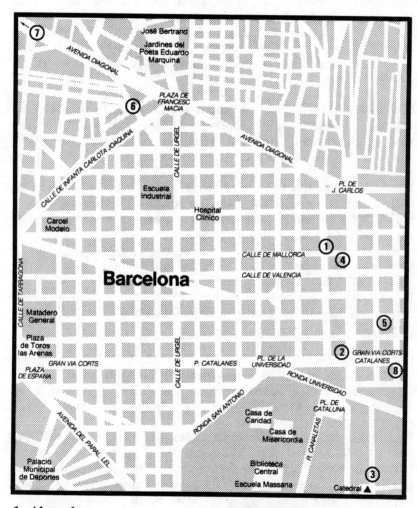

1. **Alexandra**
2. **Avenida Palace**
3. **Colón**
4. **Condes de Barcelona**

5. **Diplomatic**
6. **Gran Hotel Sarria Sol**
7. **Princesa Sophia**
8. **Ritz**

Alexandra, 251 Mallorca. Tel.: 215-3052. Telex: 51531. Fax: 216-0606. Rooms/suites: 75. Small, new, luxurious, central. Specializes in business meetings for up to 30 people.

Avenida Palace, 605-607 Gran Via de las Cortes Catalanes. Tel.: 301-9600. Telex: 54734. Fax: 318-1234. Rooms/suites: 229. A classic, built in 1952, recently renovated, and highly popular with its business clientele. First-class seminar and conference facilities.

Colón, 7 Avenida de la Catedral. Tel.: 301-1404. Telex: 52654. Fax: 317-2915. Rooms/suites: 161. Traditional comfort and elegance, but with full air-conditioning.

Condes de Barcelona, 75 Paseo Grácia. Tel.: 215-0616. Telex: 51531. Fax: 216-0835. Rooms/suites: 102. Opened in 1986 in a turn-of-the-century building, the Condes is an architectural gem. Noteworthy: friendliness and helpfulness of the staff.

Diplomatic, 122 Calle Pau Claris. Tel.: 317-3100. Telex: 54701. Fax: 318-6531. Rooms/suites: 213. All rooms are soundproofed—a considerable plus in noisy Barcelona—and there are five bars, a good restaurant, a swimming pool, and conference rooms.

Gran Hotel Sarria Sol, 50 Avenida Sarria. Tel.: 410-6060. Telex: 51638. Fax: 321-5179. Rooms/suites: 353. One of the city's tallest buildings (21 floors); very much a hotel for businesspeople, close to many bank and corporate headquarters. Meeting facilities for up to 600 people. Excellent restaurant.

Princesa Sofia, 4 Placa Pius XII. Tel.: 330-7111. Telex: 51032. Fax: 330-7621. Rooms/suites: 445. Modern, efficient, packed with extras; business center, pool, gymnasium, and so on. Barcelona's best? Some people say so; others say it could be the best anywhere in the world.

Ritz, 668 Gran Via de las Cortes Catalanes. Tel.: 318-5200. Telex: 52739. Fax: 318-0148. Rooms/suites: 208. A great hotel that fell on hard times but is now back to its *fin-de-siècle* standards of service and cuisine, thanks to a big investment and mighty management efforts. An automatic choice for anyone who relishes classic hotels.

▷ Restaurants

Catalán cuisine is both original and deeply influenced by neighboring Provence and by Italy, with which Catalonia has immemorial trade and cultural links. The result is a gourmet's paradise, with hundreds of restaurants offering an encyclopedic choice of national and regional dishes. From those hundreds we have winnowed the best and most authentic. At most, reservations are necessary; at others, they are not required but recommended.

Agut d'Avignon, 3 Calle Trinitar. Tel.: 302-6034. New owners are trying to imprint their own personality on a restaurant founded and run by a colorful character. They're succeeding. Catalán, Basque, and Provençal dishes.

Alt Berlin, 54 Calle Sabino de Arana. Tel.: 339-0166. Solid, filling, and reasonably priced German food. Avoid it in the summer unless you enjoy the sound and sight of jolly German tourists.

Ara Cata, 33 Dr. Ferran. Tel.: 204-1053. A Barcelona landmark that serves Aragonese, Catalán, and classic French dishes. Highly recommended for seasonal foods.

Azulete, 281 Via Agusta. Tel.: 203-5943. Elegance in a conservatory in the garden of a mansion in the residential part of the city. The adventurous cuisine leans toward the *nouvelle* end of the gastronomic spectrum.

Botafumeiro, 81 Mayor de Grácia. Tel.: 218-4230. A Galician restaurant named for the huge incense burner in Santiago Cathedral. One of the city's best seafood places. For those in a hurry, there's a bar that serves oysters, prawns, and other dishes, washed down with a glass or two of Galician wine.

Eldorado Petit, 57 Dolors Monserda. Tel.: 204-5506. Many connoisseurs think this is one of the half-dozen best restaurants in Spain. Cuisine is both traditional and *nouvelle*. Try the Palafrugell, a local version of paella colored by squid's ink. Sounds disgusting? Tastes delicious!

▷ Spotlight ◁

Escuela de Restauración y Hostelería, 70 Calle Muntaner. Tel.: 253-2903. Superb value and good food at this hotel and catering school: serious, earnest students practice their new-found skills on guests.

Guria, 95 Casanova. Tel.: 253-6325. We've been going to this traditional Basque restaurant for more than a quarter of a century, and it's as good as ever. Beautiful waitresses wear severe black and white uniforms; many marry well. Meanwhile, they serve superb Basque food. One of Barcelona's best.

La Rosa del Desierto, 7 Placa Narcis Oller. Tel.: 237-4590. Excellent *couscous* and *tajine* at this Moroccan restaurant, one of few in the city commemorating Moorish occupation.

▷ *Spotlight* ◁

La Barceloneta is near the port and beach and is the home of dozens of simple, family-run restaurants that serve fresh fish and other home-cooked local dishes. Value-for-money ratio is extraordinary. Don't expect to wine and dine in less than two hours.

Among the best in this distinctive neighborhood are Can Majo, 23 Almirante Baluerta (tel.: 319-5028) and Casa Costa, 124 Calle Baluarte (tel.: 319-5028). Both serve fish, shellfish, crustacea, and rice dishes.

Los Caracoles, 14 Calle Escudellers. Tel.: 302-3185. Here in a narrow street in the city's Gothic quarter is a crowded and lively restaurant. The way in is through the kitchen, where the cooks' cleanliness and devotion to duty are on display. Specialties include paella, roast suckling pig, and fish soups and stews.

Neichel, 16 bis Avenida Pedralbel. Tel.: 203-8408. The owner is French; so is the cuisine, which is of the *haute* rather than *nouvelle* variety. One of the largest cheese selections in Spain. Desserts are also famous. Barcelona's best? Some say so.

Siete Puertas, 14 Paseo Isabel. Tel.: 319-3033. The decor of this brasserie-style restaurant has changed little since its doors first opened in 1836. Famous and recommended is the *zarzuela,* a traditional shellfish and fish stew in a rich, dark sauce.

▷ *Spotlight* ◁

Zarzuela is a Castilian word with several meanings. It's the name of a royal palace in Madrid, a generic term for operettas, and a general description for seafood stews. Which came first is the subject of a lexicographers' lively

debate, though it seems unlikely that a royal palace was ever a seafood stew. Or perhaps *zarzuelas* both gastronomic and musical originated in the royal palace? Divining the answer will keep etymologists busy for many a year.

Senyor Parallada, 37 Plateria. Tel.: 315-4010. Owned by a member of the Siete Puertas ("Seven Doors") restaurant family. His hobby is studying old recipes and culinary methods. Consequently, the restaurant offers highly original and very Catalán cuisine. Popular with politicians, writers, and practitioners of the visual arts.

Taj Mahal, 89 Calle de Londres. Tel.: 322-3233. The first and probably best Indian restaurant in Barcelona. Northern Indian cuisine, which is fairly mild, with good *tandoori*. If you want it strong, just ask.

Tramonti, 501 Diagonla. Tel.: 250-1535. More than "just another Italian restaurant," with pastas and pizzas and a Ligurian emphasis; wines to match.

Via Veneto, 10 Calle Ganduxer. Tel.: 200-7024. Smart, even trendy; frequented by senior civil servants and visiting businesspeople. Catalán, French, and international dishes.

▷ Tipping

The bar or restaurant check almost always includes the tip and taxes. But, of course, staff appreciate a little extra. Taxi drivers don't expect a tip, but you'll make somebody's day if you add between 5 and 10 percent to the metered fare.

▷ Doing Business

After what they saw as the repression of the long Franco era, Cataláns seized eagerly the autonomy the democratic Spanish government offered in 1979. Under this, the Catalán Generálitat has jurisdiction over economic and physical planning, public works, health, education, civil law, tourism, research and development, and the media, and has partial control of regional savings banks. Madrid retains responsibility for foreign relations, defense, monetary policy, police, criminal law, and customs and excise. Even that wide-ranging autonomy isn't enough to satisfy some nationalists. The Catalán separatist group Terra Lliure (Free Land) will settle for nothing less than independence and tries spasmodically to prove its point and advance its cause with bombings and shootings; it has little popular support.

Catalán businesspeople are more practical. They are pragmatic, careful with their money, and drive a hard bargain. The Office of Foreign Trade and Investment bends over backwards to encourage foreign investment and has an entire Japanese-speaking department to woo Japanese companies. Among those wooed and wed: Nissan, Matsushita, Sony, Sanyo, Mitsubishi, Honda, Yamaha, Hitachi, Kao Corp., and Yoshida.

What attracts Japanese and other foreign investors? Tax and other financial incentives, to be sure, but mainly Catalonia's skilled labor force, Spain's membership in the European Community, and fast, efficient deliveries from and to the rest of the continent. Barcelona is also a bustling financial center with its own stock exchange—but, ironically, no bank of its own. Cataláns, it seems, are good traders and managers, but not born commercial bankers. We stress the word "commercial" because Catalán savings banks hold no less than a third of all Spain's savings deposits, which suggests that Cataláns are thrifty savers and less-than-adventurous lenders.

▷ Spotlight ◁

A *statue of Christopher Columbus* stands atop a pillar on the harbor of Barcelona, pointing an arm over the Mediterranean. Below him is a replica of the *Santa Maria*, the ship in which he sailed to discover America. Columbus was from Italy, not from Catalonia; and the *Santa Maria* didn't sail from Barcelona. No matter. The statue is a reminder that Spain is still a major maritime trading force.

Although the province has three other major ports—Tarragona, Palomos, and Sant Feliu de Guixoles—it is Barcelona that serves Catalán industries. Spain's busiest port offers one of the largest container terminals in the Mediterranean, regular links to more than a hundred countries, 17 kilometers (10 miles) of wharves, more than 300 cranes, and specialized equipment to handle natural gas, petroleum products, grain, cement, bulk commodities, and frozen goods. More than 50 million tons of freight pass through the port each year.

▷ Useful Phone Numbers

Emergencies		Local Information	
Fire	080	Airport	370-1011/325-5829
Police		City hall	318-2525
National	091	Radio taxis	330-0850
Municipal	092	Tourism	250-2594
		Trains	319-2791/322-4142

Generálitat de Catalunya (Autonomous Regional Government)

CIDEM (business development
   center)   215-8582/215-7178
Commerce department 237-9045
Economy and finance 302-5020
Industry and energy 237-3645

Chambers of Commerce

Council of Chambers of Commerce	319-2412
Barcelona	219-1300
Metropolitan and regional	
Manresa	872-4222
Sabadell	725-4911
Terrassa	784-4911
Foreign chambers	
American	321-8195
Arab-African	317-9783
Argentine	237-5320
Belgian	237-9464
Brazilian	322-1021
British	317-3220
Chilean	230-9055
Dutch	217-5985
French	317-6738
German (West)	218-8262
Indian	318-8411
Israeli	230-8442
Italian	317-5999
Mexican	215-4560
Moroccan	302-4982
Nigerian	301-4700
Paraguayan	317-3000

Portuguese	318-5200
Venezuelan	212-0450

Consulates

Argentina	317-5882
Austria	236-3544
Belgium	318-9899
Bolivia	250-7324
Brazil	301-4900
Canada	209-0634
Chile	318-8586
Colombia	254-0248
Costa Rica	245-7405
Cuba	318-1936
Denmark	310-2091
Ecuador	209-5731
El Salvador	209-3658
Egypt	212-8550
Finland	318-1838
France	209-6722
Gabon	228-3207
Germany (West)	218-4750
Greece	246-2290
Guatemala	330-6559
Honduras	317-7580
India	201-8755
Indonesia	317-7531
Ireland	330-9652
Italy	215-1654
Japan	310-2097
Jordan	254-4850
Lebanon	209-0399
Liberia	213-8150
Luxembourg	237-3701
Madagascar	309-1258
Malaysia	315-0011

Morocco	215-3470	Thailand	317-9593
Mexico	321-4400	Tunisia	231-5379
Monaco	209-7588	United Kingdom	322-2151
Nepal	314-7309	United States	319-9550
Netherlands	217-3358	Uruguay	317-4183
Nicaragua	209-7278	Venezuela	215-0112
Norway	215-0094		
Pakistan	257-4230		
Panama	253-6911		
Paraguay	215-0526		
Peru	230-1242		
Philippines	318-8436		
Portugal	318-8150		
Senegal	200-9722		
South Africa	318-0797		
Sweden	218-1566		
Switzerland	330-9211		

Airlines

Air France	215-2870
British Airways (toll free)	900-177777
Iberia (Spain)	325-1202
Lufthansa German Airlines	379-3766
Pan Am World Airways	301-7249
SAS Scandinavian Airlines	215-3244
Swissair	215-9100

▷ Shopping

Barcelona is Spain's design capital—designs for everything from fashion to furniture, crystal to jewelry, and kitchenware to kitsch. Paseo de Grácia is the main shopping street; most of the elegant and expensive boutiques and larger stores are located there. Many others cluster in the neighborhood. Among the emporia that more than merit a visit:

Adolfo Dominguez, 89 Paseo de Grácia and 245 Calle Valencia. Twin homes of Dominguez's "rumpled look," famous (or notorious) from Toronto to Tokyo and back again. Definitely not for the executive climbing the corporate ladder, but possibly for his or her son or daughter.

Artespana, 75 Rambla de Catalunya. Part of the state-owned chain selling a high-quality range of handicrafts, ranging in size and cost from an earthenware plate to a dining-room table.

Ediciones de Diseno, 291 Calle Mallorca. Top quality and original furniture displayed in a very attractive modern building designed by Domenech i Muntaner, one of the store's owners.

Groc, 100 Rambla de Catalunya. Clothing by top designer Toni Miro and jewelry by equally top Chelo Sastre. His abstract, geometric shapes make popular, unusual, and easy-to-carry souvenirs.

▷ Spotlight ◁

Lace. Barcelona is home of a long tradition of lacemaking. The best examples are in small, specialized stores. Among them: *Caroline Curriu i Caral*, 2 Calle Duquesa d'Orleans; *Montserrat Coll*, 48 Calle Pelayo, second floor; and *Rose Abello i Francoli*, 2 Pasatge Torastre, second floor.

Many of the city's mercantile deals are done in street markets. Try these—and don't hesitate to haggle:

Encants, Plaza de las Glorias Catalanas. Mondays, Wednesdays, Fridays, and Saturdays. Objects of all kinds, from antiques to junk.

Mercadillos de Anticuarios de la Catedral. Thursday mornings in the square fronting the cathedral. Many gems, few bargains.

Mercado Dominical de San Antonio. Sunday mornings in the San Antonio market, corner of the calles Urgel and Tamarit. Huge selection of old magazines, newspapers, postcards, cigarette cards, books.

Mercado Filatelico y Numasmatico de la Plaza Real. Sunday mornings. Stamp and coin collectors swap and buy everything from individual items to albums and complete collections. *Note:* Colonnaded Plaza Real bars and cafés serve cheap snacks (*tapas*) and beer or wine. Stroll, select, snack, enjoy.

▷ Spotlight ◁

Mercado de la Bougeria. Anyone who thinks that cucumbers grow their own plastic wrappers or that corn on the cob is born on a polyethylene tray should sneak a look at this place along Rambla de San Jose. This wonderful fish, fruit, and vegetable market has been selling to housewives and restaurateurs since 1217. Gastronomically orgasmic.

▷ After Hours

Flashy or fleshy, disco or decorous, sedate or seductive—Barcelona has it all, and more. It's a seaport city, and when sailors roll ashore, they tend to roister. Residents, on the other hand, love opera and concerts.

The Liceo Theater on the Ramblas draws some of the world's best singers, if only because many of them started their careers here. Among them are soprano Montserrat Caballe and tenor José Carreras. The Palau de la Musica, a *fin-de-siècle* building, offers both good concerts and acoustics.

Vaudeville is alive and well in Barcelona at *La Scala,* 47 Paseo de San Juan, a vast and polished place. Two other large, gilded, and slightly tarnished homes of light entertainment are *La Belle Epoque,* 246 Calle Muntaner, and *El Molino,* 99 Calle Vial. Dinner comes with the shows, which are large and daring, featuring tall showgirls whose costumes are so skimpy that they shouldn't have cost more than 10 pesetas.

Bars and Discos

So many that they cater to every taste.

Berimbau, 17 Paseo del Born, specializes in exotic cocktails, mainly Latin American; live music.

Ideal Cocktail Bar, 89 Calle Aribau, is another cocktail haven. Order from the extensive list or ask one of the skilled bartenders to shake you up a special to your own specifications.

The Up and Down 179 Calle Numancia, is a rather formal disco: suit and tie are required on the upper floor.

Otto Zutz, 13 Calle Lincoln, rations smiles at the door. Hard to get in unless the gatekeepers think you will fit in. Once in, expect a dressy and fashionable crowd of youngish people.

Studio 54, 54 Paralelo, named for its Manhattan look-alike, is high-tech and noisy. It also has a swimming pool, and some people cool off by plunging in fully clad.

▷ Sights and Sounds

Barcelona itself is a series of sights and sounds that you discover by walking and looking. Museums cover everything from postage stamps to funeral carriages. Among the best of them—but check opening hours with your hotel concierge:

Fundacion Joan Miró, Parque de Montjuic. Barcelona architect José Luis Sert designed this gallery to house the works of Catalán painter Joan Miró, who is one of this century's greatest abstract or nonrepresentational artists.

Museo de Carrozas Funebres, 2 Sancha de Avila. Dozens of hearses and funeral carriages of all sizes and periods. A morbid museum? Not really. More a social history of death and people's commemoration of it.

Nao de Santa Maria del Mar, Muelle de la Paz. An exact reconstruction of one of Christopher Columbus' three ships.

Museo Picasso, 15 Calle Montcada. Catalonia would like to claim Pablo P. as one of its own, but can't: he was born in Malaga. However, he did spend much of his early life in Barcelona, and this unique collection includes early and little-known works.

▷ Out of Town

Golf

Although Spain has nurtured great golfers of the likes of Severiano Ballestoros and José Maria Olzabel, the game hasn't yet gained mass support. Even so, many good courses are within easy reach of Barcelona. Among them:

Club de Golf Llanvaneras, San Andres de Llanveras. Tel.: 792-6050. Nine holes; 34 kilometers (21.25 miles) from the city.

Club de Golf de Pals, Playa de Pals, Gerona. Tel.: (972) 636006. Eighteen holes; 40 kilometers (25 miles) from the city.

Real Club de Golf "el Prat," El Prat de Llobregat. Tel.: 379-0278. Championship, 27-hole course. Excellent country club as well.

Club de Golf Cugat, San Cugat del Valles. Tel.: 674-3958. An 18-holer 20 kilometers (12.5 miles) from Barcelona.

Club de Golf Terramar, Sitges. Tel.: 894-0580. Close to a popular coastal resort 37 kilometers (23 miles) from the city; 18 holes.

Club de Golf Vallromanas, Montornes del Valles. Tel.: 568-0362. Fifteen kilometers (9.5 miles) from the city; 18 holes.

Coastal Beauty

Barcelona is the gateway to ruggedly beautiful scenery and coasts. In the high season (July and August), tourists almost outnumber natives, highways are crowded, and beaches smell of barbecued bodies. North of Barcelona, along the coast road leading to France, is the *Costa Brava* ("Wild Coast"), much of it spoiled by mass tourism, though some isolated beauty spots remain, particularly inland. *San Feliu de Guixols,* 105 kilometers (66 miles) north, has memorable views from its famous cliffs. Close by at S'Agaro is the *Hostal de la Gavina* [Tel.: (3472) 321100]. Each of the 144 rooms and suites is decorated differently, has its own terrace, and looks out on parkland or the sea. The exemplary standards of food, service, and comfort combine to make this one of the world's greatest resort hotels. We've been visiting it since 1964 and cannot recommend it too highly.

BELFAST

Forget the Flak Jacket, but Bring the Business

Population: 318,600 (1984). Capital and largest city of Northern Ireland (population: 1.58 million). *Location*: in the east of Northern Ireland, on shores of Belfast Lough, a bay at the mouth of the River Lagan. *Economy*: aerospace, automotive components, banking and insurance, brewing and distilling, electronics, printing and publishing, shipbuilding, textiles and textile machinery, tobacco products, tourism. Northern Ireland is part of the United Kingdom (Great Britain), which is a member of the European Community. Britain is also a member of the Organization for Economic Cooperation and Development (OECD) and a signatory to the General Agreement on Tariffs and Trade (GATT). Northern Ireland is ruled directly from London, but a number of government departments operate with a high degree of autonomy.

▷ Background Briefing

There's no getting away from it: Northern Ireland has a terrible image abroad. For 20 years, prime-time television news and front-page headlines have portrayed Belfast as a Beirut without sun, Northern Ireland as a province stretched on the rack of terrorism. What's the reality? Very different. To be sure, terrorists strike too often, the British army is there in force, and communal divisions are strong. But everyday life is surprisingly normal. Visitors who expect high drama and hair-raising stories of violence return home disappointed—or relieved. A flak jacket is just excess baggage.

Violence is sporadic rather than continuous, and confined largely to west Belfast, some distance from the city's banking and business center.

Violence reached its peak in the early 1970s, when much of the central city was deserted after 10:00 p.m. Since then, the so-called "Golden Mile" of Great Victoria Street, Shaftesbury Square, and Botanic Avenue has blossomed with new restaurants and refurbished theaters. Some half-billion dollars of new construction is under way or planned.

As recently as 1980, barely 20 restaurants were to be found in the city, and none was in the center. Today there are more than 100. Fast-rising rents for city-center shops and offices confirm the revival, and so does the Castle Court shopping mall near St. Anne's Cathedral, a $105-million project.

Most Belfast residents read with a mixture of bafflement and anger reports in the popular press that portray them and their city as living in a state of siege. The packed crowds of shoppers on Saturdays and on the late-opening nights of Tuesdays and Thursdays don't feel besieged and are not.

Foreign investors' confidence is returning, spurred by generous European Community and government incentives for new businesses. Throughout the troubles that erupted in the early 1970s, it's been almost business as usual in Northern Ireland. Most of the problems have been caused by Europe's general economic malaise rather than sectarian violence in the province.

▷ *Spotlight* ◁

Understanding the conflict. What are the reasons for communal conflict? Ask any three Irishmen, and you're likely to get five answers. The short one is that the six counties of the province are inhabited by peoples of different ethnic and religious origins. About 60 percent are nominally Protestant, most of them of Scottish ancestry; about 40 percent are nominally Roman Catholic. The conflict is more tribal than religious, though; more about differing political and cultural loyalties.

These have ancient roots. Britain occupied Ireland more than 700 years ago and at various times "planted" the country with English and Scottish settlers. The purpose, in the view of most of the indigenous Irish, was to provide the British with a permanently loyal garrison. In 1922, the British government granted the south of Ireland—today's Republic of 26 counties—a political halfway house known as the Irish Free State. The six counties of the north remained British. The immediate result was a civil war in the south between those who supported the compromise and those who opposed it bitterly. The south became a republic only in 1949.

By and large, the Protestants in the north think of themselves as British—that is, they owe their allegiance to the Crown. By and large, the Catholics believe that the two Irelands, north and south, should be united politically, or at least should be in some kind of confederation. Even so, most people in Northern Ireland live together amicably—or, rather, work together, for the two groups tend to cluster in their own neighborhoods, even if they work in the same plant or office. A tiny percentage, perhaps a tenth on each side of the sectarian divide, believe that they advance their respective causes with violence or support for it. A key difference is, of course, that the so-called Nationalists are advocating revolutionary change; the so-called Loyalists, those who regard the link with Britain as indissoluble, are fighting to retain the *status quo*.

Most people agree on one thing:

democracy doesn't flower out of the barrel of a gun. And democracy is what all but a tiny minority want. Extremists operate upon both sides of the divide. The Provisional Irish Republican Army, or Provos, claims that it is in the honorable tradition of the IRA that helped to liberate the south. In fact, many of the Provos are Marxists who would like to see a one-party state in all of Ireland.

Just to ravel a political skein already tangled enough, the constitution of the Republic calls for the reunification of north and south. However, the major political parties in the south appear no more keen to take on the problems of the north than the Protestants there are willing to be integrated into the Republic.

▷ Arriving

By Air

Belfast has two airports. The main one, the International (formerly Aldersgrove), has a simple and logical layout, ample parking space, and is only 20 minutes from the city by cab or 30 minutes by bus. It's quietly efficient, and though security is strict, it is not obtrusive. There are frequent direct or connecting flights from and to all major European cities and some lesser ones, including Aberdeen, Birmingham, Blackpool, Bristol, Cardiff, Exeter, Glasgow, Leeds/Bradford, Liverpool, Manchester, Newcastle-upon-Tyne and Teeside.

The Executive Jet Center at International has its own customs and immigration facilities, lounge, and crew rest area. The airport's business center is in three connected, soundproofed, air-conditioned rooms, and it offers full secretarial services, photocopying, and good telecoms. There's also a wide range of sophisticated audiovisual equipment; the main conference room seats up to 120 people and serves lunch, dinner, and snacks.

Belfast Harbor Airport, only a few minutes from the city center, is used mainly by commuter airlines serving Scotland, the Isle of Man, and the midlands of England.

By Sea

The main link with Britain is through Larne, a half-hour drive north of Belfast. Sealink and P & O European ferries operate short sea crossings to Scotland; Sealink times its arrival and departure times to link with British Rail trains from Stranraer to Glasgow and London. Time at sea is 2¼ to 2½ hours.

Using a terminal close to the city, Belfast Ferries operates a daily service to and from Liverpool. The voyage takes nine hours, but for passengers whose destination is in the midlands of England, this is faster than taking the ferry from Larne to Scotland and a train the rest of the way. The terminal in Liverpool is only a 15-minute bus or cab ride to the city's main railroad station, Lime Street.

By Rail

Most businesspeople use the train for trips from Belfast to Dublin. Reasons: the highway is crowded; Dublin is a terrible city for parking; and young Dubliners aren't too fussy about whose car they drive home in (Northern Ireland plates a specialty). The fastest train trips last about 2¼ hours. It's worth going first class: there's more space and comfort, and meals are served at your seat. Another advantage of the train is being able to enjoy the superb scenery.

▷ *Spotlight* ◁

Cab customs. Don't be surprised if the cabdriver at the airport, railroad station, or harbor suggests you share a ride with other passengers. It cuts the cost and speeds the journey. Northern Ireland is a friendly country, whatever its reputation.

▷ Money

Currency: the British pound. International code: GBP (for further details, see London entry). The Republic of Ireland's *punt* is worth less than the British pound. If you're coming from the republic, change your punts at a bank rather than hotel.

▷ Language

English—but often with a strong accent. There are subtle differences in the idioms and accents of Nationalists and Loyalists. For example, the city and county of Londonderry are simply Derry to most Nationalists.

Loyalists are likely to call Northern Ireland Ulster, but Nationalists argue that the province today excludes part of the ancient province of that name. They tend to call Northern Ireland the Six Counties.

▷ Communications

County code: 44. City code: 232. Quality is generally good. But remember that Belfast is on an island, with limited telecommunications connections to the British mainland and to the rest of Europe. As in all other cities, check with your hotel on the markup it charges on telecoms. This can be substantial, and you will save money if your office calls you.

▷ Getting To Know the City

Belfast was built in a hurry, its population rising from 50,000 to 350,000 in the second half of the 1880s. Few people claim that the result is beautiful—although the city's location, on the shores of Belfast Lough, is spectacularly attractive. There are many landmark buildings, including St. Anne's Cathedral and Queen's University, but on the outskirts there are also miles of nineteenth-century row houses, drearily alike, and huge, modern apartment blocks that suggest the architects' primary talent was for the design of breakfast-cereal boxes. Some of these are now being torn down.

Business Belfast is fairly compact, mainly concentrated in or close to Donegall Square, where stands the impressive City Hall. Most of what you need can be found within this district.

▷ Moving Around

Visitors new to the city may find the bus routes confusing at first; a better bet is to use taxis, which are cheap and plentiful. The so-called black cabs, similar to London's, mainly serve the Catholic and Protestant areas of north and west Belfast as cheap and flexible alternatives to buses, but don't expect to have the cab to yourself. Sharing rides is common.

▷ *Spotlight* ◁

Safety afoot. While the city is safe to explore on foot during the day, it's best to avoid side streets after dark. If you want an evening stroll, stay with the crowds on Great Victoria Street or Shaftesbury Square. If you're in a restaurant or pub late, ask the staff to call a cab for you.

▷ Hotels

There never was much choice of good hotels in Belfast's business district. Most of the best hostelries are now in the suburbs, which doesn't mean a long trek, for Belfast is small. Because tourism has languished, all hotels set lures for the business traveler.

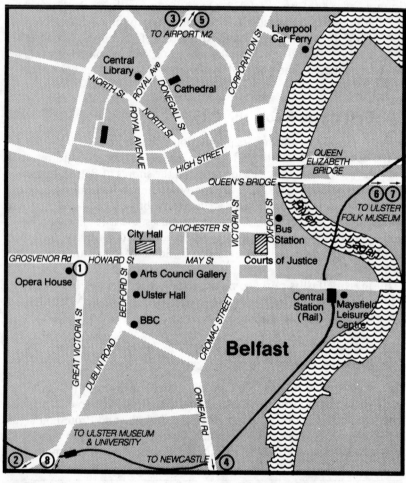

1. **Europa**	5. **Dunadry Inn**
2. **Conway**	6. **La Mon House**
3. **Culloden**	7. **Stormont Hotel**
4. **Drumkeen**	8. **Wellington Park**

Conway, Dunmurry. Tel.: 612101. Telex: 74281. Fax: 626546. Rooms/ suites: 78. Set among woods and well-kept gardens; delightful.

Culloden, Holywood. Tel.: (02317) 5223. Telex: 74617. Fax: 6777. Rooms/suites: 70. A bishop's former residence. Quiet and elegant with manicured grounds; one of Belfast's best restaurants.

Drumkeen, Upper Galwally. Tel.: 491321. Telex: 692949. Fax: 692949. Rooms/suites: 28. At the top end of Ormeau Road, within easy reach of the city center.

Dunadry Inn, Dunadry, Muckamore. Tel.: (08494) 32474. Telex: 747245. Fax: (08494) 333 89. Rooms/suites: 64. Beautifully appointed; handy for the airport.

Europa, Great Victoria Street. Tel.: 327000. Telex: 77491. Fax: 227800. Rooms/suites: 200. The great survivor, frequently bombed, never closed. Under new owners and a new manager (from the renowned Hong Kong Mandarin), it has invested some $10 million to restore itself to former grandeur and add a convention center.

La Mon House, The Mills, 41 Gransha Road, Comber, County Down. Tel.: 448631. Fax: 448026. Rooms/suites: 30. About 20 minutes' drive south of the city, in a pleasant rural setting. Indoor heated pool, Jacuzzi, sauna, solarium, gymnasium.

Stormont Hotel, Upper Newtownards Road. Tel.: 658621. Telex: 748198. Fax: 480240. Rooms/suites: 67. Directly across the road from the Northern Ireland Parliament House, the Stormont has been improved recently and has an excellent restaurant.

Wellington Park, Malone Road. Tel.: 381111. Telex: 747052. Fax: 0232 66547. Rooms/suites: 50. About 1.5 kilometers (1 mile) from the center, in the university area. Many hearty—and noisy—young people in the bars at night.

▷ Restaurants

There are many places to choose from, but do not expect gastronomy of the highest order. Expect instead high-quality meat, game, fish, and vegetables in large quantities, and friendly service. Here's the pick of the crop within the city limits:

Ashoka Indian Restaurant, 363 Lisburn Road. Tel: 660362.

La Belle Epoque, Great Victoria Street. Tel.: 323244.

Moghul Indian Restaurant, Great Victoria Street. Tel.: 243727/226677.

Oscar's, Bedford Street. Tel.: 247757.

Restaurant 44, Bedford Street. Tel.: 244844.

Saints and Scholars, University Street. Tel.: 325137.

Strand Restaurant, Stranmillis Road. Tel.: 682266.

Thompson's, Arthur Street. Tel.: 323762.

Vico's Italian Restaurant, Brunswick Street. Tel.: 321447.

The Welcome Inn (Mr. Wong's), Stranmillis Road. Tel.: 681359.

▷ Spotlight ◁

Pubs. There are pubs for every taste: for quiet contemplation, for measured conversation, for "a jar and a crack" (a drink and stimulating talk). Some pubs, it must be said, are better avoided by strangers, since they are closely associated with one faction or another. You'll be safe and happy enough in any of the following.

Start with the city's most famous and most photographed watering-hole, the magnificent *Crown Bar*, across from the Europa Hotel. *The Roost* in Church Lane (closes at 8:00 p.m. Monday through Thursday), *Madden's* in Smithfield, and the *Beaten Docket*, next to the Crown Bar, are all within walking distance of each other if you fancy a pub crawl.

Slightly further out, on the Dublin Road, is the *Elbow Inn*, popular with yuppies, some of whom also favor *Bob Cratchit's* on the Lisburn Road, part of the Russell Court development. Around the university area are several rather boisterous establishments; definitely not for a quiet night out. Among them are *Lavery's* and *The Elms*, on University Road; the *Botanic Inn* and the *Eglantine* ("*the Bot and the Eg*"), which face each other across Malone Road. Marginally less frenetic is *The Fly* in Lower Crescent. At the corner of Lower Crescent and Botanic Avenue is the staider *Regency*. Opposite the Regency is the *Empire*, where they show silent movies on a big screen at one end of the bar; if they haven't got a silent, they turn the sound off. For live music, go to the *Errigle Inn* on Ormeau Road or the *Rotterdam* in Pilot Street.

▷ Doing Business

Terrorism makes the headlines. Manufacturing delivers the goods—and the jobs. To be sure, the unemployment rate in 1988 was close to 17 percent—almost twice the United Kingdom's national average—but many sectors of the economy were performing well, with a record number of new jobs created.

Even so, gross domestic product (GDP) per capita is only about three-quarters of the United Kingdom average of $11,765, making Northern Ireland the poorest region. The figures would be far worse if the British government did not pour money into the province. No less than 65 percent of the GDP is accounted for by public spending, compared with less than 40 percent for Britain as a whole. To support this level, Northern Ireland receives a block grant from Britain of about $2.8 billion a year. Of the 98,000 manufacturing jobs that still remain after the recession of the 1970s and early 1980s, almost 90,000 are supported directly or indirectly by the state at a cost of about $66 a week for each worker.

The two largest manufacturing employers in Belfast are Short Brothers, the international aerospace company, and shipbuilders Harland and Wolff. Harland and Wolff's future is uncertain. To compete, the company would need subsidies approaching 40 percent of turnover, but EC rules limit them to 28 percent. Just to keep the yards open and 4,000 people employed (down from 8,000 as recently as 10 years ago) costs taxpayers about $100 million a year. But the government in London cannot be as ruthless with the Belfast yard as it has been with other state-owned chronic money-losers: the political and economic consequences of closure are almost incalculable.

Short Brothers is in a happier and healthier state, with the number of workers up by a thousand or so to more than 7,000 over the past five years. The company makes the highly successful Shorts 360 commuter aircraft as well as a number of derivatives for civil and military use; manufactures the Tucano jet trainer; holds lucrative airframe contracts with Boeing; and has substantial orders for its missiles division. In 1989, the government sold Short's to private-sector buyers.

With Harland and Wolff in possibly terminal trouble, Northern Ireland badly needs new jobs. Much of the responsibility for enticing firms to the province lies with the Industrial Development Board (IDB) and Local Enterprise Development Unit (LEDU), the small-business agency. Between them, they offer remarkably generous help, including 40 percent research and development grants; up to 50 percent of factory, machinery, and equipment costs; and total temporary freedom from rates (real-estate taxes). Some critics argue, though, that the IDB and other agencies pamper manufacturers while neglecting, relatively, the service industries.

The IDB has been fighting an uphill battle. Who wants to locate in a province riven by sectarian strife? The answer is a surprising number. Among them: Du Pont, Hughes Tool, Ford, Hyster, Michelin, United Technologies, General Motors, Coca-Cola, McDonnell Douglas Information Systems, and AVX Corporation, a U.S. company that is a pioneer in development and application of multilayer ceramic and hybrid surface-mount capacitators.

The presence of so many high-technology companies belies another legend about Northern Ireland: that it's stuck in traditional, heavy industries. Certainly, the largest single sectoral employer of labor is textiles and clothing, with 28,000 people on the payroll, but this is no low-wage, low-value-added business. Good design and intensive investment in new plant and equipment are helping to restore Northern Ireland to its role as a world leader in fine linens.

Undoubtedly, generous grants and tax holidays have attracted many foreign companies to Northern Ireland, but magnets just as powerful are the province's hard-working labor force and its access to the European Community. And though it's not the kind of thing that would be given formal weight in a company's location planning, the province's superb countryside and sports facilities do influence executive thinking. World-class sea and freshwater fishing and 72 golf courses, as well as riding and shooting, are more-or-less on the doorstep.

Armed with such quality-of-life statistics, the IDB has targeted the Far East as a potentially rich source of new investors and has offices in Hong Kong and Tokyo. In Europe, the IDB has a new office in the World Trade Center in Amsterdam, has doubled its presence in Düsseldorf, and runs a business center in London. Staff there report having made more than 500 high-level contacts in 1988 and 40 presentations to influential delegations. Also on the IDB's prospects list: the Nordic countries.

The IDB and the Belfast city authorities will do much to plan your trip. Quickest and easiest point of contact is through the British consulate or embassy in your city.

▷ Useful Phone Numbers

Emergencies

Ambulance, fire, and police 999

Local Information

Airport:

Belfast Harbor	457745
International	(08494) 22888

Buses 220011

Ferries

Belfast Ferries (to and from England)	320364
P & O European Ferries (to and from Scotland)	(0574) 73616
Sealink (to and from Scotland)	327525

| Tourist office | 246609/231221 |
| Trains | 230310/230671 |

Business Information

Belfast City Hall (public relations)	320202
European Community	240708
Industrial Development Board	233233
Local Enterprise Development Unit	242582

Airlines

Air Ecosse (Scotland)	(08494) 22888
British Airways	230150
British Midland	241188
Danair (Denmark)	(08494) 22049
Jersey European Airways	233425
Loganair (Scotland)	247979
Manx Airlines	232061
NLM Dutch Airlines	793486

▷ **Shopping**

Irish linen, Tyrone crystal, Belleek pottery, handwoven tweeds, pure woolen sweaters, lace, silverware, and small decorative objects made from polished granite are among the temptations to be found in Belfast stores. In the center, stores are open from 9:00 a.m. until 5:30 p.m., with late-night shopping until 9:30 p.m. on Tuesdays and Thursdays. Local products are best buys. Consult the *Guide to Northern Ireland's Crafts and Craftsmen* (published by Local Enterprise Development Unit, 17 Linenhall Street, Belfast BT2 8BS. Tel.: 242582).

▷ *Spotlight* ◁

Recommended plant tours. Nowhere is very far from anywhere else in Northern Ireland, so you can see how it's made before you buy it—and then buy it on the spot.

Check out the following:

Augher Creamery, 3 Crossowen Road, Augher, County Tyrone. Tel.: (06625) 48214. Starts with the milk, ends with the cheesemaking.

Belleek Pottery, Belleek, County Fermanagh. Tel.: (036565) 501. Fine, well-crafted porcelain.

Old Bushmills Distillery, Bushmills, County Antrim. Tel.: (02657) 31521. From water to very fine whiskey.

Tyrone Crystal, Dungannon, County Fermanagh. Tel.: (08687) 25335. Mouth-blown and handcut crystal.

▷ **After Hours**

Nightlife is scarce. Some pubs are open until 1:00 a.m. on certain nights and many hotels open their discos on weekends. Among the pubs and discos are *Pip's* at the Elbow Inn, on the Dublin Road; the *King's Head,* a pleasant pub opposite the King's Hall in Balmoral; and the *Pink Flamingo* at the Regency, corner of Lower Crescent and Botanic Avenue. The *Dome* and the *Limelight* are on Ormeau Avenue. Down Amelia Street, next to the Crown Bar, is *Shadows.* Around the corner in Brunswick Street, near Vico's Italian Restaurant, is *Stringfellow's.*

▷ **Sights and Sounds**

Stand by City Hall and look along Howard Street or Wellington Place: green hillsides are in your view. Change your perspective, and there are a shipyard's huge gantry cranes, proof that the salt waters of Belfast Lough are only a few hundred yards or meters away. Ponder now the paradox: Belfast is a divided city—divided by sectarianism, even tribalism—yet remains one of the liveliest cities in Europe, with a rich cultural legacy. Queen's University has a worldwide reputation for excellence; the far-newer University of Ulster has two of its four campuses in Belfast.

The *Grand Opera House,* next door to the Europa on Royal Avenue, is one of Britain's most beautiful theaters, a Victorian extravaganza that is highly gilded and topped by a painted ceiling with ornate cornices. Look here for everything from grand opera to vaudeville. Still on the serious side is *Ulster Hall,* with its huge Hammond organ and the Ulster Orchestra, which is rapidly making a good name for itself among the musically literate. The *Group, Arts* and *Lyric Theaters* present both professional and amateur productions, the latter often acclaimed more than the former.

For film buffs, the choice is limited—and that's putting it mildly. There are only three movie houses: on Great Victoria Street near the Europa, on Ormeau Road, and on Holywood Road (that's pronounced Hollywood). Each has three screens, in theory giving a choice of nine films, right? Wrong! For reasons that are obscure, they all show more or less the same three movies. A better bet is the *Queen's Film Theater* on the Queen's University campus. It's down a lane, University Square mews, alongside Saints and Scholars Restaurant on University Street; or you can enter the mews from Botanic Avenue. Call 244857 for program details.

Among the city's outstanding attractions:

Belfast Public Library, Royal Avenue. Early printed books, photographs, maps.

Belfast Zoo, Antrim Road. Small but interesting collection.

Harbor Office, Corporation Square. Paintings, sculptures, stained glass. Reserve your place in a tour by calling 234422, extension 205 (administrative officer).

Linen Hall Library, 17 Donegall Square. Founded in 1788 "to improve the mind and excite a spirit of general enquiry." It does.

Public Record Office, Balmoral Avenue. Search here for your Ulster roots (Ronald Reagan was one U.S. president who found them.) Helpful staff.

Ulster Museum, Stranmills Road (in Botanic Gardens). Records life in Ireland over 9,000 years. Includes recent recoveries of artifacts from Spanish Armada wrecks.

▷ Out of Town

The Giant's Causeway is Northern Ireland's most famous natural sight, a lunar landscape of which the British poet Thomas Thackeray wrote:

> When the world was moulded and
> fashioned out of formless chaos,
> this must have been the bit over
> —a bit of chaos...

The Causeway is a mass of basalt columns packed tightly together, the tops forming stepping-stones leading from the foot of a cliff to the sea. Most of the 40,000 stones are hexagonal, but some have up to eight sides. The tallest are about 13 meters (40 feet) high, and in places the solidified lava is 28 meters (90 feet) thick. Buses from Belfast travel to the site and include a visit to the Old Bushmills Distillery. Check with your hotel concierge or the local tourist authority.

County Fermanagh includes *loughs* (lakes) Erne and Macnean, where many anglers have claimed world records for their catches of trout, salmon, grilse, pike, roach, and char. (Char is an Ice Age ancestor of the trout; look also for trout relatives such as the gillaroo and sonaghan.)

County Tyrone is rich in prehistoric and Celtic remains. Belfast's two main highways lead west, skirting Lough Neagh. Highway M1 will take you to County Tyrone's windswept moors. Look for the thousand or so standing stones that are testaments to the ancient people who lived here. From the 600s to the 1100s, early Christians erected crosses, many of which remain.

▷ **Spotlight** ◁

The **Ulster-American Folk Park** at Camphill, Omagh, grew up around the cottage in which Thomas Mellon was born in 1813. His family took him to the United States when he was five; he became a professor of Latin and law—and a judge, a banker, and a millionaire. His son, Andrew, was a U.S. Treasury Secretary, ambassador to London, and a steel magnate. Mellon money helped to build the Waldorf As-toria Hotel in New York, the Golden Gate Bridge in San Francisco, the locks and gates of the Panama Canal, and the Folk Park at Camphill.

Also in County Tyrone, near the town of Strabane, is the ancestral home of Woodrow Wilson, twenty-eighth President of the United States. Wilson kith and kin will show callers around the house.

Golf

Golf is a passion in Northern Ireland, a passion testified to by the number of courses and links. Among those close to Belfast—none more than a half-hour's drive away—are the following. All rent equipment except those noted.

Balmoral, 518 Lisburn Road. Tel.: 381514. Holes: 18. Bar and meals.

Belvoir Park, 73 Church Road, Newtownbreda. Tel.: 491693/646113. Holes: 18. Bar and meals.

Cliftonville, 44 Westland Road. Tel.: 744158. Holes: 9. Bar; meals in summer.

Dunmurry, 91 Dunmurry Lane. Tel.: 610834. Holes: 18. Bar, snacks, meals; no equipment rental.

Fortwilliam, Downview Avenue. Tel.: 370770. Holes: 18. Bar and meals; no equipment rental.

Gilnashirk, Mann's Corner, Upper Braniel Road, Gilnashirk. Tel.: 448477. Holes: 9. Putting green, practice nets, pool table.

Knock, Summerfield, Dundonald. Tel.: (02318) 3251. Holes: 18.

Knockbracken, Ballymaconaghy Road, Newtownbreda. Tel.: 792108/702811. Holes: 18. Lunch, snacks, evening meals. Floodlit driving range, bowling alley, skiing.

Malone, 240 Upper Malone Road, Dunmurry. Tel.: 612758. Holes: 9 and 18. Bar, snacks, and meals.

Ormeau, 149 Ravenhill Road. Tel.: 641069. Holes: 9. Bar; no equipment rental.

Shandon, 73 Shandon Park. Tel.: 401856. Holes: 18. Bar, meals.

BRUSSELS

Bidding for European Capital Status

Population: Metropolitan area: 1.2 million (estimated). Capital of the Kingdom of Belgium (population: 9.85 million). *Location*: on Senne river, Brabant province, north-central Belgium. *Economy*: banking and financial services, brewing, chemicals, electrical equipment, machinery, textiles, tourism. Administrative and executive headquarters of the European Community and of the North Atlantic Treaty Organization (NATO). Belgium also is a member of the Organization for Economic Cooperation and Development (OECD) and a signatory to the General Agreement on Tariffs and Trade (GATT).

▷ Background Briefing

"Welcome to the Capital of Europe" read signs at Zaventem Airport—in English. Well, Brussels isn't officially Europe's capital, and the widespread use of English in advertisements is an ironic underlining of the divisions that still cleave Europe. Brussels is a French-speaking enclave in the Dutch-speaking province of Brabant, and English has become a kind of compromise language. Most of the frequent changes of government are caused by linguistic hostilities, which are themselves expressions of the tribal and economic rivalries between Belgium's two main language groups. Indeed, it's significant that King Baudouin is King of the Belgians—not of Belgium. He, of course, is fluent in both French and Dutch and in the minority language, German.

In actuality if not by right, Brussels *is* Europe's capital. To be sure, the European Parliament still deliberates in Strasbourg, France—despite the majority's wish to move to Brussels—but for the moment that is more of a talking-shop than a legislature. The European Community's executive powers are vested in the Commission, which sits on the top floors of the Bâtiment Berlaymont in Brussels. The Council of Ministers, which makes the big decisions, usually meets in a building nearby—though treaty obligations force it to move now and then to Luxembourg, just as parliamentary committees often meet in Brussels rather than Strasbourg.

Merely the small capital of a small country a quarter of a century ago, Brussels is now at the center of the world stage, since EC policies and decisions profoundly affect the international financial and trading systems, for better or for worse.

In many ways, though, Brussels remains simply one community in a collection of small towns. There are 19 *communes* (cities and towns) in the province of Brabant, each with its own elected council, and the *burgomaster* (mayor) of Brussels carries no more clout than any other town leader. This lack of pretension has preserved at least some of the city's pleasant diversity, though huge areas of interesting old buildings have fallen to the wrecking ball and the bulldozer as real estate developers have sought to cash in on the European future.

Fortunately for the rest of us, the developers have built too many apartments and offices, so that Brussels remains one of the European capitals where it is easiest and cheapest to find space. And the Bruxellois have retained their sense of humor (often aimed at themselves), their welcome for foreigners, and much of their traditional quality of life. Brussels is a comfortable city, a livable one, with uncounted pubs, bistros, and neighborhood stores where you're recognized on your second visit and considered a regular on your third.

From a business standpoint, Brussels is not just the European Community, either. Exports of goods by the Belgium-Luxembourg Economic Union account for no less than 58 percent of the gross domestic product. Of the 24 OECD countries, only the Netherlands comes close, with 46 percent. Belgium eagerly welcomes foreign investment. Fierce competition between the French-speaking Wallonia region in the south and the Dutch-speaking provinces of Flanders in the north gives the potential investor or business partner two chances instead of one of pulling off a deal with official development agencies. (Wallonia investment: tel. 211-5511 in Brussels or 248-611 in Namur, prefix 81. For Flanders: tel. 218-1210.)

▷ **Arriving**

By Air

Zaventem International Airport, 14 kilometers (8 miles) from the city center, is compact and "user-friendly" but has been coming apart at the seams, with escalators and baggage conveyor-belts breaking down too often. The airport authorities started a big, expensive face-lift and overhaul in 1988, and a new terminal is on the way. Private-sector management has replaced the previous bureaucracy, and the avowed intention is to make Zaventem at least as good as Amsterdam's gleaming, efficient Schiphol.

Buses, fast trains, and taxis link Zaventem with the city center.

▷ Spotlight ◁

The Sabena-Eurocity business-class special links Zaventem with London's City Airport (in the newly developed Docklands area) using the quiet, short takeoff and landing Dash-7 aircraft. Check in ten minutes before flights; they serve superb breakfasts. You'll gain at least half an hour in center-to-center journey time.

By Rail

The two main railroad stations are Midi (South) and Nord (North); both are large, cavernous, and shabby. However, fast and comfortable trains run to and from them to the rest of Belgium and to most parts of Europe. Highly recommended for shorter journeys are the Inter-City expresses: door-to-door, they're often faster than flights. Change at the two main stations for the Gare Centrale.

▷ Money

The standard unit of currency is the Belgian franc. International symbol: BEF. Bank notes come in denominations of 50, 100, 500, 1,000, and 5,000 francs. *Bureaux de change* are located at the airport, railroad stations, and most bank branches. On weekends, you can change money at Paul Laloy, 6 Rue de la Montagne, open Saturdays from 10:00 a.m. to 6:00 p.m. and Sundays (June through September) from 11:00 a.m. to 1:00 p.m.

▷ Language

French in Brussels itself, Dutch (Flemish) in most outlying communes. Street signs and store windows include both languages. Note that there are many *Belgicismes*—usages different from those of "proper" French. For example, the number 70, *soixante-dix* in France, is *septante* in Belgian French. English is very widely spoken.

▷ Communications

Among the best. Country code: 33. City code: 2. You don't use the city code within the metropolitan area. Phone-book instructions and the Yellow Pages' index are in English and German as well as French and Dutch.

▷ Getting To Know the City

Brussels has no clearly defined center—no equivalent of the Champs-Elysées in Paris, Piccadilly Circus in London, or the Plaza de Mayor in Madrid, from which streets spoke out as from a hub (even if the spokes are usually far from straight). For most visitors, the handiest reference point is the Grand' Place, with its magnificent Hôtel de Ville (city hall) and gilded medieval and renaissance buildings. Around the Grand' Place is a maze of narrow streets, many of them now reserved for pedestrians, with a delightfully bewildering selection of shops and restaurants. In this section of the city, too, is the Théâtre Royal de la Monnaie, a small, elegant opera house with performances so good that it draws audiences from as far away as Paris. Close by is the *bourse* (stock exchange), housed in a pillared, ornate building.

Neither does Brussels have a compact business center. Bank and corporate offices are strung out along the Avenue des Arts, the Avenue de la Loi, the Avenue Louise, and the Rue Royale, which leads from the grand park fronting the Royal Palace. As the American banks cut back, the Japanese arrive in force. New corporate buildings have sprung up around the Gare du Nord and, increasingly, companies are moving to air-conditioned offices set in landscaped gardens in the suburbs. But nowhere is very far from anywhere else: "a bunch of suburbs in search of a city" Brussels may be, but it's no Los Angeles, to which that quip was first applied.

Berlaymont, the European Commission's home; Charlemagne, where the Council of Ministers meets; and offices of the "permreps" (member-countries' permanent representatives to the EC) are all close to the Parc Cinquantenaire which, with its victory arch, celebrates the restoration of Belgium's independence in 1830. Close to this cluster of buildings are the offices of the many trade associations and other lobbying groups that seek to influence the Eurocrats as they formulate policies and recommendations for the Council of Ministers.

Brussels is host city also to NATO; its headquarters are on the main highway to the airport.

▷ Moving Around

Brussels has good bus, subway, and streetcar systems: fast, clean, and relatively inexpensive. Don't be surprised when streetcars plunge into tunnels, because some double as subway trains. Taxis are plentiful, but not cheap; however, the metered fare includes the tip.

▷ *Spotlight* ◁

Car rental. If you rent a car, be careful. Drivers are aggressive and usually have priority when entering a street from the right; some don't even bother to check whether there's any oncoming traffic. Many a tombstone should be engraved with the epitaph, "He entered from the right, he was in the right, but. . . ."

▷ Hotels

Too many rooms chasing too few guests, that's the Brussels story. And competition is increasing, thanks to an ambitious building program. As a result, rooms are available at most times of the year, and prices can be negotiated. Says the manager of one luxury hotel, "Anyone who pays the rack (full) rate is out of his mind. For anything more than a night, except at the busiest time, we're always willing to bargain, particularly with a business guest who is likely to return. Weekends, we usually charge half the posted rate." His advice: always ask about so-called corporate tariffs. The result could be a cut in the cost of a room or upgrading to a suite at no extra cost. All the hotels listed are out to capture a business clientele. Most offer secretarial and translation services as well as TV reception from several countries, including satellite programs, a channel from Paris, and two British stations. Channel flipping is great fun, if you have time for it.

Amigo, 1-3 Rue de l'Amigo. Tel.: 511-5910. Telex: 21618. Fax: 513-5277. Rooms/suites: 194. Looks old but in fact dates from the 1950s. Calm, hospitable, with impeccable service. Just off the Grand' Place's tourist bustle, but a world away in atmosphere.

Bedford, 135 Rue du Midi. Tel.: 512-7840. Telex: 24059. Fax: 514-1759. Rooms/suites: 275. A modern grand hotel downtown near the bourse. Good, unpretentious, but pleasant bar and restaurant.

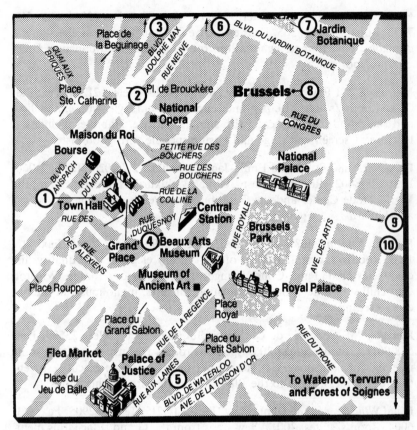

1. Hotel Amigo
2. Hotel Metropole
3. World Trade Center
4. Hotel Royal Windsor
5. Hotel Hilton
6. Hotel Sheraton
7. Hotel Scandic Crown
8. Hotel Pullman Astoria
9. EC Building
10. Hotel Europa

City Garden, 11 Rue Joseph. Tel.: 230-0945. Telex: 63570. Fax: 230-6437. Rooms/suites: 100. A few minutes from the EC's Berlaymont. Comfortable rooms have kitchens and can be used as service apartments.

Europa, 107 Rue de la Loi. Tel.: 230-1333. Telex: 25121. Fax: 230-3682. Rooms/suites: 240. This Inter-Continental Forum hotel is across the street from European Community headquarters. Popular with senior politicians, diplomats, business executives, and journalists.

Hilton, 38 Boulevard de Waterloo. Tel.: 513-8877. Telex: 22744. Fax: 513-7233. Rooms/suites: 365. Four executive floors have express checkin and checkout; club lounge, health club, rooftop dining and dancing. Great ground-floor bar.

Metropole, 31 Place de Brouckere. Tel.: 217-2300. Telex: 21234. Fax: 218-0220. Rooms/suites: 410. A grand hotel in the old style, with chandeliers and fine woods; famous café with summer terrace. Habitués include celebrities of screen and stage and businesspeople with good taste.

President, 180 Boulevard Emile-Jacqmain. Tel.: 217-2020. Telex: 21066. Fax: 218-8402. Rooms/suites: 308. New, luxurious hotel next to the World Trade Center and the Gare du Nord. Penthouse gym with sauna and billiards.

Pullman Astoria, 103 Rue Royale. Tel.: 217-6290. Telex: 25040. Fax: 217-1150. Rooms/suites: 125. Turn-of-the-century elegance and quality discreetly restored. Palm Court lounge; quiet, luxurious rooms. Winston Churchill stayed here. Sunday-morning concerts; piano music in the bar every evening.

Ramada, 38 Chaussée de Charleroi. Tel.: 539-3000. Telex: 25539. Fax: 538-9014. Rooms/suites: 206. Spacious rooms recently renovated, some reserved for nonsmokers. A special welcome for female executives. Central for business; close to the Place Stephanie with its chic shops.

Royal Windsor, 5 Rue Duquesnoy. Tel.: 511-4215. Telex: 62905. Fax: 511-6004. Rooms/suites: 300. A few steps from the Grand' Place, this member of the Warwick hotel group has refurbished all its rooms. Personal computers available. Duke of Wellington pub, Crocodile Club disco.

Scandic Crown, 250 Rue Royale. Tel.: 219-4640/217-1234. Telex: 61871. Fax: 217-8444. Rooms/suites: 315. Ultra-modern, large rooms; skilled, pleasant service; good bar. On a noisy street, so try for a room at the back.

Sheraton, 3 Place Rogier. Tel.: 219-3400. Telex: 26887. Fax: 218-6618. Rooms/suites: 406. Rooms are large, comfortable, blessedly quiet, and fully air-conditioned. The Sheraton Towers (189 rooms and suites) is a hotel within the hotel for executives; fast checkin/checkout. Good coffee-shop; health club, indoor heated pool.

Airport/Outskirts

Brussels Airport Sheraton, National Airport. Zaventem. Tel.: 725-1000. Telex: 27085. Fax: 725-1155. Rooms: 298. A brand new hotel convenient for NATO headquarters. Two restaurants, piano bar. Six meeting rooms, eight function rooms.

Holiday Inn, 7 Holidaystraat. Tel.: 720-5865. Telex: 24285. Fax: 720-4145. Well-established favorite 5 kilometers (3 miles) from airport; free shuttle service. Large beds, work-desks. Indoor pool, tennis.

▷ Restaurants

Brussels offers more choice for its size than any other European city, from *haute cuisine* through *brasseries,* to notably good small and neighborhood restaurants serving everything from home cooking to food from exotic, faraway places. Belgian specialties abound: seafood, particularly mussels, which come in a dozen or more ways; *faisan à la Brabanconne* (pheasant with braised Brussels chicory), *lapin à la biére* (rabbit cooked in beer); and, in a short spring season, *jets d'houblon* (buds of hops in a rich creamy sauce with poached eggs: delicious). There are 300 Belgian beers, ranging from very light and pale to very heavy and dark. As for Belgian *pommes frites* (French fries, if you'll excuse the confusion), they're the best in the world.

▷ Spotlight ◁

Frites. Belgians have a passion for the humble *pomme frite* (French fry). Understandably. This is how they're cooked—and why they're unforgettably good: First, of course, choose your potato. Second, peel. Third, put it through a machine that slices it into potential *frites*. Fourth, put the raw *frites* in a bowl and run cold water over them gently for at least an hour; this removes most of the starches. Fifth, dry in a cloth. Sixth, place in a wire basket, and immerse it in the hot vegetable fat of an electric *friteuse.* The dial shows the correct temperature for this first cooking phase. Seventh, when the *frites* are beginning to brown, raise the basket so that it drips into the fat, and turn up the temperature. Eighth, replace the basket in the fat and cook until the *frites* are nicely browned. Ninth, again raise the basket and let the fat drip from the *frites* until they are almost dry. Tenth, serve. The eleventh and final step comes the next day: weigh yourself. But don't think about that the night before!

Amigo, Hotel Amigo. Tel.: 511-5910. Exceptionally fine hotel restaurant serving traditional cuisine; good for business meals because it's quiet and the tables are large and spaced well apart.

Aux Armes de Bruxelles, 13 Rue des Bouchers. Tel.: 511-2118. Business-people, politicos, and a wide range of Brussels' most dedicated gourmands gather in this colorful brasserie in the old town. Try the *moules au vin blanc* and the thick Waterzooi soup with chicken.

Bruneau, 73-75 Avenue Broustin, Ganshoren. Tel.: 427-6978. Away from the center, but worth the journey. *Patron* Jean-Pierre Bruneau is an inventive master of gastronomy, the service is friendly and informed, and the Louis XVI decor is luxurious. Eclectic wine list.

Comme Chez Soi, 2 Place Rouppe. Tel.: 512-2921. Homey decor, with the kitchen in full view. Bistro food elevated to world status, thanks to the combined talents of Pierre and Marie-Therèse Wynants. Try the ham or salmon mousse, the *filet du sole au Riesling,* the wild duck in season, and the pigeon stuffed with truffles.

Francois, 2 Quai des Briques. Tel.: 511-6089. After more than half a century, this fish restaurant (with fishmongery attached) is still doing a great job. Large choice of mussel dishes: champagne, curry, white wine, and many others.

Hugo's, Scandic Crown Hotel. Tel.: 219-4640. Sober, restful decor; cloistral calm makes this a good place for business entertaining. Fish a specialty, but steaks are also excellent: large, either plain broiled or with a choice of sauces.

La Maison du Cygne, 9 Grand' Place. Tel.: 511-8244. Classic elegance, attention to detail, care of guests: a place in which to savor the atmosphere as well as the food and wines. The menu stresses seasonal foods, such as wild boar, venison, game birds, and hare (try the *rable,* or saddle). Oysters so fresh that they wince at a drop of lemon juice.

L'Ecailler du Palais Royal, 18 Rue Bodenbroek. Tel.: 512-8751. Green-aproned waiters serve with suitable reverence fruits of the sea that are among the best—possibly *the* best—in Brussels. Choice: lobster soufflé and grilled turbot with Sancerre butter.

Les Comtes de Flandres, Hotel Sheraton. Tel.: 219-3400. Within the impersonality of a very large, modern hotel, a restaurant of character. Cuisine is light, tasty, with ingredients allowed to speak for themselves. Service cannot be faulted.

L'Oasis, 9 Place Marie-Josée. Tel.: 648-4545. A gastronomic temple with an international reputation that recently changed chefs. The new one (actually the previous one's assistant) is on his mettle to show what he can do—which is much.

Palais Royal, Pullman Astoria Hotel. Tel.: 217-6290. Small, luxurious: solid-silver tableware. Sauces are light and complement rather than smother the dishes. Waiters seem to know what you want before you do. Game when in season (wild boar, pheasant, partridge); good fish and steaks year-around.

Taverne du Passage, 20 Galerie de la Reine. Tel.: 512-3731. Bourgeois Brussels at its best, opening from a nineteenth-century shopping arcade. The Taverne spends its customers' money on food rather than decor, so that it doesn't look like much. A hangout for politicians and bankers who like its understated comfort and extensive wine cellar.

Villa Lorraine, 75 Avenue Vivier d'Oie. Tel.: 374-3163. Without doubt one of the best kitchens in Belgium—and equally without doubt the most beautiful setting of any restaurant in Brussels, in gardens with trees, shrubs, and abundant flowers. Definitely for the expense-account set and the independently wealthy.

▷ Tipping

Bar and restaurant checks and taxi fares include tips, but leave small change.

▷ Doing Business

The welcome mats are out—in the plural, because the Brussels, Wallonia, and Flanders regions compete for foreign investment. Their officials, and those of the Belgian government itself, are usually approachable and friendly, and virtually all are fluent in English.

Many and good are the sources of information. The American Chamber of Commerce (50 Avenue des Arts, B-1040 Brussels. Tel.: 513-6770) publishes the best guide, *Doing Business in Belgium*. At BEF 950 to nonmembers, it's a bargain. Many of the top business consultants and tax specialists are among the chamber members. Its monthly luncheon with guest speaker is a good place at which to meet expatriate executives in the Belgian know.

There are plenty of these. Brussels claims to be the headquarters of no fewer than 841 international institutions and organizations.

Plant Location International (Industrial Research Park, B-1120 Brussels. Tel.: 268-0030. Telex: 25127) is headed by renowned investment adviser Marcel de Meirleir and has a huge data bank.

Comark Europe (27 Chaussée de Charleroi, B-1050 Brussels. Tel.: 538-9114) focuses on public purchasing and other "buried" opportunities. Many U.S. states have offices in Brussels and offer good commercial information.

Groupe Bruxelles Lambert (24 Avenue Marnix, B-1000 Brussels. Tel.: 517-2111) publishes a comprehensive free guide to business.

Belgian industry has special entrée to the Soviet Union and the rest of Comecon (the East bloc's equivalent of the European Community) through joint trading companies. Best first contact: Belgian Office for Foreign Trade, 162 Boulevard Emile, B-1000. Tel.: 219-4450. Fax: 217-6123.

If you're thinking of settling in Brussels, or stationing an executive there, *The Bulletin* is indispensable. Published in English, this long-established magazine-format weekly covers local and expatriate affairs in sprightly style, and in its classified advertisements you will find apartments, houses, babysitters, cars, garage sales, and much else. The magazine's monthly business supplement, *Prospects,* is also useful. Both are published by Ackroyd Publications, 329 Avenue Molière, B-1060 Brussels. Tel.: 343-9909. Telex: 65049.

What about entertaining your business contacts? An invitation to lunch seldom goes amiss. Both the Bruxellois and most expatriates who have lived in the city for any time have developed a hearty appetite for good food and welcome someone else's offer to pick up the tab for it.

▷ *Spotlight* ◁

Clubs. Captains of industry, blue-bloods, EC commissioners, Eurocrats, business and banking executives, and diplomats often meet at private and semiprivate clubs. Visitors and would-be residents should check fees and sponsorship before showing up at the door. The most influential clubs are:

Cercle des Nations, 25 Avenue Franklin Roosevelt. Tel.: 649-8393. Close to the university; very cosmopolitan, very "in."

Cercle Gaulois, Rue de la Loi. Tel.: 511-6750. Very much an "establish-ment" club. Some people think it old hat, others say it's more powerful than ever.

Club Européen de Val Duchesse, Chateau Sainte-Anne, Rue de Vieux Mouln. Tel.: 660-2900. Country club (but a quarter-hour from the city center) with tennis and pool.

Club Ommegang, Maison des Cygnes, Grand' Place. Tel.: 511-8244. The place for drinks with Belgian aristocrats (one or two on the board of directors is sometimes a good idea).

▷ Useful Phone Numbers

Emergencies

Ambulance	424-2329
Car rescue/police	901
Fire	900
Standby doctor	479-1818
Standby dentist	426-1026

Local Information

Flight information	720-7167
Foreign telegrams	986
Taxis	242-2222
	512-3123
Saturday currency exchange	511-7217
Tourist office	513-8940
Tourist office, airport	722-3000

Chambers of Commerce

American	513-6770
Belgium-Africa	512-4100
Belgium-Canada	511-5227
Belgium-Germany	218-5040
Belgium-Greece	647-3495
Belgium-Italy	230-1123
British	219-0788
Brussels	648-5002
Dutch	219-1174
Portuguese	647-7846
Spanish	230-2240
Swiss	217-5543

Commercial Organizations

Belgian Business Federation	511-5880
Brussels Business Federation	219-3223
Cement Industry	649-9850
Clothing Federation	230-8890
Construction Industry	771-6108
Metalworking, electro-mechanical industries	513-8634
Steel Federation	513-3820
Textiles (Febeltex)	230-9330
Woodworking Federation	217-6465

Consulates/Embassies

Algeria	343-5078
Angola	344-4986
Argentina	647-7812
Australia	231-0500
Austria	649-9170
Bangladesh	640-5500
Bolivia	217-3554
Brazil	640-2015
Canada	735-6040
Chile	648-5881
Colombia	649-5679
Czechoslovakia	647-5898
Denmark	648-2525
Egypt	345-5253
Finland	648-8484
France	512-1715
Gabon	343-0055
Germany (East)	734-9100
Germany (West)	770-5830
Ghana	649-0163
Greece	648-1730

Hungary	343-6786	Tunisia	771-7394
India	640-9140	United Arab Emirates	640-6000
Indonesia	771-2014	United Kingdom	217-9000
Iran	762-3745	United States	513-3830
Iraq	374-5992	Venezuela	649-0417
Ireland	513-6633	Vietnam	524-5063
Israel	374-9089	Yugoslavia	647-2941
Italy	649-9700	Zaire	513-6610
Japan	513-9200	Zambia	771-2110
Jordan	640-7755	Zimbabwe	230-8551
Kenya	230-3065		
Kuwait	647-7950		
Lebanon	649-9460		
Libya	649-2112		
Luxembourg	733-9977		
Malawi	217-4370		
Malaysia	762-6767		
Mexico	648-2671		
Morocco	647-3452		
Mozambique	736-2632		
Netherlands	230-3020		
New Zealand	512-1040		
Nigeria	762-9831		
Norway	230-7865		
Pakistan	673-8007		
Peru	733-3319		
Poland	733-7748		
Portugal	539-3691		
Saudi Arabia	649-5725		
Senegal	672-9051		
Singapore	660-3098		
Soviet Union	374-3406		
Sri Lanka	230-4890		
Sweden	649-2158		
Switzerland	230-6145		
Tanzania	640-6500		
Thailand	640-6810		

Commission of the European Community 235-1111

U.S. States Offices

Note: Prefix (03) indicates Antwerp office.

Arkansas	649-6024
Georgia	647-7825
Illinois	512-0105
Maryland	647-5367
Michigan	511-0732
Mississippi	380-4554
Ohio	513-0752
Pennsylvania	513-7796
Rhode Island	(03) 233-6021
South Carolina	640-5325
Texas	(03) 235-3767
Virginia	648-6179

U.S. Port Authorities

Delaware River Port	(03) 234-3960
Illinois (Port of Chicago)	512-0105
Maryland/Baltimore	648-9390
Virginia	648-8072

Airlines

Aeroflot Soviet Airlines	218-6046
Aer Lingus (Ireland)	537-2410
Aerolineas Argentinas	513-4050
Air Afrique	217-0080
Air France	219-3810
Air UK	720-7150
Alitalia	513-8808
Austrian Airlines	513-7500
British Airways	217-6000
El Al Israel Airlines	513-6564
Finnair	513-5369
Gulf Air	647-4730
Iberia (Spain)	512-1631
Japan Air Lines/JAL	640-8580
KLM Royal Dutch Airlines	720-7150
LOT Polish Airlines	217-6509
Lufthansa German Airlines	212-0922
Luxair	640-3452
Nouvelles Frontières	513-7748
Olympic Airways	649-8158
Pakistan International Airlines	511-5777
Pan Am World Airways	751-8195
Ryanair (Ireland)	647-3535
Sabena Belgian World Airlines	511-9030
SAS Scandinavian Airlines	720-5976
Saudi Arabian Airlines	218-2313
Singapore Airlines	649-9900
South African Airways	512-3137
Swissair	219-0341
Thai Airways	538-8285
Turk Hava Yollari	512-6781
UTA (France)	217-0080
Varig (Brazil)	512-5007
Zaire Airlines	513-1919
Zambia Airways	512-0586

▷ Shopping

You think shopping malls are new, the product of twentieth-century sophistication? Visit Brussels. Glassed-over, spacious, their shopfronts elegant, arcades date from the middle of the 1800s. The most famous are the *Galerie Royale Saint-Hubert* and the *Galerie de la Reine,* both close to the Grand' Place; both have inspired architects, developers, and urban planners around the world. On cold, rainy days—and many days are cold and rainy—those and other arcades are welcome cover from the weather.

Stores and boutiques bulge with goodies from all over the world. Distinctively Belgian are pralines and chocolates; the thin, spicy cookies known as *speculoos;* and lace, crystalware, pewter, and diamonds. Brussels is also a storehouse of arms and military memorabilia from many countries. Uptown are the antique shops in and around the Place du Grand Sablon, featuring antiquarian books, crystal, porcelain, swords, and stamps. On the Grand Sablon and streets leading from it are dozens of good, inexpensive restaurants; browse and enjoy.

Moving up the social and price scale, you can discover what Belgian royalty wears by visiting *Valens,* 240 Avenue Louise, and *Louis Mies,* at 261, who dresses Princess Paola, the king's glamorous, Italian-born sister-in-law. The *Galeries Louise,* on the same fashionable avenue, is lined with boutiques that sell both prestigious, world-class branded goods and the imaginative products of local designers. At *Socodiam,* also in the Galerie, there's a large selection of diamonds. Also for gold and diamonds: *Jacques Emmer,* 1b Rue Auguste Orts; and *Joaillerie Schepens,* 35-37 Rue au Beurre, between the Grand' Place and the Bourse.

On the same street, at No. 21, is the *Belgian Lace Manufactory:* close by, at 6 Rue de la Violette, is the *Belgian Lace Museum.* Above it is the atelier of Colette van Steyvoort, a famous designer.

In this downtown area is the city's largest department store, *Inno,* on the Rue Neuve, featuring multilingual hostesses, top brand names, on-the-spot tax-free shopping. The *Anspach Center,* 30-36 Boulevard Anspach, has some 40 boutiques and is a contemporary, imaginative version of the beautiful nineteenth-century arcades.

Brussels is world capital of comic strips, or *bandes dessines,* with specialized shops all over town. One, *Fil à Terre,* 198 Chaussée de Wavre, is open from 10:00 a.m. to 1:00 a.m. In its reading room are some 2,000 comic strips. For English-language books and newspapers, go to *W.H. Smith,* 71-75 Boulevard Adolph Max.

▷ After Hours

Many Bruxellois seem to think that an evening in a crowded tavern is a good way to start—or end—a night on the town. At the *Mort Subite (Sudden Death),* Rue Montagnes-aux-Herbes-Potageres, buxom waitresses serve more than 200 brews to thirsty customers seated at rows of tables. The *Moeder Lambic,* 68 Rue de Savoie, tempts with an even longer list: 1,100 beers, from such places as China and Zaire as well as Europe; but the local cherry beer on tap is the most popular variety. *Au Vieux Spijtigen Duivel,* 621 Chaussée d'Alsemberg, is one of the oldest taverns. Some taverns have dancing. One is *Taverniers,* 12 Rue Paul Devaux.

For a more sedate evening, try some of the hotels that offer dancing with dinner. Among them are the *Pavillon* at the Sheraton (Fridays and Saturdays), and *En Plein Ciel* at the Hilton (every night except Sunday). Saturday is the night at the Ramada's *Garden.*

Cabarets:

Must Club, 10 Rue de Cirque. Tel.: 217-8091. Strippers and other such entertainers.

Show Point, 344 Place Stephanie. Tel.: 647-7530. Beautiful girls circulate; show proper at midnight.

Clubs and Discos:

Crocodile Club, Royal Windsor Hotel. Tel.: 511-4215. One of the best: comfortable, amiable clientele.

Drug Opera, 51 Rue Gretry. Tel.: 218-1837. Tucked away at the top of the building: leather, wood, best for the over-30 crowd.

Funny Horse, 37 Rue de Livourne. Tel.: 538-5910. Classy, as the saying goes; right for all ages.

▷ *Spotlight* ◁

Many an innocent, seeking to rest his weary feet and irrigate his parched throat, has spied what appears to be a nice little watering-hole with a pretty barmaid rather scantily clad. But, it turned out, a drink was only a prelude. We have known brave men who have run into the street and others who... but that's another story. The red-light areas are:

Uptown: Rue de Stassart, Rue des Chevaliers, Rue des Drapiers, Rue de la Grosse Tour, Rue de la Concorde.
Parliament district: Rue du Nord, Rue de l'Association, Rue Croix de Fer, Rue de l'Enseignement, Rue du Moniteur.
Gare du Nord district: Rue du Marche, Rue du Progres, Rue d'Aerschot, Rue du Pont, Rue Verte, Rue Linne, Rue des Plantes.
City center: Rue de Colombier, Rue du Pont-Neuf, Rue du Cirque, Boulevard Jacqmain, Rue des Malines.

Brussels, obviously, is well supplied with female "social workers" determined that male visitors shall not languish for lack of companionship. Some of these "girls behind windows" take credit cards.

▷ Sights and Sounds

The Manneken Pis is the city's oddest sight. It is a small bronze statue (52.5 centimeters or 21 inches high) of a little boy who for at least 300 years has been "urinating" into a basin. He can be found at a street corner close to the Grand' Place, on Rue de l'Etuve. Usually he is naked, but on festive occasions is dressed in one of the 447 costumes donated since the Elector of Bavaria gave the first in 1698.

Antoine Demol, president of the Order of Friends of Manneken Pis, says the little lad is not obscene. Rather, "to the citizens of Brussels he symbolizes resistance to fanaticism—simple civil disobedience." Other ancient fountains nearby illustrate the medieval sense of fun: The Three Virgins spout water from their breasts, and The Spitter is a man with water cascading from his mouth.

All this watery fun apart, Brussels has sights and sounds for almost every taste. Even the Metro (subway) system offers art in the form of murals and sculptures in some stations; find details in a tourist office leaflet. More formal museums and art galleries:

Museum of Classical Art, 3 Rue de la Regence; *Museum of Modern Art,* 1 Place Royale. These adjoining museums provide an impressive vista of art from the 1300s to the present. Highlights are works from the southern Low Countries. The Dutch, German, Italian, and French schools are well represented. Includes works by Rubens, Van Dyck, David, Delacroix, and—closer to our own time—the local Magritte and Delvaux. Closed Mondays. Tel.: 513-9630.

Royal Art and History Museum, 10 Parc du Cinquantenaire, Etterbeek. Exceptionally rich panorama of ancient civilizations. Check opening days. Tel.: 733-9610.

Royal Museum of Central Africa, 13 Leuvensesteenweg, Tervuren. Synthesis of parts of Africa associated with Belgium. Tel.: 767-9384.

Royal Museum of the Army and Military History, 3 Parc du Cinquantenaire. Arms and the men from ancient times until the present, including aircraft dating from 1912.

Autoworld, 11 Esplanade du Cinquantenaire. Some 500 cars, including ones powered by steam and electricity; examples of the automotive arts of such makers as Hispano Suiza, Delahaye, and Rochet Schneider.

Beer Museum (Maison des Brasseurs), 10 Grand' Place. Tel.: 512-2696. The national drink is honored in this seventeenth-century brewery, and you get to drink the stuff, too.

City of Brussels Museum, Maison du Roi, Grand' Place. Tel.: 511-2742. The city's history is laid out here. Check opening times.

Théâtre Royale de la Monnaie, Place de la Monnaie. Tel.: 217-2211. An architectural delight, immaculately maintained, with good acoustics in which resident and visiting opera and ballet companies sound at their best. Guided tours when there are no performances.

For movie buffs: Films are usually shown in the language in which they were made, with French and Dutch subtitles, so you don't have to listen to Laurence Olivier or Eddie Murphy opening and closing their mouths like landed fishes while somebody else—often the same actor—speaks for them in another language.

▷ Spotlight ◁

The Atomium. Brussels has long hankered after a place on the world's center stage. The Atomium, built for the 1958 World's Fair, is a permanent and dramatic reminder of that ambition. Towering 100 meters (335 feet), with nine atoms represented by huge metal balls, the Atomium houses exhibitions linked by escalators and elevators within the connecting metal tubes. A half-hour ride by streetcar or bus from the city center. Next door is the royal residence of Laeken, with beautiful grounds and Japanese and Chinese pavilions. Check hours and days of opening through your hotel concierge.

▷ Out of Town

Brussels is no Paris, no London, when it comes to rush and bustle. Even so, after a few days of meetings and dashing from one appointment to another, most business visitors will need to relax, at least for a few hours. Many, pleasant, and varied are the choices.

The Bois de la Cambre   joins the Forêt de Soignes, which stretches to the suburb of Waterloo: a glorious stretch of forest, glades, lakes, jogging trails, two racetracks, and restaurants. Waterloo itself, 20 kilometers (12 miles) from the center, is where Napoleon fought his last battle; there are museums, historic farms, and other sites and monuments to visit. Every now and then a bloodless, miniature version of the battle is staged.

Golf

Many golf courses are near the capital. The closest (and some say the best) are:

Royal Golf Club de Belgique,   Chateau de Ravenstein, Tervuren. Tel.: 767-5801. The king plays here; consequently chic.

Royal Waterloo Golf Club,   Ohain. Tel.: 633-1850. Belgium's biggest: 450 holes.

For further information, contact the Federation Royale Belge de Golf. Tel.: 633-2496.

▷ *Spotlight* ◁

A *town by any other name*... When you drive out of Brussels, you will find that some towns have vanished—or appear to have. Don't worry, they're still there; they've merely undergone a linguistic change. For example, Anvers in French becomes Antwerpen in Dutch (Antwerp in English); Louvain becomes Leuven; Bruges becomes Brugge (Bruge in English). Brussels it- self is Bruxelles in French and Brussel in Dutch. In the section on places to visit, we've entered cities and towns in English first, with their variants in pa- rentheses. Note also that in Flanders, street names are different: *rue* be- comes *straat* and is a suffix instead of a prefix, as in Hoogstraat. All the places listed are served by good high- ways and fast trains.

Places to Visit

Antwerp (Anvers in French, Antwerpen in Dutch). Distance from Brus- sels: 47 kilometers (28 miles). Belgium's second-largest city, with a 1981 population of 186,000. Seaport, industrial center, diamond-cutting, and dealing. Many Gothic buildings to see; important museums and art col- lections. Birthplace of Peter Paul Rubens. World-famous zoo. Telephone city code: 3.

HOTELS

Alfa Congress, 136 Plantin en Moretuslei. Tel.: 235-3000. Telex: 31959. Fax: 235-5231. Rooms: 66. Modern hotel geared to executive needs.

    Alfa Empire, 31 Appelmanstraat. Tel.: 231-4755. Telex: 33909. Fax: 233-4060. Rooms: 70. Ultra-modern; in the heart of the diamond center.

    Crest, 10 Gerard Legrellelaan. Tel.: 237-2900. Telex: 33843. Fax: 216- 0296. Rooms/suites—Lady Crest: 254. Comfortable tower hotel near the Singel auditoriums and Bouwcentrum Exhibition Center. Excellent res- taurant, the "Land-juwell." Good meeting facilities.

    De Keyser, 66-70 De Keyserlei. Tel.: 234-0135. Telex: 34219. Fax: 232- 3970. Rooms/suites: 117. Flagship of the Alfa chain. Night club and res- taurant.

    Pullman Park, 94 Desguinlei. Tel: 216-4800. Telex: 33368. Fax: 216- 4712. Rooms/suites: 220. Futuristic design. City's most high-tech hotel, next to Singel and Bouwcentrum. This Pullman is an eye-opener.

Rosier, 21-23 Rosier. Tel.: 225-0140. Telex: 33697. Fax: 231-4111. Rooms/suites: 10. Vast, seventeenth-century town house, lovingly and tastefully restored. One of the best restaurants in town.

Switel Antwerpen, 2 Copernicuslaan. Tel.: 231-6780. Telex: 33965. Fax: 233-0290. Rooms/suites: 330. A very deluxe hotel; heated pool.

RESTAURANTS

De Kerselaar, 22 Grote-Pieter-Potstraat. Tel.: 233-5969. Inventive cooks in the kitchen, solicitous waiters at the tables.

t' Fornuis, 24 Reynderstraat. Tel.: 233-6270. A survival of seventeenth-century patrician life. Hard to better anywhere in Belgium.

Laurent, 5 Korte Klarenstraat. Tel.: 233-4485. One of the most comfortable and restful of Antwerp's restaurants.

Sir Anthony Van Dijck, 16 Oude Koornmarkt. Tel.: 231-6170/233-9125. Simple, and for that reason impressive, decor in a seventeenth-century building close to the Cathedral of Our Lady, Belgium's largest church. Stylish, discreet service; cuisine of the grand variety.

Bruge (Bruges/Brugge); 97 kilometers (58 miles) from Brussels. Population: 120,000 (estimated). One of Europe's architectural masterpieces, the virtually unspoiled center and canals are straight out of a Dutch Old Master painting. Beautiful churches and museums. Explore the winding medieval streets on foot. Famous for handmade lace. Telephone city code: 50.

HOTELS

't Bourgoensche Cruyce, 41 Wollestraat. Tel.: 337926. A mere six rooms, all comfortable. Restaurant is rightly noted for fish and seafood; on a canal.

De Orangerie, 10 Kartuizerinnenstraat. Tel.: 341649. Rooms: 19. Magnificent old building; bedroom windows open on a canal. Bar with no restaurant.

Europ Hotel, 18 Augustijnenrei. Tel.: 337975. Telex: 82490. Rooms: 30. Recently renovated, on a canal bank. Bar; no restaurant.

Ter Heyde, 620 Torhoutsesteenweg. Tel.: 383858. Rooms: 5. One of the town's most charming hotels, on the edge of a huge park. Restaurant serves refined, satisfying food with appropriate dignity. Veal cooked in many ways is one of the house's strengths.

Genval. A suburb 20 minutes from Brussels airport: not-so-plain country living. Hotel: *Chateau du Lac,* 87 Avenue du Lac. Tel.: 654-1122.

Small (32 rooms, 5 suites), luxurious; tennis, golf nearby (putting in the grounds). The hotel's *Le Trefle à Quatre* restaurant earns high marks for cuisine and service.

Ghent (Gent/Gand); 56 kilometers (34 miles) from Brussels. Population: 250,000 (estimated). Rather like Bruge, Ghent is a town that exemplifies Flemish life as it was—and to some extent still is. Many medieval buildings, with one vivid reminder of the inhabitants' age-old commercial instincts: the fish market. A town in which to wander and wonder. Make time for the cathedral, the Chateau des Comtes de Flandres, and the Musée des Beaux-Arts, with its unrivaled collection of Flemish paintings. Ghent has become famous for its horticulture industry, and it hosts a huge international flower show in the Flanders Expo Hall every five years. Shows are scheduled for April of 1990 and 1995. Telephone city code: 91.

HOTELS

Alfa Flanders, 121 Koning Albertlaan. Tel.: 220065. Rooms: 43. Central; large rooms; bar and restaurant.
   Gravensteen, 35 Jan Breydelstraat. Tel.: 251150. Rooms: 14. Suites: 3. Close to the imposing Chateau des Comtes de Flandres. Day-making breakfasts, served on the terrace in good weather. No restaurant.

RESTAURANTS

Apicius, 8 Maurice-Maeterlinckstraat. Tel.: 224600. One of Belgium's best tables. People travel from far away to savor the welcome of Nicole Slawinski and the culinary art of her husband, Willy.
   De Drabklok, 30 Drabstraat. Tel.: 251110. Serious food here from the *chef-patron,* Gino Decock, an honors graduate of Comme Chez Soi, Brussels.
   Jan Van Den Bon, 43 Koning Leopold II laan. Tel.: 219085. More Comme Chez Soi influence. First-rate ingredients; light, delicate sauces.

Knokke-Heist, 108 kilometers (65 miles) from Brussels. Population: 65,000 (estimated). This seaside resort is to Brussels as Deauville and Brighton are to Paris and London: smart and popular. Many Brussels businesspeople have vacation and weekend homes there. Long, sandy, but pebbly beach; casino; golf. Telephone city code: 50.

HOTELS

Elysée, 39 Elisabethlaan. Tel.: 611648. Rooms: 5. Suites: 5. Elysian indeed, if you like very small hotels that resemble a private home run by a very hospitable family. Restaurant: Serge Dubois. Wine-list good but limited; few limits to the kitchen's imaginative efforts.

Fairway, 9 Tuinfluiterspad. Tel.: 611-1467. Telex: 81273. Rooms: 9. Suites: 3. Sumptuous decor. On the golf course. Restaurant: Saint-Bernard. One of Belgium's youngest master chefs, Eddy Jonckheere, has made this a magnet for gourmets. His *anguilles* (eels), a Belgian gastronomic passion, are just a sample of delights to follow.

Golf Hotel, 175 Zoutelaan. Tel.: 611614. Telex: 82508. Rooms: 22. Suites: 5. All rooms are exceptionally large; good restaurant; huge terrace.

La Réserve, 160 Elisabethlaan. Tel.: 610606. Telex: 81657. Rooms: 103. Suites: 10. Faces the casino, backs on a lake with waterskiing. Sybaritic comfort; restaurant.

RESTAURANTS

Aquilon, 70 Bayauxlaan. Tel.: 601274. Highly rated: try the *mousse de poissons* (fish pâté) and the *boudin de fruits de mer* (seafood sausage).

Ter Dycken, 137 Kalvekeetdijk. Tel.: 608023. Rustic charm, sophisticated cooking, warm welcome from owners Marc and Jacqueline Boxstael. For those who like desserts, a must.

COPENHAGEN

Wonderful! But What About the Economy?

Population: 640,000 (1986). Metropolitan area: 1.4 million. Capital and leading commercial and industrial center of the Kingdom of Denmark (population 5.12 million). *Location*: east coast of Sjelland (Zealand) Island and Amager Island. *Economy*: banking and financial services, brewing and distilling, ceramics, food processing, marine engineering, maritime services, tourism. Denmark is a member of the European Community (EC) and the Organization for Economic Cooperation and Development (OECD) and is a signatory to the General Agreement on Tariffs and Trade (GATT).

▷ Background Briefing

Most people who have never been there think they know some facts about Copenhagen (*København* in Danish). First, its most famous citizen was Hans Christian Andersen, writer of fairy tales. Second, the statue of *The Little Mermaid,* a character from one of his stories, is a monumental tribute to his genius. Third, Copenhagen is the sex capital of Europe. As we'll discover, there's both truth and falsehood in those legends. What's indubitably true, however, is that Danny Kaye did sing "Wonderful Copenhagen" in a Hollywood musical. But first to more serious matters.

When it was a small fishing village, what is now the city was called *Kopmannaehafn,* or merchants' haven, and that mercantile tradition remains strong. Founded in the mid-1000s, Copenhagen later was harassed by pirates, invaded by the Swedes, twice devastated by fires in the 1700s, and twice bombarded by the British in the 1800s. When Britain's Lord Nelson turned his blind eye to the telescope, in an act that has become an idiom, it was to an order to stop shelling the Danish fleet in Copenhagen harbor.

During World War II, the Germans occupied Denmark, and the Danish king protested against Nazi anti-Semitic measures by wearing the yellow Star of David. That was a simple but brilliant riposte: if everyone pretended to be Jewish, who were the real Jews? While the Nazis pondered that conundrum, most of the real Jews were smuggled out of the country. The Danes may be friendly, but they're also feisty. Their wartime resistance record was almost without parallel in occupied Europe.

They are resilient, too. In the 1970s and early 1980s, the economy was in serious trouble, thanks in part to two oil-price shocks and an international recession. In 1982, the government introduced a comprehensive stabilization program designed to improve competitiveness in world markets, reduce both the external balance-of-payments deficit (and eventually turn it into a surplus) and the budget deficit, and create new jobs.

Most of the targets were met. The budget deficit was turned into a surplus, unemployment fell, and productive capacity expanded rapidly. But the current-account external deficit rose, forcing the government to impose yet stricter measures that cut real GDP by around 1 percent in 1987. The GDP stagnated in 1988 and is forecast to have grown by only .5 percent in 1989.

Even so, Denmark remains one of Europe's richest countries and may be over the hump of its most pressing problems, with the OECD projecting a slowing in the rise of wages and inflation during the rest of this decade. Government and business both emphasize the urgent need to increase exports to the rest of the European Community and to other countries, implying opportunities for importers who want to handle high-quality Danish goods ranging from food through specialized iron and steel products to electronics.

▷ Arriving

By Air

Kastrup International Airport is user-friendly: clean, efficient, pleasant. Buses leave frequently for the city, about 25 minutes away. Taxis cost up to four times more. The duty- and tax-free shopping center (for use on your way out, of course) is elegant and well designed after a two-year construction program and offers both high-grade buys and real savings.

By Rail or Sea

Express rail services connect Copenhagen with other major European cities. Regular ship service runs between the city and ports in England, Norway, Sweden, and West Germany.

▷ Money

The basic unit of currency is the Danish kroner. International code: DKK. The kroner is divided into 100 öre; but as the smallest coin is 5 öre, all prices are rounded up to the nearest 5 öre. Banknotes are beautiful, featuring flora and fauna. Best exchange rates are at banks. Currency exchanges at the airport and Central Railway Station stay open beyond banking hours.

▷ Language

Danish. English is the second language. You'll have quite a job finding somebody who doesn't speak at least some.

▷ Communications

Exemplary. County code: 45. City codes: 1 (inner area) and 2 (outer area). Important note: you have to use the area code even within the city.

▷ Getting To Know the City

For a capital that can trace its origins back to the mid-1000s, Copenhagen doesn't look particularly old. That's the result of the wars and fires we've mentioned already. Even so, many reminders of old Copenhagen remain, most of them in stone. King Christian IV (1577–1648) was a vigorous monarch who came to the throne when he was 11 years old and grew up to have an "edifice complex." Most of Copenhagen's finest old buildings date from his long reign.

Central Copenhagen is compact, bordered to the west by a series of neat, rectangular lakes that are remains of the old defensive moats and to the east and south by inlets from the Øresund seaway. Within this area are the headquarters of many banks and corporations as well as parks; the famous Tivoli Gardens; dozens of museums, art galleries, and churches; and the royal palace of Rosenborg.

But though the center is compact, it is also confusing, a maze of winding streets with few landmarks to guide you. The first thing to do is to buy a street map, study it, and remember to take it with you when you leave your hotel for a day of appointments.

▷ Moving Around

There are extensive and efficient bus and local railroad systems (harbor ferries are mainly for sightseers). For fare purposes, the metropolitan area is divided into zones, which are complicated for the visitor. The simplest and probably cheapest solution is to buy the Copenhagen Card, a pass valid for one, two, or three days. This provides unlimited travel by bus and rail and free admission to no fewer than 36 tourist attractions, including the Tivoli Gardens. You can buy the card at your hotel, railroad stations, travel agencies, or the City Tourist Office, 22 Hans Christian Andersens Boulevard (Tel.: 33.11.13.25).

Taxis are expensive but fast. Tip is included in the fare.

Thousands of people ride bicycles around the city. If you want to emulate them, rent one. Among firms offering them: *Danwheel-Rent-a-Bike,* 3 Colbjornsensgade (Tel.: 31.21.22.27); *Kobenhavans Cyclebors-Velonia,* 157-159 Gothersgade (Tel.: 33.14.07.17); and *Rent a Bicycle and Jet-Cycles,* 71 Istedgade (Tel.: 31.23.17.60). Some railroad stations also rent out bicycles.

▷ Hotels

Copenhagen's hotels are among the best in Scandinavia. We list those that are particularly suitable for the traveling executive because they are in or close to the commercial districts and offer a good range of business-related services. Note that in the low season, November through April, most hotels drop their rates considerably, so bargain. In the high season, May through October, reserve your room well in advance. If you do arrive without a reservation, there are Room Service desks at Kastrup Airport and at the Central Railway Station (Kiosk P). The postal address is Hotelbooking Copenhagen, Hovedbanegarden, DK-1570 Copenhagen V. Tel.: 33.12.28.80.

Admiral, 24 Toldbodgade. Tel.: 33.11.82.82. Telex: 15941. Fax: 33.32.55.42. Rooms/suites: 366. Facing the Nyhavn passengership terminal, the Admiral is an eighteenth-century former granary discreetly rebuilt inside; mysteriously, the sturdy wooden beams harmonize well with the ultramodern decor. French restaurant; nightclub.

d'Angleterre, 34 Kongens Nytorv. Tel.: 33.12.00.95. Telex: 15941. Fax: 33.12.11.18. Rooms/suites: 139. One of Europe's best hotels, with spacious rooms, immaculate service, and good food. There's music in the restaurant, and the sidewalk terrace café is a popular rendezous point year-round. Conference hall.

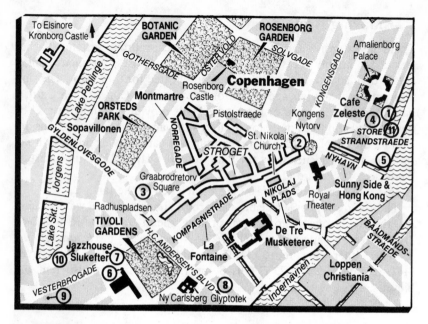

1. **Admiral**
2. **Angleterre**
3. **Kong Frederik**
4. **Neptun**
5. **Nyhavn**
6. **Plaza-Royal Classic**

7. **SAS Royal**
8. **SAS Scandinavia**
9. **Savoy**
10. **Sheraton-Copenhagen**
11. **Sofie Amalie**

Kong Frederik, 25-27 Vester Voldgade. Tel.: 33.12.59.02. Telex: 19702. Fax: 33.93.59.01. Rooms/suites: 109. Good-sized rooms, stylish restaurant, English pub bar.

Neptun, 18 Sankt Annae Plads. Tel.: 33.13.89.00. Telex: 19554. Fax: 33.14.12.50. Rooms: 60. A Best Western hotel close to the royal palace, the harbor, and the opera. No restaurant.

Nyhavn 71. Tel.: 33.11.85.85. Telex: 27558. Fax: 33.93.15.85. Rooms/suites: 82. Handsome and quiet, converted from a 200-year-old warehouse on the harbor. Outstandingly good restaurant.

Plaza-Royal Classic, 4 Bernstoffsgade. Tel.: 33.14.92.62. Telex: 15330. Fax: 33.93.95.62. Rooms/suites: 98. Paintings, antiques, Library Bar, restaurant, conference hall. Adjacent to main railroad station and city-center air terminal.

SAS Royal, 1 Hammerichsgade. Tel.: 33.14.14.12. Telex: 27155. Fax: 33.14.14.21. Rooms/suites: 275. An exemplar of the best in Danish architecture, art, and furniture. The result: luxury. The conference hall is equipped with the latest audiovisual aids. Close to railroad station and air terminal.

SAS Scandinavia, 70 Amager Boulevard. Tel.: 33.11.23.24. Telex: 31330. Fax: 31.57.01.93. Rooms/suites: 543. A huge tower between the airport and the city that faces the old moats.

Savoy, 34 Vesterbrogade. Tel.: 31.31.40.73. Telex: 27215. Fax: 31.31.31.37. Rooms: 119. Another Best Western, this one in the heart of the city, close to the Tivoli Gardens and the air terminal. Breakfast-only restaurant.

Sheraton-Copenhagen, 6 Vester Sogade. Tel.: 33.14.35.35. Telex: 27450. Fax: 33.32.12.23. Rooms/suites: 474. Very much for the business traveler, with fully equipped conference rooms, bar, and restaurant.

Sophie Amalie, 21 Sankt Annae Plads. Tel.: 33.13.34.00. Telex: 15815. Fax: 33.32.55.42. Rooms/suites: 134. No restaurant, so guests use that of the adjoining Admiral. The Sophie Amalie (formerly the Codan) is value for money: recently renovated, quiet, comfortable.

▷ Restaurants

At last count, Copenhagen had some 2,000 restaurants. Clearly, the range is wide, from modest little eateries to temples of *haute cuisine*. Note that by law restaurants must display their menus outside, with prices, and that even the grandest of them usually offer a fixed-price menu. Always reserve.

▷ *Spotlight* ◁

Danish meals and mealtimes — indeed, restaurants throughout Scandinavia—are different from those in the rest of Europe. Breakfast is a hearty repast featuring eggs, cheese, cold meats, herrings prepared in a number of ways, fruit, jams, and a huge variety of breads. Most hotels also serve British or American breakfasts, with porridge, cereals, bacon and eggs, and toast with marmalade. By noon, many business executives are eating at their desks, usually sandwiches with a glass of milk. Is that a second breakfast—or lunch? At home there are often two evening meals, one starting as soon as people get home from work, the other just before bedtime. This last supper, or *natmad*, may be as frugal as coffee and cakes or as lavish as a complete cold buffet. Business dinners can start as early as 7:00 p.m., but that doesn't mean they always end early.

Smørrebrød means "butter-bread," but that's only the foundation—literally. Unlike sandwiches, as they're known elsewhere, those in Scandinavia are piled high with fish, seafood, cold meats, cheeses, sausages, eggs, and salads. There's no bread on top,

which is why they're known as open-faced sandwiches. At lunchtime, many people eat three of these monsters and wash them down with a cold lager. Danes, like other Nordic peoples, are fond of *akvavit*, a clear liquor flavored with caraway seeds, also known in Denmark as *snaps*. It's always consumed with a beer chaser, and the results can be alarming for the novice. To be sure, the Danes are more relaxed about booze than any of their Nordic neighbors, but that doesn't mean they respect guests who show obvious signs of intoxication. If you haven't a head for the hard stuff, stay away from it.

Den Sorte Ravn, 14 Nyhavn. Tel.: 33.13.12.33. Cuisine: Franco-Danish. Sample the seafood and imaginative sauces. Eighteenth-century building.

Els, 3 Store Strandstraede. Tel.: 141341. Nineteenth-century decor, emphasis on fresh food cooked simply.

Fiskekaelderen, 18 Ved Stranden. Tel.: 122011. Seafood only apart from two meat dishes; daily change of menu.

Gilleleje, 10 Nyhavn. Tel.: 125858. Piquant food; decor from the old sailing-ship days.

Joanna's, 11 Laederstraede. Tel.: 145323. Small French-Polish restaurant in city center. Tempting cuisine and charming hostess, Joanna in person.

Kong Hans Kaelder, 6 Vingardstraede. Tel.: 116868. Gourmets head for this restaurant, which is remarkably luxurious—and expensive.

L'Alsace, 9 Ny Østergade. Tel.: 145743. Fish and seafood *à la français*. Picturesque setting in an old courtyard.

La Tour, 3 Jarmers Plad. Tel.: 130001. Beirut transplanted; wide variety of Middle Eastern dishes.

Reine Pedauque, Hotel d'Angleterre, 34 Kongens Nytorv. Tel.: 120095. International cuisine; all the wine you can drink when you choose the fixed-price menu.

Sankt Gertruds Kloster, 32 Hauser Plads. Tel.: 146630. No lunch here, but meals from 4:00 p.m. in an old ecclesiastical building with cloisters and 1,200 candles.

Skovshoved, 267 Strandvejen, Charlottenlund. Tel.: 640028. Worth the quarter-hour drive or taxi ride out of town; gourmet food served in a conservatory.

▷ Tipping

Tips are included in bar, hotel, restaurant, and taxi charges. Only if you've enjoyed exceptionally good service should you add anything.

▷ Doing Business

The 1980s weren't kind to the Danish economy, to some major businesses, and to the banking system. One medium-sized bank crashed in 1984; two more very small banks went under in 1987. All were victims of breakneck expansion, unwise lending to customers with whom the bigger banks refused to do business, and Denmark's general economic stagnation. The head of the bank inspectorate spoke of unprecedented "criminal behavior," the central bank acted swiftly to impose stricter discipline on the banking system, and the Folketing (parliament) passed legislation requiring external auditors to be tougher and for deposits to be insured.

All this was a nasty shock for Danish bank and business executives, coming as it did at a time when foreign observers were already wondering how Denmark could continue to finance its external deficits by borrowing abroad on a scale that was huge for so small a country. The authorities insisted that the banking system was fundamentally sound and efficient. (They would, wouldn't they?) And, certainly, there were few signs that lenders regarded the kingdom as anything less than a good risk, though bankers with a taste for history did recall that it went bankrupt in 1813.

The focus now is on the two biggest banks, Den Danske Bank and Handelsbank, which occupy nearby eighteenth-century mansions in the city center and have long been slogging it out for top place. In 1987, Den Danske Bank pulled ahead in terms of share capital and reserves. Both are minnows, though, when measured against the European giants, let alone the Japanese and American ones.

The Danish economy as a whole may need some restructuring. Manufacturing accounts for about a fifth of gross national product (GNP), and a third of the industrial sector is concentrated in machinery and instruments. Most firms are small, specialized, niche producers. Indeed, Danish industry as a whole is characterized by a large number of small and medium-sized companies: about 6,500 employing six or more people. Only four or five Danish companies are among the top 500 in Europe.

A salient question is whether the country's many small enterprises can compete successfully in the "Europe without frontiers" of the 1990s. A wave of national and transnational mergers has created gargantuan corporations elsewhere, able through subsidiaries to eat into smaller and weaker firms' markets, thanks to economies of scale and heavy investment in new products and marketing. Although the public sector is large, employing about 30 percent of the labor force, private enterprise is left largely to get on with its job of creating the wealth; government interferes little. The corporate tax rate is a standard 50 percent on profits declared after depreciation allowances.

Personal income taxes are onerous. The highest marginal rate, about 68 percent, is applied to incomes that are just 20 percent above the average for a blue-collar worker; the lowest rate is 51 percent. There is also a personal wealth tax that is paid by about 100,000 people—triple the number in 1982—who have been caught by an inflationary increase in the value of real property. The 2.2 percent levy starts at a net wealth of DKK 1.3 million. As if that were not enough, value-added tax (VAT) on goods and services is charged at a flat 22 percent, with additional levies on certain goods. In all, government revenues are about 58 percent of GDP, a level that is second only to Sweden's (61 percent) among the 24 OECD countries. The main cause of that burden: heavy spending on cradle-to-grave welfare programs and the huge bureaucracy needed to administer these transfer payments.

As in most small countries, doing business in Denmark can be pleasant and friendly. All the movers and shakers know each other; introduced to one, you're likely to be passed on to others if you make a good impression and your deal appears sound. Foreigners can invest in all types of Danish securities. Denmark is a high-wage, high-cost country, but labor is skilled and profits can be repatriated as of right.

There are some do's and don'ts for the visiting executive. The Danes value punctuality, and they start work early: 8:00 or 8:30 a.m. is common. Most do not welcome business dinners; family life is cherished. Business lunches tend to be short. On the other hand, business breakfasts have caught on to some extent, though they're not yet popular.

▷ *Spotlight* ◁

Drinking etiquette. Danish life is far from starchy, but there are a few ceremonies. At more-or-less formal meals, you're likely to be confronted with one glass of *snaps* and another of beer. Wait until the host has welcomed you and other guests before lifting either glass to your lips. If the speech is in Danish, you'll recognize the end by the word *skal!* And so say all of us.

Many official, quasi-official, and other bodies stand ready to help the visitor with advice, research, and introductions; we list them in the Business Information section of Useful Phone Numbers. The Bella Center stages between 25 and 30 fairs and exhibitions every year, as well as congresses and conferences for up to 4,200 people. The emphasis is chiefly on Nordic affairs and business, though many companies from elsewhere also participate.

▷ Useful Phone Numbers

Note: All Copenhagen numbers are changing to eight digits. Generally, the initial 01 becomes 31 or 33, followed by the six figures given below. There are quite a few exceptions, so check at your hotel or the tourist board. The numbers should "settle down" by 1990.

Emergencies

All-night pharmacy	148266
Ambulance, fire, and police (01 not needed)	000
Doctor (01 not needed)	0041

Local Information

Airport flight information	541701
Air taxis	(02) 391114
Lost and found	161406
Airport	503260
Buses	147478
Trains	442011
Taxis	
Central area	353535
Suburbs	(02) 353535
Trains	141701
Tourist office	111325

Business Information (add 31 as prefix)

Agriculture Council and Marketing Board	145672
Danish Bankers' Association	120200
National Bank of Denmark	141411
Chamber of Commerce	155320
Congresses, conventions, and exhibitions	
Bella Center	518811
Convention bureau	111415
Industries' Board of Trade fairs	144346
Customs Board	157300
Export Council	231444
Federation of Danish Industries	152233
Foreign Ministry	920000
Handicrafts Council	123676

National Association for
  Promotion of Danish
  Enterprises   225222

Embassies

Note: Be sure to first check that these numbers now have 31 as a prefix and not one of the limited number of variations.

Argentina	158082
Australia	262244
Austria	124623
Belgium	260388
Brazil	206478
Canada	122299
Colombia	112603
Cuba	420515
Finland	3313-4214
France	155122
Germany (West)	261622
Greece	114533
Iceland	159604
India	182288
Ireland	423233
Israel	626288
Italy	260400
Japan	263311
Kuwait	(02) 885020
Luxembourg	121271
Mexico	208600
Norway	388985
Poland	627245
Portugal	131301
Saudi Arabia	621200
Soviet Union	425585
Spain	422266
Sweden	142242
Switzerland	141796
Turkey	205500
United Kingdom	264600
United States	423144

Airlines

Aer Lingus (Ireland)	126055
Aeroflot Soviet Airlines	126338
Air Canada	121155
Air France	127676
Alitalia	128850
Austrian Airlines	117725
British Airways	146000
Canadian Pacific	129523
Cathay Pacific	154033
Czechoslovak Airlines/CSA	120121
Danair (Denmark)	515055
Finnair	120855
Iberia (Spain)	122222
Icelandair	123388
Japan Air Lines/JAL	113300
KLM Royal Dutch Airlines	113334
Kuwait Air Ways	150915
Lufthansa German Airlines	126511
Northwest Airlines	148899
Olympic Airways	126100
Pan Am World Airways	241555
Qantas Airways (Australia)	118911

Sabena Belgian		European	154877
World Airlines	123027	Overseas	158188
SAS Scandinavian Airlines		Saudi Arabian Airlines	155588
First and business classes		Singapore Airlines	143456
Domestic	136266	Thai Airways	155152
European	137277	Turk Hava Yollari	144499
Overseas	138288	TWA	328088
Economy class		Varig (Brazil)	119122
Domestic	155266		

▷ Shopping

Quality and prices are both high, but many stores offer tax rebates on purchases totaling more than DEK 1200 (U.S. residents) and DEK 2300 (European Community residents). Look for the distinctive red and white sign, and take your passport with you when you go shopping.

As in other European cities, try to avoid imports and concentrate instead on distinctive products of the country. Denmark is famed for excellent design work quality, which is to be found in everything from traditional arts and crafts through contemporary glassware to porcelain and silverware. For a comprehensive display of design visit *Den Permanente,* near the main railroad station, a national showcase. All exhibits are for sale. *Illum,* 52 Østergade, is sometimes described as the Neiman-Marcus or Harrods of Copenhagen. Its 70 or so departments stock the most famous names in glassware, porcelain, textiles, furs, jewelry, and furniture (they'll ship that for you). Confusingly, there's also an *Illums Bolighus* at 10 Amagertorv, which specializes in furniture as well as furnishings.

The name in silverware known best outside Denmark is probably *Georg Jensen,* and at 40 Østergade is the world's largest collection of the firm's varied wares. New, used, and antique items are for sale. A far smaller but almost equally interesting silversmith is *Hans Hansen* at 16 Amagertorv. Peter Hertz, 34 Kobmagergade, is one of the oldest silversmiths, specializing in place settings and discreetly beautiful jewelry.

Now a shop on the original site, the *Royal Copenhagen Porcelain Manufactory,* 6 Amagertorv, is three floors of dazzling exhibits ranging from single figurines to hand-painted dinner services. Second-quality items, what the British call "export rejects," are sold at reduced prices, and most people would never notice the difference. Next door is *Bing and Grøndahl,* with a similar reputation for quality. You can buy B&G "seconds" direct from the factory at 149 Vesterbrogade.

Magasin du Nord, Kongens Nytorv, is Denmark's largest department store, with excellent selections of jewelry, silver, furs, and ceramics.

▷ After Hours

We shall now kill a myth. Copenhagen is Europe's sex capital. Yes or no? Answer: no. Back in the 1970s it might have been, though Amsterdam and Brussels must have run it a close second, and all three were puritanical when compared with Manila or Bangkok. In the postAIDS world, Copenhagen is a reformed city. Mark you, its sexy reputation always was grossly exaggerated. So let's look at life today—or tonight.

Those seeking certain pleasures can still find them in some of the cafés lining Nyhavn and around Nikolaj Kirke. A few of these provide rooms upstairs for customers who become tired and emotional and wish to discuss matters privately with sympathetic young ladies, or even young gentlemen, while reclining comfortably. Escort services are also available.

Most of the larger hotels feature nightspots with live or disco music, or both (though not at the same time). Other night-owl places include: *La Fontaine Jazz Club,* 11 Kompagnistraede; *Jazzhus Montmartre,* 1 Norregade; *New Daddy's/Cafe Rio,* 5 Axeltorv; *Three Musketeers,* 25 Nikolaj Plads; *Vin and Olgod,* 45 Skindergade; *Wonder Bar,* 69 Studiestrade.

▷ Sights and Sounds

During a quick visit, it's not possible to do more than sample very selectively, even skimpily, the vast cultural wealth of this small city. Let's start with three of the most obvious features: Hans Christian Andersen, one of whose fairy tales inspired the sculptor of the Little Mermaid, and the Tivoli Gardens.

The Little Mermaid (den Lille Havfrue) is indeed little, a bronze statue that since 1913 has been sitting pensively on a rock on the edge of the Lystbadehavn, a park at the northern end of the harbor. A quarter of a century ago, a vandal decapitated her; Copenhagen mourned, and so did much of the world. She was soon restored to her rather prim pose, prim in spite of her being naked. The long waterfront is a pleasant bustle of craft large and small, and for much of its length there are charming old buildings looking out over the wharves and water.

▷ *Spotlight* ◁

Hans Christian Andersen (1805–75) was a poor shoemaker's son born in the town of Odense on the island of Funen (Fyn in Danish). As a young and struggling poet he went to Copenha-gen, tried successively to become an actor and singer, failed, but achieved some success with his poetry. He found his real talent with children's stories, among the most famous being

"The Emperor's New Clothes," "The Snow Queen," "The Ugly Duckling," and of course "The Little Mermaid." He was a convivial egotist, a frequenter of taverns, and a genuis.

Andersen and the Tivoli Gardens did much to inspire Walt Disney, and the gardens are, indeed a nineteenth-century forerunner of Disneyland. George Carstensen, an architect and literary figure, persuaded King Christian VIII to let him turn the site of old fortifications into an amusement park, arguing in effect that "bread and circuses" would keep the populace happy. The gardens have, ever since, but Carstensen died bankrupt 12 years after they opened in 1843. The splendid grounds include flower gardens, lakes, and restaurants. Tivoli is open from May through September, attracts some 4 million visitors in those few months, and on many nights is enlivened by fireworks displays. More than 100,000 colored lights illuminate the park at night. The Tivoli Guard, a group of boy soldiers (the oldest is 17), marches twice daily through the gardens to the music of its own band. A concert hall on the grounds attracts internationally known artists.

Amalienborg Palace is really four royal mansions. When Queen Margrethe is in residence, as she usually is in fall and winter, there is a daily noontime changing of the guard, complete with band.

Art Galleries and Museums

Copenhagen has plenty to offer. Admission is free unless otherwise noted. Check days and times of opening with the tourist office or hotel concierge.

Davids Samling, 30 Kronprinsessegade. Fascinating collections of medieval Islamic pottery and European decorative art from the 1700s onward.

Frihedsmuseet, Esplanaden. How the Danish Resistance operated in World War II.

Glyptotek, Dantes Plads. Eclectic range of Egyptian, Etruscan, Greek, and Roman collections; French and Danish art, including works by Paul Gauguin.

Den Hirschsprungske Samlin, 20 Stockholmsgade. A very superior collection of nineteenth-century Danish impressionist works.

Kobenhavns Bymuseum, 59 Vesterbrogade. Depicts the capital's history from earliest times.

Kunstindustrimuseet, 68 Bredgade. Museum of decorative and applied arts, including European and Oriental handicrafts. Admission charge on Sundays and in July and August.

Nationalmuseet, 12 Frederiksholm Kanal. Danish civilization from the Stone Age through recent times; also has prehistoric and Greenland collections.

Statens Museum for Kunst, Solvgade. Features Matisse and other European artists.

Tojhsmuseet, 3 Tojhusgade. Weapons and uniforms displayed in a royal arsenal built about 1600.

Louisiana. One of Europe's best modern art collections. Out of town; check trains with hotel concierge.

Historic Places

Again, check days and hours when these are open.

Amalienborg Palace has been the residence of the Danish royal family since 1794. Its four identical buildings were completed in the mid-1700s. They form a courtyard with a superb equestrian statue in the center. Access to the interior is limited.

The Borsen, or stock exchange, is on Slotsholmen, dates from the early seventeenth century, is in Danish Renaissance style, and is noted for a spire of entwined dragons' tails. Closed to the general public, but business visitors can usually arrange an unofficial guided tour.

Christiansborg Slot, also on Slotsholmen, is a palace that includes the Folketing (parliament), state apartments, the knights' hall, and some romantic ruins.

Det Kongelige Bibliotek, the royal and national library, is at 8 Christians Brygge; entrance from Christiansborg courtyard. The *Radhuset,* or city hall, is topped by a tower 105 meters (350 feet) high and is a monument to civic pride at the dawn of the twentieth century.

Rosenborg Slot, 4a Øster Voldgade, is another example of King Christian IV's building mania. See the crown jewels here.

Runde Taarm, Kobmagergade, was Christian IV's observatory, completed in 1642. There's an internal spiral ramp, and Peter the Great of Russia is reputed to have driven to the top in a horsedrawn carriage.

▷ Spotlight ◁

King Christian IV was one of the most amazing men of his century—or, indeed, of any century. King of Denmark and Norway and Duke of Schleswig-Holstein, he was elected successor to his father in 1588, when he was only 11 years old, assumed government of the duchy in 1593 and of the kingdom in 1596, and fought two wars with Sweden in the 1600s. The first gave him an advantageous peace, the second cost him territory.

In the Thirty Years War, he became chief of the Protestant Union, but his military disasters were so great that in 1629 he handed over power to Gustavus Adolphus. Christian IV's enduring legacies to Denmark are his agricultural, administrative, and educational reforms, and his encouragement of international trade. These helped to turn Denmark from a poor, obscure country into a regional power.

Music and Theater

Pick up a copy of *Copenhagen This Week* to discover what's on. The answer usually is a lot. *Det Kongelige Kapel,* the Royal Theater's Orchestra, is often conducted by international stars with guest soloists. Address: Kongens Nytorv. Tickets from Wilhelm Hansen (Tel.: 155457). From May through September there are nightly concerts at the Tivoli Gardens. Not surprisingly, the city's theaters present plays in Danish. At the Mermaid, however, all performances are in English. Location: 7 Ny Vestergade.

Sports

Few capital cities offer as many sports within such easy reach. Bicycle races, horse races, and soccer (*fodbold*) matches are popular. Other sports:

Golf. Contact Dansk Golf Union. Tel.: 131221. Among the many courses: *Copenhagen Golf Club,* Eremitagesletten, about half an hour away by car or train; *Rungsted Golfklub,* also a half-hour away; *Helsingor Golfklub,* Hellebaekvej; *Hillerod Golfklub,* Ny Hammersholt, about forty minutes' drive. The tourist information office publishes a golf pamphlet.

Sailing. Contact Copenhagen Amateur Sailing Club. Tel.: 207172.

▷ Out of Town

Arhus is Denmark's second-largest city, with a population of 250,000. On the Jutland peninsula's east coast, Arhus is handsome and varied, a combination of ancient and modern architecture. *Den gamle By* (the old town) is an open-air museum of 61 houses, each furnished and equipped for its period. The thirteenth-century *Domkirke,* with copper roof and red-brick walls, is a landmark in this flat countryside. So is the *Radhuset* (city hall), built between 1938 and 1942 as a demonstration of Danish architectural skills. Some people think it a masterpiece, others condemn it as an eyesore, and few are lukewarm in their views.

You can get to Arhus by air, bus, ferry, boat, and train. It's hardly a day trip. Telephone city code: 06. Recommended hotels are the *Atlantic,* 12-14 Europlads (Tel.: 131111); *Marselis,* 25 Strandwejen (144411); and the *Scanticon,* Ny Moesgarsvel, just outside town in Hojbjerg (273333). For further information contact the Arhus Tourist Office at 121600.

Silkeborg is the modern town west of Arhus on the banks of the Gudena river. This is a great center for visiting the lake district. Tour it by canoe, rowboat, or a paddle steamer built in 1861. It's an unspoiled wonderland capped by a tower on top of *Himmelbjeret,* 147 meters (483 feet) above sea level; great views of one of Denmark's loveliest landscapes.

Odense (population: 170,000) is the country's third-largest city and birthplace of Hans Christian Andersen—and, of course, there's a museum dedicated to the man and his works. Odense is on the island of Funen (*Fyn*), known as "the Garden of Denmark," where there's much to see and relish. *Den fynske Landsby* (Funen Village), just south of Odense, is an open-air museum of country buildings that include a watermill and an open-air theater where Andersen plays are performed in the summer. Hotels: *H.C. Andersen* (09-147800) and *City Hotel* (09-121258). Tourist office: (09) 127520.

Helsingor, a 40-minute train ride from Copenhagen, is Shakespeare's Elsinore, where Hamlet roamed the ramparts uttering soliloquies of the "to be or not to be" variety. Whether Shakespeare wrote the play or somebody else did is a matter of lively debate in scholarly circles; so is the accuracy of the play's historical description and context. Indubitably, though, the castle is there.

DUBLIN
Fair City, Fair Future

Population: 423,000 (1981). Metropolitan area: 1 million (estimated). Political, administrative, and commercial capital of the Republic of Ireland (population: 3.5 million). *Location:* east of Ireland at the mouth of the River Liffey on Dublin Bay. *Economy:* banking and financial services, brewing and distilling, electronics, food processing, glassware, maritime services, shipbuilding, tourism. Ireland is a member of the European Community (EC) and the Organization for Economic Cooperation and Development (OECD) and is a signatory to the General Agreement on Tariffs and Trade (GATT).

▷ Background Briefing

For more than a thousand years, Ireland has been invaded, fought over, and occupied by foreign powers: the Norsemen, the Danes, the Normans, and the British. In 1922, after a five-year rebellion against the British, the country attained autonomy as the Irish Free State. Not until 1949 did it become a fully independent republic. Even then, its writ ran only to 26 of the 32 counties on the island. The remaining six counties make up the nation of Northern Ireland, which is part of the United Kingdom (Great Britain).

The republic's constitution calls for the unification of all Ireland, north and south, but most politicians think that is no more likely to happen than the joining together of East and West Germany. Meanwhile, the two Irelands must get on together as best they can, and that isn't easy. Any politician in the Republic of Ireland who is thought to be too close to the British endangers his or her electoral future. On the other hand, the

United Kingdom—including Northern Ireland—is the republic's major trading partner.

The north-south Irish conflict makes headlines and prime-time television news around the world, particularly in Britain and the United States—Britain because it holds the power in the north, and the U.S. because of its large population of Irish origin. But Anglo-Irish politics are not the dominant issue in the south; the economy is. In the 1980s, inflation and unemployment were high, the country's foreign debts rose alarmingly, and economic growth lagged. Candidate Charles Haughey, leader of the Fianna Fáil party, campaigned vigorously against an austerity program initiated by his main opponents, the Fine Gael party. As *taoiseach* (prime minister), Haughey clamped down heavily on public spending.

He had little choice. For more than a decade, the Irish had lived well beyond their means. In an effort to break that bad habit, the government raised taxes in draconian fashion, but one result was an exodus of qualified people. In all, about 100,000 people emigrated between 1985 and 1987, a huge and worrisome figure for a small country. Three times that number, perhaps, are planning to leave.

Frustration is building among those left behind, particularly among the under-25 age group that makes up half the population. Most don't see a solution to their nation's economic problems apart from further belt-tightening. Neither of the mainstream parties offers radical or hopeful recipes. In the conventional left-right terms of other countries, there is not much to choose between Fine Gael and Fianna Fáil: on that spectrum, they are fighting for the middle.

History lies heavy in Ireland, however; and Fianna Fáil is the party that rejected the Anglo-Irish settlement and partition of the island more than six decades ago. Ireland doesn't suffer from future shock, but from past shock; the old and bitter battle between descendants of those who signed the treaty with Britain and those who didn't. The result was a bloody civil war and a political heritage that is still hard for outsiders to understand.

Quite rapidly, though, Ireland is transforming itself from a nation shrouded in the mists of Celtic mysticism into one determined to live in the modern world while retaining the best of its traditional values. That delicate balancing act isn't easy. The republic remains heavily dependent on agriculture for its living. No less than 15.3 percent of the labor force works on the land or in forestry and fishing, the highest ratio in the European Community, with the exceptions of Greece (27.0 percent), Portugal (21.9 percent) and Spain (15.1 percent). On the other hand, the fast growth of the new economy is shown by other figures. Over the last decade, the share of meat and live animals in total exports has fallen from

19.7 to 8.8 percent, while that of office machinery has risen from 4.8 to 18.7 percent.

Much of that transformation has been achieved with the help of foreign investors, who provide about 80,000 of the 200,000 jobs in manufacturing. More than 300 U.S. subsidiaries employ some 37,000 people. Of 21 companies on four industrial estates near Dublin, all but two are American. Asian interest is perking up, with Japanese, Taiwanese, and South Korean companies already manufacturing in Ireland or planning to open plants.

The Asians, like the Americans before them, are attracted as much by the quality of life as by the financial carrots the Irish dangle before them. Ireland may be poor by European standards, but it's not impoverished. Furthermore, money isn't the only measure of the quality of life. Dublin is a small city when compared with other capitals, its cultural life is vibrant, and within easy reach are unspoiled beaches and countryside. As if all that were not enough, and it's quite a lot, Dubliners have an unquenchable spirit; they never give up.

▷ *Spotlight* ◁

Terrorism—or as some see it, fighting for freedom. Does it make Dublin a dangerous city? No, it does not. The Provisional Wing of the Irish Republican Army (IRA) operates mainly in the six counties of Northern Ireland. After all, the terrorists want Ireland to be unified politically, so it wouldn't make much sense for them to hit targets in the south. That would be fouling their future nest. They do, very occasionally, attack in the republic, but the visitor's chances of being caught in the crossfire are roughly equal to those of being knocked down by a drunken donkey in a blizzard—and blizzards in Ireland are as rare as heat waves in Antarctica.

▷ Arriving

By Air

Dublin's Collinstown Airport, 9.5 kilometers (6 miles) from the city center, handles some 3.5 million passengers a year, usually with few delays. There are direct and connecting flights from and to major European and transatlantic destinations as well as to other parts of Ireland, including Belfast and Shannon. Buses to the Central Bus Station in downtown Dublin leave about every 20 minutes. Taxis are usually waiting.

Shannon Airport, near Limerick, in the west of Ireland, also serves destinations worldwide. Many transatlantic flights stop over for the famous duty-free shopping and local tourist attractions.

By Sea

Fast and frequent ferries connect Dublin with British and continental European ports. Schedules vary with the time of year; check with your travel agent.

By Train

Iarnrod Éireann (Irish Rail) runs clean, modern trains on such routes as Dublin-Cork, Dublin-Galway, and Dublin-Belfast. They're a good way to see the countryside in comfort.

▷ *Spotlight* ◁

Car rental. If you rent a car at the airport or docks, you'll find that the steering wheel is on the right—enough of a reminder, we hope, that the Irish drive on the left side of the road. Ireland accepts a valid U.S. driver's license. Car rental is popular, and major companies such as Avis, Hertz, and National operate in Ireland. Consult the Irish Tourist Board or your travel agent for further details.

▷ Money

The basic unit of currency is the punt, or Irish pound. International code: IEP. Banknotes are in denominations of 1, 5, 10, 20, 50, and 100 punts. Coins are in units of 1, 2, 10, 20, and 50 pence (100 pence = 1 punt). Best exchange rates are at banks.

▷ Language

English and Gaelic (Irish) are the two official languages. Except in a few remote places, chiefly in the west of the country and on islands, everyone speaks English. Irish, a member of the Goidelic group of the subfamily of Indo-European tongues, is taught in all schools. In its classical form, Irish was written in the *ogham* script; today the alphabet is an uncial variant of the Roman, but with only 18 letters. Most towns and cities have an official name in Irish. Dublin, for example, is *Baile Átha Cliath,* Cork is *Corcaigh,* and Limerick is *Luimneach.*

▷ **Spotlight** ◁

Vocabulary. Here are a few basic Irish words, just in case you don't see the English ones.

Irish	English
an lar	city center
fleadh	festival
fir	gentleman
garda	police
mna	ladies
offig an phoist	post office

▷ Communications

Country code: 353. City code: 1. Quality is generally good, but not up to the highest Western European standards. Don't expect everyone to be on the telecoms network. There are only 235 phones for each thousand people, compared with 521 in neighboring Britain and 650 in the U.S.

▷ Getting To Know the City

The River Liffey flows gently through the city center on its way to the sea. On both banks are quays that are less commercially important than they were half a century ago, but still are crowded with the country's exports and imports. Bisecting the northern and southern sections of the city are several bridges, the most notable being O'Connell's. This leads from the university and administrative districts to the busy commercial heart of Dublin, concentrated around broad O'Connell Street and to the east and west.

Most of business Dublin can be walked within an hour, but not all of it. Some companies have moved to the suburbs, so check addresses very carefully.

▷ Moving Around

Ireland's national bus and rail transport company is the Coras Iompair Eireann (CIE). Dublin also has an efficient city bus and rail system, called the Dublin Area Rapid Transit (DART), which connects north Dublin from Howth with the south of the city, Killiney. If you're going to be traveling a lot, it's worth buying a weekly commuter ticket at *Bus Átha*

Cliath, 69 O'Connell Street; this is valid on both buses and trains. Taxis are usually plentiful.

▷ Hotels

One slogan of the Irish Tourist Board (*Borde Fáilte* in Irish) is "Ireland of the Welcomes." For once, there's truth in advertising. For all we know, a secret hospitality center in a remote part of the island trains people to smile and generally bid welcome to visitors, but we prefer to think that the warmth is natural. Dublin has hotels for every taste and pocket, though it's not cheap. We've selected those that go out of their way to help the business traveler. If the hotel of your choice is full, contact Central Reservations Service (14 Upper O'Connell Street, Dublin 1. Tel.: 735209. Telex: 32462). This official organization will handle reservations for hotels and other accommodations throughout the Irish Republic.

Berkeley Court, Lansdowne Road. Tel.: 601711. Telex: 30554. Fax: 617238. Rooms/suites 200. Modern, but with traditional standards of service. Outstandingly good restaurant and grillroom. Pool, sauna, shopping arcade.

Bloom's, Anglesea Street. Tel.: 715622. Telex: 31688. Fax: 715997. Rooms/suites: 86. Right in the center of things. Small, cozy, intimate; such thoughtful touches in the rooms as garment presses.

Burlington, Upper Leeson Street. Tel.: 605222. Telex: 93815. Fax: 605064. Rooms/suites: 420. In the main business district, the Burlington offers so many distractions that you may be reluctant to venture out. Among them: late-night dancing and dining, cabaret, shops; indoor heated swimming pool.

Gresham, 23 O'Connell Street. Tel.: 746881. Telex: 32473. No Fax. Rooms/suites: 180. O'Connell Street is Dublin's Fifth Avenue or Champs-Elysées, with a statue of Donald O'Connell himself, The Liberator (1775–1847), to remind one of Ireland's revolutionary past. The Gresham is in the top echelon of Dublin hotels.

Jury's, Pembroke Road, Ballsbridge. Tel.: 605000. Telex: 93723. Fax: 605540. Rooms/suites: 300. Large rooms, lots of Irish people making merry in the three bars; two restaurants. There's an outdoor pool—and a hot whirlpool. *Slainte!* (That's Irish for cheers, in case you didn't know.)

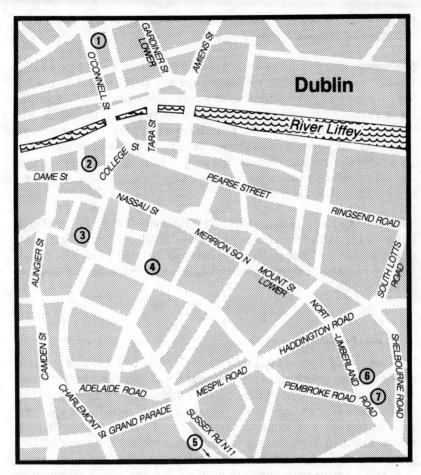

1. **Gresham Hotel**
2. **Blooms Hotel**
3. **Westbury Hotel**
4. **Shelbourne Hotel**
5. **Montrose Hotel**
6. **Berkeley Court**
7. **Jurys Hotel**

Montrose, Stillorgan Road. Tel.: 693311. Telex: 91207. Fax: 691164. Rooms/suites: 190. The green campus of University College is just across the street; about 10 minutes' drive from city center. Good food (in the hotel, that is); health center, boutiques, bank.

Royal Dublin, 40 Upper O'Connell Street. Tel.: 733666. Telex: 32568. Fax: 733120. Rooms/suites: 101. A Best Western/Irish Welcome hotel,

►113

the Royal Dublin sets out its traps for executives with better-than-average telecoms and meeting-rooms.

Shelbourne, St. Stephen's Green. Tel.: 766471. Telex: 93653. Fax: 616006. Rooms/suites: 172. We put the Shelbourne to a test: Could it dine, wine, and take care of friends who weren't even staying there—and send the check to us? We reserved by phone from far away, and the Shelbourne passed the test with honors. Our friends reported, "From the moment we walked in the door, we thought we were royalty. *Everyone* seemed to know who we were, and the food and service were sublime. They even got our names right—and our names aren't easy." The Shelbourne vies for the title of Dublin's best hotel.

Westbury, Grafton Street. Tel.: 791122. Telex: 91091. Fax: 797078. Rooms/suites: 150. Dublin's newest top-level hotel, the Westbury is a subtle and interesting blend of Irish and international styles. Features include a Georgian-pastiche shopping mall, Chinese and Indian restaurants, and a seafood bar.

▷ Restaurants

Time was—and it wasn't too long ago—that you couldn't find a decent meal except at an expensive international hotel, and even there it wasn't always good. Today it is, or almost always. Ireland grows some of the best food in the world; the problem in the past was that too often it was over-cooked. *Nouvelle cuisine* hasn't taken Ireland by storm. Why, after all, should a sensible Irishman pay twice as much for half the portion he expects? But cooking has become more refined.

If you want to have lunch, don't start the day with a typical Irish breakfast, which usually includes cornflakes (Cornflakes? They're not Irish!), bacon, sausage, eggs, and toast with marmalade. You may even find yourself eating smoked herrings, or kippers. Do specify soda bread: it's delicious.

▷ *Spotlight* ◁

Drinks. Ireland has long been a discerning buyer of imported wines and liquors. Where, after all, did such names as Château Lynch-Bages, Château Haut-Brion (O'Brien) and Hennessy and Martell originate? But Ireland has its own good drinks as well. Among them is the world-famous Guinness, and people who have drunk only the bottled, pasteurized version have a treat in store when they sample the real thing, which is out of the wood. Irish whiskeys are subtly different from the Scottish versions. A barman at Shannon Airport invented Irish Coffee, or so one version of the story goes—and it is delicious there. What- ever the truth, Irish Coffee is usually better in Ireland than anywhere else.

Chez Beanos, 37 Lower Stephen Street. Tel.: 776384. Reserve at least a week ahead. The restaurant is small, the clientele is loyal, and the food is both excellent and inexpensive.

Le Coq Hardi, 35 Pembroke Road. Tel.: 684130. Politicians and tycoons mingle here to wheel, deal, and eat some of Dublin's finest (and most expensive) food, washed down by wines from owner John Howard's extensive cellar. Private dining rooms provide seclusion for those who don't want to be seen carving up the country among them.

George's Bistro, 29 South Frederick Street. Tel.: 603177. No gastronomic awards—but one for "crack," which in Ireland means getting high on fun and talk. Moderate prices, by Dublin standards.

Locks, 1 Windsor Terrace, Portobello. Tel.: 652025. Former banker Richard Douglas attracts business executives and diplomats to this lively place, which addicts swear is the city's best. French and Scandinavian dishes. Reserve well ahead.

Lord Edward Seafood Restaurant, 23 Christchurch Place. Tel.: 542420. Just that: seafood, and very good indeed.

Old Dublin, 90 Francis Street. Tel.: 542346. Pleasantly retrospective; emphasis on Irish dishes; usually crowded.

Patrick Guilbaud, 46 James Place. Tel.: 764192. Bright, airy rooms, flawless service. Guilbaud's sauces are light and smooth, and his *nouvelle cuisine* is delicious.

Whites on the Green, 119 St. Stephen's Green. Tel.: 751181. Peter White, a real-estate tycoon, started this elegant place, with its interesting decor and elegantly good French cuisine. A hangout for politicians, senior civil servants, celebrities famous for being celebrated, and people with long expense accounts.

Away from the City Center

Dun Laoghaire (pronounced "Dun Leery"). Trudis, 107 Georges Street. Tel.: 805318. Trendy Trudis is having a long and successful run: that says something.

King Sitric, Howth. Tel.: 326729. Just north of Dublin is the pretty fishing village of Howth (pronounced "Hoath"). Jean and Aidan McManus pride themselves on serving the freshest fish and lobsters, prawns, and scallops.

▷ Spotlight ◁

Pub life. Talking and drinking; drinking and talking. Dublin's pubs are the loquacious center of a lively and distinctive culture. Certainly, drink lubricates the Irish brain and tongue, but less than it did a few years ago, when taxes on alcohol were lower than they are now. Even so, pubs are still social and cultural magnets. *The Bailey* and *Davy Byrnes*, both in Duke Street, evoke the city of James Joyce's youth (read his *Dubliners*). Sunday nights at O'Donohue's in Merrion Row feature traditional music and sawdust on the floors. In the same street is *Doheny and Nesbitt*, much favored by politicians and civil servants. A pint of Guinness at *The Dawson Lounge*, Dawson Street, comes with a shamrock on the froth. The Dawson claims to be Ireland's smallest pub; extensive research hasn't yet refuted that curious boast. A "snug" is a tiny room partitioned from the rest of the pub. *William "Bongo" Ryans*, Parkgate Street, has a fine selection of snugs.

▷ Tipping

The European Community might one of these days turn its passion for harmonizing everything to imposition of a uniform tipping code on all 12 member countries. Until it does, confusion and chaos reign. Some Dublin restaurants include a tip in the check, others do not. The basic rules are: examine the check, and if it doesn't include a tip, add 10 percent at least. You do not have to tip in pubs, but nobody will object if you do. A more tactful way of tipping in a bar is to offer the barman or barmaid a drink. He or she will probably promise to drink it later—and charge you for a large one.

For taxis, add 10 percent to the metered fare. *Note:* Outside Dublin and other cities, taxis may not be metered. It's up to you, then, to negotiate a fare with the driver, preferably before you start your trip.

▷ Doing Business

Ireland is open for business—but don't be misled by all that charm, otherwise known as blarney. The Irish are shrewd, and they've learned over the years to tell the difference between people who are serious about doing business in their country and those who are not.

▷ **Spotlight** ◁

Romancing the stone. In the wall of Blarney Castle near Cork, close to the top and difficult to reach, is a triangular stone. Tradition has it that anyone who kisses the Blarney stone will be given wonderful powers of persuasion. Most Irish people haven't kissed the stone; many are wonderfully persuasive even so.

For what is Ireland looking? Above all, export opportunities and inward investment. What attractions does it offer? An educated labor force, a green and pleasant land, and many tax and other concessions to investors. Some of these concessions are provided by the government, others by official agencies, and still others by the European Community.

The type and generosity of investment incentives change, so before setting out for Ireland, it's a good idea to check the position with its embassy or consulate in your own country. Our experience is that the Industrial Development Authority takes excellent care of the business executive researching investment possibilities in Ireland, providing exhaustive research and even arranging appointments and travel schedules.

▷ **Spotlight** ◁

Avoiding duty. Back in the prejet days, transatlantic flights stopped at Shannon Airport to refuel. Somebody came up with the brilliant idea of opening a duty-free shop there. It was almost the first of the breed and soon was more of a department store than a shop. A few years later, somebody had another good idea: to create a duty-free zone for manufacturers. Again, it was a first, or almost a first. More than 7,000 people work in the airport complex, and the companies in the duty-free zone export goods and services worth about $420 million a year.

Some adventurous Dublin entrepreneurs, with quasi-official backing, are trying to turn their city into a major international financial center. A fantasy? Possibly, but not necessarily. After all, financial markets these days are really a set of electronic ganglia rather than a physical marketplace. The plan is the brainchild of Prime Minister Charles Haughey. When he returned to power in 1987, he established a committee of financial and economics experts. Within weeks the group produced a plan for a $250-million project. By the following year, no fewer than 31 companies had committed themselves to opening offices in the financial center, being built around the old, classical Custom House on the waterfront.

Among attractions for pioneers and those following them: the prospect of business from the 900 multinationals with operations in Ireland. They are obvious candidates for such services as financing and treasury management. It helps, too, that Ireland levies only a 10 percent corporate tax on financial services; in Britain it's 35 percent. Planned developments include offices, a hotel, restaurants, a conference center, museums and art galleries, and apartments. For information, contact Custom House Docks Development Co. Tel.: 683791. Fax: 680265.

▷ Useful Phone Numbers

Emergencies

Ambulance, fire, and police	999
Lost and found	999

Local Information

Airports	
Cork	(021) 865388
Dublin	370011
Shannon	(061) 61666
Buses	
City	720000
Country	363333
Ferries	
B&I	788077
Irish Ferries	610511
Sealink British Ferries	807777
Taxis	
Allied Taxis	557777
Blue Cabs	761111
Metro	683333
Tourist information	747733
Trains	787777

Business Information

Chamber of Commerce of Ireland	612888
Dun Laoghaire Chamber of Commerce	803013
European Community	712244
Government ministries and departments	
Industrial Development Authority	686633
Industry and Commerce	614444
Information Service	607555
Labor	765861
Foreign chambers	
American	793733
Arab-Irish	605276
Chinese	782241
German-Irish	789344

Embassies and Consulates

Argentina	691546
Australia	761517
Austria	694577
Belgium	692082
Canada	781988
China (People's Republic)	692707

Denmark	756404	**Airlines**	
Egypt	606566	Aer Lingus (Ireland)	377777
France	694777	Aeroflot Soviet Airlines	425400
Germany (West)	693011	Air France	778899
Greece	767254	British Airways	610379
India	970843		
Iran	880252	Club Air	787599
Italy	601744	Danair (Denmark)	428311
Japan	694244	Delta Airlines	794744
Netherlands	693444	Iberia (Spain)	779846
Nigeria	604366	Iona National Airways	379900, Ext. 4254
Norway	783133		
Portugal	884416	Lufthansa German Airlines	761595
Soviet Union	975748	Manx Airlines	423555
Spain	691640	Ryanair (Ireland)	774422
Sweden	715822	Sabena Belgian World Airlines	716677
Switzerland	692515		
Turkey	685240	SAS Scandinavian Airlines	491922
United Kingdom	695211	TAP Air Portugal	377777
United States	688777	Virgin Atlantic Airways	7333388

Note: All airlines using Shannon are represented by one of these two handling agents: *Aer Lingus,* telephone (061) 61666, or *SRS Aviation,* (061) 61544.

▷ **Shopping**

Ireland is justly famous for its tweeds and woolens and for glassware. It's also gaining a name for well-crafted jewelry, much of it the work of young, adventurous designers.

Linen. The city's four major department stores are *Arnotts* and *Clerys* on the north side and *Switzers* and *Brown Thomas* on the south. All specialize in Irish linens and woolens and carry good stocks of Waterford and Galway crystal. Irish linen is now high fashion (and about time, too); it's a favorite of the Princess of Wales. Paul Costelloe uses it very imaginatively, and his clothes for men and women can be seen at Brown Thomas in Grafton Street. Two other master craftsmen in the medium are John Rocha, of Chinatown Clothing Company, at the Powerscourt Townhouse Center; and Michael Mortell, 1 Cope Street. Ib Jorgensen (good Irish name, that) is at 53 Dawson Street and dresses the cream of Irish society.

Antiques. Dublin has a plethora of antique shops, not all of them offering value for money (whatever that may be in this idiosyncratic trade). It's a good idea to stick to shops that are members of the Irish Antique Dealers Association. Reliable stores in the Grafton Street neighborhood are *Alexander Antiques,* 10 Duke Street; *Dillon Antiques,* 27 South Anne Street; *McDonald,* 16 Kildare Street; and *Jane Williams* in the Westbury Hotel, Grafton Street. *The Grafton Gallery,* 3 Anne's Lane, South Anne Street, offers contemporary Irish, British, and European art. Other interesting commercial galleries include: *Hendriks,* St. Stephen's Green; *Oliver Dowling,* Kildare Street; *Solomons,* Powerscourt Townhouse Shopping Center; *Taylor,* Dawson Street; and *Tom Caldwell,* Upper Fitzwilliam Street.

Clothing. Dublin tailoring is well up to London standards—though Savile Row would deny it—and far, far cheaper. Highly recommended are *Joseph Monaghan,* 98 St. Stephen's Green; and *Louis Copeland,* 30 Pembroke Street. *Alias Tom's,* Duke Lane, off Grafton Street, stocks the best of Irish linen shirts in classic and designer styles.

A tax-free shopping scheme allows you to claim refunds of up to 25 percent. Keep your receipt, have it stamped by customs when you leave the country, and mail it back to the shop where you bought the goods.

▷ After Hours

Dublin's night life doesn't scintillate, to be frank. You may find that your hotel offers more glamor at lower cost than some of the tourist traps.

Leeson Street is known as "the strip"—which probably derives from the stripping of customers of their money. In most of the basement clubs the wine is horrible—and horribly expensive. One of the better Leeson Street places is *String's* (Tel.: 613664), frequented by a rather intellectual blend of lawyers, economists, and computer buffs; wines only. *Buck Wailey's,* also in Leeson Street, is usually crowded with amusing people (Tel.: 761755). *Frank Conway's Joys,* 127 Lower Baggot Street (Tel.: 766729) is for the mature set. *Le Cirque,* 16 Merrion Road, Ballsbridge (Tel.: 602236) is for younger people looking for a local version of London's Annabel's or of a Regine's anywhere. In South Frederick Street is the *Pink Elephant* (Tel.: 712428), popular with trendy Dubliners—television personalities, actors, models, and the like. Full restaurant and bar; hard to get into. Music is the specialty of the house at *Gigi's,* a nightclub in the Harcourt Hotel, Harcourt Street (Tel.: 752013). Good food, too.

▷ Sights and Sounds

Dublin has charm. Though developers have put up some dreadful buildings, the heart of the city remains, with graceful Georgian squares and terraces. The best way to see the city is on foot, with a stroll along the banks of the slow-moving Liffey included. Among the most imposing buildings are the Custom House and the Four Courts, on the river; and Trinity College, with its large and beautiful grounds.

Many and mostly delightful are the open spaces, the largest being Phoenix Park, which the president of Ireland and the American ambassador share with the zoo and a herd of free-roaming red deer.

Horses are part of the Irish way of life, so there are many racetracks. The two closest to the city are *Phoenix Park* and *Leopardstown,* 9.5 kilometers (6 miles) south of the city. In August, the Dublin Horse Show attracts entries from many countries. It is not a race meeting, but a celebration of equine glories and the crowning event of the city's social season.

Golf. An hour or so from the city center are no fewer than 38 golf courses. Ask the hotel concierge or phone the tourist office (747733).

▷ Spotlight ◁

Hurling and Gaelic football are boisterous games that are exciting to watch and extremely bewildering for the novice. Hurling is played with what appear to be outsized hockey sticks; Gaelic football may have inspired the much newer game of rugby (except that the ball is round, not ovoid).

Rugby is also popular in Ireland, though widely identified with the British, who invented it. Ireland's most famous businessman, Tony O'Reilly, chairman of H.J. Heinz, the U.S. and multinational food manufacturer, was one of his country's greatest rugby stars.

Cultural life is bewilderingly rich and varied for a city of Dublin's size. But, of course, the Irish have an intellectual influence out of all proportion to their population. George Bernard Shaw, Oscar Wilde, James Joyce, W.B. Yeats, J.M. Synge, Oliver St. John Gogarty—all those and many more writers, poets, and playwrights have walked down Sackville Street (now O'Connell Street) and into literary history.

Theater. Ireland's theatrical traditions live on at the *Abbey*, the *Peacock* and the *Gate*—the latter an architectural gem—and at the *Olympia* and *Gaiety*. At the *National Concert Hall* there are lunchtime as well as evening performances.

Art. For lovers of art there is a trove of treasures, starting with the illustrated eighth-century Book of Kells in the library of Trinity College. The *National Museum* houses remarkable evidence of Ireland's cultural sophistication in the Celtic era; and in the slightly shabby *National Gallery* is a fine collection of European Old Masters. Spend time also to see there the paintings of Irish artist Jack B. Yeats. The *Hugh Lane Municipal Gallery* exhibits contemporary Irish and international art, as well as a collection of French Impressionist works.

▷ Out of Town

Ireland is one of Europe's most beautiful countries, with lakes, mountains, spectacular cliffs rising sheer from the sea, and dozens of small towns and villages where time seems to have been banished. Ireland is also one of the few European countries left in which driving can be a pleasure. Except in and around the cities, highways are often empty and drivers are seldom aggressive.

Suburban Dublin rises southwest into the foothills of the Wicklow Mountains, which by Swiss standards are mere hills. Once up there, though, you are in a wonderland of flora and fauna, most of it less than an hour's drive from the city center. Make one of your destinations *Glendalough,* a monastic center of learning since about 800 A.D., and there see what remains, including the Gaelic crosses and a small, beautiful church. Recommended hotel: *Royal.* Tel.: (0404) 5135. Good restaurant serving both traditional dishes and *nouvelle cuisine.*

South of Dublin are the coastal towns of *Bray, Wicklow,* and *Arklow,* with long beaches stretching on either side of them. Except at the height of the summer season, they are almost deserted, and even then are not really crowded. Recommended hotels: In Bray: *Royal,* Main Street. Tel.: (01) 862935. Old but modernized hotel on the southern tip of Dublin Bay. In Wicklow: *Old Rectory Country House.* Tel.: (0404) 67048. Pretty bedrooms, quiet gardens, gourmet meals. In Arklow: *Arklow Bay Hotel.* Tel.: (0402) 32309. Lively is the word for this modernized hostelry. Nightclub, leisure center, pool, sauna, tennis.

DÜSSELDORF

Office of the Ruhr

Population: 580,000. Capital of the West German state of North Rhine-Westphalia (population: 17 million). *Location*: On the Rhine River, 50 miles north of Bonn. Business and financial center of the *Ruhrgebiet*, the traditional industrial area around the Ruhr River, which runs into the Rhine. *Economy*: chemicals, engineering, branches of iron and steel, vehicles, paper, electrical engineering. Major banking center. Second-largest West German stock exchange, after Frankfurt. Trade Fairs for industry and the fashion world. Leading federal city for advertising and public relations agencies. West Germany is a member of the European Community (EC) and the Organization for Economic Cooperation and Development (OECD) and is a signatory to the General Agreement on Tariffs and Trade (GATT).

▷ Background Briefing

Düsseldorf recently celebrated 700 years as a city, having received its first charter in 1288. It became a capital of duchies in the 1500s, but only the *Schlossturm* (Castle Tower) and the restored town hall remain from this epoch. A later, popular duke collected art, drank with his subjects in the *Altstadt*—the half-square-mile old city—and so launched Düsseldorf's reputation as the West German city with the light touch, the city with style. The way the city organized its layout and the kind of architecture it encouraged raised it above provincial status. The magnificent *Hofgarten* park with its sculptures and fountains was built 200 years ago and was followed by the Königsallee, a kilometer-long, scaled-down version of the

Champs-Elysées with one advantage over the Parisian triumphal way: a central canal with swans and ducks.

The Prussians may have absorbed Düsseldorf after the Congress of Vienna, but the French occupied the city twice (first under Napoleon and then during a four-year period after World War I) and lay some claim to having safeguarded Düsseldorf's sophistication while Duisburg, Dortmund, and Essen had their hands black from the Industrial Revolution. Düsseldorf had its share of ironworks and steel mills, but it was also the place to be seen—and to spend. It helped finance Nazi Germany's war machine of the 1930s and was largely destroyed in the course of 243 air raids during World War II.

The city changed course and ambitions after the war and developed as an international center for trade, services, and administration, the latter after its designation as capital of the newly established West German federal state of North Rhine-Westphalia. A new airport, a major exhibition center, banks, foreign newcomers such as the Japanese, new industries such as computers and fashion, and the geographical location at the gateway to the Ruhr—all contributed to Düsseldorf's renaissance, which accompanied the fall of those working in manufacturing from 52 percent in 1950 to less than 30 percent today. The other 70 percent now work in the new division of labor. The steel mill next to the main train station has made way for a modern office block. Across the Rhine, another mill in Oberkassel is today the site of an industry park and not far from the largest Japanese school in Europe. While the children play under the imported cherry tree, their parents strive in the big Japanese trading houses across from their big German rivals—Thyssen-Handelsunion, Krupp Handel, Mannesmann-Handel, Teekanne, and others.

Advertising account executives, PR consultants, and beautiful fashion models have given Düsseldorf a new look, sometimes *nouveau riche,* a clamour for glamour. The city remains second only to Frankfurt in high finance, while regions farther south have attracted more new industries than the Ruhr, which has benefitted from the turnaround of steel. However, as Napoleon Bonaparte, a one-time visitor, might have remarked, "Düsseldorf does have *élan.*"

▷ Arriving

By Air

The modern Rhein-Ruhr airport, the second-largest in West Germany, is adjacent to the trade fair grounds and the fashion house complex. A taxi to the city center, six miles away, usually takes 15 minutes. The *S-Bahn* (commuter subway) leaves every 20 minutes (30 minutes in the evening) and takes less than a quarter of an hour to the *Hauptbahnhof* (central station). Lufthansa German Airlines maintains senator and frequent flier lounges. Duty-free shopping does not equal the city center cornucopia. The adequate top-floor *Stockheim* restaurant offers reasonably priced meals. Excellent connections to other West German cities, notably Munich and West Berlin.

By Train

The renovated *Hauptbahnhof* (central station) is linked by intercity trains to other West German cities and those in Western Europe, but it will have to wait till the end of the century before it is hooked up to the future European TGV network. However, the West German high-speed train will be operational before then. Currently, trains also provide connections to East Germany and Poland. The Hauptbahnhof is the center of the U-Bahn and S-Bahn metro and suburban networks. There is a U-Bahn link to the fairgrounds. The railroad station has a wide selection of cafés, restaurants, and food shops. The *Vekehrsverein* (city tourist office) in Konrad Adenauer Platz is opposite the station exit. Open from 8:00 a.m. to 6:00 p.m. on weekdays and on Saturday mornings, it offers a business service including chauffeurs and multilingual guides.

By Car

Düsseldorf is in the middle of a motorway system, on the right bank of the Rhine with the Frankfurt-Cologne-Oberhausen Autobahn and the parallel Autobahn to Leverkusen, and on the left bank of the Rhine the connection to the Ludwigshafen-Cologne-Krefeld Autobahn. Be prepared before venturing onto the Autobahn: there is no speed limit, and the traffic is *fast*.

▷ Money

Currency: the Deutsche mark, or D-mark. International code: DEM. Banknotes issued in denominations of 10, 20, 50, 100, 500, and 1,000 marks. Coins in 1, 2, and 5 marks and 1, 2, 5, 10, and 50 pfennigs (100 pfennigs = 1 mark). Banks offer the best exchange rates. The airport's foreign exchange counter is open from 6:30 a.m. to 10:00 p.m. The counter at the Hauptbahnhof is open from 7:30 a.m. to 8:00 p.m.

▷ Language

German, of course, but wide use of English given the importance of the financial, advertising, and fashion sectors.

▷ Communications

Country code: 49. City code: 211. The strength of the German economy has put a strain on the telephones. Bankers, dealers, and traders are swamping the lines, particularly in the morning. Be warned: it is difficult often to get through from Düsseldorf to London or Paris and vice versa. Have patience. The other bad news is that the 20-pfennig cost of a call box call is now 30—and a ridiculous 70 in the smart shopping galleries. There are no locally purchased phone cards (as in Paris).

▷ *Spotlight* ◁

Japanese companies flocked to Düsseldorf and the Ruhr more than two decades ago to learn from German chemical, electrical, engineering, and steel firms. "We go where the competitors are," said one Mitsubishi director at the time. Today, there are some 300 Japanese companies in the city or nearby—banks and trading houses in Düsseldorf itself with manufacturing companies close to hand. The result: a two-to-one trade balance in favor of the former pupil.

Immermannstrasse, a few minutes walk from the railway station, is the core of Japanese business activity. The large Deutsch-Japanisches Center is run by Marubeni in association with the Bank of Tokyo, Dai Showa paper, Japan Air Lines, Tokyo Marine Insurance, and Yasuda Fire Insurance. The center houses nearly 80 Japanese tenants plus seven shops, one of which is a branch of Mitsukoshi, the leading Tokyo department store. A JAL Nikko Hotel, more than a dozen restaurants, and *karaoka* sing-along bars complete the picture.

The Japanese are within Düsseldorf and the European Community—and that makes them well-placed to tap the city's expertise in East-West trade. Munich with Siemens and a high-tech sector has attracted some Japanese investment of late, but Düsseldorf remains the favorite.

One of the city's leading officials looks after the Japanese, introducing them into the business clubs, such as the Industrie and the Rotary, or arranging land deals. Most of the 6,500 Japanese live in the Oberkassel quarter across the Rhine. The Japanese describe it and the rest of the city as possessing the added qualities of cleanliness and calm. They form a city within the city with a large 900-pupil school, travel agencies, grocers, hairdressers, doctors, and a theater director who has also brought the two business communities together and helped negotiate deals. One problem: the Germans are reluctant to allow the Japanese in numbers into their golf clubs. So the Japanese community has built its own course and given the city a garden to balance matters.

▷ Getting To Know the City

Düsseldorf's sobriquets are "Little Paris" and "Garden City" because of innercity greenery, broad avenues, fashionable shops, and terrace dining in the summer. Two questionable chunks of modern architecture—the 234-meter-high TV and radio Rhine Tower and the 95-meter-high Thyssen building—are blots on the skyline. Otherwise, the city proper on the east bank of the Rhine is easy to grasp, with its somewhat grid-style layout. From the station and avenue swinging across the southern part of the city, one walks north along parallel avenues—Berlinerallee, Königsallee, Breitestrasse-Heinrich Heine Allee—towards the extensive *Hofgarten,* Düsseldorf's central park. The northwest route across the city, directly from the Hauptbahnhof, is via Friedrich-Ebert-Strasse and Steinstrasse. Between the Hofgarten and the river is the *Altstadt* (old city), with museums, city hall, and 300 pubs. Three bridges cross the Rhine leading to the fashionable suburb of Oberkassel. There's a "diplomatic row" along Cecilienallee on the west bank, with the fairgrounds just beyond. The *Bilk,* or harbor district, in the southeast corner by the Rheinkniebrücke, is becoming smarter with the new Parliament building.

▷ Moving Around

The bus, tram, and subway systems (U- and S-Bahns) are centered on the Hauptbahnhof, the main station. The city's subway and bus map is confusing for a visitor. Your concierge will guide you. For example, the 722 bus goes from the station to the fashion house complex and fairgrounds for a couple of Deutsche marks (the ride would cost 12 to 15 marks by taxi). The Rheinbahn transit authority has an information line (58228— German only) and information booths in half-a-dozen stations. Tickets are transferable between buses, trams, and local trains, and there are bargains such as a special 24-hour ticket or a discount-priced book of 10 tickets. Tickets must be punched and retained. You can also buy them on the buses. Having said all that, it must be added that taxis across town are fairly inexpensive.

▷ Hotels

Düsseldorf has 11,000 hotel beds (the Germans calculate in beds rather than rooms) and 4,000 of these are in the luxury bracket. In addition, there are 40,000 more beds within 30 miles, a radius that takes in Essen, Germany's fifth-largest city. Rooms are difficult to obtain during the larger trade fairs. Remember that the winter boat show is the world's largest, that the spring printing and paper fair is huge, and that the fashion shows are swelling, particularly those in March and September. The Hilton and Inter-Continental double as fairgrounds and airport hotels. The following is a choice of the very best for businesspeople, plus some more moderately priced hotels.

Luxury Hotels

Breidenbacher Hof, Heinrich Heine Allee 36. Tel.: 1330. Telex: 8582630. Fax: 1303830. Rooms/suites: 156. Situated in the heart of the city, the hotel has been updated to combine antiques and business facilities. Meeting as well as banquet rooms. Grand Grill Royal restaurant.

Hilton, Georg-Glock-strasse 20. Tel.: 43770. Telex: 8584376. Fax: 4377650. Rooms: 379. Suites: 8. Close to the fairgrounds. Restaurants, lounges, disco, pool, fitness room, and 24-hour business facilities.

Inter-Continental, Karl-Arnold Platz 5. Tel.: 45530. Telex: 8584601. Fax: 4553110. Rooms: 309. Overlooking the Rhine in the same area as the Hilton. Room and business services around-the-clock. Excellent pool, Jacuzzi, and fitness facilities. Noted locally for its restaurants. Lufthansa checkin.

Nikko, Immermannstrasse 41. Tel.: 8340. Telex: 8582080. Fax: 161216. Rooms: 301. A Japanese-German delight. A mixture of Oriental comfort—the top floor health club with *shiatsu* massage—and German efficiency. Center of Japan-on-the-Rhine, the Nikko has brought an exotic touch to the city.

Steigenberger Park, Corneliusplatz 1. Tel.: 8651. Telex: 8582331. Fax: 131679. Rooms/suites: 160. Next to the Opera and the Hofgarten park, the Steigenberger Park is a superb traditional hotel that has been renovated. Rotisserie restaurant with summer terrace. Function rooms. The Park is a noted business and social meeting place.

Moderately Priced Hotels

Eden, Aderstrasse 29-31. Tel.: 38970. Telex: 8582530. Fax: 3897777. Rooms: 106. This centrally located Best Western hotel calls itself "classic first class," a fairly accurate description. The Eden is very pleasant and efficient.

Graf Adolf, Stresemannplatz 1. Tel.: 360591. Telex: 8587844. Fax: 354120. Rooms: 102. More reasonable rates than its sister hotel, the Eden. Near the station and Königsallee. Convenient for banking district.

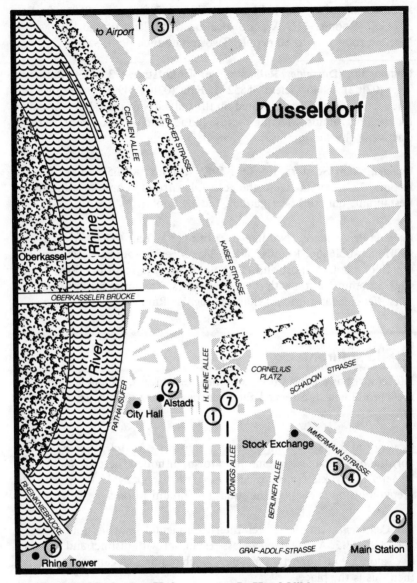

1. **Hotel Breidenbacher Hof**
2. **City promotion office**
3. **Fairgrounds**
4. **Japan Center**

5. **Hotel Nikko**
6. **State Parliament**
7. **Hotel Steigenberger Park**
8. **Tourist office**

Holiday Inn, Graf-Adolf-Platz 10. Tel.: 38730. Telex: 8586359. Fax: 3873390. Rooms: 177. A good location at the end of the Königsallee. Meeting rooms up to 80 people. Two restaurants, pool, sauna.

Holiday Inn (Düsseldorf-Ratingen), Broichhofstrasse 3, 4030 Ratingen. Tel.: (02102) 46046. Telex: 8585235. Fax: (02102) 499603. Rooms: 199. The former Crest Hotel, located on the outskirts of town but convenient for the fairgrounds. Meeting rooms. Indoor and outdoor pool. Very attractive in the summer.

Ramada, Am Seestern 16. Tel.: 591047. Telex: 8585575. Fax: 593569. Rooms: 222. Not far from the colorful Altstadt. Large meeting room. Restaurant, bar, and beer garden. Indoor pool.

Ramada Renaissance, Nordlicher Zubringer 6. Tel.: 62160. Telex: 17-211-4001. Fax: 6216666. Rooms/suites: 245. Meeting rooms. Restaurant and top-floor pool. Airport and fairgrounds nearby. Top-floor Renaissance Club accommodation with rooms and suites. Amenities for business travelers. Fancier (and pricier) than the regular Ramada.

▷ Restaurants

Düsseldorf has a good variety of ethnic restaurants, Japanese among the most prominent. It offers a lighter contrast to the typically heavy German fare.

Benkay, in the Hotel Nikko, Immermannstrasse 41. Tel.: 834-2621. Probably the best Japanese restaurant in town, although there are many challengers. Sukiyaki, tempura, and raw fish. Teppanyaki table with the preparation on show plus the squatting Tatami Rooms.

Les Continents, in the Hotel Inter-Continental, Karl-Arnold Platz 5. Tel.: 4553-1315. A new luxury-class restaurant with distinct and imaginative salons. If an important business lunch requires elegant surroundings, then this is the place.

De Medici, Amboss-strasse 3. Tel.: 594151. An excellent Italian restaurant across the Rhine in Oberkassel. This is the suburb for Germans (and Japanese) who have "arrived" and for whom gastronomy is important.

Grill Royal, in the Breidenbacher Hof Hotel, Heinrich Heine Allee 36. Tel.: 13030. This grand hotel today has a wide choice of eating places—

the quick "Eck," even a Trader's. The Grill Royal is for the connoisseur with time. *Nouvelle cuisine.*

Im Schiffchen, Kaiserswerther-markt 9, Kaiserwerth. Tel.: 401050. Frenchman Jean-Claude Bourgueil's noted, award-winning establishment just outside of town. Düsseldorfers save up to make a pilgrimage there.

Kai4-Maasen, Kaistrasse. Tel.: 304547. Local color in the old harbor district. This French-style fish restaurant has a simple downstairs section with menu on the wall and a more expensive restaurant upstairs. It is fashionable.

Nachrichtentreff, Königsallee 27. Tel.: 132311. A cross between a New York bar, a British pub, and a French-style drugstore. News on the ticker, a "smell of ink" from the *Westdeutsche Zeitung* above. A lively scene all day.

Orangerie, Bilker-strasse. Tel.: 373733. A very good French-style restaurant in the bustling Altstadt.

Rosati, Felix Klein-strasse 1. Tel.: 4360503. Further proof that the Düsseldorfers appreciate good Italian cuisine as much as—or even more than—the native variety.

Rotisserie, in the Steigenberger Hotel, Corneliusplatz 1. Tel.: 8651. International cuisine. Fish and lamb specialties. The famous summer terrace is heated for winter.

▷ Tipping

The restaurant check includes the standard tip, so don't add more than a few coins unless the service was particularly outstanding. Tip the hatcheck or coatcheck attendant. The concierge or doorman should receive between $3 and $5 for such services as reserving a restaurant table or concert tickets or getting you a taxi. Tip cabdrivers about 10 percent on top of the metered fare.

▷ Doing Business

Düsseldorf is second to Frankfurt in the financial league, but the visiting business executive receives a better welcome from a city that is evidently "trying harder." The city's promotion office, or *Werbeamt*, at 29 Mühlenstrasse, is highly efficient. Officials direct visitors to the most appropriate bank, the right venture capital outlet, as well as the finest or the most "in" restaurant. The NOWEA organization for the many Düsseldorf fairs is also fast with information and help.

In a way, Düsseldorf tries to deny its industrial past in its efforts to paint a picture of a gleaming world of trade and services, fashion and advertising. The much-sought-after Japanese banker and trader, particularly if he likes a bit of style, is the chief beneficiary of this charm campaign. One of the city's leading officials—*stadtdirektor* level—looks after Japanese interests and creature comforts on an almost permanent basis.

▷ Spotlight ◁

The fashion industry. "Paris and Milan design, we sell." This slogan of the Düsseldorf—and West German—fashion industry has a lot of truth. The six annual fashion shows (and four shoe shows) add up to one of the biggest, if not *the* biggest, concentrations of thousands of designers and salespeople (and the media). Some 200,000 buyers from 70 countries attend. The year kicks off with CPD (Collections Premieres Düsseldorf), followed by the bigger Igedo shows in March and September (Igedo-Internationale Modemessen Kronen KG, which works with Düsseldorfer Messegesellschaft NOWEA). The big Igedos are held in the exhibition center, the smaller versions in the Fashion Haus complex nearby.

This is unique in Europe: two big buildings packed with designers and wholesalers who show year-round.

Success depends on the size of the West German consumer market, but another key to success has been the designers' middle-of-the-road approach, leaving haute couture to the Latins. (Writer Heinrich Heine, Düsseldorf's most famous son, describes his mother's longing for elegant—and if possible Parisian—clothes. That was pre-Igedo.)

The fairgrounds stage 30 specialized fairs a year.

The biggest ones besides the fashion shows are K (International Plastics and Rubber); Drupa (printing and paper); Interpack (packaging machinery); Interkama (measurement and automation engineering); Gifa (foundry trade); Metec (metallurgical engineering); Boot (boat show); and GDS (footwear). In all, 1.5 million visitors come to the fairs.

Foreign business activity in the city is not all Japanese. Less visible, but substantial in numbers and trading volume, are the 2,700 branches and subsidiaries of other foreign firms; 350 Americans and a similar number from the Netherlands; 250 British companies; 150 French; and today more than 30 Taiwanese concerns.

There's a rich, local consumer market. The city population may be dwindling, but the suburbs grow and now total 1.5 million. The Rhine-Ruhr economic region numbers 8 million. The larger state unit of North Rhine-Westphalia produces 27 percent of the gross national product (GNP). Yet, most foreigners are in the city because of financing and trading opportunities. Düsseldorf is a gateway to Eastern Europe and the Soviet Union, a market that is bound to grow, perhaps in an irregular fashion. Countries like China and Taiwan, as well as Japan, see Düsseldorf as a natural place to be—to buy and sell machinery and raw materials.

Düsseldorf is home to heavy industry trade associations: the Association of German Engineers; the Business Union of Iron and Steel; the Association of German Iron-Works Engineers; Business Union Metals; Association of the Chemical Industry and others. There are also the offices of the Business Association of German Advertising Agencies and the Retail Trade Association North Rhine. Last, but not least, Düsseldorf has a concentration of several hundred local and foreign management consulting companies, international auditing firms, attorneys, and tax consultants.

Watch out for business and social "traps" in this seemingly free-and-easy, swinging business scene. True, the normally austere Deutsche Bank has trees, a cafeteria, and a nice lounge in its main banking hall on the Königsallee. True, Dresdner Bank, not to be outdone, has a hall resembling the atrium of a Miami hotel with a safe that is visible and can be touched—why else design it and polish it like a gleaming diamond? However, there are *grafs* (counts) and other aristocrats in this apparent financial Disneyland. They represent the old money, the discreet founding families of Ruhr industry in both good times and bad times. Take the Industrie Club, Heinrich Heine Allee. The city lists it as a meeting place. The club, which is a sanctum for captains of industry and aristocratic *freiherrn,* does not like this one bit. Introductions are needed to get in, particularly for receptions there and at the Rotary Club. Younger bankers can be seen in the pseudo-French fish restaurants, but some of their elders prefer to remain out of public view.

▷ Useful Phone Numbers

Emergencies

Ambulance	621126	Motorcar emergency	19211
Chemist	1141	Police	110
Dentist	666291		
Doctor	597070	**Local Information**	
Fire	112	Airport	4211
Lost/found property	8993285	Information	421223

Customs	4216927	Italy	387990
Railway info	19419	Japan	369001
Rhine cruises	326072	EIAJ (Electronics)	369816
Shiatsu center	678639	Jetro	136020
Time	1191	Korea	362044
Tourism/		Netherlands	4987201
accommodation	350505	Norway	45890
Weather	1164	Singapore	499269
		Spain	480621

Business Contacts

City economic	
promotion	8995500
Economy/technology	
ministry	83702
Igedo fashion fairs	8584823
NOWEA (trade	
fair HQ)	8584853
Venture capital	878974

Sri Lanka	593053
Sweden	452074
Switzerland	434488
Taiwan	84811
United Kingdom	43740
Northern Ireland	719011
United States	596798
Missouri	592025
North Carolina	320553
U.S. Embassy,	
Bonn	(0228) 3391

Chambers of Commerce

Düsseldorf chamber	35571
Austria	324036
Canada-British	
Columbia	353471
Quebec	320816
China	8662905
Denmark	392035
East Germany	391031
France	139920
Sopexa food	498080
India	360598
Indonesia	452908
Iran	451018
Ireland	353951
Israel	325272

German Business Associations

Boilers, power plants	485006
Chemical industry	83890
Construction	67031
German foundry	68711
German steel	370094
German welding	154040
Glass industry	168940
Iron, steel union	8291
Iron, tin, metal	454930
Ironworks engineers	67070
Publishers	363333
Retail trade	498060

Consulates

Argentina	324205
Austria	434141
Belgium	498987
Canada	353471
Denmark	131400
Finland	367204
France	499077
Ghana	682858
Greece	499246
Iceland	2509441
Japan	353311
Jordan	80075
Korea	365939
Lebanon	431512
Luxembourg	4981366
Malawi	(0203) 741224
Mauritius	356754
Monaco	4979141
Morocco	451041
Netherlands	3613055
Norway	45890
Pakistan	329266
Peru	667839
Philippines	370366
Portugal	80633
South Africa	452627
Spain	434777
Sweden	324632
Switzerland	434601
Thailand	8382247
Tunisia	371007
Turkey	450999
United Kingdom	43740
United States	490081
Yugoslavia	673067
Zaire	353643

Airlines

Aeroflot Soviet Airlines	320491
Aer Lingus (Ireland)	80231
Aerolineas Argentinas	365083
Air Canada	80451
Air France	38907
Air India	369835
Alitalia	388631
Austrian Airlines	84423
British Airways	80021
Finnair	353373
Iberia (Spain)	370103
Japan Air Lines/JAL	329070
Korean Air	340491
KLM Royal Dutch Airlines	325066
Lufthansa German Airlines	8885
Olympic Airways	84941
Pakistan International Airlines	370361
SAA	320611
SAS Scandinavian Airlines	89070
Sabena Belgian World Airlines	327048
Singapore Airlines	350631
Swissair	87977
TAP Air Portugal	80737
Turk Hava Yollari	374089
TWA	84814
UTA (France)	84927
Varig (Brazil)	84746

▷ Shopping

French, Italian, Japanese, and British designers have their names in the windows of the Königsallee shops. Going north, the shops are more or less on the right, the banks and finance houses on the left. The Königsallee—Kö for short—gallery is a luxurious German version of a U.S. mall with probably more high-class foreign goods. There are smaller boutiques tucked away in the side streets off the Kö. It is worth a trip if only to see the face of West German consumerism.

Nearby *Schadowstrasse* is also a highly concentrated shopping region. *Friedrichstrasse* has books as well as clothes, whereas antiques are to be found in the Altstadt. Naturally, the range of Japanese shops is wide, and a list can be obtained from the Nikko hotel.

▷ After Hours

Nightlife has two distinct compartments. The first is the noisy, beery, but generally harmless scene in the Altstadt, with its roughly 300 pubs (no one knows for sure). It is an area which Düsseldorfers boast is "the longest bar in the world" and which is the center for the very German carnival held on and off from November to February. The second is a "beautiful people" scene for the self-conscious fashion world and its satellites.

In the Altstadt, the specialist is the bitter *Altbier,* which has little foam and is served in simple cylindrical glasses. Top ale houses include *Uerige,* Bergerstrasse 1, with its old seamen's saloon; and two in the colorful Bolkerstrasse: *Zum Schlussel,* at No 47, and *Im Goldenen Kessel,* at No 44. There's also one near Little Japan, *Schumacher Brau,* Oststrasse 123. (The Hotel Nikko management supplies a full list of Japanese bars and sing-alongs.)

The beautiful people flock to *Sam's West* disco, Königsallee 27 (say "Kö 27"). A similar, elegant disco is *Checkers,* Kö 28. Recommended: *Club 1001* at the Hilton. Best jazz: *Down Town*, Mertensgasse 8. Good piano bar with night beauties: *Front Page,* Mannesmannufer 9. There's also *Marktwirtschaft on the Karlplatz,* Altstadt, a pub with some food. Here one can join or observe the Düsseldorf trendsetters. This is a place where clothes outrank gastronomy.

▷ Sights and Sounds

Leading architects recreated Düsseldorf's cultural centers after the wartime destruction. The new buildings are among the most admired, modern structures in Germany. A superb hall houses the *German Opera on the Rhine,* on Heinrich Heine Allee. Another stunning building is the *Tonhalle,* Hofgartenrampe, the center of the city's concert world—Yehudi Menuhin to Oscar Petersen. Plays are in German at the *Schauspielhaus,* Jan-Wellem Platz. The decor is one of the most dazzling in the country and therefore international.

The unmistakeable TV tower is worth a visit for the view towards Cologne—and Holland—on a clear day. An even better view is offered by Rheinland Air Service from the airport.

▷ Out of Town

One can drive, or even take a tram, to look at the slow beautification process underway in the Ruhr. A surer way of relaxing is a trip on the Rhine. Düsseldorf is the headquarters of the Köln-Düsseldorfer Rheinschiffahrt Ag—KD for short—the largest and oldest passenger shipping line on the river. Information and tickets are available from the KD Agent at the downtown port of call, Rathausufer (tel.: 326072).

Düsseldorf is a stopover point for cruise ships between Switzerland and Holland. Shorter one- or two-day trips to Rotterdam or Amsterdam and back are available. There are also day excursions (some in conjunction with German Railways) past meadows complete with sheep.

In summer the river is alive with sailboats. Ten miles upriver is *Schloss Benrath,* an eighteenth-century pleasure seat of the local prince set in a formal garden. A work of art.

EDINBURGH

New Life in Auld Reekie

Population: including Port of Leith: 440,000. Administrative capital of Scotland (population: 5.2 million). *Location*: southeast Scotland, on south shore of Firth of Forth. *Economy*: commerce, banking and financial services, publishing, marine engineering, glassware, chemicals, education, government, and tourism. Scotland is part of the United Kingdom of Great Britain and Northern Ireland, and as such is within the European Community.

▷ Background Briefing

Edinburgh and Glasgow have long been keen rivals for investments in business and jobs. So it says much for Scottish honesty and fairness that a Glasgow University study done in 1988 put Edinburgh at the top of 38 British cities for "quality of life." Survey respondents cited Scotland's capital for its good race relations, as well as its health, leisure, and sports facilities.

These findings will surprise few people who know *Auld Reekie,* the affectionate if critical nickname bestowed when Edinburgh was enveloped in the fog and fug from uncounted coal fires and chimneys of industrial plants. Central heating has replaced most of the coal fires, and virtually all of the plants have gone, they and their workers victims of wrenching economic change.

Edinburgh today is an important commercial, banking, and arts center, its annual festival drawing tourists by the thousands. Once a provincial capital, it is now cosmopolitan. Yet Edinburgh remains distinctively Scottish. Nobody, except a foreigner or naive *Sassenach* (Gaelic for Englishman), raises an eyebrow at the sight of a kilted man striding the hilly streets—and, as likely as not, entering a bank, there to negotiate a big-bucks deal. That mingling of tradition with modernity typifies the city that is often called "the Athens of the North."

Like its Greek counterpart, Edinburgh is built on a series of hills, some of them steep. And though it has been capital of Scotland only since the twelfth century (long enough, in all conscience), Edinburgh has a venerable and diverse cultural history. Economist-philosopher Adam Smith and historian-philosopher David Hume were only two of the luminaries who · made Edinburgh a magnet for scholars in the 1700s.

For most people, though, what gives Edinburgh its unforgettable distinction is its Scottish and English royal heritage and dramatic mixture of architectural styles and periods. The city doesn't have the physical luminosity of Paris, Rome, or Athens: many of its buildings are of granite, which is grayly durable. What Edinburgh does have is a livable, human scale, with only half a million people or so; and the bustle and vigor of a nation proud of itself and determined to maintain its identity while adapting to the modern world.

Within the city limits are no fewer than 28 golf courses, and close at hand are world-renowned sea- and freshwater fishing, empty and unspoiled countryside with first-class hunting (shooting in British terminology), and much else for the outdoorsperson.

One of the first things to know about Edinburgh is that it's quite far north. Summer days are long; winter days are very short. The second thing to remember is obvious but worth underlining: Scotland isn't England.

The Scots are justly proud of their lineage, culture, and history. Although most Scots now accept that union with England (hence the name United Kingdom) is probably an irreversible political fact, all Scots cherish and nurture their differences from (and with) the English. There's also a rising popular demand for more autonomy from England—a demand nurtured by the Scottish National Party and endorsed, albeit reluctantly, by the dominant Labour Party.

Scottish law is distinct from English law, though both are branches of the great trunk of Roman jurisprudence, which has spread its influence throughout the English-speaking world. Edinburgh is no puppet capital. It is, rather, the capital of a nation that has its own language, Gaelic (though few people speak it now), and its own literature, some of it written in one of the many Scottish dialects.

▷ Arriving

By Air

Edinburgh airport is international but small, which means that when all goes well, and it usually does, the traveler is in or out within half an hour or so, and in the city within another half hour—it's only eight miles (14 kilometers) away. The maddening wait for baggage common at larger airports is virtually unknown. There are frequent flights to and from London and other major destinations. But remember that during the three weeks of the Edinburgh International Festival in August, seats are hard to find—reserve well in advance for this period.

By Train

British Rail runs a fast service from London to Edinburgh: the city-center to city-center time of less than six hours compares well with the total journey time by air. Trains are comfortable and the food is usually good —or at least ampler and more varied than that provided by the airlines. *Hint:* Inter-City trains are popular and often overcrowded. Best to reserve both your seat and your meal. Waverley Station, built in a tunneled cavern just off Princes Street, is an architectural sight not to be missed— even if you are not traveling by train.

▷ Money

The British pound sterling is the currency. Do not be surprised, though, if you find a beautiful but unfamiliar bill in your change: some Scottish banks retain the right to issue their own currency. Indeed, something rather odd has happened. The Bank of England (founded by a Scot, naturally) has replaced pound notes with pound coins. The English do not like them; Scottish banks are exporting their pound notes south of the border.

But it isn't a good idea to go south with too many Scottish pound notes, since some stores and hotels look at them askance in England (and we shan't even try to guess how Scottish notes would be received outside the British Isles). New and crisp, however, Scottish banknotes make good souvenirs. Changing foreign currency: as in all cities you get the best rates at banks, the second best at non-bank *bureaux de change,* and the worst at hotels.

▷ Language

English. Most Scots speak with a recognizable "burr"—an emphasis on certain consonants, particularly *r,* and pronounce some vowels and diphthongs differently from the English. Many Scots use dialect words— though not, usually, with visitors. *The Concise Scots Dictionary* (Editor in chief Mairi Robinson; Aberdeen University Press, 1985) is a good (or *guid*) guide to dialect and variant spellings.

Which is the correct adjective: Scots, Scottish, Scotch? Grammarians disagree. We've chosen to use Scots as a noun and Scottish as an adjective, with one exception: whiskey is Scotch (though one famous brand does describe itself as Scots).

▷ Communications

Good. Country code: 44. City code: 31 (031 if you are calling from within the United Kingdom. You don't need to use the code when dialing within the Edinburgh area). Telephone dialing is direct to most cities in the world. All hotels charge a markup for outside calls. Check what it is before placing intercontinental calls. Usually, it's cheaper to have your correspondent call you back (and at least your expense report looks better).

▷ Getting To Know the City

Princes Street is to Edinburgh what the Avenue des Champs-Elysées is to Paris, or Fifth Avenue to New York; and there comparisons end, for few streets anywhere match the grandeur of the city's principal thoroughfare. For much of its length, the shops and restaurants of Princes Street face well-tended gardens. Across from them are the castle on its great, frowning rock, and the spires and turrets of the medieval city.

Many-floored houses cling to the steep hillside, the spine of old Edinburgh. The Law Courts and the Advocates' Library are in the buildings that once housed the Scottish Parliament, abolished by the Act of Union with England in 1707.

▷ *Spotlight* ◁

Government. Scotland sends elected members to the House of Commons in London and hereditary and life peers to the House of Lords. A small but vigorous nationalist party calls for restoration of the Scottish Parliament; that doesn't seem likely to happen soon, though support for the movement may be growing. The Secretary of State for Scotland, a member of the House of Commons and of the Cabinet, administers Scottish affairs, with offices and staff in both London and Edinburgh.

Much of Edinburgh's business and banking life is concentrated in what is still called the New Town, the eighteenth-century streets, squares, and crescents north of Princes Street. This graceful neighborhood is an early example of town planning, the dream come true of George Drummond, one of a long line of imaginative lord provosts (mayors). Drummond and architect John Adam chose the plan of James Craig for a town on a grid-iron plan, each street ending in a massive square at either end. The result was what the Pelican *History of Art* describes as "the most extensive Romantic Classical city in the world."

For the visiting executive, the result is a compact business district complete with hotels and restaurants.

▷ Moving Around

Because Edinburgh is small, moving around is easy. Remember, though, that it is built on hills: flabby legs will feel the strain. Public transportation is frequent, cheap, and clean; taxis are readily available, except during rush hours. There are three of these: morning, lunchtime (when many people go home), and early evening. And, of course, taxis are hard to find during the three-week Edinburgh International Festival in August.

As in any other city, allow plenty of time between appointments— though the problem is less acute in Edinburgh than in larger cities. However, Edinburgh businessmen do value punctuality, believing that time is money.

▷ Hotels

Hoteliers have invested no less than $35 million over the past four years in both new and existing properties. The results: more comfort—and more rooms. Except at peak seasons, Edinburgh is (temporarily at least) glutted with beds. The list that follows is selective—and, as for other cities profiled in this book, hotels have been selected for their suitability for business travelers.

Caledonian Hotel, Princes Street. Tel.: 225-2433. Telex: 72179. Fax: 225 6632. Rooms/suites: 252. A rather grand hostelry, built early this century, and recently refurbished to its original Edwardian elegance. It looks out on busy (and noisy) Princes Street, but the walls are thick. Good views of Edinburgh Castle and its gardens. Scottish *fin-de-siècle* living at its best.

Carlton Highland Hotel, North Bridge. Tel.: 556-7277. Telex: 727001. Fax: 556 2691. Rooms/suites: 220. The building is old, with conical turrets; the hotel is new, opened in 1985. Lures include a leisure center with swimming pool, Jacuzzi, squash courts, sauna and Turkish baths, snooker, and gymnasium.

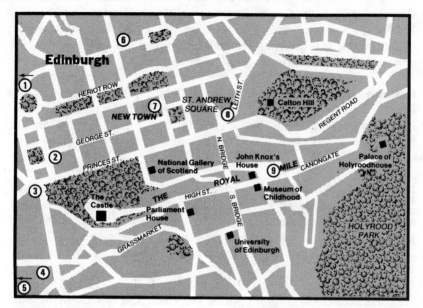

1. **Crest Hotel**
2. **Roxburghe Hotel**
3. **Caledonian Hotel**
4. **Edinburgh Sheraton**
5. **Post House**
6. **Howard Hotel**
7. **George Hotel**
8. **King James Thistle Hotel**
9. **Carlton Highland Hotel**

Crest Hotel, Queensferry Road. Tel.: 332-2442. Telex: 72541. Fax: 3323408. Rooms/suites: 120. About twenty minutes from the city center by car or taxi, the Crest is blandly modern—but does have spectacular views of the Firth of Forth and the Pentland Hills.

Edinburgh Sheraton Hotel, 1 Festival Square. Tel.: 229-9131. Telex: 72398. Fax: 228-4510. Rooms/suites: 279. You'll suffer little or no culture shock when you wake up at the Sheraton. The hotel's restaurants volunteer various tastes of Scotland, however. Location: handily central.

Forth Bridge's Moat House, South Queensferry. Tel.: 331-1199. Telex: 727430. Fax: 3191733. Rooms/suites: 108. A new leisure center provides swimming, Jacuzzis, squash courts, snooker tables, and a health and beauty studio. Location: five miles from the airport and a 15-minute drive from the city center.

George Hotel, 19-25 George Street. Tel.: 225-1251. Telex: 72570. Fax: 226-5644. Rooms/suites: 203. In the heart of the New Town, the George is comfortable and quiet, and though refurbished has an Edwardian air to it—which isn't surprising, given its history.

Howard Hotel, 32-36 Great King Street. Tel.: 557-3500. Telex: 727887. Fax: 727 887. Rooms/suites: 25. Staying at the Howard is rather like staying at somebody's home. Not surprising: it's actually three Georgian houses turned into a hotel. Food has a Scots accent—a skirl of the pipes, so to speak.

King James Thistle Hotel, Leith Street. Tel.: 556-0111. Telex: 727200. Fax: 557-5333. Rooms/suites: 147. One of the city's newer hotels, this sets out to attract the business executive with first-class telecommunications and meeting rooms fitted with state-of-the-art audiovisual systems. Good location: bang in the city center, but in a tranquil street.

Ladbroke Dragonara Hotel, 69 Belford Road. Tel.: 332-2545. Telex: 727979. Fax: 332 3805. Rooms/suites: 146. Interesting mixture of old and new: one of the bars is in a former granary. The hotel's frontage overlooks the turbulent river known as the Water of Leith.

North British Hotel, Princes Street. Tel.: 556-2414. Telex: 72332. No Fax. Rooms/suites: 172. When Britain's railroad pioneers built, they really built. The North British is testimony to their belief that a chap couldn't have a good night's sleep unless he was in a high-ceilinged, thick-walled bedchamber, with a bathroom the size of a ballroom. The North British is a splendid example of what might be called the "edifice complex."

Post House Hotel, Corstorphine Road. Tel.: 334-8221. Telex: 727103. Fax: 334-9237. Rooms/suites: 207. Owned by Trusthouse Forte, the Post House is within 10 minutes' drive of the airport and city center—though let's make that 15 minutes when the highway is crowded. It's also next to the zoo. The Post House is very much the business executive's hotel, with good telecoms and a variety of small and large meeting rooms.

Roxburghe Hotel, Charlotte Square. Tel.: 225-3921. Telex: 727054. Fax: 220 2518. Rooms/suites: 77. Privately owned, the Roxburghe resembles a country house come to town. But it could hardly be more central: Charlotte Square is the very heart of the city's business district. Good, snug bars and restaurants; all-night room service.

Stakis Grosvenor Hotel, Grosvenor Street. Tel.: 226-6001. Telex: 72445. Fax: 220 2387. Rooms/suites: 138. Five minutes' walk from Princes

Street, the Grosvenor isn't exactly the Ritz, but is quietly comfortable, with two restaurants, one distinctively Scottish, the other—well, international.

▷ Restaurants

There was a time, and not so long ago, when the best you could hope for in Edinburgh was a steak or a mixed grill. No longer. The city now claims (who can prove or disprove it?) that "per head of population, Edinburgh has more restaurants listed by gourmet guides than any other city in the country." What's sure is that the adventurous eater-out can find almost any cuisine he or she wants—Chinese, French, Greek, Italian, Indian, Pakistani, Turkish, and even Scottish. A sampler:

Abbotsford Bar and Restaurant, 3 Rose Street. Tel.: 225-5276. Victorian hostelry featuring four cask-conditioned Scottish traditional beers. Bar lunches include such Scottish desserts as Plum Duff and Scotch Trifle. Upstairs restaurant offers poached salmon and "Cullen Skink" soup.

Bar Italia, 100 Lothian Road. Tel.: 228-6379. Businesspeople have come to value this restaurant for its comprehensive Italian menu and extensive wine list—as well as for its late-night (or early-morning) hours: until 3:00 a.m. Close to the city center, too.

Cramond Inn, Cramond. Tel.: 336-2035. Just a quarter of an hour from the city by car, or half an hour by bus, Cramond is a fishing village of stone, whitewashed houses that was the site of a Roman fort (the original name was *Caeravon:* the fort on the river). The inn, dating from the seventeenth century, specializes in Scottish dishes, with a strong emphasis on fish and seafood. Copious servings; short but good wine list.

Handsel, 22 Stafford Street. Tel.: 225-5521. Edinburgh is so far north that it's hardly surprising to find a Nordic restaurant within the city limits —this one being Danish. Elegant decor; elegant young business and banking executives, too.

Howtowdie, 27a Stafford Street. Tel.: 225-6291. Like the Handsel, situated in the handsome Georgian New Town district; popular with businesspeople. Good French and Scottish cuisine—a reflection of the Auld Alliance between Scotland and France.

La Potiniere, Gullane, near Edinburgh. Tel.: (0620) 843214. Regularly listed as one of Scotland's finest restaurants. Small, intimate, elegant; reserve well ahead.

Loon Fung Seafood Restaurant, 32 Grindlay Street. Tel.: 229-5757. Chinese seafood delicacies. The city's Chinese eat here, surely a very good recommendation.

Old Boathouse, Old Post Office Lane, 19 High Street, South Queensferry. Tel.: 331-1155. Scottish food with a French influence; seafood and vegetarian dishes are specialties. High-quality gift shop with a nautical flavor.

Prestonfield House, Prestonfield Road, Newington. Tel.: 667-8055. Peacocks primp and pipers play in and around this magnificent seventeenth-century house. Certified associations with King James II, Bonnie Prince Charlie, Benjamin Franklin, and others of that ilk and era, or thereabouts. Pleasures of the table are memorable.

Tattler, 23 Commercial Street. Tel.: 554-9999. A friendly Victorian restaurant with an extensive menu that includes French, Italian, and—increasingly popular in Scotland—vegetarian dishes.

Witchery by the Castle, 352 Castlehill. Tel.: 225-5613. For a shivery *hors d'oeuvre,* take a short guided tour of the haunted parts of the nearby city. Extensive wine list and menu, and nothing spooky about the food or the service.

▷ Tipping

Confusion reigns. Let us organize it. First, you don't have to tip in a bar —though no barman or barmaid objects to a few coins left on the counter. Second, some restaurants do include a service charge in the check total—and some do not. If a gratuity is included, don't add more unless you feel that the service was exceptionally good—and then not more than a few coins. The Scots guard their own *bawbees,* and expect you to be frugal with yours. "A fool and his money are soon parted" is a saying that may well have originated in Scotland. If a tip is not included, and you have enjoyed good service, add between 10 and 15 percent. Cabbies expect about 10 percent on the fare shown on the meter.

▷ Doing Business

Scotland is looking for two main kinds of business: capital investments in job-creating enterprises and export opportunities.

Although Scotland is part of the United Kingdom, it retains some autonomy, which locally based administrators stretch to the utmost. Like other regions of the UK, Scotland dangles tax and other incentives before foreign investors—which helps to explain why so many computer, software, and other information-technology companies have located there that California's Silicon Valley has its tartan counterpart, Silicon Glen. Some localities and industries are beneficiaries also of development grants from the European Community. But any company investing for the long haul is as much attracted by the availability and quality of local management and labor—and Scotland scores high on those counts.

Scots pride themselves upon being blunt and straightforward in business. Do not take that claim at face value. They bargain just as hard and subtly as business executives anywhere—but do favor getting down to business without too much of a decorative preamble. Which means, in practice, that they don't want to waste their time—or yours.

That means you can usually do business quickly: most movers and shakers know each other. Business executives and bankers tend to have brisk manners, but that doesn't mean they accept bad manners. And, of course, the Scots have turned skepticism into a minor art form: the hard sell backed only by soft facts and figures has all the appeal of a burst *haggis.*

When the project is good, and the presentation is persuasive. Edinburgh's wheels can move remarkably quickly. The visiting business executive needs a new plant, a grant for training of workers, a loan? Within a week or so, all can be arranged—but read the footnotes and the small print carefully.

▷ Useful Phone Numbers

Emergencies

Ambulance, fire, police	999
Seven-day pharmacy	225-6757

Local Information

Airport	333-1000
Buses	226-5087
Rail	556-2451
Radio taxis	229-5221/228-1211
Chamber of Commerce	225-5851

Tourism/arts

Festival	226-4001
Edinburgh	557-2727
Teletourist information	246-8041

Business Information

Chamber of Commerce	225-5851
City Economic Development	225-2424

European			**Airlines**	
Community	225-2058		Air Canada	226-6560
			Air France	333-5050
Consulates			British Airways	225-2525
			British Midland	
Note: for further consulate/			Airways	447-1000
embassy entries, see London.			KLM Royal Dutch	
American	556-8315		Airlines	225-7208
Belgian	554-3333		Northwest Airlines	(041) 226-4175
French	225-7954		Pan Am World	
commercial section	225-5468		Airways	(041) 248-5744
Swiss	667-1011		TWA	(0345) 333333

▷ Shopping

You can buy almost anything in Edinburgh. The question is what. The obvious answers are to avoid the international brand-name goods and go for the local products: plaids, knitwear, food, and whiskey (you can buy this at the airport duty-free shop, but won't find there the huge selection available in Edinburgh). We're tempted to list antiques as local products, because more than 200 shops now sell them in the Royal Mile, Grassmarket, and New Town districts (see map). What is the provenance of all these antiques? Were they antiqued in the afternoon? Or is there an inexhaustible supply of the real stuff from impoverished Highland lairds?

We found that the best bargains were without doubt Scottish clothing and food. Whether clerks resent selling a clan tartan to somebody who has no right to wear it, we never have discovered, and perhaps never will. As for food, Scotland offers much, including smoked salmon—the best in the world—and fruit-rich cakes of the variety known generically as Dundee. We like also Dundee marmalade—though another mystery yet to be solved is why Dundee should import Spanish oranges, turn them into marmalade, and re-export them to Spain. And then there is *haggis,* the minced heart, lungs, and liver of sheep boiled with suet and oatmeal contained in a sheep's stomach. An acquired taste? Yes, but one acquired easily—and cheaply, for haggis was originally humble fare.

▷ *Spotlight* ◁

Haggis. *Sassenachs* and other foreigners tend to joke about the haggis, asking such fatuous questions as whether one shoots or traps it. The Scots take the haggis seriously, and the poet Robert Burns (1759–96) wrote an ode to it. At the January Burns Night dinners held wherever

Scots gather, the haggis is piped in ceremonially and the ode recited. But we shan't quote from it: the verses are in Ayrshire dialect.

The most interesting shopping areas—because the most varied—are Princes Street, the Royal Mile, the Grassmarket, Rose Street, the St. James Center, and the ultra-modern Waverley Market, just above the main railroad station. Around Charlotte Square, and in other parts of the New Town, are the city's most elegant (and costly) clothing stores.

Among purveyors of genuine Scottish garb and gear, guaranteed not be imported from Taiwan:

The House of Macpherson, 17 West Maitland Street, Haymarket. Tel.: 225-4008. Kilts, skirts, clan tartans, bagpipes, drums, ties, scarves, sashes, stoles, pipe-band uniforms, dance pumps—everything one needs to become an instant Scot.

Discount Highland Supply, 7 Cowgateshead, Grassmarket. Tel.: 225-2390. This emporium will sell you complete Highland garb as a package deal: worsted kilt, Argyle jacket, leather sporran, belt and buckle, hose, flashes, *sigan dubh* (ceremonial dagger), and *gillie brogues* (shoes). Bagpipes come extra.

Clan Bagpipes, 13a James Court, Lawnmarket, Royal Mile. Tel.: 225-2415. Some people, Shakespeare wrote, will "laugh like parrots at a bagpiper." He was a Sassenach, of course, and it's not a good line to quote at this shop, where they make the pipes and demonstrate and sell them.

▷ *Spotlight* ◁

Bagpipes. You probably can't avoid taking a sauna in Helsinki or drinking an A*pfelwein* in Frankfurt, and you almost certainly can't avoid hearing the bagpipes in Edinburgh. Like the sauna and apple wine, they're an obsession. From the beginning of July through the end of September, a "Welcome Piper" in full fig marches along Princes Street while playing stirring Scottish airs. Blast-off time: 11.00 a.m. Military pipers in even fuller fig feature in the Edinburgh Tattoo. Information: 225-1188.

Kinloch Anderson, John Knox House, 45 High Street, Royal Mile. Tel.: 556-6491. This firm holds royal warrants as tailors and kiltmakers to the Queen, the Duke of Edinburgh, and the Prince of Wales. As though that were not enough, the firm also makes and sells sweaters, scarves, and berets.

The Whisky Shop, Waverley Market, Princes Street. Tel.: 558-1588. An Aladdin's—or Fingal's—Cave for "The Water of Life" (the word whiskey comes from the Gaelic *uisge* = water and *beatha* = life). The shelves and stockroom hold about 700 brands, from obscure single malts to well-known blends. Huge range of miniatures, too.

Museum Shop, National Museum of Scotland, Chambers Street. Tel.: 220-0237. Arts, crafts, textiles, Scottish jewelry, books, and cards. *Art nouveau* scarves based on late nineteenth-century Scottish designs; glass, pottery, and decorative stained glass.

James Thin, 56 South Bridge. Tel.: 556-6743. Near the Royal Mile, this claims to be Scotland's largest bookstore. Knowledgeable, helpful staff.

Charles Burns, 367 Royal Mile. Tel.: 225-4827. Opposite the famous St. Giles' Cathedral, just down from the Castle. Continental European, Middle East, and U.S. newspapers and magazines—plus all of Scotland's daily output.

Royal Mile Curios, 363 High Street. Tel.: 226-4050. Antique Scottish brooches, cairngorm stones, and silver. A collector's gem. Near St. Giles' Cathedral and Castle.

Les Cadeaux, 121 Rose Street. Tel.: 225-9120. On the pedestrians-only Rose Street precinct, just behind Princes Street. Features Edinburgh crystal, Caithness glass paperweights, bronze art sculptures from the Scottish borders, and ceramic miniatures of such famous buildings as Burns' Cottage, Holyrood House, and Edinburgh Castle.

▷ After Hours

Don't expect a glittering night life in Edinburgh; there isn't one, except at festival time. Nightclubbing has never really caught on this far north. Gaming has. Here is a selective list of places with green baize, soft lights, and sharp-eyed croupiers that offer most of the popular money-losing games. Most are open seven days a week; check times by phone.

Berkeley Casino Club, 2 Rutland Place. Tel.: 228-4446. Private club, free membership: 48 hours' joining notice required. Bar and restaurant.

Casino Martell, 7 Newington Road. Tel.: 667-7763.

Royal Chimes Casino, 3 Royal Terrace. Tel.: 556-1055.

Stakis Regency Casino, 14 Picardy Place. Tel.: 557-3585. Restaurant open until 3:15 a.m. Door membership, but 48-hour delay until it becomes valid.

▷ Sights and Sounds

The most famous sight and blaring sound comes from the Edinburgh International Festival, along with its companion, the Edinburgh Festival Fringe. For those three August weeks, many good burghers absent themselves, leaving their city to the tourists—and some their homes to performers, thereby earning many a bawbee. The festival features theater, opera, dance, and music from top-notch entertainers. During the rest of the year there is still much to do and to see. A sampling:

History and Architecture

These are mingled inextricably. The *Palace of Holyroodhouse* is the Queen's official residence when she is in Edinburgh. The palace began as a guesthouse for the Abbey of Holyrood in 1128. The present structure was begun in 1498, enlarged in the next century, and in 1671 rebuilt on the orders of Charles II—though there is no record of his having stayed there. Mary Queen of Scots spent six years of her reign in the palace; Bonnie Prince Charles held a ball there when he occupied the city in 1745. Open to the public—but confirm days and times either with the tourist office or with the hotel concierge.

Every day except Sunday the "one o'clock gun" is fired from the Castle battlements—a time-check you cannot miss if you are anywhere within a mile (it's not as accurate as an atomic clock, but much more interesting). The very name Edinburgh probably comes from the Gaelic *Din Eidyn,* which means a fortress, and from *burg,* the Anglo-Saxon for a stronghold or town. There has been a fortress on this hill since at least 600 A.D. Much history has been made there. The Crown Room houses the Honours of Scotland—the Crown, the Scepters, and the Sword of State. The Crown is made of Scottish gold and is said to contain the circlet with which Robert the Bruce was crowned at Scone in 1306.

St. Giles' Cathedral hasn't been a cathedral since 1688, when the Church of Scotland did away with bishops, but few people would know what you meant if you asked the way to the High Kirk of Edinburgh. There has been a church on the site at least since 854; the present building, imposingly Gothic, is basically fifteenth-century.

Art Galleries and Museums

Edinburgh's cultural heritage is rich and is reflected in the many collections and visiting exhibitions. Hours and days of opening vary from time to time; check with your hotel concierge or the tourist office.

City Art Center, Market Street. The City collection covers Scottish painting through the centuries. There are also visiting exhibitions, usually with a Scottish flavor.

National Gallery of Scotland, The Mound. One of the most important smaller galleries of Europe, with works by continental European and English masters from the 1300s onward; a good section of Scottish artists.

Royal Scottish Museum, Chambers Street. Houses the national collections of decorative arts, archaeology, ethnography, natural history, geology, technology, and science.

Scottish National Gallery of Modern Art, Belford Road. Picasso, Matisse, Giacometti, Moore, and Hepworth are among the modern artists represented here. Also a fine selection of contemporary Scottish works.

Talbot Rice Art Centre, corner of South Bridge and Chambers Street. Houses the Torrie Collection of sixteenth- and seventeenth-century European painting and sculpture; changing exhibitions in adjacent gallery.

Theaters and Concert Halls

As one might expect of a city that is home to one of the world's most famous arts festivals, Edinburgh is generously supplied with theaters and concert halls. Among them:

King's, Leven Street. Edwardian decor, neo-baroque frontage. Plays and musicals; operas during the Festival. *Leith Theatre,* Ferry Road. Two auditoria, the larger seating 1,440. Used for concerts and mass entertainment. *Playhouse,* Greenside Place. Originally a movie house, now also the venue for large-scale shows—everything from rock and pop to grand opera. *Queen's Hall,* Clerk Street. A former church; home of the Scottish Chamber Orchestra and the Scottish Baroque Ensemble. *Royal Lyceum,* Grindlay Street. Built in the Victorian Renaissance style, with an ornate interior and three tiers of galleries on cast-iron columns. *Usher Hall,* Lothian Road. Fine acoustics, full air-conditioning; used for conferences of up to 2,700 people, as well as musical and artistic events.

For programs, consult daily listings in *The Scotsman* (morning) and the *Edinburgh Evening News.*

▷ Out of Town

Much of Scotland's heritage is on Edinburgh's doorstep—and that heritage includes *lochs* (lakes or near-landlocked inlets from the sea), rivers, moorlands, forests, and the sea. Edinburgh itself is on the southern side of the Firth of Forth, a long inlet from the North Sea with road and rail bridges west of the city. Straddling the Firth is the area known as the Forth Valley, which runs west from Edinburgh to Glasgow and north to Stirling. Within the Forth Valley is a huge variety of things to do and to see—from golf and fishing to stately homes and towns and cities.

One easy and cheap way to discover the Forth Valley—and to go further afield—is to buy an Explorer Ticket from Historic Buildings and Monuments. Address: 20 Brandon Street. Tel.: 244-3101. The tickets, available for 7 or 14 days, are valid for all 330 historic sites in the care of the Secretary of State for Scotland—abbeys, castles, palaces, Stone Age villages, and much else.

Among the Forth Valley's many attractions:

Almondell and Calderwood Country Park, near Mid Calder. Tel.: (0506) 882254. Walks, picnic and barbecue sites, aquarium.

Balbardie Park of Peace, Bathgate. Tel.: (0506) 633048. Par 3 golf course, decathlon athletics area.

Beecraigs Country Park, near Linlithgow. Tel.: (0506) 844516. Trout and deer farms, target and field archery, water sports, angling.

Bo'ness Steam Railway. Tel.: (0506) 822298. Steam locomotives lovingly restored by enthusiasts haul trains from Bo'ness to Kinneil Halt and back again. Railroad memorabilia on view.

Carnegie Birthplace Museum, Dunfermline. Andrew Carnegie (1835–1918) was born in this weaver's cottage, became America's "Steel King," and gave away $350 million. Memorial Hall tells this classic rags-to-riches story.

Dalmeny House, near Queensferry. Tel.: (031) 331-1888. Built in Tudor Gothic style, beautiful grounds and shore walk; home-made teas.

▷ *Spotlight* ◁

Gleneagles. North of Edinburgh is Gleneagles, sometimes called the Pride of Perthshire. A hotel internationally renowned, it is the nineteenth hole, so to speak, for no fewer than five golf courses. Gleneagles Hotel, Auchterarder PH3 1NF. Tel.: (07646) 2231. Telex: 76105.

Other local attractions: Strathallan Aircraft Museum, Glenruthven Weaving Mill, and the Tullibardine Distillery. More information: Auchterarder Tourist Information Center. Tel.: (07646) 3450.

Inchcolm Island and Abbey. Gray seals can often be seen here; Alexander I built St. Colm's Abbey in the 1100s.

Kinneil House, Bo'ness. James Watt invented the steam engine—or at least was one of its discoverers—in the outhouse of this stately home.

Livingston Mill Farm, Livingston. Tel.: (0506) 414957. See how farm families lived in the 1700s (badly, is the answer). Working farm, agricultural museum, cafeteria.

Polmonthill Ski Slope, Polmonthill. Tel.: (0324) 711660. Dry ski slope, instruction, equipment rental.

Union Canal, Linlithgow. Tel.: (0506) 844916. The *Victoria* carries passengers and can be chartered (how about that for an unusual promotional party?). Museum records the Canal's history.

FRANKFURT

The Deutsche Mark's Home Town

Population: 615,000. Metropolitan area: 2.5 million. Unofficial financial capital of the Federal Republic of Germany (population: 61 million). Political capital: Bonn. *Location:* on the Main river, in the state of Hesse in southwest Germany. *Economy:* Seat of the *Bundesbank* (central bank) and the three biggest West German commercial banks: Commerzbank, Deutschebank, and Dresdner. City's stock exchange is West Germany's largest. Newspaper, magazine, book-publishing, and printing center; road, rail, and air hub. Site of international fairs, including those for books, food, furs, automobiles, and capital goods. West Germany is a member of the European Community (EC) and the Organization for Economic Cooperation and Development (OECD) and is a signatory to the General Agreement on Tariffs and Trade (GATT).

▷ Background Briefing

Outside Frankfurt am Main's cavernous Hauptbahnhof, one of Europe's largest railroad stations, an enterprising travel agent has put up a prominent sign that reads: "It's better in the Bahamas." Even the serious bankers and managers, advancing relentlessly along streets that are often wet or icy, raise a wistful smile in the comfort of their BMWs, Mercedes-Benzes, and Porsches. Then it's back to battling the traffic on their way to skyscraper offices and the making of more D-marks—or any other currency, for Frankfurt is second only to London in the European foreign-exchange business.

Banks, banks, and more banks. There are 370 altogether, 230 of them foreign, most of them clustered around the huge Bundesbank complex of buildings. There are also 128 insurance companies, and the city is head-quarters as well for such giant industrial concerns as AEG and Hoechst. Just outside of town are grouped the major foreign corporations. Beyond them, the massive, modern airport disgorges and engulfs thousands of business travelers each day.

▷ *Spotlight* ◁

The Rothschilds, one of the world's most famous banking families, got their start in Frankfurt in the late 1700s. Mayer Amschel Rothschild (1743–1812), son of a moneychanger in the Jewish ghetto, founded the family fortune with his skillful operations as financial agent for the Landgrave of Hesse-Kassel, later Elector William I. The founding father had five sons, and by the 1800s, the Rothschilds were running banks in London, Naples, Paris, and Vienna, and had agents in many other cities. In 1822, Emperor Francis I of Austria bestowed baronies on all five brothers in recognition of their services to the House of Habsburg—and, indeed, of their pivotal role as financiers to many European governments.

The Rothschilds' relative power as bankers declined as government financing became increasingly sophisticated during the second half of the nineteenth century. However, the family found new opportunities in trade and industry. Their humble original home in the Jewish ghetto was destroyed in World War II, but the city has recently honored one of its most celebrated families—and the Jewish contribution to Frankfurt's prosperity and cultural life—by restoring part of that section of town.

And then in 1989, after an 88-year absence, the Rothschilds decided to return with a rep office of both N.M. Rothschild & Sons, of London, and Bank Rothschild A.G., of Zurich.

Trade has been Frankfurt's lifeblood ever since it was known as the "ford of the Franks," first mentioned in dispatches by the Emperor Charlemagne in 794 A.D. By 1361, rich traders were using some 117 houses for the annual autumn trade fair. A chronicler wrote, "The fair has the same significance as the flooding of the Nile, except that what is left behind on the banks of the Main is not silt, but gold." It's pretty much the same story today whenever thousands of exhibitors and visitors leave after one of the big trade fairs that follow each other throughout the year, except in July.

German kings and emperors were crowned in Frankfurt from the middle of the 1500s, and the first German national assembly met in 1848 in a building on the ancient Romerberg square. Most of the central city was flattened by Allied bombing during World War II, but the burghers have built replicas of many of the old houses that give some character to a city nicknamed "Bankfurt" and "Mainhattan."

▷ *Spotlight* ◁

Local politics. Frankfurt has the reputation of being a tolerant town, particularly among the French who have a special eye for a place's lifestyle. The Franco-German political activist Daniel Cohn-Bendit, Danny the Red, retired to Frankfurt when his presence became undesirable in Paris after the street clashes and uprising of students in May 1968. Danny returns to Paris for TV talk shows but today is more associated with the so-called realistic wing of the German "green" movement and more recently as a city councillor. His newspaper, *Pflasterstrand*, shocks some but is printed on glossy paper.

Danny is likely to drop in on Karl Trebes, former student leader of the ultra-radical SDS movement, now owner of the Gargantua, a smart restaurant for "yumpies" (Young Urban Marxist Professionals) and a wine bar, Le Vin Divin, for the advertising teams from the West End. Trebes, who has been a lawyer, actor, and cabarettist, denies he "sold out to the establishment," claiming, "We never wanted just a social-democratic desert of work. We wanted everything, but subito." In his case, it has taken a little more time.

Business Frankfurt isn't pretty, or even architecturally impressive. Its style is modern monolithic. If the typical office building says anything at all about the owners and occupiers, it is that they're too busy making money to make cultural statements. Frankfurt thus lacks the chic of Munich or even Düsseldorf, but it does rival Hamburg as the richest city in West Germany—or Europe, for that matter. The locals' sartorial style is cut from the same cloth as their architecture, so to speak: it's expensive rather than adventurous.

Even so, Frankfurt is rapidly acquiring some cosmopolitan polish. The big banks have bought a lot of real estate in the old red-light Kaiserstrasse district, and as the girls have moved out, the gourmet food stores and fashionable boutiques have moved in. The Alte Oper, the opera house seriously damaged in the war, has been rebuilt; and there is now an impressive parade of museums and art galleries on the Main river's southern bank.

Few wartime scars now remain, except in the mental and political senses. Most Germans do not forget World War II and the fact that theirs is a divided country, its border with East Germany disfigured by a high, wire-mesh fence designed to prevent that communist state's citizens from defecting (that is, emigrating) to the West. Frankfurt is, furthermore, a

U.S. Army garrison town, its commanding general and his staff housed in the former headquarters of I.G. Farben, the giant chemicals combine dismantled by the Allies after World War II.

▷ *Spotlight* ◁

Berlin Wall. The symbol of East-West divisions most publicized is the Berlin Wall, built by the Communist regime to pen its citizens in. Berlin, of course, is deep in East Germany. Less notorious, but a symbol equally potent, is the fence that keeps the two Germanies apart. Built by East Germany at an estimated cost of half a billion dollars, the fence is backed on its side by concrete revetments designed to prevent drivers from crashing through to freedom, a no-man's land of dirt regularly dosed with herbicides so that escapers cannot hide in undergrowth, and by tall watchtowers manned 24 hours a day. East German border villages are surrounded by more fences, and farmers are guarded as they work in the fields. Although the East German authorities say they have removed the mines and automatic machine-guns that fired when the fence was touched, doubts remain in the West. It isn't a statement you want to put to the test. Now, Frankfurters and other West Germans want to see if the trumpets of glasnost will bring down the wall.

▷ Arriving

By Air

If your city is one big counting house, your airport should be a *hubsche* (pretty) hub. Frankfurt is up there with Amsterdam's Schiphol and deserves high praise. It's the second largest in Europe, after London Heathrow—and planned much better, since it is all one building, with adjacent hotels and business center and, above all, easy metro and intercity railroad links. The Frankfurters have also had some fun with the airport, as if they wanted to temper their renowned efficiency with a touch of levity. Among the attractions: 100 shops, including ones that sell Harrods clothes and fine wines, 30 restaurants and bars, three movie theaters, an aviation museum, an imaginative observation deck, Europe's largest airport hotel (a Sheraton), and two sex shops. The airport is like a not-so-small city, and some business executives arrive, meet, sleep, and depart without ever going into Frankfurt.

The *S-Bahn* (commuter subway) runs every 10 minutes to the *Hauptbahnhof* (central station); line S14 arrives below ground and line S15 above ground. S-Bahn trains leave every 20 minutes for the Hauptwache/Konstablerwache downtown section. Traveling time to downtown points is between 10 and 15 minutes. In contrast, a rush hour journey by automobile can take up to an hour and a half. There are also fast trains from the airport to such major cities as Cologne, Bonn, and Düsseldorf.

By Train

The state-owned *Bundesbahn* railroad is making a big effort to capture more business travelers for its fast, comfortable, intercity services. Many long-distance trains offer mobile phones, secretaries, and interpreters, even offices. Food is usually good. Among German cities served are Bonn, Cologne, Düsseldorf, Essen, Dortmund, Hamburg, Munich, and Nuremberg.

International trains run from and to such major centers as Amsterdam, Basle, Brussels, and Paris. The overnight train from Paris, for example, arrives at Frankfurt's Hauptbahnhof at 7:00 a.m., and the train back leaves at 11:00 p.m. The traveler can thus spend a full day in Frankfurt, have dinner, and be back in the Paris office bright and early the following morning. Particularly in the summer, when the skies are crowded with charter flights and airport delays become severe, it's comforting to know there's an alternative that runs on schedule.

▷ Spotlight ◁

Safety. Are Frankfurt's mass-transit systems and the Hauptbahnhof safe? Police with dogs patrol the metro, and there are police posts throughout the system. But like most big railroad stations, the Hauptbahnhof becomes a bit beery at night and is an unofficial market for the "rent-a-boy" trade. However, the streets around the station are safe for an evening stroll. That doesn't mean, though, that one should throw caution to the night winds.

By Car

Autobahnen (freeways) link Frankfurt with cities throughout Germany and the rest of Europe. Before deciding to drive to or from Frankfurt, though, note these hazards. First, the metropolitan area is approaching the gridlock stage, and parking is extremely difficult. Second, in the fall and winter, weather can be foul: foggy, frosty, snowy. Third, there is no speed limit on the *Autobahn,* so don't be surprised if somebody overtakes you when you're driving at 160 kilometers an hour (100 mph). West Germans tend to drive well, fast—and ruthlessly.

▷ Money

Currency: the Deutsche mark, or D-mark. International code: DEM. Notes: 10, 20, 50, 100, 500, 1,000, and—wait for it—5,000. Coins 1, 2, 5, 10, and 50 pfennigs (100 pfennings = 1 mark). Also 1, 2, and 5 marks. Banks offer the best exchange rates.

▷ Language

German. Many people speak two versions: *Hochdeutsche* (High German) or *Schriftdeutsch* (Written German), which is "correct" and formal German; and the local dialect, which is a variant of *Plattdeutsch* (Low German). Virtually all banking and business executives also speak English.

▷ Communications

Country code: 49. City code: 69. (See also Düsseldorf for further information.)

▷ Getting To Know the City

Essential Frankfurt is small—that is, if we define "essential" as being the districts that include banking, business, and major hotels. Many of these neighborhoods fan out from the Hauptbahnhof area, recently cleaned up both physically and morally. Kaiserstrasse and Münchenerstrasse, until recently notorious, have had a scrub, and together with Taunusstrasse provide convenient links with the Romerplatz neighborhood. In and around Romerplatz are city hall, the tourist offices, the Gothic cathedral, and restored medieval Frankfurt. In the nearby Hauptwache district are banks, the stock exchange, chambers of commerce, and department stores.

▷ *Spotlight* ◁

The Burostadt. Many companies and several industry associations have their offices in the Burostadt, a high-rise office park located in Niederrad on the south side of the Main, west of downtown Frankfurt. Bull, Nixdorf, Honeywell, Wang, and the West German Machine Builders Association and many others can be found here. Burostadt can be reached by S-Bahn. But if you are leaving after business hours, have your host order a taxi, because the area turns into a ghost town.

The left or south bank of the Main river is where citizens find their fun in apple-wine taverns, discos, and clubs that make Frankfurt Germany's jazz capital. This is the Sachsenhausen area, capital of *gemütlichkeit,* for which in this context the translation is "conviviality."

▷ Spotlight ◁

Who are the Frankfurters? At least a quarter of them are *Gastarbeiter* (immigrants): Turks, Italians, Yugoslavs, Greeks—the list could run on. Many went to the city to find work that paid well by standards back home; some have saved their pay so as to open businesses. By so doing, they have greatly enriched the city's cultural variety with restaurants, food markets, and clothing stores. Racism isn't dead in Frankfurt, but slumbering, and many people agree that the immigrants have added zest, effervescence, and gaiety to the city's life.

▷ Moving Around

Public Transportation

The *U-Bahn,* or subway system, serves the city and links with the S-Bahn commuter network at three downtown stations: Hauptbahnhof, Hauptwache, and Konstablerwache. At ground level there are also streetcars and buses. During major fairs, it's best to use one or more of the mass-transit systems rather than wait interminably for a taxi that then gets stuck in a traffic jam. You can buy tickets good on both trains and buses at change-making vending machines, which are a distinctive blue, and at stations. Bus drivers sell tickets valid on their route only. A special ticket valid for 24 hours allows the rider to travel throughout the city. Kiosks sell tickets known as *Mehrfahrten* or *Streifenkarten* that are valid for 12 rides on streetcars. The transportation system is efficient and clean.

Car Rental

Car rental is available from a number of major companies, but we don't recommend it for getting around the city. If you do choose to drive, familiarize yourself with street signs and terms before climbing behind the wheel. One executive who had figured out that *strasse* means "street" became very confused and frustrated nevertheless because he kept running into the same street no matter which direction he drove. What he didn't understand was that the ubiquitous *Einbahnstrasse* was simply "one-way street!"

▷ *Spotlight* ◁

Business correspondence. German tradition is to address a business letter like this:

An Herrn Heinrich Muller,
D-5000 *Romberg,*
Kantstrasse 3.

Many business houses, however, are conforming increasingly to common European usage, but do not be surprised or confused if your correspondent adheres to the traditional version.

▷ Hotels

Frankfurt has never been a great hotel city. To be sure, its numerous hostelries have provided comfortable rooms at the inn, but without the flair of Paris or the discreet luxury of London. That's changing, thanks in part to international hotel chains that by sharpening competition have shaken local rivals into refurbishing their properties physically and improving their standards of food and service. Rooms are scarce when major trade fairs are being held—and impossible to find in October, the month of the International Book Fair.

Frankfurt Plaza, Hamburgerallee 2. Tel.: 79550. Telex: 416745. Fax: 79552432. Rooms/suites: 600. This Canadian Pacific tower hotel is opposite the main fairgrounds entrance; popular with delegates to the book, fur, and other trade shows. Restaurant, bars, coffee shop, Blue Infinitum nightclub.

Frankfurter Hof, Am Kaiserplatz. Tel.: 20251. Telex: 411806. Fax: 215900. Rooms/suites: 360. Historic, luxurious, and the most central of the major hotels, this asset compensates for somewhat unimaginative decor. The Steigenberger chain, headquartered here, has made sure that food and service in the four restaurants are just right. A big plus: SAS Scandinavian Airlines checkin at the hotel.

Gravenbruch Kempinski, Neu-Isenburg. Tel.: (06102) 5050. Telex: 0417673. Fax: 505445. Rooms/suites: 317. The famous Kempinski chain has combined elegance with rural charm: the hotel is in a large park only a 15-minute drive from the city. Excellent restaurants, indoor and outdoor pools, beauty and fitness farm. Suitable for high-level meetings and often so used.

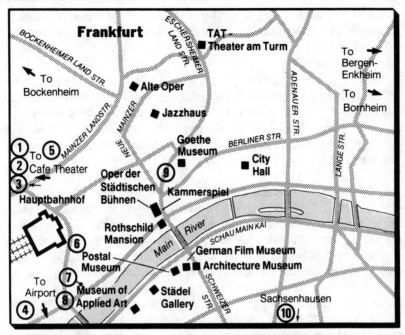

1. Hotel Hessicher Hof
2. Hotel Frankfurt Plaza
3. Fairgrounds
4. Airport
5. Hotel Pullman Savigny
6. Hotel Park
7. Hotel Inter-Continental
8. Hotel Savoy
9. Hotel Frankfurter Hof
10. Hotel Holiday Inn

▷ *Spotlight* ◁

American Express has Consul Clubs in Frankfurt and some other European cities (Brussels, London, Paris, and Rome) to cater to the needs of business travelers in the way of telecommunications, secretarial help, meeting rooms, or just relaxation. Frankfurt's Consul Club is at Bürohaus, an der Alten Oper, Neue Mainzer Strasse 68-75. Tel.: 2980070. It's on the 20th floor, with a view matching the services. The Consul Clubs around Europe are open weekdays from 9:00 a.m. to 7:00 p.m.

Hessicher Hof, Friedrich-Ebert-Anlage 40. Tel.: 75400. Telex: 411776. Fax: 7540924. Rooms/suites: 160. Handy for the Messeglande, or fairgrounds. The world's biggest publishers huddle in the bar and lounge to do megabucks deals during the book fair. Not much to admire on the outside, but plenty on the inside.

Holiday Inn, Mailanderstrasse 1. Tel.: 68020. Telex: 411805. Fax: 6802333. Rooms/suites: 404. They include 28 rooms especially for female executives, 42 for nonsmokers, and 34 business suites on the Club Europe executive floor. Hotel is across the river from the rest of Frankfurt, in Sachsenhausen, but is a self-contained conference center. Restaurant, bar, indoor pool, and fitness center.

Inter-Continental, Wilhelm-Leuschner-Strasse 43. Tel.: 230561. Telex: 413639. Fax: 252467. Rooms/suites: 800. Overlooks the river and is close to the business, banking, theater, and shopping districts. This is one of the best in the chain, with just about everything for the executive: business services, 24-hour room service, airline checkin, restaurants (both moderately priced and exclusive), pool, health club, and meeting rooms.

Park, Wiesenhuttenplatz 28. Tel.: 26970. Telex: 412808. Fax: 26978849. Rooms/suites: 279. These include 30 for nonsmokers. A stone's throw from the Hauptbahnhof; five minutes by streetcar to the fairgrounds. This is really two hotels. Movenpick, the Swiss owner, has overhauled the whole place, right down to the public toilets; inspectors cast their expert eyes over them every hour and sign their names to displayed certificates. Apart from all that, a symbol of care and attention, the hotel is efficient and cozy. La Truffe Restaurant is one of the city's best, and the Casablanca Bar is a favorite rendezvous for American and other executives.

Pullman Savigny, Savignystrasse 14-16. Tel.: 75330. Telex: 412061. Fax: 7533175. Rooms/suites: 126. Part of the well-run Franco-Belgian hotel group. Walking distance from the fairgrounds. Comfortable rooms, bar, and restaurant. A good example of the French drive to capture an important segment of the German market.

Ramada Frankfurt Caravelle Hotel, Oeserstrasse 180. Tel.: 39050. Telex: 416812. Fax: 3808218. Rooms/suites: 236. Adjacent to a pleasant wood. A mile from fairgrounds. Ten meeting rooms. Secretarial services.

Scandic Crown, Weisenhuttenstrasse 41. Tel.: 230511. Telex: 273960. Fax: 273-96795. Rooms/suites: 144. Modern, well-equipped, and close to the Hauptbahnhof. Good grill restaurant, bar, and disco.

Sheraton, Rhein-Main International Airport. Tel.: 69770. Telex: 4189294. Fax: 69772209. Rooms/suites: 820. One of Europe's largest and best airport hotels; connected to the arrivals section by footbridge and adjoining the business center. Excellent service: the whole place is geared to the executive. Several restaurants, including the *haute cuisine* Papillon, many bars, pool, fitness center. Above all, superb communications.

Steigenberger Airporthotel, Flughafenstrasse 300. Tel.: 69851. Telex: 413112. Fax: 69851. Rooms/suites: 350. Modern, efficient, and determined to spoil the visiting executive with thoughtful caring. Bus shuttle to the airport. There is an outdoor summer restaurant, and one can dance in the Montgolfiere club.

Moderately Priced

Arcade, Speicherstrasse 3. Tel.: 273030. Telex: 6997510. Rooms: 200. Modern and comfortable, but with no special trimmings. Breakfast is memorable; bar and restaurant are good; conference rooms. Central.

Schwille, Grosse Bockenheimerstrasse 50. Tel.: 283054. Telex: 4170572. Rooms: 60. Pleasant, pedestrians-only street near main squares, chambers of commerce, and the stock exchange. Airy rooms; lots of local flavor in the big *cafe-konditorei*. Terrace seating, weather permitting.

Westend, Westenstrasse 15. Tel.: 746702. Rooms: 20. Calm and tasteful with pretty garden; in a chic area. Popular with publishers and journalists. Reserve well ahead.

▷ Restaurants

Frankfurt will probably never be known as a gastronomic mecca. Typical Frankfurt specialties are *Handkäs mit Musik,* a yellowishly translucent, wrinkled, gelatinous cheese served with vegetable oil and raw onions, one of the try-it-once-and-call-it-an-experience dishes; and *Frankfurter Würstchen*—these long, slender, spicy pork sausages are known around the world and celebrated their 500th birthday in 1987. Legally speaking, a sausage can only be called a *Frankfurter* if it is produced in the city or the surrounding area. Another culinary tradition is *Grüne Sosse,* or green sauce, a thin cream sauce containing six varieties of fresh herbs, usually served with hard-boiled eggs or boiled ox breast and boiled potatoes. If one is going "native," all this is washed down with *Apfelwein* (apple wine).

The city does offer a broad array of other cuisines, ranging from American "soul food" to Japanese sushi. The high proportion of foreigners living in the city has resulted in a better-than-average selection of national cuisines to choose from.

High Class

Bistro 77, Ziegelhüttenweg 1-3. Tel.: 614040. French *nouvelle cuisine,* rated highly by customers but less so by some professional critics. One of the best kitchens in Frankfurt with an excellent wine list. Tables spaced far enough apart for sensitive conversation. Don't be put off by a bunkerlike exterior. Decor inside is postmodern pastel pink and grey. Extremely attentive service.

Bettina-Eck, Bettinastrasse/Erlenstrasse. Tel.: 749652. Tucked behind a high-rise bank, this is one of the Frankfurt banking community's favorite lunchtime hideaways. Food and wine are very good. And, unlike some "big name" restaurants in the banking district, the prices are right, too. Small and popular. Reservations a must.

Erno's Bistro, Liebigstrasse 15. Tel.: 721997. French cuisine. A long-time lunch and dinner favorite with the bankers. Small, cozy, wood-paneled, it's Frankfurt's version of a Parisian bistro. Lamb is outstanding. Good lunch. Quality has declined since Erno's death, but still very good.

Gargantua, Friesengasse 3. Tel.: 776442. Fine food and wine at this small, warm restaurant catering to successful young urban types. Owner is former political streetfighter Klaus Trebes.

Le Gourmet, Hotel Gravenbruch-Kempinski. Tel.: (06102) 5050. If you are not staying in the hotel, the restaurant is worth the trip. Has earned a Michelin star. Intimate and comfortable, excellent service, and superb French cuisine, both classic and *nouvelle.*

Hessler, Am Bootshafen 4, Maintal-Dörnigheim. Tel.: (06181) 492951. Twenty minutes east of Frankfurt on the Main bank, Frau Hessler's restaurant features one of the region's best wine lists and pricy—but very good—food, mixing regional and French specialties.

Humperdinck, Grüneburgweg 95. Tel.: 722122. *Nouvelle cuisine* variations on the classic French. Luxurious decor and good service within walking distance of the banking district. Located in the former Westend villa of composer Humperdinck, famous for the opera "Hansel and Gretel."

Le Midi, Liebigstrasse 47. Tel.: 721438. French-international cuisine with the *nouvelle* touch. Pleasant and comfortable, in the heart of the Westend banking area. Expensive to the point of being overpriced.

Sängers Restaurant-im "Weissen Turm," Hugenottenstrasse 121, Friedrichsdorf. Tel.: (06172) 72020. If you are seeking a break from the urban environment, Klaus Sänger's highly rated restaurant in the Taunus Hills outside Frankfurt is worth an excursion, with an original, eclectic menu including fixed price "surprise" menus of five or seven courses.

Weinhaus Brückenkeller, Schützenstrasse 6, Tel.: 284238. The most famous of the old Frankfurt restaurants. Interesting mix of well-prepared international and regional cuisine. Evenings only. Located in the still-unpretentious east side of Frankfurt, it provides one of the last remaining tastes of the prewar city. Elegant, 360-year-old, multilevel, vaulted cellars with valuable antiques. House musicians. Can get smoky.

Chinese

Lain-Yi, Niddastrasse 39. Tel.: 235915. Centrally located and considered one of the best Chinese restaurants in the city.

Greek

Alexandrion, Weckmarkt 13. Tel.: 288287. A popular place near city hall.

Italian

Da Mario, Moselstrasse 12. Tel.: 251194. A good and moderately priced restaurant.

Napoli (Golfo di), Leipzigerstrasse 16. Tel.: 776566. Also good and inexpensive.

Pittore, Zeisselstrasse 20. Tel.: 599134. Excellent fresh food, including fish and seafood. Inexpensive.

Japanese

Kikkoman, Friedberger Anlage 1. Tel.: 232541. Part of the Japanese chain. Central situation. Recommended by book fair PR chief Peter Czerwonka who publishes a small guide (*Börsenverein des Deutschen Buchhandels*) for fair visitors.

Turkish

Taverna Kervansaray, Abtsgasschen 8. Tel.: 626310. The Turks, along with the Greeks, Spanish, Yugoslavs, and other foreigners, form close to a quarter of the population and have considerably enlivened the gastronomic scene. This restaurant also features belly dancing.

▷ Tipping

The check includes the standard tip, so don't add more than a few coins unless you're particularly pleased with the service. Tip the hatcheck attendant, of course, and the concierge and doormen for such services as reserving a restaurant table or concert tickets for you and finding you a taxi. Between $3 and $5 is the going rate. Tip cabdrivers about 10 percent on top of the metered fare.

▷ Doing Business

Frankfurt is the dominant city of the *Land* (state) of Hesse, and the Hessian character is serious and solid, even stolid. Formality is one keynote of business life. After a quarter-century of working in the same office, colleagues still refer to each other formally as "Herr Weber" or "Frau Klinke." Visitors should never use first names unless invited to do so, and such invitations are rare. Address senior managers as "Herr Doktor" or "Herr Direktor," but check beforehand which is which. There are even "Herr Professor Doktors," believe it or not—men with two higher-educational degrees.

Business is done in offices, not over lunch or drinks, and is done with great thoroughness. The typical German company is looking for a relationship that will last 10, 15, or more years, not a here-today-gone-tomorrow deal.

Frankfurt business and banking executives arrive at meetings well briefed, and visitors should be equally well informed. The typical Frankfurt executive does not like to be hurried. One American with long experience of the city says that it's counterproductive, possibly fatal, for a visitor to say, in effect: "Let's sign this—I have a flight to catch." That won't move the German: he is likely to schedule another meeting. Details and more details—that is the *Leitmotiv* (recurring theme). A stereotype of the Teuton? Perhaps, but most members of the army of foreign business executives living in Frankfurt stress over and over again certain linked themes: be prepared, be patient, be a master of facts and figures.

If you are trying to introduce a new product, remember that West Germany is the home of technical standards. The *Deutsche Industrie Normen* (DIN) lists no fewer than 25,000 of them, ranging from aeroengines to electrical sockets. Industrial trade associations assign numbers to products; without a number, you cannot sell yours. You'll need a lawyer to guide you through the jungle. Help may be at hand, though, in the form of the European Community, which takes the view that national standards imposed in West Germany and elsewhere are often nontariff barriers to trade.

A good place at which to introduce a new product or process is at one of Frankfurt's innumerable trade fairs. The huge fairgrounds, recently extended and modernized, are busy year-round. Expositions range from the International Fair, held in spring and fall and claimed as the world's largest for consumer goods; through the automobile show, held every two years; to lesser but still huge and impressive unveilings of the latest in publishing, musical instruments, textiles, and computer technology. For further information, contact *Messe Frankfurt GmbH,* Ludwig-Erhard-Anlage 1. Tel.: 75750 or 757-5276.

Buses and streetcars will get you to and from the fairgrounds faster than cars and taxis. The streetcar routes are 16 and 19, the bus routes 32, 33, and 50. If you must drive, there is a bus shuttle between the Rebstock parking lot and the fairgrounds.

▷ Spotlight ◁

Banking. West Germany's big banks are major players in the industrial field, holding the pursestrings of many manufacturing giants—and sometimes a strategic shareholding. The banks are also dealmakers, putting together mergers and acquisitions and financing them wholly or partly. The system is known as "universal." In short, what would be known in the United States as commercial or retail banks are also investment banks, new-issue underwriters of stocks and bonds, and providers of a wide range of other financial services. This freedom to compete extends also to the *Landesbanken*, which can be likened to central banks for the *Lander* (states') savings banks.

Representatives of the banks sit on the boards of every major company, and a business of any size without a solid connection to a bank is in for a very rough time. The "Big Three"— Deutsche Bank, Dresdner Bank, and Commerzbank—have high-rise headquarters within shouting distance of each other on the west side of Frankfurt's city center. Deutsche's twin towers of reflective glass at Taunusanlage 12 outshine the smaller rivals on the rare sunny day, reflecting also its position as the nation's largest commercial bank and the 11th largest in the world, with total assets of DM 250 billion.

The Bundesbank, West Germany's powerful central bank, is located at Wilhelm Epsteinstrasse 14. The massive, modern building, set in an immaculate park dotted with swan-filled lagoons, looks like a cross between an edge-of-town hotel and an insurance company headquarters. From the 13th floor, Karl Otto Pöhl, the president, and the other members of the six-man directorate have a clear view of the city's banking district, one mile to the south in downtown Frankfurt. They really do have their fingers on the pulse of national monetary policy, for under West German law, the Bundesbank is a completely independent institution, and Herr Doktor Pöhl is not required to answer to anyone. In the cold light of banking reality, it is the most powerful central bank in Europe, dominating the European Monetary System. Pöhl is also the senior statesman of the so-called Group of Seven, which is comprised of the finance ministers and central bank chiefs of Britain, Canada, France, Italy, Japan, the United States, and West Germany.

The bank's monetary policies have kept West German inflation low and made the Deutsche mark the second most important reserve currency after the U.S. dollar. Critics say the bank is headed by a corps of hard-core monetarists with an almost obsessive fear of inflation, who are often rigidly nationalistic in their outlook.

Now, during Pöhl's second seven-year term, that image is changing. The bank president is a tough, but witty and urbane, pragmatist. He is not an enthusiastic supporter of a European central bank, which France and Italy have been promoting as a prerequisite to the European Community's single, frontierless market of 1992. Pöhl thinks such a central bank is a long way off but does joke that its natural site would be "Frankfurt-sur-la-Main."

Tradition and formality both argue against business breakfasts. Lunch with wine is a social occasion, and documents should not be spread on the table or napkins used for scribbling. Business dinners are rare. Managers prefer to head for their homes in such smart suburbs as Bad Homburg, Königstein, and Kronberg, and they're not to be disturbed. It's a bad idea, too, to phone your business contact over the weekend.

Your Frankfurt host may well take you to one of the many apple-wine pubs in the Sachsenhausen district. Foreigners often find apple wine too tart, but it's good manners to pretend that you enjoy it.

Does all that has gone before make Frankfurt sound dour and joyless? Perhaps. The impression is wrong, however. Though it doesn't have the charm of Rome, the champagne fizz of Paris, or the majesty of London, Frankfurt does have certain virtues, and one of them is its commitment to doing business. Old hands will tell you, too, that when in an unbuttoned mood, Frankfurt executives have a distinct, if wry, sense of humor.

▷ *Spotlight* ◁

West Germany's 16 labor unions are strong, rich, and disciplined. About 42 percent of nonagricultural workers are union members, and union representatives sit on the supervisory board of all large companies (the companies' other board, management, deals with day-to-day matters). Employers fought hard to defeat this legal requirement, the so-called *Mitbestimmung*, introduced by the Social Democratic Party government in the 1970s, but seem now to accept it as both permanent and even desirable. After all, labor union board members have learned some of the facts of economic life, one of them being that their country's prosperity rests largely on exports—and that means that it must remain competitive.

How do labor union leaders view *Mitbestimmung*? One of them described his tactics as "antagonistic cooperation" with the bosses. He contrasted this favorably with what he saw as the more hostile approach to union-management bargaining in Britain, France, and Italy. Whether that view is right or wrong, and whether the system is chiefly responsible, the facts are that half of all workers now enjoy working weeks of fewer than 40 hours, along with pay and fringe benefits that are the highest in the entire European Community.

Employers and unions alike are committed to the value of training future workers and retraining people already in the labor force. About 1.8 million apprentices attend special schools—10 times more than in France, for example. This means that employers can often recruit directly from the schools rather than placing help-wanted advertisements in the newspapers.

The high skills of West German workers counterbalance their high cost by world standards. There's a cloud on the horizon, though, and that's the looming European Single Market of the 1990s. When all barriers to intra-European trade are removed—if they indeed are—West Germany will feel the full force of competition from such relatively low-wage countries as Spain and Portugal. Many West German labor leaders are advocating the formation of transnational unions that would raise wage and employment standards elsewhere.

▷ Useful Phone Numbers

Emergencies

Accident assistance	233364
Ambulance	490001
Fire, first aid	112
Helicopter rescue	441033
Police	110

Local Information

Airport	6901
Schedules	690-3501
Tourist Office	212-8849
Congress service	212-4137
Trains	212-8849/51

Business Sources

Bundesbank (central bank)	1581
German Chambers of Commerce	
Industrie und Handelskammer	21970
Handwerkskammer Rhein-Main	710-0010

►171

▷ **Spotlight** ◁

The **American Chamber of Commerce** in West Germany, headquartered at Rossmarkt 12, has about 2,200 members, some of them German firms with a presence on both sides of the Atlantic. American members' investment in West Germany is $28 billion, roughly equal to West Germany's investment in the United States. The chamber has representatives in many parts of West Germany, including Berlin, Baden-Wurttemburg, Bavaria, and Nord Rhein-Westfalia.

Overseas Chambers/Economic Offices

American	283402	South Africa	(06172) 31181
Australia (Victoria)	666-6028	Spain	638031
Austria	720866	Taiwan	610742
Connecticut State	282055	Thailand	281091
Finland	728148		
France	729353		
Ghana	234313		

Consulates

Greece	291879
Hong Kong	740161
India	252254
Iowa State	233858
Israel	722821

Argentina	233644
Austria	707-2558
Belgium	590578
Bolivia	728205
Brazil	290708
Cameroon	254-2311

Italy			
(Mezzogiorno)	708024/294151	Chile	550194
Japan (Jetro)	283215	Denmark	770391
Old West (North		Egypt	590557
and South Dakota,		Finland	728148
Montana, Nebraska,		France	740137
Wyoming)	20516	Greece	595750
Louisiana State	591808	India	271040
Mauritius	284348	Indonesia	(06105) 76003
Penn's Southwest	(06174) 1055	Iran	714-0050
Philippines	748048	Italy	75310
Puerto Rico	721242	Japan	770351
Singapore	233838	Kenya	2825512

Korea (South)	563051	Alitalia	633-4140
Luxembourg	236611	Austrian Airlines	230991
Mexico	235709	Avianca (Colombia)	236251
Morocco	231737	Balkan-Bulgarian	
Netherlands	752021	Airlines	295167
Norway	411040	British Airways	250121
Philippines	627538	Canadian Pacific	
Peru	20301	Air Lines	294044
Portugal	702066	Cathay Pacific Airways	230192
South Africa	723741	Continental Airlines	748081
Spain	638071	Czechoslovak Airlines/	
Sweden	230479	CSA	233559
Switzerland	725941	Delta Air Lines	233024
Tanzania	745989	Eastern Airlines	287459
Thailand	20110	Egyptair	235509
Turkey	772048	El Al Israel Airlines	20326
United Kingdom	720406	Ethiopian Airlines	250077
United States	753040	Garuda Indonesian	
Uruguay	518510	Airways	232956
Venezuela	287284	Gulf Air	295242
Yugoslavia	439923	Iberia (Spain)	717201
		Iran Air	232067

Airlines

		Iraqi Airways	235227
		Japan Air Lines/JAL	136-0136
Aer Lingus (Ireland)	292054	KLM Royal Dutch	
Aeroflot Soviet Airlines	230771	Airlines	740811
Aerolineas Argentinas	238-3219	Korean Air	239201
Aeromexico	747981	Kuwait Air Ways	234074
Air Afrique	590936	LAN-Chile	235640
Air Algerie	233281	LOT Polish Airlines	231981
Air Canada	250131	Lufthansa German	
Air France	230501	Airlines	25701
Air India	230241	Malev Hungarian	
Air Lanka	281395	Airlines	234043
Air New Zealand	291897	Northwest Airlines	234344
Alia Royal Jordanian	231853	Olympic Airways	75345

Pakistan International		South African Airways	13691
Airlines	238-5311	Swissair	26026
Pan Am World		TAP Air Portugal	720435
Airways	256-5222	Thai Airways	740286
Philippine Airlines	230416	Turk Hava Yollari	253031
Qantas Airways		TWA	770601
(Australia)	230041	United Airlines	239221
Sabena Belgian World		UTA (France)	590936
Airlines	294061	Varig (Brazil)	26991
SAS Scandinavian		Wardair (Canada)	230056
Airlines	26461	Western Airlines (USA)	291011
Saudi Arabian		Yugoslav Airlines/JAT	20956
Airlines	273-3111		
Singapore Airlines	724-0204		

▷ Shopping

Frankfurt scores high on prices, but also on variety. The city's best stores are packed into a small area around the main square, the *Hauptwache.* On the square itself is a wide variety, both above and below street level, with the emphasis on groceries, flowers, clothing, tobacco products, photographic equipment, and bookstores. There are also plenty of cafés.

Next to the Hauptwache is the *Zeil* pedestrian zone, which claims to hold the all-German record for spending per square foot or meter of retail space. Where else is champagne dispensed on the street to entice buyers? Department, clothing, and footware stores predominate, but the *Kleinmarkthalle* is a covered, lively market for international food. *Schillerstrasse,* near the stock exchange, is thronged with men's and women's fashion boutiques. *Steinweg* offers jewelry and perfumes, and *Goethestrasse* goes for top-mark elegance and exclusivity. *Fressgasse,* or gourmet alley, has cafés with terraces, delicatessens, and wine shops. Nearby *Kaiserstrasse* is dominated by the BFG skyscraper and its galleries of restaurants and *haute couture* stores.

▷ After Hours

Frankfurt is the jazz capital of West Germany, and possibly of Europe. Prominent soloists and groups play at the *Alter Oper,* the *Frankfurter Festhalle,* and the *Jahrhunderthalle Hoechst.* There are hundreds of clubs, discos, and bistros as well featuring German and foreign groups. In the summer, open-air concerts are staged in parks and squares. Among leading clubs:

Der Jazzkeller, Kleine Bockenheimstrasse 18a: Tel.: 288537. Modern, hot, and free jazz.

Down by the Riverside, Mainkai 7. Tel.: 292150. Quaint and interesting.

Jazzhouse, Kleine Bockenheimerstrasse 12. Tel.: 287194. Disco and live jazz.

Jazzkneipe, Berlinerstrasse 70. Tel.: 287173. Noted for swing.

Jazzlife Podium, Klein Rittergasse 22. Tel.: 626346. Dixieland and swing.

Niddapark-Terrassen, Woogstrasse 52. Tel.: 520522. New Orleans and Country.

Schlachthof, Deutscheherenufer 24. Tel.: 623261. Dixieland and swing.

Sinkkasten, Bronnerstrasse 9. Tel.: 280385. Jazz rock, blues, and fringe groups.

▷ Sights and Sounds

Johann Wolfgang von Goethe (1749–1832) is Frankfurt's most famous citizen. Poet, novelist, scientist, dramatist, theater director, ducal courtier—he was a man of many parts and talents. Goethe represents the romantic, liberal, and kindly part of the German *Weltanschauung* (world view), and in his reworking of the medieval legend of Faust foreshadowed with uncanny accuracy the demonic pact that led to the Nazi era and its horrors. In the *Goethehaus-Goethe Museum,* Grosserhirschgraben 23, are the desk at which he worked, many documents, and a rare view of how a prosperous eighteenth-century German family lived.

Schaumainkai is Museum Row. At number 23 is the *Staedel Art Institute,* a repository since 1878 of a superb collection covering six centuries. Painters represented include Fra Angelico, Botticelli, Picasso, and members of the Flemish, French, and German classical schools. At number 17 is the *Museum für Kunsthandwerk,* the arts and crafts museum; at 29 the *Museum für Völkerkunde,* the ethnology museum; at 41 the film museum; at 43 the architecture museum; and at 71 the *Liebieghaus,* the sculpture museum.

Another source of local pride is the *Rathaus,* or city hall, on Romerberg. Completely rebuilt after almost total destruction during World War II, the Rathaus and the square are both physically impressive and a symbolic link between past and present. In the history museum is a model of prewar Frankfurt, and nearby are the restored *Dom* (cathedral), where the Holy Roman emperors were crowned; and *Paulskirche,* site of the first German national assembly about 150 years ago.

Henninger Turm, Hainer Weg 60-64, is the city's tallest building at 120 meters (390 feet), with a panoramic view from the observation platform. It also houses restaurants and a brewery museum. *Palmengarten,* Palmengartenstrasse, is more than a memorably admirable botanical garden. It's a place where one can relax and recharge batteries run down by Frankfurt's relentless business pressures.

▷ Out of Town

Mountains (or are they hills?), the Rhine River, vineyards, forests...All these and more are close to the city. Among the many choices: a weekend cruise on the Rhine in great comfort, or a visit by coach to the chic wine-making villages of the Taunus hills or to the Black Forest, with castles along the way. The tour business is admirably well-organized and often combines tours by river and road. Your hotel concierge will help. If you prefer to arrange your own tour, the main bureau is located in the Hauptbahnhof.

Some travel agencies specialize in visits to East Germany and Eastern Europe. Two of those offering comprehensive services are *DER Deutsches Reisebüro* (Tel.: 156-6289) and *Deutsche Touring* (Tel.: 790-3219).

For information on horseracing, riding, swimming, tennis, squash, fitness centers, golf, and other sports, call *Sport und Badeamt* on 212-3565.

▷ Spotlight ◁

The villages and towns of the Taunus mountains, northwest of Frankfurt, are the most prestigious bedroom suburbs of Frankfurt. Virtually all bankers from middle manager level upwards live in the Taunus, where the air is noticeably clearer. Königstein, Kronberg, and Bad Homburg are the most select. Kronburg's Schloss Hotel has been the site of high-level meetings of international monetary leaders. Bad Homburg features the castle that was the summer residence of Germany's Kaisers. The Taunus region is also a favorite local recreation area, with its fir-covered hills crisscrossed by hiking paths. It's reachable by bus, subway, S-Bahn or auto in 20 minutes.

GENEVA

City of Secrets

Population: 157,000 (estimated). Capital of Swiss *canton* (state) Geneva (population: 350,000). *Location*: southwestern Switzerland, at southernmost tip of Lake Geneva, on Rhône river. *Economy*: banking and financial services, chemicals, clocks and watches, international organizations, jewelry, precision instruments, surgical appliances, tourism. Switzerland is a member of the European Free Trade Association (EFTA) and the Organization for Economic Cooperation and Development (OECD) and is a signatory to the General Agreement on Tariffs and Trade (GATT).

▷ Background Briefing

Two distinct Genevas live as neighbors but rarely meet. On one side is the bureaucratic world of the United Nations agencies and their cousins, a multitude of international organizations. On the other side is the very closed world of Geneva banking.

Members of the first group, thousands strong, are drawn from as many countries as there are UN members—more than 155 at last count. Ironically, Switzerland is not one of them: it is barred from membership by its own constitution, which mandates neutrality. Members of the second group, the bankers, are *Genevois*—a handful of families with strong, cohesive cultural and consensual ties. The international functionaries tend to describe the Genevois as stiff, formal, and standoffish; the Genevois return that compliment by regarding the functionaries as overpaid, underworked, and—above all—over here.

Yet neither can really do without the other. The UN and other bodies pump untold billions of Swiss francs into the local economy each year;

and the career functionaries, who pay no taxes, are only too glad to use the banks and other financial institutions to squirrel savings away. And though many complain about Geneva, the Genevois, the climate, and the cost of living, few choose to leave. Why should they? Geneva is one of Europe's most pleasant cities, with watersports almost at residents' doorsteps and skiing close by.

▷ Arriving

By Air

Geneva-Cointrin Airport (part of it is in France) is fast and efficient. The authorities claim that passengers can usually be out of the airport with their baggage within a quarter-hour. Buses to the city center take about 20 minutes, taxis a little less.

Going the other way, one should check in for international flights at least an hour ahead of departure (allow more time during the post-Christmas ski rush). Swissair, the national airline and one of the world's best carriers, has a lounge for business-class passengers, and the airport offers a VIP welcome service. Call 7981122 if you think you qualify.

Swissair is upgrading baggage handling and sorting, partly to handle new door-to-door services linked to hotel and railroad station checkins. Swissair has also introduced what it claims is the world's first automatic ticket-issuing system, incorporating checkin and baggage formalities. First, reserve a seat by phone. Second, find the ticketing machine at the airport—and indicate whether you want to communicate in English or French. Third, insert your credit card. Fourth, choose a seat in the smoking or nonsmoking section, window or aisle. The machine does the rest.

By Rail

Geneva is well served by trains. The super-fast French TGV takes you right into the city center; Swiss trains are notably clean and punctual. (But if you're traveling from Geneva to Zurich and are pressed for time, a Swissair flight is far faster. Though a small country, Switzerland is corrugated by mountains and valleys, and the only way to get from Point A to Point B in a hurry is by air.) If you have the time, the rail journey is enjoyable, with superb scenery from your window, and good food.

▷ Money

The standard unit of currency is the Swiss franc. International code: SFR. Banknotes are works of art and come in denominations of 10, 20, 50, 100, 500, and 1,000 Swiss francs. Don't worry if a banknote's color rubs off in your billfold: it's an artful way of making forgery harder (the ink formula is a secret). Coins are minted in denominations of 10, 20, and 50 centimes (100 centimes = 1 franc) as well as 1, 2, and 5 francs. Banks offer the best exchange rates.

▷ Language

French—of a kind. Parisians in particular delight in telling jokes in what they imagine is Genevois dialect, which is slow. Note that while in Parisian French the figure 90 is *quatre-vingt-dix,* in Swiss French it's *nonante;* and there are other language variations. Sophisticated Genevois are perfectly capable of speaking "pure" (Parisian) French when they want to. The city's name is *Genève* in French. Many people in Geneva speak English. German and Italian may also be heard, as they are official languages of Switzerland along with French.

▷ Communications

Among the best in Europe. Country code: 41. City code: 22. You don't need to dial the city code within the city. Listed hotels make a point of keeping guests happy with good telecommunications and message-taking. Indeed, we recall vividly that the concierge at one hotel tracked us from the UN Palais des Nations to a lakeside restaurant, and from there to a friend's home, with an urgent call from New York.

▷ Getting To Know the City

The lake and the French border have determined the city's topography; indeed, Geneva is almost completely surrounded by France. The business district is concentrated where the lake narrows and is dominated by the *Jet d'Eau,* a large fountain which shoots a huge vertical spray high into the air, its slightly dirty water being illuminated at night. Geneva has few grand buildings. It was, after all, the home for many years of John Calvin (1509–64), the French-born Protestant reformer who in the 1540s established a stern and intolerant local theocracy that frowned upon earthly show of pomp and circumstance.

That Calvinistic principle meshes nicely with—or perhaps fostered—the Genevois dislike of conspicuous consumption. Geneva bankers dwell not in marbled halls; but even if they believe in their heart of hearts that heavenly treasures are more enduring than earthly ones, they spend a lot of money on building impenetrable bank vaults and safety-deposit boxes.

▶179

Going out of the central city, along the lake toward Lausanne, one comes to the area dominated by buildings of the UN, its agencies, and nongovernmental international organizations, many of them lobbyists. The largest of these monuments to the hope that springs eternal in the human breast is the Palais des Nations, a vast complex that dates from League of Nations days from 1920 to 1946. Though the league collapsed, the building remains, with its high, echoing corridors, cavernous conference rooms, and bars, lounges, and restaurants for delegates. The main restaurant is excellent: don't refuse an invitation to it. The press bar on the ground floor is crowded, cheerful, and the place to go to hear the stories that don't get into the papers.

In all, there are more than 200 international organizations in Geneva. The most useful, perhaps, is dedicated to extermination of the tsetse fly. At least that's not a political issue—yet.

▷ Moving Around

Geneva has a good, efficient mass transit system, but it can be confusing to people who don't know the city well and aren't avid mapreaders. Taxis are easier, though somewhat expensive. Rental car rates are among the highest in Europe.

▷ Hotels

Geneva has no fewer than 16 five-star hotels—a disproportionately high number for a city of its modest size. Most are close to the lake, and some are still family-owned; all pride themselves on their restaurants. Many of these hotels offer services long abandoned elsewhere: a complimentary shoeshine, messages slipped under the door for guests who do not want to be disturbed, a linen cloth for the guest to step on when getting out of bed. Old-fashioned? Yes, delightfully so. But new-fashioned, too, behind the unchanging, aristocratic façade. The top suite at the Hotel des Bergues is air-conditioned and has a private balcony, a Jacuzzi, a solarium, plugs for telefax, telex, and computers—and bullet-proof windows.

The "Palaces"

Hôtel des Bergues, 33 Quai des Bergues. Tel.: 7315050. Telex: 23383. Fax: 321989. Rooms/suites: 123. In the banking and business center. Trusthouse Forte has spent some $6 million on refurbishment; the hotel is officially designated as a historic monument. Superb restaurant.

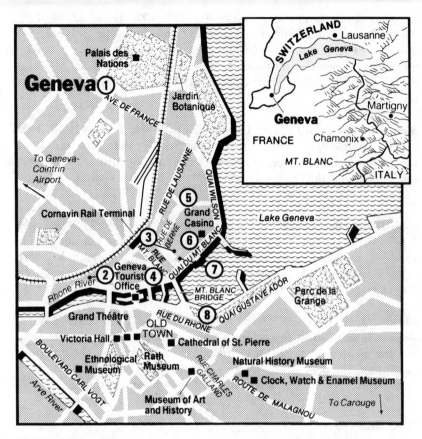

1. **Hotel Inter-Continental**
2. **Hotel du Rhone**
3. **Hotel Richemond**
4. **Hotel des Bergues**

5. **Hotel Ramada**
6. **Hotel Noga Hilton**
7. **Hotel Beau Rivage**
8. **Hotel Metropole**

Inter-Continental, 7-9 Chemin du Petit Sacconex. Tel.: 7346091. Telex: 23130. Fax: 342864. Rooms/suites: 377. Located ideally for any business connected with the UN and other international agencies. Shopping arcade, many business services, large heated pool.

Le Beau Rivage, 13 Quai du Mont Blanc. Tel.: 7310221. Telex: 23362. Fax: 786-7841. Rooms/suites: 120. A gem, carefully and tastefully modernized, but with a staff that venerates the old values of quiet, thoughtful service.

Le Richemond, Jardin Brunswick. Tel.: 7311400. Telex: 22598. Fax: 316709. Rooms/suites: 104. The Armleder family has owned this hotel for more than a century, and the current generation says its idea is to dissociate Geneva from Calvinistic austerity. Done—with the help of Rolls-Royces for the guests. Particularly recommended: *Le Gentilhomme* restaurant.

Metropole, 34 Quai General Guisan. Tel.: 211344. Telex: 421550. Fax: 211350. Rooms/suites: 140. Owned by the city, the Metropole was closed for six years and, after being entirely renovated, opened again in 1982. Once again, it is the top hotel in the left bank business section. Café, restaurant *l'Arlequin,* grillroom.

Noga Hilton International, 19 Quai du Mont-Blanc. Tel.: 7319811. Telex: 289704. Fax: 348612. Rooms/suites: 316. Relatively new, but not brashly so; decor and comfort are outstanding. Theater and conference hall with translation booths. Well-appointed fitness club with saltwater pool. *Le Cygne* restaurant is outstanding.

Rhône, Quai Terrettini. Tel.: 7319831. Telex: 22213. Fax: 324558. Rooms/suites: 280. A top business hotel, just across from the old town and the major private banks. One floor for nonsmokers. The luxurious sixth floor, the *Belle Etage,* features marble bathrooms, wall safes, telex and telefax plugs, electrically controlled shutters and curtains.

Also Starred

These properties are not quite as heavily acclaimed as the hotels listed above but still of high quality.

Century, 24 Avenue de Frontenex. Tel.: 7368095. Telex: 23223. Fax: 786-5274. Rooms: 138. On the left bank of the Rhône/lake. Comfortable, central.

Ramada Renaissance, 19 Rue de Zurich. Tel.: 7310241. Telex: 289109. Fax: 337961. Rooms: 219. Suites: 8. Studios: 30. Contemporary comfort in a lively part of the city; nicely designed; two restaurants.

Royal, 41 Rue de Lausanne. Tel.: 7316600. Telex: 27631. Fax: 786-7085. Rooms: 153. Central, quiet, friendly: tumble out of the train from France and straight into bed.

Warwick, 14 Rue de Lausanne. Tel.: 7316250. Telex: 23630. Fax: 738-9935. Rooms: 180. Close to the central station.

Airport

Holiday Inn, 26 Voie de Moens. Grand Saconnex. Tel.: 7910011. Telex: 415695. Fax: 989273. Rooms/suites: 305. Next to exhibition center, close to UN. Meeting rooms, pool, sauna, disco.

Penta, 75-77 Avenue L-Casai, Cointrin Airport. Tel.: 7984700. Telex: 27043. Fax: 798-7758. Rooms: 308. Better than the usual run of airport hotels; soundproofed rooms.

▷ Spotlight ◁

The Hotel du Lac at Coppet, 13 kilometers (8 miles) from Geneva, on the lakeside road to Lausanne is a place not many visitors know. Not many should: it's tiny, with only 31 rooms. Family-owned and run, the hotel is exquisite, with a first-class restaurant looking out on the lake. *Spécialité de la maison*: freshwater fish. Thoughtful selection of local wines. Try for one of the lakeside rooms; some have terraces. Tel.: 7761521. The charming little town of Coppet features a castle and a park.

▷ Restaurants

France's *Michelin Guide* gives one or two stars to 15 Geneva restaurants. *Gault-Millau,* Michelin's quirky and less authoritative rival, also rates Geneva highly. Cuisine is strongly influenced by that of France but does have a character of its own, with succulent recipes for freshwater fish, particularly the rare (and therefore costly) *omble chevalier.*

Sample the local wines. Most are light-bodied whites, with growths from Lavaux, Dezaley, and Saint-Saphorin usually dry. Many enophiles think that the Clos des Abbayes at Dezaley is Switzerland's best vineyard. Neuchatel is a slightly bubbly, very light wine that is at its best when served cold on hot days. There are some interesting reds, too, again light-bodied.

In Geneva

Amphitryon, 33 Quai des Bergues (in the Hôtel des Bergues). Tel.: 7315050. One of the city's best and most elegant restaurants, offering a subtle choice of classic and contemporary cuisine. Eat on the terrace on warm, dry days.

Chez Bouby, 1 Rue Grenus. Tel.: 7310927. An "in" bistro where bankers and artists mix. Food's not bad, either.

Chez Francis, 8 Boulevard Helvetique. Tel.: 463252. Restaurant on one side, piano bar on the other; open until 1:00 a.m.

Huissoud, 51 Rue du Stand. Tel.: 282583. Probably the best fondue in town. For those who don't know it, fondue is self-service: melt for yourself a variety of cheeses, often flavored with *kirsch* (cherry liqueur).

Le Bearn, 4 Quai de la Poste. Tel.: 210028. Warm, welcoming atmosphere; 20,000 bottles of wine in the cellar; memorable food on the table. *Patron* Jean-Paul Goddard does wonders with fish and seafood.

Le Cygne, 19 Quai du Mont-Blanc (in the Noga Hilton). Tel.: 7319811. Creative French dishes on the *nouvelle cuisine* side; fish and shellfish are specialties; melt-in-the-mouth desserts. Excellent selection of cigars.

Le Saint-Germain, 61 Boulevard Saint-Georges. Tel.: 282624. A haunt for the private bankers who relish both its proximity and its fish and seafood.

Lipp, Confederation Center. Tel.: 293122. Geneva branch of the famous Paris brasserie. Good cooking, reasonable prices, fast service—but crowded. Reserve.

Parc des Eaux-Vives, 82 Quai Gustave-Ador. Tel.: 7354140. Classic cuisine in a magnificent setting.

Farther Out

Away from the city are many good restaurants, both on the lake and inland. A selection, with distances from Geneva in parentheses:

Domaine de Chateaux-Vieux, 15 Chaussée du Chateau-Vieux, Peney-de-Sus (15 kilometers/9 miles). Tel.: 7531511. Charming, romantic eating among vineyards.

La Closerie, 301 Route de Lausanne, Bellevue (6 kilometers/3½ miles). Tel.: 7741741. Set in a park, with lake views, this restaurant offers a combination of rural tranquility and reasonably priced but ambitious dishes.

Le Leman, 287 Rue d'Hermance, Anieres (10 kilometers/6 miles). Tel.: 7512020. Rustic decor, sophisticated food, personal attention from *patron* Jean-Marie Claudel.

Le Lion d'Or, 5 Place Gauthier, Cologny (3.5 kilometers/3 miles). Tel.: 7364432. Splendid lake views; much favored by UN people for those and for a memorable menu.

▷ Tipping

Service is included in bar, restaurant, and taxi prices, but it's polite to "round off" with small change. Hotel bills cover tips—except those for the concierge and his or her staff. The minimum for small tasks is $5, such as reserving a restaurant table, and 10 percent of the cost of theater tickets. Leave at least $20 when you depart. Most concierges are members of an international fraternity, *Les Clefs d'Or*—so demanding guests who don't tip may find that their reputation has preceded them to their next port of call.

▷ Doing Business

The Swiss are rich because they're good businesspeople, and they're good businesspeople because they have a nose for a deal. They also work hard: banking and other executives are often at their desks at 7:30 a.m. They and many groups in both the private and public sectors are ready to help the visitor with information, advice, and introductions to potential partners. Among these groups:

Association of Private Banks *(Groupement des Banquiers Genevois)*, 67 Rue Saint-Jean. Tel.: 7313136. Banks can provide excellent statistics and background information. Once accepted by a private bank, a foreign client will find many doors open that were previously shut.

Cantonal Department for the Public Economy, 14 Rue Hôtel-de-Ville. Tel.: 272805. Cantonal officials can help investors with work permits for essential foreign personnel and industrial sites for rent—and with tax breaks. FIPA, a private foundation set up by the canton, can help with land.

Office for the Promotion of Geneva Industry (OPI), 9 Rue Boissonas, 1227 Carouge (this in the Acacias industrial zone). Tel.: 424244. Telex: 429080. OPI helps local industry to adapt to changing conditions and seeks to attract foreign industry. Highly efficient; will even meet visitors on Saturdays and outside normal working hours.

World Economic Forum, 53 Chemin des Hauts-Crets, 1223 Cologny-Geneva. Tel.: 7360243. Telex: 27973. The Forum organizes high-level meetings with politicians and business executives, most notably at Davos in the winter; and publishes an interesting study of the comparative competitiveness of the twenty-four member-countries of the Organization for Economic Cooperation and Development (OECD).

World Trade Center, PO Box 306, 1215 Geneva Airport. Tel.: 7989989. Telex: 289950. Mail and message services, multilingual staff, advice on startups, law, and taxes.

Let's sweep away a hoary old myth right now—the one about Swiss banking secrecy. It's had a long life; it's overdue for retirement.

First, bankers have *always* been required to cooperate if a prosecutor has cause to believe that a customer's money comes from crimes committed in Switzerland. That's how one of the authors of this book helped to unmask Clifford Irving as the forger of the alleged autobiography of American millionaire Howard Hughes: Irving's wife had used a stolen identity card to open one of the bank accounts in which she stashed the loot. The bank in question didn't even wait for a prosecutor's order before dropping hints so heavy that they clanged loudly on the floor like horseshoes.

Second, a numbered bank account protects a customer's identity, wealth, and dealings only from bank staff—and not from the law's prying eyes. A numbered account, in short, ensures privacy only within the bank, where the customer's identity is known only to two executives.

Third, though tax evasion is not a criminal act in Switzerland, the authorities are cooperating increasingly with their counterparts in the United States and elsewhere, particularly if there is a strong suspicion that deposits represent "laundered" proceeds from organized crime—and a belief that a tax-evasion prosecution will nail the criminal back home. A new Swiss law also allows the banks to cooperate with the SEC in insider-trading cases.

None of this means, of course, that Swiss bankers are blabbermouths: they imbibed discretion with their mothers' milk. It does mean that they are even more careful about with whom they do business than they were a few years ago. If you want real secrecy, go to Austria.

A quiet revolution is taking place on Rue de la Corraterie where the spacious mansions house Geneva's more exclusive private banks, the so-called Protestant Six and Roman Catholic Three. Old-money banks, such as Hentsch (1796) and Lombard, Odier, established more recently in 1798, specialize in "capital preservation" for rich clients worldwide. The Swiss Big Three—Union Bank of Switzerland, Swiss Banking Corporation, and Credit Suisse—manage close to half of the staggering $900 billion Swiss private banking market, but the nine members of the inner circle handle a very nice $70 billion.

Serious private money has always flowed to Geneva rather than Zurich. The revolution concerns advertising. One private banker explained: "Our institutional clients thought we were too discreet." Name plaques with just initials remain, however. A visitor asks if the division into Protestant and Catholic has much meaning today. The simple answer is "Yes." Other big players are: American Express, Paribas, and Safra Republic Holdings.

▷ *Spotlight* ◁

CERN. Scientists from around the world, led by Italian Nobel physics prize winner Carlo Rubbia, are engaged in pure, long-range nuclear research at the European Laboratory for Particle Physics (CERN), near Geneva. Fourteen leading European countries are members, with the EC, Poland, Turkey, and Yugoslavia as observers. A new 27-kilometer (16-mile) accelerator, or tunnel, serves as a covered bobsleigh run for atoms. Upcoming: a large proton collider. CERN has given European high-energy physics a world lead. It attracts thousands of scientists and engineers from the world over. Tel.: 7834101 and 7836397. Telex: 419000 CERN.

Business life isn't all hard, grinding work. The Genevois like their food and drink, and they appreciate an invitation to one of the city's better restaurants. Many are also gamblers. "Let's have dinner in France" isn't the adventurous invitation it sounds. The resort town of Divonne-les-Bains is only 19 kilometers (12 miles) away and offers the formal glitter of a French casino, where the loudest noise is the click of the ball in the roulette wheel. The restaurant most starred is the *Château de Divonne,* with its park and terrace. Telephone: (33 for France) 5020-0032. Always check with the concierge or with the consulate about the current French entry visa situation.

A good way to get to know other non-Swiss business executives is to go to one of the many luncheon clubs. The *American International Club* meets at the Hotel Inter-Continental. Tel.: 7330180.

▷ Useful Phone Numbers

Emergencies

Dentist	216022
Doctor	202511
Lost/found	7876111/7993335
Night pharmacy	111
Police	117

Local Information

Airport	7981122

Cantonal government	272805
Chamber of Commerce	215333
Highway conditions/snow	163
Industrial promotion	424244
Legal advice	282411
Railroad station	455200
Taxis	141
Tourist information	287233
Weather	162

Business Clubs

Rotary, Geneva	7315050
Professional Women's Club	7360120

Transportation Arrangements

Aeroleasing	7984510
Executive car service	7377977
Executive jet	7984480
Heli-transport	7984481
Palexpo exhibition center	7981111

International Organizations

European Broadcasting Union	7987766
European Free Trade Association (EFTA)	7349000
General Agreement on Tariffs and Trade (GATT)	7395111
Intergovernmental Committee for Migration	7980066
International Air Transport Association (IATA)	7983360
International Labor Office	7996111
International Organization for Standards	7341240
International Red Cross	7346001
International Telecommunications Union	7995111

International Trade Center	7300111
United Nations	7310211/7346011
UN agencies	
Commission on Human Rights	7310211
Conference on Trade and Development	7300111
Economic Commission for Europe	7310211
International Law Commission	493545
World Health Organization	7912111
World Council of Churches	7916111
World Meteorological Organization	7346400

Chambers of Commerce/ Commercial Offices

Geneva

Arab-Swiss	473202
Chinese-Swiss	422010
Franco-Swiss	7356540
Japan (Jetro)	7321304
Portugal	7357410
South Korea	454920
Turkey	7323488

Basel (061)

Franco-Swiss	225600
Latin America-Argentine	7523222
Venezuela	7361111

Lausanne (021)

Franco-Swiss	261767
Swiss-Brazil	207482
Taiwan	7335005

Consulates

Australia	7346200
Austria	478213
Bahrain	7582102
Bangladesh	7325940
Belgium	7338150
Brazil	7320930
Cameroon	7362022
Canada	7339000
China	7922537
Netherlands	7356611
Peru	7311912
Portugal	7311980
Qatar	7988256
South Africa	7357803
Soviet Union	7347955
Sweden	7351946
Syria	7325658
Thailand	294666
Turkey	7361440
Uruguay	7315013
West Germany	7335000

Airlines

Aer Lingus (Ireland)	7321656
Aeroflot Soviet Airlines	7311643
Air Afrique	216844
Air Algerie	7315180
Air Canada	7314980
Air France	7310400
Alitalia	7316650
American Airlines	7942111
Austrian Airlines	7315730
British Airways	7314050
Crossair (Switzerland)	7982121
El Al Israel Airlines	7320550
Finnair	7312530
Iberia (Spain)	7317650
Japan Air Lines/JAL	7317160
KLM Royal Dutch Airlines	7983777
Lufthansa German Airlines	7319550
Olympic Airways	219621
Pan Am World Airways	7323834
Qantas Airways (Australia)	7320450
Saudi Arabian Airlines	7319150
Sabena Belgian World Airlines	7326620
SAS Scandinavian Airlines	216522
Singapore Airlines	7322205
South African Airways	7316740
Swissair	7982121
TAP Air Portugal	7317350
Turk Hava Yollari	7316120
TWA	450350
Varig (Brazil)	7317730

▷ **Shopping**

Geneva is the natural place to look for watches—and for chocolates and cuckoo clocks. Swiss watch exports total about $2.5 billion a year, solid evidence that in the era of the cheap, throwaway timepiece, some people care about quality. Places to look for watches:

Benoit de Gorski, 86 Rue du Rhône. Tel.: 281430. An institution on the waterfront.

Bucherer, 45 Rue du Rhône and 22 Rue du Mont-Blanc. Tel.: 216266. A famous name which has equally famous repair service.

Golay Fils et Stahl, 1 Place des Bergues. Tel.: 7315400. This firm set up shop in 1837 and sells a wide range of both watches and jewelry.

Gubelin, 60 Rue du Rhône. Tel.: 288655. A prestigious company on the prestigious watch street.

Patek Philippe, 41 Rue du Rhône. Tel.: 200366. One of the world's great watchmakers; in Geneva since 1839.

Vacheron et Constantin, 1 Rue des Moulins. Tel.: 283133. Another world-famous maker of superb timepieces. For antique watches, clocks, and jewelry, try *Lattes,* 29 Rue de la Cité.

▷ *Spotlight* ◁

Rolex is the quintessential Swiss watch, right? In fact, the firm was founded in London, but it has long had its headquarters in Geneva. As a private company, it doesn't publish financial results, but it is said to account for a quarter of Swiss watch exports— no less than $625 million by value. Rolex chronometers are tested for 15 days and nights in five positions and at three different temperatures.

Chocolates. *Hautle,* 21 Place du Bourg-de-Four; and *Michelli,* 1 Rue Michelli-du-Crest.

Cigars. *Davidoff,* 2 Rue de Rive. Huge selection, all in prime condition.

Feminine fashions. *Blondino,* Rue Fontaine/Rue Purgatoire.

Knives—the famous Swiss Army design, and others. *Wenger,* 4 Rue du Port. Tel.: 213179.

Souvenirs, linens, music boxes, and other miscellaneous items: *Swiss Art,* Rue du Mont-Blanc. Tel.: 7867962.

▷ After Hours

The city of Calvin is hardly the city of night. There are no clubs with lavish floor shows. Note also that clubs are really clubs: ask your hotel concierge for advice about temporary membership. A sampling:

Grafiti, 7 Route de Saint-Julien. Tel.: 425498. Private club, with chic clientele.

Griffin's, 36 Boulevard Helvetique. Tel.: 7351218. Top (private) club frequented by "beautiful people"—models, entertainers, and the merely rich.

King's Club, 92 Rue du Rhône. Tel.: 214587. Self-styled "international bar club."

Pussy Cat Saloon, 15 Rue des Glacis-de-Rive. Tel.: 7351515. Good cabaret, affable staff and clients.

Regine's and Jimmy's, both at the Hotel Noga Hilton, 19 Quai du Mont-Blanc. Tel.: 7319811. Superior discos.

▷ Sights and Sounds

Geneva has a long and distinguished literary, musical, and artistic history, thanks in part to its having been a refuge for Protestants in the war-torn and intolerant period of the 1500s to 1700s. Philosopher Jean-Jacques Rousseau was born there. Among world-famous men and women who lived in and around Geneva for a while were Voltaire, Lord Byron, Jean-Baptiste-Camille Corot, Victor Hugo, Alexandre Dumas, Honoré de Balzac, George Sand, and Franz Liszt.

Closer to our own times, Ernest Ansermet founded Geneva's international musical ambassador, the *Orchestre de la Suisse Romande,* which gives frequent concerts at *Victoria Hall.* For opera and dance, there is the 1500-seat *Grand Theater,* which has a ballet of its own and welcomes such companies as the Bolshoi and that of Maurice Bejart, the master of modern dance who moved recently from Brussels to Lausanne.

The city is rich in museums and art galleries, some 30 of them. Recommended are:

Museum of Art and History, 2 Rue Charles Galland. Tel.: 290011. Civilization traced from prehistory to the present, with masterpieces by Quentin de la Tour gracing the first floor.

Natural History Museum, Route de la Malagnou. Tel.: 7359130. At the top of its category when judged by the most rigorous criteria.

Barbier Mueller Museum, 4 Rue Ecole de Chimie. Tel.: 200253. A jewel-box of art from Africa and the South Seas.

Watch and Clock Museum, *(Musée de l'Horlogerie),* 15 Route de Malagnou. Tel.: 7367412. Timepieces through the ages, enamel work, antique miniatures.

▷ Spotlight ◁

The United Nations complex, which is as large as the Château de Versailles (though not half as pretty) has been the site of some important historical events. Recently, UN Secretary General Javier Perez de Cuellar brought representatives from Iran and Iraq together in the same room to negotiate a peace settlement. Letters mailed from the *Palais de Nations* will bear UN stamps; there's a good selection of them at a shop in the main lobby. The Visitors' Service offers guided tours daily. Tel.: 7346011, extension 4539.

Geneva's old town, or *Vielle Ville,* has art galleries, antique shops, bookstores, and tiny bistros. There's also a big, recently excavated architectural site. Rousseau's house is at 40 Grand Rue.

▷ Out of Town

Lake District

Good highways and fast, frequent trains bring within easy reach Geneva's lakeside neighbors, *Lausanne, Montreux,* and *Vevey,* the latter the world headquarters of the globe-girdling Nestlé food group. Elizabeth Taylor has moved on, and Vladimir Nabokov has passed on, but this golden strip along Lake Geneva is still home to stars and millionaires. Steamers tour the 45-mile-long lake with stops at castles, ports, and parks. For details, contact Mouettes Genevoises, 8 Quai du Mont-Blanc. Tel.: 7322944.

Lining the lakeshore and inland are many unspoiled villages, along with vineyards and woods. Most of the rustic inns serve good, hearty "peasant food" with local wines. Among places to visit: *Hermance,* on the lake; the wine-growing villages of *Russin* and *Dardagny* (good train service); and *Jussy*.

Golf

There are plenty of golf courses near Geneva and across the French border. Among them:

Domaine Imperial Golf and Country Club, Route Cantonale 1, Gland. Some 15 miles from Geneva. Tel.: 644545. A luxurious private club on former royal grounds. An 18-hole Pete Dye course. Hotel and sports facilities. Membership and entry details: Cotrasa, 31 Rue du Rhône, Geneva. Tel.: 212622.

Golf Club de Genève, 70 Route de la Capité, Cologny. Tel.: 7522041.

Club de Golf du Domaine de Bonmont, Cheserex. Tel.: 691012.

Skiing

Within range are ski resorts, from celebrity-studded *Gstaad* in Switzerland to *Chamonix* and *Megeve* in France. Information about French resorts: *Comité Regional de Tourisme Savoie-Mont Blanc,* 9 Boulevard Wilson, 73100 Aix-les-Bains, France. Tel.: (33) 7988-2341. Telex: 980306.

HELSINKI

Hands Across the Gulf

Population: 484,000 (1981). Metropolitan area: 950,000 (estimated). Capital of the Republic of Finland (population: 4.9 million). *Location*: southern coast of Finland, overlooking the Gulf of Finland on the Baltic Sea. *Economy*: banking and financial services, ceramics and glassware, chemicals, clothing, electronics, engineering, foodstuffs, pharmaceuticals, printing and publishing, shipbuilding, textiles; country's largest seaport. Finland is a member of the Organization for Economic Cooperation and Development (OECD), an associate member of the European Free Trade Association (EFTA), and a signatory to the General Agreement on Tariffs and Trade (GATT). The country has agreements with the European Community (EC) and the Council for Mutual Economic Assistance (COMECON), the Soviet and East European Common Market.

▷ Background Briefing

Helsinki is a very Western city, but with strong architectural reminders of former Russian dominance. Indeed, film crews have used it as a stand-in for Moscow. But there is nothing Russian about the way the city functions. Streets are clean, service is excellent, stores are jammed with high-quality goods, and even in the harsh winter everything works. And unlike most other Western capitals, Helsinki has no street crime worth mentioning, there is virtually no drug abuse (though alcoholism is a problem), and there isn't even a red-light district.

Worthy, dull? Not at all. Once you get to know them, the Finns tend to be friendly, hospitable, warm, and funny—and certainly are eager to do business. Helsinki may not be a world center of culture, but let's not forget the composer Jean Sibelius, the architect Saarinen, the philologist-poet Elias Lonnerot, who compiled the mighty *Kalevala* epic, and a recent crop of Finns who have made their nationality synonymous with good design. Culture apart, Helsinki has much to please the visitor: first-class hotels and restaurants, clean air, and around a great many corners the sea and inlets from it.

The Finns are fiercely independent, and with good cause. Freedom has taken a long time to achieve. Finland was a Swedish colony for centuries. Then in 1807, without a word to the Finns, Tsar Alexander I and Napoleon Bonaparte agreed in the Treaty of Tilsit that Finland was in the Russian sphere of influence. The country became a grand duchy, with the tsars as grand dukes, and something of a showcase for Russian imperialism, with its own administration, elected assembly, legal system (still Swedish) and currency. In all this, there was more calculation than generosity: Russia wanted a reliable buffer between itself and the West. Lightly ruled, and encouraged in their sense of national identity, the Finns would be more loyal to Russia than to Sweden, in those days a regional great power.

Finland gained its independence in 1917. A mere three weeks after the Russian revolution, the Commissar of Nationalities arrived in Helsinki to tell the Social Democrats' congress, "Full freedom to shape their own life has been given to the Finns...No tutelage, no control from above over the Finnish people." The speaker was Joseph Stalin. Some historians have suggested that Lenin, then Stalin's boss, was sentimental about Finland because he had been sheltered there from the tsarist secret police. A more likely explanation is that he and Stalin thought they would achieve more in Finland with a magnanimous gesture than with repression—a theory that, if correct, is an interesting illustration of the continuity of tsarist and Soviet policy.

In 1939, Stalin demanded that Finland cede islands in the Gulf of Finland and the southern part of the Karelian isthmus in return for forests in eastern Karelia, deeming this exchange vital for the Soviet Union's defense. Finland refused. The Winter War was the result. For three months the Finns held out against the numerically superior Red Army, winning a decisive defensive victory when Stalin agreed to talk about territorial concessions and dropped his idea of installing a puppet government of exiled Finnish communists.

In 1941, when Hitler attacked the Soviet Union, German troops were already in Finland, and it entered the war on Germany's side, though not as a formal ally. In 1944 and 1945, the Finns had to fight to rid themselves of German forces. Stalin exacted his revenge after World War II: Finland had to pay the Soviet Union reparations of $525 million (in 1952 dollars) and cede territory, from which every Finn fled.

The reparations, a painful burden for a small, poor nation impoverished by war, put Finland's feet firmly on the road away from unduly heavy reliance on agriculture, fishing, and forestry, and toward diversified industrialization. Finland today has an advanced economy, its people are among the most educated in the world, and its major banks and corporations are expanding aggressively, in part by foreign mergers and acquisitions.

But what about its neutrality? The 1948 Treaty on Friendship, Cooperation, and Mutual Assistance provides that Finnish territory cannot be used for aggression against the Soviet Union, and it requires Finland to oppose such an attempt and call on the USSR for help. "Finlandization" has entered the political vocabulary as a synonym for the vassalage of small countries to the Soviet Union, much to the Finns' annoyance. They argue that they are not neutral on anyone's side except their own and could mobilize 700,000 men in 48 hours.

▷ *Spotlight* ◁

"Finlandization." Writer and former diplomat Max Jakobson has noted with some asperity that "Finland is forever at the mercy of the itinerant columnist who after lunch and cocktails in Helsinki is ready to pronounce himself upon the fate of the Finnish people." Such practitioners of parachute journalism usually are obsessed by a single aspect of the Finnish situation, relations with the Soviet Union. Jakobson describes the word "Finlandization" as "a kind of character assassination denoting supine submission to Soviet domination." Supine, after the Winter War and later battles against the Germans, which together cost 100,000 Finnish lives?

The Soviet Union and Finland have both benefited from trade links. The USSR has a reliable purveyor of high-quality goods right on its doorstep—everything from icebreakers, through complete new manufacturing plants, and even cities, to pharmaceuticals—which is willing, furthermore, to accept Soviet commodities instead of cash for exports. Finland, in turn, has found the Soviet Union to be a reliable trading partner, and during the world recession of the 1970s and early 1980s suffered less than most industrialized nations.

▷ Arriving

By Air

Helsinki-Vantaa airport is a hint of what's to come: clean, efficient, friendly. A long way from town, so it's a good idea to take the bus to the city; the trip takes about 40 minutes. Some hotels run shuttle services.

By Sea

If you're not in a tremendous hurry, you can sail to Helsinki from these and other ports: Leningrad, Stockholm, Tallinn (Soviet republic of Estonia), Travemunde (West Germany), and Gdansk (Poland). Most ferries are really floating hotels, carrying up to 2,500 passengers and offering a choice of restaurants from gourmet to self-service.

▷ Money

Currency is the *markka* or Finnmark. International code: FIM. Banknotes come in denominations of 10, 50, 100, 500, and 1000 markkas. There are coins of 5, 10, 20, and 50 pennies and 1 and 5 marks. Try to change your foreign money or travelers' checks at a bank, though Helsinki hotels tend to offer a better rate of exchange than their counterparts elsewhere. Some even have a bank branch right in the lobby.

▷ Language

Finnish—with a Swedish-speaking minority. Even the Finns admit that the native tongue is baffling and obscure, with a complicated grammar and little resemblance to any other language, the closest relative probably being Estonian. You can't puzzle out a word by searching for its Greek or Latin root, because there usually isn't one. Restaurant is *ravintola,* the plural is *ravintoloita,* and a coffee shop is *kahvila.* Only a few words show any sign of foreign origin, usually with an *i* at the end. Thus: hotel becomes *hotelli,* bar *bari,* and film *filmmi.* As for "Helsinki Tourist Office," that's a tongue-twisting, jaw-breaking *Helsingin kaupungin matkailuoimisto.* Finland itself is *Suomi.*

Swedish comes to the rescue of baffled foreigners. At least a hotel is a hotel and a restaurant a *restaurang.* Since signs are in both languages, look for the Swedish version, hope for the best, and remember that Helsinki in Swedish is *Helsingfors.*

If it's hard for the rest of us to learn Finnish, it's just as hard for the Finns to absorb any other language, since there is no etymological relationship to help them. The fact that most speak good English, at least in the big cities, is a token of their determination to play a part in the world.

▷ Communications

First class. Country code: 358, followed by 0 for Helsinki (which you don't use within the city, of course). International dialing code from Helsinki: 990. Hotels levy a stiff surcharge.

▷ Getting To Know the City

Helsinki is on a peninsula surrounded by islands. The center, stretching north from the main harbor, is compact. Most banks, business headquarters, and government offices are in this area and are within walking distance of each other. But remember that Helsinki is very far north: winters are bitter and the days very short. In the summer, in contrast, Helsinki can be very warm, and nights are a mere dimming of the sun for a couple of hours.

The main artery is Mannerheimintie (*Mannerheimvägen* in Swedish), for most of its length a handsome street, all of it named for the great Marshal Carl Gustav Emil, Freiherr von Mannerheim (1867–1951), whose forces fought the Red Army to a standstill in the Winter War. On or close to this street are most of the fashionable stores, hotels, restaurants, and leading businesses and banks. When you stand at the intersection with Aleksanterinkatu, you are at the very heart of the city. Do not expect architectural grandiosity, because there isn't any. Instead, there are many impressive buildings, both old and new, with the later ones showing classic Nordic restraint.

▷ Moving Around

As we've noted, Helsinki is small, but some businesses have moved to the suburbs. Good streetcar, bus, and train services reach the parts to which your legs won't take you. Use public transportation when you can, because taxis are notably expensive, perhaps not surprisingly if you consider that most are large Mercedes-Benzes, Volvos, and Audis, with luxurious Japanese models making up the balance. Tip is included. The Helsinki Card, which you can buy at most hotels and at tourist offices, is good for unlimited travel on buses, streetcars, and the metro.

▷ Hotels

No great palaces here. Instead, some very comfortable, well-run establishments with large rooms, good service, and first-rate telecommunications. That they go out of their way to attract the business traveler is proved by a feature in most of the hotels listed: spacious desks, usually under the window, with plenty of working space and a telephone. All hotels have good restaurants; people don't charge around Helsinki on a blizzardy night looking for the ideal meal. They stay in the warm hotel. All listed hotels have a sauna.

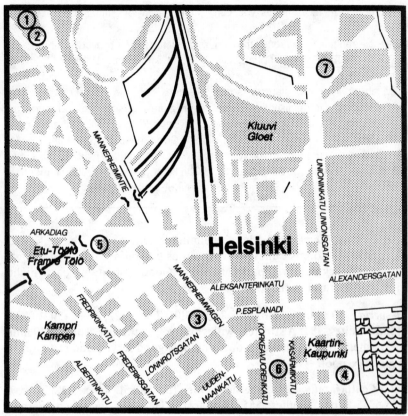

1. **Hesperia**
2. **Inter-Continental**
3. **Marski**
4. **Palace**
5. **Ramada Presidentti**
6. **Rivoli Jardin**
7. **Strand Inter-Continental**

Arctia Hotel Kalastajatorppa, 1 Kalastajatorpantie. Tel.: 488011. Telex: 121571. Fax: 458-1668. Rooms/suites: 235. Luxurious is the word for this hotel, set at the water's edge and among lawns and trees, but only 10 minutes by car or taxi from the center. Restaurant with floor show, nightclub, bank.

▷ *Spotlight* ◁

Keeping in touch with the world. Just because you can't understand a word of Finnish, and papers in other languages tend to arrive a day late, don't feel cut off. In most hotels you can choose from at least 10 television channels, ranging from French through Swedish, with the international satellite channels in between. There are also about 40 radio stations, some with broadcasts in English. For instant news in English, dial 040; for tourist information, 058.

You can even pick up programs from Tallinn, capital of the Soviet republic of Estonia. Do the Estonians really watch long films about love in a tractor factory or heroic workers overfulfilling their production norms? We don't know, but Estonian TV does show them. To be fair, it also shows some lively news and current-affairs programs—or so we're told by friends fluent in Russian or Estonian, or both.

Good news for monolingual visitors: foreign-made programs shown on Finnish TV are subtitled rather than dubbed.

Arctia Hotel Marski, 10 Mannerheimintie. Tel.: 68061. Telex: 121240. Fax: 642377. Rooms/suites: 164. About as central as you can get, right opposite Stockmann's department store. Good restaurant, bars, nightclub, bank, travel agency.

Hesperia, 50 Mannerheimintie. Tel.: 43101. Telex: 122117. Fax: 431-0995. Rooms/suites: 384. A streetcar will whisk you to the city center in 10 minutes. Fine, modern hotel with outstandingly good service and restaurants; nightclub, pool.

Inter-Continental, 46 Mannerheimintie. Tel.: 40551. Telex: 122159. Fax: 405-5255. Rooms/suites: 555. Next to the Hesperia and of comparably high quality; perhaps a little more cosmopolitan, thanks to its being part of an international chain. One of the best restaurants in town. Nightclub.

Ramada Presidentti Hotel, 4 E. Rautatiekatu. Tel.: 6911. Telex: 121953. Fax: 694-7886. Rooms/suites: 500. Another international hotel with a high reputation among frequent visitors to Helsinki. Tennis, pool, nightclub.

Rivoli Jardin, 40 Kasarmikatu. Tel.: 177880. Telex: 125881. Fax: 656988. Rooms/suites: 53. A small hotel, well kept, with friendly, helpful staff.

Seurahuone Socis, 12 Kaivokatu. Tel.: 170441. Telex: 122234. Fax: 664170. Rooms/suites: 118. Pleasant, comfortable, recently renovated; immaculate service. Finnish specialties in the restaurant.

Strand Inter-Continental, 4 John Stenberginranta. Tel.: 39351. Telex: 12610. Fax: 761362. Rooms/suites: 194. Helsinki's newest, opened in fall 1988. Modern luxury facing the water; specialty restaurant, informal atrium restaurant and bar; business center; 3 kilometers (1.8 miles) from city center.

▷ Restaurants

Fish from sea, lake, stream, and river dominate Finnish cuisine, along with reindeer meat—which is delicious (and low in both fat and cholesterol). In summer, many dishes include a sauce with Arctic berries, served also as dessert. That having been said, Helsinki isn't the culinary capital of Europe: look for good, basic food rather than sophistication. The quantity would choke a mammoth moose, so try the *voielipäpöytä*— Finland's equivalent of the Swedish *smörgasbörd,* or buffet. This allows you to sample without overeating. If you're still hungry after your first attack upon the culinary ramparts, you're allowed to go back for more, no questions asked.

Russian cuisine is better in Helsinki than it is in Moscow or Leningrad, according to connoisseurs who include Russians stoking up for a long, cold winter. (Of course, it isn't hard for almost any restaurant to be better than one run by surly oafs on the state payroll, but even Moscow is looking up.) Here's a highly selective (and subjective) listing of restaurants, or *ravintoloita.*

▷ *Spotlight* ◁

Alcohol consumption. Here's a joke that says it well. A Finn and a Swede are sitting on adjacent barstools. After the fifth round, the Swede raises his glass and says: "S*kal!*" The Finn downs his tipple before asking, "What are we doing, drinking or talking?" Booze is a touchy subject in Finland. Cocktails at lunchtime are almost unknown, but watch out for the flow at dinner, especially at weekends. Many Finns tend to tackle a bottle assiduously, not to say enthusiastically. Dinner may well start with a cocktail, continue with beer and vodka, glide into white wine, followed by red, and end with what the French call, euphemistically, a *digestif*—a cognac or something similar. Note that wine lists usually show the prices for alcohol exclusive of the service charge of 14 percent on weekdays and 15 percent on Sundays, but this is added to the check. N*ever* drink if you're going to drive. Finland's drunk-driving laws are extremely tough.

Aleksander Nevski, 17 Pohjoiseplanadi. Tel.: 639610. A new, top-class Russian restaurant with decor as authentic as you can find outside the Soviet Union (or could have done under the tsars).

Amadeus, 4 Sofiankatu. Tel.: 626676. A new place for gourmets; French accent.

Bellevue, 3 Rahapanjankatu. Tel.: 179560. Both Finnish and Russian fare here.

Golden Onion, 3 Kanavaranta. Tel.: 179900. Lavish decor, lavish French cuisine.

Havis Amanda, 23 Unioninkatu. Tel.: 666882. Neptune rules: seafood addicts gather.

König, 4 Mikonkatu. Tel.: 171271. Large, varied Finnish menu; a rendez-vous for businesspeople.

Mikadon Salongit, 6 Mannerheimintie. No reservations. More a pub than a restaurant; known as "the back office" for its banker clientele.

Palace Gourmet, 10 Etelaranta. Tel.: 171114. A place for senior business executives. Rather serious, like the prices.

Säkkipilli, 2 Kalevankatu. Tel.: 605607. A cuisine to remember; quiet, comfortable, and with several small rooms. Rather English decor and atmosphere.

Savoy, 14 Eteläesplanadi. Tel.: 176571. Very formal, favored by top business executives; almost certainly the best Finnish food in town.

Svenska Klubben, 6 Maurinkatu. Tel.: 628706. Outstandingly good Swedish food. Historic building, club atmosphere.

Walhalla, Souemenlinna. Tel.: 668552. On an island reached by ferry from the South Harbor; summer only.

▷ Tipping

Service is included, and extra tips are not expected in bars or restaurants or by cabdrivers.

▷ Doing Business

Finland is often called the most capitalistic of the Nordic countries, and there's something in that description. State-owned companies account for only 16 percent or so of industrial production, and government seldom interferes in their operation. The small but bustling stock market and a central bank committed to liberal policies provide a good platform for private enterprise.

The Finnish specialty is filling the gaps left by larger nations. By so doing, it eloquently has refuted the notion that to be rich, a nation needs abundant natural resources, a favorable climate, and a large home market. It has none of those things, apart from forests that cover two-thirds of the country and a few minerals. What Finland has instead is an educated, energetic population and a stable political system that encourages business enterprise and the work ethic.

Finland has built its prosperity on forest products, which still account for more than a third of exports. But the interest and the excitement are in the building of new industries and the attack on new markets. Finland is almost a Nordic NIC—a newly industrialized country—the northern counterpart of Singapore, Taiwan, South Korea, and Hong Kong. The mix of products is different and Finland doesn't rely on cheap labor, but like those NICs, it has concentrated on market niches.

The Finnish hallmarks are good design, high quality, and technical sophistication; and thanks to them, manufacturing output since 1980 has risen substantially more than it has on average in the OECD Europe area. To be sure, the Moscow connection has played its part, but both government and business are trying hard to reduce their reliance on the Soviet Union for export orders.

▷ *Spotlight* ◁

Finland's trade balance with the Soviet Union. Between 1973 and 1981, Finnish manufactured exports to the Soviet Union soared from $378 million to $2.9 billion, an annual average increase of 29.3 percent. In the same period, exports of manufactures to OECD countries rose by a relatively dismal average of 14.1 percent, from $2.1 billion to $6.2 billion.

So what has the price of crude oil got to do with this snug trading relationship? Much. The Soviet Union will take almost everything the Finns have to offer, and would take more if it had the money, but it doesn't. So the Russians pay in kind, chiefly in oil, the price of which is related to that in world markets for crude of comparable grade. When the free-market price of crude falls, so does the Soviet Union's purchasing power in Finland.

In theory, the Soviet Union's imports and Finland's exports balance; in practice they don't, or haven't recently. So the Finno-Soviet clearing account shows a huge imbalance in Finland's favor. What to do? Finland has taken to importing more Soviet oil than it can consume, refining the surplus, and exporting it. But that's a losing game in a glutted world market. Meanwhile, Finnish exporters to the Soviet Union are still getting what they want, cash paid by their central bank—but the country's new aggressiveness in other markets is based in part on a realization that the Soviet bonanza years are over, at least for the time being. *Perestroika* has left its mark on Finland as well as the Soviet Union. Over the decades, Finnish companies built a valuable network of Soviet contacts. Recent abolition of some ministries and streamlining of others have fractured that web of influence. Business was simpler and easier when Soviet economic power was concentrated in a few hands.

Waning trade with the Soviet Union is one reason for Finnish banking and business executives' receptiveness to new contacts, ideas, joint ventures, and other forms of cooperation. The second main reason is that Finland is not a member of the European Community and fears that the so-called European Single Market of the 1990s and beyond will be just that—a single market for companies within the EC. So Finland's largest companies are busily stitching together strategic alliances within the EC and buying companies there.

In all this the banks are leading players. As in Japan, they have formed groupings that include insurance and industrial companies. The biggest of them, Kansallis-Osake-Pankki (KOP) and Union Bank of Finland, already have their "families." Skopbank is busily building its empire; bank competition is intense. Finland has been barren ground for foreign banks, though. Chase Manhattan has pulled out; Citibank of the United States, Indosuez of France, and PKbanken of Sweden have limited operations there.

Most foreign companies don't find investment in Finland either exciting or profitable: they account for only 5 percent of industrial output. The domestic market is small. Even if Sweden, Norway, and Iceland are regarded as a single market, the total population is only 13 million or so (that addition is legitimate: the non-EC Nordic countries have created their own internal market). And there's no doubt that the Finns are a clannish lot.

▷ Spotlight ◁

Are the Finns racist—In the nicest possible way, of course? Some say they are, pointing to the country's very restrictive immigration policies. Look not for immigrants sweeping the streets, making hotel beds, washing the dishes in restaurant kitchens, or doing any of the other menial jobs in which millions of immigrants from Africa, the Caribbean, and Asia sweat for a living in such former imperial powers as Belgium, Britain, and France. Finland has never had a colony; instead, it *was* a colony. For first-time visitors, it's usually a shock to find that Finns are doing the hard and dirty jobs that are left to immigrants elsewhere. Why is that beautiful blonde girl sweeping the gutter?

So is Finland racist? The question raises another one, rather than provoking an immediate answer. How can Finns be racist when most of them have never seen a black, an Arab, or an Asian in their lives, except on television or while on vacation? Immigration policy is based on the indisputable fact that a lot of people would like to move to Finland, but it has a population so small that it could easily be swamped. Furthermore, if Finland opens its doors to one group, how can it close them to another without being accused of racism?

So why go to Finland in the first place? For a start, it's a good market, if a small one, with imports accounting for some 35 percent of gross domestic product. It's also a keen exporter. And Helsinki is probably the best place in Europe in which to discover what *perestroika* means in practical terms for companies in the West that want to do business with the Soviet Union and Eastern Europe.

▷ Spotlight ◁

Take a large supply of business cards, and remember to shake hands. Finns exchange cards on the flimsiest of pretexts, and if you don't hold out your hand, you're an oddity.

A small capital, a small nation: making business contacts is easy. Without too much difficulty, indeed, you can arrange a meeting with a government minister or a very senior civil servant. It's best to line up meetings before you leave, of course, and Finnish embassies and consulates around the world are usually eager to help. In many of them you will find a representative of the Finnish Foreign Trade Association (FFTA), a very lively body that is charged with promoting exports, imports, and joint ventures.

▷ Spotlight ◁

Saunas. A few words about a national institution. The rest of the world has baths. The Finns have saunas—more than a million of them, at last count. Of course, they have baths, too, but the shower or tub is devoid of ritual and magic. The sauna is redolent with them, the equivalent of bagpipes for the Scots, bullfights for the Spanish, pasta for the Italians, and cheese for the French: a symbol of their culture and national identity.

Visitors can hardly avoid a sauna, even if they want to. As the Finnish Sauna Society puts it in a publication, "Finnish businessmen and politicians take their adversaries to the sauna. Hostility melts in the steam as the birch whisks swish, and stubborn minds accept compromise. Rank and protocol are shed in the dressing room with one's clothes, and it is hard to maintain pompous dignity in a birthday suit. Statesmen from both East and West, blue bloods and com-

moners, have been given the same sauna treatment. . . . It is just part of the Finnish tradition of hospitality." And, perhaps, bargaining techniques.

▷ Useful Phone Numbers

Emergencies

Ambulance, fire, police	000
Hospital for foreigners	4711
Lost and found	1891
Pharmacy (24-hour service)	415778

Local Information

Airport	653756
Long-distance bus schedules	602122
Ship/ferry schedules	631251
Train schedules	659411

Business Information

Central Chamber of Commerce	650133
Confederation of Finnish Industries	18091
Finnfacts Institute	642980
Finnish Foreign Trade Association	69591
Helsinki Chamber of Commerce	644601
Ministry for Foreign Affairs	134151
Ministry of Trade and Industry	1601

Consulates and Embassies

Argentina	607630
Austria	634255
Belgium	170412
Brazil	177922
Bulgaria	661707
Canada	171141
Czechoslovakia	171051
Denmark	641948
France	171521
Germany (East)	688138
Germany (West)	694-3355
Greece	645202
Hungary	484144
Israel	175177
Italy	175144
Japan	644206
Netherlands	661737
Norway	171234
Poland	688077
Portugal	171717
Romania	413624
Soviet Union	661876
Spain	647351
Sweden	651255
Switzerland	649422
Turkey	406058

| United Kingdom | 647922 | Kar-Air (Finland) | 82501 |
| United States | 171931 | KLM Royal Dutch Airlines | 646645 |

Airlines

		LOT Polish Airlines	640613
Aeroflot Soviet Airlines	659655	Lufthansa German Airlines	694-9900
Air France	625862	Malev Hungarian Airlines	646116
Austrian Airlines	171311		
British Airways	650677	Pam Am World Airways	694-2422
Czechoslovak Airlines/ CSA	647786	SAS Scandinavian Airlines	177443
Finnair	410411		
Interflug (East Germany)	170833	Swissair	647335

▷ Shopping

Prices are at the upper end of the European scale, but there are two tax-rebate schemes for people living outside the Nordic nations. The first allows you to pay a tax-free price, but the goods have to be mailed to you. The second requires you to pay tax when you buy, but enables you to claim the rebate when you leave the country. Both schemes save you about 10 percent.

There are many good things to buy in Helsinki, among them elegantly designed glass; ceramics; textiles; coats, hats, and stoles in mink, fox, and lamb; and collectors' items in wood. Finnish jewelry is also outstandingly attractive.

The best neighborhood in which to shop is the city center; both Aleksantinkatu and Pohjoiseplanadi are famous for their boutiques. The newish Forum arcade houses a range of stores.

If you haven't much time to shop around, go to the *Finnish Design Center,* 19 Kasarmikatu (scheduled to move, so check). Here is a permanent but ever-changing exhibition of the best in Finnish design. Not likely to move is the huge *Stockmann's* department store, founded in 1862 and filling a city block between Aleksanterinkatu, Mannerheimintie, and Keskuskatu. Stockmann's has also overflowed into nearby streets. In all, there are about 50 departments staffed by knowledgeable clerks wearing lapel badges with national flags showing the languages they speak.

▷ *Spotlight* ◁

Stockmann's is Finland's version of Harrods of London, Bloomingdale's of New York, or Galeries Lafayette of Paris. But how can a small city support such a big store? One answer is that Stockmann's has a huge trade with diplomats and other expatriates in Moscow and Leningrad—and with well-to-do Soviet bureaucrats who have hard currency to spend. The store sends railroad cars full of goodies every week to the Soviet Union, the goodies including thousands of liters of milk. Visiting Westerners, it seems, don't think Soviet milk hygienic enough. Stockmann's barbershop is quite something for men: it's staffed entirely by women.

Other stores worth a visit:

Fashions. *Arola,* 36 Aleksanterinkatu. Tel.: 652522. *Diorina,* 21 Pohjoiseplanadi. Tel.: 627467. *Marimekko,* 31 Pohjoiseplanadi. Tel.: 177944.

Furs. *Furni,* 1 Mikonkatu. Tel.: 628371. *Grunstein Boutique,* 27 Unioninkatu. Tel.: 602682. *Tarja Niskanen,* 30 Unioninkatu. Tel.: 652386.

▷ *Spotlight* ◁

Arabia. If ceramics are your passion, visit Arabia at 135 Hämeentie, a little way out of town. Arabia is a working factory famous for porcelain, a museum, an art gallery, and a shop, all on the same site. For a guided tour, call 790211. Arabia is owned by the Wärtsilä shipyard—not such an odd couple when you think of it, since ships do need ceramics, don't they?

▷ After Hours

Gambling

Many restaurants and nightclubs offer the visitor a chance to gamble. Thanks to strict rules, however, the maximum stakes are small, and so are the winnings. Even so, there's much excitement when somebody is on a high roll by Finnish standards. The nearest international-class gambling is aboard the *George Ots* cruise liner, which plies between Helsinki and Tallinn across the Gulf of Finland. No upper limit to stakes. Because Tallinn is in the Soviet Union, you'll need a visa except on Tuesdays and Saturdays in summer, when the ship returns the same day. Details: Estonian Shipping Company/Oy Saimas Lines. Tel.: 651011.

Nightlife

Nightlife doesn't exactly glitter in Helsinki, but is usually enjoyable. For the mature set:

Adlon, 14 Fabianinkatu. Tel.: 664611. *Cafe Metropol,* 17 Mikonkatu. Tel.: 175433. *Groovy Restaurant,* 4 Ruonalandenkatu. Tel.: 694-5118. *Pressa Night Club,* Ramada Presidentii Hotel, 4 Etelainen Rautatiekatu. Tel.: 6911. Check your own hotel for a nightclub; many hotels have one.

For the disco set:

Alibi, 14 Hietaniemnkatu. *Club Anna and Eric,* 3 Eerinkinkatu. *Harald's,* 40 Kasarmikatu. *Ky--exit,* 21 Pohj. Rautiekatu. *Tavastia,* 4-6 Urho Kekkosenkatu.

▷ Sights and Sounds

One of the most colorful and cheerful sights is at *Kauppatori* (Market Square), just by the South Harbor, where a lively open-air food market is held every morning. On summer afternoons, the emphasis is on arts and crafts.

Museums

Culture of a different kind is offered by a good range of art galleries and museums. Among the best of them:

Ateneumin Taidemuseo, 3 Kansakouluk. Tel.: 694-5933. Some foreign and Old Masters; mainly paintings, drawings, and sculptures by Finnish artists.

Helsingin Kaupunginmuseo, 2 Karamzininkatu. Tel.: 169-3444. The city museum specializes in art, furniture, and artifacts explaining Helsinki's history and development.

Helsingin kaupungin Taidemuseo, 6 Tamminiementi. French and Finnish twentieth-century art.

Seurasaaren ulkomuseo is an open-air museum on Seurassari island. It features farm and manor buildings from different parts of the country.

Music

There is plenty of music in Helsinki. Watch for programs at these places:

National Opera Theater, 23-27 Bulevardi. Performances of international and Finnish operas and ballets.

Finlandia Hall, a superb example of the architecture of Alvar Aalto; frequent concerts.

Still on the music front, try to see the magnificent monument to Finnish composer Jean Sibelius (1865–1957), designed by sculptor Eila Hiltunen and welded out of hundreds of steel pipes. The monument is in the impressively beautiful Sibelius Park on Mechelininkatu. Take the number 18 bus from the railroad station.

Architecture

Other interesting architecture:

Temppeliaukion kirkko, 3 Lutherinkatu; a church carved out of the living rock to the plans of Timo and Tuomo Suomalainen.

Uspenkin Kathedraali, 1 Kanavankatu. Completed in 1868 and the most important Orthodox church in Finland.

Toumiokirkko, Senaatintori, is a fine cathedral by Engel dating from the 1830s.

Tanhakaupuni, reached by streetcar number 6, is the original site of the city founded in 1550.

Eduskuntatalo, Mannerheimintie, is the parliament building designed by Siren and completed in 1931. Don't miss it.

Islands

Many of the city's interesting sights are on islands, the most prominent being the fortress of *Suomenlinna,* once called the Gibraltar of the North. Today the fortress houses several museums and is surrounded by lovely gardens. Ask your hotel concierge or the tourist office for details of cruises around Helsinki's islands.

▷ Out of Town

More than 30,000 islands form a magnificent archipelago in the Gulf of Finland and the Baltic Sea. Some are tiny, others are large, and on many are summer homes, often modest wooden structures. In summer, with birch trees shimmering green in the sunlight, the water glittering, and the landscape empty apart from an occasional farm, this part of Finland has a tranquil beauty all its own. In winter, it glistens white for months on end, and the soft glow from a farmhouse window is something out of a Nordic folk tale.

Porvoo. On the coast 50 kilometers (31 miles) east of Helsinki is Porvoo (*Borga* in Swedish), one of the country's oldest towns. The cathedral is the major landmark. Here in 1809 met for the first time the Finnish *Diet* (assembly) called by Tsar Alexander I to proclaim Finland an autonomous grand duchy. The town today is the home of many writers and painters; Porvoo's most illustrious son was J.L. Runeberg, the national poet. His home, kept as it was when he lived in it, is at the corner of Runeberginkatu and Aleksanterinkatu.

Hvittrask, 28 kilometers (17 miles) west of Helsinki was the lakeside home of the famous architects Eliel Saarinen, Armas Lindgren, and Herman Gesellius. Today it is a museum with an excellent restaurant. Bus no. 166 from Helsinki or train to Masala, and then by taxi. Tel.: (297) 6033.

Turku (*Abo* in Swedish) is Finland's third-largest city, with a population of about 165,000, and is a major industrial center. Founded in the 1200s and the country's capital until 1812, Turku has a harbor that is more easily freed of ice than Helsinki's during the winter, which has helped to make it into a leading seaport. You can reach Turku by road, rail, and air from Helsinki and by ferry from Stockholm. Telephone area code: 921. Tourist information: 336366.

Recommended hotels, all with restaurant, conference rooms, sauna, pool, and nightclub or dancing:

Cumulus Turku, 28 Eerikinkatu. Tel.: 514111. Telex: 62406. Rooms: 208.

Hotel Ruissalo, Ruissalo. Tel.: 306222. Telex: 62314. Rooms: 132.

Marina Palace, 32 Linnankatu. Tel.: 336300. Telex: 62355. Rooms: 182.

Rantasipi Ikituuri, 7 Pispalantie. Tel.: 376111. Telex: 62315. Rooms: 150.

ISTANBUL

Waiting at the Crossroads

Population: 5.5 million (1985). Metropolitan area: 7 million (estimated). Commercial capital of the Republic of Turkey (population: 52.8 million). *Location*: northwestern Turkey, straddling the Bosporus strait that connects the Sea of Marmara with the Black Sea and divides southeastern Europe from northwestern Asia. *Economy*: banking and financial services, metalworking, maritime services and shipbuilding, textiles, tobacco products, tourism. Turkey is a member of the Organization for Economic Cooperation and Development (OECD), an associate member of the European Community (EC), and a signatory to the General Agreement on Tariffs and Trade (GATT).

▷ Background Briefing

Istanbul has two faces, one European and the other Middle Eastern. In the mid-600s B.C., Greeks founded the city and called it *Byzantium*. It was one of the many Greek-speaking city-states of antiquity. In 330 A.D., Byzantium was renamed *Constantinople* and became capital of the Roman Empire under Constantine I. During the 500s A.D., much of the city was destroyed in riots but beautifully rebuilt by emperor Justinian I. Over the course of several hundred years, Constantinople was attacked by various invaders and crusaders. Finally, in 1453, the powerful Ottoman Turks conquered the city and made it the capital of their empire. They called the city *Istanbul*. Although the Ottomans ruled much of Europe, a dichotomy remained: was Turkey occidental or oriental? Its rulers backed the wrong horse during World War I, and after Germany and its allies were defeated, the remaining vestiges of the Ottoman Empire collapsed.

The country's great nationalist and reforming leader, Mustafa Kemal (1881–1938), came to power in the postwar chaos. He "Westernized" Turkish society with zest and zeal, abolishing religious orders, disestablishing Islam as the state religion, forbidding polygamy, banning veils for women, and replacing with hats the *fez* that men traditionally wore. Kemal also substituted the Latin alphabet for Arabic script and forced all Turks to take surnames (the Grand National Assembly decided that his should be *Atatürk,* meaning "father of the Turks," so he became known as Kemal Atatürk). In 1930 the assembly formally changed the city's name from Constantinople to Istanbul.

Most of Istanbul's people accepted the Western reforms without protest. Yet 97 percent of Turkey is in Asia, and mass migrations from the rural areas to Istanbul in the 1950s and 1960s strengthened its Middle Eastern flavor. Even so, most Turks from all walks of life believe that their future lies in Europe rather than the Middle East. The government underlined that belief in 1987 by applying formally for full membership of the European Community, but the Turks weren't accepted in a rush of enthusiasm by the EC Twelve.

There is, for a start, the difficult issue of agriculture. About 55 percent of the Turkish labor force is in farming, forestry, and fisheries and could pose a major threat to the EC's complicated and heavily subsidized Common Agricultural Policy. Rightly or wrongly, EC opponents of Turkish full membership argue also that Turkish democracy is still fragile. Since 1960, there have been three military coups d'etat, with one democratically elected prime minister hanged for alleged crimes against the state.

The most recent coup, in 1980, ended a virtual civil war between extremists of left and right but made Turkey an outcast in the eyes of many Western politicians. Among the charges against Turkey's rulers were their denial of basic freedoms, including those of the press and peaceful assembly, and the widespread use of torture. Amnesty International, which monitors such abuses, reported in 1988 that torture and political repression continued, though on a lesser scale; the government launched a vigorous campaign to contest the allegations.

The current government, headed by Prime Minister Turkut Özal, came to power in 1983 under the shadow of a military regime. It moved rapidly to reintroduce democracy and in 1987 won a five-year mandate in relatively free elections. Only alarmists now fear another military intervention in civil affairs.

Of more pressing concern to foreign observers is the future of Islamic fundamentalism. About 98 percent of Turks are Muslems, but there's little evidence that most of them see in neighboring Iran a model for their country. (Turkish Muslims are in the majority Sunni sect of Islam, while Iranian Muslims follow the more fundamentalist Shiite teachings.) Although Prime Minister Özal was a member of the most radical religious party in the 1970s, made the *haj* (the pilgrimage to Mecca), and remains devout, he is also devoted to Atatürk's Westernizing reforms. Indeed, he has taken them much further than the Father of the Turks ever did. Özal's free-market policies have opened Turkey to the world economy for the first time, encouraged Turkish business executives to look beyond their country's borders, and stimulated competition.

Özal has been equally bold with his foreign policies. He and his ministers have cemented ties with Western Europe; had frank-but-friendly talks with Turkey's traditional antagonist, Greece; and strengthened relations with another neighbor, the Soviet Union. At the same time, though, Turkey has stressed its Islamic commitments. It is a member of the Organization of the Islamic Conference.

Rather like President Mikhail Gorbachev across the Soviet border, Prime Minister Özal now has to convince ordinary people that far-reaching reforms will benefit them. Although economic expansion has been rapid by world standards since Özal's Motherland Party first came to power, so has population growth, at an average annual rate of 2.2 percent in the 1980s. If this growth rate continues unchecked, there could be 100 million Turks by the third or fourth decade of the next century. Unemployment remains high, the public schools are overcrowded, and Özal's aim of leaping "from one age into another" is for most people still a political slogan rather than a promise likely to be honored soon.

▷ Arriving

In 1986, Atatürk International Airport replaced the wholly inadequate Yeşilköy, now used only as a customs shed. Arrivals and departures at Atatürk are swift and painless and should become even smoother when a current expansion program is completed. The airport is only 15 kilometers (9.4 miles) from the city, buses are frequent and air-conditioned, and taxis are cheap.

▷ Money

The Turkish lira. International code: TUL. Banknotes of different sizes and colors come in denominations of 100, 500, 1,000, 5,000, 10,000, 20,000, and 50,000 lire. You can change foreign currency and travelers' checks at banks, *bureaux de change,* and hotels. Hotels charge a premium, usually 1 percent, and most provide money-changing services only for registered guests.

▷ Language

Turkish, the official language spoken by more than 90 percent of all Turks, is neither Indo-European nor Semitic in origin but is related to the Ural-Altaic group of languages, which includes Finnish, Hungarian, Korean, Japanese, and—in the view of some scholars—Eskimo and Navajo. The country's official name in Turkish is *Türkiye Cumhuriyeti*. Most educated Turks speak English or another European language, many taxi drivers and waiters speak German, and hustlers in the bazaar speak everything from Arabic to Chinese.

▷ Communications

Country code: 90. City code: 1 (not needed for calls within the city). Quality is generally good, though it does depend upon the time of the day and the weather. All first-class hotels have telex machines and most have faxes as well, both of which are today standard equipment in nearly all offices.

▷ Getting To Know the City

Istanbul isn't one city: it's three or even four. The most obvious division and topographical feature is the Bosporus strait: on one side is Europe, on the other Asia. The European side is also divided by an arm of the Bosporus, the Golden Horn, which many first-time visitors assume to be the Bosporus itself because of the number of bridges crossing it. The best-known of these bridges is the Galata, which spans the Horn where it opens into the Bosporus near its confluence with the Sea of Marmara.

Traditional or touristic Istanbul is south of the Horn on Seragelio Point, and includes the Topkapi Palace, the St. Sophia Museum, the Blue Mosque, and the Grand Covered Bazaar.

North of the Horn are Pera/Beyoğlu, the old Levantine quarter, distinguished by the conical Galata Tower; Taksim/Harbiye, center of the modern downtown area, where the Hilton, Sheraton, and Pullman-Etap hotels are located; Nişantaşi/Sişli, the commercial and shopping heart of the city; and, much further up the Bosporus, the fashionable residential areas of Bebek/Etiler, Rumeli Hisar, and Tarabya.

Perhaps surprisingly, the Asian side is in many ways more modern and "Western" than the European city. You reach the Asian part of Istanbul by driving over one of the two suspension bridges (to be avoided during the rush hours), by hydrofoil, or by one of a score of quaint old ferryboats that ply the Bosporus.

The fourth section of the city, which few business travelers and tourists visit, is Gaziosmanpasa and Merter. Here are hastily built housing for workers and sprawling *gecekondu,* slums built almost overnight on any vacant land.

▷ Moving Around

Buses are usually crowded to the point of suffocation, so taxis are a better choice for the business traveler. There are two kinds. In the first, you ride in solitary splendor; in the second, you share with other passengers. The latter, called *dolmuş,* or route taxis, cruise the streets like small buses to pick up and deposit passengers. Most of the *dolmuş* are Packards, Studebakers, or Fords of vintages that would merit them a place in a museum in other countries. Most have been stretched with an additional midsection that makes room for more passengers.

Don't ignore the ferryboats, either. During rush hours, they can be faster and much more enjoyable than taxis, *dolmuş,* or private cars.

▷ Hotels

A recent boom in tourism has been answered by a boom in hotel construction. There are hotels for a wide range of tastes and pockets. We've listed those suitable for the traveling executive—and added a few cautionary notes. Because Istanbul sprawls, we've also listed them by location.

Central

Büyük Surmeli Oteli (Grand Surmeli), 3 Saatcibayiri Sokak, Gayretepe. Tel.: 172-0515/172-1160. Telex: 26203. Rooms/suites: 220, plus four apartments. Sauna, outdoor and indoor swimming pools, lobby bar, nightclub, small and large conference room.

Dedeman Oteli, 50 Vildiz Posta Caddesi, Esentepe. Tel.: 174-8800. Telex: 28217. Fax: 175-1100. Room/suites: 394. Although slightly out of the downtown area, the Dedeman is a good place to stay, with roof and lobby bars, a large restaurant, a casino, and a sauna.

Divan Oteli, 2 Cumhuriyet Caddesi, Elmadağ. Tel.: 131-4100/4070. Telex: 22402. Fax: 131-4100. Rooms/suites: 188. Smallish, centrally located, with a justly famous restaurant specializing in Turkish cuisine. The Divan Pub is popular for drinks and snacks, and the streetside coffeeshop is a favorite spot for watching the world go by.

Hilton Oteli Istanbul, Cumhuriyet Caddesi, Elmadag. Tel.: 131-4650. Telex: 27027. Fax: 140-4165. Rooms/suites: 536. Virtually everything the

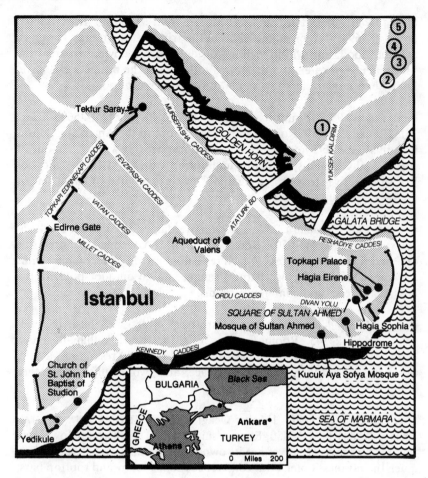

1. **Pera Palas**
2. **Etap Marmara**
3. **Sheraton**
4. **Divan**
5. **Hilton**

business traveler wants, from excellent telecommunications to limousine service and helicopter pad. Many small-to-medium-sized meeting rooms and two 1,600-seat conference halls. There are extensive gardens, an outdoor pool, three tennis and two squash courts, a shopping arcade, and a Bosporus tour boat. Services include a rooftop restaurant, another that serves Turkish dishes, a third (under separate management) offering Chinese cuisine, and a basement casino.

►217

Maçka Oteli, 35 Eytan Caddessi, Maçka. Tel.: 134-3200. Telex: 28002. Fax: 140-7694. Rooms/suites: 181. On the fringe of the trendy Nisantasi neighborhood, and within walking distance of the downtown area, the Maçka tends to cater to tour groups rather than the business executive. Lobby bar, large restaurant, sauna, three conference rooms.

Pera Palas, 98 Mesrutiyet Caddesi, Tepebaşi. Tel.: 151-4560. Telex: 24152. Fax: 151-4089. Rooms/suites: 145. Close to the American Consulate, this venerable hostelry is full of atmosphere. It was a hang-out of British and German spies before and during World War II; the ghost of British detective-story writer Agatha Christie is reputed to haunt one of the rooms, though she died elsewhere.

Pullman Etap Maramara Oteli, Taksim Meydani, Taksim. Tel.: 151-4696. Telex: 24137. Fax: 145-0503. Rooms/suites: 417. A Vienna-style streetside café and the Orient Express French restaurant are the hotel's main claims to fame. There's a Turkish bath, a sauna, and an outdoor pool. In the basement are several conference rooms.

Pullman Istanbul Tepebaşi Oteli, Meşrutiyet Caddesi, Tepebaşi. Tel.: 151-4646. Telex: 24345. Rooms/suites: 210. More tourists than business-people stay here. Even so, it boasts one good (French) restaurant, a café, two bars, an outdoor pool with terrace, and two smallish conference halls.

Sheraton Oteli Istanbul, 1 Asker Ocaği Caddesi, Taksim. Tel.: 131-2121. Telex: 22728. Fax: 131-2180. Rooms/suites: 479. The Sheraton Tower section for business executives has its own reception desk and elevator. Very much the business hotel, with conference rooms, lobby and rooftop bars, a coffee shop, and two restaurants.

Away from the Center

Büyük Tarabya Oteli (Grand Tarabya), Kefeflikoy Caddesi, Tarabya. Tel.: 162-1000. Telex: 26203. Fax: 162-2260. Rooms/suites: 244, plus nine apartments (two of them billed as "King's") and nine other "special" rooms. A fine, quiet hotel if you want to escape the downtown bustle: it's about 20 kilometers (12 miles) from the center. Attractions include a sauna, Turkish bath, tennis court, indoor and outdoor pools, and gardens. Indoor and outdoor restaurants, too.

Çinar Oteli, 35800 Fener Mevki, Yeşilköy . Tel.: 573-2910. Telex: 28861. Fax: 573-5701. Rooms/suites: 168. Not quite an airport hotel, but not quite a city-center hotel, either. Sauna, outdoor pool, two conference rooms, bar, and restaurant.

Historic Istanbul

Ramada Otel Istanbul, 226 Ordu Caddesi, Laleli. Tel.: 513-9300. Telex: 30222. Fax: 512-6390. Rooms/suites: 276. A lovely restoration of a 1920s art deco-style housing project. Opened only in 1988, the hotel is already a firm favorite for banquets and receptions. Bedrooms are smallish but cozy; there are three restaurants and a popular wine bar, and tea and cakes are served in alcoves scattered around the labyrinthine lobby.

Yeşil Ev (Green House), 5 Kabasakal, Sultanahmet. Tel.: 511-1150. Telex: 31041710. Rooms/suites: 20. A pretty and comfortable renovation of old buildings. Rooms are small; the compensation is that the hotel is within sight of the Topkapi Palace, the Hagia Sophia Museum, and the Blue Mosque. A perfect hotel for a honeymoon—not, perhaps, ideal for a lone business traveler.

▷ Restaurants

Many gourmets rank Turkish cuisine with French, Italian, and Chinese for its variety, subtlety, and distinction. That is hardly surprising. Modern Turkish cooking is a wonderful blend of ingredients and culinary traditions inherited from Central Asia, Persian court kitchens, Arabia, the Balkans, and Western Europe. For this glorious melange we have to thank Byzantium and the Ottoman Empire: their cohorts both taught and learned.

The Turks love to eat—and to eat out. Istanbul is rich with restaurants, both large and small. There are so many, indeed, that we can't list more than a sampling—and if you cannot find a table at one, try around the corner. All the places we recommend are highly suitable for business entertaining. Few are expensive; the possible exceptions are mostly those we have designated International. Even these are expensive only by Turkish standards.

Meat (Grills)

Beyti, 33 Orman Sokak, Florya. Tel.: 573-9373.

Gelik, 68-70 Sahil Yolu, Ataköy. Tel.: 571-3732.

Turkish

Abdullah, 11 Emirgan Koru Caddesi, Emirgan. Tel.: 163-6400.

Pandeli, 1 Misir Çarsisi, Eminönü (lunch only). Tel.: 522-5534.

International

Ambassadeurs, Bebek Hotel, Bebek. Tel.: 163-3002.

Four Seasons, 509 Istiklal Caddesi, Tünel/Beyoğlu. Tel.: 145-8941.

Park Şamdan, 18 Min Kemal Öke Caddesi, Nişantaş. Tel.: 140-8368.

Ziya, 21 Min Kemal Caddesi, Nişantaş. Tel.: 147-17089. Summer: 109/1 Muallim Naci Caddesi, Ortaköy. Tel.: 161-6005.

Chinese

China, 17/1 Lamartin Caddesi. Tel.: 150-6263.

Peking, 3 Aytar Caddesi, Levent. Tel.: 169-9017.

French

La Bouffe, 13 Karakol Boston Sokak. Tel.: 146-9943.

Italian

Ristorante Italiano, 131 Cumhuriyet Caddesi, Elmadağ. Tel.: 147-8640.

Japanese

Yumeya, 39/1 Cumhuriyet Caddesi. Tel.: 156-1108.

Korean

Seoul, Niapetitye Caddesi, Etiler. Tel.: 163-6087.

Russian

Rejans, 15 Olivo Cikmazi, Galatasaray. Tel.: 144-1610.

▷ Tipping

Most bars and restaurants include a 15 percent service charge—but you should add another 10 to 15 percent. If that seems excessive, remember that Turkey's rate of inflation is high, but wages do not rise at the same rate. As in other cities, tip also hotel and restaurant staff who probably do not share in the *tronc* (trunk) system run by the maître d'hôtel: for example, the hatcheck attendants and the doormen who fetch you a taxi. As for cabdrivers, add about 10 percent to the metered fare.

▷ Doing Business

A quarter of a century ago, even a decade ago, a Turkish government official, banker, or businessman might have forgiven you for being late for the date you had made at his favorite belly dancing club. No longer. Today he wants to see you on time, at his office. Nor does he expect you to sweeten the deal by "putting sugar in his coffee"—small-denomination bills, preferably in Swiss francs or West German Deutsche marks. Indeed, such sweeteners always were less rampant than rumor and legend had suggested.

Turkish businessmen today are almost without exception more Western or international in outlook than many Westerners themselves, converts are often more devout than those born into the faith. Be punctual, be precise, be ready with the answers to pointed and prescient questions. Turkey may be poor, but the executive with whom you are dealing, or his company, or both, is likely to be rich—and that means neither he nor it is foolish. Forget any ideas you may have about Turkish concepts of time and morality that are different from those in the West. Office hours are those of the rest of Europe, generally Monday through Friday from 9:00 a.m. until 6:00 p.m., with lunch between noon and 1:00 p.m. Leave plenty of time between appointments, unless they're in nearby offices: Istanbul can teach Manhattan a few things about gridlock.

Hospitality is a strong tradition. If you get on well with your business contact, he is likely to ask you to his tennis or squash club. He will then take you to a members-only bar or to a luxurious restaurant along the Bosporus for dinner. He will almost certainly insist upon picking up the tab. Turks believe they should be the hosts on their own territory.

▷ *Spotlight* ◁

ENKA, STFA, *Koc,* and *Sabanci* may be Greek, so to speak, to most foreigners, but these names and acronyms are household words in Turkey, being among the few remarkably powerful and usually family-owned holding companies that dominate Turkey's domestic and foreign economy. ENKA, the construction giant active throughout the Middle East and lately in the Soviet Union, is the abbreviated form of the Turkish words for "brother-in-law" and "brother." Run by Şarik Tara, a Turkish emigrant from Yugoslavia, the company ranks in the top 20 construction firms worldwide by value of contracts. STFA, another construction giant, combines the initials of its two partners, Sezai Türkeş and Feyzi Akkaya.

Since 1980, official policy has been to galvanize the economy by giving market forces more play, liberalizing the financial system, and ending subsidies to lame-duck (or lame-turkey) companies and industries. On the face of it, those and other measures have been successful. In 1987, real gross national product (GNP) expanded by 7.4 percent and is estimated to have grown by another 5.9 percent in 1988, with further strong growth forecast for 1989. Unemployment, though, remained stubbornly high, at an official 16 percent in 1988 and 16.5 percent in 1989. Some observers suggest that a vast "underemployed" sector disguises the true figures. Inflation rose from about 70 percent in 1987 to more than 80 percent the following year. A tight-money policy is designed to reduce the burden to a more tolerable 50 percent in 1990 and beyond.

One of Turkey's problems is that it's a low-wage, low-productivity country short of managerial and technical skills. More than half the labor force works in agriculture, fishing, and forestry, yet this sector contributed only 17.4 percent to total gross domestic product (GDP) in 1987, the latest year for which firm figures are available. Most of the 8.8 million workers in the sector are miserably poor by Western European standards.

Turkey's prosperity is clearly dependent upon exports. However, it is far from the only poor country that sees its salvation in foreign markets, hence its determination to join the European Community, so that it can benefit from financial grants and other assistance and enjoy tariff-free access to a rich market of 323 million people. Greece's attitude is crucial: it could veto Turkey's application to join the EC when the Council of Ministers decides to decide, which could be as late as 1992.

An intractable problem in this regard is Cyprus, where there has been long and bitter conflict between ethnic Greeks and Turks. After a Greek coup in 1974 inspired by Greece's then-rulers, a junta of colonels, Turkey invaded and divided the island into two sectors. Talks about a future federal system of government broke down repeatedly, and in 1985, the Turkish-speaking northern enclave declared independence unilaterally, though only Turkey recognizes this Turkish Republic of Northern Cyprus. However, recent better relations between Greece and Turkey have eased tensions somewhat on the island, and optimists hope that with United Nations help, the two sides will soon find a solution.

▷ *Spotlight* ◁

Turkey and the European Community. Turkey formally applied in April 1987 to become a full member of the EC. But will it be allowed into the club, to become the thirteenth member? Some expert commentators doubt it; others think the EC Twelve will drag their feet rather than reject Turkey outright.

The Turkish application presents the Twelve with sensitive, ticklish challenges. On the one hand, Turkey is a staunch member of NATO, and of the Twelve, only Ireland is not a signatory to that military alliance. Turkey's military contribution to Western security and its geographically strategic position weigh heavily in its favor. Along with Norway, it is the only NATO member bordering the Soviet Union.

If Turkey is blackballed, the political consequences could be disastrous. Public humiliation of its political and economic elite could greatly strengthen Islamic fundamentalists who argue that Turkey should look East rather than West for its destiny, and no Western politician wants a hostile Islamic power sitting on Europe's doorstep.

Weighing against Turkey in the political scales is the fact that as citizens of a full EC member, the country's 50 million Muslims would have the right to live and work in the rest of the EC. Only a tiny proportion would choose to do so, of course, but the mere hint of mass immigration is enough to frighten some Western European politicians and is grist to the mills of others who play the racist card.

There's also the economic balance. Turkey is more populous than all but four of the EC Twelve, but it is poor. It's thus seen as an economic threat, since though membership is a two-way street, the immediate result would be a larger market for Turkish exports than for EC sales to Turkey.

Özal's conclusion? He's on record as saying that Turkey will be a full EC member by the year 2000.

Özal and his ministers believe not only that their country's future is in Europe, but also that its economic development depends upon rapid expansion of industry. Indeed, between 1980 and 1987, exports of manufactured goods rose from 35 percent of the total to almost 80 percent. Some people, perhaps visionaries, contend that Turkey could become Europe's own NIC (newly industrialized country), a Hong Kong, South Korea, or Taiwan within the EC. That isn't a view likely to appeal to governments fighting high and apparently chronic unemployment.

Looking beyond their usual four- or five-year terms in office, however, politicians may see the logic of Turkey's case. Population trends in Western Europe mean that by the end of the century, there will be shortages of labor, with the service and manufacturing sectors competing for a shrinking pool of young recruits. When Western Europe last suffered labor shortages, in the 1950s and 1960s, the solution was to import workers, with Turkey providing a sizable proportion. The future solution may be to take the jobs to where the workers are, and Turkey is likely to have an abundant supply well into the next century.

▷ Useful Phone Numbers

Emergencies

All-night pharmacies
(directory assistance)   011
Ambulance: (better to hire a
taxi or call the police)

Fire, police

Asian Istanbul	366-6666
Old city and airport area	566-6666
Taksim and European Bosporus	166-6666

▷ *Spotlight* ◁

Hospitals. Istanbul is well supplied with hospitals for foreigners. Phone numbers: American, 131-4050; Arme-nian, 148-4762; French, 146-1020; German, 143-8100; Italian, 149975.

Business Information

Istanbul Chamber of
Commerce 526-6215/528-1800
Istanbul Chamber of
Industry   145-4130
Middle East Trade and Export
Center   166-9945

Consulates

Austria	140-0506
Bangladesh	165-0672
Belgium	143-3300
Bulgaria	166-2605
Canada	172-5174
Chile	145-0183
China (People's Republic)	172-5200
Costa Rica	575-1585
Czechoslovakia	147-5030
Denmark	140-4217
Egypt	163-6033
Finland	143-3775
France	143-1852
Germany (West)	143-7220
Greece	145-0596
Hungary	140-4275
India	141-7372
Indonesia	163-8008
Iran	512-0090
Iraq	160-5020
Israel	146-4125
Italy	143-1024
Japan	145-0290
Jordan	130-1221
Korea (South)	146-7643
Lebanon	140-5599
Libya	143-3760
Malaysia	147-1728
Mexico	144-0691
Netherlands	144-9096
Norway	149-9753
Pakistan	172-1636

Peru	146-8809	Egyptair	146-7191
Poland	140-7956	El Al Israel Airlines	146-5303
Portugal	150-1130	Emirates Airlines	131-2044
Romania	144-3555	Finnair	141-3636
Saudi Arabia	172-4396	Gulf Air	131-3450
Soviet Union	144-1693	Iberia (Spain)	150-5478
Spain	140-3444	Interflug (East	
Sweden	143-5770	Germany)	140-4878
Switzerland	148-5070	Iran Air	141-1916
Syria	148-2735	Iraqi Airways	146-0170
Thailand	131-1585	Istanbul Airlines	570-3400
Tunisia	144-9611	Japan Air Lines/	
United Kingdom	144-7540	JAL	141-7366
United States	151-3602	KLM Royal Dutch	
Yugoslavia	148-1004	Airlines	130-0311
		Korean Air	146-7643
		Kuwait Air Ways	140-4081

Airlines

		Libyan Arab	
Air Afrique	155-3050	Airlines	133-0228
Air Algerie	141-0246	LOT Polish Airlines	140-7927
Air France	155-3050	Lufthansa German	
Alia Royal Jordanian	133-0744	Airlines	146-5130
Alitalia	131-3391	Malev Hungarian	
American Airlines	130-2211	Airlines	141-0309
Austrian Airlines	140-2247	Middle East Airlines	148-2241
Balkan-Bulgarian		Olympic Airways	146-5081
Airlines	145-2456	Pakistan International	
British Airways	148-4235	Airlines	146-9409
CAAC (China)	132-7111	Pan Am World	
Cathay Pacific		Airways	131-2339
Airways	167-4649	Qantas Airways	
Canadian Pacific		(Australia)	140-3100
Air Lines	141-7366	Sabena Belgian	
Cyprus Turkish		World Airways	150-6026
Airlines	133-0055	SAS Scandinavian	
Czechoslovakian		Airlines	146-6075
Airlines/CSA	148-3811	Saudi Arabian	
Eastern Airlines	141-7366	Airlines	156-4805

►225

Singapore Airlines	147-8111	Tunis Air	141-6833
Syrian Arab Air	146-1781	Turk Hava Yollari	146-4017
Swissair	131-2844	TWA	141-0246
Tarom (Romania)	143-6514	Yugoslav Airlines/JAT	148-2904

▷ Shopping

The *Kapali Çarsi* (Grand Covered Bazaar) is the city's most exotic and memorable shopping area for the visitor, a labyrinth of more than 5,000 stalls and stores, where everything is sold, including rugs, jewelry, copper, onyx, Meerschaum pipes, and even locally produced Calvin Klein jeans. Many of the more fashionable items are in hotel boutiques as well, so price them before descending on the bazaar. Remember to haggle: it's worth the time and trouble, and merchants expect it.

▷ Spotlight ◁

Rugs. Few people can resist entering one of the city's myriad carpet stores, there to sip tea or coffee and watch the merchant roll out a dozen or more rugs for inspection. Most will look antique. Now for the truth about these "magic" carpets. Most were made to order a few weeks before by village women who followed a standard pattern and then dipped the rugs in a chemical bath to "age" them. Of course, some stores do sell genuine antique rugs, but prices are high. If you're looking for a bargain that will last, insist that you want a new rug, not an "aged" one, and try another store if the first one protests it has none.

Fashionable and sophisticated people crowd the streets and avenues of the Şisli-Nişantaş-Teşvikiye neighborhoods, where stores and boutiques are only a day or two behind Italian and French designers' latest in clothing and leather goods. No haggling here. Another interesting addition to the shopping scene is the *Galleria* mall, where several hundred stores and shops are ranged around an ice rink, à la Rockefeller Center. Galleria is Turkey's first Western-style mall, and it is the only one-stop arcade where one can find both Italian roast coffee beans and smoked ham without rushing all over town.

▷ After Hours

Late-night clubs are known generically as *casinos,* which doesn't necessarily mean you can gamble. The standard entertainment is a belly dancer whirling around in a revealing, silky costume. Those in the know gather at the two best places. The first is *Maksim's,* Taksim Square, which offers a full floor show and meal. The second is on the top floor of the *Galata Tower* in Karaköy. Rather more earthy is *Les Parisiennes* on Cumhuriyet Caddesi, near the Hilton.

Those with a taste for adventure will sample the many clubs off Isiklal Caddesi in the Beyoğlu district. This is where the action is: bigger bellies, wilder dances, larger and cheaper drinks, louder music, and more of almost everything.

There is a fascinating and legal red-light district, but we cannot recommend it to anyone except the very brave.

▷ Sights and Sounds

As the former capital of both the Byzantine and Ottoman empires, Istanbul is the inheritor of architectural and other riches dating back to the 300s A.D. Constantine the Great, properly Flavius Valerius Aurelius Constantinus (c. 274–337), first Christian emperor of Rome, made his capital in what is now Istanbul, and many monuments of the ancient world were moved to the new city of Constantinople.

Among the city's glories was the *Hagia Sophia,* a Christian cathedral built by emperor Justinian in the 530s A.D. Furious mobs sacked the cathedral several times, but the authorities always rebuilt. Also known as Saint Sophia, the structure remains one of Istanbul's—and possibly the world's—most stupendous monuments. Converted into a mosque in 1453, Hagia Sophia was an Islamic spiritual center until it was converted into a museum in 1935.

Behind Hagia Sophia is the *Topkapi Palace,* home of the Turkish sultans during their days of near-absolute power. Displays of jewelry and the old harem—a world of its own—are the palace's primary attractions, along with a section devoted to holy relics. These include traces of what is believed to be the Prophet Muhammed's beard, along with weapons used by the first Muslim caliphs. Just outside the Topkapi walls are the *Çinili Kösk,* or Tiled Pavilion, with incredible wall tiles, and the *Archaeological Museum,* where many pre-Byzantine relics are displayed.

Across the square from Hagia Sophia is the *Sultan Ahmet Mosque,* also called the Blue Mosque. With Saint Sophia, it serves as a backdrop for the city's sound and light shows in summer. The mosque is in classical Ottoman style, with a towering dome and wonderful tiles, primarily blue. Visitors must wear decent attire—no short-sleeved shirts or miniskirts, for example—and remember that the mosque is off-limits at prayer times.

Just to the left of the Sultan Ahmet Mosque is the *Mosaic Museum,* built around the tattered fragments of the Blacherne Palace, residence of the Byzantine emperors. The few traces of mosaic that remain are vivid reminders of the palace's remarkable luxury, which the European Crusaders sacked in 1204. The famous golden horses that once formed part of the decoration were taken to the Basilica of San Marco in Venice.

Another fascinating trace of old Byzantium is the *Basilica Cistern,* across the main street from the Blue Mosque and Hagia Sophia. Carefully restored in the 1980s, the huge underground chambers once formed part of the city's water supply system—and may have been a watery grave for inconvenient corpses.

The great architect Sinan (c. 1489–1578) designed many of Istanbul's impressive mosques, and examples of his distinctive work are still found from Damascus in Syria to central Europe. Most experts agree that Sinan's masterpiece is the great *Süleymania* complex behind the university and the Grand Covered Bazaar. This took more than 10 years to complete, and the cost was huge.

Sinan set the style and pace; others followed. The work of other architects includes the so-called *New Mosque,* at the foot of the Galata Bridge and next to the fragrant Spice Bazaar. Built in the 1500s, the mosque is hardly new, taking its name from its sponsor, the *Yeni Valide* or "New" Mother Sultan. Another mosque not to be missed is *Eyüp,* on the upper reaches of the Golden Horn. Set in a vast cemetery of Ottoman tombstones, the mosque is frequented by young lovers, athletes, and even businessmen seeking the blessing of Eyüp, one of the companions of the Prophet Muhammed, who fell outside the city's walls during the first (and unsuccessful) Arab siege in the 600s A.D.

Try also to visit the *Dolmabahçe Saray,* on the other side of the Golden Horn and down the hill from Taksim Square. A rococco-style palace built by Sultan Abdulmedic, it is said to have been so costly that it was a main cause of the Ottoman empire's bankruptcy in the late 1800s.

▷ *Spotlight* ◁

The Ottoman Empire. The terms "Ottoman" and "Turkish" are often used interchangeably. They shouldn't be, as it's the equivalent of referring to the English as Windsors or the Germans as Hohenzollerns. The Ottoman Empire was a multiethnic, multinational, and multireligious state founded by a Turkish warlord named Osman in the late 1200s.

His heirs reigned first from Bursa in Asia Minor and then Edirne in Thrace until the armies of Osman's descendant, Mehmet the Conqueror, stormed Constantinople in 1453. The city became the new capital. For the next 200 years, Ottoman armies, directed from the imperial seat of power at the Topkapi Palace, seemed nearly invincible. At its height, in the 1600s, the empire covered most of the Middle East, North Africa, and eastern and southeastern Europe.

In 1683, a huge Ottoman army besieged Vienna, but the expedition failed, and the Treaty of Karlowitz in 1699 cost the Ottomans Hungary and other European territories. The tide had turned at last, and Ottoman fortunes started a 200-year slide as province after province fell to rival imperial powers, particularly the Habsburgs of Austria and the Romanovs of Russia.

Even at its height, though, the Ottoman Empire was economically, socially, and militarily stagnant, a medieval state that resisted change. The sultans sank into decadence, indolence, and depravity. Until the early 1600s at least, each ruler's sons fought their rivals to the succession, and the victor habitually had the losers killed. Obsessed with the formality, pomp, and circumstance of power, the sultans unwittingly handed actual management to the *grand viziers*, in effect, senior civil servants. The empire added to its problems by taxing citizens heavily while the sultans lived in ostentatious luxury. Corruption and inefficiency became rampant.

By the 1800s, the Ottoman Empire was known as the Sick Man of Europe. Despite attempts to reform, the social fabric continued to disintegrate, with religious and ethnic minorities in a near-constant state of revolt. Chunks of the empire broke away to become independent states. Even so, it limped into the 1900s, when the Young Turk movement wrested power from the despotic Abülhamid and reduced the sultanate to a figurehead role.

Turkey backed the losing side in World War I, and the victorious allies reduced the once-great empire to the city of Istanbul. There followed the War of Liberation, expulsion of the occupying forces, and the sending of the last sultan into exile. The Sick Man of Europe was dead and buried at last, and in his place emerged the new Republic of Turkey.

▷ Out of Town

Istanbul is crowded and noisy. For a change of pace and balm for battered ears, try the *Princes' Islands.* You can reach these by ferry or hydrofoil. No cars are allowed on the islands, and the only modes of transport are horse-drawn carriages, bicycles, and your own two feet.

Istanbul's Black Sea beaches, *Kilyos* on the European side and *Şile* on the Asian, are close to the crowded city. Both are an hour or so away, depending on the traffic. If you don't have time even for this brief break, simply jump on a ferry and cruise up and down the Bosporus, passing palaces, pavilions, castles, and quaint fishing villages. Very restful.

LIECHTENSTEIN
Where a Secret Is a Secret

Population of country: 27,000 (17,000 with citizenship). Capital: Vaduz (population: 5,500). *Location of country*: west-central Europe; borders with Austria and Switzerland. *Economy*: agriculture; banking and financial services; light industry, including false teeth, sausage skins, textiles, and precision engineering; tourism.

▷ Background Briefing

In the pastures of this mountainous little country cowbells clatter, while in the village capital of Vaduz computers hum, for this is a land of contrasts. Since World War II, the head of state, Prince Franz Josef II, now in his eighties, has helped to transform his tiny domain into a tax haven that is famous—or notorious—around the world.

With Crown Prince Hans Adam taking over more day-to-day duties, Liechtenstein is showing new vigor in its search for foreign business—and it has much to offer. Indeed, even the Swiss go to the principality when they want total, impenetrable anonymity and freedom from all taxes. To be sure, the Liechtensteiners do not offer this out of the goodness of their hearts: government, banks, and lawyers have become rich from registration fees, foreigners' bank deposits, and legal work.

▷ Arriving

The nearest airport is Kloten in Zurich, 112 kilometers (70 miles) away. See Zurich entry for more information on the airport. Trains run from the airport to the Liechtenstein border. From there, travelers continue by bus to Vaduz, a 20-minute journey, or by taxi.

There are also good highway connections with Zurich. Switzerland and Liechtenstein are in a customs union, so there are no border formalities; entry points from Austria are handled by Swiss officials.

▷ Money

The Swiss franc is the basic unit of currency. See Geneva or Zurich entries for further details.

▷ Language

Local version of Swiss German. See Zurich entry for details. English is widely spoken.

▷ Communications

Country code: 41 (same as Switzerland). City code: 75. Well up to Swiss standards, which are among the best in Europe.

▷ Getting To Know the City

Well, town. Vaduz consists of a single main street, the Städtle, with the princely castle dominating it from a rocky crag; nobody can get lost. The three banks and the lawyers' offices are all within walking distance of each other.

▷ Hotels

Small it may be, but Liechtenstein is cosmopolitan, thanks to the constant flow of foreigners checking on their wealth. Many expect the best—and get it. The brothers Emil and Felix Real, who run the second and third hotels listed, trained at Maxim's in Paris.

Engel, Städtle, Vaduz. Tel.: 21057. Good, friendly, inexpensive by local standards.

►231

Parkhotel Sonnenhof, just outside Vaduz. Tel.: 21192. Quiet, pleasant gardens, fine mountain views, sauna, indoor pool.

Real, Städtle, Vaduz. Tel.: 22222. Hospitable, comfortable, good bar, relaxed atmosphere.

▷ Restaurants

The Real brothers' hotel restaurants compete for accolades; both are excellent, specializing in local game, fish, and fungi with delicate, imaginative sauces. The Parkhotel Sonnenhof has the decor edge, the Hotel Real the edge for sociability.

Try also the *Torkel,* owned by the Prince of Liechtenstein Foundation, set amid the princely vineyards. Vaduzer wine is a full-bodied red.

▷ Tipping

Service charges are included, but, as elsewhere, a few coins extra won't come amiss.

▷ Doing Business

How many tax-haven entities are registered in Liechtenstein? Only a few people know, and they're not telling; an informed guess is more than 10,000. Banking secrecy is officially enshrined and waived only in criminal proceedings—and tax evasion is not considered criminal. But how does anybody act against an entity of which there is little or no public record? There are three main kinds of corporate entity.

An *Anstalt* (establishment) must have at least one director and a legal representative living in the principality. A local lawyer usually wears both hats. An *Anstalt's* capital is not usually divided into shares; this exempts it from local withholding tax and allows the founder to allocate profits as he or she wishes. Public filing of accounts is not normally required; neither is the name of the founder listed.

The *Stiftung* (foundation) protects and administers family assets. It is formed by settling any type of asset permanently on the recipient. The articles of association may specify that a beneficiary who challenges the allocation of capital or income or defaults on debts automatically loses all rights. These provisions are designed to settle family quarrels before they start and to protect assets from being plundered by prodigal children.

The principality also has its own specific trust entities, the *enterprise* (or registered) and *settlement* (or relationship) trusts. These can be required to comply with the laws of any country with developed trust legislation, the choice being the founder's.

▷ **Spotlight** ◁

Robert Maxwell, a British (by naturalization) publishing tycoon, vested control of his international media empire in a Vaduz charitable trust in 1982. Nothing wrong in that, perhaps. He reduces his tax bill, thereby benefiting recipients of his charity, and operates behind a veil of financial secrecy.

He soon found, though, that anonymity comes at a price—perhaps a high one. At least three companies he tried to acquire trumped his Liechtenstein ace by asking, in effect: What is he hiding? Shareholders rejected his bids. Trying to dispel the mystery, Maxwell allowed a respected merchant bank to inspect the trust documents, but it reported that no beneficiaries were listed. The mystery thickened.

That there were no names is no surprise. Liechtenstein law allows a trust's founder to specify a nominee for the ultimate beneficiaries.

The three Vaduz banks come under the eye of the Swiss central bank, but in matters of secrecy they remain independent. Agreements between Switzerland and the U.S. Securities and Exchange Commission about insider trading do not apply in Liechtenstein; Ivan Boesky should have known. The principality has just one double taxation treaty, and that's with Austria, not Switzerland. Taxes on holding companies are specifically excluded.

Increasingly, though, Liechtenstein wants to be known as more than just another tax haven, albeit the tightest and rightest of the fiscal shelters. Recently it has been stressing the range and quality of the financial services it offers, with much of the running being made by Christian Norgren, Swedish chairman of the Bank in Liechtenstein, of which the ruling family owns some 95 percent.

▷ **Spotlight** ◁

Don't call the movers. Some tax havens welcome foreign residents, provided they're rich enough. Not Liechtenstein. Immigration rules are extraordinarily tough, and citizenship qualifications even tougher. Not even marriage to a citizen automatically guarantees a passport.

▷ Useful Addresses and Phone Numbers

Banks

Bank in Liechtenstein, 12 Herrengasse, FL-9490 Vaduz. Tel.: 51122.

National Bank of Liechtenstein, 44 Städtle, P.O. Box 384, FL-9490 Vaduz. Tel.: 68811.

Private Trust Bank Corporation, 6 Auelenstrasse, FL-9490 Vaduz. Tel.: 56655.

Chamber of Commerce

Liechtensteinische Industrie-und Handelskammer, P.O. Box 232, 5 Gerberweg, FL-9490 Vaduz. Tel.: 22744.

Government

Press and Information Office, Regierungsgebaude, FL-9490 Vaduz. Tel.: 66111.

Tourism

National Tourist Office, P.O. Box 139, 37 Städtle, FL-9490. Tel.: 21443.

▷ Shopping

Watches, clocks, and jewelry aplenty are sold along the main street of Vaduz. For philatelists, the post office on the main street offers a comprehensive selection of the famous stamps that Liechtenstein issues so profitably. The stamps really are quite beautiful, many of them larger than U.S. commemoratives. This is the place to mail postcards if you want to impress the folks back home. Also be sure to ask for a catalog and about subscribing to first-day covers (philatelists will know what that means).

It is also worth buying a few bottles of the principality's best wines, direct from the vineyards; they're virtually unobtainable elsewhere.

▷ After Hours

What do you expect in a town of 5,500? Nightlife is staid.

▷ Sights and Sounds

Parts of the ruling family's castle are open to the public. Housed in magnificent medieval architecture is a world-famous collection of arms and armor, paintings, and sculptures.

Down in the town, more treasures from the princely art collection are on show. They represent only a fraction of the entire collection—it's one of the world's largest, and the oldest in the world in continuous private possession. Earlier princes bought direct from the studios of such painters as Rubens. The total value is incalculable.

▷ Out of Town

In winter, enjoy the many ski slopes and trails. In spring and summer, savor the alpine flowers and plants in the mountains. Many are rare and protected, however, so do not pick them.

Despite its small size, Liechtenstein is topographically varied, and in the foothills are villages and farmhouses that seem lost in time. *Eschen* has two prehistoric settlements, and the *Schellenberg* community has several archaeological sites dating back to the New Stone Age. Nearby *Mauren* has the remains of a Roman bath. Medieval chapels are found in *Nendeln* and *Schaan,* the latter village just 3 kilometers (2 miles) north of Vaduz. *Triesenberg* is a charming Alpine village south of the capital. A bit farther south is *Balzers,* home of the fictional Heidi and the very real and impressive Gutenberg Castle.

LISBON

The Second Revolution

Population: 812,000 (1981). Administrative and commercial capital of the Portuguese Republic (population: 10.2 million). *Location*: western coast of Portugal, on the Atlantic Ocean at the mouth of the Tagus River. *Economy*: banking and financial services; fishing and fish processing; food processing and distribution; manufacturing; petroleum refining; shipping, shipbuilding, and maritime services; textiles; tourism. Portugal is a member of the European Community (EC) and the Organization for Economic Cooperation and Development (OECD) and a signatory to the General Agreement on Tariffs and Trade (GATT).

▷ Background Briefing

Lisbon is an ancient city. It was colonized successively by the Greeks, Carthaginians, and Romans. The Visigoths took Lisbon from the Romans in the 400s A.D., and the Moors captured it in the 700s. Christian forces led by King Alfonso I retook the city in 1147, and it became Portugal's capital in the late 1200s. Lisbon was a key port for the traders who made the Portuguese empire strong and widespread during the 1400s and 1500s. Portugal has seldom experienced democracy. Sitting as it does on the western edge of the Iberian peninsula, Portugal has been occupied by Spain, fought over by Spain's enemies, and during intervals was a kingdom. A republic replaced the monarchy early this century. In the 1930s, Antonio Salazar became dictator, and his regime lasted until April 25, 1974, when his chosen successor was finally overthrown by an unlikely and temporary alliance of young military officers, hard-line communists, socialists, liberals, and people with lukewarm political allegiances but red-hot disenchantment with the Salazar years.

The 1974 revolution, almost bloodless, raised hopes and created chaos—economic, political, social. Communist labor unions and self-appointed local committees seized vast tracts of farmland. In the cities, the extreme left and its allies nationalized banks, insurance companies, factories, shipyards, transportation companies—all the commanding heights of the economy, in fact. Furthermore, the expropriators offered little or no compensation and seldom paid what they had promised.

Some former owners were jailed for crimes vaguely specified and seldom tested in court. Once released, the "economic criminals" followed many other middle-class Portuguese who had fled abroad, depriving the country of its few skilled managers. The new constitution was avowedly Marxist and was enforced by the so-called Council of the Revolution, a combination of watchdog and supreme court manned by the young officers who had led the coup d'etat.

Compounding the country's problems, the governments that followed each other in rapid succession during the 1970s dismantled the empire, notably the colonies of Mozambique and Angola, causing hundreds of thousands of people to flee to Portugal. Already a poor country by European standards, Portugal became poorer as it grappled with the overlapping problems of political turmoil, a flood of *ritornados* from the former colonies, a drying up of foreign investment, and a ballooning and parasitic bureaucracy.

So why today is Portugal a favored destination for foreign investment? There are three answers. First, since the turbulent 1970s, Portugal has tackled most of its problems, if not solved them, and the people have voted into power middle-of-the-road governments. Second, political stability and the return to private ownership of former state-owned companies have boosted production. Third, Portugal's membership in the European Community has opened new markets—and the floodgates to EC development aid.

Lisbon today is a bustling city, very much a European capital. And that, too, is a sign of change. A decade ago, deprived of its empire, Lisbon was an imperial city without a role, to paraphrase the famous (or notorious) description of Britain by former U.S. Secretary of State Dean Acheson. But Lisbon still bears the scars of its revolutionary years in the form of political graffiti and peeling posters.

However, there's no doubt that Lisbon—and Portugal—is in the throes of a second revolution. Instead of looking to Africa and to Brazil, as it did for centuries, the city is looking to Europe for its future—a future, by the way, that many hundreds of thousands of Portuguese workers voted for with their feet by moving to France and West Germany long before the Salazar regime fell.

▷ Spotlight ◁

Portugal's biggest export has long been people. This tiny country pioneered European exploration of the Americas, Africa, and India, founded colonies, and spread its culture wherever its fleets touched shore. The achievement was astonishing, even if one disagrees strongly with the very concept of colonialism. But Portugal paid a price, of course, and that price was the loss of so many of the best and brightest people to the colonies.

▷ Arriving

Portugal is rapidly knitting itself into the European pattern, but the airport remains reminiscent of one in the third world: crowded, hot, inefficient, subject to inexplicable bureaucratic delays. In the summer, hordes of tourists worsen those delays, so do not count on getting out of the airport with your baggage in less than one hour. Do not expect the airport staff to smile, because they don't; foreign visitors are vital to the country's economy, but also a nuisance. Once you have extricated yourself, take a taxi to the city. It's not far, and taxis are plentiful and priced reasonably.

▷ Money

Currency: the *escudo*. International code: PTE. The escudo is further divided into a hundred centavos. Don't be surprised if somebody mentions a *conto*: that's 1,000 escudos (usually pronounced "skewds"). As in all cities, try to change your foreign currency at a bank rather than at a hotel or restaurant; you'll get a better rate. But be prepared to wait. Grossly overstaffed, Portugal's banks invent paper-shuffling to keep their bureaucrats busy.

▷ Language

Portuguese. The language isn't easy to learn. One of the Romance tongues, it resembles in written form both Spanish and Italian. Spoken, though, it's entirely different. Most native speakers swallow whole syllables, so that *vinho tinto* (red wine) becomes "vin tint."

A surprisingly high proportion of Portuguese speak another language, usually English. One possible reason: Salazar decreed that all movies and TV programs be shown in their original form, with Portuguese subtitles. As a result, several generations of Portuguese have learned English from the screen, if not at school.

▷ Communications

Country code: 351. City code: 1. Quality is patchy. The telecommunications system is notably better than it was a few years ago, but still not up to Western European standards. If you cannot dial a foreign number—or even a Portuguese one—at first try, do not blame the hotel. The switchboard operator spends a considerable proportion of his or her time trying to explain to guests why the world doesn't answer, or seems not to.

▷ Getting To Know the City

Lisbon is built on hills facing the estuary of the River Tagus. Virtually destroyed by an earthquake in 1755, Lisbon today is an architectural mixture of the few medieval buildings that survived, the visionary urban planning of the Marquès de Pombal after the quake, and, alas, the miserably narrow vision of today's commercial developers. Teotonia Pereira of the Association of Portuguese Architects said recently that "the people of Lisbon need to become aware of the fact that the architectural heritage of Lisbon is a public calamity. Today...everything is for sale. Advertising, for example, has taken over every public space."

That having been said, Lisbon is still an attractive city, if one closes one's eyes to the pervasive billboards and flashing neon signs. It has character, even if such critics as Senhor Pereira think that character is bad. It's also very obviously a poor city, with peddlers and beggars infesting the main streets. And on the outskirts are the shanty towns of the chronically impoverished, many of them immigrants from the countryside, gypsies, or Cape Verde islanders who moved to Portugal to work in the construction industry.

How then does one account for the traffic jams, the smart shops, the excellent restaurants, the well-dressed people who stroll the wide *avenidas*, the vivid contrasts of poverty and wealth? The answer is that incomes are distributed very unevenly, as in most third-world countries. Portugal is the nearest thing Europe has to a developing nation.

Business Lisbon is compact, though more and more companies are locating their headquarters on the outskirts, thanks to skyrocketing real estate prices in the central neighborhoods. Some of the best hotels are also in the city center, along with most of the outstanding restaurants. The easiest way to visualize the city is to imagine one is landing from the Tagus at the *Estação Fluvial Sul e Sueste* (see map).

To the right, rising steeply to a peak, is what remains of medieval Lisbon, the picturesque and crowded Alfama neighborhood topped by churches and monasteries. This was the old Moorish quarter.

Straight ahead, again looking from the sea, is the "new" city built by

Pombal. The huge *Praça do Comércio* (Commercial Square), open to the sea at the front, is flanked by impressive, pinkish buildings at left and right, and leads through arches to another vast square, the *Praça Don Pedro IV*, known popularly as the Rossio. The area between these squares is known as the *Baixa* and is the central commercial and shopping district. The dominant building in the Rossio is the National Theater, with its classical-style, colonnaded facade. That square leads into *Praça dos Restauradores* and then the *Avenida da Liberdade*, which ends at the *Praça Marquès de Pombal*. Immediately beyond is the greenery of the *Parque Eduardo VII*.

Back to the waterfront. Left, looking inland, are more hills and a maze of streets, some wide, some narrow, some of them extremely steep. This is the *Bairro Alto*, home of *fado* houses and some of Lisbon's best restaurants. If one looks sharply left, the coast stretches along the Tagus to Estoril and Cascais, two fashionable resorts, the first with an elegant casino. Although not administratively part of Lisbon, these two resort towns and others in between are integral parts of the metropolitan area, which has an estimated population of more than a million.

Now turn your back on the city of Lisbon and look across the river's broad mouth. There are some of the most important industrial suburbs, with shipbuilding, shiprepairing, and other maritime services. There also are some good, crowded, and noisy popular restaurants specializing in fish and seafood. To reach this part of the Lisbon metropolis, either take one of the cheap and frequent ferries or drive across the *Ponte 25 de Abril* (25th of April Bridge), one of the longest suspension bridges in Europe, with a span of 1,013 meters (3,300 feet).

▷ Moving Around

Lisbon has a subway system called the Metropolitano, as well as buses (some of them British double-deckers) and streetcars. Most are crowded; all are cheap.

Taxis are plentiful, except when you need them, and inexpensive by Western European standards. Many drivers speak English, or at least understand it.

We do not recommend taking a taxi—or driving yourself—along the coastal highway, the *Marginal*, to Estoril and Cascais. Recent studies have shown it to be one of the most dangerous highways in Europe. Instead, try the fast and frequent commuter trains, which start from a station near the ferryport on the river. The Estoril stop, for example, is only five minutes' walk from the casino, which you approach through well-tended gardens. There and back, the train will give you a magnificent view of the sea and the busy shipping.

▷ Spotlight ◁

Lisbon's streetcars, many of them old and beat-up, grind up and down hills that seem impossibly steep. But a streetcar ride gives the visitor a unique view of the city. The transit company has preserved immaculately some streetcars that are the better part of a century old. These can be rented, complete with smartly garbed crew, for the day or half-day—an unusual venue for an office party or hospitality for customers. The trip can start with a tour of the old city, continue along the coast, and include a stop for lunch or snacks. For more information, check with your hotel concierge.

▷ Hotels

Lisbon lacks a truly great hotel in the grand European tradition. What it does offer is a range of good to excellent hotels. Those listed specialize in business travelers, but that doesn't mean that vacationers are excluded or greeted as less than welcome. All the listed hotels serve good food, are fully air-conditioned, and provide both local and satellite TV.

Alfa Lisboa, Avenida Columbano Bordalo Pinheiro. Tel.: 726-2121. Telex: 18477. Fax: 726-3031. Rooms/suites: 355. Billing itself as a combination of "the most advanced technology with traditional knowledge of the hotel industry," the Alfa is close to the city center, yet only a claimed 10 minutes from the airport. Shopping gallery and guarded garage.

Méridien, 149 Rua Castilho. Tel.: 690900/690400. Telex: 64315. Fax: 693231. Rooms/suites: 353. Fronting Parque Eduardo VII. Another newish hotel; business center offers secretarial, translation, photocopying, and telex services.

Palácio, Estoril. Tel.: 268-0400. Telex: 12757. Fax: 268-4867. Rooms/suites: 227. Many business visitors choose the Palácio, even though it's 40 minutes or so from Lisbon. Understandably. Recently refurbished, the hotel is in the grand style; has a pool, sauna, and steam baths; and its own golf courses; and is close to Estoril Casino.

Ritz (Inter-Continental), Rua Rodrigo da Fonseca. Tel.: 692020. Telex: 12589. Fax: 691783. Rooms/suites: 360. Few faults, many virtues. Rooms are elegant, comfortable, and maintained immaculately. Decor is superb. One floor reserved for nonsmokers. Restaurants offer classic French and Portuguese cuisines. Meeting rooms accommodate up to 800 people. Executive Service Center provides secretarial, translation, and telecommunications services.

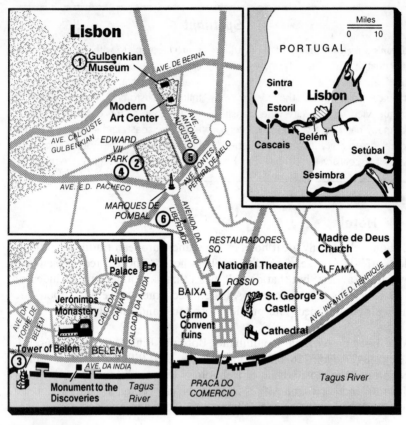

1. Alfa Lisboa
2. Méridien
3. Palácio

4. Ritz (Inter-Continental)
5. Sheraton
6. Tivoli

Sheraton, 1 Rua Latino Coelho. Tel.: 575757. Telex: 12774. Fax: 547164. Rooms/suites: 400. Some suites are designated Presidential (and some presidents actually stay in them). Within walking distance of the business, shopping, and entertainment neighborhoods. There's a swimming pool, a health club, and a sauna. So numerous are the shopping, laundry, and other facilities that one needs hardly to leave the hotel. Outstandingly excellent bars and restaurants.

Tivoli, 185 Avenida da Liberdade. Tel.: 530181/521101. Telex: 12588. Fax: 579461. Rooms/suites: 329. In the center of business Lisbon. The Tivoli

Club offers tennis, a solarium, a bar, snacks, and a beautiful garden. Valet parking.

▷ Restaurants

Portuguese cuisine is not Europe's most elegant or subtle. More than a fifth of the labor force still works on the land—a high proportion by Western European standards—and most native dishes are earthy and filling rather than imaginative, evidence of the country's deep peasant roots. That doesn't mean Portuguese dishes should be scorned. Fish and seafood are toothsome and fresh, and the best restaurants have honored Portuguese traditions while refining the recipes.

Wines are an adventure. The very best—which are not cheap—rival those of France, Italy, and Spain. And, of course, Portugal is the home of—you guessed it—port. You can drink a white port as an aperitif, but it's better to wait until the end of a meal for the red. Another good aperitif is Madeira, which comes from the island of that name.

▷ *Spotlight* ◁

Port. Much pretentious nonsense is talked and written about port wine—which is, after all, merely a desperate measure invented by the British in the 1700s for making Portuguese wines palatable. At that time rough, dry, and almost black, those wines were not to British tastes. So somebody (probably a British wine-shipper) had the brilliant idea of stopping fermentation and keeping the wine sweet by adding brandy.

To this day, the principle of making port is as simple as that. The practice is a little different, since port takes a long time to settle down in the cask.

Port varieties:

Ruby is young (10 or so years old), full of color, rich, and sometimes a little raw. Best as an aperitif.

Tawny has faded after 10 to 15 years in the wood, gaining smoothness and a nutty flavor. Complements cheese or fruit.

Vintage is declared by shippers when all has gone well with the vines and the weather has been perfect.

Matured vintage is anything from 20 to 40 years old, a mere stripling as port chronology goes. Usually has a crust; decant carefully.

Avis, 12B Rua Serpa Pinto. Tel.: 328391. A *Belle Epoque* restaurant of extraordinary distinction: quite the best in Lisbon in our view. Lapped in luxury, one is served food of outstanding quality by a staff that cannot be faulted.

Bonjardim, 10 and 11 Travessa de Santo Antao. Tel.: 327424/324389. Two bustling restaurants facing each other and offering wonderful value. *Frango na brasa* is the high point: chicken charcoal-grilled and accompanied by a fiery chili sauce.

Bota Alta, 3 Travessa da Queimada. Tel.: 327959. A cheerful bistro in the bohemian Bairro Alto quarter. Not for a serious business lunch, but definitely for relaxation after a day of successful negotiations.

Casa da Comida, 1 Travessa das Amoreiras. Tel.: 685376. A rising star in the Lisbon gastronomic galaxy, said by many knowledgeable people and professional food critics to serve the best international cuisine. Tables set around a charming enclosed garden.

Convêntual, 44 Praça das Flores. Tel.: 609196. Delicacies are based on convent and monastery recipes dating back to the 1500s. Vows in those days obviously didn't include bread-and-water diets.

Cozinha Velha, Palácio de Queluz. Tel.: 950232. The former royal kitchen has been turned into an interesting restaurant, with high stone arches, walk-in fireplace, and walls lined with gleaming copper utensils. Fine Portuguese and other European dishes.

Gambrinus, 25 Rua das Portas de Santo Antao. Tel.: 321466. Many small rooms in which are served fish and crustacea famous for their quality and variety. Open, blue-tiled kitchen; popular with the business crowd.

Ô Lacerda, 36 Avenida Berna. Tel.: 774057. A former butcher's shop across the street from the Gulbenkian Museum. Steaks are among Lisbon's best. Informal.

Pabe, 27 Rua Duque de Palmela. Tel.: 535675. English pub-style decor: dark wood paneling, solid masculine comfort. Top lunchtime venue for executives, politicians, newspaper editors, and media people.

Papa 'Açorda, 57 Rua Atalaia. Tel.: 364811. Açorda is a hard-to-describe combination of seafood, bread, and eggs. Potted palms, air-conditioning, friendly service, reasonable prices.

Porto do Abrigo, 16 Rua dos Remolares. Tel.: 360873. A tiny culinary landmark specializing in simple Portuguese dishes. Crowded at lunchtime; reservations recommended.

Tàgide, 18 Largo da Biblioteca Pública. Tel.: 320720. A great view of the Tagus estuary may be this place's best point, though the food is good and the service exemplary.

Tavares, 37 Rua da Miséricorda. Tel.: 321112. Mirrors, crystal, and brocades are a gilded setting for sumptuous food and wines, which have been served here since the 1700s. Lisbon's oldest restaurant. Expensive.

Varina da Madragoa, 34 Rua Madres. Tel.: 665533. A traditional tavern converted into a restaurant, close to the legislative assembly, the Palacio São Bento. Simple, traditional fare served politely. Popular with embassy officials and journalists.

Cascais and Estoril are resort towns along the coast from Lisbon. Here's a list of the best places in which to eat.

Cascais

João Padeiro, 12 Rua Visconde da Luz. Tel.: 280232. One of the oldest restaurants in the area. Appetizing, middle-level Portuguese food.

Ô Pescador, 10 Rua Flores. Tel.: 282054. Probably the area's best fish restaurant. Decor is forgettable—dishes are not.

Estoril

English Bar, Estrada Marginal. Tel.: 2681254. Close to the Hotel Atlântico. Oak beams, stucco, large dining room, candlelit comfort. Kitchen offers a melange of international and Portuguese dishes. Excellent wines.

Four Seasons, next to Hotel Palácio. Tel.: 2680400. One of the few luxury restaurants to be found outside the five-star hotels. Servitors pamper guests; valet parking.

▷ Tipping

Gratuities are usually included in the check, but it doesn't hurt to add a few *escudos* on top, particularly if you want to return to the bar or restaurant. Metered taxis fares do *not* include a tip; add about 10 percent. For journeys out of town, there are plenty of limos. Ask your hotel concierge to negotiate a price—and then try to bargain it down. You don't need to add a tip to the agreed fare.

▷ Doing Business

Government bureaucracy is powerful. And because there are so many functionaries, they have to justify their existence. This means, in practice, that getting official agreement to almost anything is slow, cumbersome, and sometimes infuriating.

Labor unions and laws protecting workers are strong. Although Portugal needs and encourages foreign investment and trade, there are laws, regulations, and plain old stubborn customs firmly in place; they're not easy to bend or circumvent. The government is trying, though, to make life easier for business in general and foreign investors in particular.

Portugal's private sector has an entrepreneurial enterprise that is surprisingly energetic. Increasingly, the most successful firms are looking far beyond Portugal's borders to the rest of Europe, and moving away from low-cost, low-technology industries and products into those with high added value. However, they must often seek foreign technology and partners: Portugal, to put it mildly, has lagged behind the rest of Western Europe in research and development.

Local banks, nationalized after the 1974 revolution, are far from noted for adventurous loan policies. Recent regulatory changes have allowed foreign banks to set up shop. In general, they are more willing and able than local banks to listen to investment propositions.

Portugal is a big recipient of European Community aid, and the government has also created a number of regional development programs. Well worth talking to are both the EC local office and chambers of commerce. Talk first, though, to people who know the lay of the land and the thrust of politics, among them the commercial attachés at embassies.

▷ *Spotlight* ◁

The Anglo-Portuguese News (APN) is a valuable guide for people who don't read Portuguese—and even for some of those who do. A weekly newspaper, the *APN* covers in detail the doings of foreign residents and, more important for the visitor, key political and economic events. The *APN* is a must for anyone thinking of settling in Portugal, since its news and advertising columns chart and price everything from education to the housing market. *APN*, Apartado 113, 2765 Estoril. Tel.: 244-3115.

Business hours are similar to those of the rest of Europe. The Portuguese do not take a siesta, like their Spanish neighbors do. Why they don't is an interesting speculation.

▷ Useful Phone Numbers

Emergencies

Fire Brigade	606060
National emergency services	115
Poisoning	761176
Police	366141
Red Cross	783003

Travel

Airport	802060
Long-distance buses	545826
Railways	876025

Business Information

European Community	541144
Portuguese Industrial Association	644161

Chambers of Commerce

American	572561
Arab	547312
Argentinian	774207
Australian	574104
Belgian	572502
Brazilian	367729
British	661586
Canadian	577562
Chinese	771317
French	549748
Indian	574104
International (ICC)	363304
Italian	778663
Japanese	689632
Moroccan	692277
Netherlands	365629
Portuguese	364133
South African	553208
Spanish	536758
Venezuelan	557180

Embassies and Consulates

Angola	767041
Algeria	616356
Argentina	522094
Australia	522094
Austria	547609
Belgium	549263
Bolivia	613536
Brazil	535639
Bulgaria	671713
Canada	563821
Chile	528054
China (People's Republic)	611947
Colombia	557096
Costa Rica	669767
Cuba	616411
Czechoslovakia	549838
Denmark	545099
Ecuador	776689
Egypt	687143
Finland	607551
France	526206
Germany (East)	803887
Germany (West)	563961
Greece	616991
Hungary	610281
Iceland	546078

India	683203	Venezuela	573803
Iran	610871	Yugoslavia	615311
Iraq	607012	Zaire	536211
Ireland	661569		
Israel	570251		

Airlines

Italy	546144		
Japan	562177	Aeroflot Soviet Airlines	561296
Libya	616301	Air France	562171
Luxembourg	881177	Air Zaire	579704
Mexico	570683	Alitalia	536141
Morocco	679193	British Airways	363307
Mozambique	771994	Canadian Pacific	539511
Nigeria	616191	El Al Israel Airlines	576593
Norway	615344	Finnair	576148
Pakistan	538486	Iberia (Spain)	562016
Panama	825830	Iraqi Airways	774416
Peru	570005	KLM Royal Dutch Airlines	579110
Poland	808650	LAM (Mozambique)	578254
Romania	666463	Lufthansa German Airlines	573852
Singapore	370319	Royal Air Maroc	574031
South Africa	535041	South African Airways	536102
Soviet Union	562424	Sabena Belgian World Airlines	365572
Spain	549605		
Sweden	606097	SAS Scandinavian Airlines	557116
Switzerland	673121		
Thailand	805359	TAP Air Portugal	575020
Turkey	614275	TWA	539541
United Kingdom	661191	Varig (Brazil)	563841
United States	726660	Viasa (Venezuela)	530969
Uruguay	689265		

▷ Shopping

There's much to buy in Lisbon—and much not to buy. Avoid the aggressive street hawkers of seemingly genuine brand-name goods: they're all counterfeits. Concentrate instead upon local arts and crafts: jewelry, leather goods, textiles, and ceramics, particularly tiles (*azulejos*).

▷ *Spotlight* ◁

A *tile* is a tile is a tile—except in Portugal. There, this distinctive form of art is both ancient and surprisingly fresh. Subtly colored, *azulejos* can depict a scene on one tile or tell a story spread over many tiles. Some craftworkers will make tiles to order, working from the customer's basic design. A tile set into a wall or table will last forever, or almost. Certainly, some of the tile murals in Lisbon's older public buildings date back centuries, and some even survived the 1755 earthquake.

In September 1988, a fierce fire fanned by strong winds devoured most of the *Chiado*, one of Lisbon's two most famous shopping areas. At least two people died, more than 50 were taken to hospitals, 300 people lost their homes, 200 businesses were destroyed, and 2,000 people were put out of work. The disaster was Lisbon's worst since the earthquake of 1755, which killed about 50,000 people and destroyed most of the city.

Some of the Chiado neighborhood survived the fire, so it's still worth window-shopping in the area between the Rossio and *Praça Luis de Camoes*. Antiques and old books and prints are in *Rua da Misericordia*, which leads to *Rua São Pedrode Alcantara*. Untouched by the fire was the *Baixa*, popular name for the grid of narrow streets between the Praça do Comercio, on the river, and the Rossio square. The Baixa offers almost everything, but there is a particularly high concentration of gold- and silversmiths and shoe stores.

The place to hunt for junk and bric-a-brac is the *Feira da Ladra* (Thieves' Market), held Tuesdays and Saturdays in the Campo de Santa Clara in the Graça quarter. However, the most significant development in recent years has been the rise of the modern shopping mall, *centro comercial* in Portuguese. The largest and most fashionable of these is in the *Amoreiras* complex on the edge of town on the way to Estoril/Cascais. If you can stand the rather overpowering decor—Knossos as designed by Walt Disney—you will find that the shopping is good.

Recommended for quality and value:

Books/prints/maps. *Livrarira Historica e Ultramarina*. 28 Travessa de Queimda. Tel.: 368589. Special focus on Portugal's imperial past. *Mundo do Livro*, 11 Largo Trinidade. Tel.: 369951. Great for browsing.

Fashions. *Ana Salazar*, 87 Rua do Carmo. Tel.: 372289. Lisbon's trendiest designs: love 'em or hate 'em.

Handicrafts. *Arestenao Arameiro*, 62 Praça Restauradores. Tel.: 320238. Wide variety of regional ceramics, brassware, rugs, blankets, filigree, and so on.

Jewelry/silverware. *Joalharia Mergulhão*, 162 Rua São Paulo. Tel.: 360013. One of the oldest and best practitioners of the craft. *Torres*, 235 Rua Doro. Tel.: 323196. A leader; expensive but excellent.

Lace and linens. *Madeira House*, 131 Rua Augusta. Tel.: 320557. Old-established supplier of Madeira and other laces; also superb linens.

Porcelain. *Vista Alegre*, 52-54 Rua Ivens, and 18 Largo Chiado. Tel.: 328612 and 361401. Both in the Chiado; enormous selection of Portugal's best porcelain.

Rugs. *Casa Quintão*, 30 Rua Ivens. Tel.: 355837. Specializes in rugs from Arrailoas, so if you don't have time to visit that small town, this is the place to find them.

Shoes. *Sapateria Charles*, 105 Ruad do Carmo. Tel.: 320700. High-fashion brand-name shoes sold in Paris are often made in Portugal. Buy them here and save mightily.

Tiles. *Fabrica Ceramica Viuva da Lamego*, 25 Largo do Intendente Pina Manique. Tel.: 521401. Modern designs and reproductions of old ones. *Fabrica Santa'ana*, 95 Rua Alecrim. Tel.: 322537. Huge selection; factory will make tiles to order.

▷ **After Hours**

Nightclubs tend to run from the sleazy to the very sleazy. Exceptions are the *Estoril Casino* and the *Carroussel*, attached to the Ritz. Both are glamorous. Most of the rest are pickup joints that feature tired strippers and jazzed-up *fado* singers.

Among the less objectionable: *Night and Day*, 49 Avenida Duque de Loulè. Tel.: 574976. *Scarlaty Club*, 111 Rua de São Marçal. Tel.: 369733.

The casino at Estoril offers what is probably the most glittering—in the sense of glitzy—floor show in Portugal, perhaps in the Iberian peninsula. The casino makes much of its money from suckers who think they can beat the bank odds, a mathematical impossibility in the long run. But, as the economist John Maynard (Lord) Keynes once wrote, in the long run we'll all be dead. Until then, let's enjoy ourselves—if losing money is a form of enjoyment. The Estoril casino provides what is best called international fare, including young ladies who wear more smiles than clothes.

Fado

For the discerning, though, the Lisbon area offers much more than bare bouncing breasts and buttocks. As the flamenco is to Spain, the tango to Argentina, so is the *fado* to Portugal. The difference is this: the word *fado* means "fate"—and the fate is always dire. You may not enjoy the fado, but only if you hear it will you understand the melancholy that throbs in the Portuguese soul.

Once confined to Portugal, fado became world-famous because of the genius of Amàlia Rodrigues. She now sings seldom in public, and nobody has replaced her as the undisputed queen of fado or Portugal's unofficial ambassador of song. Even so, fado flourishes. Before we list some of the better fado houses, a few words of warning. Fado is a form of art—a working-class form, perhaps, but still art. In the more serious fado houses, nobody dares even to whisper while the *fadista* is singing. We should stress that *fadistas* do not dance, throw themselves around the stage, or in other ways play to the audience. They stand up straight, keep their arms by their sides, and use their voices, which are usually deep.

Adega Machado, 91 Rua do Norte. Tel.: 360095. A big fado house that features singing and dancing as well as classical fado. Medium-to-good food; an excellent introduction for people who are not quite sure they want their fado undiluted.

Ô Faia, 48 Rua da Barroca. Tel.: 369387. Pure, undiluted fado. Listen; do not speak.

Senhor Vinho, 18 Rua do Meio a Lapa. Tel.: 672681. Must be the best fado house in town because it's always crowded. Classical fado.

▷ Sights and Sounds

Museums and Landmarks

Lisbon—indeed, Portugal—possesses and has embellished a long and distinctive patrimony. Name a part of the world that the Portuguese navigators did not discover for Europe: it's hard to find. Start at the riverside suburb of Belèm, rich with monuments to the great explorers, Vasco da Gama prominent among them. The *Torre de Belèm*, built between 1515 and 1521, is a masterpiece of Manueline architecture, that being the term

▶251

for buildings designed during the reign of King Manuel I. Once a watch-tower, it is now a museum.

In the same neighborhood are the *Museu do Marinha* (naval museum), obligatory for lovers of the sea, and the *Museu Nacional dos Coches*, which houses what may be the world's finest collection of coaches. The *Mosteiro dos Jerónimos* (Hieronymite Monastery Church), also in the Belèm area, is the most notable example of Manueline architecture. The style is characterized by a profusion of ornate stonework featuring marine motifs such as ropes and coral. The cloisters are exceptionally beautiful.

Closer to the city center is the *Castelo São Jorge* (Saint George's Castle), a hilltop fortress built in the 400s A.D. and since extended and much changed by the Romans, the Moors, and early Portuguese kings. A challenging climb, but a clanking little streetcar will carry you most of the way.

Calouste Sarkis Gulbenkian (1869-1955) was known as the "Mr. Five Percent" of the oil industry. When he died, he left some $70 million garnered from his various deals in the Middle East and shrewd investments elsewhere. A chief beneficiary was the Gulbenkian Foundation, endowed with money and vast art collections. The foundation sets the tone and the pace for the visual and performing arts in Portugal, its museum and modern art center set in a manicured park bordered by the Avenidas de Berna and Antonio Augusto.

Sintra is 32 kilometers (20 miles) northwest of Lisbon, along the coast road that leads first to Estoril and Cascais. Two royal palaces make the journey worthwhile. In the town itself is the *Palácio Nacional*, a former summer residence of the royal family. Nearby is the *Pena Palace*, a romantic nineteenth-century folly that crowns a hill. The art-loving German consort of Queen Maria II built the palace; mad King Ludwig of Bavaria and Walt Disney could hardly have mixed more architectural styles if they'd joined forces.

Sports

Two golf courses are within each easy reach, both at Estoril. One is the eighteen-hole *Estoril Golf Club*, Avenida de Republica. Tel.: 2680176. The other is the smaller, nine-hole course owned by the *Estoril Sol Hotel*. Tel.: 923-2461. Both clubs rent equipment and caddies can be hired.

▷ Spotlight ◁

Beaches. Between Lisbon and Cascais are long stretches of tempting beaches. Don't be tempted unless you're a good swimmer. This is the Atlantic, not the Mediterranean: tides surge, waves are strong, and the un- dertow can be lethal. The water's usually cold and often polluted.

The Portuguese don't kill bulls in public, they merely worry them to death. The *cavaleiros* canter into the ring on horseback wearing splendid eighteenth-century costumes. Men on foot, *forcados*, incite the bull to charge. Ideally, the leader of this intrepid band allows himself to be caught between the bull's horns. The other *forcados* then pile on the bull, sticking it with darts. When the bull is sufficiently enraged, the *cavaleiro* runs it ragged around the ring. When the bull has had enough, it is dragged off to die behind a fence in decent obscurity (to end up, no doubt, as steak). Bullfight season runs from May to October. There are bullrings in Cascais and Lisbon. If you fancy a stylish death in the afternoon, go to *Santarem*, 79 kilometers (50 miles) north of the capital.

LONDON

Capital of Britain's New Empire

Population: 6.8 million (1981). Metropolitan area: 9.4 million. Political, administrative, and financial capital of the United Kingdom of Great Britain and Northern Ireland (population: 56.9 million). *Location*: southeast England on River Thames. *Economy*: aerospace equipment and aircraft; banking and financial services; brewing; chemicals and pharmaceuticals; electrical, electronics, and scientific equipment; film and television production; optical and photographic equipment; printing and publishing; tourism. Britain is a member of the European Community (EC) and the Organization for Economic Cooperation and Development (OECD) and a signatory to the General Agreement on Tariffs and Trade (GATT). England's Queen Elizabeth II is head of the Commonwealth, a voluntary association of 48 sovereign states formerly ruled by Britain.

▷ Background Briefing

The late Dean Acheson, a former U.S. Secretary of State, jibed in 1972 that Britain had lost an empire but failed to find a new role. Back then, things did indeed look bleak for a country that had once ruled a quarter of the world but since 1947 had relinquished all of its sprawling empire, apart from a few tiny territories. For most of the period since the end of World War II, Britain had also lurched from one economic crisis to another and lagged behind other major industrialized countries' growth in prosperity.

The United Kingdom's chronic problems were dubbed "the British disease"—and when the annual inflation rate soared to more than 20 percent in the late 1970s, and the government of the day had to go cap in hand to the International Monetary Fund for a loan to pay for vital imports, the worst forebodings seemed justified.

So why was Britain able in the second half of the 1980s to register economic growth well above the major industrialized nations' average, cut the basic rate of personal income tax to 25 percent—one of the lowest levies in the world—and not only balance its domestic budget, but also show a surplus?

The party-political answer is that those were among the fruits of "the enterprise culture" nurtured by the government of Prime Minister Margaret Thatcher, which first took office in 1979, and was re-elected in 1983 and 1987 with huge parliamentary majorities.

But can Mrs. Thatcher and her government take all the credit for having cured, at least for the moment, "the British disease"? No, they cannot. A number of favorable developments helped them: continuing though falling revenues from North Sea gas and oil, growth in world trade, and membership of the European Community, which has helped to end the insular "Little England" view of the world. All is not well, though. Unemployment, though down from its mid-1980s high, is still a major social problem.

In the late 1980s came fresh cause for concern, a high deficit on foreign trade. As in the past, Britain's appetite for imports far exceeded its ability to export, and the government was able to finance the deficit only by raising domestic interest rates to levels that would attract foreigners to the pound, thereby keeping its value high against other major currencies. In the late 1980s, too, inflation rose far above government targets, and the chancellor of the exchequer (finance minister) found himself in a classic policy bind. He needed to keep interest rates high so as to finance the balance-of-payments deficit with foreigners' deposits and to dampen a retail boom in consumer-goods sales, but high interest rates also raised both the price index and industry's borrowing costs.

That dilemma and its consequences dulled some of the gloss on the Conservatives' economic performance. Even so, the Thatcher government has done much to change popular attitudes. The Tories have legislated to curb the power of the labor union "barons," the powerful officials who until recently were almost pillars of state. No longer are union leaders able to call strikes without first holding a secret ballot of their members. At the same time, a combination of unemployment and a shift from traditional heavy industries to new ones and to services has cut union membership in both absolute and percentage terms.

▷ *Spotlight* ◁

Strikes. Back in the "bad old days"— well, up until the late 1970s—the ostensible causes of many of Britain's strikes made the rest of the world wonder whether workers had taken leave of their senses. A car plant was struck because union members objected to a cat's having urinated on the assembly line; a shipyard was idle for weeks because rival unions demanded that carpenters and metalworkers should be employed to drill the same hole when it penetrated both wood and metal; highly paid newspaper production workers in a London plant walked out in an argument over which union had the right to start the presses rolling. The examples of seemingly unnecessary strikes would fill the whole of this book. These days, strikes are fewer. In 1988, though, postal workers baffled most people by striking for two weeks, weeks, reportedly because the Post Office's wanted to pay new recruits more in London and the expensive southeast of England than in the rest of the country. Mailboxes were sealed after more than 150 million letters and parcels piled up in idled sorting offices. One swift result of the strike was that businesses rushed to buy telefax machines and use private courier services, thereby threatening the Post Office profits from first-class mail and possibly, in the long run, jobs that were until then secure. Then came the 1989 train and underground (metro) strikes to remind Mrs. Thatcher of the danger to herself, and to business, of soaring inflation.

The workers' mood isn't exactly docile, but fewer labor disputes have left managers with more time and energy to get on with their real job, which is producing goods and services that people want to buy. The Thatcher government stresses individual initiative and responsibility and believes passionately that the state isn't able to run businesses effectively. The result has been "privatization" of such major state-owned firms as British Airways, British Telecom, British Gas, Rolls-Royce (the aero-engines company; the prestigious carmaker of the same name was already owned privately), and the royal armaments factories. Even Rover cars—previously British Leyland, and the very symbol of industrial decline—went on the block and found a buyer in British Aerospace, itself a privatized company. Plans are now afoot to sell off British Coal, newly profitable after decades of large losses, and other industries that had become fat and slothful under state ownership but have now slimmed. Even British Rail, or parts of it, may soon be sold to private investors.

Other countries looked at Thatcherite radicalism, and many liked what they saw. Around the world, governments decided that getting the state off people's backs was a way of unleashing energies, and "market forces" became the fashion. Indeed, some observers believe that Thatcherism has even influenced the thinking of Soviet leader Mikhail Gorbachev—"a man with whom I can do business," she has said. He apparently believes that state control has stifled his country's economic performance, but he has met stubborn resistance from the entrenched bureaucracy and vested interests in his country.

So, in Britain, has Margaret Thatcher. But though the parallels are close, the magnitudes of the two leaders' respective challenges are not. How have the British reacted to her government's reforming zeal, its determination to substitute individualism for collectivism? Some people have embraced it fervently, deciding that if money's there to be made, they should make it—and flaunt it. Others have reacted with bitter anger. In the north of England, Wales, and Scotland, the heartlands of the Labor Party, the political maps are mainly Socialist red. The Labor Party is in trouble, though, since its natural electoral base is shrinking as heavy industry declines and the once-comforting notions of state control and social collectivism sound increasingly dated.

They sound dated, in fact, to most Labor Party leaders themselves, who admit that many of the Thatcherite measures are probably irreversible. Shrewd foreign investors are betting that even if Labor does return to power at the next election, which could be held as late as 1992, nothing much will change, except at the margin. Investments are pouring into Britain, with Japanese-owned plants widely publicized. Most Japanese investors say that the productivity and quality of British labor are well up to benchmarks set back home.

Britain, in turn, has reverted to its old role as a major investor abroad. In many countries, including the United States, British companies are the leading foreign owners of local businesses. Such investments may strain Britain's external payments balance when they are made, but they do result in a flow of profits back to headquarters and thus reduce the foreign payments deficit. The Union Jack no longer flies over a quarter of the world, but British corporate names and logos are increasingly emblazoned where once the flag waved. Having lost one empire irrevocably, Britain is building another and may have found the role that Dean Acheson thought it lacked.

▷ *Spotlight* ◁

Will the real Margaret Thatcher please stand up? The Iron Lady, the Scourge of the Left, the Hard-hearted Hannah of British politics: Who is she, this first female prime minister who has served longer in that office than anyone this century?

She was born in 1925 in Grantham, Lincolnshire, a smallish town (population: 31,000) in the east of England, daughter of one Alfred Roberts, a grocer. She has degrees from Oxford in science and law, and she became a barrister.

She married oil-company executive Denis Thatcher in 1951 and has a twin son and daughter and one grandchild. Mrs. Thatcher was first elected to the House of Commons in 1959 and served in various government posts before becoming Conservative Party leader in 1975. The leader she replaced, former prime minister Edward Heath, dislikes her intensely. Labor and the other opposition parties tend to characterize her as a ruthless, opportunistic politician who cares more for the rich than for the poor.

She's certainly no soft touch. Having fought her way to the top from obscurity, Mrs. Thatcher reveres initiative and is acridly impatient with people who pine for a "nursemaid society" of abundant social programs. On the other hand, her government has steadily increased spending on health, education, and welfare.

So is she ruthless or realistic? A much-needed radical reformer or a seam ripper in the fabric of British life? A traitor to her humble origins or a heroine who has broken the caste and class fetters? The definitive biography has yet to be written, and when it is, it will almost certainly provoke as much bad-tempered dispute as the woman herself. History itself will be the final judge.

London is the central nervous system of business, financial and banking networks that stretch to virtually every country. Traditions remain strong, but London today is cosmopolitan and vibrant and ranks with Tokyo and New York as a business capital of world stature.

▷ Arriving

By Air

London has three airports: *Heathrow*, the main one, 23 kilometers (15 miles) west of the city; *Gatwick*, 45 kilometers (30 miles) southeast of London; and the brand-new *London City Airport*. Each airport has its strengths and weaknesses.

Heathrow somehow handles about 30 million people a year, billing itself as the Gateway to Europe and the world's busiest international airport. Just under half of the passengers are traveling on business. A guide to the complexity:

Terminal 1 mixes domestic and European flights, but it also takes South African Airways and El Al Israel Airlines. Features include duty-free supermarkets for passengers headed for the Republic of Ireland and rental of a mobile phone for people staying in southeast England.

Terminal 2 is used mainly for European and Mediterranean-basin airlines. Oldest of the terminals, it has been brightened recently by the Plaza on the Balcony restaurant and a new shopping area.

Terminal 3 has been renovated and handles mainly Middle Eastern, Asian, African, and North and South American carriers.

Terminal 4 is used by Air Malta, British Airways, and KLM. It houses a small communications center that offers word processing, Prestel teletext (a video-screen information system), an electronic mail terminal, worldwide direct dialing by phone, and telefax and telex machines. Nearby is a luxury, duty-free shop that is usually crowded with Japanese visitors buying obligatory expensive gifts for the folks back home.

Privatized British Airports Authority and the major airlines have spent heavily to improve Heathrow, with more business-class lounges, business centers, and restaurants. Heathrow's main business center is next to Terminal 2 and is one of the best of its kind in Europe. Facilities include telephones, telefax and telex machines, electronic mailboxes, photocopiers, executive offices, boardrooms, translation and secretarial services, and a multilingual, remarkably competent staff. All this doesn't come for free, of course. For details, phone extension 5757 within the airport, 759-2434 from outside.

Traveling to town. Try not to take taxis; they're expensive. If you do decide to cab it into central London, insist upon paying what's shown on the meter, which should be the distance/time charge and any extras: these are listed on prominent notices inside the cab. The standard tip is 10 percent of the total.

The London Underground subway system, nicknamed the "Tube," costs about a sixth of the cab fare. There is one station for Terminals 1, 2, and 3, and another for Terminal 4. However, the Tube does not serve all hotel areas, space for luggage is limited, the train fills up fast during rush hours, and there are no trolleys for your bags when you arrive.

Buses are a good alternative, though slower than the Tube: A1 goes to Victoria after passing through Chelsea, A2 to Euston after passing Marble Arch and Russell Square.

Gatwick airport is a village when compared with the sprawling city that is Heathrow, and except at peak vacation periods is less frenetic. There are two terminals, one of them new, light, and airy; they are connected by a "people-mover" automatic train running every few minutes. Its three-car units are able to carry 7,900 baggage-toting passengers every hour.

Restaurants are good. So are shops, particularly in the North Terminal. Ubiquitous British Airways uses Gatwick for some flights, mainly to Africa, but so do cost-cutting airlines such as Air Europe. In summer, the airport is jammed by the backpack and charter-tour sets.

Trains run from Gatwick to Victoria Station, in the heart of London. They leave every quarter-hour, and the journey time is about 30 minutes. Pleasant young people offer food and drinks from trolleys while the train meanders first through rural Sussex and then London's suburbs before crossing the Thames.

London City Airport is the newest, on a site bounded by the former Royal Albert and King George Docks, relics of another epoch. It's mainly

►259

for business travelers hopping over from or to continental Europe for quick visits, with Amsterdam, Brussels, and Paris the main cities served directly. Advantages: new, small, clean, close to the financial district. Disadvantage: fares to a given destination are usually much higher than those charged from Heathrow or Gatwick.

By Rail

British Rail operates fast, efficient train service throughout the UK. Trains also connect with incoming ferries, jetfoils, and hovercraft from points in Ireland, the Netherlands, Belgium, and France. The Dover-to-London express train will make your ears pop as it whizzes through tunnels, but the 1½-hour ride goes through some pleasantly green countryside and small towns and villages.

▷ *Spotlight* ◁

The Chunnel. Due to open in 1993 is the Channel Tunnel, also called the Chunnel, which will go underneath the English Channel to offer fast rail links between London and Paris (about three hours) and other cities. That is, if all goes according to plan. Though the private Anglo-French consortium is sticking resolutely to its opening date, tunneling has been slower on both sides of the Channel than forecast. Furthermore, there is a huge political battle brewing over the proposed new high-speed railroad track from the tunnel's English exit to London. Pressure groups and lobbyists are claiming that it will ruin much of the rural and small-town charm of the County of Kent, known sometimes as ''the Garden of England.''

▷ Money

The basic unit of currency is the British pound sterling. International code: GBP. Banknotes come in denominations of 5, 10, 20, and 50 pounds. You may also see a few 1-pound notes. These are no longer printed and were replaced with 1-pound coins beginning in the mid-1980s. Coins are minted in denominations of 1 and 2 pounds and 1, 5, 10, 20, and 50 pence (100 pence = 1 pound). Some of the older coins may be labeled as *shillings*, but you can ignore that term. The currency was decimalized in 1971, and all coins count as pence now.

Banks offer the best rates of exchange for foreign currency, non-bank *bureaux de change* the second best, and hotels the worst.

▷ Language

English. But don't be lulled into complacency—British English is a far cry from American, and the variety you'll hear in London is astounding. Standard Received English, or Oxford English, is what "proper" people talk. People born and raised in the East End of London speak a Cockney dialect that's thicker than *My Fair Lady* would lead you to believe. Most other Londoners speak in a generalized London accent. A quarter of the central London population is of African, Asian, or Caribbean origin; another sizable slice is continental European. These folks all have their own inflections. And then there are all the British regional accents. As a Cockney might say: "Gorblimey, myte, it's a Tower of bloody Bybel 'ere!" So keep your ears tuned.

Once your ear is tuned to the words, you may discover that they don't seem to make sense; they're loaded with idiomatic expressions whose meaning you can't quite fathom. Most Americans have enough vague knowledge of Britain to know that an elevator is a "lift" and an apartment is a "flat," but the differences are more widespread than that. One thing American businesspeople should know is that in Britain, to "call" traditionally means to pay a personal visit. For a phone call, you "ring" or "ring up." Body language also differs. *Never* hold up your index and middle finger together to order two drinks; that gesture carries the same obscene meaning as the middle finger alone in the United States. A British hand-count begins with the thumb, so the number two is signaled with thumb and index finger outstretched. An interesting guide is the paperback *British/American Language Dictionary* by Norman Moss (Passport Books).

▷ Communications

Country code: 44. City code: 1 (from other parts of the British Isles, dial 01 before the London number). Quality is generally good but patchy. Too many crossed lines, wrong numbers, clicks and buzzes.

Many hotels levy huge surcharges on calls from rooms. Check the markup before deciding to use your room as a communications center. Alternatives are to call from pay phones, found in most hotel lobbies, or from outside phones. *Westminster Communications Center*, 1 The Broadway, SW1—opposite New Scotland Yard and St. James's Park Underground—has an overseas call service open daily from 9:00 a.m. to 7:00 p.m.

Phone booths are of three types. The traditional dial phone takes only 10-pence coins. Lift the receiver, wait for the tone, and dial the complete number, including the area code. When someone answers, you will hear

► 261

rapid pips: put the coin in the slot immediately. More pips mean that you need to insert more money.

The push-button phone takes coins of up to 1 pound and is better for long-distance calls. Insert the money first, dial, and don't wait for the pips: there aren't any. A sign flashes when more coins are needed.

The Cardphone is London's latest. You buy cards at post offices or some newsstands. Insert the card in the slot; an indicator panel shows how many units you are using and, at the end of the call, how many are left in the card. The Cardphone is better than the other two types for long-distance calls.

▷ Getting To Know the City

For the business visitor, most of the action is in three main locations north of the Thames that are known collectively as Central London. *The City*, to the east, is the financial district, where the Bank of England, the Stock Exchange, and other financial institutions are concentrated. This fringes into the *West End*, rather more vaguely defined. It includes the theater district, raffish Soho, Piccadilly Circus, and Leicester Square; and dignified Mayfair and St. James's, where many of the finest hotels, restaurants, and shops are to be found. *Westminster* and *Victoria* are dominated by the royal residence of Buckingham Palace, the Houses of Parliament, Westminster Abbey, and Whitehall. There also is Downing Street, where the prime minister and chancellor of the exchequer have their official residences, at numbers 10 and 11. Further west, and slightly north, are *Knightsbridge* and *Kensington*, with more shops, including the world-famous Harrods department store, and luxury hotels. Bordering these neighborhoods is *Chelsea*, once the home of artists, but now of the rich and of trendy designers and fashionable restaurants.

Most of London wasn't planned, as Paris and New York were; and though this haphazardness has its charms, a visitor who doesn't know the territory but wants to walk or ride the bus or subway should buy a street guide. Geographers' Map Company publishes both the pocket-size *AZ* and the larger, three-color *Master Atlas of Central London*; most newsstands and bookstores stock them.

One of London's most pleasant features is the extraordinary number and variety of parks: 387 of more than 2.5 hectares (20 acres) in Greater London. It's possible to walk all the way from Holland Park in west London to the Houses of Parliament, a distance of 6.4 kilometers (4 miles) exclusively in parkland, apart from a short stretch through the streets of Kensington. The parks are also useful topographical reference points when you are making your way around London.

▷ Spotlight ◁

How safe is London? Raw statistics suggest not very. There were 10,000 street robberies in 1987. However, London is a huge, sprawling area, the total population is almost 10 million, and pickpockets and muggers concentrate in a few places. Most of their victims are frail old people living in poor, run-down neighborhoods. Street markets are also hunting grounds for purse snatchers and pickpockets. *Dips* (criminal slang for "pickpockets") also work some subway stations, particularly Oxford Circus. But lest anyone think that Londoners are prone to dishonesty, note that milkmen leave bottles on doorsteps; few are stolen. Prudence suggests that after dark one keep to busy, well-lighted streets and avoid the parks. Finally, it should be noted that handgun violence is nowhere near the problem in London—or other European cities—that it is in the United States.

▷ Moving Around

Allow plenty of time between appointments if they're not within walking distance of each other. London is increasingly clogged, and the subway is sometimes so crowded at rush hours that you cannot get on the first train that comes along. But don't despair—most run at intervals of less than five minutes. Peak periods are 7:30 to 9:30 a.m. and 5:00 to 7:30 p.m. The big, red, double-decker buses are freed from traffic jams on some main arteries by having their own lanes, but at busy times they can be slow.

London Regional Transport publishes free, easy-to-follow bus and Underground maps. Fares are charged by zone and are not cheap. There are good deals going at British tourist offices overseas, which sell Visitors' Travelcards. These are valid for three, four, or seven days, cover all zones, and include the bus to and from Heathrow. Once in London, you can also buy travel cards that cut costs, provided you use them only during off-peak times. Deals change every now and then; check with your travel agent or the British Tourist Authority office in major U.S. cities.

As you've probably heard, traffic drives on the left in Britain. London has many one-way streets, however, and on some of them buses drive in their own lanes—which may be against the prevailing traffic. Be watchful before you step off the sidewalk.

London's black cabs (though some of them are now in other colors) are legendary for their spacious size and their drivers' familiarity with London streets, however obscure. That comes from their having been "on the knowledge"—spent up to two years studying the shortest way of getting from Point A to Point Z, and all the points and permutations between. Only after passing a strict examination can they become licensed drivers. Their vehicles, too, are licensed and inspected regularly by the same agency of the Metropolitan Police. Cabs can turn on a dime, and often do, such as when the driver sees a traffic jam and does a U-turn. Virtually all cabbies are honest. Pay what is shown on the meter, which includes extra charges for luggage and for journeys started after 8:00 p.m. Permissible charges are displayed clearly inside the cab. Add a tip of not less than 10 percent to the total metered amount. You can find black cabs at ranks, or hail them in the street, and many are on radio networks.

So-called minicabs are a different story. Some are gleaming luxury cars—Mercedes-Benzes, Rovers, or Volvos, for example. Many are equipped with carphones. Others are smaller and dingier. Drivers are not subject to the licensing rules for taxicabs, so they range from highly professional to novices who can't find their way from Park Lane to Piccadilly without help (and when you look at the map, you'll see how puny that challenge is). Ask your hotel porter (concierge) to recommend a good minicab company, and if you're satisfied with the service, note the phone number. Minicabs are not allowed to pick up passengers on the street, are not metered, and are not licensed by the Metropolitan Police. A minicab may cost a little more than a black cab, but who cares when the rain is pelting down and an appointment is looming? Radio dispatchers are often overly optimistic about the time it will take for the minicab to arrive, so call at least 20 minutes ahead, and half an hour during peak periods.

We don't recommend renting a car unless you are going out of town. Traffic in the city is heavy, parking space is scarce, and unless you know London well, you can find yourself driving along a one-way street—*away* from your destination. This is to say nothing of the mental strain involved in remembering to stay on the left! If you want to travel in style, make a deal with a limousine service, asking advice from your hotel.

▷ Hotels

London real estate is among the most expensive in the world—if we leave aside Tokyo, where only a yen billionaire can afford a handkerchief-size garden. Top-of-the-range hotels are currently valued at more than $330,000 a room; and a rule-of-thumb calculation is that the daily rate should be about $1 for each $1,000 of capital cost. Hence, the $330-plus-per-night room. At the same time, London also has some of the world's best hotels, offering indubitable value for the money.

The stated, or "rack," rate is seldom the real one: there are corporate, long-stay, group, and weekend rates, among others. Remember, though, that between May and October there's a dire shortage of rooms, so you won't have much choice if you haven't reserved well ahead of arrival.

Because of the staggering variety of hotels, we have put the best into two categories: *grande luxe* and *deluxe*. We've listed airport hotels separately here.

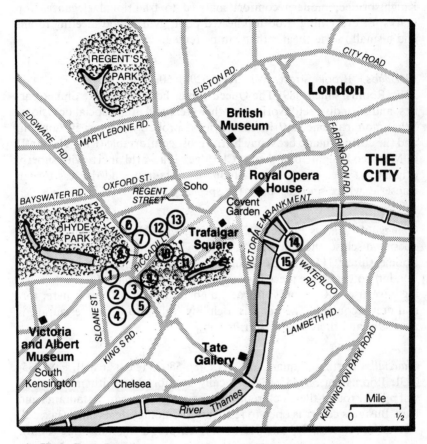

1. Hyde Park Hotel
2. Sheraton Park Tower
3. Berkeley
4. Hyatt Carlton Tower
5. Belgravia Sheraton
6. Grosvenor House
7. Dorchester
8. Inn on the Park
9. Inter-Continental
10. Meridien Piccadilly
11. Ritz
12. Connaught
13. Claridge's
14. Savoy
15. Howard

Grande Luxe

Berkeley, Wilton Place, SW1. Tel.: 235-6000. Telex: 919252. Fax: 235-6000. Rooms/suites: 160. Stylish, in the heart of Belgravia and Knightsbridge; modern comfort married to traditional elegance. Top marks for everything. Rooftop heated pool, gym. Good meeting rooms and a small movie theater that can be rented.

Claridge's, Brook Street, W1. Tel.: 629-8860. Telex: 21872. Fax: 499-2210. Rooms/suites: 189. The Queen comes here for private dinner parties, and it's a discreet favorite for other great and grand social occasions. What more can one say? Room service is probably the best in London, and the custom-made beds may be the most comfortable (King Hassan II of Morocco bought 20 of them). Claridge's is a world apart, with superb, original art deco touches. A fashionable restaurant and the less formal Causerie, where *smörgåsbord's* the specialty.

Connaught, Carlos Place, W1. Tel.: 499-7070. Telex—yes, but the hotel doesn't disclose the number, a clue to its discretion. Fax: Likewise. Rooms/suites: 114. The Connaught's manager is the envy of all other London hoteliers: the place is nearly always full in spite of its seldom being advertised. Key words: privacy, dignity. Mahogany everywhere; formal dress required. The bar has a clubby feeling to it; the restaurant is *Lucullan,* and there is also a grillroom.

Churchill, Portman Square, W1. Tel.: 486-5800. Telex: 264831. Fax: 935-0431. Rooms/suites: 485. Sybaritically comfortable, with multilingual staff. Fast, round-the-clock room service and a range of restaurants and bars. Business center is open to residents and nonresidents alike (fax, full secretarial services, TV and video services, plus a small meeting room).

Dorchester, Park Lane, W1. Tel.: 629-8888. Telex: 887704. Fax: 409-0114. The Sultan of Brunei liked this place so much that he bought it. Richard Burton and Elizabeth Taylor led the parade of stars who made "the Dorch" into London's most fashionable hostelry for the *glitterati.* Deciding that even the best wasn't good enough, the sultan closed it for a virtual rebuild costing a reputed $126 million; it is due to open again in 1990. The one thing he won't be able to change is the fine view of Hyde Park.

Grosvenor House, Park Lane, W1. Tel.: 499-6363. Telex: 24871. Fax: 493-3341. Rooms/suites: 463. If you see a small, elderly man with a mustache and twinkling black eyes scurrying through the lobby, you can say:

"Good morning, m'lord." This is the flagship of Lord Forte's TrustHouse Forte group, and very proud he is of it. The Great Room is a focal point of social and cultural life, with the annual British film and TV awards ceremony, the antiques fair, and dinners given by trade associations. The Crown Club floor is for the globetrotting business executive, and the concierge's desk can handle a planeload of demanding lawyers without blinking. Gourmet food in the *Ninety Park Lane* restaurant, good Italian trattoria (Lord Forte is Italian by origin), health club with pool.

Hilton, 22 Park Lane, W1. Tel.: 493-8000. Telex: 24873. Fax: 493-4957. Rooms/suites: 613. Four executive floors; and the 26th-floor executive lounge is the best of its kind in London, with fine views. Five restaurants, including one on the rooftop with bands, and *Trader Vic's*. A social and business hub with many services; casino next door. New owner Ladbrokes has a small hotel in an adjoining building that caters especially to traveling businesswomen.

Howard, Temple Place, WC2. Tel.: 836-3555. Telex: 268047. Fax: 379-4547. Rooms/suites: 141. On the Thames embankment and close to both the City and the West End, the Howard is one of the newer luxury hotels, with extraordinarily elegant decor and lavish furnishings. Reproduction antiques in the bedrooms.

Hyatt Carlton Tower, 2 Cadogan Place, SW1. Tel.: 235-5411. Telex: 21944. Fax: 235-9129. Rooms/suites: 233. Full-security presidential suite. Hyatt spent three years and $28 million refurbishing this handsome hotel, built in the 1960s. The *Chelsea Room* restaurant looks out on Cadogan Place Gardens, there are other restaurants and bars, and the duplex Peak Health Club is probably the only gym in London with a view. Highly rated business center; private dining rooms are geared for executive get-togethers.

Hyde Park Hotel, 66 Knightsbridge, SW1. Tel.: 235-2000. Telex: 262057. Fax: 235-2000. Rooms/suites: 186. Very English, very Edwardian, with marble-clad lobby, distinguished public rooms, and a view of Rotten Row, the part of Hyde Park along which ride both the gentry and the soldiery. Impeccable food, gracefully served; the *Cavalry Grill* specializes in English roasts (beef, lamb, pork) in the ambience of a gentlemen's club.

Inn on the Park, Hamilton Place, Park Lane, W1. Tel.: 499-0888. Telex: 22771. Fax: 493-1895. Rooms/suites: 228. Winner of many awards, the Inn is a favorite with the French, who head for the *Four Seasons* restaurant—and right they are to do so: the wine list is one of London's most eclectic. The hotel stresses service; rooms are large and luxurious.

Inter-Continental, 1 Hamilton Place, W1. Tel.: 409-3131. Telex: 25953. Fax: 493-3476. Rooms/suites: 497. The Interconti group's London exemplar of international *hotellerie* at its best. Located at the Hyde Park Corner end of Park Lane; large, comfortable, soundproofed rooms; fitness center, business services.

Marriott, Grosvenor Square, W1. Tel.: 493-1232. Telex: 268101. Fax: 491-3201. Rooms/suites: 245, including some "double doubles." Close to the American Embassy and in the heart of Mayfair. Fine *Diplomat* restaurant, top-class lounges, nonstop room service, and an efficient business center.

May Fair Inter-Continental, Stratton Street, W1. Tel.: 629-7777. Telex: 262526. Fax: 629-1459. Rooms/suites: 309. Superb location: Berkeley Square and Bond Street are close by, and it's only a few steps to Green Park. The May Fair has long been a home-away-from-home for star entertainers; real-estate developers make deals in the bars and restaurants. Luxuriousness is traditional, with lots of wood, leather, and thick carpets.

Meridien Piccadilly, Piccadilly, W1. Tel.: 734-8000. Telex: 25795. Fax: 437-3574. Rooms/suites: 284. *The* French accent in London. The result is a "Franglais" hotel of charm and character. Princess Anne pops in every now and then; tennis star Ivan Lendl strolls through the hall. Jaded executives use Champneys Health Club, undoubtedly the finest in a London hotel, with its gym, squash, and beautiful pool. Just to remind us where we are, there is a very English drawing room and library. The business center is excellent. Satellite TV.

Ritz, Piccadilly, W1. Tel.: 493-8181. Telex: 267200. Fax: 493-2687. Rooms/suites: 144. So many legends encrust this venerable tribute to César Ritz's genius that it's surprising the walls don't buckle under the weight. (They don't.) Ultimate owner is Trafalgar House, a construction company (among other things), which has poured money into restoration. Lunch and dinner in a beautiful, high-ceilinged restaurant looking out on Green Park; afternoon tea in the lounge is a showcase for Beautiful People.

Savoy, The Strand, WC2. Tel.: 836-4343. Telex: 24234. Fax: 240-6040. Rooms/suites: 202. Here Auguste Escoffier invented both peach melba and melba toast for Australian diva Nellie Melba; here Johann Strauss conducted Viennese waltzes in the restaurant and Pavlova danced in cabaret; and George Gershwin played the piano solo of his "Rhapsody in Blue" with the Savoy Orpheans. And who was manager in the hotel's early days? César Ritz, of course. In the many private dining rooms, both small and large, captains of industry and politicians make decisions that will change the world, or so they think. Strong transatlantic links include the American Bar and the huge Abraham Lincoln Room for balls and banquets.

▷ *Spotlight* ◁

Savoy and THF. Everyone loves the Savoy—nobody more than Lord Forte and his son, Rocco. Their company, TrustHouse Forte (THF), owns most of the equity in Savoy Hotels but has only a minority of the votes. That's because the Savoy company long ago created two classes of shares, with the farsighted idea of repelling bidders, of whom there have been many. So the somewhat absurd situation is that THF consolidates its proportion of Savoy results into its financial statements but doesn't have a single director on the Savoy board.

THF isn't after the Savoy alone, of course. The company also runs the Berkeley, Claridge's, the Connaught, and the Lancaster in Paris. Gilbert and Sullivan could have written a very witty operetta about the Savoy-THF corporate conflict—and staged it, naturally, in the Savoy Theater, part of the hotel complex and home of their Savoy Operas.

Sheraton Park Tower, 101 Knightsbridge, SW1. Tel.: 235-8050. Telex: 917222. Fax: 235-8231. Rooms/suites: 324. This 17-floor cylindrical construction raised eyebrows and ire when it was built: it just doesn't match Knightsbridge's staid architecture. However, the design means that every bedroom faces outward. "The Pineapple," as some people dub it, is a thoroughly international hotel liked by Arab businessmen, among others. Conservatory-style restaurant is good.

Deluxe

Belgravia Sheraton, 20 Chesham Place, SW1. Tel.: 235-6040. Telex: 919020. Fax: 000-0000. Rooms/suites: 90. Cozy, informal, clubby, and so small that it's more like the home of a hospitable friend than a hotel.

Britannia Inter-Continental, Grosvenor Square, WI. Tel.: 629-9400. Telex: 23941. Fax: 259-6243. Rooms/suites: 356. Corinthian columns outside and a Georgian atmosphere inside. Just to make sure you don't know where you are, the hotel makes your location entirely confusing by housing a Japanese restaurant, an English pub, and a Canadian bar. Business center never closes: telex and fax.

▶269

Brown's, Dover Street/Albemarle Street, WI. Tel.: 493-6020. Telex: 28686. Fax: 493-9381. Rooms/suites: 134. Proper Bostonians stay here, attracted by solicitous service and the private townhouse atmosphere; popular also with British backwoods aristocrats anxious to avoid the riff-raff. Brown's is a splendid survivor from the days when London suffered from pea-soup fogs, and Sherlock Holmes' hansom cab could be heard clattering off to confuse poor Doctor Watson with yet another mystery. No business center, no fishhooks for the executive, just good food and superb service.

Cavendish, Jermyn Street, SW1. Tel.: 930-2111. Telex: 263187. Fax: 839-2125. Rooms/suites: 254. On this site, long ago, the now-legendary Rosa Lewis ran a hotel that was greatly favored by amorous gentlemen from the Prince of Wales (later King Edward VII) on down (her story, or a romanticized version of it, was told in the British TV series *Duchess of Duke Street*). No such shenanigans now. Instead, a comfortable, modern hotel with rather small rooms, an excellent restaurant, and two bars (the one downstairs is the Sub Rosa). Valet parking.

Cumberland, Marble Arch, W1. Tel.: 262-1234. Telex: 22215. Fax: 724-4621. Rooms/suites: 907. Very large and well sited, with Hyde Park and Oxford Street adjacent, the Cumberland has been modernized and improved and fills the gap between the "to-hell-with-the-expense" properties and the budget hotels. Interesting extras include a business center and executive lounge, the clublike Duke's Bar, a top Japanese restaurant, the new *Wyvern Restaurant* for English cuisine, and well-equipped meeting and conference facilities. Power breakfasts are among the best (and most powerful).

Fenja, 69 Cadogan Gardens, SW3. Tel.: 589-7333. Telex: 934272. Fax: 581-4958. Rooms: 14. Formerly a private club for Indian visitors, the Fenja has been converted by the team that refurbished the famous Cliveden stately home. Relaxed and elegant.

Halcyon, 81 Holland Park, W11. Tel.: 727-7288. Telex: 266721. Fax: 229-8516. Rooms/suites: 44. A little out of Central London. Privacy and security are the emphases. Marble bathrooms, some with Jacuzzis; secretarial services and satellite TV. *Kingfisher* restaurant serves a wide range of dishes—but not kingfishers.

Holiday Inn, 3 Berkeley Street, W1. Tel.: 493-8282. Telex: 24561. Fax: 629-2827. Rooms/suites: 190. Nonsmoking rooms available. In the Mayfair area, one of the best locations in London, with spacious rooms, live entertainment, gift shops, secretarial services, and pleasant public areas.

Holiday Inn, 128 King Henry's Road, Swiss Cottage, NW3. Tel.: 722-7711. Telex: 267396. Fax: 586-5822. Rooms/suites: 291. Nonsmoking rooms available. Near Regent's Park, Hampstead Heath, and Lord's Cricket Ground. Live entertainment, pool, sauna, fitness equipment, shops. Though out of Central London, the hotel is close to it and easy to reach; top-floor suites for high-flying executives.

Montcalm, Great Cumberland Place, W1. Tel.: 402-4288. Telex: 28710. Fax: 724-9180. Rooms/suites: 114. Only two minutes' walk from the bustle of Marble Arch and Oxford Street, but in a calm backwater of Georgian houses. Courteous, thoughtful servitors, secretarial services. A place for the discerning rather than the flashy.

Portman Inter-Continental, Portman Square, W1. Tel.: 486-5844. Telex: 261526. Fax: 935-0537. Rooms/suites: 275. Just north of Oxford Street. The Portman was one of the first London hotels to study and then cater to business travelers' needs; some stay for weeks. Modern, competent, with pleasant bars and coffeeshop and a first-class restaurant. Sunday brunch with live jazz.

Ramada Hotel, 10 Berners Street, W1. Tel.: 636-1629. Telex: 25759. Fax: 580-3972. Rooms/suites: 232. A physically imposing hotel of Edwardian vintage just north of Oxford Street, now tastefully modernized and refurbished.

Ramada Inn, 47 Lillie Road, SW6. Tel.: 385-1255. Telex: 917728. Fax: 381-4450. Rooms/suites: 504. Close to Earls Court Exhibition Center. Two bars, *Earls Carver* restaurant. Secretarial services, conference facilities, live entertainment, in-room movies.

Royal Garden, Kensington High Street, W8. Tel.: 937-8000. Telex: 263151. Fax: 938-4532. Rooms/suites: 395. Well-equipped rooms, views over Kensington Gardens and Hyde Park, excellent bars and restaurants, multiple business services. There's dancing in the Royal Roof Restaurant.

Royal Lancaster, Lancaster Terrace, W2. Tel.: 262-6737. Telex: 24822. Fax: 724-3191. Rooms/suites: 418. Reserve Club rooms on the 15th through 18th floors have service at all hours. *La Rosette* restaurant, plus The Pavement, a brasserie-style café.

Saint James Court, Buckingham Gate, SW1. Tel.: 834-6655. Telex: 938075. Fax: 630-7587. Rooms/suites: 390. Apartments (up to three bedrooms): 97. Close to another good address, Buckingham Palace. Once a rundown Edwardian relic, Saint James Court is now smart and comfortable, the result of a $76-million refurbishment by Taj International Hotels Group. Chambers Business Center facilities include a boardroom, a committee room, five offices, multilingual secretaries, and word processors. There's also a health club. Portable phones for rent, they also send and receive fax messages and computer files. Restaurants: one French, one Chinese.

Scandic Crown, 2 Bridge Place, SW1. Tel.: 834-8123. Telex: 914973. Fax: 828-1099. Rooms/suites: 212. The new hotel in London of Scandinavia's largest group. Excellent location behind Victoria station/air terminal. 100 nonsmoking rooms. Restaurant. Health and leisure center with Finnish saunas.

Stafford, St. James's Place, SW1. Tel.: 493-0111. Telex: 28602. Fax: 493-7121. Rooms/suites: 69. Knowledgeable Americans have been staying at the Stafford for more than a century. Most of the 130 staff are long-serving, the wine cellars are capacious, and there are private rooms for eating and meeting. The hotel is tucked away in a quiet street and is hard to fault.

Tower Thistle, St. Katherine's Way, E1. Tel.: 481-2575. Telex: 885934. Fax: 488-4106. Rooms/suites: 826. One of London's largest hotels, overlooking St. Katherine's Dock, now a pleasure-boat marina, next to the World Trade Center, and close to the City financial district. Vast and therefore rather anonymous, but with good food and bars; many rooms for meetings and corporate merrymaking.

Waldorf, Aldwych, WC2. Tel.: 836-2400. Telex: 24574. Fax: 836-7244. Rooms/suites: 310. More-or-less across the street from the Savoy, and less than half the price. Rooms are comfortable, service is good, and the main bar on the ground floor is notably elegant. In the huge, high-roofed Palm Court, there's a help-yourself breakfast, and on some afternoons, music and dancing enliven afternoon tea. The restaurant deserves to be known better: After eating there at least 40 times, we have never had a meal that was less than competently cooked and beautifully served. There's also a moderately priced French-style bistro.

Westbury, Conduit Street, W1. Tel.: 629-7755. Telex: 24378. Fax: 495-1163. Rooms/suites: 243. They're smallish, but pleasant. The first West End hotel built after World War II, the Westbury has garnered a loyal clientele. The Polo Bar is a rendezvous for the international set and Mayfair types. In the small wood-paneled lounge, you can have one of the best afternoon teas in London, and the restaurant has long merited its first-class reputation.

Airport Hotels

HEATHROW

Ariel, Bath Road, Hayes, Middlesex. Tel.: 759-2552. Telex: 21777. Fax: 564-9265. Rooms/suites: 177. With its distinctive circular shape, the Ariel has become a Heathrow landmark since its 1960 opening on the airport's north side. Between Junctions 3 and 4 of the M4 London-South Wales motorway (freeway).

Excelsior, Bath Road, West Drayton, Middlesex. Tel.: 759-6611. Telex: 24525. Fax: 759-3421. Rooms: 580. Opposite the airport entrance near the spur to the motorway. International conference center.

Heathrow Penta, Bath Road, Hounslow, Middlesex. Tel.: 897-6363. Telex: 934660. Fax: 897-1113. Rooms: 670. Award-winning conference center, with 29 meeting rooms of various sizes and video theater.

Holiday Inn, Stockley Road, West Drayton, Middlesex. Tel.: 445555. Telex: 934518. Fax: 445122. Rooms/suites: 400. Indoor pool, sauna; tennis and golf nearby. Popular with executives from Stockley Technology Park.

Post House Hotel, Sipson Road, West Drayton, Middlesex. Tel.: 759-2323. Telex: 934280. Fax: 897-8659. Rooms: 607. Another TrustHouse Forte enterprise; business visitors' executive club.

Royal Berkshire, London Road, Sunninghill, Ascot, Berkshire. Tel.: (0990) 23322. Telex: 847280. Fax: (0990) 27110. A dawn chorus of birds, not Boeings; but only 20 minutes from Heathrow. Operated by Hilton.

Sheraton Heathrow. Colnbrook Bypass, West Drayton, Middlesex. Tel.: 759-2424. Telex: 934331. Fax: 759-2091. Rooms: 440. Pool, sauna, meeting rooms, and several restaurants.

Sheraton Skyline, Bath Road, Hayes, Middlesex. Tel.: 759-2535. Telex: 934254. Fax: 750-9150. Rooms: 355. Right next to the airport; 24-hour room service; conference rooms and business services; "exotic" pool with tropical gardens.

Skyway, Bath Road, Hayes, Middlesex. Tel.: 759-6311. Telex: 23935. Fax: 759-4559. Rooms: 432. Another long-established Lord Forte special. Courtesy coaches to and from London—and out to Windsor, Runnymede, and other locations.

GATWICK

Alexander House, near Gatwick Airport. Tel.: (0342) 714914. Telex: 849169. Fax: (0342) 717328. This former private estate is now an all-suite hotel. Trout fishing, golf, and other "escapist" activities. Conferences and meetings, too.

Chequers Thistle, Brighton Road, Horley. Tel.: (0293) 786992. Telex: 877550. Fax: (0293) 820625. Rooms/suites: 78. A former Tudor coaching inn greatly enlarged but with much of its original character retained.

Copthorne Hotel, 2.5 kilometers (4 miles) from airport. Tel.: (0342) 714971. Telex: 95500. Fax: (0342) 717375. Rooms/suites: 223. Set in spacious grounds; rooms are pleasantly large, and the atmosphere is that of a rambling country house. Two restaurants, two bars, squash, gym—and the ancient game of croquet.

Crest Hotel, Langley Drive, Crawley. Tel.: (0293) 29991. Telex: 877311. Fax: (0293) 515913. Rooms/suites: 231. Designed specifically for the business traveler, with secretarial services and some rooms reserved for women and nonsmokers.

Gatwick Hilton International. Tel.: (0293) 518080. Telex: 877021. Fax: (0293) 28980. Rooms/suites: 552. Four minutes' walk from the terminal. Among architectural and design features are a plant-filled atrium from which is suspended a replica Gypsy Moth airplane; a garden; indoor swimming pool; and a smart, split-level coffeeshop open around the clock.

Ghyll Manor, Rusper, 11 kilometers (7 miles) from Gatwick. Tel.: (0293) 84571. Rooms/suites: 28. Gracious country living straight out of a travel brochure: half-timbered building; every room furnished differently; large, landscaped gardens with lake and peacocks; well-stocked library.

▷ Restaurants

London offers a wide variety of ethnic restaurants, and if we listed even half of them, this book would be in two volumes. Instead, we're going to be selective, starting with establishments that make a point of offering the best of British cuisine and then moving on to the best of the rest. In all of the places we list, gentlemen must wear tie and jacket, and in the evenings it's advisable to wear a suit. Ladies enjoy more latitude in their dress. Even so, the emphasis in fashionable London is on elegance, or at least formality.

Reservations are essential at most listed restaurants. Some may ask for your credit card number before granting you a table. Others don't take plastic, so it's a good idea to check (we don't list the holdouts because policies change).

Lunch is still the business meal; dinner tends to be more social. The business breakfast is increasingly used to lengthen the working day and is usually eaten at a hotel; few other good restaurants are yet willing to open their doors before lunchtime. Among those that are: *Fox and Anchor* pub, 115 Charterhouse Street, EC1, open from 6:00 a.m.; *La Brasserie,* 272 Brompton Road, SW3, open from 8:00 a.m.; and *Langan's Bar and Grill,* 7 Down Street, W1, also open from 8:00 a.m.

British

Bentley's, 11-15 Swallow Street, W1. Tel.: 734-4756. In a narrow street close to Piccadilly Circus, Bentley's is one of the grand old places: fish, seafood, wide selection of wines, particularly white.

Berkeley, Wilton Place, SW1. Tel.: 235-6000. Lots of French dishes on the menu, but also British ones. Try the smoked Scotch salmon; the pheasant, grouse, and partridge when they're in season; and roasts from the trolley. Cheeses include cheddar, Double Gloucester, Stilton, and Wensleydale. This hotel dining room is coolly elegant.

▷ *Spotlight* ◁

Port. We're not urging anyone to imbibe heartily. However, we do recommend vintage port. Britain has a historical claim on the stuff, which means that it's better here than anywhere else, including Portugal. The British eat their dessert—if they have it—before their cheese, so they drink their port with or after the cheese. Remember that port is a "fortified" wine—in short, it has a high alcoholic content. Always ask the *sommelier* for his recommendation. Cheers!

Brown's Hotel, Albemarle/Dover Streets, W1. Tel.: 493-6020. The restaurant floor creaks slightly; also creaky are many of the waiters. They love their work, and you'll like the food, if not love it: a good selection of English dishes, including those inevitable roasts and heavy puddings.

Green's Restaurant and Oyster Bar, 36 Duke Street, SW1. Tel.: 930-4566. Tempting seafood, a wide selection of wines, including champagne by the glass. Oysters (when there is an *r* in the month) are so fresh that they wince when you squirt them with lemon juice.

Leith's, 92 Kensington Park Road, W11. Tel.: 229-4481. Smooth-running restaurant on the ground floor of a Victorian house that is popular for business dinners. Separate vegetarian menu.

Lockets, Marsham Court, Marsham Street, SW1. Tel.: 834-9552. Members of Parliament dine off English classics such as roast lamb while keeping ears pricked for the division bell that sends them running to vote in the nearby House of Commons. Lobbyists stay on to pick up the tab.

Manzi's, 1 Leicester Street, WC2. Tel.: 734-0024. One of the oldest seafood restaurants, always bustling; in the heart of the theater district. Friendly, informal atmosphere; better for social than business occasions.

Rule's, 35 Maiden Lane, WC2. Tel.: 836-5314. A collection of crowded rooms upstairs and downstairs. Seasonal specialties include *jugged hare* (hare stewed in an earthenware pot), game birds, and venison; steak-and-kidney pie is a staple. As English as English could be, except for the staff.

Savoy Grill, The Strand, WC2. Tel.: 836-4343. Open a *Who's Who,* either American or British (or even international), pick a name at random, and almost certainly he or she has eaten at the Grill. We haven't seen Gorbachev here lately, but he's been busy with *glasnost, perestroika,* and other pressing matters. Speaking of which, the Grill does a great pressed duck.

Savoy Restaurant, The Strand, WC2. Tel.: 836-4343. We've spent many enjoyable lunchtimes and evenings here. The restaurant is rather cavernous, but if you can grab one of the window tables, you'll have a superb view of the Thames. Very nice for a relaxed Sunday lunch.

Simpson's-in-the-Strand, 100 The Strand, WC2. Tel.: 836-9112. Dignified men carve *joints* (roasts) on the trolley with loving care and load clients with enough carbohydrates and cholesterol-inducing foods to keep a convention of cardiologists happy until retirement. Author J.B. Priestley ate here often but did not succumb until the age of 90.

Waltons, 121 Walton Street, SW3. Tel.: 584-0204. Very fashionable, rather starchy; much is made of the English and French dishes' presentation. The leather-bound wine list is an encyclopedia of good vintages.

Wheeler's, 19 Old Compton Street, W1. Tel.: 437-2706/7661. There are many Wheeler's. This one is in Soho and is the *only* Wheeler's for devotees of English seafood and fish—no matter that many of the cooks are Chinese and most of the waiters hail from somewhere well south of Dover. Regulars include painters Francis Bacon and Lucien Freud, and various theater producers and thespians. Having spent enough money at Wheeler's in the past 30 years to buy the place several times over, we can recommend it highly.

Wilton's, 27 Bury Street, SW1. Tel.: 930-8391. If you believe that a typical English restaurant should be quiet and dignified, with no voice raised above a discreet hush, then Wilton's is your place. The decor is so quiet as to be virtually invisible unless you look very closely. And that isn't an ectoplasm at your table, it's your waiter.

▷ *Spotlight* ◁

Pub grub is becoming high fashion. Reasons: it's increasingly good and relatively cheap—relative, that is, to the food in most restaurants. Watch out particularly for wine bars, many of which are run by youngish enthusiasts. The pub and wine bar crowds tend to be distinctly different, the first being older and a little rougher, the second being there more for the conversation than for the booze.

English liquor laws, long a bafflement for tourists, were relaxed in 1988. Both pubs and wine bars can stay open now on weekdays from 11:00 a.m. to 11:00 p.m. Not all do. Some still follow the traditional closing from 3:00 p.m. to 5:30 p.m. Hotel residents always have been able to drink for as long as the staff deigned to serve, and so have residents' guests. So why the previously tough restrictions on pub hours? They were introduced during World War I to discourage munitions workers from getting bombed instead of making bombs.

Best of the Rest

A l'Ecu de France, 111 Jermyn Street, SW1. Tel.: 930-2837. Large, spacious, formal, long established. Classic French cooking served with grace; extensive, interesting wine list. Five private rooms for parties.

Alastair Little, 49 Frith Street, W1. Tel.: 734-5183. Fish and meat with subtle sauces; small but well-chosen selection of wines; lots of youngish media people entertaining informally and trading the "who's in, who's out" gossip of the day.

Auberge de Provence, St. James Court, Buckingham Gate, SW1. Tel.: 821-1899. An accent so French you could "cut eet wiz ze knife." Food is southern French, so is the choice of wines, predominantly; and the service is highly professional.

Bombay Brasserie, Bailey's Hotel, Courtfield Close, SW7. Tel.: 370-4040. From a Bombay beach snack (yes, there's a pool here) to a Parsi wedding breakfast, the food is memorable, and possibly the best of the Indian variety in town.

Boulestin, 1a Henrietta Street, WC2. Tel.: 836-7061. Rich, classic French cuisine, with some deference to the *nouvelle*. A reassuring temple of high standards maintained for many years.

Café Royal, 68 Regent Street, W1. Tel.: 437-9090. Rococo decor in the famous Grill Room, where royals, nobles, and *fin-de-siècle* literati once held court, Oscar Wilde being among the latter. The eight floors include a bar, brasserie, and private dining and meeting rooms. Food critics' findings vary. Ours is that the basically French cuisine lacks sparkle. Superb wines, though.

Clarke's, 124 Kensington Church Street, W8. Tel.: 221-9225. Californiae in Kensington in this pretty restaurant on two floors. What one might call *nouvel Californie,* with fresh herbs and fine oils among the ingredients of the nicely varied menu.

Fakhreldine, 85 Piccadilly, W1. Tel.: 493-3424. Lebanese opulence with views of Green Park. Exemplary food and service: a reminder of Beirut when it was a city and not a battlefield. Lebanese wines are interesting.

Gay Hussar, 2 Greek Street, W1. Tel.: 437-0973. Downstairs is the place to be, and the place where regulars have been for most of the 35 years that have passed since Victor Sassie opened this roost for the literati and left-wing politicians. Long menu, with carp, beetroot, hare, dumplings, and goose strongly featured (Sassie was trained in Hungary).

Ho-Ho, 29 Maddox Street, W1. Tel.: 493-1228. Sophisticated Chinese food, with all the main regions represented on the extensive menu.

Inigo Jones, 14 Garrick Street, WC2. There's a choice of 250 wines in this bare-brick restaurant with large windows. The food is pure *nouvelle cuisine.* Good at any time, but particularly for pretheater dining, since it's right in the district. Supper starts at 5:30 p.m.

Joe Allen, 13 Exeter Street, WC2. Tel.: 836-0651. East Side New York in London, right down to the chalked menu boards and chili con carne (that's New York?). Famous faces, slowish service until the smaller hours; on the fringes of Covent Garden, a short walk from the Strand, and close to many theaters. Nearly always crowded.

Langan's Brasserie, Stratton Street, W1. Tel.: 493-6437. The late Peter Langan was a wild eccentric; the combination of his personality, the talents of chef Richard Shepherd (also an owner), and the opulent, *fin-de-siècle* decor have made Langan's *the* place to be seen—if that's your style. The third owner, by the way, is actor Michael Caine, himself a bit of a character.

La Tante Claire, 68-69 Royal Hospital Road, SW3. Tel.: 352-6045. One of the best French restaurants: food, wines, and service are all stylish, evidence of Pierre Koffmann's exuberant flair. Reserve well ahead, particularly for lunch.

Le Caprice, Arlington House, Arlington Street, SW1. Tel.: 629-2239. Opened in the 1930s, the Caprice stumbled in the 1970s, found its footing in the 1980s, and now attracts everyone from royalty to pop stars. Inventive cocktails are a specialty. Maximum of eight people to a table. Just around the corner from the Ritz.

Le Gavroche, 43 Upper Brook Street, W1. Tel.: 408-0881. *Patron* Albert Roux still slaves over a hot stove in spite of his having earned fame and riches—and the first three-star rating the *Guide Michelin* ever awarded to a London restaurant. French cuisine, of course; half the *corps diplomatique* at the tables. An impressive place for business entertaining.

Rue St. Jacques, 5 Charlotte Street, W1. Tel.: 637-0222. Advertising and media people power-lunch here and strut while sitting down. Fish, game, and sauces are the French menu's strengths. Wine prices are on the high side.

Suntory, 72 St. James's Street, SW1. Tel.: 409-0201. Lots of Japanese executives eat here—and if they don't know Japanese food, who does? Suntory is one of about 30 restaurants in London from the Land of the Rising Sun, and its star (forgive the mixed metaphor) has been in the ascendant for a long time.

White Tower, 1 Percy Street, W1. Tel.: 636-8141. Much frequented by publishers, authors' agents, advertising executives, and people who simply appreciate the (mainly Greek) food, wine, decor, and service. A happy place.

Ziani, 45 Radnor Walk, SW3. Tel.: 352-2698. Italian food, Chelsea chic. Better for socializing than dealmaking; perhaps the place to celebrate the signing. One of the few London Italian restaurants where the cuisine matches the decor's promise.

The City of London (Financial District)

The City was for years a gastronomic wasteland—unless, that is, one was invited to eat in a directors' private dining room. Then, in 1986, *Le Poulbot* opened, setting new standards. A clutch of competitors decided that if the Roux brothers of Le Gavroche fame could succeed in the City, so could they.

Café Rouge, 2c Cherry Tree Walk, Whitecross Street, EC1. Tel.: 588-0710. Set in a rather ugly shopping mall, but good and sophisticated once one gets inside.

Corney and Barrow's, 109 Old Broad Street, EC2. Tel.: 638-9308/920-9560. Distinguished kitchen, with Central European accent; clublike atmosphere.

Le Champenois, Cutlers Gardens Arcade, 10 Devonshire Square, EC2. Tel.: 283-7888. Urbane and Gallic; a deal with every meal.

Le Poulbot, 45 Cheapside, EC2. Tel.: 236-4379. Another operation of the Roux brothers, this one in the heart of the City financial district. High-powered business lunches (closed for dinner); upstairs café serves soups and sandwiches.

Sweetings, 39 Queen Victoria Street, EC4. Tel.: 248-3062. No Roux influence here, because it wasn't needed. Dickensian atmosphere: you sit at long tables to eat superbly fresh fish simply cooked.

▷ Spotlight ◁

Bloom's. Close to the City is an institution almost as famous as the Bank of England in some circles: Bloom's. Probably the best-known kosher restaurant in Britain, it's a big, bustling place where the specialties are a huge variety of mainly Eastern European dishes—and talk. Sunday lunch is the best time to see Bloom's in full swing. Address: 90 Whitechapel High Street, E1. Tel.: 247-6001. Sunday reservations are essential.

▷ Tipping

Chaotic. Most restaurants add a service charge of between 10 and 15 percent; others do not, so check. Few people leave tips in pubs or wine bars, unless they are served food at a table. The standard then is about 10 percent. It's customary to tip doormen for small services, such as finding you a cab; somewhere between 50 pence and a pound is about right (the more generous you are, the more likely it is that he'll find you a cab quickly next time you need one). Be generous with the hall porter (concierge); he can be helpful in a dozen ways.

▷ Spotlight ◁

A *club* was traditionally an Englishman's refuge from his wife, his children, and even his mistress. Children are still barred from most clubs; women are not. The Saint James's and Mayfair districts of the West End are classic clubland. Each club is different in architecture, decor, membership, and that elusive quality, character. The best all offer tranquility in the center of a busy, noisy city, with soft-footed servants, deep, comfortable armchairs, and the assurance that all members, if not congenial, at least are not obnoxious. The food isn't usually brilliant but is reliably filling, and many clubs have superb wine cellars from which bottles are fetched reverently for prices that would make a commercial restaurateur feel faint. Many clubs have bedrooms.

To enter a club, you have to be a member, a guest, or a member of a club with what are called reciprocal arrangements. Dress is always formal, and the flourishing of spreadsheets and other business documents is usually forbidden or at least very bad form. Among the most noted clubs:

Athenaeum, 107 Pall Mall, SW1. Judges, ambassadors, bishops, Oxbridge dons. Extensive library; so-so food.

Beefsteak, 9 Irving Street, WC2. Not in clubland proper. No women admitted. Members address all club servants as "Charles."

Brooks's, 61 St. James's Street, SW1. Started in the 1700s for people who didn't like White's. Still less starchy.

Buck's, 18 Clifford Street, W1. Strong business membership; women like it for friendly atmosphere. Small; better-than-average club food.

Carlton, 69 St. James's Street, SW1. A Conservative Party bastion; meet members of the government and Tories who wish they were.

Cavalry and Guards, 127 Piccadilly, W1. Officers of grand regiments, both serving and retired, compare campaigns and trade tales. Favorite tipple: champagne.

Garrick, 15 Garrick Street, WC2. In the theater district, it attracts actors, publishers, lawyers, journalists—and Prince Charles. Lively talk.

Mark's, 46 Charles Street, W1. Smart, glossy, used by jetsetters and tycoons. Many are not gentlemen. Food and wine are good but costly. Service is obsequious.

Reform, 104 Pall Mall, SW1. Magnificent building; members come from the thinking left of the political center. Intellectual tone; superb dining room.

St. James's Club, 7 Park Place, SW1. Created by ostentatious millionaire Peter de Savary. Members are extroverted and wealthy.

Turf, 5 Carlton House Terrace, SW1. Very horsey and energetic. Members include owners, trainers, and gentlemen jockeys; many are peers of the realm.

White's, 37 St. James's Street, SW1. The Dukes of Edinburgh and Kent are members of London's most famous club; so, according to legend, are the heads of MI5 and MI6, Britain's intelligence agencies.

▷ Doing Business

Some paradoxes here. The British are often accused of being insular, yet they acquired a globe-girdling empire. Britain joined the European Community (EC) late, in 1973, yet it has become one of the dominant countries within it. Prime Minister Margaret Thatcher has criticized what some people call "Europhoria," yet is committed politically to the European Single Market that is supposed to be born at the end of 1992. Behind those apparent paradoxes is the fact that London was a hub of world trade and finance even before the Industrial Revolution of the 1700s and remains one, mentioned in the same breath as New York and Tokyo.

Major British banks, other financial institutions and corporations are mighty overseas investors, and about 2 million people visit London each year on business—quite apart from the other millions who go there from the British provinces.

The heart of financial activity is the district called the City of London, the famous "Square Mile" that has its own Lord Mayor, municipal authority, and police force. Here are the Stock Exchange; the Bank of England, Britain's central bank; Lloyd's insurance market; the headquarters of all the major banks and hundreds of subsidiaries or branches of foreign banks; most of the merchant (investment) banks; and markets that deal in precious and base metals, commodities, and financial futures. Just west of the City proper is the wholesale diamond center, concentrated in and around Hatton Garden. And either in the City or close to it are the offices of such ancillary professions as accounting and law.

Competition is intense, and it comes not only from within the City, but also increasingly from other financial centers around the world. Until a few years ago, many senior executives in the City took three-hour lunches and left early on Friday afternoons to play golf and spend long weekends at their country homes. Some still do, but not as many. The old style was gentlemanly, leisurely; the new one is often brash, sometimes abrasive, and always energetic.

The cause of this new style is the globalization of financial markets, with London a vital link between the Tokyo and New York time zones, and globalization is in large part the result of information technology. Appropriately, one of the world leaders in the supply of financial information, Reuters, has long had its headquarters in the City.

Back in what now seem like halcyon days to nostalgics, City functions were in neat compartments. There were commercial and merchant banks, stockbrokers and stockjobbers, foreign-exchange dealers and money brokers, and so on. But the old divisions have almost gone, and some of the biggest City names are parts of financial conglomerates, offering a wide range of services under one corporate umbrella.

Until very recently, the City was virtually self-regulating. Today there are tougher laws, more official investigation of a person's or firm's fitness to handle other people's money, and stiffer penalties for transgressors.

Even so, the City has been rocked by some nasty scandals in the second half of the 1980s. These have included huge frauds on investors in the Lloyd's insurance market, corporate takeover battles tainted by allegations of large-scale share-price rigging and insider dealing, and multimillion-dollar losses suffered by people who put their money into funds supposedly investing solely in government stocks (they didn't).

Strictly speaking, the City played little or no part in some scandals, but the Square Mile has become a popular—or unpopular—shorthand term for all British financial activity. One affair that left egg on the City's face that it didn't deserve involved a bank headquartered in an offshore tax haven that was alleged by U.S. and British prosecutors to have laundered Colombian drug barons' money. The wonder is not that scandals surface; rather, that there are so few of them compared with the gigantic sums of money that pour in and out of the City every day, mostly in electronic form.

London, next to New York, is the best place to look for venture capital. Tax incentives have encouraged people with high incomes and few deductions to invest in new or young businesses and financial institutions quickly grasped the potential of this source of capital.

The commercial banks, once very cautious lenders, have become more liberal, and merchant bankers are always willing to listen to soundly based propositions. Like their Wall Street counterparts, London merchant banks don't have huge capital of their own. Instead, one of their functions is to structure deals and bring together potential investors and companies that need capital, either to start new businesses or expand existing ones.

Not so long ago, one of the first questions a banker asked a would-be borrower was about asset backing; now it's just as likely to be about cash-flow projections. That may seem a small change, but in terms of attitude it is large. Most of today's new businesses don't have or need many physical assets. Their investment is in ideas and people rather than in plant.

City real estate prices and rents are among the world's highest, if we exclude Tokyo, so "the City" is spreading beyond its municipal boundaries and becoming a term in the Hollywood or Wall Street sense: it describes a multiplicity of related businesses and a state of mind.

▷ *Spotlight* ◁

London Docklands. In the early 1980s, land in the derelict port area sold for around $160,000 an acre (.4047 hectare). In 1988, it was changing hands for up to $6.4 million. London Docklands has become Europe's largest and most costly urban development, and it is all happening remarkably fast.

When the last ship sailed in 1981, it left behind a wasteland of empty warehouses and motionless cranes. Since then, under the aegis of the London Docklands Development Corporation, the 22 square kilometers (8.5 square miles) have been transformed into an area of luxury apartments and towering office buildings. As well, many of the old warehouses and other structures have been turned over to new uses: concert halls, shopping precincts, sports and leisure centers, and restaurant areas.

When completed in the 1990s, the development will include 81 kilometers (50 miles) of new roads, several million square meters of office space, and 25,000 homes. For every dollar of public funds invested, Docklands has attracted nine dollars of private money, the project's planners say.

Already the automated Docklands Light Railway is running over a 12-kilometer (7.5-mile) route, most of it elevated, giving passengers scenic views along the Isle of Dogs, a peninsula formed by a loop of the Thames. Open for business, too, are the London City Airport and a fleet of waterjet-powered catamarans for commuters to points east and west alongside the Thames.

By far, the most spectacular scheme is at Canary Wharf, in the former West India Docks, where the Canadian company Olympia and York is planning what it claims is the world's largest commercial development: more than 1 million square meters (12 million square feet) of office and retail space in 22 separate buildings. The centerpiece will be Britain's tallest skyscraper, at 280 meters (840 feet), clad in stainless steel or orange granite. Total cost of the Olympia and York scheme: an estimated $6.6 billion.

Although the business center of London seems to be shifting east to Docklands, the West End is likely to remain important. Many major corporations, both British and foreign, are headquartered in Mayfair and St.

James's, and the ancillary professions and occupations cluster around them: advertising and public relations agencies, law firms, accountants, and so on.

As in the City, the style of doing business is brisker than it was a few years ago. Some things have changed little, though. First, there's the question of dress. In advertising and similar "creative" businesses, designer casual is okay; it is not at the point where people sign checks and deals. A suit and tie are obligatory, even on warm days. Second, there's the question of offering and receiving hospitality. Much business is done over lunch, and your choice of restaurant is important. This may seem a trivial point—and perhaps is, since neither clothes nor restaurant make the man or woman—but in London more than in some other cities, there is a restaurant snobbery. In the Restaurants section, we've indicated the kinds of people who frequent different establishments. Always try to choose a rendezvous close to your guests' office; lunchtime traffic can become horribly snarled.

You'll find that decisions are fast and relatively free of what the British call red tape: bureaucratic entanglements. Relatively free, that is, compared with those in some other European countries. You can buy an "off-the-rack, ready-to-wear" company for about $250 in 24 hours or less with a guarantee from the vendors that it has done no business. Formation of a company takes a little longer and costs more; many firms offer company-formation services.

▷ Useful Phone Numbers

Emergencies

Ambulance, fire, police   999

Hospitals with 24-hour casualty
   departments

Charing Cross, W6	748-2040
Guy's, SE1	407-7600
London, E1	377-7000
Royal Free, NW3	794-0500
St. Bartholomew's (Bart's), EC1	601-8888
St. Thomas's, SE1	928-9292
University College, WC1	387-9300

Rape crisis center	837-1600
Samaritans	283-3400

Local Information

Directory inquiries (information)

London	142
Outside London	192
Highway conditions	246-8021
Weather	246-9091
London Regional Transport inquiries	222-1234
London Tourist Board	730-3488
Teletourist	730-0791

Train information (main
destinations served)

Charing Cross (southeastern
suburbs, Kent)   928-5100

Euston (Birmingham,
Liverpool, Manchester,
Glasgow)   387-7070

King's Cross (Aberdeen,
Edinburgh, Leeds,
Newcastle)   278-2477

Liverpool Street (Cambridge,
Ipswich, Norwich,
and eastern
England)   283-7171

Paddington (Bristol, Oxford,
Plymouth, Swindon, west
of England)   262-6767

St. Pancras (northern
suburbs, Midland cities,
Sheffield)   387-7070

Victoria (southern suburbs,
southeast,
Channel ports)   928-5100

Waterloo (southwestern
suburbs, southwest
England, including
Bournemouth and
Southampton)   928-5100

British Trade and Commercial Organizations

Overseas Trade Board   215-7877

Central Office of
Information   928-2345

Central Statistical
Office   270-6363

Confederation of British
Industry   379-7400

Customs and Excise   626-1515

Department of
Employment   213-3000

Department of Trade and
Industry   215-7877

Inland Revenue   438-6622

Institute of Directors   839-1233

National Economic
Development Office   211-5953

Chambers of Commerce

American   493-0381

Association of British Chambers
of Commerce   240-5831

Belgian   434-1815

Canadian   839-1838

Dutch   405-1538

French   439-1735

German   930-7251

International (ICC)   240-5558

Italian   734-2411

Portuguese   821-5575

Spanish   637-9061

Swedish   493-9668

Consulates and Embassies

Note: HC = high commission.
Countries with high commis-
sions are members of the
Commonwealth.

Argentina   730-4388

Australia (HC)   438-8000

Austria   235-7371

Bahamas (HC)   409-4488

Bahrain   370-5132

Bangladesh (HC)   584-0081

Belgium   235-5422

Bolivia	235-4248	Lebanon	229-7265
Brazil	499-0877	Luxembourg	235-6961
Brunei (HC)	581-0521	Malaysia (HC)	235-8033
Bulgaria	584-9433	Mexico	235-0393
Burma	629-5966	Morocco	240-0393
Cameroon	727-0771	Netherlands	584-5040
Canada (HC)	629-9492	New Zealand (HC)	930-8422
Chile	580-6392	Nigeria (HC)	839-1244
China (People's		Norway	235-7151
Republic)	586-9646	Pakistan	235-2044
Colombia	589-9177	Paraguay	937-1253
Cyprus (HC)	499-8272	Peru	235-1917
Czechoslovakia	229-1255	Philippines	937-1609
Denmark	235-1255	Poland	580-4324
Ecuador	584-1367	Portugal	235-5331
Egypt	499-2401	Qatar	370-6871
Ethiopia	589-7212	Romania	937-9666
Finland	839-7262	Saudi Arabia	235-0831
France	235-8080	Senegal	937-0925
Germany (East)	235-9941	Singapore (HC)	235-8315
Germany (West)	235-5033	South Africa	930-4488
Ghana (HC)	235-4142	Soviet Union	727-6888
India (HC)	836-8484	Spain	235-5555
Hong Kong Government		Sudan	839-8080
Office	499-9821	Sweden	724-2101
Hungary	235-7680	Switzerland	723-0701
Iceland	730-5131	Thailand	589-0173
Indonesia	499-7661	Tunisia	584-8117
Iraq	584-7141	Turkey	235-5252
Ireland	235-2171	Uganda (HC)	839-5783
Israel	937-8050	Uruguay	589-8835
Japan	493-6030	Venezuela	584-4206
Jordan	937-3685	Vietnam	937-1212
Korea (South)	581-0247	Yugoslavia	370-6105
Kuwait	589-4533	Zaire	235-6137

▷ *Spotlight* ◁

Business services. Major hotels compete both with each other and with business centers to provide visiting executives with what many need: an office away from home. ABC—the Association of Business Centers—groups together for marketing and monitoring of standards independently owned operations in London and many provincial cities. Tel.: 439-0623. British Telecom's *Network Nine* (629-9999) has offices in Stratford Place just off Regent Street, in the West End, and in

other cities. Also in Regent Street is *Management Business Services* (408-1611); and in the same neighborhood is *Angela Pike Associates,* 9 Curzon Street, W1 (491-1616). *Worldwide Business Centers* (836-8918) in the Strand, WC2, claims to have offices and affiliates in more than 20 countries. All these and other business centers offer a wide range of services, with a strong emphasis on telecoms; many provide teleconferencing facilities.

Airlines

Air Algerie	487-5903
Air Canada	759-2636
Air Europe	(0345) 444737
Air France	499-9511
Air India	491-7979
Air Lanka	439-0291
Air Malta	785-3177
Air New Zealand	930-3434
Air UK	(0345) 666777
Air Zimbabwe	897-4000
Alia Royal Jordanian	734-2557
Alitalia	602-7111
American Airlines	834-5151
Ansett (Australia)	(0345) 747767
Australian Airlines	897-4400
Austrian Airlines	439-0741
British Airways	897-4000
British Midland	589-5599
Brymon Airways (England)	(0345) 717383

BWIA International (Trinidad and Tobago)	734-3796
Canadian Pacific Airlines	930-5664
Caribbean Airways	493-6252
Cathay Pacific Airways	930-7878
Cayman Airways	581-9960
China Airlines (Taiwan)	434-0707
Connectair (UK)	897-4000
Continental Airlines	(0293) 776464
Cyprus Airways	388-5411
Dan-Air Services (England)	(0345) 100200
Delta Air Lines	(0800) 414767
Eastern Airlines	(0293) 517622
El Al Israel Airlines	437-9255
Emirates Airlines	930-3711
Ethiopian Airlines	930-9152
Egyptair	734-2395

Finnair	408-1222	Piedmont Airlines	(0800) 777333
GB Airways (Gibraltar)	897-4000	Qantas Airways	
Garuda Indonesian		(Australia)	(0345) 747767
Airways	486-3010	Royal Air Maroc	439-4361
Gulf Air	408-1717	Sabena Belgian World	
Iberia (Spain)	437-5622	Airlines	437-6950
Japan Air Lines/JAL	408-1000	SAS Scandinavian	
Jet America	839-9384	Airlines	734-4020
KLM Royal Dutch		Saudi Arabian Airlines	995-7777
Airlines	568-9144	Singapore Airlines	747-0007
Korean Air	930-6513	South African Airways	734-9841
Kuwait Air Ways	935-8795	Swissair	439-4144
Lloyd Aero		TAP Air Portugal	828-0262
Boliviano/LAB	930-1442	Thai Airways	499-9113
London City Airways	511-4200	Transavio Airlines (Italy)	(0293)
LOT Polish Airlines	580-5037	38181	
Lufthansa German		TWA	439-0707
Airlines	408-0442	Tunis Air	734-7644
Maersk Air (Denmark)	623-3813	Turk Hava Yollari	499-9113
Malev Hungarian		United Airlines	(0800) 898017
Airlines	439-0577	USAir	(0992) 441517
MAS	491-4542	UTA (France)	629-6114
Middle East Airlines	493-5681	Varig (Brazil)	629-5824
Nationair	(0444) 415551	Viasa (Venezuela)	493-7287
Northwest Airlines	629-5353	Virgin Atlantic Airways	(0293)
Olympic Airways	846-9080	38222	
Pacific Southwest Airlines	(0992)	Wardair (Canada)	(0800) 234444
441517		Yugoslav Airlines/JAT	493-9399
Pakistan International		Zambia Airways	491-0650
Airlines	734-5544		
Pan Am World Airways	409-0688		
Philippine Airlines	629-6767		

▷ Shopping

London has some of Europe's best shops—and some of its worst help. Spoiled by a long-lasting consumer boom and an ever-rising flood of foreign visitors, too many stores hire novice clerks, give them little or no training in even the rudiments of trade, and seem to be run on the principle that retailing would be a delightful business if only customers didn't come in to disturb the stock. That's not true of all stores, to be sure; but do not expect to find in London, particularly in the central area, the obsequiousness of Tokyo sales clerks, the eagerness to sell of those in New York, or the encyclopedic knowledge of Parisian *vendeuses*.

The problems are worst in the great department stores, again with exceptions. They are least in small, specialized stores, often owner-managed. The clerks there may not be trained, but at least they know their merchandise—and know that the rent has to be paid. And we have to report, in all fairness, that every now and then we have encountered a clerk who has "bent over backward" (as the British say) to be helpful. In general, though, shopping in central London is not a pleasure, it's a chore.

▷ *Spotlight* ◁

You'll find few bargains in London—or, rather, you'll find few unless you come from a country with a currency that is very strong against the pound. (The U.S. dollar often isn't.) Prices usually include 15 percent value-added tax (VAT), but most visitors can claim this back if they leave the country with the goods within three months. Check that the shop operates the official Export Scheme, show your passport, and ask for VAT Form 707. When leaving Britain, show the goods to the customs official, and make sure he or she stamps the form. People living in another EC country need to have the form stamped at their port of entry. Then mail the stamped form to the store with instructions for payment. Some stores levy an administration charge; others operate the scheme only for purchases worth more than 50 pounds. Procedures are different for goods mailed to visitors.

Let's get the topography straight.

West End. *Oxford Street,* W1, runs west from the intersection with Charing Cross Road where it joins Tottenham Court Road at St. Giles's Circus, and ends at Marble Arch. Many Oxford Street stores sell overpriced schlock, but it's worth browsing. Notable exceptions to the general rule are *Selfridges* at 400, *Debenhams* at 334-338, and *Marks and Spencer* at 173. Selfridges, founded by an American, is one of the world's largest—

and most confusing—emporia. Once you've found your away around, though, Selfridges sells virtually everything, and usually at very competitive prices. Venerable Debenhams has been transformed into an American-style shopping experience, with dazzling decor. Competitive prices and a huge selection of goods. Marks and Spencer, flagship branch of a nationwide chain, specializes in high-quality, medium-cost clothing. Persistent legend has it that some members of the royal family buy their underwear here, or have it bought for them. The store's nickname is "Marks and Sparks."

About half way along Oxford Street is Oxford Circus, and leading south from it is *Regent Street.* This broad, gentle curve of dignified buildings leads to Piccadilly Circus and is lined with stores, most of them selling higher-quality goods than those generally offered in Oxford Street. *Hamleys,* 188-196 Regent Street, claims to be the world's largest toy and leisure store. Even if it isn't, Hamleys is certainly impressively gigantic. A wonderful place for parents to play with train sets they buy for their children but would rather keep for themselves. *Garrard,* at 112, has been selling beautiful silver and other *objets* since 1720; worth visiting even if you don't intend to buy. *Liberty,* also in Regent Street, has these virtues: its architecture is a choice example of the Art and Crafts movement, the stock is eclectic in its variety, and the staff is knowledgeable and helpful. An excellent place at which to buy gifts, either large or small. Keep an eye out for the famous Liberty textile prints.

South of Regent Street are Mayfair and St. James's, and Savile Row. This is where the toniest stores are to be found, along with the best (or at least most expensive) gentlemen's tailors, shirtmakers, and shoemakers. The shopping "spine" of the neighborhood is *Bond Street,* divided into New and Old, which leads from Oxford Street in the north to Piccadilly in the south. Also in the district are many of the top art and antiques dealers. *Sothebys'* main salerooms are at 34 New Bond Street (Tel.: 493-8080); *Christies,* its neck-and-neck rival in the fine arts auction business, is at 8 King Street, SW1, south of Piccadilly (Tel.: 839-9060). Both Christies and Sothebys run less grand salerooms elsewhere; check days and times, because just occasionally people pick up bargains. In the Mayfair and St. James's neighborhoods, look for the famous shopping arcades, particularly *Burlington*, where small stores offer high-quality (and high-priced) buys ranging from antiques and antiquarian books, through fashion, to jewelry.

▷ Spotlight ◁

Savile Row, roughly parallel to Regent Street, has become a generic term for superb men's tailoring. Customers include members of the royal family and the aristocracy. All Savile Row tailors are *bespoke*—that is, the customer chooses the cloth, and it is "bespoken" (committed) to him. Tailors usually insist upon three fittings before delivering the suit, but in these hectic times some will telescope them into a week or even less. Is a Savile Row suit worth the money—which can be as high as $1,700? Devotees say that it's almost cheap at the price, because with care it will last for 20 or more years. We can bear witness to that: we still wear suits made in the 1960s, and if they're out of fashion today, they're likely to be in fashion again tomorrow.

What about shirtmakers, who congregate on and near to Jermyn Street, St. James's, a five-minute walk from Savile Row? Our doubts grow. To be sure, many of these firms make bespoke shirts that are works of art, or at least are craftwork of the highest order, but prices have soared stratospherically. Expect to pay $100 to $130 for a ready-to-wear shirt at *Turnbull and Asser*, 71 Jermyn Street. *Hilditch and Key*, at 33, 37, and 87, sells both men's and women's wear, with shoes at number 87; less costly than many of its neighboring rivals.

While on Jermyn Street near Savile Row, visit three of its most famous stores. *Fortnum and Mason*, with its main entrance at 181 Piccadilly, W1, but one on Jermyn Street as well, sells everything from antiques to Zelda clothes. The street-level food hall is an epicure's delight: when in London we nearly always pick up some meat pies, English white wine (yes, there is such stuff), and cheeses. Fine selection of coffee and tea in Fortnum's distinctive boxes. If we don't find exactly the cheeses we want, we walk across Jermyn Street to *Paxton and Whitfield* at number 93. This is London's oldest cheesemonger, with sawdust on the floor and about 300 cheeses in stock, many of them British. Good choice, too, of such things as English bacon. Going east along Jermyn Street, you will reach the rear entrance of the *Simpson* department store; its main entrance is at 203 Piccadilly. Simpson features men's and women's clothing and accessories with a powerful emphasis on the tweedy, country look, but increasingly strong stress on designer casuals as well. Home of the famous Daks suits.

Knightsbridge and Kensington. *Harrods* is the standout store here, on the busy street known as Knightsbridge. (Harrods doesn't bother with the street number: it's a landmark.) With 230 departments at last count, Harrods stocks everything you can imagine—and some things you cannot. The Food Hall is particularly interesting. For a long time, we thought that the grand old place was overrated and overpriced, the management distracted by a long-running battle over ownership. Perhaps we were wrong; certainly, recent visits have shown that Harrods has recovered much of its verve and vigor. If your set of fine china is British, check here for pieces that may not be available back home. For example, teacups and coffee cups are two distinctly different items, and many American stores carry only the former. Be forewarned that Harrods is usually crowded, and *never* go there during a sale if you value your life.

Harvey Nichols, Knightsbridge, is more of a fashion than a department store. Its window displays are London's most imaginative. Stock is more classic than trendy. Beautiful chinaware, glassware, and household linens. Small gifts in the basement. There's also a pleasant restaurant. Close by, at 144 Sloane Street, is the *General Trading Company.* Twelve departments are divided into traditional, modern, and oriental. Some kitsch, but much more good design.

Sloane Street leads down to Sloane Square, and at the right is the start of *King's Road, Chelsea.* In the 1960s, when London was dubbed the Swinging City, King's Road blossomed with trendy boutiques. Some designers now famous got their start here (and some were washed into oblivion by the raging tides of changing fashion), and Flower Power became money power for men in striped suits and stiff-collared shirts. King's Road is worth a look, particularly on Saturdays, when it's crowded with members of the sixties generation remembering their lost youth. Try the Chelsea Potter and Markham Arms pubs for atmosphere. Some interesting boutiques, too.

▷ **After Hours**

Act I, Scene 1. Six girls prance onto the stage wearing next to nothing and proceed to dance clumsily to what sounds, more-or-less, like a samba. They prance off, squealing. Act I, Scene 2. To the rhythm of Ravel's *Bolero,* rather badly played, a man and a woman wearing nothing more than what the French call a *cache-sexe* (one each, of course) undulate sinuously; much of the act consists of the woman climbing the man's well-muscled body and his showing his strength by lifting her over his head. They leave. Act II, Scene 1. Girls wearing black underwear, but not much of it, adopt various postures while a woman wearing a top hat and full evening dress, minus the trousers, brandishes a whip and sings throatily in German. Act III, Scene 2...But no, we really cannot continue.

Is this nightclub in Berlin, Paris, Rio de Janeiro? No, it's in London, and the hour is two in the morning, and everyone's aching to leave, particularly the hatcheck girl. Of course, not all London nightclubs are quite as dreadful as this famous one, which the laws of libel make it dangerous to name. And so we have a duty to list only the nightspots where you may venture without suffering extreme boredom and the need to take out a second mortgage on your home when the check arrives.

Annabel's, 44 Berkeley Square, W1. Tel.: 629-3558. Bar, dining, disco. Luxurious, crowded with rich men and (usually) notably younger women.

Very much "in," so you may be out if you don't reserve. In theory, at least, you must be a member or be introduced by one.

Elephant on the River, 129 Grosvenor Road, SW1. Tel.: 834-1621. Tables overlook the Thames; dancing to a band; international cuisine; good service.

Grecian Taverna, 27 Percy Street (Tottenham Court Road), W1. Tel.: 636-8913. Very Greek, with *bouzouki* music, a five-piece band, and cabaret. Dancing.

Hamilton's, Inter-Continental Hotel, 1 Hamilton Place, W1. Tel.: 409-3131. Up on the seventh floor: dining, live music, then disco.

Limelight, 136 Shaftesbury Avenue, W1. Tel.: 434-1761. In a former church; dancing area, lounge, Japanese sushi bar. Raffish clientele.

Omar Khayyam, Mitre House, 177 Regent Street, W1. Tel.: 437-3000. Huge meals with Arabian origins; belly dancers, singers, live music.

Stork Club, 99 Regent Street (entrance in Swallow Street), W1. Tel.: 734-3686/1393/1368. Dinner, band, dancing; two different shows nightly. A good old reliable.

Stringfellow's, Upper St. Martin's Lane, WC2. Tel.: 240-5534. Dine upstairs, with trio playing; disco downstairs. Club nonmembers must pay entrance fee.

Villa dei Cesari, 135 Grosvenor Road, SW1. Tel.: 828-7453. Overlooks the river. Italian dining; dancing to live music.

▷ *Spotlight* ◁

We recommend the music at all these places—more, perhaps, than we recommend the food.

Dolphin Brasserie, 2 Dolphin Square, Chichester Street, SW1. Tel.: 828-3207. Cuisine with an English accent; British blues singer George Melly, American Slim Gaillard and others are making this a top jazz spot.

Dover Street Wine Bar, Dover Street, W1, is popular for business lunches—and for blues and jazz at night. Tel.: 629-9813.

Palookaville, 13a James Street, WC2. Jazz every night in a large, candlelit room. Tel.: 240-5857.

Ronnie Scott's club at 47 Frith Street, W1, has resounded to the music of most of jazz's big names. Tel.: 439-0747.

▷ Sights and Sounds

Royal Attractions

London's biggest tourist attractions are royalty and everything to do with it. Family members, with Queen Elizabeth II as undisputed star, are the cast of a long-running soap opera with thousands of extras. Who will marry whom? Which royal couple is on the outs? What names will the new baby have? Then there's all the pomp and pageantry, from the relatively modest Changing of the Guard at Buckingham Palace to the great occasions, all of them skillfully scripted, crafted, choreographed, and acted: the State Opening of Parliament, the Trooping the Color on the Queen's official birthday, visits by heads of state.

Royal London is neatly bounded within a triangle, the three points being Buckingham Palace, Trafalgar Square, and Westminster. Within these few hectares are not only the palace itself, the Queen's official residence when she is in London, but also Clarence House, London home of the Queen Mother; St. James's Palace, now used mainly as royal offices; and Horse Guards Parade, facing beautiful St. James's Park, with its ponds and wildfowl.

The best of sights and sounds:

Changing of the Guard, Buckingham Palace. Daily, 11:30 a.m. Canceled on state occasions and when weather is exceptionally bad. Guardsmen march in from their barracks in gorgeous, colorful red uniforms (which may be covered by grey overcoats on chillier days), with flags flying and bands playing. Impressively precise military ceremony. Crowds are huge for much of the year; get there early. There is also a miniature version of the ceremony at Horse Guards, a classical building; Queen's Life Guards are on duty.

Buckingham Palace itself is resolutely closed to the public. However, adjoining it is the Queen's Gallery, which houses regular exhibitions of material selected from the royal collections. The nearby Royal Mews are the stables and coach houses. Jewel in the crown: the sumptuous State Coach used at coronations. It was built in 1761.

Trooping the Color marks the Queen's official birthday in June (she was born in April). Date: Saturday closest to June 11. Starting time: 10:45 a.m., when the Queen rides in procession along the Mall from Buckingham Palace to Horse Guards Parade to inspect the seven regiments of the Household Division of the Army, her personal guard. The ceremony features horses, colors (flags), soldiers in immaculate, traditional uniforms, and bands. You can watch it from the Mall if you get up early to take your place—or from Horse Guards Parade if you have the pull to obtain a ticket through a friendly diplomat.

Art Galleries and Museums

From ancient to *avant-garde,* London has them all, and more. Major attractions are:

British Museum and the British Library, Great Russell Street, WC1. A majestic, Greco-Georgian-Victorian edifice that houses some of the world's greatest collections. They span the world and time: ancient Egypt, classical Greece, Roman Britain, Chaldean—Ur was Abraham's home town. The library houses original copies of the Magna Carta, which King John granted at Runnymede in 1215. By recognizing the rights of barons, church, and freemen, it laid many of the foundations of Anglo-American democracy. Other manuscripts include the original *Beowulf* and gorgeous medieval illuminations as well as handwritten drafts by authors of recent centuries, such as Lewis Carroll and George Eliot. Some Beatles lyrics scrawled by the band are also part of the collection. The huge, circular Reading Room is where Karl Marx did much of his research; now called the British Library, the books division will soon be housed in a new, horrible building between Euston and St. Pancras stations.

Institute of Contemporary Arts, foot of Carlton House Terrace, SW1 (entrance on the Mall). The wonderful and occasionally weird work of today's artists. Excellent bar and café in which to recover.

National Gallery, Trafalgar Square, WC2. King George IV fathered this great art repository in 1824 by encouraging his government to buy a famous collection. Practically every foremost European artist from the 1300s to 1800s is represented: Michelangelo, Raphael, Leonardo da Vinci, Titian, Rubens, Rembrandt, Vermeer, Goya, Davíd, Turner, and Monet are among them.

National Portrait Gallery, 2 St. Martin's Place, WC2. Just around the corner from the National Gallery. Very British—and a few foreign—faces stare down from the walls. Some portraits are by masters, others by second- or even third-rank painters: works have been chosen to illustrate the British character down through the ages. Even pop stars are included, and some of the settings are almost stage sets. Official portraits of royal family members are prominent.

Royal Academy of Arts, Burlington House, Piccadilly, W1. Founded in 1768, with King George III as patron; housed since 1868 in the Palladian mansion of Lord Burlington. Some superb small collections and many special exhibitions. The RA's summer exhibition hangs both amateur and professional works. Check what's on. Tel.: 734-9052.

Tate Gallery, Millbank, SW1. The Tate houses two famous collections: British painting from the 1500s to 1900s and an eclectic international culling of modern and contemporary art. The *Clore Gallery,* opened in 1987, is dedicated solely to works by J.M.W. Turner. Many special shows, some of them eccentric, to put it kindly: check programs. Tel.: 821-1313.

Victoria and Albert Museum, Cromwell Road, SW7. Huge and rambling: arm yourself with a free floor plan when you enter. The catholicity of exhibits is amazing: paintings by Constable, baroque jewelry, medieval ecclesiastical art, clothes from many centuries, musical instruments (some of them played in recitals), Japanese art—the list goes on and on. Many visiting exhibitions too. Discover them by phoning 581-4894.

Music

Every night there are world-class performances of ballets, operas, and classical and modern music. London's own permanent companies are famous with music lovers everywhere, if only on recordings and television, and the city's many symphony orchestras and smaller ensembles offer a rich feast, from ancient music played on original instruments to Stockhausen played on electronic devices. Check programs in *The Standard,* an afternoon paper (not published Saturdays and Sundays), and in the *What's On, City Limits,* and *Time Out* guides.

BALLET AND OPERA

The Coliseum, St. Martin's Lane, WC2. Tel.: 836-3161. The English National Opera stages English-language productions here—and if you haven't heard Wagner translated, you've missed something. Critics differ over whether the whole thing is a good idea.

The Royal Opera House, Covent Garden, WC2, is up there with La Scala in Milan and the Metropolitan in New York on the musical scale—and on the price scale, too. You can buy a cheap seat "in the gods," next to the ceiling, and see little; or pay top prices for a stalls seat, and see everything, including very fashionable people for whom one of the attractions is hobnobbing in the Crush Bar during the intervals (intermissions). Tel.: 240-1066.

CONCERTS AND RECITALS

The Barbican Center, Silk Street, EC2, is home to the prestigious London Symphony Orchestra. Visiting orchestras include the Philharmonia and the Royal Philharmonic. The Barbican also puts on chamber music concerts by such renowned executants as the Gabrielli String Quartet and the City of London Sinfonia. Tel.: 628-8795 and 638-8891.

The Royal Albert Hall, Kensington Gore, SW7, is a vast, circular, many-tiered Victorian confection with nostalgic charm. One night it can be filled with all-in wrestling enthusiasts, the next with people listening to an evangelist, and the third with a black-tie crowd at a charity concert. The hugely popular promenade concerts are held here in July and August. You can sit—or pay about half the price to stand. Tel.: 589-8212.

The South Bank arts complex on the Thames includes the large *Royal Festival Hall* and smaller *Queen Elizabeth Hall.* Phone number for both: 928-3191. Address: South Bank, SE1. Regular concerts and recitals. Be warned, though, that the complex is dismayingly dirty and that under the many walkways and bridges London's homeless congregate, some of them aggressive supplicants of alms.

Wigmore Hall, 36 Wigmore Street, W1. Tel.: 935-2141. Chamber ensembles, quartets and quintets, and solo recitals in this small, comfortable auditorium just north of Oxford Street.

London's musical life is far from confined to the major venues listed above; it pulsates also in smaller halls and churches all over the city. One leading place is *St. John's,* Smith Square, SW1. Tel.: 222-1061. Watch the papers and check the weekly guides for events.

Theaters

At last count, London had 43 theaters—and many more on the fringe, the equivalent of off-Broadway and off-off-Broadway. Some shows open and close so fast they might never have been; others run and run until they stagger with fatigue. The ones that make it big these days are usually musicals, with Andrew Lloyd Webber leading the way (*Evita, Phantom of the Opera, Cats*); light comedies with plenty of sexual innuendo; and all-star revivals of great plays of the past. Worth checking out is the longest-running play in London (over 30 years!), Agatha Christie's *The Mousetrap.* For British theater at its best, try these good old reliables:

Royal Shakespeare Company at the Barbican Center, Silk Street, EC2. Tel.: 628-8795 and 638-8891.

National Theater, South Bank Arts Center, SE1. Tel.: 928-2252.

Both the RSC and the National can be adventurous—and sometimes pompous and self-congratulatory. The RSC does not confine itself to Shakespeare, nor does the National stage only British plays.

Check the entertainment guides and *The Standard* for theater offerings. By Broadway standards, seats are cheap (assuming a halfway decent exchange rate). You can buy them at half price (plus a modest booking fee) by visiting the Society of West End Theaters' ticket booth in Leicester Square, WC2, on the day of the performance; no phone. Not all shows will have tickets available; the ones that do are listed on a board outside the booth. Expect a line. The Fringe Box Office, Duke of York's Theater, St. Martin's Lane, WC2, handles bookings for some 40 fringe establishments of various kinds. It also provides information about current productions. Tel.: 379-6002.

▷ Spotlight ◁

Vaudeville. We've never had less than an enjoyable time at the Players' *Theater,* Villiers Street, WC2. Tel.: 839-1134. Just off the Strand, hard by Charing Cross Station, the Players' cherishes the traditions of late Victorian and Edwardian music hall (vaudeville), complete with master of ceremonies. The program changes every two weeks, and though quality of the acts varies, it's usually high. Sup simple fare, including sausages, mashed potatoes, poached kippers, or a mixed grill.

The Water Rats, 328 Gray's Inn Road, WC1, is one of London's entertainment bargains, with a fixed price for dinner *and* two hours of acts with a period, vaudeville flavor. Tel.: 837-9661.

▷ Out of Town

London sprawls so much that it's hard to say what's in town and out of it. One thing's for sure, though: some attractions are far from the center, even if they're technically in London. Assuming that most of our readers are in a hurry, we are listing the closest of the choices.

The Country

Our first choice for a quiet night in the country is *The Bell*, Aston Clinton, Buckinghamshire, about 40 miles (66 kilometers) northwest of London. There's not much at Aston Clinton except The Bell, but that's enough. Dating from the 1600s, it is rustically luxurious, with 21 rooms, each comfortable and characterful. The restaurant has been renowned for decades, both for the cuisine and for the cellar. Reserve well in advance. Tel.: (0296) 630252. Telex: 83252.

If you want a restful time on the river, try the *Compleat Angler* at Marlow Bridge, Buckinghamshire, which borders the Thames and takes its name from Izaak Walton's classic work. It's very comfortable, and the Valaisan Restaurant is highly rated. There are only 46 rooms, and the restaurant seats a mere 130 people, so reserve well ahead of time. Tel.: (06284) 4444. Fax: 6388. Telex: 848644. About a hour from London along the M40 highway or by train to Maidenhead from Paddington Station.

The Sea

Brighton is London-on-Sea, just an hour by train from Victoria Station, rather more by car. The train arrives in the center of town, only 10 minutes' walk from the sea. Brighton offers an extraordinary and sometimes contradictory set of attractions: Georgian elegance and plebeian pastimes such as bingo halls; *haute cuisine* restaurants and fish-and-chip shops; grand hotels and back-street rooming houses.

All life is in Brighton and neighboring Hove: starchy and unbuttoned, refined and raffish. Just one set of architectural fantasies makes a visit worthwhile: the Royal Pavilion. Built by the Prince Regent, later King George IV, in the late 1700s and early 1800s, the pavilion is one of Europe's most visually sensational buildings, a unique concoction in which Chinese and Indian designs predominate—but are refracted through the cultural lens of English architects and artists. Recommended hotel: *Old Ship,* King's Road. Tel.: (0273) 29001. Timeless charm and hospitality on the seafront; fine restaurant with good wine list.

Stately Homes

Within easy reach of central London, by car or train, are many remarkable stately homes. For their historical interest and accessibility, we've selected four:

Arundel Castle, seat of the Dukes of Norfolk and their ancestors for more than 700 years, is a great stone structure that overlooks the River Arun in West Sussex. Rare furniture, tapestries, and clocks; portraits by Van Dyck, Gainsborough, Reynolds, and others. Tel.: (0903) 883136 or 882173. By car: 93 kilometers (58 miles) south of London on the A27 highway. By train: Victoria Station to Arundel. Recommended hotel: *Norfolk Arms Hotel,* 22 High Street. Tel.: (0903) 882101. Georgian coaching inn beneath the castle battlements.

Hatfield House, Hertfordshire, has been the home of the Cecils, the Earls of Salisbury, since the early 1600s, though the house is much older. Noble families accumulate treasures: superb paintings, furniture, armor, and various other artifacts. Queen Elizabeth I spent much of her childhood in the royal palace of Hatfield, one wing of which survives. Elizabethan banquets most nights; you can sign up for a package deal that includes roundtrip bus transportation as well as the banquet. Food is so-so, but the entertainment is rollicking. Tel.: (07072) 62823. By car: 34 kilometers (21 miles) north of London on highway A1000. By train: King's Cross Station to Hatfield.

Leeds Castle, Maidstone, Kent. Built on two islands in the middle of a lake set in wooded, rolling countryside. A favorite home of eight of England's medieval queens, the castle is now owned by a charitable foundation. Attractions include art and furniture collections, gardens and parklands, aviaries and a duckery, and a golf course. There's a conference center for up to 200 people, along with accommodations. Tel.: (0622) 65400. By car: 64 kilometers (40 miles) on the A20/M20. By rail: Victoria Station to Bearsted or Hollingbourne.

Stratfield Saye House, Hampshire, is the home of the eighth Duke of Wellington, descendant of the Great Duke—he who (with help) defeated Napoleon at the Battle of Waterloo in 1815. A grateful nation presented him with this seventeenth-century estate; among the treasures are books from Napoleon's own library. Tel.: (0256) 882882. By car: M4 highway to Reading, turn off at exit 11, and head for Basingstoke on the A33. After about 9.5 kilometers (6 miles) and the Wellington Arms Hotel, the house is signposted. By train: Waterloo Station (appropriately enough) to Basingstoke.

LUXEMBOURG

Grand Duchy, Grand Ambitions

Population: 80,000. Capital of the Grand Duchy of Luxembourg (population: 370,000). *Location:* on a plateau overlooking the Alzette and Petrusse rivers. *Economy:* agriculture, banking and financial services, chemicals, iron and steel. The country of Luxembourg is a member of the European Community (EC) and of the Belgium-Luxembourg Economic Union.

▷ Background Briefing

Luxembourg is one of those tiny countries that somehow escaped the form of cartography known as statesmanship in the peace settlements that followed wars. A mere 2,600 square kilometers (999 square miles) in area, the Grand Duchy has maintained independence of a kind, apart from occasional military occupation, ever since it became a distinct entity in the 900s A.D.

The country and its ruling family are survivors—as the European Community has learned to its cost. One of the founding members of the EC, Luxembourg ensured early on that it grabbed its share of the institutions, perhaps more than its share. The European Tower on Kirchberg Plateau, just outside Luxembourg city, is one of the three seats of the EC, smaller than Brussels but larger than Strasbourg.

No fewer than 3,000 people work in this complex, and that's not counting those at the European Investment Bank, the Court of Justice, and the Court of Auditors. All are compelling evidence of the awesome power that a small country can wield when it's run by shrewd politicians, for there is no operational reason why EC institutions shouldn't be concentrated in one place, probably Brussels. Nobody has calculated the cost of shuttling politicians and Eurocrats around the Brussels-Strasbourg-Luxembourg triangle, perhaps because nobody wants to know the cost. What's certain is that the EC pumps vast sums into the Luxembourg economy, which is one of the healthiest in Europe. Indeed, Luxembourg prospers by offering itself as a host country to all kinds of international enterprises. No less than 60 years ago, Radio Luxembourg was the forerunner of European commercial broadcasting. More recently, the Grand Duchy has become headquarters of the *Société Européenne des Satellites;* once again, Luxembourg is in the vanguard of broadcasters trying to tap the lucrative pan-European television market.

Not surprisingly, Luxembourg has long been a tax haven, its chosen corporate form being the holding company. This is exempt from local taxes on income arising outside the country, and strict confidentiality is guaranteed. As a result, banking and financial services have boomed to become the economy's dynamo, and today they account for no less than 15 percent of gross domestic product.

▷ Arriving

By Air

Findel Airport is 8 kilometers (5 miles) from the city center. Once a backpackers' paradise, thanks to cheap flights to and from the United States via Iceland, Findel today is more geared to the business traveler. Findel is very close to EC buildings on the Kirchberg Plateau. Major hotels offer free bus rides. The city is about 20 minutes away by taxi.

By Rail

Luxembourg is a bit of a backwater—if that's the right railroad term. But there are frequent, fast trains to and from neighboring Belgium, France, Germany, and the Netherlands.

By Road

Good, fast highways, usually uncrowded, leading to and from major European cities.

▷ Money

The basic unit of currency is the Luxembourg franc. International code: LUF. However, it's known locally as a Flux. Since the end of World War II, the Flux has been held at one-to-one parity with the Belgian franc.

Like the Belgian franc, the Flux is freely convertible, but ask a banker to explain the complexities of and practical differences between the so-called commercial franc and the "free" or financial franc.

▷ Language

Complicated. Luxembourg has three official languages: Letzeburgesch, French, and German. Letzeburgesch, a German dialect, is the prevailing everyday language, but French is the official language of government. Newspapers are printed mainly in German. However, English is the *lingua franca* of banking and business.

▷ Communications

The telephone dialing code for both country and city is 352. You don't, of course, need to dial the code within Luxembourg. Service is good.

▷ Getting To Know the City

With a population of 80,000 or so, Luxembourg city is a metropolis only in Grand Duchy terms. Some people find it charming, others dull.

A deep ravine divides the city. On one side is the old town, dominated by the Grand Duke's castle. This section has become newly fashionable, is being restored, and houses some fine restaurants. On the other side is commercial Luxembourg.

▷ Spotlight ◁

The Luxembourg royal family is a branch of the House of Nassau, which holds the Netherlands' throne. During World War II, the Grand Duchess Charlotte personified national identity. She ruled in all for 45 years. Her son, Grand Duke John, now reigns. His wife is Princess Josephine-Charlotte, sister of King Baudouin of the Belgians. Traditionally, Luxembourg's ruling family has been discreet, even secretive. Crown Prince Henri is changing that tradition: he likes to get out and about and smiles for photographers. His wife, the Grand Duchess Hereditary, Maria Teresa, is a bombshell by Luxembourg standards: beautiful, outspoken, of Cuban origin, with all the polish and self-assurance that a Swiss finishing school could impart.

▷ Moving Around

Efficient bus service; check hotels for shuttle buses to and from EC institutions. More taxis than riders except at peak times—when, of course, we all want taxis. Car rental is available from most of the major companies.

▷ Hotels

Not so long ago—15 years ago?—Luxembourg was a hotel desert. Now it's a green oasis. Competition is keen. When the EC Council of Ministers meets in Luxembourg, there isn't a room to be had. When it doesn't meet there, which is most of the time, rooms go abegging.

Arcotel, 43 Avenue de la Gare. Tel.: 49041. Telex: 3776. Rooms: 30. Comfortable, quiet. Close to main railroad station and city air terminal.

Aerogolf-Sheraton, Route de Treves, Findel. Tel.: 34571. Telex: 2662. Fax: 34217. Rooms/suites: 142 (some nonsmoking). Friendly bar, good restaurant; faces golf course.

Grand Hotel Cravat, 29 Boulevard Roosevelt. Tel.: 21975. Telex: 2846. Fax: 26711. Rooms/suites: 59. First class, right in the city center; an old favorite with discerning frequent visitors.

Inter-Continental, 12 Rue Jean Engling. Tel.: 43781. Telex: 3754. Fax: 436095. Rooms/suites: 344. Superb; probably Luxembourg's best. Often used for top European ministerial meetings. Restaurant, *Café Stiffchen,* has won a Michelin star. Indoor pool and fitness club, sauna, tennis.

Le Royal, 12 Boulevard Royal. Tel.: 41616. Telex: 2979. Fax: 25948. Rooms/suites: 170. Even the parking garage is heated, just one sign that this hotel pampers its guests. Famous restaurant *Le Relais Royal.* Pool and nightclub. Totter straight out into the banking district.

Pullman Luxembourg, 6 Rue du Fort-Niedergrunewald. Tel.: 437761. Telex: 2751. Fax: 438658. Rooms/suites: 256. A remodeled, refurbished, and reorganized former Holiday Inn close to the Kirchberg European center. Large, comfortable rooms; heated pool.

▷ Restaurants

Cuisine is an interesting melange of French, Belgian, and German. Curiously, for a landlocked country, there's a passion for fish. But, in season, the passion is for game—venison, pheasant, partridge, hare, and wild boar. Luxembourg borders the hilly, wooded Ardennes, where such creatures can still be shot or trapped.

▷ *Spotlight* ◁

Wine. Luxembourg isn't the first name that springs to mind when fine wines are being discussed. Yet there are good local wines, most of them very light, sharp, slightly bubbly, almost colorless—and wonderfully refreshing. They are classified as Moselle wines, products of Riesling grapes grown in the vineyards lining the river that winds out of France, through Luxembourg, and into Germany. Most of the vineyards are terraced, rising from the river banks to the peaks of hills, and they're among Europe's most beautiful.

Bouzonviller, 138 Rue Albert-Unden. Tel.: 472259. Fine cuisine presented professionally in a beautiful restaurant, with a terrace for warm-weather enjoyment. Strong emphases on fish from the sea, lakes, and streams, and on wild mushrooms. Extensive wine list.

Cafe Stiffchen, Inter-Continental Hotel. Tel.: 43781. Here on the hotel's terrace (glassed over for much of the year), good, simple, enjoyable food is served rapidly but without hurry. Salads a specialty.

Clairefontaine, 9 Rue Clairefontaine. Tel.: 462211. Physically luxurious, gastronomically inventive, with a cellar to savor: the place for a lingering meal.

Cordial, 1 Place de Paris. Tel.: 488538. Small, elegant, intimate; farm-fresh food. Fish dishes particularly recommended.

La Cigogne, 22-24 Rue du Cure. Tel.: 28250. A pleasant, restored house in the old town, with friendly service and a choice of dishes wide enough, but not so wide that one suspects they've been cooked in advance.

La Lorraine, 7 Place d'Armes. Tel.: 474620 and 471436. Classic fish and seafood restaurant with a wine list expertly chosen.

Le Relais Royal, Hotel Le Royal. Tel.: 41616. In the heart of the banking district, with a cuisine as fine and tasty as well-marinated thousand-dollar bills. The *chef de cuisine,* Daniel Perrin, learned his trade in luxury liners, and it shows. Altogether excellent—and value for (not inconsiderable) money.

Le Vert Galant, 1 Rue de la Poste. Tel.: 470822. A wide choice of seafood in a pleasant place favored by neighboring bankers.

Les Continents, Inter-Continental Hotel. Tel.: 43781. Ranks among the best tables in the whole country, with a *brigade* in the kitchen that seems always to be spurring itself on to greater effort. We can seldom resist the *ecrevisses* (crayfish)—or, indeed, most of the other dishes presented so temptingly. Michelin star.

Les Trois Glands, Pullman Luxembourg. Tel.: 437761. Very much coming up in the world, with a menu that offers both American cooking (sliced, tender steak, for example) and local.

Saint-Michel, 32 Rue de l'Eau. Tel.: 23215. The boss here is Pierrick Guillou, a Breton safely anchored in this magnificent sixteenth-century house. As a good Breton, he likes his fish—and so do his customers. But finny things are not the only pleasures here: the desserts are probably the best in town.

▷ Tipping

Service charge is included—but it's usual to leave small change and, of course, a good deal more if you've been particularly pleased and want a welcome when you return.

▷ Doing Business

In its 150 years of political independence, Luxembourg has used its geographical location to become a major steel producer, serving the neighboring German, French, Belgian, and Dutch markets in particular. But when steel fell on hard times, the Grand Duchy rapidly emphasized itself as a diversified services center. Today, industry accounts for only 32.9 percent of people in civilian employment. The vast majority, 63.4 percent, work in the services sector, with a mere 3.7 percent in agriculture, forestry, and fishing.

Six decades ago, Radio Luxembourg pioneered pan-European commercial broadcasting, and today has radio and television affiliates in Belgium, France, and West Germany. Building on that long history is *Société Européenne des Satellites,* owner of the Astra TV satellites. The

Grand Ducal family has even sold its hunting lodge outside the city to make way for an ultramodern control center.

▷ *Spotlight* ◁

Information, please! A quarter of the country's population comes from other EC countries. The English-language weekly *Luxembourg News Digest* is both a "what's on" guide and a slim compendium of the expatriates' so-cial, cultural, and business lives. The classified advertising section is a good place in which to find a home, a car, a garage sale, and much else. Address: 34 Avenue Victor Hugo, L-1750 Lux-embourg. Phone: 470052/3.

Just about the biggest employer is the banking and financial services sector, which accounts for about 15 percent of gross domestic product. All three political parties—right, center, and left—are committed to the greater glory and profit of the 125 or so banks, most of them of foreign origin.

The Luxembourg banks, led by the West German majors, *Deutsche* and *Dresdner,* grew rich with the booming Eurobond market of the past quarter-century, but a relative decline in that business forced many of them to seek more private customers. Local bankers are after investors with upwards of $25,000 to invest, as well as corporate business.

Well-trained trilingual staff (French, German, English) smooth inves-tors' and depositors' way and preach the virtues of the country's system: exemption from local taxes on income elsewhere, freedom of capital movement, and strict confidentiality. The Banking Commission has said that in virtually all cases, it refuses to cooperate with foreign tax authori-ties. Among recent recruits to the discreet charms of Luxembourg as a fi-nancial center are Hollywood and European movie and television producers, some of their stars, and entertainment groups. Re-insurance is also big business with a prominent Scandinavian presence. Recently, the government has been firm in its determination to maintain Luxembourg's special role as an offshore banking center within the European Commu-nity.

Aside from resisting EC-imposed withholding taxes, Luxembourg wants to keep tight banking secrecy. Like Switzerland, it is under fire for masking alleged fraud and the laundering of drug profits. Luxembourg says it will cooperate when there is a case brought before a national court but not when there is only suspicion.

Luxembourg is one of the two best listening posts for people keen to know what the European Community is about to perpetrate, the other being Brussels.

The small capital of a small country, Luxembourg is an easy city in which to do business. Executives are accessible, even top ones; and the whole government and its bureaucrats are virtually housed just in one building.

▷ Useful Phone Numbers

Note: Numbers run from four to eight digits. Short ones are usually reserved for important subscribers, such as ministries; eight digits normally means a direct line.

Emergencies

Police	485115
SOS	012

Local Information

Airport	47981
City tourism	27565
Taxis	
Downtown	27575
Railroad station	485868
Trains	492424

Business Information

Ministries	
Foreign Affairs	4781
Directorate, International Economic Relations	478611
Economics	479-4224
Information office	478224
Luxembourg Chamber of Commerce	435853

Banking

Bankers Association	29501
Monetary Institute	478888

European bodies

Commission	43011
Council	43021
Court of Auditors	47731
Court of Justice	43031
Parliament offices	43001
Conference center	478560
Investment Bank	43791

Embassies

Austria	26957
Belgium	442746
China (People's Republic)	436991
Denmark	20964
France	471091
Germany (West)	453444
Greece	445193
Ireland	450610
Italy	443644
Netherlands	27570
Portugal	473955
Soviet Union	21731
Spain	460255
Switzerland	27474

United Kingdom	29864	Icelandair	4798-2470
United States	460123	Lufthansa German Airlines	491627

Airlines

		Luxair	436161
Aeroflot Soviet Airlines	493-291	executive taxi	4798-2285
Air France	22643	Pan Am (cargo)	437269
Balkan-Bulgaria Airlines	28333	Sabena Belgian World Airlines	21212
British Airways	22088	Swissair	434343
Cargolux	4360211	TAP Air Portugal	494656
Finnair	487888	Thai Airways	448186

▷ After Hours

Aside from the nightclub at Le Royal and the piano bar at the Inter-Continental, there's little nightlife that can be recommended. There's plenty that cannot be. In side streets opposite the main railway station are plenty of clip joints with strip shows. A girl usually joins you immediately and the bill can be hefty. There's plenty of sleaze under the staid exterior of the Grand Duchy. Check with your worldly wise banker friend or your satellite TV company contact before entering the first door with bright lights.

▷ Sights and Sounds

There's more to see and do in this apparently dour city than first acquaintance might suggest. The old town around the Grand Duke's castle has been nicely restored and is worth a wander. The castle itself is open to the public from the middle of July until early September, during the Grand Ducal vacation.

The *Place d'Armes* and *Place Guillaume* are two central squares that bring together the twin influences of France and Germany, with terraces and good beer. Also in this downtown area, on Avenue de la Porte Neuve, is the *stock exchange,* large in terms of transactions, but the only one in Europe that's over a row of boutiques and next to a supermarket.

The Jean-Pierre Pescatore Museum (Villa Vauban), Avenue Emile Reuter, houses a collection of paintings bequeathed to the city by two nineteenth-century bankers. Painters represented include seventeenth- and eighteenth-century Flemish and Dutch masters, and Canaletto, Courbet, and Delacroix.

One of the fathers of the European Community was Luxembourg-born Robert Schuman, so a visit to the Kirchberg Plateau is appropriate. *European City* is almost that—certainly a town almost in its own right. A visitors' bureau arranges guided tours.

▷ Out of Town

Luxembourg bills itself as "the green heart of Europe," and in this tiny country there are indeed several picturesque, medieval towns.

Echternach, 34 kilometers (21 miles) from Luxembourg, is one of the earliest centers of Christianity in Europe. St. Willibrord from Northumberland, England, founded an abbey there in 698. To be seen are the rebuilt abbey, cloisters, and the graceful, eighteenth-century houses of local dignitaries.

Mondorf-les-Bains, 21 kilometers (13 miles) from Luxembourg, is where you can lose both weight and money—the first at the renowned thermal baths, the second at the casino.

Moselle River

The steamship *Princess Marie-Astrid* cruises between the vineyards. Check with your hotel concierge for sailing times.

Horseback Riding

Luxembourg has a number of trails and riding schools that offer horseback riding with or without an escort. Contact the *Fédération Luxembourgeoise des Sports Equestres* at 9 Rue du Fort Elisabeth.

MADRID

Life In the Afternoon

Population: 3.16 million (1981). Political and administrative capital of Spain (population: 38.8 million). *Location*: central Spain. *Economy*: aerospace; automotive components and assembly; banking and financial services; electronics; leather goods; optical equipment; pharmaceuticals; plastics; rubber; science and technology; tourism. Spain is a member of the European Community (EC) and the Organization for Economic Cooperation and Development (OECD) and is a signatory to the General Agreement on Tariffs and Trade (GATT).

▷ Background Briefing

The Moors built a fortress in the 900s A.D. on the site of what is now Madrid. Spanish Christians gained control of the area in 1083, and it became the capital of Spain in 1561. Madrid was one of the great cities of Western Europe in the 1500s and 1600s but later declined and failed to join the Industrial Revolution of the 1800s. After the Spanish Civil War of the 1930s, Madrid was held in the grip of Generalissimo Francisco Franco, who ruled as dictator until his death in 1975. The nation then became a parliamentary monarchy.

Today, Madrid is a city in a hurry. It's in a hurry because, as many business executives explain, they and the government want to make up for time lost during the torpor of the 36 Franco years. Europe in those days ended at the Pyrenees, or so the saying went.

Much has been achieved by the government of Prime Minister Felipe González, a pragmatic socialist government that has bolstered rather than battered business, embraced market economics with discreet enthusiasm, and reduced the once-powerful Communist Party to a rump of its former self in elections and opinion polls.

Polls also show the nation's young people aspiring to success and riches rather than espousing causes. Even so, the "born-again" Spanish need national ideals as well as "me-too" goals. Three events in Spain in 1992 will help to define those ideals: the world's fair in Seville marking Christopher Columbus' discovery of America (the fact that Columbus was an Italian and Spain's role was confined to backing his expedition financially will not blunt Spanish pride); the staging of the Summer Olympics in Barcelona; and the advent of the Single European Market.

But even if Spain is well on the way to becoming as "European" as, say, France or Belgium, the route has been bumpy. Along the way, regional pressures have forced the Spanish *Cortes* (parliament) to grant autonomy to the province of Catalonia and to the Basque region. The Basques remain the government's biggest domestic political problem. A tiny but violent minority will settle for nothing less than secession from Spain. Seeking to further that cause, Basque terrorists have bombed and shot soldiers, police officers, and civilians. But the militants, the ETA, have little popular support, and that little continues to dwindle.

Regional challenges underline a fact often forgotten or discounted by foreigners: Spain is a collection of provinces rather than a single, unified society. When a foreigner asks a Spaniard what his nationality is, he will say he is Spanish. If another Spaniard asks him the question, he will answer that he is Andalucian, Basque, Catalán, Galician, or a son of any of the country's fifty provinces; not that one Spaniard would have to ask another that question. Provincial accents, dialects, and languages make such probing unnecessary, and local patriotism is served up piping hot.

Madrid is the Spanish melting pot, a blend of native *Madrileños* and migrants from the four corners of the country, not to mention foreigners who have made the city their home and its culture cosmopolitan. In few European cities is the way of life changing as fast. Take the Spanish day—and night. Time was, not so long ago, that business executives were seldom in their offices before ten in the morning, left at one o'clock or so for lunch, took a two- or three-hour siesta, and returned—if they did—at four or five in the afternoon. Anyone who dined before 10:00 p.m. was either a foreigner or an eccentric, or both.

There's life in the afternoon now. Spain has hitched its wagon to the European star—and changed its schedule to European time.

▷ *Spotlight* ◁

Foreign investors are a sturdy pillar of today's Madrid. They and their modern buildings are everywhere, but mostly along the fashionable *Paseo de la Castellana*, a Champs-Elysées multiplied by two or three. On and around the Paseo are such major Italian new-comers as Montedison, French insurance and food processing concerns, West German computer companies, Danish brewers, and Arab investors. *Actualidad Economica*, a lively business magazine, calls the Madrid business scene *el gran festin*—the big feast. Rising foreign investment helps to explain Madrid's increasing adoption of "European" business hours. What, after all, would corporate headquarters in West Germany think if all its Madrid-based executives were away from their desks for most of the afternoon?

▷ Arriving

Marble floors give Madrid-Barajas international airport a grand air, but the best thing about it is its closeness to the city: 16 kilometers (10 miles). The nearby national terminal serves flights to and from such cities as Barcelona, Seville, and Malaga. Buses to Madrid are fast and cheap; taxis a little faster, and not nearly as cheap. Duty-free shops at Barajas are so-so. For anything except liquor and cigarettes, you'll do better in Madrid.

▷ Money

The basic unit of currency is the peseta. International code: ESP. Colorful banknotes come in denominations of 100 (brown), 200 (orange), 500 (blue), 1,000 (green), 2,000 (red), and 5,000 (violet) pesetas. Coins are minted in amounts of 1, 2, 5, 10, 50, and 100 pesetas. As in other cities, banks offer the best rates for foreign exchange, hotels the worst.

▷ Language

Castilian Spanish is the language of Madrid and most of the rest of Spain. The most noticeable difference between Castilian Spanish and Latin American Spanish is that Castilian pronunciation replaces the "s" sound with a soft "th," as in the word "thank." To American ears, Castilian Spanish can sound a bit lispy, so don't laugh if someone tells you he's from "Barthelona."

About a third of Spain's people speak also—or even primarily—one of the minority languages: Catalán, Gallego, or Basque. These languages are more regionally centered, but you may hear them in Madrid upon occasion. The Franco regime tried to suppress them, banning their teaching in schools and use in books and newspapers. That suppression failed.

Nobody expects a visiting foreigner to speak one of the minority languages, but it does help to learn some Castilian Spanish phrases before arriving in Spain. Unlike the French, who do not understand (or profess not to) a heavily accented version of their language, the Spanish adjust their ears to distortions of Castilian, perhaps because there are so many spoken versions of it. In pure Castilian, for example, the *ll* in a word such as *calle* (street) is pronounced almost as a *y* in English: "Kay-yay." In Argentinian Spanish, it is pronounced as a *j*: "Kah-jay." The Spanish taught in American schools generally follows Castilian pronunciation but often ignores the lispy "s," in part because it sounds funny and in part because Americans are more likely to converse with people from Mexico, Puerto Rico, or parts of Central and South America, none of whom use the Castilian lisp.

▷ Spotlight ◁

Spanish names can be both tongue-twisting and confusing for foreigners. Remember that the middle name is the patronym by which a person is usually called, the last name being that of the mother's family. For example, Miguel Cervantes de Saavreda, who wrote the famous Spanish novel *Don Quixote*, is known as Miguel Cervantes—not Miguel de Saavreda.

▷ Communications

Country code: 34. City code: 1. Until recently an international laughing stock, the Spanish telecommunications system is now improving. However, the telecom company, *Telefonica,* was recently privatized and has given priority to big cities and to international calls, so don't be surprised if it is easier to call home to Cleveland, Copenhagen, or Cork than it is to reach a number in a small Spanish town.

▷ Spotlight ◁

Telefonica has made ambitious deals abroad, but the telecoms system at home has been groaning under the weight of rising demand. In 1988, the waiting list for phones stood at 430,000. Thousands of villages lacked even one public telephone, and would-be users had waited six months or more for a line. Few people were impressed by Telefonica's devoting 0.1 percent of its investment budget to building up Spain's largest private art collection. Most wished Telefonica would just stick to its real business—telephones.

▷ Getting To Know the City

Madrid and its suburbs sprawl over the Castilian plain. Business Madrid is compact, though, concentrated in the center, with many government ministries housed in tower blocks to the north. Madrid boasts one of the tallest office buildings in Europe, the 46-story Torre Picasso, the new symbol of business, yet is still a charming mixture architecturally of ancient and modern, and socially of dynamism and courtliness.

▷ Moving Around

Madrid has good bus and subway systems. The subway is called the Metro. Most business visitors will find taxis easier and faster, however, if they are not familiar with the city's layout. Taxis are cheap by European standards, drivers do not expect a tip, and many speak English or understand even a mangled version of Spanish street names. Taxis are white with a diagonal red line. They display a green light when they are free, and behind the rear window is a meter that, by law, must show when the driver is on or off duty.

▷ Spotlight ◁

Safety at night. Progress has a price. Part of that price is a jump in street crime, much of it committed by drug addicts desperate for the money for their next fix. Areas to avoid after dark are the corner of *Gran Via* and *Calle Hortaleza* (that's where the Telefonica building with the big clock stands). The Gran Via can be risky after midnight. So can the *Puerta del Sol, Plaza Mayor,* and *Plaza Santa Ana.* The *Malasana* and *Chueca* neighborhoods should be shunned when dusk falls.

▷ Hotels

Madrid has long had some fine hotels, but until recently most were geared to tourists' needs. Many still are, of course, but others have set out to lure the more profitable business traveler. What follows is a selective list of those that have gotten this equation right, even if they have failed to control prices.

Eurobuilding, 23 Padre Damian. Tel.: 457-7800. Telex: 22548. Fax: 457-9729. Rooms/suites: 516. Situated in the business-ministerial section of northern Madrid, it is a favorite with Americans, in part because it offers

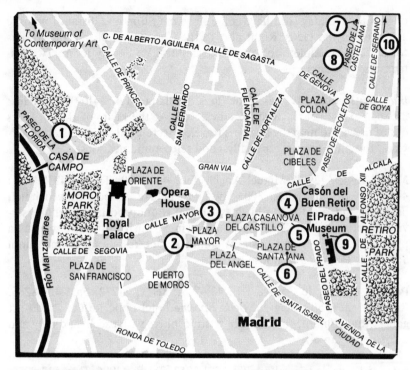

1. **Main Station**
2. **Foreign Ministry**
3. **Madrid Region hq**
4. **Cortes (Parliament)**
5. **Hotel Palace**

6. **Tourist Office**
7. **Hotel Inter-Continental**
8. **Hotel Villa Magna**
9. **Hotel Ritz**
10. **Hotel Eurobuilding**

some of the city's best long-stay rates. A second building has corporate offices and apartments. Among other facilities: 20 meeting rooms, pool, sauna, shops, multilingual secretarial and advisory staff.

Holiday Inn, 4 Plaza Carlos Trias Bertran. Tel.: 456-7014. Telex: 44709. Fax: 597-0292. Rooms/suites: 313. Some nonsmoking rooms. A reminder

►317

of how far Holiday Inns have come since their dim and distant founding as motels in the 1950s. Right next to the Congress Hall; meeting rooms for up to 500 people; rooftop pool; satellite TV in every room. Two restaurants, two bars.

Inter-Continental, 49 Paseo de la Castellana. Tel.: 410-0200. Telex: 27686. Fax: 419-5853. Rooms/suites: 305. At the heart of things. Goes out of its way to help the business traveler: secretarial and translation services, function rooms, especially good telecommunications.

Miguel Angel, 29-31 Miguel Angel. Tel.: 442-8199. Telex: 44235. Fax: 442-5320. Rooms/suites: 300. The latest deluxe, air-conditioned hotel, designed and run for top businesspeople: soundproofing, attentive service, meeting rooms. Has a reputation in Spanish business circles as a place to take wives and business contacts. One restaurant is open until 3:00 a.m. Pool and in-house barber.

Palace, 7 Plaza de Cortes. Tel.: 429-7551. Telex: 22272. Fax: 429-8266. Rooms/suites: 508. A great *Belle Epoque* hotel opposite the Prado art gallery that combines a Palm Court atmosphere with excellent dining and a cosmopolitan air.

Ritz, 5 Plaza de la Lealtad. Tel.: 521-2857. Telex: 43986. Fax: 532-8776. Rooms/suites 156. One of the best European hotels—a gem. Now run by the British TrustHouse Forte group, the Ritz would probably please the eponymous César Ritz himself, what with its hand-woven carpets, immaculate service, and superb food, served in a restaurant with decor that vies with the cuisine for attention and, when the weather is good, on the terrace. In season (and when the weather is good), guests can go hunting ("shooting," that is) on the Duke of Fernan Nunez's estate.

Villa Magna, 22 Paseo de la Castellana. Tel.: 261-4900. Telex: 22914. Fax: 275-9504. Rooms/suites: 182. An elegant, cool hotel with all modern facilities. Just right for chief executive officers.

▷ **Restaurants**

Madrid businesspeople spend a lot of time in restaurants. The most fashionable (though not necessarily the best) are crowded. Reserve a week ahead for some, at least a day ahead for all. And remember that though Spain is coming into line with the rest of Europe, lunch and dinner tend still to be late: 1:30 p.m. at the earliest for lunch, 9:30 p.m. for dinner. Forget breakfast; the "power breakfast" hasn't yet caught on in Spain.

Choose Spanish wines if you are the host. They are ranked with the world's finest. Among them: *Marqués de Murietta, Marqués de Riscal,* and the white *Monopol.* And you cannot go far wrong if you order any red wine from the *Rioja* region. Meals are to be savored, not hurried; count on two hours at least.

Though he or she might not drink it, your Spanish guest will be flattered if you order a *DYC* whiskey for your aperitif: not as good as a Scotch, but close to it. And if you fancy a brandy, try one of the Spanish best, a *Torres Imperial.* Even better, ask the wine waiter for his recommendation—and insist upon a Spanish distillation. After all, you can get a French cognac or armagnac anywhere.

▷ Spotlight ◁

Wine. Spain is one of the world's greatest producers of wines—and they remain one of the world's great bargains, given their quality. They are usually stronger and fuller-bodied than wines from other countries, because Spain enjoys more sun and heat than, say, its rival French producers in Bordeaux and Burgundy. Spain invented sherry (*jerez*), now imitated by other wine-producing countries. It makes a good, palate-clearing aperitif, and in Spain is usually served chilled. Again, though, be aware that sherry is high in alcoholic content.

Cabo Mayor, 11 Juan Hurtado de Mendoza. Tel.: 250-8776. A well-planned menu featuring dishes from the Cantabria region. Open until midnight; closed Sundays.

Carmencita, 16 Libertad. Tel.: 231-6612. A famous and typical Madrileñian restaurant serving classical dishes. Closed for Saturday lunch and on Sundays.

Club 31, 58 Alcala. Tel.: 231-0092. One of the best; Spanish and French cuisine, with fresh, seasonal products a specialty. It is closed on public holidays.

Horcher, 6 Alfonso XII. Tel.: 522-0731. Central European specialties have earned Horcher's an international reputation. Open until 11:30 p.m.; closed Sundays.

Jockey, 6 Amador de los Rios. Tel.: 419-0310. One of the greats. Superb service and decor. Open until midnight. Closed Sundays, holidays.

La Dorada, 64-66 Orense. Tel.: 270-2004. High-quality seafood, salted and dried fish, and stews. Open until midnight; closed Sundays.

Sacha, 11 Juan Ramon Jimenez. Tel.: 457-5952. Catalán cuisine, which means plenty of tasty fish and piquant stews. A place in which to eat extremely well and be pampered by solicitous service. Closed Sundays and holidays.

▷ Spotlight ◁

Tapas bars. If your stomach can't wait for a late lunch or dinner, join the Madrileños (and Madrileñas) at a tapas bar. *Tapas* is the generic term for a huge selection of dishes, hot and cold—in the more ambitious places, up to a hundred—that are served in tiny portions. But they add up, so if you are going on to a meal, resist the temptation of gorging. Tapas bars are everywhere. Some offer music on the menu, often a group playing and singing the gypsy music of Andalusia, the flamenco. If you've enjoyed it, or even if you haven't, drop a few pesetas into the high-crowned, wide-brimmed hat when it's passed around.

▷ Tipping

Most people render services without expecting a tip. Moderate tips (5 percent of the bill) are greatly appreciated. Airport porters have fixed fees and don't expect a tip on top; neither do cabdrivers on the metered amount. Give hotel doormen between 100 and 200 pesetas, a concierge 1,000 pesetas at the end of your stay. Restaurant checks include a service charge; add 5 percent if you are happy.

▷ Doing Business

Don't think that Spain's somewhat eccentric business day is the result of laziness. Traditionally, government employees have held down two or even three jobs so as to make ends meet financially. So have many bank workers (they voted recently against "European" hours of opening). Here's a checklist of current business hours:

Banks. Open weekdays from 9:00 a.m. to 2:00 p.m. and on Saturdays from 9:00 a.m. until 1:00 p.m.

Businesses. Usually from 9:00 a.m. to 2:00 p.m. and from 4:30 to 7:30 p.m. International firms: 9:00 a.m. to 5:30 p.m., with an hour for lunch.

Lunches are becoming shorter—say, 2:00 to 4:00 p.m. Which, of course, is still long by standards elsewhere. Some foreigners advise that one should never mention business before the cigars arrive. A top Spanish marketing man counsels visitors to wait at least until the second course. All experts agree that the first lunch or dinner with a potential partner or client is largely introductory. Afterward, contacts and deals can be less formal, and done by phone, telex, and telefax.

Until recently, Spanish business executives were coy about their companies' sales and profits. More and more are coming out of the financial closet, impelled in part by their need to raise capital in the international money markets and to tap loans from banks that demand full disclosure. Many medium-sized Spanish companies need also to find merger partners if they are to prosper after Europe becomes a single market in the 1990s.

Gone—or at least going—are the days when Spanish companies kept three sets of books: one for the tax authorities, one for the shareholders, and one for the directors—that being the set that showed the company's true position. All the major international accounting and auditing companies have offices or associate partnerships in Madrid, and all are very good sources of up-to-the-minute information about the Spanish economy, both macroeconomic and by sector.

So what does Spain need from the rest of the world? Technology is high on the list. The country has a skilled and energetic labor force—and unemployment. Government ministers, civil servants, and forward-looking business executives all agree that Spain's future lies in its being able to add high value to raw material inputs rather than being a low-cost, low-wage producer of low-technology goods. Spain is looking also for foreign investment in a wide variety of business sectors, including tourism. With more than 40 million tourists each year, it is second only to the United States as a vacation destination.

Who you know is more important in Madrid than in many other business centers. *The* place at which movers and shakers congregate is the *Club Financiero Genova,* 14 Marqués de la Ensenada. Tel.: 410-4900. The style is that of a London gentlemen's club—plus such extras as rooftop pool and golf putting links. Below this fourteenth-floor haven are an apartment hotel, a sauna, more swimming, squash courts, a library, and meeting rooms. The club really is a club: members only. However, the Financiero has reciprocal arrangements with, among others, the East India Club, London; the Baur au Lac, Zurich; Gremio Literario, Lisbon; the Royal Bachelors, Stockholm; and many clubs in Latin America. And your Madrid business contact almost certainly will be able to arrange temporary membership for you. The best temporary office space: Lynx, International Business Center, Paseo de Recoletos 4. Tel.: 542-7039. Fax: 542-7306.

Some 50 of Spain's leading industrial and financial groups (aerospace, banking, construction, electronics, insurance, nuclear, oil, public services, telecommunications, and other sectors) are profiled in the *Spanish Company Handbook,* available from the International Herald Tribune, 181 Ave. Charles de Gaulle, 92521, Neuilly Cedex, France (Tel.: 4637-

9396), or locally through La Ley SA, Goya 15, Madrid 28001 (Tel.: 431-5479, Fax: 276-3492). The handbook contains industry-by-industry evaluations and phone numbers of a wide range of ministries, trade federations, and ports. A practical dictionary of financial and business terminology is a bonus.

Madrid is building new fairgrounds close to the airport. Planned for 1990, they will offer twice the space currently available at the Casa del Campo site. Heading the project is the city/government body, *Refemasa* (Tel.: 435-8765). Major Madrid fairs include *Fitur* (tourism), *Los Cibeles* (fashion), *Simo* (office equipment), *Tecnova* (do-it-yourself), and *Arco* (contemporary art).

▷ Useful Phone Numbers

Emergencies

Lost property	441-0214
Medical	734-2600
	734-5500
Police	091 or 092

Local Information

Highway conditions	445-7222
Municipal information	266-4874
Airport flight information	205-4372
Automobile Club	447-3200
City Center	429-4951
PTT telegraph	221-4004
Renfe (railways)	733-2200
Security/passports	410-3521
Tourist information	205-8656

Government

Commerce, State secretariat	458-8664
Economy, State secretariat	468-2000

Ministries

Labor	253-6000
Industry, energy	458-8010
Transport	456-1144

Administration

Customs	254-3200
Foreign Trade	458-0016
Investments	458-0016
Small Business Institute	450-8048

Madrid Community (region)

Employment	410-5092
Industry, energy	402-5150
Labor, commerce	419-8048
Technology park	803-3550
High council, chambers of commerce	275-2303
IMADE (foreign investment)	410-2063
Madrid chamber of commerce	429-3193

Convention bureau	463-6334	Iraq	455-5528
Stock exchange	521-4790	Ireland	276-3500
Town hall	242-5819	Italy	402-5436
European Community	435-1700	Ivory Coast	261-1607
		Japan	262-5546

Consulates and Embassies

		Jordan	419-1100
Algeria	411-6065	Korea (South)	410-0439
Argentina	442-4500	Kuwait	450-2900
Australia	279-8504	Lebanon	457-1368
Austria	456-5315	Libya	458-0458
Belgium	401-9558	Mexico	456-1263
Bolivia	270-9858	Morocco	458-0950
Brazil	270-9858	Nicaragua	456-6216
Cameroon	458-7423	Nigeria	458-0650
Canada	431-4300	Norway	401-6262
Chile	431-9160	Malta	262-1200
China (People's Republic)	413-4889	Netherlands	458-2100
		Pakistan	431-5441
Costa Rica	441-6767	Panama	276-2747
Cuba	458-2500	Paraguay	435-8858
Denmark	431-8445	Peru	431-4242
Ecuador	262-7215	Philippines	419-5962
Egypt	401-9600	Poland	209-1605
El Salvador	262-8002	Portugal	261-7800
Finland	419-6172	Qatar	418-8400
France	435-5560	Romania	250-4436
Gabon	279-9740	Soviet Union	262-2264
Germany (West)	419-9100	Sweden	419-7550
Greece	411-3345	Syria	239-8558
Guatemala	457-7827	Thailand	250-3872
Haiti	410-0055	Tunisia	447-3508
Honduras	279-0251	Turkey	419-5554
Hungary	413-7011	United Arab Emirates	270-1004
India	413-6161	United Kingdom	419-0200
Indonesia	458-0668	United States	276-3600
Iran	457-0112	Uruguay	248-7035

Venezuela	455-8455	Kuwait Air Ways	242-0317
Yugoslavia	262-8292	LAN-Chile	247-6433
Zaire	262-4710	LAP (Paraguay)	241-4975
		LOT Polish Airlines	248-1373

Airlines

		Lufthansa German Airlines	247-1905
Aer Lingus (Ireland)	241-4216		
Aerolineas Argentinas	247-4700	Pan Am World Airways	248-8535
Aeroflot Soviet Airlines	241-9934	Philippine Airlines	242-3711
Aeromexico	247-9900	Pakistan International Airlines	248-1241
Air Algerie	242-0801		
Air France	247-2000	Qantas Airways (Australia)	241-9736
Air India	248-9897	Royal Air Maroc	247-7905
Alia Royal Jordanian	247-9436	Sabena Belgian World Airlines	241-4809
Alitalia	247-4603		
Austrian Airlines	247-1600	SAS Scandinavian Airlines	247-6936
Avianca (Colombia)	247-9626		
British Airways	248-7801	South African Airways	205-4108
Cubana Airlines	242-2923	Swissair	247-9207
Egyptair	221-3406	TAP Air Portugal	242-0000
Finnair	247-0778	TWA	248-0004
Iberia (Spain)	411-2011	Varig (Brazil)	242-0208
Iraqi Airways	445-7908	Viasa (Venezuela)	242-3716
Japan Air Lines/JAL	248-8126	Yugoslav Airlines/JAT	247-9715
KLM Royal Dutch Airlines	241-8807		

▷ Shopping

Spain is famous for its high-quality leather goods, such as shoes, coats, and luggage. Many come from craftworkers following a centuries-old tradition. Keep an eye out also for jewelry. Designs are imaginative, and quality can be superb. Do *not* be tempted, though, by brand-name bargains hawked on the streets; those cut-price Lacoste shirts at the Goya subway station are counterfeits. So are what appear to be Rolex or Cartier watches sold from stalls.

The Salamanca district, east of Castellana, is packed with the main boutiques for men and women, the key streets being Serrano and Velazquez.

Adolfo Dominguez, creator of a line that has renovated Spanish fashion, has several boutiques, notably at 4 Ortega y Gasset and 98 Serrano. *Loewe,* at 26 Serrano, is famous for its classic leather goods and recently moved into women's ready-to-wear. *Multicentro Serrano,* 88 Serrano, has 30 shops for men and women. Two large department stores, *El Corte Ingles* and *Galerias Preciados,* offer discounts. Most shops will also arrange for value-added tax (in effect, a sales tax) to be refunded to visitors living outside the European Community.

The Gran Via and Almirante neighborhoods are less chic than Salamanca, but increasingly are the home of new fashion stores. For men's and women's clothes, try *Jesus de Poszo, Ararat,* and *Enrique P.,* all on Almirante. Another "in" boutique is *Francis Montesinos,* 8 Argensola.

There are some marvelous jewelry stores and silversmiths in and around *Calle de Zaragoza,* near the Plaza Mayor. Among the best: *La Onza de Oro, Agrufia,* and *Perez Fernandez.*

Engravings and lithographs are sold on Saturday mornings under the Plaza Mayor arches. Don't pay the first price asked; vendors enjoy a bit of skillful haggling.

▷ After Hours

Madrid's night life is sparkling and varied, and continues into the wee hours. As one veteran put it, "I can stand late nights and early mornings, but in Madrid I have early mornings and early mornings." Best to arrive and depart by taxi. As we have noted, street crime thrives in some of the neighborhoods.

Arco de Cuchilleros Flamenco Club, 7 Arco de Cuchilleros. Good, authentic flamenco acts.

Café Central, 10 Plaza del Angel. Jazz, folk, classical, and South American music. Popular with "alternative" types. Must reserve. Tel.: 468-0844.

Café de Chinitas Flamenco Club, 7 Calle Torija. Top flamenco spot (with prices to match). Good food. Must reserve. Tel.: 248-5135.

Clamores Jazz Club, 14 Calle Albuquerque. Famous for excellent music—and equally excellent champagne cocktails. Best to reserve. Tel.: 445-7938.

Corral de la Moreria, 17 Moreria. This is the real flamenco dancing, with a superb, 90-minute show. Reserve well in advance. Tel.: 265-8446.

La Fidula, 57 Calle Huertas. Live classical music, usually soloists and chamber music quartets. Attracts young professionals and university academics. Tel.: 429-2957.

Whiskey Jazz Club, 7 Calle de Diego de León. Located in the elegant Salamanca area, the Whiskey is popular with fans of traditional jazz. Tel.: 261-1165.

DISCOS

Joy Eslava, 11 Calle Arenal. Tel.: 266-3733. Madrid's most opulent disco. Latest international and Spanish hits and live acts.

Oba-Oba, 4 Calle Jacometrezo. Just off the Gran Via. Brazilian music until dawn, with live salsa Caribbean bands on weekends. Lots of rum and fruit juice concoctions.

Pacha, 11 Calle Barcelo. Tel.: 446-0137. The capital's hippest disco, much frequented by local and visiting celebs.

▷ Sights and Sounds

The Prado. Not to be missed by anyone with an eye for painting is the Prado, which houses one of the world's finest collections, with strong emphasis on Spanish artists and those who have made Spain their own—with El Greco well represented. The Prado is almost next door to the Ritz and three minutes' walk from the Palace. Madrid offers humbler pleasures as well:

City strolling. Sunday morning in the *Rastro* flea market can lead the observant buyer to a painting, a Gothic statue, a piece of furniture, or a bullfighter's "suit of lights." A famous Sunday morning attraction is the stamp and coin market under the historic arcades of the *Plaza Mayor.* Another choice Sunday spot is the *Casa de Campo,* a huge park across the Manzanares from the Royal Palace. Boats cruise the lake, and there are also a zoo and an amusement park.

City sport. *Bullfights* are held on Sunday afternoons at the big ring in the *Plaza Monumental de las Ventas* from early spring until the middle of fall. In the summer, if you don't want to be blinded by the cruel sun of central Spain and swelter in the heat, try to get tickets for the shady side of the ring: they're more expensive, but worth the extra.

Real Madrid, the renowned soccer club, plays at the *Estadio Santiago Bernabeu* on Castellana, in the city center.

Outskirts. *Horse racing* takes place at the *Hipodromo de la Zarzuela,* near the Puerta de Hierro.

For *golf,* try the *Real Club de Puerta de Hierro* or the *Real Sociedad Hipica Espanola.* There are other fine courses near the city. Details are available from the Spanish Golf Federation, Capitan Haya 9, Madrid. Tel.: 455-2682.

▷ Out of Town

The *Costa del Sol,* sunniest (and hottest) of Spain's many coasts, is a one-hour flight, with Malaga the airport. Much of the coast's previous charm has been spoiled by the real estate boom. The millionaires' enclave, *Marbella,* has become the residence of Arab sheikhs, international businessmen, and arms dealers. Notorious British criminals have also chosen the golden mile for their enforced exile and are relatively safe from the law, thanks to a loophole in the Anglo-Spanish extradition treaty.

Hotel Byblos at Mijas, behind the coastal resort of Fuengirola, has superb, Moorish-style architecture, fountains, a French seawater cure establishment, and its own golf course (there are many more courses in the region). Tel.: (52) 460250.

Winter skiing. This can be found only 50 kilometers (30 miles) from Madrid at *Sierra of Guararrama* and the *Navacerrada* ski center. Good road and rail connections (station: Navacerrada). Most travel agents offer attractive ski packages.

MILAN
Italy's Economic Powerhouse

Population: Milan and suburbs: 3.9 million. Province of Milan: 16 million. Capital of Lombardy and of Milano province; (financial and commercial center of Italy. *Location:* northern Italy, near a pass through the Alps. *Economy:* banking and financial services; automotive products; chemicals; electrical engineering and electronics; fashion and textiles; machinery; a leading conference and trade-fair center. Italy is a member of the European Community (EC) and the Organization for Economic Cooperation and Development (OECD) and is a signatory to the General Agreement on Tariffs and Trade (GATT).

▷ Background Briefing

Italy, ah, Italy! Land of smiling, singing gondoliers and waiters; carefree, flashing-eyed, flirtatious girls; and a great many other characters straight out of Central Casting. Milan is the other Italy, the country's Frankfurt or Zurich, even its Chicago. Milan is dedicated to commerce and industry, a proud city that is the unofficial capital of the financial-manufacturing complex that has helped to make Italy a leading industrial power.

Milan is thus the nexus of economic influence, where old money and new meet; where wheeler-dealers wheedle money out of banks, stock-market players (and each other), where today's *condottieri* (renaissance mercenaries) lay the foundations of fortunes that tomorrow will make them acceptable socially—for Milanese patricians, though a starchy lot, admire greatly a self-made man who has acquired manners and grace as well as wealth. Why not? After all, what were their ancestors except *condottieri* with deep pockets and persuasive biographers?

Ambrose, the city's patron saint, set the serious tone in the 300s A.D. in his role as governor of Liguria and Aemilia, with Milan as their capital. A superb administrator, and a very firm one, Saint Ambrose saw no inherent conflict between religious duty and temporal power, or if he did was not unduly worried. The great Milanese families of Visconti and Sforza and their successors in the Middle Ages clearly believed that the storing up of earthly riches was no obstacle to their achieving a credit balance in heaven.

To be on the safe side, though, the great Milanese families built churches and laid their dead to rest in cemeteries of remarkable opulence—indeed, of remarkable vulgarity in the eyes of some visitors. Ancestry still counts for much in Milan. The Milanese have a phrase for the venerable families: *Salotto Buono.* This can mean, variously, "Old Guard," "Old Drawing Room," or, in a word, "Establishment."

▷ *Spotlight* ◁

Monumentale cemetery. Sheer weight of money and the strength of family ties are to be seen in the Monumentale cemetery, which ranks with Paris's Pere Lachaise as the most incredible resting place in Europe. It's the ultimate—literally and figuratively—in bourgeois burial. A tomb in the Monumentale, a small box at the Quartetto musical society, and a family place in the country—those are the visible signs of old money.

No institution is more establishment than *Mediobanca,* the merchant bank that controls a web of corporate and banking cross-holdings. Generally agreed to be the prime mover in Mediobanca's affairs is the Agnelli family. The Agnellis run not only Fiat, the country's sole major automotive manufacturer, but also a network of lesser-though-still-mighty enterprises, including *La Stampa,* if not Milan's leading daily newspaper, *Corriere della Sera.* The Agnellis have what the Italians call *strapotere,* or all-encompassing power. But they're not the only ones.

Though ancestry still counts for much in Milan, nimble-footedness counts for even more. Milan is renowned for entrepreneurs who create or seize opportunities zestfully—not just in Italy, but all over Europe and, indeed, the world. Whether in banking, manufacturing, services, or financial dealing, the Milanese look outward for new markets and new ways to make money.

▷ *Spotlight* ◁

Rome vs. Milan. For the visitor drawn into the Rome vs. Milan debate: the Romans resent the attitude of superiority they think the Milanese have toward them. There's a tendency to think of the Milanese as rather stupid for working so hard and not relaxing, *alla romana*. The Milanese, in turn, resent having to carry much of the financial weight of all those Roman bureaucrats. The Milanese can be terribly presumptuous, in Roman eyes, about how much more efficient they are than people to the south, when the difference isn't really all that great. As the Romans say, "When all is said and done, they are still Italians." True—but with strong Germanic and American streaks.

▷ Arriving

By Air

As airports go, Milan's *Linate* isn't bad—physically. Getting in or out is another story. The Alps, immediately to the north, mean clouds for most of the year and often fog. Sometimes the weather blocks flights for days. When that happens, aircraft use *Malpensa,* more than an hour's drive away, or *Genoa,* much further. Even when the weather is good, internal flights—to Rome every half-hour at peak times—are often delayed for several hours. Add to the weather the occasional wildcat strikes, and what does one have? A mess.

Before flying to Milan, the traveler already in Europe (or even on another continent) will be prudent to check conditions. If they're bad, time may be saved by flying to Rome, Paris, or Zurich and going by train to Milan.

On the plus side (yes, there is one), baggage retrieval is usually rapid; the restaurant is goodish, if not good; and Linate airport is only 10 kilometers (just over 6 miles) from the city center, about 20 minutes drive. Cabs are abundant, except on weekends, and drivers pride themselves on their honesty and knowledge of the city, though not, alas, on their knowledge of alien tongues.

By Rail

Milan is easily accessible by rail from other cities in Italy and throughout Europe. Your travel agent can help with the itinerary.

By Car

Speed limits on Italian highways vary with the season or the day, depending on the amount of traffic, and parking in the cities is a real problem. In Milan, part of the city center is closed to traffic.

▷ Money

The basic (and only) unit of currency is the lira. International code: ITL. Colorful banknotes come in denominations of 1,000, 2,000, 5,000, 10,000, 50,000, and 100,000 lire. (You feel rich carrying all that money until you find out that a beer from a street vendor costs 1,000 lire!) The commonest coins are 50, 100, 200, and 500 lire. Coins are always scarce; hold on to them for phone calls. Change money and travelers' checks at banks if you can—and always avoid street-corner moneychangers.

There has been talk in recent years of revaluing the currency by knocking off a couple zeroes, but it will probably be a while before such a change is made.

▷ Language

Italian—but there is a Milanese dialect. In a large city heavily reliant upon foreign trade and the international fashion business, the Milanese are surprisingly weak in English and other languages. However, they're tolerant of mangled Italian, so try to learn a few key phrases before you arrive. You may also want to carry a pocket phrasebook for solo forays in public.

▷ Communications

Country code: 39. City code: 2 (not needed within the city). Service is dreadful. As one executive put it, "Italy is a rich, industrialized country with Nigerian telecommunications and postal systems." Unfair to Nigeria. Despairing of the government's will or ability to solve the problem, some major companies have set up their own telecom networks. The postal service is almost totally unreliable. The corporate response has been to turn to private mail carriers.

▷ Getting To Know the City

The *Piazza del Duomo,* or Cathedral Square, is the core of Milan, a short walk from the famous La Scala opera house, the financial district, the smart shopping area, and arcades and galleries of boutiques. Shopping in the center rivals that in Paris and London.

Close to the Cathedral neighborhood is the distinctly different area surrounding the *Piazza della Repubblica,* with a concentration of such leading hotels as the Principe and Palace. Just beyond is the main railroad station.

A third area, again not too far from the center, is the canal district. For centuries, a network of canals served Milan, and the docks were still working in the 1950s. Most of the network is now dry and covered, but some canals remain and the area, *La Zona dei Navigli,* is full of students, artists, craftworkers, designers, good bars and restaurants—and lots of jazz.

Downtown today is also fashion, a business worth about a billion dollars a year; design, particularly of furniture and consumer products; advertising, with no fewer than 683 agencies; and *Italtel,* the telecom company, which has been run by a woman, the late Marisa Bellisario, once called "the Italian Mrs. Thatcher."

▷ Moving Around

Much of business Milan is within walking distance of the Cathedral—except during the torrid summer or frigid winter. Taxis are fast because in most important streets, they use lanes reserved for them.

Mass transit systems are good. There is a subway, the *Metropolitana Milanese* (MM), and on the surface there are buses and streetcars. The Metro is basically an east-west system that includes the main railroad station, the San Babila stop (with its bus connection to Linate airport), the *Duomo* (Cathedral), Cordusio (for the financial district), and the fairgrounds. You can buy metro, bus, and streetcar tickets at cigar stores or by playing the slots at stations with 100- and 200-lire coins.

▷ Hotels

Milan's best hotels are very much attuned to the business traveler; unlike Rome, the city isn't a major tourist attraction. All the hotels listed either have secretarial and translation services on the premises, or can arrange for them. Always reserve well in advance if you can: Milan is a city of trade fairs and conferences. Top of the tops:

Admiral, Villa Domodossola 16. Tel.: 349-2151. No telex. Fax: 349-8434. Rooms/suites: 60. Well placed for people attending trade fairs: it's right opposite the main fairground gates.

Antares Hotel Concorde, Viale Monza 132. Tel.: 289-58853. Telex: 315805. Fax: 656802. Room/suites: 84. One of the city's two Best Western Antares hotels (the other is near the fairground); modern comforts and satellite TV; excellent public transportation.

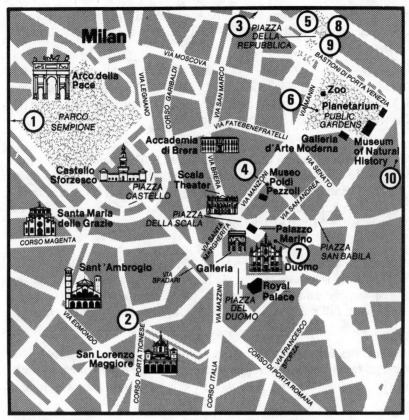

1. Fairgrounds
2. Hotel Pierre
3. Main Station, Hotel Hilton
4. Grand Hotel
5. Hotel Palace

6. Hotel Manin
7. Hotel Grand Duomo
8. Hotel Principe di Savoia
9. Hotel Duca di Milano
10. Hotel Diane Majestic

Diane Majestic, Viale Piave 42. Tel.: 203404. Telex: 333047. Fax: 276072. Rooms/suites: 94. Run by the Ciga chain, this hotel is first class without being deluxe. Most rooms look onto the private garden—important in noisy Milan.

Duca di Milano, Piazza Repubblica 13. Tel.: 6284. Telex: 325026. Fax: 6555966. Rooms/suites: 60. Most of the accommodation consists of suites with working salons for businesspeople. This prestigious hotel provides a range of business services—and facilities at the Monticello Golf Club.

Grand Duomo, Via San Raffaele 1. Tel.: 8833. Telex: 312086. Fax: 872752. Rooms/suites: 161. This is the place if you want to be near the Cathedral; executive suites look out on it.

Grand Hotel de Milan, Via Manzoni 29. Tel.: 870757. Telex: 334505. Fax: 872526. Rooms/suites: 102. Originally famous because opera composer Giuseppe Verdi lived and received homage here. Now a favorite with the cinema, theater, and fashion set, and with the harried people who do business at the MIFED television market.

Hilton International, Via Galvani 12. Tel.: 69831. Telex: 330433. Fax: 6071904. Rooms/suites: 339. In the heart of the business section, by the central station, and also convenient for Linate international airport. Smart, with full business services, including free use of a typewriter.

Hotel des Iles Borromees, Stresa, Lake Maggiore. Tel.: (0323) 30431. No telex, no fax. Rooms: 115. Suites: 56. Easy to reach by rail or car. A magnificent establishment for meetings; superb health and sports facilities.

Manin, Via Manin 7. Tel.: 659-6511. Telex: 320385. Fax: 655-2160. Rooms/suites: 110. Comfortable and calm, so important for business travelers; rooms on a courtyard. Restaurant, bar. Within a block of La Scala.

Monte Bianco, Viale Monte Rosa 90. Tel.: 4697941. Fax: 490658. Rooms/suites: 44. Next to the fairgrounds and accustomed to business needs; try for a room on the courtyard.

Palace, Piazza della Repubblica 20. Tel.: 6336. Telex: 311026. Fax: 654485. Rooms: 173. Suites: 10. Modern, with excellent restaurants, piano bar, medical care, roof garden. Cigahotels jet rentals.

Pierre, Via de Amicis 32. Tel.: 805-6220. Telex: 333334. Fax: 805-2157. Rooms/suites: 47. New, calm, and *avant garde,* with electronic message system and lots of remote-control gadgetry.

Principe di Savoia, Piazza della Repubblica 29. Tel.: 6230. Telex: 310052. Fax: 6595838. Rooms: 271. Suites: 18. Elegant, efficient; outdoor summer restaurant, *La Bella Fontana.* Very chic bar scene during the fashion fairs. Cigahotels Business Club privileges: double room for the price of a single, reduced-price limousines, access to the exclusive Monticello Golf Club (pool, gym, restaurant, disco, and, almost as an afterthought, 36 holes).

▷ Restaurants

There's no such thing as "Italian" cuisine. There is, rather, a family of cuisines. Milan has its own dishes, so does Lombardy. Both are richer, heavier, and more varied than typical fare found further south, for the north has long been rich—and local ingredients and relative wealth are among the historical determinants of cuisine. Milanese cuisine also reflects the Germanic influence of nearby Switzerland and Austria.

Milan's restaurants offer the full range of Italian food, and these are among the best. Note, however, that many restaurants are closed on Sundays.

Al Porto, Piazza Candore. Tel.: 832-1481. Family-run restaurant offers fish so fresh, they would jump off the plate if they hadn't been cooked. Closed Sundays.

Antica Brasera Meneghina, Via Circo 10. Tel.: 580-8108. Ancient (dates from 1672), popular with a wide range of Milanese; full range also of Lombardy specialties.

Aurora, Via Savona 23. Tel.: 835-4978. City's most famous Piedmontese restaurant, featuring truffles and porcini mushrooms.

Bagutta, Via Bagutta 14. Tel.: 702-2767. Arty and popular, famous for offering its own literary prize as well as delectable food.

Berlin Café, Via G.G. Mora 9. Tel.: 839-4336. Milan tends to be deserted on Sundays, but here the stranded visitor can find friendly faces and an interesting, Italian-style brunch.

Biffi Scala, Via Filodramatici 2. Tel.: 876332. The Biffi, part of the world-renowned La Scala opera house, is a "monument" with a famous terrace. International and Milanese cuisine. Reservations recommended. Closed Sundays.

Don Lisander, Via Manzoni 12a. Tel.: 790130. Salmon, *chicchi alla crema di pomodoro* (literally, "grain with tomato cream") and many other delicacies. The most beautiful restaurant garden in Milan.

Giannino, Via A Sciesa 8. Tel.: 545948. Grand yet friendly. Everyone, or so it seems, has eaten in the great dining halls with beams: artists, politicians, Hollywood stars, and a few kings.

Gualtiero Marchesi, Via Bonvesin de la Riva 9. Tel.: 741246. *La nuova cucina (nouvelle cuisine)* here—which in some other places translates into half the normal portion for twice the money. Not here. Expensive, to be sure, but not because the kitchen is skimping; rather, because food, preparation, cooking, and presentation are impeccable.

Savini, Galleria Vittorio Emanuele 11, 16. Tel.: 8058343. This ancient establishment (1867) is very much back in favor with prominent Milanese businessmen and attracts an elegant post-Scala evening crowd. The winter garden opens onto the gallery. The chandeliered dining room inside is imposing. Traditional northern Italian dishes a specialty. Reservations are now essential—as even the Aga Khan discovered. Closed Sundays.

Stendhal/Café Stendhal, Vias San Marco and Ancona. Tel.: 655-5587. New, but looks to the past with imported French woodwork. A favorite with the fashion and theater crowd.

Suntory, Via Verdi 6. Tel.: 869-3022. Best Japanese restaurant in town, with memorable tempura and sukiyaki.

Un Altro Malstrana, Via Solferino 12. Tel.: 655-9672. Soft lights, pink linen, modern art, tasty but light food. The fashion and financial worlds meet here.

▷ Tipping

Largesse for the staff is included in hotel and restaurant bills—but, of course, you can always add a few hundred lire. Hatcheck attendants in top hotels and restaurants expect a tip of not less than 8,000 lire—which sounds a lot, but really isn't.

▷ Doing Business

Milan has been a business and banking center for centuries. In banking, indeed, it was an early innovator: Lombard Street in London is now a generic term for the British money market. That commemoration of Lombardy's (and Milan's) enterprise symbolizes the city's outward-looking bent. This has helped it to become a business and financial center that is disproportionately influential and prominent, given its size. The television, media, and advertising power of Milan is personified by the tycoon Silvio Berlusconi.

Helping Milan to achieve a prominence beyond that based on the clout of the big industrial and financial families have been two rather recent developments. One is the result of sheer entrepreneurial energy and specialized talent: Milan's rise as a fashion center. The fashion Big Six are Georgio Armani, Laura Biagotti, Gianfranco Ferre, Mariuccia Mandelli, Franco Moschino, and Gianni Versace. One fashion writer, gushing no doubt, claims that the Big Six "live like royalty, earn like corporate raiders, and roam the globe with the influence of diplomats." The second development, of a more cooperative and official nature, is Milan's energetic growth as a trade fair and conference center.

Visitors to the 80 trade fairs held each year see, among other things, the best of Italian products. But they can see much else.

▷ Spotlight ◁

Eighty fairs a year —with no fewer than 22 of them in each November alone. Many sell Italy and Italian products to the world, others are international in scope.

In October, MIFED brings together makers, buyers, and sellers of movies and television programs. Industry leaders debate such hot issues as video piracy, protection of authors' and producers' rights, and international coproductions. MIFED is held at the original fairgrounds on the edge of the city, *Fiero Milano*, Largo Domodossola 1.

South of Milan is *Il Girasole* ("The Sunflower") fairground, hub of the new commercial center at Lacciarella, known as the City of Fashion. That's where buyers from many countries look at the latest ready-to-wear clothes and accessories.

Among other important shows: home furnishing; gardening equipment; leather goods; food, drink, and catering; franchising; textile technology; do-it-yourself gadgetry; chemical and medical equipment; motorcycles and scooters. The BIT travel show is second only to West Berlin's. On display are "products" in the form of tourist destinations.

April is the month of the *Great Milan Fair*, "mother" of all the others. It usually attracts more than 3,000 exhibitors and a million visitors.

For information about the many shows, consult the English-language guide to Milanese events, *What's On In Milan*, published monthly. Editor: Marina Borri. Address: Piazza San Simpliciano 7. Tel.: 870078.

Milan rivals Paris as a fashion capital, so it's no surprise that people take much care over their appearance. That having been said, they do not indulge in conspicuous consumption. Though they spend heavily on clothes, as shown in winter by the large number of fur coats, their style is conservative. Currently, this often means dressing like an English gentleman: dark suits and striped shirts in the financial sector, dark trousers, striped or check shirts and hard-wearing brogue shoes in the other businesses.

People put a premium on punctuality and a brisk, though polite, coming to the point. Milanese businesspeople appreciate being invited to lunch but are equally willing to pick up the check. Most are moderate drinkers, often accompanying both lunch and dinner with sparkling mineral water. Particularly at lunch, cocktails are a rarity. When wine is consumed, it's usually a white in summer and a red in other seasons, with Piedmontese or Tuscan wines preferred.

More than 7,400 U.S. companies are in the Italian market. The only guide covering them is the *American Chamber of Commerce in Italy Directory* available from the Chamber, Via C. Cantu 1, 20123 Milan, Tel.: 8690661.

▷ Spotlight ◁

Money talks in Milan just as it does in the city the Milanese most admire, New York. Old money, however, still controls the city's most exclusive club for business and society leaders, the *Circolo dell'Unione* (Union Club), Via Borgonuovo 11. Tel.: 869-2569. Founded by aristocrats in the late 1800s, the Unione's membership is still restricted to 450. The club president decides whether guests may be admitted. Contact Dr. Vincenzo de Vera, Cigahotels. Tel.: 62661.

▷ Useful Phone Numbers

Emergencies	113	Local Information	
All-night pharmacy	192	Central post office	869-0735
Ambulance	7733	Highway conditions	7740-2974
Fire	3190	Hotel reservations	706095
Police	62261	International Business	
Red Cross	3883	Center	545-6331

Public transportation information	875495
Radio taxi	8388/6767/8585
Stock exchange	853-4650
Telex (open night and day)	877628
Tourism	809662

Business Information

EC office	801505
Lombardy Trade Board	88231
Milan Chamber of Commerce	85151
Milan trade fairs	49971
Industry federations	
Building	6571861
Chemicals	63621
FAI (Federazione Associazioni Industriali)	324846
Leather, skins	7750
Machinery	8242101
Office machinery/ electronics	878941/32641
Pharmaceuticals	879087
Rubber	4988168
Textiles, clothing	8053536

Foreign Chambers of Commerce

African	483456
Arab	208225
Argentina	490571
Australia	659-8727
Austria	866168
Belgium	498-7647
Brazil	4396011
Canada	657-0451
Chile	864093
China (People's Republic)	862765
Cuba	670-2551
Czechoslovakia	220741
Denmark	498-5251
Egypt	860697
Ethiopia	436411
European Community	801505
Finland	545-6585
France	805-3890
Germany (East)	546-0016
Germany (West)	652651
Greece	670-2779
Hungary	498-4471
India	344945
Ireland	709068
Israel	873000
Japan	865546
Korea (South)	876806
Latin America	805-9373
Netherlands	498-0581
Poland	524-2241
Portugal	470659
Romania	581078
South Africa	433697
Soviet Union	670-5621
Spain	861137
Sweden	875666
Switzerland	794475
Tunisia	548-9096
Turkey	545-9227
United Kingdom	670-2870
United States	869-0661

Consulates

Argentina	864184
Australia	659-8727
Austria	481-2937
Bangladesh	869-0161
Belgium	659-0668
Bolivia	381-9127
Brazil	780851
Canada	657-0451
Chile	407-5976
China (People's Republic)	271-6469
Cyprus	289-6232
Colombia	879408
Costa Rica	784422
Denmark	498-1441
Ecuador	271-9603
Egypt	20129
France	794341
Germany (West)	655-4434
Greece	659-8624
Iran	805-5852
Israel	349-8606
Luxembourg	331-9162
Malta	659129
Mexico	790541
Morocco	669-3898
Netherlands	434557
Norway	801139
Portugal	650230
South Africa	809036
Soviet Union	404-6741
Spain	481-2337
Sweden	803688
Switzerland and Liechtenstein	795515

Tanzania	877857
Thailand	799846
Turkey	573370
United Kingdom	869-3442
United States	652841
Venezuela	654136
Zaire	864188

Airlines

Aer Lingus (Ireland)	783565
Aeroflot Soviet Airlines	655-9985
Aerolineas Argentinas	871957/805-8929
Air Afrique	657-2351
Air Algerie	873811
Air Canada	270829
Air France	77381
Air India	860565
Air Lanka	873428
Air Malta	867773
Air Zaire	864188
Alitalia	62811
American Airlines	655-7720
Austrian Airlines	807795
Avianca (Colombia)	809021
Balkan-Bulgarian Airlines	866671
Birmingham Executive Airways (UK)	271-0056
Brazilian Airlines	871533
British Airways	809041/809892
Canadian Pacific Air Lines	879121

Cathay Pacific Airways	805-0643	Middle East Airlines	545-6486
Cyprus Airways	545-5970	Olympic Airlines	802404
Czechoslovak Airlines/CSA	869-0246	Pakistan International Airlines	867773
Egyptair	865777	Pan Am World Airways	877241/877262
El Al Israel Airlines	866151	Philippine Airlines	872153
Ethiopian Airlines	805-6562	Qantas Airways	
Finnair	865568	(Australia)	807551
Garuda Indonesia Airways	809736	Royal Air Maroc	652418
Iberia (Spain)	8899/864244	Sabena Belgian World Airlines	876787
Interflug (East Germany)	805-2873	SAS Scandinavian Airlines	867541
Iran Air	879270	Saudi Arabian Airlines	877495
Iraqi Airways	860277	Singapore Airlines	780916
Japan Air Lines/JAL	869-0251	South African Airways	804779
KLM Royal Dutch Airlines	807846	Swissair	659-8341/655-9141
Kenya Airways	865865	TAP Air Portugal	809691
Korean Air	803320	Thai Airways	867541
Kuwait Air Ways	878190	Tunis Air	805-7753
Libyan Arab Airlines	870269/878120	Turk Hava Yollari	805-6233
Loftleider Icelandig	805-3031	TWA	77961
LOT Polish Airlines	805-5897	Varig (Brazil)	345-2151/878921
Lufthansa German Airlines	85581	Viasa (Venezuela)	875792
Malev Hungarian Airlines	872474	Yugoslav Airlines/JAT	866859

▷ Shopping

Expensive boutiques dot the streets of central Milan, particularly the vias *Manzoni* and *Montenapoleone;* both are synonymous with luxury. Of the newer, hotter streets (in fashion terms, that is) the best known is the *Via della Spiga,* crowded with boutiques bearing such famous names as *Gianfranco Ferre, Gianni Versace, Gian Marco Venturia, Krizia, Gio Moretti, Lancetti,* and *Spiga 31* (for sweaters by Umberto Ginocchietti). The shoe and leather stars are also on the Via della Spiga: *Prada, Gherardini,* and *Diego della Valle.*

For some discerning Milanese ladies, the rage is the *Naj-Oleari* boutique on Via Brera. The noted jewelers, *Bulgari* included, are on Via Montenapoleone. *Pellini,* on Via Moriggi, has jewelry from the 1940s and 1950s. *Era l'Ora,* on Via del Bollo, is for antique watches; art deco items can be found at *Roberta e Basta* or *Carlo Zonco* on Via Fiori Chiari.

The *Emporio Armani,* a temple to the great designer, is at Via Durini 23-24. A few doors away is the *Caffe-Moda-Durini,* a shopping center on three floors with 24 name boutiques. For high-quality furs in contemporary style try *Daylyne,* Via Manzoni 24.

You can, of course, buy the products of Milan's designers in many cities, so a good idea is to look at the products of lesser-known and therefore cheaper houses that cannot be found so easily elsewhere, if at all. Many of these firms are building their reputations for flair, quality, and workmanship. One place to try is *G. & C. Scalf,* Via Mercato.

Milanese businessmen tend to wear handmade shirts with monograms. One excellent address is *Vittorio Siniscalchi,* Via Gesu 8, where the craftsmanship is impeccable.

Shops that follow tradition may close between 1:00 and 4:00 p.m. but remain open until 7:30 or 8:00 p.m. Stores are usually closed on Sundays.

In a town where not everyone speaks a second language, it's good to know the location of those expatriate meeting places, the foreign book and newspaper stores: *Marco, Galleria Passarella,* on the Corso Vittorio Emanuele; *Algani, Galleria Vittorio Emanuele,* Piazza Scala; and the aptly named *American Bookstore,* Via Camperio 16.

▷ After Hours

Milan "lacks an Annabel's," lamented a well-traveled financial journalist, referring to the glitterati's favorite nightspot on London's Berkeley Square. Hmm...Annabel's isn't our favorite place, but we see what he means: Milan does lack wee-hours watering holes with international chic, so people who don't speak Italian may encounter various linguistic problems.

There are two distinct nocturnal areas: the fashionable *Brera* in the center, with what the smart Milanese call "pubs," and the more down-to-earth *naviglio* (canal district) on the southwest side of the city. Such as it is, here is Milan's nightlife:

Angelo Azzurro (Naviglio Grande), Ripa Porta Ticinese 11. Tel.: 350992. Live jazz some nights; very varied selection of drinks.

Biblos (Brera), Via Madonnina 17. Tel.: 805-1860. Guitarists play nostalgic Italian favorites, country and western, and pop rock. Friendly staff; English spoken.

Ca' Bianca Club (Naviglio Grande), Via Lodovico il Moro 117. Tel.: 813-5260. Members only—but you can join at the door. Chic, with live music, cabaret, international guest stars.

Cin Cin Bar, Via Felice Casati 45, near the Piazza Repubblica. Tel.: 650476. Vast range of stiff drinks; restaurant; piano; showbiz people tend to drop in after entertaining elsewhere.

Cristal (Naviglio Pavese), Via Ascanio Sforza 11. Tel.: 835-3951. A heady mixture of ice-cream parlor, beer hall, wine bar, and live classical music. Has to be seen and heard to be believed. Popular also for Sunday brunch.

El Brellin (Naviglio Grande), Vicolo Lavandai/14 Alzaia Naviglio Grande. Tel.: 835-1351. The after-the-theater crowd dines on Milanese cuisine while singers offer Italian and other tunes—hundreds of them. Sophisticated and pleasant.

Il Banco (Brera), Via Pontaccio. Tel.: 805-3083. The longest bar in town, with beer the main tipple. Very "in."

Il Patuscino (Brera), Via Madonnina 21. Tel.: 807264. Lots of live music with a little food—mainly macaroni and sauce. Friendly, English-language welcome.

Il Ragno (Brera), Via Madonnina 11. Tel.: 805-3643. Live music from visiting American, British, and Italian musicians, explained by the fact that one of the owners is a former pop star manager.

Scimmie (Naviglio Pavese), Via Ascanio Sforza 49. Tel.: 839-1874. Air-conditioned barge on the canal, one of the most popular joints in town. Full range of jazz, with some big-name groups. English is spoken—when it can be heard above the noise.

▷ Sights and Sounds

La Scala

A famous sound comes from La Scala. Fans like to think of themselves as the world's most knowledgeable operagoers. Perhaps they are. Certainly, any hopeful young singer or conductor who wins applause at La Scala and good notices from the critics will not be short of bookings thereafter. Conversely, when the La Scala audience erupts into noisy rage, as it does sometimes, the offending performer has a lot of explaining to do— though audiences can be fickle and wrong-headed.

Purchase of a ticket seven days before a performance is theoretically possible, but in practice is *im*possible. So how does the visitor from abroad obtain seats? The answer is long and complicated, so we'll put it in a box for those whose love of opera and determination to hear a performance are of equal strength.

▷ Spotlight ◁

Teatro alla Scala, the full name, is closed in the summer. Concerts are held in September, October, and November. December 7 is usually the start of the lyric season. Reservations start a week before each production. In the following cities, La Scala has agencies: Los Angeles (Tel.: 938-2821); Montreal (845-9101); New York (397-2666); Paris (266-0090); Zurich (221-2664). Elsewhere, check with the local Italian tourist office, CIT (*Compagnia Italiana Turistica*).

Art and Architecture

Milan is rich with art and architecture, and a mere skimming of the surface takes days.

Il Duomo, or Cathedral, is 600 years old, has 135 Gothic spires, and is one of the most remarkable ecclesiastical edifices in Europe. It is the third largest church in Europe, after St. Peter's in Rome and the cathedral in Seville. The cathedral museum, Piazza Duomo 14, tells the full story of its fourteenth-century origins and centuries of construction. Tel.: 860-3588.

Leonardo da Vinci's *The Last Supper,* recently restored, is in the refectory of the *Santa Maria delle Grazie* church and convent, Piazza delle Grazie 2. Tel.: 498-7588. Quite apart from this great painting, there is much to see in this cluster of conventual buildings.

The fifteenth-century *condottiero* (mercenary) Francesco Sforza built the *Castello Sforzesco* on the Piazza Castello. Tel.: 6208-3284. It has towers, courtyards, a moat and drawbridge—and a superb museum with Michelangelo's unfinished *Rondanini Pietà* probably its main attraction.

There's more art at the *Pinacoteca Ambrosiana,* Piazza Pio XI. It includes, notably, drawings by Raffaello and the only Caravaggio in Milan. Tel.: 800146. Milan's leading gallery is *Pinacoteca di Brera,* Via Brera 28. Tel.: 808387. The permanent collection of hundreds of masterpieces ranges in period from the 1300s to the present day. The *Museo Poldi Pezzoli,* Via Manzoni 12, is the mansion of a nineteenth-century collector turned into a museum. Tel.: 794889.

The Galleria

Between the Cathedral and La Scala is the *Galleria Vittorio Emanuele II:* glass-domed, elegant, with restaurants, cafés, and stores selling everything from books to silverware. Developers of shopping malls should see what good taste can achieve—and has been achieving for a very long time.

▷ Out of Town

The northern Italian lakes—Como, Garda, and Maggiore—are ringed with mountains and lined with historic towns, most with art collections. *Maggiore,* northwest of Milan, is the watery link with Switzerland and Locarno. *Stresa,* on the west bank, is a well-known health and watersports resort. *Garda* lies to the east of Milan on the way to Verona and Venice by direct *autostrada.*

Milan's favorite lake is *Como,* to the north, which can be reached by way of Bergamo, where many wealthy Milanese have villas. The lake's three sections meet at Bellagio, where you will find one of Italy's finest hotels, the *Grand Hotel Villa Serbelloni,* Via Roma 1. Tel.: (031) 950216. Telex: 380330. Rooms/suites: 82. Closed mid-October through mid-April. Here one can best enjoy the mild climate and leisurely life of the lakes. The hotel is set in a park, commands spectacular views of the lake and snow-capped mountains, and has a private beach. Golf is twenty minutes away at Grandola.

At Cernobbio, on Como's western shore, is the *Grand Hotel Villa d'Este.* Tel.: (031)511471. Telex: 380025. Rooms/suites: 182. Closed November through March. Once owned by royalty, the Villa d'Este is truly grand. On the veranda is a grillroom that serves enticing meals; in the hotel and grounds are many sports facilities.

Golf. Milan is a business city, golf is a business executives' game, and, *ecco!,* the city is surrounded by courses. Among them:

Parco di Monza, 15 kilometers (9 miles) away. Tel.: (039) 303081/2/3.

Barlassina, 22 kilometers (13.5 miles) from the city. Lentate sul Seveso Fraz Biargo. Tel.: (0362) 560621/23.

MOSCOW

Gorbachev's Crucible

Population: 7.9 million (1979; estimated). Political and administrative capital of the Union of Soviet Socialist Republics USSR, population 262.5 million. *Location*: west-central Russia on the Moskva river. *Economy*: automotive components and assembly; chemicals; clothing; electrical equipment and electronics; food processing; footwear; household appliances; paints and dyes; printing and publishing; movie and TV production; textiles; tourism; transportation. The Soviet Union is the dominant member of the Council for Mutual Economic Assistance (COMECON), the economic bloc of Communist states.

▷ Background Briefing

No city listed in this book is more in a state of flux than Moscow. After 70 years of relative political immobility, the great Soviet glacier is melting under the blowtorch of reform wielded by President Mikhail Gorbachev. Many Western observers question whether he will remain in power; others theorize that by melting the glacier he has unleashed forces that could sweep away the icefloes of communism and the Soviet empire itself.

Russian history has shown a pattern of seeking the future in models adapted alternately from its own Asiatic heritage or from Europe. The revolution of 1917 didn't end those cultural swings. Indeed, it's possible to argue that Vladimir Ilyich Lenin and Leon Trotsky, who had spent many years in European exile, represented a Westernizing influence, albeit a Marxist one, whereas their successor, Josef Stalin, clamped upon the Soviet Union an Asiatic view of the outside world: suspicious, cautious, byzantine.

After the great dictator's death in 1953, Nikita Krushchev softened some of the more totalitarian aspects of Stalinism and tried modest economic and political reforms, but even those were too much for the party apparatus. In a bloodless coup in 1964, Krushchev was ousted as Soviet leader by Leonid Brezhnev, who preferred economic and social stagnation to risky experiments. By the time he died in 1982, Brezhnev had perfected a system designed to keep the vast bureaucracy happy—or if not happy, at least docile.

At every level, from the lowest to the highest, carrots were dangled—and sticks wielded. The carrots ranged from minor privileges, such as subsidized vacations for some workers at Black Sea resorts, to luxuries such as chauffeur-driven limousines, *dachas* (country houses), and shopping at hard-currency stores for goods denied to all except the most powerful. The stick was withdrawal of such privileges and a kick off the career ladder—which was at least less bloody than Stalin's ruthless use of terror.

During the Brezhnev years and those of his immediate successors, graft and corruption were rife, both in Moscow and in the fiefdoms carved out by party leaders and their friends in the republics. The late leader's son recently paid the price—a long jail sentence. The ordinary people, meanwhile, stood in line for their daily needs, and all too often the shelves were empty. For years there were rumors, seldom confirmed, of strikes and demonstrations and of troublemakers' subsequent imprisonment or confinement to psychiatric clinics.

Like their tsarist predecessors, the Soviet Union's rulers were haunted by the fear of revolution, of a popular uprising; and Mikhail Gorbachev's elevation to power in 1985 may have been a desperate expedient meant to give the people hope while keeping the party's rule intact. If that was the party's intention, it must have been sorely disappointed.

Hopes raised must be fulfilled if frustration is not to turn to burning anger. Gorbachev has raised hopes, but his promised *perestroika* (restructuring) has yet to put more food on the table or generally raise living standards. *Glasnost* (openness) has been his one great domestic success: people and the media are speaking out in ways that would have been unimaginable only a few years ago. In 1989, Soviets had more than one candidate per seat to choose from on their election ballots, the first time that had happened since the 1917 revolution.

Glasnost is levying a price, though, and it may yet prove to be higher than the communist hierarchy is willing to pay. In 1988, the three Baltic republics—Estonia, Latvia, and Lithuania—demanded virtual autonomy. The Armenians demanded the return of Nagorno-Karabakh, an ethnic enclave in neighboring Azerbaijan, and huge demonstrations in both republics presaged civil strife, with thousands of people fleeing bloody ethnic violence, which has also hit Kazakhstan. The fires of nationalism, it turned out, had been merely damped down by Stalin and Brezhnev; under Gorbachev, they burst into flame. In a televised address, Gorbachev warned in June 1989 that such outbreaks were endangering the state. Just as serious was the wave of strikes starting in the coal fields.

On the international front, the Soviet Union has become both conciliatory and constructive. The Cold War seems over, the iron curtain to be rusting away. Is it a genuine change of heart, a commitment to democracy, Soviet-style? Or a belated realization that the Soviet Union cannot afford or win an arms race?

Some Western leaders, most notably Britain's Margaret Thatcher, urge caution. Though she gets along well personally with Gorbachev, Thatcher wants to see more evidence of fundamental and permanent change before she is willing to accept that the Soviet Union is no longer a threat to the West. Reductions in nuclear arms are not enough for her and for like-minded Western leaders. They await large cuts in Soviet conventional forces and evidence that in the future, these will be designed for defense rather than offense. Gorbachev grabbed headlines in December 1988 with promises before the United Nations General Assembly of unilateral cuts in troops and armaments over the next two years. Western leaders are anxious to see if he'll keep his word. Gorbachev has earned a measure of credibility with the West for withdrawing all Soviet troops from Afghanistan by February 15, 1989, in accordance with a timetable he had established a year earlier.

In Moscow, gaps between promises and performance on the domestic front are striking. Eight-lane highways sweep past majestic buildings gone to seed and seedy buildings gone seedier. Cabbage-carrying trucks move aside for luxurious Chaika limousines carrying top bureaucrats to and from their offices. What was great—the Moscow Circus, the Bolshoi Ballet—still is. What was awful—hotel food, retail service, deafening bands in state restaurants—remains awful.

Whatever your expectations, they are likely to be confounded. There is the shock of the new: teenagers with purple and green hair pump out rock music from Japanese boomboxes bought during rare and coveted weekend trips to Helsinki; there is sex in films such as the acclaimed Malienkaia Vera (Little Vera), the cult film of the new generation with the sensational Natalia Negoda; anger in the theater; sidewalk artists line the *Arbat,* the pedestrian mall. There is the torpor of the old: the monumental buildings, the surliness of servitors, the scarcity of all but approved Western newspapers and magazines, the rounded shoulders and resigned expressions of Muscovites waiting to buy foodstuffs or goods that may be sold out before people at the back of the line even enter the store. Moscow is the crucible for Gorbachev's reforms.

▷ Arriving

You know you've arrived in the Soviet Union before you've landed at She-ryemetovo II airport. You know it when a voice on the plane's loud-speaker system announces, "We have now crossed the Soviet border. Taking pictures is forbidden." Why, heaven knows; there are plenty of observation satellites up there.

The airport is far from welcoming. Passport officials stare hard at arriving passengers. Their expression says, "I shan't forget you." At customs, you have to show a form listing all the money you're taking in, as well as such valuables as jewelry and watches. Don't lose the form. You must show it when you're leaving if you want your valuables to leave with you. If you take out more money than you brought in, be ready to show official bank records justifying the transaction.

The organization you're doing business with should have sent a car to meet you. If it hasn't, your hotel should have. If both have failed, go to the Intourist counter on the arrivals level between the two wings of the airport. An official can help to get you a taxi and will point you toward the currency exchange window across the hall.

▷ Money

The basic unit of currency is the ruble (also spelled *rouble*). International code: ROU. The ruble is divided into 100 kopeks. Exchange rates are fixed, and the ruble is not convertible into other currencies. You are not allowed to take rubles in or out. Hard currencies, particularly the dollar, are highly prized in the Soviet Union. If you're willing to take the risk, you'll get more rubles for your money from a black-marketeer than from a bank. Always keep plenty of foreign currency and travelers' checks. You'll need them to pay your hotel bill, in some restaurants, and in the Beriozka stores for visitors—which do not take rubles.

▷ Spotlight ◁

Computer regulations. Check before leaving home that your portable computer is not banned by Western export regulations. All members of the North Atlantic Treaty Organization (NATO), minus Iceland but plus Japan, are members of Cocom, which regulates technology transfers. Rules are applied by the Commerce Department or its equivalent. If you do take a portable computer to Moscow, be sure you have a surge protector; the power supply is far from stable.

▷ Language

Russian—though many of the Soviet Union's 100 ethnic groups have their own languages or dialects. The alphabet is Cyrillic. Except at the airport and in major hotels and some stores, there are no translations for visitors, so it's best to learn the Cyrillic alphabet—not a task as daunting in practice as it is in imagination. English is quite widely spoken, often with an American accent.

▷ Communications

Country code: 7. City code: 095. Quality is poor. A pre*glasnost* peculiarity of Moscow is that there's no official phone book, even if you can read Russian. However, your embassy should be able to provide you with an unofficial one. Note that we have listed several numbers for some hotels, consulates, and airlines. That is because something taken for granted in the West, a multiline private automatic branch exchange, is less common in the Soviet Union. If you cannot reach your party on the first number, try the second, the third, and so on.

▷ Getting To Know the City

Moscow's five major sections form concentric circles, of which the innermost is the *Kremlin,* a walled city in itself that occupies 36.4 hectares (90 acres). East of the Kremlin is the huge *Red Square,* once a marketplace that is now used as a parade ground and for (officially sanctioned) demonstrations. East of Red Square is the old district of *Kitaigorod* (Chinatown), originally the merchants' quarter, later the banking section, and now an administrative hub with government offices and ministries.

North from the Kremlin is *Gorky Street,* a main thoroughfare lined with modern buildings, including the headquarters of the Council of Ministers. Gorky Street connects with the Leningrad highway, which passes the huge Dynamo sports stadium and the airport. Near the start of Gorky Street is *Sverdlov Square;* here are the Bolshoi and Maly theaters.

Traditionally the most elegant part of Moscow, *Bely Gorod* (White City) is now a commercial and arts area. Bely Gorod, Zemlyanoy (Earth City—named for the earthen and wooden ramparts that once surrounded it)—and the inner suburbs encircle both the Kremlin and Kitaigorod.

▷ *Spotlight* ◁

Maps. Openness has also meant accurate city maps for the first time in 50 years. Stalin's paranoid policy of secrecy led to falsified maps to confuse real or imagined enemies—just as the dictator used to dispatch decoy cars carrying false Stalins. Tass agency admitted in the summer of 1989 that maps showing theaters, monuments, shopping, and transportation were inaccurate. New maps will presumably kill off the old Moscow saying: "If you don't know where you are, you don't belong there."

▷ Moving Around

Traffic can be heavy, but never as snarled as it is in European cities of comparable size. The reason is that, by Western standards, there are few cars. All but a fortunate minority of Muscovites—those with official cars or with the patience to wait years for delivery—use public transportation. There's a fairly good bus system and an excellent subway, most of its stations elegant in a richly somber way.

These days you can rent a car—and then wish you hadn't. Drivers are fiercely competitive, and traffic flows are complicated by the prohibition of virtually all left turns. If you do rent a car, remember to remove the windshield wipers when you park. They're chronically scarce, commanding a high price on the black market.

In good weather you can walk to many appointments, but remember that Moscow is bitterly cold in winter. Be prepared with warm, thick clothes and footwear—and a hat or cap with earflaps. Moscow is humidly hot in summer; take lightweight clothes. In the fall or spring, do not look up for snow but down for mud. March and April, months of the spring thaw, are known in rural areas as "The Time of No Roads," so thick is the slush. Parts of Moscow are little better; wear sturdy, waterproof boots or shoes.

▷ Hotels

The era of *glasnost* and *perestroika* has made Moscow a desirable destination for foreigners of all kinds—tourists, businesspeople, scholars, politicians, delegates to conferences on this and that. One measure of rooms' scarcity: the story of a Bulgarian airline captain who walked into a visitor's room at 3:00 a.m. looking for a bed. Intourist guides, meanwhile, were sleeping in closets.

In 1989, modernization took hold with the transformation of the Berlin-turned-Savoy and improvements at the Metropole and National. The bad news was the leap in prices, leading business travelers to say that Moscow was as expensive as Thailand but without Thai service. The Savoy's promise of 24-hour room service is considered the test of whether

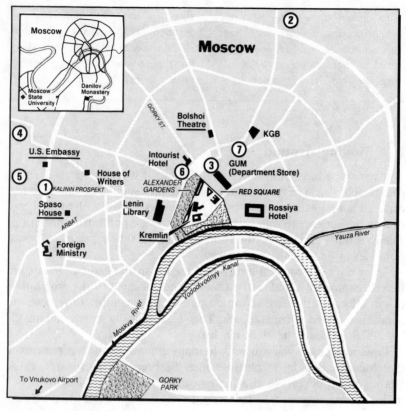

1. Hotel Belgrade
2. Hotel Cosmos
3. Hotel Metropole
4. Hotel Mezhdunarodnya

5. Hotel Mozhaiskaya
6. Hotel National
7. Hotel Savoy, ex Berlin

Moscow is entering a new hotel era; this will hopefully be achieved before the convertible ruble planned for the end of the 1990s.

Reserve well ahead through your local Intourist office or its agent. Even better, pull strings so that you can get into either the *Mezhdunarodnya* or the *National*. The first, "the Mezh" to resident foreigners, isn't in the center but does have air-conditioning and most of the comforts of home. The National, fading grandeur overlooking the Kremlin, is a Moscow institution. Things are changing, but Intourist still won't guarantee you a room in a specific hotel unless you have VIP status or something close to it. Try to avoid staying in hotels in the suburbs if your appointments are in the center.

Wherever you stay, you will be segregated from Soviet citizens—at the Mezh and the National because they are for foreigners only, at the mammoth (and less desirable) *Rossiya* by floor. You'll also pay about 10 times more for a room than a Soviet would.

All hotels have many things in common. As you try to enter, a doorman will ask for your *propusk* (pass). You won't get in without it unless you make an enormous fuss and thus raise hackles. With the Mezh and the National as exceptions, hotels work on the key-lady principle: a *dezhurnaya* (key-lady) sits at a desk on your floor or corridor. You show her your *propusk*; she gives you your key; she may not give you a smile. Rooms may be large, but bath towels will be tiny, and there seems to be a permanent shortage of plugs for baths and washbasins. Food in hotel restaurants is mediocre, and servitors are lackadaisical at best. Most hotels list a wide range of services that in theory take care of all your needs, but don't expect them to work to European or American rhythms.

Belgrade, 5 Smolenskaya Square. Tel.: 248-7848/6692/1643. Rooms/ suites: 920. Opened in 1973, the Belgrade is in two buildings, each 20 floors high, and its chief virtue is its central location. The atmosphere is impersonal, but the hotel offers plenty of services.

Cosmos, 150 Mir Prospekt. Tel.: 217-0785/215-8680. Rooms/suites: 1,767. A late 1970s monster with all the cozy appeal of an airport departure lounge.

Intourist, 3/5 Gorky Street. Tel.: 203-4007/4008. Rooms/suites: 458. A vast rectangle built in 1970, Intourist is sandwiched between two nostalgic reminders of what architecture used to be. Handily central.

Metropole, 1 Marx Prospekt. Tel.: 225-6212/6677. Rooms/suites: 326. A gracious building that opened its doors in 1905 and retains some of its elegant luxury in the public rooms. Bedrooms decorated and furnished by people with little sense of stylistic harmony. However, the Metropole is being modernized.

Mezhdunarodnya, 12 Krasnopresnenskaia Neb. Tel.: 253-2382. Moscow's best, its closest counterpart to a top-class Hilton or Sheraton. Nearly always full; if you want to stay here, you will have to pull strings and be insistent with Intourist.

Mozhaiskaya, 165 Mozhaiskoye Highway. Tel.: 447-3434/3435. Rooms/ suites: 152. A 1970s creation 20 kilometers (12 miles) from the center. Rooms are brightly modern in the international style.

National, 14/1 Marx Prospekt. Tel.: 203/6539/6083. Rooms/suites: 199. Turn-of-the-century grandeur in the city center with a wide range of services. Due for renovation.

Rossiya, 6 Ul Razina. Tel.: 298-5409. Rooms: 3,000. One of the world's largest hotels, it can accommodate 6,000 guests. Of the nine restaurants, the best is on the 21st floor overlooking the Kremlin. Disco and dollar shop. Improving the service at the Rossiya will be one of the main tests of Soviet hotel policy in the 1990s.

Savoy (formerly the Berlin), 3 Rozhdestvenka Street. Tel.: 928-9169. Telex 411620. Fax: 2302186. Rooms: 86. The fading, prerevolutionary Berlin, close to the Bolshoi Theater, the Kremlin, and Red Square, has been completely redone by a Finnair-Intourist joint company. It's the city's first hotel with 24-hour room service. Secretarial and translating services, modern communications, and 10 limousines. The restaurant has been refurbished but the fountain retained. The English built the new Ermitage bar.

Sevastapol, 1a Bolshaya Yushunskaya Street. Tel.: 318-2827/3536. Rooms/suites: 1,287. Dating from the late 1970s, these four buildings are 20 kilometers (12 miles) from central Moscow and are virtually a city of their own. Close to the university.

▷ Restaurants

Until 1987, there was good reason to hibernate your taste buds and wear earplugs when eating in Moscow. The food was terrible, and in most restaurants a band made conversation almost impossible—which may have been the idea. But in 1987, a change in the law allowed cooperatives to open their doors, and the lonely islands of decent cuisine and service have become an archipelago in an otherwise dismal culinary sea. Today there are three types of restaurant.

The first is *state-run*—and there's at least one for each of the 15 republics, as well as a few more honoring fraternal socialist states. These eateries are a poor lot. Don't be surprised if the *maitre d'* blandly maintains "Mest nyet" ("There are no seats") even when the place is only a fifth full—or four-fifths empty.

The second category is the *foreigners-only* restaurant, also state-run and usually in or near large hotels. These places are expensive and seldom worth the money—which you must pay in foreign currency.

Third, there are the *cooperatives*. These would be Gorbachev's gift to gourmets if it were not for one thing: they range from expensive to very expensive. However, they offer real value for money, which most of the state-run places do not. Furthermore, they welcome customers; no "mest nyet" when there obviously are empty tables. These private sector restaurants—for that's what they are if one strips away the Marxist-Leninist façade—are opening so rapidly that a list of them is out of date before it's printed. We've mentioned only those that seem to be here to stay. Who knows? The state-owned restaurants may feel the brisk breezes of competition and decide that customers are a value instead of a nuisance.

Contrasting cuisines abound, from Armenian through Georgian to Ukrainian—with stops on the way for Chinese, Indian, and Italian. Reservations are essential, particularly at the cooperatives.

▷ *Spotlight* ◁

Drinking. The United States discovered it the hard way in the 1920s and the Soviet Union in the 1980s: prohibition doesn't work. One of Gorbachev's first acts in 1985 was to make alcohol more expensive and harder to find. The Soviet Union has from time immemorial been a hard-drinking society, however, and an edict from Moscow could not wean people overnight from their bottle. Instead, millions of tipplers—there's no knowing how many—started to make their own hooch. The linked results were disastrous: spasmodic shortages of sugar became chronic as people bought huge quantities for their home brew, rotgut liquor made hangovers worse, and the state's revenues from drink taxes plunged. Gorbachev, a pragmatist if ever there were one, relaxed the rules in 1988. Foreigners with hard currency never did notice any shortage of liquor. Now they won't notice any shortage of drunks, either, though most obedient bureaucrats have sworn off the stuff, at least in public.

State-run

Aragvi, 6 Gorkova Street. Tel.: 229-3762. The best in this category because it's Georgian. Try the *chicken satsivi* with its spicy, nutty sauce. Also roast sturgeon. Good Georgian wines.

National Hotel, Tel.: 203-5550. The restaurant specializes in Russian cuisine and is certainly worth a visit.

Praga, 2 Arbat. Tel.: 290-6170. Close to the Kremlin, and some of the clientele come from the No. 1 office block. The chicken dishes are recommended. Rather grand.

Rus, Saltykovskaya Stn, 12 Krasnozyvozdnaya. Tel.: 528-0778. About 50 minutes from town, with a delightful country flavor—mushroom dishes, soups, sour-cream-and-mushroom bakes, and hearty meat-and-potato basics. In winter, one-horse sleigh rides are available for customers.

Ruskaya Izba, Ilinskoye, near Arkhangelskoye. Tel.: 561-4244. A similar, equally pleasant country restaurant.

Hard Currency

Delhi, 23-b, Krasnaya Presnya Street. Tel.: 252-1766. A joint-venture restaurant serving Indian food—for rubles in one room, for hard currency in another.

Riviera, Krasnopresnenskaya Na, on board the "Alexander Blok." Tel.: 253-2639. A good French restaurant anchored in the Moskva.

Sakura, 12 Krasnopresnenskaya Nab. Tel.: 253-2894. Moscow's leading Japanese restaurant.

Cooperatives

Aist. Tel.: 291-6692. Russian cuisine with a splendid veal main course. Prices, however, tend to be staggering.

Atrium. Tel.: 137-3008. Recommended, particularly for the stuffed pork.

Kolkhida, 6 Sadovaya-Samotechnaya. Tel.: 299-6757. Georgian cuisine. The chef puts pomegranate seeds in the *shashlik*—when he can.

Lasagna. Tel.: 231-1085. A rare and good Italian eating place.

Myikhua, 2/1 Rusakovskaya Street. Tel.: 264-9754. One of the best of the city's Chinese restaurants, also known as the Plumblossom.

Pirosmany. Tel.: 247-1926. Excellent Georgian food is served in this lovely wooden dining room, overlooking the Novodevichy Lake, with swans in summer and sledders and skaters in winter. Full-bodied Georgian wines.

Razgulyai, 11 Spartakovskaya Street. Tel.: 267-7613. Excellent entrées and a fine gypsy band. Russian cuisine.

Skazka, Yaroslavkoye Chaussee, 41st km. Tel.: 271-0998. Former Secretary of State George Schultz ate here. Recommended for its Russian cuisine—and its evening act by a contortionist.

Yakimanka. Tel.: 238-8772. Uzbek food with an Armenian accent. Try the *plov* or the *dolma-stuffed grape leaves.*

▷ Tipping

"This capitalistic relic is degrading and illegal." So goes the official line, even today. In fact, it's essential to tip for a table in a supposedly crowded restaurant. Moscow old-timers offer a packet of Western cigarettes rather than dollar bills—the handing over of foreign currency in this way is forbidden. However, it has been known for cut-price caviar to be available for cash. The attitude towards open tipping may change with the growth of some kind of service industry, but that dawn has yet to break.

▷ Doing Business

Frescoes in a Kiev church depict with all the vividness of primitive art the torments of souls in limbo. One of these is the Perpetual Gnashing of Teeth. That is a peculiarly Russian punishment now reserved for people who arrive in the Soviet Union bearing Western assumptions about the value of time and money. Many Soviet trade officials can be polite, informed, helpful, and efficient—but they are swimming against the tide rather than with it.

The system is inherently slothful, cautious, conservative, and bureaucratic. Recent attempts to reform it have compounded the problems, at least in the short run. In 1987, the Ministry of Foreign Trade lost its monopoly. In 1989, all enterprises were given the right to import, export, and negotiate joint ventures. In 1988, the Ministry of Foreign Trade combined with the Committee on Foreign Economic Relations to become the Ministry of Foreign Economic Relations.

The goal: a leaner and more flexible system. The result: confusion and widespread uncertainty about who can do what and to whom. The confusion is almost as bad for foreign firms as it is for Soviet officials. Western companies had spent untold sums and innumerable executive hours in making and strengthening Soviet contacts; much of the investment has now turned out to be wasted.

Three precepts are valuable:

- Deal with the top official, or as close to the top as you can get.

- Plan ahead, triple-checking all arrangements for travel, hotel reservations, and appointments.
- Relax. Go for a walk in Red Square. The unforeseen is routine.

Communications are usually a problem. Letters often go unanswered. The telephone lacks a device taken for granted in the West: a hold button. As an official rises in eminence, he needs more phones on his desk. Some he answers, some he doesn't; some his secretary answers; others nobody answers. Even when the secretary picks up the phone, she is often unable to make an appointment with her boss: all too often, he keeps his schedule to himself.

There's a national reluctance to say no. A secretary won't say that her boss is too busy to see you or—perish the thought—doesn't want to see you. She'll ask you to call back. If you agree, you will suffer all over again the frustrations of making calls that are never answered or, if you're lucky, speaking to secretaries who might as well be answering machines. Invoke higher authority, the higher the better. Write letters and memoranda and have them delivered by hand—you cannot rely upon the postal system.

▷ *Spotlight* ◁

Restrictions. When KGB chiefs dine with Americans, as has been the case, then the era of John Le Carré and his Moscow Center has faded. The average business executive can safely leave the paranoia at home. However, the economic espionage arm of the secret police remains very active, both abroad and at home, so don't leave vital documents lying around, any more than you would in London, New York, or Paris. This large-scale economic espionage has been accompanied by a Soviet diplomatic campaign against the Cocom list, the one that restricts sensitive, high-tech exports to the Eastern Bloc. There are still plenty of secrets the Soviets would like to get their hands on—and their techniques have grown more sophisticated since agents hid the plans for the Concorde supersonic airliner behind the toilet on the Warsaw Express train.

Your visa will be just for Moscow and the immediate surroundings. A special Intourist pass, for example, is required for the monasteries at nearby Zagorsk. If in doubt, don't just set off in a car. Ask Intourist or your embassy. Or John Le Carré himself. He has been allowed in and has been busy on the streets doing his new-style, on-the-spot research.

Is the course of business never smooth? Answer: Some visits are productive and go without a hitch. Others build to a peak of frustration and then, as one Western executive puts it, "the clouds part and the sun shines." You are led into an office, usually with an L-shaped table for visitors and an imposing desk for the official, or into a ceremonial room suitable for a tsarist banquet. Bottled water, fruit juices, and candies await; so do tea and coffee. Vodka is out, a victim of Gorbachev's antialcohol campaign.

The pleasantries completed, negotiations start. There are two barriers to surmount. The first is linguistic. Be sure an interpreter is there who is fully fluent in your language. The second is cultural. Terms such as "rate of return" and "bottom line" are foreign to the official Soviet mind. There is a conceptual gap between the two cultures, between the two economic and social systems, and you will have to bridge it tactfully.

An official may even become bewildered by your concern with the cost of a raw material or component. As an American economist has explained, for most Soviet citizens, price is a philosophical issue. A bureaucrat or factory manager wants to know whether the commodity or component is available and whether what is ordered is what will finally arrive. The price usually has scant relationship to cost—for the simple reason that the cost itself is unknown. *Perestroika* is supposed to change all that, but hasn't yet. How can change be rapid in a system based in part upon the labor theory of value—but lacking anything except the most arbitrary methods of determining the value of different kinds of labor and skills? Cost accounting and allocation in the Western sense exist only in vestigial forms, though managers are studying them increasingly.

▷ *Spotlight* ◁

Selling. Western advertising executives have followed in the footsteps of Italian TV tycoon Silvio Berlusconi, whose subsidiary, *Publitalia*, signed with Channel Two for the twice-monthly show with the hardly snappy title, "Progress, Information, Advertising." The Soviet-Hungarian joint venture *Risza* is also involved. *Burda*, of West Germany, and *Publicitas*, of Switz-erland, now handle *Izvestia's* advertising. The European group TBWA is in Moscow, as are the Americans *Young and Rubicam* (working with Vneshtorgreklama, the State advertising organization) and *Ogilvy and Mather*. Main activities of the newcomers are consultancy services to Western companies doing business in the Soviet Union.

Do not think, though, that the official or manager with whom you are negotiating is a fool blinded by dogma. He is not. He doesn't look in his shaving mirror every morning and say: "I am a Marxist-Leninist, and the Communist Party is the fount of all wisdom." High officials are educated men; factory managers are at least as competent as many of their Western counterparts—and have to deal with problems that are almost unimaginable in the West, where managers take for granted on-time deliveries, quality control, market-led demand, and competition. In the Soviet Union, by contrast, the system has produced—or not, as the case may be—goods that the *apparatchiks* (powers-that-be) have deemed necessary, and a factory's success has been judged by its volume of output rather than quality and consumers' reactions. Everyone knows that the system doesn't work, everyone from Gorbachev down to a *babushka* (grandmother) waiting patiently in line at a grocery store with shelves almost bare. The question is whether any other politically conceivable system will work better.

▷ Spotlight ◁

Businessman's Moscow is the best short reference guide. It is published by Vneshtorgreklama and sold in the West at Soviet trade legations for $20. In Moscow, it's available (sometimes) at the bookstore in the Mezhdunarodnaya Hotel. If you don't read Russian, the English-language edition of the weekly *Moscow News* will open your eyes wide to what *glasnost* has wrought. A lively tabloid, the paper throws darts at plump targets, the editors obviously delighting in the hiss as the fat cats deflate.

The Soviet Union produces few goods that other countries want to import. It is rich in oil and gas, but world prices have fallen since the heady days of the first and second oil shocks in the 1970s and 1980s. It is rich in gold, but its price also faltered. Like all countries that depend heavily on basic commodities for foreign exchange earnings but need to import both food and capital goods, the Soviet Union has had to resort to bartering. Soviet-made goods that do appear on Western markets are often there as the end of a complicated chain of barter deals.

What business is the Soviet Union looking for today? And is it worth pursuing? At the top of the shopping list are Western technology and management. Ever since World War II, the Soviet Union has committed so high a proportion of its gross domestic product to the armed forces that the civil sector has been starved. Plants are antiquated; technology is outdated; management techniques are skewed by doctrine and bureaucratic rigidity; and for those and other reasons, labor productivity is low by the standards of major industrialized countries.

▷ Spotlight ◁

Selling technology. You may not be allowed to "export" your portable computer. You may also run afoul of Cocom regulations covering the sale and licensing of many kinds of technology. Check the position before you make even a tentative approach to a Soviet ministry or other potential buyer.

The place to start is with your own government's department dealing with international trade. If your product or technology is on the "sensitive" list, you will have to apply formally for permission to export to the Soviet Union (and to countries in Eastern Europe). Your application will be considered both by your own government's relevant agency and by Cocom in Paris. Rules have become less stringent recently, but still are strict; and you will be wasting time and money—and wearing out the welcome mat in Moscow—if you promise but then cannot deliver because of Cocom rules.

Even if your country is not a member of Cocom, you can still be caught. The rules forbid the export from all countries of technologies and products licensed to them by firms in the Cocom states. Penalties can be severe, ranging from heavy fines and even prison sentences to denial of scientific and technological developments. Generally speaking, Cocom prohibits the export of goods and knowledge that might benefit, even potentially, the armed forces of the Soviet Union and other members of the Warsaw Pact.

Soviet leaders are determined to drag their state into the modern world—kicking and screaming if necessary. But how can they pay for the imports they need: goods, technology, turnkey projects? Barter trade is one way. Loans from the West are another. Even in the iciest days of the Cold War, the Soviet Union had a good reputation among western bankers for paying its debts on time. Now it is looking for large loans and trade credits from the West. It is seeking also joint-venture partners for everything from fast food outlets to machine-tool factories and has passed and is preparing legislation guaranteeing repatriation of profits. As a gesture of its good intentions, the Soviet Union recently redeemed—at a huge discount—bonds sold in the West in tsarist times.

The hopes, doubts, and complexities of doing business with the Soviet Union have given birth to an industry of seminars and trade conferences. A senior Soviet diplomat will state that there is no automatic uniformity in the treatment of either joint ventures or their foreign partners. The following was heard at a typical get-together in Chicago: "We do not presume all will operate equally. Some might have a tax deduction, in some cases others might have more privileges in hiring and firing people." Another diplomat will add that free economic zones are on the horizon (along with the convertible rouble). Useful advice can be gleaned: Better to deal with a state enterprise than a cooperative; more sophisticated partners are to be found in the Baltic republics with their industrial culture; the Soviet Union is now party to all trademark and patent protection agreements; the hardest thing remains finding an office and place to live.

▷ *Spotlight* ◁

Advice from a pro. Samuel Pisar is a noted, Paris-based international lawyer who specializes in East-West trade, investments and commercial transactions—skills that take him on occasion to the General Secretary's table. He has negotiated many deals with the Soviets, including ones for CocaCola, Seagram's, Rank Xerox, Occidental Petroleum, and Pechiney. Pisar's latest book, *Dealing with Russia*, is to be published by Macmillan. A distillation of his advice:

What they're like. We are dealing with a new generation, a new type of individual. At all levels, Soviet officials are remarkably young, compared to their predecessors. There is no more sentimental reminiscing about World War II, no more vodka toast contests. The Soviet president has a splendid table but does not serve liquor. The new people are more educated, pragmatic, and businesslike. They are more preoccupied with economics than ideology. One should still be concerned about hidden motives. Even so, business dialogue with them is becoming more understandable, normal, and comfortable. These days, they are surprisingly profit-oriented, and it's amusing to see them struggle with balance sheets, cost accounting, asset valuation, and joint ventures.

How to approach them. Lay the groundwork carefully. Get advance knowledge of the Soviets' needs from their commercial attachés abroad, from official economic plans, from purchasing and selling schedules. Also collect data about chronic production shortfalls. It's here that very good deals indeed can be struck. Be creative: try to conceive joint ventures in manufacturing and marketing—these are the coming things—as well as various forms of business cooperation. Creativity is still needed in counterpurchase (barter) transactions. The Soviets' shortage of hard currency dictates them.

Buy or sell? One way to make the Soviets snap to attention is to put the accent on prospects of buying from them—and only afterwards to introduce selling. A detailed and lavishly illustrated brochure in Russian for circulation among selected decision-makers will make them come to you, not the other way around. It will also make them aware of your strengths, your geographic reach, the range of your products, and your state-of-the-art technology.

Support staff. Field someone who speaks Russian and knows the system, can monitor the interpreting, and will generally help to smooth misunderstandings caused by linguistic, cultural, and political differences. Such support is expensive—but cost-effective. Lastly, bear in mind that the abolition of the old monopoly of the Foreign Trade Ministry means that there are now many more players to deal with, and the Western business executive can in fact negotiate directly with Soviet suppliers or the end-users of the products. Also, to overcome bureaucratic inertia, you have to deal at the highest levels. Only there can rapid decisions be made.

A good, reliable, and comprehensive source of information on who's who is the Soviet Union is in Paris. *SOVT* is a computerized data bank started by *Le Monde* Kremlinologist Michel Tatu. SOVT has two sections. The first, BIOG, lists some 23,000 people: everyone from Gorbachev down to plant managers. The second, EVTS, has about 6,000 texts on the leaders' speeches and details of their foreign trips. Tatu and his team update SOVT daily. Clients include governments, banks, multinational corporations, the CIA, and the Pentagon. Access to SOVT costs about $250 an hour. *SOVT*, c/o *Le Monde*, 5 rue des Italiens, 75427 Paris Cedex 09. Tel.: 4247-9638. Fax: 4523-0681.

▷ Useful Phone Numbers

Emergencies

Ambulance	03
Fire	01
Police	02

Medical

Doctor (the British, French, Japanese, U.S., and other embassies have their own doctors)

Botkin Hospital (with diplomatic block)	255-0015
Diplomatic Polyclinic	237-5933
Tourists Clinic	254-4396

Local Information

Aeroflot (internal flights)
245-3877/238-7786/238-8791
Intourist

Information	203-6962
Excursions	298-1753/
253-2362/253-2347/243-2690	

Business Contacts

Atomenergo-export	220-1436
Avioexport	202-5806
Avtoimport	202-8337
Energomashexport	203-1571
Expotsentr	268-6352
Exportkhleb	244-4701
Litsenzintorg	145-1111
Mashinoexport	147-1542
Medexport	331-8200
Neftkhimpromoexport	220-1109
Promashimport	220-1505
Promsyrioimport	203-4446
Selkhhozpromexport	220-1692
Sovintsentr	256-6303
Sovrybflot	208-4057
Sovtransavto	292-4462
Sovtransavtoexpeditsiya	143-7867
Soyuzgazexport	220-2440
Soyuzkhimexport	244-2284
Soyuzagranpribor	229-6110
Tekhmashexport	147-1562
Tekhmashimport	202-4800
Tekhpromexport	220-1523

Vneshtorgreklama	331-8311	Singapore	241-3702/3913/3914
Vneshtorgbank		Spain	
	253-2349/232-5300		202-2161/2180/7772/6181

Embassies

Sweden 147-9009

Australia 246-5011/16

United Kingdom
231-8511/8512/241-1035

Austria
201-7307/7317/7379/2166

United States 252-2452/59

Belgium
203-6566/6529/6557/6568

Denmark 201-7860/7868

Airlines

Finland 246-4027/33

Aeroflot Soviet Airlines
245-3877/238-7786/238-8791

France
236-0003/237-8740/237-8755

Air France 237-2325/3344/6777

Germany (West) 252-5521

Alitalia 923-9840/0576

Greece 290-2274/291-8900

Austrian Airlines 253-1670/1

Indonesia 239-9549/50/51

British Airways 253-2481

Ireland 288-4101/4192

Finnair 292-8788

Italy 241-1533/38/248-3152

Japan Air Lines/
JAL 221-6448/6648

Japan 291-8500

Malaysia 147-1514

KLM Royal Dutch
Airlines 253-2150/1/230-2304

Netherlands
291-2999/2948/2954

Lufthansa German
Airlines 923-9840/9856

New Zealand
290-3485/1277/5704

Pan Am World
Airways 253-2658/9

Norway
290-3872/3874/202-3484

Swissair 253-8988

▷ **Shopping**

The Soviet authorities still have a somewhat schizophrenic attitude toward foreigners who want to go on a shopping spree. On the one hand, the Soviet Union needs hard currency; on the other, prices are high and formalities are tough. Take caviar, which is nothing more than the eggs of the sturgeon fished on the Caspian Sea—the world's largest inland body of water (373,000 square kilometers, or 144,000 square miles), shared by the Soviet Union and Iran. While in Moscow, you may feel yourself awash in the stuff; it is routinely served as an appetizer even in railroad station buffets. Try to take the stuff out, though. First, you must buy it at one of the state-run *Beriozka* stores, paying hard currency. Second, you must present customs officials with a form confirming the purchase's legality.

The Beriozka stores sell a great variety of goods, but we cannot pretend that they are Soviet versions of Harrods in London, Printemps in Paris, or Stockmann's in Helsinki. *GUM,* the huge department store complex on the eastern side of Red Square, is the place to go for fashion goods (such as they are) and for fur hats and furs of every kind. Most GUM goods are far too expensive for all but a tiny minority of Soviet citizens, and the staff tend to think their job is to guard the stock rather than to sell.

The *Arbat,* the downtown pedestrian mall, is lined with sidewalk artists—some good, some mediocre, some downright bad. You may find something there that is startingly vivid. Savor also the *Izmailovsky* weekend art bazaar—like Arbat, a jumble-sale of varying quality. Much kitsch, but some really excellent work as well.

▷ Sights and Sounds

Some of Moscow's best sights seem always to be under wraps and wrapped in scaffolding. The *Tretyakov Gallery* closed in 1986 and is not scheduled to open until 1991 or so; the *Bolshoi Theater* is undergoing a multiyear restoration; other places are also either closed or due to be renovated. The Intourist office at your hotel should know what is happening where, and how to get tickets for the ballet, opera, and symphony.

A word here about Intourist. Many of its people, perhaps most, are genuinely helpful; some are charming; and all speak at least one language other than Russian, usually well. If they can't give you an instant answer to a request for ballet tickets, for example, don't blame them as much as the system: they, too, find it hard to get through on the phone.

If you have time for only a few hours of sightseeing, head for the Kremlin churches. Intourist will arrange a guided tour. If you want to wander and wonder by yourself, go to the *Kremlin's Trinity Gate* (the metro stop is Ploshchad Marksa). Just outside in the Alexander Gardens, a cashier sells tickets for all the churches and museums, and in each there is a consultant to answer your questions. The Kremlin sights are open from 10:00 a.m. to 5:00 p.m. but are closed on Thursdays.

The architecture is magnificent. Try at least to see *St. Basil's Cathedral* in Red Square; within the Kremlin walls the *Cathedral of the Archangel,* where early tsars, including Ivan the Terrible, are buried; and the *Cathedral of the Annunciation,* where icons include one reputedly painted by the indisputable master, Andrei Rublyov. Just outside Red Square proper is the *Lenin Museum,* a fascinating look at myth rendered as fact.

▷ Spotlight ◁

Religion. In 1988, Russia (we use the word advisedly) marked with some embarrassment and hesitation the millennium of its conversion to Christianity. With some embarrassment, because the state's official creed is atheism. However, a high official proclaimed at the end of the year that atheism was a distortion of Marxism, and religious belief was a private concern. Undoubtedly, most of the Soviet peoples are deeply religious—and Marxism-Leninism has its equivalent of saints and sinners, or gods and anti-Christs. Once there were three in the pantheon: Marx, Lenin, and Stalin. Then Stalin was, so to speak, cast out like Lucifer. Leon Trotsky, murdered in Mexico, almost certainly by Stalin's agents, remains in limbo. Seek in vain for any memorials to him. *Glasnost* may yet restore him to his place as an important revolutionary leader and founder of the Red Army.

▷ Out of Town

Leningrad

Saint Petersburg became Petrograd and is now Leningrad, with an estimated population of more than 4 million. Peter the Great (Tsar Peter I, 1672–1725) built it in the early 1700s—with some help from many thousands of laborers, some of whom died as they raised a new city on the marshlands of the Neva river and the islands of its delta at the head of the Gulf of Finland. Moscow is a hodgepodge; Leningrad is planned and classical, a city of grand boulevards and vistas. The best way to get there from Moscow is by train, and the best of the trains is the overnight Red Arrow Express, which takes about eight hours.

Leningrad has some good hotels, but check. The *Yevropaiskaya* and the *Astoria* have been closed for renovations but are due to reopen in the early 1990s (which could mean the middle of the decade).

Leningrad's jewel in the crown is the *Hermitage* art gallery and museum in the old Winter Palace. The collection includes Scythian gold artifacts dating from the pre-Christian era, Italian Renaissance art, and French Impressionist works. Intourist offers guided visits; try to spend a second day reviewing your favorite works.

Across the Neva river is the old fortress of *Saints Peter and Paul,* the first buildings completed on the swamps. All the tsars from Peter the

Great onward are buried in the church, apart from Nikolas II. He was shot by revolutionaries in 1918, along with his wife and children, and his body was burned.

▷ Spotlight ◁

Peter the Great reigned nominally from 1682, as joint tsar with Ivan V, and as supreme ruler from 1696 until his death in 1725. Influenced strongly by his visits to Western Europe and by European friends, Peter saw in Western models the future of his country—though he strongly resisted democratic ideas. Instead, Peter thought that he could harness European technology to the needs of an autocratic state. Like many other Russian rulers, he failed to see that slavery or serfdom was a foundation no more substantial than the marshes upon which Leningrad was built. Even so, Peter's rule was decisive in transforming Russia from a medieval into a modern state.

He was far from an admirable man, however, displaying all the contradictory traits of his race and class. Huge and hairy, he drank himself into stupors—though usually could rouse himself in an emergency; took many mistresses; and concluded that ruthless reform was necessary if Russia were to be rescued from its cultural and economic backwardness.

He remains a controversial figure. Commentators who believe the Soviet Union's future is essentially European praise him for his foresight; those who think that the country is unique and neither European nor Asiatic criticize him for diverting it from its own, unique path of cultural and social development. Leningrad is his monument: a European city on the marshes.

Further Reading

The Russian Revolution of 1917 started in what is now Leningrad, with the storming of the Winter Palace. Those events were stirring and changed the world—but if you want to understand their causes and consequences, you should consult many versions to arrive at a synoptic view.

A good, scholarly work is Bertram D. Wolfe's two-volume *Three Who Made a Revolution* (Dial Press, New York; paperback edition Time-Life Books, New York and Arlington, Virginia). This is a biographical triptych of Lenin, Trotsky, and Stalin—with Stalin playing a role far less important than that described by his biographers. Trotsky's own account, *The Russian Revolution: The Overthrow of Tsarism and the Triumph of the Soviets,* is a brilliant eyewitness narrative with portraits of the leading actors (Doubleday Anchor Books, New York). A succinct history of the revolution is in *The New Columbia Encyclopedia* (Columbia University Press, New York). See also entries for Russia, the Union of Soviet Socialist Republics, and Engels, Marx, Marxism, Lenin, Stalin, and Trotsky. All entries include reliable bibliographies.

For those who want to understand communism's historical roots, failures, and probable future, we recommend Leszek Kolakowski's three-volume *Main Currents of Marxism* (Oxford University Press). Kolakowski, a Warsaw University professor of history, was expelled from Poland for his political views in 1968 and became a fellow of All Souls College, Oxford. In the epilogue to his third volume, *The Breakdown,* Kolakowski writes, "Marxism has been the greatest fantasy of our century." He goes on, "The influence that Marxism has achieved, far from being the result or proof of its scientific character, is almost entirely due to its prophetic, fantastic, and irrational elements. Marxism is a doctrine of blind confidence that a paradise of universal satisfaction is awaiting us just round the corner." Kolakowski concludes: "The self-deification of mankind, to which Marxism gave philosophical expression, has ended in the same way as all such attempts, whether individual or collective: it has revealed itself as the farcical aspect of human bondage."

MUNICH

Life After Strauss

Population: 1.28 million (1985). Administrative and business capital of the West German *Land* (state) of Bavaria (population: 10.96 million). *Location*: on the Isar River in southeastern West Germany, 80 kilometers (50 miles) north of the Bavarian Alps. *Economy*: automotive components and assembly; banking and insurance; brewing; electrical and other engineering; electronics; fashion and textiles; movie and television production; printing and publishing; tourism. West Germany is a member of the European Community (EC) and the Organization for Economic Cooperation and Development (OECD) and is a signatory to the General Agreement on Tariffs and Trade (GATT).

▷ Background Briefing

More than most of the ten *Länder* (states) that make up the Federal Republic of Germany, Bavaria has kept its character. A land of rich plains and valleys and high Alpine peaks, its people vigorous, hearty, and proud, Bavaria is today a distinctive mixture of old and new—of castles and villages, of baroque, rococo, and modern architecture, of agriculture and high technology. All of Bavaria's contrasts and contradictions are to be found in Munich, a city founded in the mid-1100s and ruled by the royal House of Wittelsbach until the end of World War I.

Badly damaged during World War II, Munich has been rebuilt in a way that retains its stylish, baroque look, inherited from its royal past. The Maximilian and Ludwig kings had sponsored both fine buildings and the arts; the mentally unbalanced Ludwig II built fantasy castles that inspired adaptations at Disneyland in California and Disney World in Florida. Munich was also the birthplace of another fantasy: the Nazi party.

▶369

For such a down-to-earth people, the Bavarians have endured more than their fair share of dreamers. Adolf Hitler, a native of neighboring Austria, made Munich his political base, staged his disastrous attempted Beer Hall Putsch of 1923 in the city center, and served his prison sentence in the fortress jail of Landsberg, where with much help from Rudolf Hess he wrote *Mein Kampf* ("My Struggle").

The Bavarians' dream after World War II was to turn their state into a rich democracy. They have succeeded; and much of the credit must go to one man, Franz-Josef Strauss, longtime leader of the right-of-center Christian Social Union (CSU). Strauss was a potent figure in federal politics until bribery and other scandals—in which he always denied any part—forced him back to his Bavarian stronghold. There he competed energetically and often ruthlessly with other cities for business investment and a slice of the European Community cake. One monument to his enterprise: the rapidly expanding European Patents Office.

Strauss was Bavarian to the tips of his stubby fingers: unabashedly fat, a hearty eater fond of his bottle, a roisterer. He was also shrewd and cunning; and under his somewhat coarse exterior hid (when it suited him) a first-class political brain. No wonder, then, that men in traditional costume wept openly when his funeral procession passed with regal pomp through Munich's main streets in 1988. Were they mourning not only the passing of a man they admired, but also of an era? Strauss built well, though, and the CSU party machine has its own momentum.

He did leave a power and leadership vacuum, however, and the city could be heading into an uneasy future. Real estate costs, already the highest in West Germany, have been soaring to new heights, threatening to scare off investment. There's also the question of whether the swing toward a high-tech economy is unduly risky, with too many of Munich's chips on the same number.

That swing started after the war, notably with the relocation of the electrical and electronics giant, Siemens, from Berlin to Munich. More recently, such multinational corporations as Hewlett-Packard, Texas Instruments, and Digital Equipment Corporation have crowded in. Bavaria is also the home of BMW's three plants and headquarters of Audi, a subsidiary of Volkswagen. The MBB aerospace giant has also set up shop in the area. Strauss's policies included encouragement of smaller and medium-sized German companies with start-up loans. At the same time, Munich became a major center for trade and industrial fairs, with no fewer than 5 of the 15 held annually devoted to electronics and computer systems. Significantly, there's now no room for the food and wine fair: it has moved to Stuttgart.

Munich has remained a pleasant city in spite of all the changes. People work hard—but they also play hard. Tradition still rubs shoulders with the avant-garde; students still share their backstreet tavern tables with elderly intellectuals; and the price of a mug of beer is still a factor in the official cost-of-living index.

▷ Arriving

By Air

Munich's one commercial airport, Riem, is due to be supplemented in 1991 by a much larger one, further out and to the northwest. Until then, Riem is struggling to cope with ever-rising numbers of passengers. Delays are common, particularly in summer, and the arrivals hall is often chaotic. If you're being met, arrange to be picked up outside the main doors, not inside. Opening of a new charter terminal in late 1988 did little to organize the chaos.

Transport from and to the airport is equally tiresome. There is no direct rail service to the city, and the shuttle buses from the airport to the station of Riem are crowded. Buses direct to the city are nonstop and drop passengers on the north side of the main railroad station, the *Hauptbahnhof,* opposite the Hotel Deutscher Kaiser. Taxis take just as long, particularly at peak times: about half an hour. They cost about four times more than buses.

By Train

The newly refurbished Hauptbahnhof is central and served by hourly InterCity and EuroCity trains to and from all major German cities and some foreign ones. Frankfurt is 4¹/₂ hours away, Hamburg 8. If you're traveling first class, reserve a place in a *Grossraumwagen,* which offers very comfortable compartments with food and drink served at your seat. Many trains have telephones and secretarial services. InterCity and EuroCity diners offer good food of high quality, and it's not expensive by European railroad standards.

▷ Money

The standard unit of currency is the Deutsche mark, or D-mark. International code: DEM. Banknotes come in denominations of 10, 20, 50, 100, 500, and 1,000 marks. Coins are minted in amounts of 1, 2, 5, 10, and 50 pfennigs (100 pfennigs = 1 mark). Banks offer the best exchange rates.

▷ Language

German—but there's also a strong Bavarian dialect. Many people speak or understand English.

▷ Communications

Country code: 49. City code: 89.

▷ Getting To Know the City

Munich sprawls. The center, though, is small and can be walked within an hour or so, even if you pause to gaze at the city's historic heart. This central area is about one mile square, and a shopping or sightseeing tour can be packed into a morning or afternoon. A pedestrian zone about 1¹/₂ miles long begins opposite the Hauptbahnhof (main railway station) and encompasses most of the city's important shopping streets. The purchase of goods is a major pastime in a city rated their favorite by the majority of West Germans. The Hauptbahnhof, on the western side of downtown, faces the Bahnhofplatz, and beyond are the streets leading to the main squares: the *Karlsplatz,* also known as *Stachüs,* and the *Marienplatz,* the oldest part of Munich with daily bell-ringings in the tower of the *Neues Rathaus* (city hall).

Slightly to the north is the glitzy area of the *Promenadeplatz* with the Bayerische Hof Hotel. A short distance to the east is *Max-Joseph-Platz,* with the Residenz complex of palace and theater—the pride of the city— and the elegant *Maximilianstrasse,* where the Hotel Vier Jahreszeiten sets the moneyed tone. A little bit farther to the north is the *Englischer Garten,* the local equivalent of Central Park, the Bois de Boulogne, or Hyde Park. A number of leading hotels are in this extremely pleasant area of the city. Continuing counterclockwise, the visitor reaches *Schwabing,* the former artists' quarter now too expensive for much of the bohemian crowd that made it famous. Munich, however, still has strong ties with the film world, and more recently that of television, and this imparts a flavor to the city's working and social life. The pink baroque building on Wittelsbacher square, the headquarters of Siemens, perhaps represents best the modern and growing industrial importance of Munich.

▷ Moving Around

The transit system is efficient, reasonably priced, and clean. It includes the *U-bahn,* a sleek subway; *S-bahn* high-speed suburban trains; buses; and slow, noisily nostalgic streetcars, which nostalgics are fighting to keep on the rails. The self-service business of buying a ticket from one machine and canceling it in another defeats many visitors (and some residents): buy instead a 24-hour ticket. The first version covers you for all travel within the central area, the second for the whole metropolitan area. Taxis are costly, but most are Mercedes-Benzes, and drivers are both courteous and knowledgeable (cultural information is part of the service).

▷ Hotels

Munich is both a business and a tourist destination, and rooms are scarce during the carnival, or *Fasching* (January 7 through Shrove Tuesday, date of which varies); the summer festival season (mid-July through early August); and *Oktoberfest* (September through the first Sunday of October). On the business side, there are fairs throughout the year—construction, fashion, computers, electronics, and others.

Luxury

Bayerischer Hof, Palais Monteglas, Promenadeplatz 2-6. Tel.: 21200. Telex: 523409. Fax: 212-0906. Rooms/suites: 440. The same family has owned this hotel since 1897. It's in the shopping and banking district, and service is excellent. Rooftop pool, lobby bar, nightclub, shops. Restaurants are undistinguished unless you fancy a Bavarian *Trader Vic's*. Associated with SAS Scandinavian Airlines.

City Hilton. Rosenheimer Strasse. Tel.: 3845-0. Telex: 5215740. Fax: 3845-1845. Rooms: 460. Suites: 27. A second, brand-new Hilton just across the Isar River, part of the Gasteig cultural center and close to the European Patent Office. Business service center with personal computers. Extensive meeting facilities. Three restaurants.

Grand Hotel Continental, Max-Joseph-Strasse 5. Tel.: 551570. Telex: 522603. Fax: 55157500. Rooms/suites: 157. Not much to look at from outside, but lavish inside with period decoration. Popular *Conti Grill,* a second restaurant, and bar-lounge. A Best Western enterprise.

Hilton, Am Tucherpark. Tel.: 340051. Telex: 5215740. Fax: 38451845. Rooms/suites: 518. Facing the famous Englischer Garten, this Hilton features Belle Etage and Sunshine rooms with Laura Ashley decor. Two restaurants, nightclub, pool, health club, and business center.

Königshof, Karlsplatz 25. Tel.: 551360. Telex: 523616. Fax: 55136113. Rooms/suites: 106. A pleasant blend of traditional and modern on one of

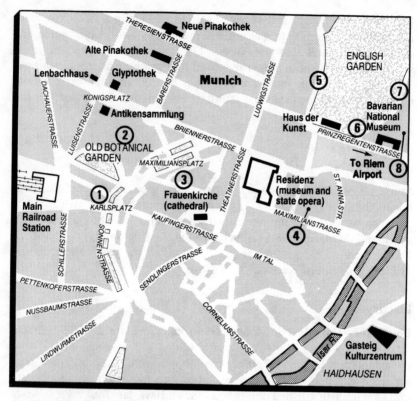

1. **Hotel Königshof**
2. **Grand Hotel Continental**
3. **Hotel Bayerischer Hof**
4. **Hotel Vier Jahreszeiten**

5. **Hotel Ramada**
6. **Hotel Hilton**
7. **Hotel Crest**
8. **Hotel Sheraton**

the city's main squares (also known as Stachus). Munich executives favor the several restaurants.

Ramada Parkhotel, Theodor-Dombart-Strasse 4. Tel.: 360990. Telex: 5218720. Fax: 36099684. Rooms/suites: 260. A little out of the center. Comfortable rooms, five restaurants.

Sheraton and Towers, Arabellastrasse 6. Tel.: 924011. Telex: 523754. Fax: 916877. Rooms/suites: 635. Four restaurants, a biergarten, a nightclub, bars, outdoor pool, fitness center. Separate lounge in the Towers.

Vier Jahreszeiten, (Four Seasons), Maximilianstrasse 17. Tel.: 230390. Telex: 523859. Fax: 23039693. Rooms/suites: 341. Top hotel on the top street, a Munich institution popular with executives—and with divas from the nearby opera house. A huge rotunda has stained glass for the four seasons. Ambience is that of a gentlemen's club, yet with modern and practical touches such as pullout desks in the rooms. The *Walterspiel* restaurant is great for food, wines, service, and atmosphere. Run by the Kempinski chain.

First Class

Crest, Effnerstrasse 99. Tel.: 982541. Telex: 524757. Fax: 983813. Rooms/suites: 154. The Crest chain is making a big effort in West Germany, and the results show here. There are Crest Lady, nonsmoking, and executive rooms, two restaurants, and excellent conference facilities. Handy for the airport.

Drei Löwen, Schillerstrasse 8. Tel.: 595521. Telex: 523867. Fax: 55104905. Rooms/suites: 130. Close to the main railroad station and not far from the fairgrounds. Pleasant lobby and accommodations.

Eden-Hotel Wolff, Arnulfstrasse 4-8. Tel.: 551150. Telex: 523564. Fax: 55115555. Rooms/suites: 215. Opposite the main station and known as a well-managed hotel with a good restaurant and a variety of meeting rooms.

Excelsior, Schutzenstrasse 11. Tel.: 551370. Telex: 522419. Fax: 55137121. Rooms/suites: 116. Comfortable, stylish, and close to the station. The *Hubertus Grill* is popular with businesspeople.

Holiday Inn, Leopoldstrasse 194. Tel.: 340971. Telex: 17-897930. Fax: 3617119. Rooms/suites: 363. Away from the center, 3.2 kilometers (2 miles) from Marienplatz. Noteworthy selection of restaurants and bars; nightclub, pool, sauna, fitness center, meeting rooms.

Novotel, Rodolf-Vogel-Bogen 3. Tel.: 638000. Telex: 522030. Fax: 631309. Rooms/suites: 254. A touch of France close to the airport, but the stress is on business as well as cuisine: there are ten conference rooms. Pool and fitness facilities.

Prinzregent, Ismaninger Strasse 42. Tel.: 4702081. Telex: 524403. Fax: 470-2392. Rooms: 67. Probably the best of the smaller hotels. Central location, Bavarian decor, and a very warm welcome. Superb breakfasts.

Regent, Seidlstrasse 2. Tel.: 551590. Telex: 523787. Fax: 551-59154. Rooms/suites: 222. Also two apartments. A modern hotel, near the station, with French period decor in the bedrooms. Three restaurants, health and fitness club.

▷ Restaurants

The prosperity that has come with the high-tech and service industries has swollen expense accounts and raised awareness of fine eating, particularly *nouvelle cuisine*. There are still the traditional Bavarian restaurants with their wurst, sauerkraut, pig's feet, and plenty of beer, but a number of other restaurants, such as *Aubergine, Tantris,* and *Walterspiel* have won the critics' stars, including the coveted Michelin. A selection of the best:

Deluxe

Aubergine, Maximilianstrasse 5. Tel.: 598171. This is top-of-the-scale *nouvelle cuisine*. Owner-chef Eckart Witzigmann runs what is the most sophisticated restaurant in the city. The decor is rather modern, but the service is impeccable. Specialties: turbot in champagne, breast of pigeon with artichoke and truffle salad. Reservations are imperative in this and other Munich gastronomic temples.

Boettner's, Theatinerstrasse 2. Tel.: 221210. The dark paneling and pleasant bar are what you might expect in the oldest of Munich's top restaurants—Boettner's has been around since the beginning of the century. It's a haven with seafood, notably lobster and sole, predominating. Again, it is essential to reserve.

Dallmayr, Dienerstrasse 14. Tel.: 21350. Downstairs is West Germany's most famous food store, often likened to Paris' Fauchon or London's Fortnum and Mason. Upstairs a fine restaurant.

Le Gourmet, Ligslazstrasse 46. Tel.: 503597. Gastronomic critics have heaped praise on this restaurant, now member of the Relais and Chateaux chain. Specialties: oxtail in champagne sauce, zucchini and truffle salad.

Käferschänke, Schumannstrasse 1. Tel.: 41681. Like Dallmayr, this culinary landmark is a high-class charcuterie on the ground floor, while upstairs are connecting rooms in rustic decor with fine antiques. Fish flown in daily from the French Riviera. Specialty: grilled prawns in sweet-sour sauce.

Sabitzer's, Reitmorstrasse, 21. Tel.: 298584. Attractive nineteenth-century dining room, but more *nouvelle cuisine* of the highest order (although with more local influences). Try the venison, lamb, or salmon dishes. Important to reserve.

Tantris, Johann-Fichter-Strasse 7. Tel.: 362061. Situated in the "artistic" quarter of Schwabing, Tantris is, in the opinion of many, Munich's finest restaurant. *Nouvelle cuisine* is served with flair. The modern decor leaves something to be desired, but not the food, notably the pigeon breast, venison, caviar terrine.

Walterspiel, Maximilianstrasse 16. Tel.: 230390. Softly lit, extremely comfortable banquettes, crisp tablecloths, beautiful china. The food is good, too. The Walterspiel also has Germany's finest wine list—national whites as well as French and the others.

First Class

Austernkeller. Stollbergstrasse 11. Tel.: 298787. Cellar restaurant with vaulted ceilings and baroque fittings. Noted for *austern* (oysters) and many other forms of shellfish.

Bouillabaisse, Falkenturmstrasse 10. Tel.: 297909. Beams and chandeliers give this restaurant a distinctive air, but the real distinction (and rarity) is to find the famous French fish stew in Bavaria. A person from Marseilles would feel at home.

Gratzer's Lobby, Beethovenplatz 2-3. Tel.: 531154. A library setting, wood fires, very British in many ways. The locals use it for cocktails. Good for intimate discussions.

Preysing Keller, Innere-Wienerstrasse 6. Tel.: 481015. The sixteenth-century cellar has been ruined by restoration, but the seven-course meal is highly rated. Excellent wine list.

Offbeat

Der Kasladen von Tölz. Westeriederstrasse 16. Tel.: 226322. Cheese dishes and wine at this charming chalet-style restaurant. Lunch, but not dinner.

Goldene Stadt, Oeranger 44. Tel.: 264382. This is the place for Bohemian cooking from next-door Czechoslovakia. Roast duck, goose, and dumplings.

▷ Spotlight ◁

Beer and pig's feet. Haxnbauer, Platzl, and Hofbrauhaus: this trio in and around the Munzstrasse offers traditional Bavarian fare of pig's feet and calves' knuckles served by waitresses in dirndls. Platzl has lederhosen-clad musicians and yodellers. The Hofbrauhaus is a very big, rather gray beer hall where vast quantities of beer are consumed by local and foreign visitors. Restaurant upstairs.

For beer lovers, autumn brings the Oktoberfest at the Theresienwiese grounds, southwest of the main railway station. Some 1.5 million gallons of beer and mountains of sausages are consumed. The fun of the fair includes merry-go-rounds, parades, and folklore. A different crowd from the schickeria, or the "schickie-mickies," or fast set, in the Maximilianstrasse.

▷ Tipping

The restaurant check includes the standard tip. If the service was particularly outstanding, you might want to add a few coins. The hatcheck or coatcheck attendant should receive a tip. Give the concierge or doorman between $3 and $5 for such services as reserving a restaurant table or concert tickets or finding you a taxi. Cabdrivers should receive a tip of about 10 percent on top of the metered fare.

▷ Doing Business

Bavarians are reputed to be open, carefree, easygoing, and even naïve. Perhaps they are, but they turn over every pfennig before parting with it. They also examine every deal with painstaking and sometimes frustrating caution. There's a lot of the peasant in the Bavarians—and we don't mean that rudely or pejoratively. Peasants know how to bargain, and all that carefree charm is part of the technique.

Most of the bargaining is done in offices, but the Bavarians do like their food and drink. So do not be surprised if your business contact suggests a first meeting over lunch—or even over a beer in a local tavern. In summer you can find yourself talking big bucks under the chestnut trees of a beer garden, so pack some casual clothes.

English is spoken widely, as we've noted—almost universally by people doing international business. You'll delight them, though, if you try even a few words of German, however bad your accent.

Aside from the tripling of investment in electronics in the past few years, Munich also has seen the growth of aerospace activities around

Messerschmitt-Bölkow-Blohm (MBB), jet fighters and space satellites, and Motoren-und-Turbinen Union (MTU), aero and industrial engines (both are now with the Daimler-Benz group).

Not all is big in the manner of the aerospace, electronics, and insurance groups (Allianz, Europe's largest, and others). The Bavarian Act for the Promotion of Medium and Small Business has meant firms with less than 500 employees occupying the dominant position.

▷ Useful Phone Numbers

Business Contacts

Bavarian Chamber of Industry-Trade	51160
Bavarian Foreign Trade Association	5577701
Munich city information	23911
Trade fairs	51070/500610
European Community	2021011

Emergencies

Police	110
Fire	112
Medical	558661
Pharmacy info	594475

Travel

Airport	92112127
Automobile service	19211
Railways	592991
S-bahn	557575
Ski info	294940

Consulates

Argentina	263787
Austria	921090-0
Belgium	397096
Brazil	227985
Canada	558531
Denmark	220441
Finland	221493
France	475016
Greece	4701061
Indonesia	294609
Ireland	985723
Italy	4180030
Japan	471043-5
Jordan	282953
Luxembourg	20242(0)202
Malaysia	1232178
Mexico	981617
Morocco	476031
Netherlands	594103
Norway	224170
Philippines	400482
Portugal	299932
Spain	985027
Sweden	264089
Switzerland	347063
Thailand	781997
Turkey	176093
United Kingdom	394015
United States	2301-1

Airlines

Aeroflot Soviet Airlines	288261	Olympic Airways	224148
Air Canada	288451	Pan Am World Airways	558171
Air France	21067	Qantas Airways (Australia)	292071
Air India	296831	Sabena Belgian World Airlines	555845
Alitalia	2380031	SAS Scandinavian Airlines	908021
American Airlines	2285018		
Austrian Airlines	226666	Singapore Airlines	596654
British Airways	292121	South African Airways	265071
El Al Israel Airlines	296888		
Finnair	281023	Swissair	23633
Iberia (Spain)	558491	TAP Air Portugal	598086
Japan Air Lines/JAL	225255	Turk Hava Yollari	539415
KLM Royal Dutch Airlines	268026	TWA	597643
Lufthansa German Airlines	268026	Varig (Brazil)	554901
		Yugoslav Airlines/JAT	554561
Malev Hungarian Airlines	293434		

▷ Shopping

Several multifloor department stores offering a cornucopia of goods from fashion to food, plus a cluster of streets lined with trendy boutiques and interspersed with smart *Konditorei* (cafés), make Munich West Germany's best city for shopping. The larger stores are along the *Neuhauserstrasse* and *Kaufingerstrasse,* which together form a long, pedestrian-only thoroughfare between the main city center squares, the *Karlsplatz* and the *Marienplatz.*

One store, *Karstadt,* has three buildings, and shoppers will find an excellent food department and porcelain from Meissen, East Germany. The *Hertie* store specializes in *loden* (the distinctively heavy woolen cloth)—and more food—while the *Kaufhof* store has just about everything from shoe repairs to a rooftop restaurant and beer garden. Another, *Ludwig Beck am Rathauseck,* on Marienplatz, sponsors young designers. Just off the square is the picturesque *Viktualienmarkt* beneath the trees of Old Munich.

More fashionable shops are situated along *Maximilianstrasse, Residenzstrasse, Theatinerstrasse,* and the block around the Bayersicher Hof

Hotel. The first named is the most noted, with French, Italian, and American quality—and high price tags—as well as furs, leather, porcelain, silver, hunting clothes, and antiques. Residenzstrasse has the *Bogner* store for ski clothes and the *Wallach-Haus für Volkskunst* which, as its name suggests, has Bavarian crafts and clothing. A similar store is *Ingo* on Leopoldstrasse.

Munich's renowned *Nymphenburg porcelain* is sold at an outlet in the Nymphenburg Palace itself and in another at Odeonsplatz by Theatinerstrasse. One can buy individual pieces or services, but be warned that prices are high. Near the Odeonplatz shop is another selling Meissen china at Briennerstrasse 6. All in all, one can find an extremely large variety of local and international goods in the city.

▷ After Hours

More beery than bawdy—that's the after-hours scene. Clustered around the Hofbrauhaus, where people go to drink beer, more beer, and yet more beer, are some good-value bars and clubs. In the area are an original *Harry's New York Bar,* at Falkenturmstrasse 9; and the city's best singles bar, *Schumann's,* Maximilianstrasse 36, where some of the *fräuleins* (young women) are stunning.

Stunning in a different sense is the area south of the Hauptbahnhof, the main railroad station. Particularly in Schillerstrasse, insist on paying for each drink as it arrives.

For jazz, try the *Allotria,* Turkenstrasse 33, and the *Scwainger Podium,* Wagnerstrasse 1. The top clubs for Munich's Beautiful People and "buppies" (upwardly mobile Bavarians) are *Pl,* Imhause der Kunst, Prinzregentstrasse 1, where a tie is obligatory; and *Park Café,* Alter Botanischer Garten, Elisenstrasse 2, where the decor is 1940s and a younger crowd congregates.

▷ Sights and Sounds

Alte Pinakothek, Barerstrasse 27. Tel.: 23805215. The former kings launched this remarkable museum, one of the best in Europe (certainly for the works of Rubens, who is represented by 30 paintings). A Dürer self-portrait, a stunning display of the great Italian masters, and Rembrandt works complete the collection.

Asamkirche, Sendlingerstrasse. Situated near the city center, this small jewel of religious art is considered to be the most beautiful of all Munich's churches.

Bayerische Staatsoper, Max-Joseph-Platz. Tel.: 2185-1. The opera house, within the National Theater, was rebuilt after the war like many of Munich's cultural centers. Opera, ballet, and orchestral concerts. Advance planning needed to obtain tickets.

Deutsches Museum, Auf der Isarinsel. Tel.: 21791. This island museum on the Isar River is the largest technical show in the world. A staggering display of planes, locomotives, cars, metal and mining machines, even sewing machines.

Frauenkirche, Frauenplatz. Built in 1488 and rebuilt after World War II. Its onion-shaped domes are the symbol of the city. Resting place of royalty and Cardinal Faulhaber, opponent of the Nazis.

Haus der Kunst, Prinzregentstrasse 1. Tel.: 222651. Likened to the Grand Palais in Paris. Contains the *Staatsgalerie Moderner Kunst* (State Museum of Modern Art) with West Germany's finest collection of twentieth-century art. Works of German artists hang near to 14 Picassos and Americans such as Warhol.

Neue Pinakothek, Barerstrasse 29. Tel.: 23805195. Nineteenth century works, including Turner and Goya, German romantics plus Cezanne and Gaugin.

Nymphenburg Schloss, St. Callerstrasse. Summer residence of the Bavarian kings, a kind of Bavarian mini-Versailles. Plenty of baroque and rococo. A display of the famous Nymphenburg porcelain. One must allow half a day.

Residenz (Royal Palace), Max-Joseph-Platz. A tremendous feat of reconstruction for the Residenz was a major complex of sixteenth to nineteenth century buildings. The different epochs live again—in the palace itself; the *schatzkammer,* or treasury, with jewels and other artistic treasures; and the theater.

▷ Out of town

Alps

A few stops on the *S-bahn*, the fast suburban railway, and one is in lush, rolling Bavarian meadowland and forest. The Alps are only one hour away by car or train. Bavaria's Alpine "capital" is *Garmisch-Partenkirchen,* at the end of the southbound Autobahn 95, close to the

Austrian border and at the foot of Germany's highest mountain, the 10,000-foot Zugspitze. There's glacier skiing on an open bowl of treeless terrain near the summit, while lower slopes and nearby peaks are connected by a large network of trails and ski lifts. In summer and autumn, the area is a hiker's paradise. Luxury accommodation: *Clausing's Posthotel,* Marienplatz 12. Tel.: (08821) 58071. Rooms: 31. Open all year. There is also a Holiday Inn.

Castles

Beyond the Ammer mountains are two of the exotic castles built by the flamboyant King Ludwig II in the late 1800s. *Schloss Neuschwanstein,* a medieval-style, turreted fairy castle, clinging to the rocky pinnacle above West Germany's "Romantic Road," was the inspiration for a Disney cartoon film setting—and later Disney real estate. *Schloss Linderhof,* a short local bus ride from Oberammergau, of Passion Play fame, is more traditional on country house lines set in a forest park. Ludwig's third palace, *Herrenschiemsee,* stands in unfinished splendor on an island in the Chiemsee lake, 60 miles west of Munich, one hour by car on the Salzburg bound Autobahn 8. Bus excursions to all three can be booked in Munich.

The small castle where Ludwig was detained before his mysterious death, *Schloss Berg,* is on the shores of Lake Starnberg. The Starnberg resort town is half an hour from Munich by S-6 suburban line. Best see Visconti's remarkable film on Ludwig before embarking along these historical paths.

Dachau

The S-2 suburban line runs 12 miles to Dachau. The concentration camp site is now a memorial to the victims of Nazism, who died there both before and during the war. It is open Tuesday to Sunday from 9:00 a.m. to 5:00 p.m., and an English-language documentary film on the camp is shown twice daily at 11:30 a.m. and 3:30 p.m. Bus 722 runs there from the railway station. Dachau is a hilltop town of great beauty, bearing forever the stamp of death.

OSLO

Is There a Fjord In Your Future?

Population: 452,000. Administrative, commercial, and political capital of the Kingdom of Norway (population: 4.18 million). *Location*: southeast coast of Norway at the northern end of Oslo Fjord. *Economy*: banking and financial services, chemicals, dairy products, electronics and electrical equipment, forest products, machine tools, maritime services, textiles, shipyards. Norway is a member of the Organization for Economic Cooperation and Development (OECD) and a signatory to the General Agreement on Tariffs and Trade (GATT).

▷ **Background Briefing**

King Harald III (Haardraade) founded the city in 1050; it became the capital in the 1300s and was destroyed by fires in 1567 and 1624. King Christian IV of Denmark (that country then ruled Norway) rebuilt the city, and with due modesty named it Cristiania. And so it was called until 1925.

Oslo today is a metropolis modest in population but rather larger in its economic ambitions. Norway is, after all, a major exporter of oil and gas through its share of the North Sea fields and for centuries has looked outward from its mountains, valleys, and spectacular fjords to the rest of the world. Norway was one of the homes of the Vikings, who from the 800s A.D. onward colonized many parts of northern Europe. Some Norsemen settled in what is now Normandy, France, became known as Normans, and conquered England in 1066.

▷ **Spotlight** ◁

Vikings in America. Who were the first Europeans to land in America—a name derived from that of *Americus Vespucius*, the Latinized name of Florentine explorer Amerigo Vespucci (1451–1512)? Almost certainly, neither he nor the Genoese Christopher Columbus were the first Europeans to set foot in "the new world." That honor may have belonged to the Norsemen Leif Ericsson in about 1000 A.D. and Thorfinn Karlsefni in 1004–06.

All that sort of conquest having been over long ago, Norway nowadays is peaceful and politically stable: the rush at election time is toward the middle ground. But like all neighboring countries that are not members of the European Community, Norway is worried by the potential impact of "1992," the year in which the last barriers to intra-Community trade are supposed to fall. Soon after, Norway's oil bonanza may slow to a trickle. The Oil and Energy Ministry has warned of declining prospects for new discoveries, prices stable or falling in real terms, and consequent little chance of maintaining investment levels after the first half of the 1990s.

Norwegian business ears are therefore eager to hear of foreign alliances that will reduce the country's reliance on oil and gas and strengthen manufacturing and service companies' competitive position in the post-1992 era.

▷ Arriving

Oslo has two airports, Fornebu and Gardermoden. The first is between 15 and 30 minutes from the city center by taxi, depending on the time of day and the weather; Fornebu handles most scheduled flights from Europe. Gardermoden takes all North American scheduled flights and international charter traffic; allow up to an hour to or from the city. Taxis are expensive; the far-cheaper bus takes little longer.

▷ Money

The basic unit of currency is the krone. International code: NOK. The krone is further divided into 100 ore. Most banks are open from 8:15 a.m. to 3:30 p.m. Monday through Friday; some stay open until 5:00 p.m. on Thursday. All are closed on Saturday. The Foreign Exchange Bureau at Oslo Central Station is open from 8:30 a.m. until 8:30 p.m. Monday through Friday and from 8:00 a.m. until 2:00 p.m. on Saturday; closed Sunday. Opening hours are longer during the summer, so phone to check, tel.: 420769. Airport banks are usually open from early in the morning until late at night.

These post offices change foreign banknotes and certain traveler's checks: *Central,* 15 Dronningenst.; *Vika,* 7 Klingenberggt.; *Egerfortet,* 25 Ovre Slottgst.; *Kringsja,* Panorama Summer Hotel, 218 Songsvn.

▷ Language

Norwegian, a member of the North Germanic or Scandinavian group of languages. Virtually all educated Norwegians speak English and/or German, as well as Danish. There are two reasons for that linguistic versatility. First, English is the *lingua franca* of business. Second, there isn't one single form of Norwegian. Instead, there are two official versions: *bokmal* (book language) and *nynorsk* (new Norwegian). *Bokmal* is greatly influenced by Danish, reflecting that country's rule of Norway from 1397 until 1814. *Nynorsk,* also known as *landsmal,* or country language, stems from the native Norwegian dialects that evolved from Old Norse and were little affected by Danish. For many years, politicians and educators have urged that *bokmal* and *nynorsk* be fused into a common Norwegian tongue, *samnorsk.* They haven't yet succeeded.

▷ Communications

Country code: 47. City code: 2. Quality of service is good. You can dial most countries in the world directly from your hotel—though watch the markups. Many hotels have a telefax machine as well as a telex. The public telecommunications office is open daily from 8:00 a.m. until 9:00 p.m., providing telephones, telex, fax, and telegraphic facilities. Address: Kongens Gate (entrance on Prinsens Gate).

▷ Getting To Know the City

Easy—if you want to know the bare topography. The city covers 445.97 square kilometers (about 175 square miles), of which more than half is forest or parkland. The map in this chapter shows the city center—and with it Oslo's huge frontage to the water. That's an inescapable reminder of both the city's and the country's long involvement with international trade.

From a visitor's viewpoint, then, the waterfront is the perspective from which to start. At right is the finger of land pointing toward the sea, with piers to which tie up the ferries to and from Denmark. Move your gaze left, past the parks and their museums, and there's another dent in the land, caused by the sea's remorseless pounding; and so it goes to the top left hand of the map, to the end of the stretch of water known as the *Frognerkilen*. Inland from the waterfront—waterfronts, really—are the streets that make up Oslo's business districts.

Gratitude goes to urban planners of bygone ages who interspersed and surrounded the city with parks large and small; nowhere in Oslo is one far from an open space or the water. Grandeur is natural rather than manufactured. Oslo offers no victory arches, few arabesques frozen in stone commemorating half-forgotten military victories over foes who have long since become friends. Oslo is a city on the human scale.

▷ **Spotlight** ◁

Communing with nature. Without leaving the city limits, you could get lost in the wilderness of forests, lakes, streams, and waterfalls, mountains and valleys. Oslo is home to moose, deer, foxes, and lynx, just 4 of the 20 species that roam the woods. Black grouse and ptarmigan as well as 150 species of migratory birds make Oslo a nesting-box for ornithologists. For botanists, there are about a thousand kinds of wild flowers. How best to see all this? There are safaris in four-wheel-drive vehicles; meals include trout that clients have caught for themselves. Details from the Tourist Information Office, City Hall.

▷ Moving Around

Easy—in theory, since the center is compact. But Oslo is a northern city. It can be hot in summer and bitterly cold in winter. Often, there are strong winds as well. Get the weather forecast before deciding that the business district is small enough for you to walk to and from your appointments.

The public transportation system is efficient, with *T-Banen* (subways), streetcars, and buses, and ferries to and from islands in the harbor. As one might expect in a Scandinavian country, all are clean and run on time. Well worth buying is the Oslo Card, available at most hotels and at tourist information offices, the central railroad station, and many other places. Cards—valid for 24, 48, or 72 hours—entitle holders to free travel on public transportation, free admission to museums and art galleries, car rental discounts, and other benefits.

Taxis can be picked up at ranks or cruising when their signs are lit: most drivers understand English. You can call a radio taxi by phoning 388090. For reservations at least an hour ahead, call 388080.

Car rental is available from major American and European companies. It's good advice anywhere, but especially in Norway: do not drink before driving. Laws are tough and enforcement is strict.

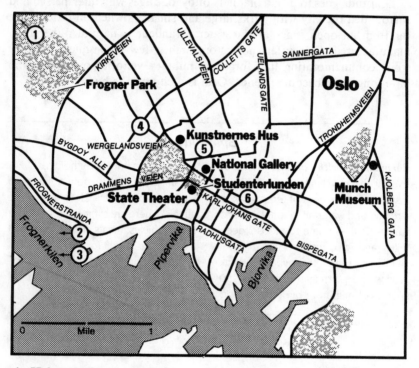

1. **Holmenkollen Park, Hotel Rica**
2. **Sheraton Hotel, Oslo Fjord**
3. **SAS Park Royal Hotel**
4. **Hotel Ambassadeur**
5. **SAS Scandinavia**
6. **Bristol Hotel**

▷ Hotels

Oslo's hotels are comfortable rather than grandiose, the other side of that coin being that they tend to be friendly rather than starchy. That's no criticism: Paris palaces and London luxury often demand as much stiff-backed dignity from guests as they do from the staff.

Ambassadeur, 15 Camilla Collettsvei. Tel.: 441835. Telex: 71446. Fax: 441835. Rooms/suites: 54. Central, in the diplomatic quarter near the Royal Palace; notably comfortable. Indoor pool.

Bristol, 4 Kristian IV's Gate. Tel.: 415840. Telex: 71668. Fax: 428651. Rooms/suites: 220. On a quiet, central side street. The grill is excellent; the *El Toro* is a Spanish restaurant with dancing and floor shows; and there are a nightclub and disco.

Continental, 24-26 Stortingsgate. Tel.: 419060. Telex: 71012. Fax: 429689. Rooms/suites: 318. In the business, ministerial, and legislative district. *Annen Etage* restaurant is one of the city's best.

Grand, 31 Karl Johansgate. Tel.: 429390. Telex: 71683. Fax: 421225. Rooms/suites: 350. Grandness without pomp, polished for a century; popular with business travelers and out-of-town Norwegian legislators. Five restaurants and three bars, indoor pool and solarium.

▷ Spotlight ◁

For watersports enthusiasts is the Holmen Fjord, 64 Slemmestadveien, Nesbru. Twenty minutes west of Oslo on the E18 highway, the Holmen has a marina with sailboats, motorboats, and windsurfers for rent. Comfortable rooms, sports facilities, restaurant, nightclub. Tel.: 847280. Telex: 78786.

Holmenkollen Park Hotel Rica, 26 Kongeveien. Rooms/suites: 200. Tel.: 146090. Telex: 72094. Fax: 146192. "Very special" is how an Oslo business executive describes the Holmenkollen. Slightly out of town on a hill; built in old Norse log cabin style and set in gardens, with superb views; ski jump nearby. Nightclub, disco, indoor pool, whirlpool, gym, squash court, curling rink.

SAS Park Royal Hotel, Fornebuparken, Lysaker. Tel.: 120220. Telex: 78745. Fax: 120011. Beds: 500. Suites: 10. One of the larger hotels, but service is personal and comforts are many.

SAS Scandinavia Hotel, 30 Holbergsgate. Tel.: 113000. Telex: 79090. Fax: 113000. Rooms/suites: 476. You think SAS is an airline? You're right. But it's also a hotel company, and the Scandinavia is a good example of the care it takes of business and first-class travelers once they've touched down. Spectacular smörgasbörd, nightclub with disco and live music, indoor pool, shopping center—and round-the-clock room service.

Sheraton Fjord, 130 Sandviksveien. Tel.: 545700. Telex: 74345. Fax: 542733. Rooms/suites: 245. Luxurious elegance 15 minutes from the city center, 10 minutes from Fornebu airport, with shuttle buses to and from both. Restaurant, piano bar, nightclub, health studio.

West Hotel, 15 Skovveien. Tel.: 554030. Telex: 72058. Fax: 557704. Beds: 79. Favored by business travelers on a tight budget: central, comfortable, excellent value for money.

▷ **Restaurants**

Norway is one of the world's great fishing nations. You can hardly go wrong if you choose to dine on creatures caught in rivers, streams, lakes, or the sea. The salmon are particularly fine. Norwegian cuisine stresses fresh, first-quality fish, meat, and fowl rather than elaborate sauces and other preparations. Watch out for the right-hand column of the wine list: prices are high.

Annen Etage (The Second Floor), Hotel Continental, 24-26 Stortingsgate. Tel.: 419060. Fancy food, fancy prices, but good value.

Bagatelle, 3 Bygdoy Alle. Tel.: 419060. Some people say this is the best restaurant in Oslo; it has a star in the *Guide Michelin*.

Etoile, Grand Hotel, 31 Karl Johansgate. Tel.: 429390. French cuisine, extensive wine list, panoramic views of the city.

De Fem Stuer (Five Rooms), Holmenkollen Park Hotel Rica, 26 Kongeveien. Tel.: 146090. Norwegian food and atmosphere are specialties, and very pleasant they are.

Det Gamle Raadhus (The Old Town Hall), 1 Nedre Slottsgate. Tel.: 420117. Oslo's oldest restaurant, or so it's said, the building dating from 1641. Up-to-date, too: there's a piano bar. Much to offer in atmosphere and nostalgia.

Hos Thea, 11 Gabelsgate. Tel.: 446874. Named in a 1987 poll as the "business restaurant of the year." Later, independent checks support that finding.

La Mer, 31 Pilestredet. Tel.: 203445/69. *La Mer* (that's *Norwegian?*) means "the sea"—and seafood sweeps in a tidal wave over the menu.

L'Orchidée, Sheraton Hotel Oslo Fjord, 184 Sandviksveien. Tel.: 545700. Large, widely spaced tables; cool elegance; excellent for business meals.

▷ Tipping

Some bar and restaurant checks include the tip, some don't. The safe and prudent thing to do is to add between 5 and 10 percent to the total. That goes for taxis, too.

▷ Doing Business

When oil and gas prices slid in the 1980s, so did the Norwegian economy. In 1987, total domestic demand declined, after an aggregate increase of 20 percent in the previous two years, and the current external deficit was equivalent to 5 percent of gross domestic product (GDP). Consumer price inflation reached an annual rate of about 7 percent in 1988, though the OECD forecasts a fall starting in 1989 or 1990.

If the economy does indeed recover soon, that will be due in part to the government's prompt and severe reactions, which included rigorous monetary policy spearheaded by interest rate rises. Clearly, Norwegians will have to learn to like tightened belts until world energy prices rise substantially, or until it is able to enlarge the nonoil economy. That it is certainly trying to do, with increasing emphasis on such relatively high technologies as computer hardware and software and telecommunications equipment.

With a tiny home market, however, Norway must rely heavily on exports, which in the period 1983–87 accounted for no less than 48.5 percent of GDP, high by OECD standards. There is also a looming challenge: the European Community's plan for an integrated, barrier-free internal market after 1992. Norwegian voters rejected EC membership in a 1972 referendum, but now most business leaders and many politicians wish with fresh fervor that their country was inside what could soon become Fortress Europe instead of outside gazing at the ramparts.

If Norway does reapply for EC membership—and the "if" is still big—it will have to pass a number of tests before being accepted as a member of the club. One of them is the level of government subsidies for both private- and public-sector businesses: the EC has strict rules (even if they are not always applied strictly) that are designed to guarantee fair competition.

Like those in other Nordic nations, Norwegian industrialists are niche players, seeking—and often finding—commercial crannies ignored by larger companies. But companies that are small by world standards cannot always afford the research that will keep them in the scientific and technological vanguard. One popular solution is the forging of commercial and research-and-development links with foreign partners. Another is the banding together of Norwegian companies to finance R&D.

Minds and doors are open to new projects, ranging from licensing of patents and copyrights, through investment in the country, to import-export agreements. Visitors will discover that Norway is one of the easiest countries in which to find a business partner, due to Norwegian executives' eagerness to do deals and their informality.

You usually can phone the top man in a department or even a company (female executives are still rather rare) without a lot of time-taking ritual. No layers of bureaucracy, no ranks of gatekeepers. Give your name and that of the executive to whom you wish to speak, and you're usually on the line within a few minutes.

You'll often find that your host, however high in rank, will serve the coffee or tea personally. The Norwegians neither stand on ceremony nor value it.

What they *do* value (and in that they differ little from executives in other countries) is a succinct presentation of the deal. For all their relaxed manners, coffee-serving Norwegian executives are smart cookies.

Punctuality is almost a fetish; time your appointments accordingly. If you absolutely must be late, phone ahead to apologize. Business hours are from 8:00 a.m. through 4:00 p.m. in the summer, through 3:00 p.m. in the winter (it's almost dark by then). Lunch usually starts at noon and lasts no longer than half an hour. Don't be surprised if it's no more than a sandwich in the office or a snack in the company cafeteria. As a visitor, though, you're likely to be invited out for at least one lunch or dinner. Your return invitation will be valued, but try not to issue it for the weekend. Norwegians like to spend spare time at their seaside summer homes or mountain cabins. If you're invited for a family weekend, accept—because you've been accepted.

▷ Useful Phone Numbers

Emergencies

Accident/ ambulance	003 or 201090	Fire	001 or 114455
All-night pharmacy	412482	Lost property	669865
Car rescue	232085	Medical center (*Oslo Akutten*)	412440/412409
Dentist	674846	Police	002 or 669050

Local Information

Guided tours	414863
Tourism	
City Hall	427170
Central Station	416221

Business Information

Association of insurance companies	555000
Bankers association	411830
Chamber of Commerce	557400
Conventions and expositions	
Central bureau	422982
Congress center	546090
Oslo University Congress Service	455055
Export council	437700
Shipowners association	416080

Foreign Chambers of Commerce

American	114030
French	203721
German (West)	447079
International (ICC)	437000
Italian	437700
Japanese	558611
Spanish	437700
Swedish	440630

International Organizations

European Community	331040
Nordic Cooperation Council	506900

Embassies and Consulates

Argentina	552448
Belgium	552215
Brazil	552029
Bulgaria	554040
Canada	466955
Chile	448955
Colombia	556579
Denmark	441846
Egypt	447767
Finland	430400
France	441820
Greece	442728
India	552229
Indonesia	441121
Iran	552408
Israel	448094
Italy	557250
Japan	551011
Korea (North)	559575
Korea (South)	552018
Mexico	431165
Netherlands	602193
Poland	430161
Portugal	606225
Romania	441512
Soviet Union	553278
Spain	552015
United Kingdom	552400
United States	448550

Airlines

Air France	421045
British Airways	418750
Lufthansa German Airlines	200836

Northwest Airlines	112010	City office	429970
SAS Scandinavian Airlines		Domestic/Scandinavia	427900
Fornebu airport	596050	Europe/intercontinental	427550

▷ Shopping

The most distinctive goods are those of Scandinavian origin—for example, handknitted woolens, handwoven table runners and rugs, reindeer pelts and horns, sheepskin and sealskin clothing, and (unavoidably) trolls and dolls. Many of the larger stores are in the cathedral area and near the *Stortinget* (parliament). In the *Hegdehaugsvan/Bogstadvn,* which runs from the upper part of the Royal Palace park to Majorstuen, are both large stores and small boutiques. The *Gamlebyen* neighborhood is noted for its antiques dealers. *Aker Brygge* is a new quarter with shops, bars, and restaurants lining the inner harbor.

Some 450 stores offer tax-free shopping for people living outside the Nordic countries. Ask for a tax-free check when you pay, and present this with the goods and your passport to the "tax-free representative" at the airport, border crossing, or ferry—*not* to the customs office. For further details, contact Norway Tax-free Shopping A/S. Tel.: 592650.

▷ After Hours

Oslo's nightlife is dominated by jazz; the summer festival attracts international stars. There's jazz almost every night at these places:

Guldfisken, 2 Radhus Gate. Tel.: 411489.

Jazz Alive, 2 Observatorie Gate. Tel.: 440745.

Jeppe's Kro, Vinederen. Folksong club meets Tuesdays.

New Orleans Workshop, 5 Christies Gate.

Oslo Jazzhus, 69 Toftsgate. Tel.: 383765.

Stortorvets Gjaestgiveri, 1 Grensen. Tel.: 428863.

There are discos too, of course, but they tend to drift in and out of popularity. Ask the hotel concierge which ones are currently "in."

▷ Sights and Sounds

In few other capital cities is there such a rich variety of sea, scenery, and culture—all within minutes of the center.

The Sea

The most pervasive sight is the sea, and a visit to Oslo isn't complete without at least one trip by boat, if only a ferry ride. The forest comes right to the city limits, and down to the water's edge at some points. For joggers or energetic walkers, a good idea is to go by taxi to *Sognsvann* and hike around the lake, returning by train from Gaustad station—something you can do between breakfast and your first appointment (in the summer, that is; winter days are short). There is good bathing on the east side of the lake. In winter, you can make the same tour, but on skis.

Sports

Two golf courses are within easy reach of the city. *Oslo Golfklubb* (tel.: 240567) welcomes members of other clubs, but charges green fees; it rents clubs and equipment. *Kjekstad Golfklubb* (tel.: [03] 855850) is a 10-hole course.

Tennis courts are crowded in the summer, but visitors can usually find a game. The leading locations are *Frogner Parken* (no telephone inquiries— ask at the kiosk); *Jordal* and *Volslokka* in the Sagene district; *Njardhallen,* at 106 Sorkedalsvn (tel.: 141592), with indoor and outdoor courts; and *Valle Hovin,* where the courts are asphalt.

Cross-country skiing is the most popular winter sport, and there are hundreds of good trails; some are floodlit. As well, there are about 30 slalom slopes close to the city. To find out more, call the Association of Skiing (*Skiforeningen*) at 360796. For information about buses to and from the ski areas, phone 141690. Ski rentals may be arranged through *Skiservice A/S Tomm Murstad Jnr.,* Voksenkollen Station. Tel.: 144124 and 149678.

▷ Spotlight ◁

Ice fishing. If you wonder why those chaps are sitting on stools in the middle of an icy, snowy wilderness, the answer is that they're fishing. Practicing the piscatorial art through holes in the ice on lakes and even Oslo Fjord itself is very popular—when the ice is thick enough to be safe. Equipment cannot be rented, but a gentle hint to your business associates might be enough to get you out on the ice, if that's what you really want.

Cultural Attractions

Oslo's cultural life is suprisingly intense for a city of its size, with opera, ballet, and concerts. The Oslo Philharmonic Orchestra has won a deserved reputation internationally. For details, pick up a copy of *Oslo This Week,* available at most hotels and newsstands.

Not to be missed, if you have the time, are the *Akershus* castle and fortress, the oldest parts of which date back to the 1300s, and the *Vigeland-sparken,* a park full of sculptures. Most city halls are places to avoid, except on business. Not Oslo's: its attractions include rich decorations done by Norwegian painters in the 1930s and 1940s. Well worth visits also are:

Norsk Folkemuseum (Norwegian Folk Museum), Bygdoy (tel.: 437020). Indoor and outdoor exhibits, including farm buildings. Shows how the Norwegians lived of old—and how some still live today.

Polarskipet Fram (Fram Museum), Bygdoynes (tel.: 438370). See the Polar exploration vessel *Fram,·* built in 1893 and used by Nansen and Amundsen on Arctic and Antarctic expeditions.

Kon-Tiki Museum, Bygdoynesveien (tel.: 438050). The balsa raft used in Thor Heyerdahl's epic *Kon-Tiki* expedition; a papyrus boat; statues of gods from Easter Island; other objects.

Nasjonalgalleriet (The National Gallery), just by the university, was founded in 1836 and today houses some 4,000 paintings—a quarter by Norwegian artists—as well as about 40,000 other works, including engravings, drawings, prints, and watercolors (tel.: 200404). The country's most famous modern artist, Edvard Munch (1863–1944), is well represented. He is celebrated also at the *Munch Museum,* 53 Toyengate, his gift to the nation in 1940 (tel.: 673774).

Ski Museum, Kongeveien (tel.: 141690). The world's oldest collection on the subject, or so it's claimed; includes some of Nansen's and Amundsen's polar equipment.

Viking Ship Museum, Huk Aveny, Bydoy (tel.: 438379). How the Vikings lived, sailed, and conquered. Ships and artifacts dating from 800 to 900 A.D.

▷ Out of Town

The nearest mountain resort is *Norefjell,* 110 kilometers (66 miles) away. Above Norefjell is the Hogdevarde, with a view of about an eighth of all Norway on a clear day. In the summer, the Norefjell offers not only swimming and fishing in Kroderen and other lakes, but also exciting rambles in the clear mountain air.

Further afield is *Bergen,* a small city on the coast surrounded by seven mountains. From Oslo, you can reach Bergen by car, bus, plane, or train—and the train ride offers spectacular views. Information: Tourist Office, Slottsgate 1, N-5000 Bergen. Tel.: (47) 313860. Telex: 42934.

PARIS

New Hues for the City of Light

Population: 2.06 million (estimated). Metropolitan area: 8.2 million (estimated). Administrative, political, and commercial capital of the French Republic (population: 55.6 million). *Location*: north-central France, on the Seine River, about 180 kilometers (107 miles) from the English Channel. *Economy*: wide range of manufacturing and service industries both in the city and in suburbs; banking and financial services, including the *Bourse* (stock exchange); one of the world's top tourist destinations; home to several dozen international organizations, large and small; European hub for trucking, railroad freight system, the highspeed TGV passenger trains, and inland waterways. France is a member of the European Community (EC) and the Organization for Economic Cooperation and Development (OECD) and a signatory to the General Agreement on Tariffs and Trade (GATT).

▷ Background Briefing

Paris has long been a city that visitors either love or hate, or perhaps love to hate. Probably the most architecturally stunning of all European capitals, it is noted also, perhaps unfairly, for being inhabited by some aggressive and unlovely people. They drive their cars like lethal weapons and their bargains like nails into an opponent's coffin. A business relationship all too often is adversarial.

And yet, and yet...If New York's the city that people like to visit but wouldn't like to live in, then Paris is the city that many foreign residents wouldn't trade for any other. What the stranger sees as rudeness, the expatriate veteran views tolerantly as part of the game that Parisians play with passion and verve—a game in which they deliberately perpetuate the myth that Parisians are a ruthless, hard-hearted bunch who wait until they see the whites of a little old lady's eyes before stamping on the gas pedal and running her down.

French writer and pundit Jean Cocteau described Parisians as "bad-tempered Italians." On the other hand, the American jurist and essayist Oliver Wendell Holmes wrote that "good Americans, when they die, go to Paris." Or, more accurately, many Americans go to Paris in the justifiable hope that before they die they'll learn how to live.

Much about Paris seems unchanging, almost eternal: the broad boulevards, the splendid buildings, the silvery skein of the Seine winding through the city center, the sidewalk cafés. Illusion, of course. Central Paris, as we've come to know and love it (or some of us have) is largely the creation of one Georges Eugene Haussmann (1809–91), a financier and urban planner who under Napoleon III's approving eye imposed his own grand vision on the city.

But even if central Paris hasn't changed much since Baron Haussmann's time, what goes on behind those elegant façades is excitingly effervescent. A new entrepreneurial and international spirit is blowing away the cobwebs of tradition. Once content to be the capital of France and of a colonial empire, Paris now aspires to be the center, if not the capital, of a powerful, unified Europe.

This new vigor expresses itself in dozens of ways, among them the bold, expansive mergers and acquisitions of many French companies, emergence of a new generation of entrepreneurs and chief executives who think in European and global terms, and the increasing aggressiveness of banks.

Surprisingly, this has been happening under a socialist president, François Mitterrand. Elected in 1981, with a handy majority in the National Assembly, Mitterrand at first embarked on a bout of doctrinaire policies: a state takeover of all large banks and of some major manufacturing companies, an expansionary economic strategy, and increases in government spending, particularly on social services.

Within 18 months, the cost of those and other measures was plain for all to see. Mitterrand did a screeching U-turn, had to devalue the franc, and in 1986 lost his legislative majority to a rag-tag conservative coalition. Re-elected in 1988, Mitterrand called new National Assembly elections; no single party won a majority, but a left-leaning coalition enabled him to form a government which pursued a middle-of-the-road program geared to 1992.

Since then, the government has pursued economic policies that can offend only extremists of the left and right. Mitterrand, it turns out, is more of a pragmatist than a socialist. For *grandeur,* a preoccupation with all French leaders, he has paid as much attention to a few spectacular new buildings (the Arch at La Defense, the pyramid at the Louvre) as traditional empire-building.

▷ Arriving

By Air

Paris is served by two major international airports: Charles de Gaulle-Roissy, north of the city, and Orly, to the south. Roissy or CDG, as it's usually known, is an austere example of people management at its best. Thanks to a design that treats passengers almost as though they were inanimate objects on a conveyor belt, the airport never seems crowded, though it often is.

European competition between major "hub" airports has meant revamped duty-free shops at CDG 1 and a new roof restaurant, while passenger-friendly CDG 2 has just been extended. Preparations are underway for a TGV express train station at the airport. Business services? The present "2a Service" is limited but improving—CDG: 4862-2290; Orly Sud and Ouest: 4975-1233. Orly, now used mainly for internal flights and for those to and from French-speaking Africa, is bustling and noisy. However some U.S. carriers prefer it. Both Roissy and Orly are served by fast subway lines to the city (although both stop short of the terminals), clean and comfortable buses, and taxis.

An important note: Citizens of most countries outside of Europe need visas to enter France. This requirement began in 1987 as an antiterrorist measure. Check your status with a French Consulate before leaving. You cannot obtain a visa at either Roissy or Orly, and you could be denied entry to the country without it. The requirement has been dropped for Americans.

By Rail

If you're going to Paris from a major city in Belgium, the Netherlands, or Switzerland, you may find that the train takes less time than a flight. That's particularly likely in the summer, when European skies and airports are clogged by tourist traffic or hit by strikes. French trains—and, indeed, those in most parts of Europe—are fast, comfortable, and clean. Many also serve excellent food, particularly the Euro City expresses.

Before boarding a train in France, make sure that you have punched your own ticket. You do that by putting it into an orange-colored machine close to the departure barrier. Failure to do this could cost you a fine, though inspectors are usually tolerant of flustered foreigners.

▷ **Spotlight** ◁

TGV—*Train à Grande Vitesse*—is a potent set of initials. Looking rather like urgent, streamlined centipedes with wheels instead of feet, TGVs speed across France at up to 260 kilometers an hour (162 mph). Best to reserve a seat, and a meal at your seat if you want one. Airline-style food; also snack bars.

▷ Money

The basic unit of currency is the French franc. International code: FRF. Big, beautifully colored banknotes come in denominations of 20 francs (which are now being phased out), 50, 100, 200, and 500 francs. Coins are minted in amounts of 1, 2, 5, and 10 francs, and 5, 10, 20, and 50 centimes (100 centimes = 1 franc). The best exchange rates are at banks; next best are *bureaux de change.* Hotels will change money, though the clerks can sometimes get a little sniffy about the inconvenience.

▷ Language

French—and don't forget it. Most French people are almost inordinately proud of their mother tongue. The official *Académie Française* guards its purity, and laws forbid the use of imported words and phrases except as translations of the French original—if there is one. None of which does one whit, of course, to slow the spread of "Franglais," a horrid hybrid that spawns such monstrosities as *le look,* sales slogan for a French car, and *le top-niveau* (the top level). *Le parking, le weekend, le fast food,* and *le self-service* have been absorbed into the polluted mainstream of the French language.

Vive l'Académie Française! It and government committees have hit back. Officially, cash should be *comptant,* royalties must be *redevances,* rate fixing becomes *fixage,* marketing has to be *mercatique,* and so on. More amusing than serious. After all, *savoir-faire* is prettier than "know-how."

Americans who complain about the French being snooty are invariably the ones who don't bother to learn a single word of French and expect the locals to willingly converse in English. Major mistake. Even a feeble attempt at the language will work wonders toward assuaging the pride of the French. The Parisian businessperson may still sneer a bit, but he or she will inwardly remember that you at least gave it a try.

▷ Communications

Country code: 33. City code: 1. Telecoms are good. To phone the provinces from Paris, first dial 16. Buy a *Telecarte* if you're going to be calling from public phone booths. Sold at *tabacs* (cafés licensed to sell cigarettes and stamps) and post offices, the Telecarte incorporates a microprocessor that entitles you to a stated number of telephone units. Phone booths provide instructions in English as well as French; a video display tells you how many units you have left in your card. Some phone booths take coins, but they are increasingly rare—and often vandalized. You can also make a phone call from most cafés, but many restrict calls to the Paris area and charge a markup.

▷ Spotlight ◁

Telecommunications. Only a decade or so ago a wry joke had it that while half of France waited for the dial tone, the other half waited for the telephone. No longer. Thanks to a huge investment program that still continues, France has one of the best telecommunications systems in the world.

A potent symbol is the unique *Minitel* interactive videotex service. The small, lightweight portable terminals with screen and keyboard are supplied free of charge to most telephone subscribers; they can call up about 6,000 different services. These range from up-to-the minute stock market quotations, through games, to what are delicately called *messageries roses*—pornographic electronic talk and dating. Providers of services charge, of course. The Minitel can be used as an electronic mailbox and hooked up to a printer. The Minitel now is rapidly adding business information services—companies' whereabouts, turnovers, the copyright situation. Some of the best come from the French copyright-trademark association, INPI, 26 bis, Rue Leningrad, 75008. Tel.: 4294-5252.

▷ Getting To Know the City

The Seine River snakes sinuously through Paris, dividing it into left and right banks. On the *Rive Gauche*—the Left Bank—are the Latin Quarter, the Sorbonne University, the National Assembly and Senate (parliament), government ministries, wide boulevards, and a maze of narrow, winding streets (Baron Haussmann didn't get his hands on much of the Left Bank). Dwarfing everything is the Eiffel Tower, the very icon of Paris. The view from the top is remarkable.

The *Rive Droite*—the Right Bank—is dominated by the Avenue des Champs-Elysées, a century old in 1989, with the Place de la Concorde at one end and the Arc de Triomphe at the other. Beyond the arc, going west, is the equally grandiose though lesser-known Avenue de la Grand-Armée, Neuilly with its advertising agencies, and then the newish office development of *La Défense,* home to many multinational companies. La Défense has its own, contemporary Arc de Triomphe—and a diminished version it is of the original one, and a new exhibition center and World Trade Center. Other, increasingly popular business centers are Marne la Vallée, to the east, and in satellite towns: Saint-Quentin-en-Yvelines, Cergy Pointoise, and Evry.

Paris is divided into twenty *arrondissements*—administrative districts with their own *mairies* (town halls) that answer to the mayor and elected council of the city. The most fashionable and therefore expensive *arrondissements* are the eighth, which includes the Champs-Elysées; the seventh, particularly around the neighborhoods known as Invalides, close to the river, and the nearby Ecole Militaire; parts of the first and second; and virtually all of the sixteenth, west of the center. The sixteenth borders the large and famous Bois de Boulogne, a stretch of wooded parkland, within which are two racetracks, Longchamp and Auteuil; some excellent restaurants; a lake; and a bevy of excessively friendly (at a price) "ladies." The sixteenth's dignified and calm next-door neighbor is the suburb of Neuilly, a coveted address: close to the city center, to La Défense, and to the Bois de Boulogne.

▷ **Spotlight** ◁

Cruising the Seine. One of the best ways of getting a feel for Paris topography is to go aboard a boat that plies the Seine. Known generically as *bateaux mouche,* these range in size from long, glassed-in monsters to more modest older vessels. Some offer lunch or dinner aboard; all provide skilled commentaries in several languages. Ask the hotel for a brochure. New *bateaux-bus,* or water-buses have been launched recently.

▷ Moving Around

Paris has one of the best rapid-transit systems in Europe, perhaps in the world. Taxpayers foot a high bill, in the form of massive subsidies from employers, central government, and the city of Paris. But—and it's a very important but—the result is a coordinated subway, bus, and railroad network that offers riders clean, fast transportation and notable value for money.

The subway system—the *Métro*—and the RER, which is run by the state-owned French railroad company, together offer the fastest transportation from Point A to Point B. Use the Métro for shorter distances, the RER for longer ones. At any Métro station you can buy *carnets* of ten tickets valid within the Paris area on subway and RER trains and on buses. Clear, detailed maps of the subway, RER, and bus routes are free. Note that though one ticket takes you all over Paris by Métro, you may have to use two tickets for a long bus journey; check the map at bus stops and in buses themselves. If you're staying in Paris for a few weeks, it's worth buying a Métro and bus pass entitling you to unlimited travel. Ask your hotel concierge for details.

Taxis are hard to find in rush hours, and too many drivers seem to be either off duty or determined to go in the direction opposite to yours. Most drivers will take only three passengers. Try to avoid unmetered limos lingering at airports and railroad stations; they are very expensive unless there are four or five people in your party and you bargain hard.

Rental cars from major American and European firms are available, but expensive. We don't recommend driving in the city. Traffic is a headache, parking is scarce. There's really no reason to drive in a place that has such excellent public transportation.

▷ Hotels

Paris is what people in the trade call over-hotelled—too many rooms chasing too few guests except at certain times of the year. The result is intense competition. The total of 70,000 rooms is divided among what the French describe as the palaces; the luxurious international-style and usually chain-operated hotels; smaller top-class hostelries stressing superb service; and cheaper places that also take care of the business traveler.

Space is tight at Christmas because of the boat show; in the last week of January because of the *haute couture* collections; in June in odd-numbered years because of the Le Bourget air show; in the last week of July, *haute couture* again; in September and October of even-numbered years, when the auto show is held; and every September, when the men's fashion and women's *prêt-à-porter* (ready-to-wear) marts coincide.

Because there are so many good hotels, and because they vary greatly in style, we've listed them in two sections: classic and modern luxury. All the hotels mentioned feature outstandingly good bars and restaurants and provide prompt room service and excellent telecommunications. Digits after the address indicate the *arrondissement*.

Classic

Balzac, 6 Rue Balzac, 8me. Tel.: 4561-9722. Telex: 290298. Fax: 42252482. Rooms/suites: 82, including the Presidential and the Royal.

Just a few steps away from the Champs-Élysées and the Arc de Triomphe, the Balzac is an old hotel recently refurbished in classic style. Its *Le Sallambier* restaurant deserves special mention. Exceptionally elegant basement disco.

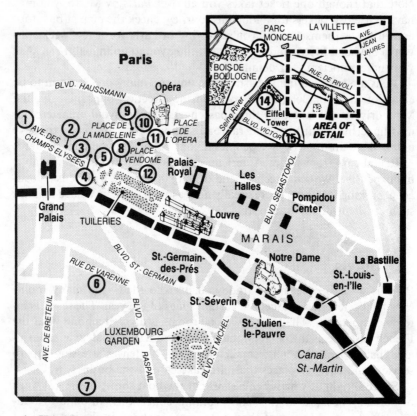

1. **Hotel Balzac**
2. **Hotel Bristol**
3. **Elysée Palace**
4. **Hotel Castiglione**
5. **Hotel Crillon**
6. **Prime Minister's office**
7. **Hotel Meridien/Montparnasse**
8. **Hotel Meurice**
9. **Hotel Scribe**
10. **Grand Hotel**
11. **Hotel Ritz**
12. **Hotel Inter-Continental**
13. **Palais des Congres**
14. **Hotel Hilton**
15. **Exhibition Center, Porte de Versailles**

Bristol, 112 Rue du Faubourg St-Honoré, 8me. Tel.: 4266-9145. Telex: 280961. Fax: 42666868. Rooms/suites: 200. Four salons for conference/ banquets that can be combined. Three other salons. Long a favorite with top West German business executives, the Bristol is now also a haunt of the Japanese. Sybaritically luxurious; good location.

Castiglione, 38 Rue du Faubourg St-Honoré, 8me. Tel.: 4265-0750. Telex: 240362. Fax: 42651227. Rooms/suites: 114. On the most fashionable shopping street, much favored by fashion industry designers and also executives.

Crillon, 10 Place de la Concorde, 8me. Tel.: 4265-2424. Telex: 290204. Fax: 47427210. Rooms/suites: 205. The best location in Paris, next to the American Embassy, a walk away from the British one, just across the river from the National Assembly. World statesmen have been using the Crillon for generations. Superb decor; large, luxurious rooms.

George V, 31 Avenue George V, 8me. Tel.: 4723-5400. Telex: 650082. Fax: 47204000. Rooms/suites: 341. Seven salons for 30 to 600 people. TrustHouse Forte's Paris flagship, with expensively loving care lavished on the furnishings and decor. Just off the Champs-Elysées, the George V is among the grandest of the grand. Long a favorite of Americans.

Grand, 2 Rue Scribe, 9me. Tel.: 4268-1213. Telex: 220875. Fax: 42661251. Rooms/suites: 535. Meetings and functions can accommodate up to 1,000 people. An oasis of calm in a bustling neighborhood, right next to the Opera district and big bank headquarters. Some modern suites are duplexes; traditional suites are furnished with antiques.

Inter-Continental, 3 Rue Castiglione, 1er. Tel.: 4260-3780. Telex: 220114. Fax: 42611403. Rooms/suites: 450. Meeting facilities for up to 2,500 people. Classic architecture. Overlooking the Tuileries gardens and close to the Louvre art gallery, the Interconti is a favorite of French politicians. The National Assembly is just across the Seine, and the presidential palace is 10 minutes' walk away. It's also a favorite of international business travelers.

Lancaster, 7 Rue de Berri, 8me. Tel.: 4359-9043. Telex: 640991. Fax: 42892271. Rooms/suites: 70. Just off the Champs-Elysées, but sedate. If it resembles a luxurious private home, that's not surprising. The previous owner regarded it as such, and London's Savoy Hotel group has carried on the tradition. Every room and suite is different, furnished with antiques. More staff than guests. Famous, "I-want-to-be-alone" movie stars appreciate it.

Marriott Prince de Galles, 33 Avenue George V, 8me. Tel.: 4723-5511. Telex: 280627. Fax: 47209692. Rooms/suites: 301. American management has renovated and improved a famous hotel that had fallen on slightly hard times. A great place for "power breakfasts."

Meurice, 228 Rue de Rivoli, 1er. Tel.: 4260-3860. Telex: 230673. Fax: 40159231. Rooms: 151. Suites: 36. This nineteenth-century palace is probably the most sumptuous of the city's grand hotels, and the new owner, the Aga Khan, plans to improve existing business and convention facilities. Salvador Dalí, a difficult man to please, practically lived at the Meurice for long periods.

Plaza Athénée, 25 Avenue Montaigne, 8me. Tel.: 4723-7833. Telex: 650092. Fax: 47202070. Rooms/suites: 262. Full of Beautiful People; probably the top Paris hotel in the social sense. Bar and restaurants very fashionable. Close to the Champs-Élysées and many of the best-known *haute couture* houses.

Ritz, 15 Place Vendome, 1er. Tel.: 4260-3830. Telex: 670112. Fax (Reservation): 42860091. Messages: 42602371. Rooms/suites: 209. Yes, the César Ritz original, now owned by the Egyptian Al-Fayed brothers (who also own Harrods in London). More a way of life than a hotel, the Ritz is a place in which servitors collide—quietly, of course—as they compete to carry your luggage or light your cigarette.

Royal Monceau, 37 Avenue Hoche, 8me. Tel.: 4561-9800. Telex: 650361. Fax: 45632893. Rooms: 180. Suites: 40. The hotel has been refurbished. It has a top Italian restaurant, another in the covered garden, plus a bar popular with businesspeople. A super health club for guests.

St. James Club, 5 Place du Chancellier Adenauer, 16me. Tel.: 4704-2929. Telex: 643850. Fax: 45530061. Rooms/suites: 48. The owner is Peter de Savary, a British business executive who has spent a fortune on trying to win the America's Cup. He has also spent a fortune on this club, and it has been winning international accolades. Technically, the St. James is a club, but the management has found an ingenious way around that hurdle for people it really wants to house.

Scribe, 1 Rue Scribe, 9me. Tel.: 4742-0340. Telex: 214653. Fax: 42653997. Rooms/suites: 228. A grand hotel opposite to the Grand Hotel. Owned by Canadian National Railways, the Scribe goes out of its way to lure business executives. Close to the financial district.

Tremoille, 14 Rue de la Tremoille, 8me. Tel.: 4723-3420. Telex: 640344. Fax: 40700108. Rooms/suites: 111. Another TrustHouse Forte hotel. Calm: no rush, no bustle. Great comfort; skilled and friendly staff. Right in the center of things, but a world away from them. If some of the guests' faces seem familiar, that's probably because they are. Many well-known business leaders stay at the Tremoille.

Modern Luxury

Concorde La Fayette, Place du Général Koening, 17me. Tel.: 4758-1270. Telex: 650892. Fax: 47575321. Rooms/suites: 1,000. Soundproofed, air-conditioned skyscraper hotel next to an air terminal opposite the Palais des Congrès exhibition and conference center. Top Club: three tower floors with special services for the international business executive. Within the building are 80 shops, four movie theaters, two discos, and a marvelous health club. Indoor golf.

Hilton, 18 Avenue de Suffren, 15me. Tel.: 4273-9200. Telex: 200955. Fax: 47836266. Rooms/suites: 495. Meeting facilities for up to 1,000 people. Almost in the shadow of the Eiffel Tower; the first major, foreign-owned hotel built after World War II. Rooms by famed designer Raymond Loewy. Excellent roof restaurant with music and dancing.

Holiday Inn Paris, 10 Place de la République, 11me. Tel.: 4355-4434. Telex: 210651. Fax: 47003234. Rooms/suites: 339 (including non-smokers). An old hotel completely refurbished in discreetly modern style. Good location for visits to the garment industry and the great department stores. Sauna baths, fitness club.

Méridien, 81 Boulevard Gouvion Saint-Cyr, 17me. Tel.: 4758-1230. Telex: 290592. Fax: 47576070. Rooms/suites: 1,041. Across from the Palais des Congrès; near La Défense and Champs-Elysées business districts. Run well—and lively. Famous for brunches and cocktails with jazz. Business center. Best TV selection in town: 24 channels, including Soviet and Saudi programs.

Meridien Montparnasse, 19 Rue du Commandant Mouchotte, 14me. Tel.: 4320-1551. Fax: 43206103. Telex: 200135. Rooms/suites: 950. Conference and banquet facilities for up to 1,400 people. In the expanding Montparnasse business section, an area tilting from arts to management.

Nikko, 61 Quai de Grenelle, 15me. Tel.: 4575-6262. Telex: 260012. Fax: 45754235. Rooms: 779. The home-away-from-home for Japanese travellers. Japanese restaurant. Riverside location. French restaurant and brasserie. Beauty parlor, excellent health facilities, barbers, and pharmacy.

PLM Saint-Jacques, 17 Boulevard Saint-Jacques, 14me. Tel.: 4589-8980. Telex: 270740. Fax: 45888393. Rooms/suites: 812. Large adjoining conference hall. Slightly out of the center, but with easy access to Orly Airport and main highways to the south.

Sofitel, 8 Rue Louis Armand, 15me. Tel.: 4060-3030. Telex: 200432. Fax: 45570422. Rooms: 635. A modern hotel next to the Porte de Versailles exhibition park and convenient for Orly airport. Some 37 meeting rooms. Good backup facilities for businesspeople. Special features: exterior bubble elevators, pool and health club, and late night dancing.

Airport Hotels

CHARLES DE GAULLE-ROISSY

Sofitel. Zone Centrale. Tel.: 4862-2323. Telex: 230166. Fax: 48627849. Rooms: 344. Suites: 8. The top airport hotel geared for arrivals and departures at all hours. Conference and function rooms. Pool, sauna, tennis. Top-floor "gourmet" restaurant.

Novotel, Unité Centrale-RER station. Tel.: 4862-0053. Telex: 232397. Fax: 48620011. Rooms: 203. Suites: 2. Four rooms for handicapped guests. The latest of the airport hotels and the best placed, particularly for the Villepinte exhibition park down the RER line.

ORLY

Hilton Orly, near terminal. Tel.: 4687-3388. Telex: 250621. Fax: 49.78.06.75. Rooms: 380. Situated right next to both Orly Sud and Orly Ouest terminals, with shuttle services. Comfortable and, above all, soundproofed.

Holiday Inn Orly, 4 Avenue Charles Lindbergh. Tel.: 4687-2666. Telex: 204679. Fax: 45609125. Rooms: 171. Meeting facilities for up to 300. Bar, indoor tennis. Free airport transportation.

LA DÉFENSE

Ibis La Défense, 4 Boulevard Neuilly. Tel.: 4778-1560. Fax: 47789416. Rooms/suites: 284. A modern, two-star hotel of the Accor group right next to La Défense. Easy exit to Paris. Restaurant.

Novotel Paris La Défense, 2 Boulevard Neuilly. Tel.: 4778-1668. Telex: 630288. Fax: 47788471. Rooms/suites: 276. Occupies the same building as the Ibis but has an extra star. These two Accor hotels are forerunners of coming hotel development at La Défense, including a new Sofitel at the World Trade Center. Restaurant.

▷ Spotlight ◁

World Trade Center. The latest World Trade Center with practical (and hedonistic) services has been built under the vaulted roof of the CNIT exhibition hall, La Défense. It offers a permanent, Dallas-style Infomart, conference rooms, business center, and more convivial touches such as the Cercle Europe executive club (pool, restaurant, even putting green); a new 160-room Sofitel hotel with restaurant (Tel.: 47764443. Telex: 612189. Fax: 47737274); and TV studios for businesspeople who want to make news. WTC: Tel.: 47736644. Fax: 47761632.

▷ Restaurants

You can eat a bad meal in Paris. You can also eat an overpriced meal. But you'll have to be exceptionally unlucky to suffer both flaws at the same time. A good tip is to stay away from the Champs-Elysées—though even there, some exceptions disprove the rule that tourist areas are full of tourist traps. If you're entertaining for business purposes, of course, you may want to go to top restaurants; but you may also want to sample some less prestigious and costly delights. For that reason, we've listed five categories of restaurant: classic, bourgeois, exotic, open-air, and late-night. Each category needs a few words of explanation.

Those dubbed *classic* are the very best of their kind—and, we need hardly add, the most costly. At none of them will you find less than superb food, wine, and service. *Bourgeois* restaurants are more modestly priced, but often the food is as good as it is in the classic establishments. Under the label *exotic* we group the best of the restaurants offering a cuisine that isn't French. Although the French serve up their culinary chauvinism steaming hot, the large number of exotic restaurants wouldn't exist if nobody went to them—and most of their customers are French. *Open-air* restaurants are those with gardens, and we have chosen the ones that are not right on the street; who wants carbon monoxide in the salad? As for *late-night* places, they're the ones where you can expect to find a reasonably good meal in the wee hours of the morning.

For all the places listed, a reservation is necessary—at some, essential.

We have not listed separately restaurants in the recommended hotels. All are good, particularly those in the classic hotel category.

▷ *Spotlight* ◁

The Paris hotel concierge is often a miracle-worker; he (it's almost always a he) can find the unfindable. So it's a good idea to ask him to reserve you a table at a restaurant. Phoning out of the blue, with a foreign name the French find hard to pronounce, let alone spell, you may be disappointed. Your concierge, in contrast, may be able to cajole and persuade a reluctant restaurateur to let you have a table. That the concierge may gain a commission is a matter entirely between him and the restaurant.

Classic

Jamin/Robuchon, 32 Rue de Longchamp, 16me. Tel.: 4704-2453. Small and intimate, Jamin is one of the most fashionable places. Reserve at least a week ahead for dinner, more for lunch. *Maître chef de cuisine* and *patron* Joël Robuchon has created a gem, with 34 staff for a maximum of 45 customers at any one time. He's also an exceptionally pleasant fellow, and modest withal.

L'Ambroisie, 9 Place des Vosges, 4me. Tel.: 4278-5145. Sumptuous decor and food. The Place des Vosges is an ancient square that has come up in the world recently, a rise both confirmed and hastened by this restaurant's move there from an earlier location. Noted for fish and seafood.

Lasserre, 17 Avenue Franklin D. Roosevelt, 8me. Tel.: 4359-5343. Stars of the theater, screen, and politics favor Lasserre, a great showcase in which people strut while sitting down. Although they are there to be seen, more serious customers are also there for the food, for which there's only one word: *magnifique!*

La Tour d'Argent, 15 Quai Tournelle, 5me. Tel.: 4354-2331. Claude Terrail runs this famous and ancient establishment with great friendliness and good humor. The restaurant is high over the Seine; the cellars are in the basement. Duck is the house's most celebrated specialty, but not its only one by far. Taking their cue from *Patron* Terrail, the waiters are friendly—and patient with foreigners.

Laurent, 41 Avenue Gabriel, 8me. Tel.: 4723-7918. Set in gardens, Laurent has been the canteen of Sir James Goldsmith, an Anglo-French financier. Hordes of businesspeople crowd in hoping to see him—or, even better, to hear of his latest deal before the rest of the world does. Their consolation prize if he doesn't show (he's been buying in London recently) is a cuisine prepared to classic standards.

Le Grand Vefour, 17 Rue de Beaujolais, 1er. Tel.: 4296-5627. Some people swear that this is the best restaurant in Paris; others argue that it is overpriced and overrated. We think it lies somewhere between those extremes. Certainly, it has charm, and the Taittinger champagne family which owns it has lavished money on maintaining the eighteenth-century decor. Private rooms are good for business meals.

Lucas-Carton, 9 Place de la Madeleine, 8me. Tel.: 4265-2290. If Brillat-Savarin and Auguste Escoffier never presided over the kitchen, that was their bad luck. Lucas-Carton nurtures and perpetuates French gastronomic traditions as few others places do, even though it is now Japanese-owned. The wine cellar is exceptional—but check the price before ordering one of the rarer bottles, such as a 1928 Margaux. The triple or even quadruple digits are no misprint.

Le Taillevent, 15 Rue Lamennais, 8me. Tel.: 4563-3994. Don't look for mere cooking here, look for (and enjoy) culinary art, from the choice of raw materials to their treatment and presentation. Taillevent is a club passionately devoted are its *habitués*—and you might as well reserve before leaving home, for the widely spaced tables are nearly always full. Louis XVI furnishings add elegance to this nineteenth-century mansion.

Maxim's, 3 Rue Royale, 8me. Tel.: 4265-2794. This famous and venerable eatery has had its ups and downs recently. The respected *Guide Michelin* doesn't list it; that brash relative newcomer, *Gault-Millau,* does so with "ifs" and "buts." So what's the truth about Maxim's? The decor is as good as ever—after all, owner Pierre Cardin *is* a fashion designer. Eating fashion has swung to lunchtime and Maxim's Business Club sometimes looks like a French version of the Young Presidents Club in the U.S.

Bourgeois

Beaujolais d'Auteuil, 99 Boulevard Montmorency, 16me. Tel.: 4743-0356. Slightly far from the center, but worth a visit. Warm welcome; good and ample food; emphasis (as name suggests) on wines and cuisine from the Beaujolais region.

Brasserie Lipp, 151 Boulevard Saint-Germain, 6me. Tel.: 4548-5391. President François Mitterrand is reputed to like this place when he isn't in his presidential palace. It's hard to see why anyone else likes Lipp, which is overpriced, overrated, and over on the crowded Left Bank. We list it because it's a Paris landmark.

▷ Spotlight ◁

The Bistro de la Gare at 59 Boulevard du Montparnasse (Tel.: 4222-2255) isn't a place to which you would take a pompous business contact (if you were wise). The Bistro bustles. But it has an extraordinary 1900's decor, beautifully restored, so that the tiles glisten; the young waiters and waitresses smile so much that they appear to enjoy their jobs; and the (cheap) food is excellent. Just the place for the business executive who is running out of budget.

Chiberta, 3 Rue Arsène-Houssaye, 8me. Tel.: 4563-7790. Elegant, modern decor; pleasant, smiling service; menu emphasizes southwestern Basque dishes. Good value for (not inconsiderable) money.

Fouquet's, 99 Avenue des Champs-Elysées, 8me. Tel.: 4723-7060. Right on the corner of the Champs-Élysées and the Avenue George V, Fouquet's is a landmark—and a question mark hung over it recently. The owners of the real estate wanted to raise the rent; the owners of the restaurant said they couldn't afford it, which may surprise people who pay Fouquet's prices. The government stepped in; Fouquet's is safe for the time being at least.

▷ Spotlight ◁

The Avenue des Champs-Elysées (the name means Elysian Fields) has long been a synonym for architectural elegance and all that's best about France. No longer does the reality match the myth. To be sure, some elegance remains, but it's being replaced by fast-food eateries and stores selling international schlock. Avoid the cafés if you can: they're vastly overpriced and staffed by waiters (and waitresses) of the kind for whom a mordant wit wrote a mock epitaph: "He was a waiter, and God caught his eye—at last." By all means, stroll the Champs-Elysées, but if you must have a coffee, or anything stronger, go to a side street café, where you'll pay half as much. One exception—and a cool haven in summer: Copenhague Restaurant at No. 142.

Jules Verne, second floor, Eiffel Tower, 7me. Tel.: 4555-2004. Take the private elevator, and leave sweaty tourists far below. But reserve well ahead of time: this restaurant has a deserved reputation for excellence. Almost incidentally, it also has one of the best views of Paris.

Le Bonaventure, 35 Rue Jean-Goujon, 8me. Tel.: 4225-0258. World headquarters of the International Chamber of Commerce is just across the courtyard, so many senior business executives eat in this comfortable restaurant. The service is good, if not fast, and the food is palatable, if not exciting.

Lamazère, 23 Rue Ponthieu, 8me. Tel.: 4359-6666. We've long admired this place. *Patron* Roger Lamazère and his *chef de cuisine,* Daniel Tricaud, pamper their clients with delicacies from Perigord: try the *confit de canard* or *d'oie*—duck or goose preserved in their own grease, but then cooked and dried to a pleasantly moist consistency. The result is delicious. M. Lamazère has a superb stock of very old Armagnac.

La Sologne, 164 Avenue Daumesnil, 13me. Tel.: 4307-6897. The Sologne, south of Paris, is famous for its game: birds, hares, rabbits. So La Sologne specializes in them and in wild boar (no longer to be found in the Sologne). Sauces are subtle.

Le Bourdonnais, 113 Avenue de la Bourdonnais, 7me. Tel.: 4705-1654. Madame Micheline Coat runs this quiet, elegant restaurant with a warm smile and a will of steel. The cuisine stresses fish and herbs, but there's much else to tempt and distract. Very much of a neighborhood restaurant—which says a lot for the variety to be found on Mme. Coat's menu.

Le Train Bleu, Gare de Lyon (first floor), 20 Boulevard Diderot, 13me. Tel.: 4343-0906. The art déco style dazzles: murals, sculptures, painted ceilings. Waiters wear starched shirts and aprons, and there's nothing false about it: the restaurant was designed for the Paris Exposition of 1901. The food? Ah, the food! Yes.

Exotic

Food follows the flag—the flag in retreat, that is. Britain is full of Chinese, Indian, and Pakistani restaurants, Portugal of African ones, France of Vietnamese and North African ones—all vestiges of their colonial heritage. What follows is a very selective sampling—but a rich one, we hope—of restaurants that may be called, interchangeably, exotic or ethnic (though we flinch from the term "ethnic," since even French restaurants are ethnic).

▷ *Spotlight* ◁

Should you invite to lunch or dinner a French executive you barely know? To lunch, yes; wait until you're better acquainted before suggesting dinner. When you do, include the spouse in the invitation. She or he may not accept, particularly if you don't have a language in common, but the gesture will be appreciated.

AMERICAN

Joe Allen, 30 Rue Pierre-Lescot, 1er. Tel.: 4236-7013. Spareribs, hamburgers, fried chicken, apple pie—you could be back in Manhattan, an illusion strengthened by the bustle and the dominance of American accents.

Marshal's, 63 Avenue Franklin Roosevelt, 8me. Tel.: 4563-2122. California *patron,* West Coast decor, American clientele. Recommended: Caesar salad, baby spareribs, pecan pie.

CHINESE

Chez Vong, 27 Rue du Colisée, 8me. Tel.: 4359-7712. Luxurious, with excellent service. Decor is both impressive and unobtrusive, all of it imported from China or Hong Kong. High-backed chairs, far-apart tables; ideal for business lunches and dinners.

Le Château de Chine, 9 Rue de la Tremoille, 8me. Tel.: 4723-8090. Quiet elegance, wide selection of distinguished Chinese cuisines; exemplary service.

GERMAN

Au Vieux Berlin, 32 Avenue George V, 8me. Tel.: 4720-8896. They probably don't serve better food in new Berlin—and certainly don't in the eastern sector. Guaranteed to change any prejudices against German cuisine.

INDIAN

Indra, 10 Rue du Cdt-Rivière, 8me. Tel.: 4359-4640. Elegant with specialties from the Punjab. A forerunner of the Indian restaurant boom of the past decade or so. Still one of the best, as its gastronomic prizes attest.

Masheed-Mahal, 138 Blvd du Montparnasse, 14me. Tel.: 4320-6809. Another prize-winner. Noted for its curries and tandoories.

JAPANESE

Kinugawa, 9 Rue Mont Thabor, 1er. Tel.: 4260-6507. Many Japanese eat here, which must be a recommendation. Comfortable; good service; *tempura* a specialty of the house.

Shogun, Bateau "le Nomadic," opposite 24 Avenue de New York, 16me. Tel.: 4720-0504. A successful attempt to revive the River Seine restaurants. Classical Japanese dishes in a luxurious setting.

JEWISH

Jo Goldenberg, 7 Rue des Rosiers, 4me. Tel.: 4887-2016. A picturesque deli-style restaurant in the old Jewish quarter of the Marais neighborhood. Warm, welcoming atmosphere; tremendous selection of central European dishes.

LEBANESE

Fakhr el Dine, 30 Rue de Longchamp, 16me. Tel.: 4727-9000. Beirut chic; lots of Lebanese businessmen and families noshing away until late at night. Superb service; deals done at all hours. Try the Lebanese wine.

NORTH AFRICAN

Martin Alma, 44 Rue Jean-Goujon, 8me. Tel.: 4359-2825. For more than half a century, the Martin Alma has been serving sophisticated versions of North African cuisine (and, on Wednesdays, an excellent Spanish *paella*). Sample the North African wines.

PORTUGUESE

Saudade, 34 Rue des Bourdonnais, 1er. Tel.: 4236-3071. If you like Portuguese food—and there are those who do—the Saudade is a find: faithful to its traditions, interestingly decorated. Good selection of Portuguese wines.

RUSSIAN

La Datcha Lydie, 7 Rue Dupleix, 15me. Tel.: 4566-6777. Since the advent of *glasnost* and *perestroika,* even Soviet diplomats have been glimpsed at this shrine to old Russia. Enjoyably nostalgic.

Ludmila (Pavillon Russe), 45 Rue François 1er, 8me. Tel.: 4720-6069. Food, wine, service, and decor for the pampering of grand dukes and duchesses. Ukrainian culinary emphasis.

►415

VIETNAMESE

La Riviére des Parfums, 36 Rue Poncelet, 17 me. Tel.: 4763-4197. Delectable dishes, pleasantly calm and unhurried atomsphere. Fifteen minutes' walk from the Place Charles de Gaulle (Arc de Triomphe), which is just enough to work up an appetite for this excellent food.

Open-air

Of course, they do serve indoors as well...

La Grande Cascade, Bois de Boulogne. Tel.: 4527-3351. Fine food since 1880; only the prices have changed. Good even in the winter; better on a sunny day under the umbrellas on the terrace.

Le Pré Catelán, Bois de Boulogne. Tel.: 4524-5558. Fish and seafood are the specialties—along with assiduous service and beautiful gardens. On the city's outskirts, but a million miles away in ambience.

Late-night

Andrée Baumann, 64 Avenue des Ternes, 17me. Tel.: 4574-1666. Last orders: 1:00 a.m. Run-of-the-mill French cuisine.

Le Boeuf sur le Toit, 34 Rue du Colisée, 8me. Tel.: 4359-8380. Last orders: 2:00 a.m. First-class beef and other meats.

Vaudeville, 29 Rue Vivienne, 2me. Tel.: 4233-3931. Last orders: 2:00 a.m. Close to the Opéra, facing the stock exchange; popular and bustling.

With a few francs in your pocket and enough determination, you'll never starve in Paris. Though few restaurants stay open very late (or open very early), many cafés do, and most serve food of some kind.

▷ Tipping

Don't tip in bars and restaurants—unless you're really impressed. Then leave some small change. The check always includes a 15 percent service charge, noted as *servis compris.*

Taxis are different: add about 10 percent to the metered amount. Note that cabdrivers are entitled to charge extra for picking you up at an airport or railroad station and for luggage in the trunk. Allowable extras are shown (in French and English) inside the taxi.

▷ Doing Business

A British real estate developer had a very good deal in the major provincial city of Lyons. But he needed bridging finance, and so he went to a Paris bank. The bank's executive started his speech—and it was no less—with the ominous words, *"En principe"* (in principle). Fifteen minutes or so later he uttered the magic words *"Mais, en pratique. . . "* (But in practice. . .) Blinking in the sunshine outside, the British developer shook his head in disbelief and asked the interpreter plaintively: "Well, do I have the loan, or don't I?"

Well, yes, he did have it—but he had first to pay the price, a philosophical statement of the difference between principle and practice. Senior business executives are well-educated, usually fluent in at least one language other than French, and products of an educational system that stresses intellectual achievement. Many, indeed, are graduates of one of *les grandes écoles*—the prestigious establishments that turn out the country's future top civil servants and chief executives. Often, graduates shuttle back and forth happily between the public and private sectors, and some end up in government. Newspapers often refer to a person's educational background in the headline.

An incestuous, nepotistic system riven by conflicts of interest? Perhaps. But it works, and though there is a Washington-style sleaze factor, nobody talks about it very much. For the visiting business executive, the challenge is to use the system. How?

Business and government are close—indeed, are intertwined at national, regional, and local levels. France has no fewer than 36,000 municipalities; a high proportion of legislators are also mayors or members of regional authorities. Jacques Chirac managed to be both prime minister and mayor of Paris in 1986-88—and continued as mayor after losing the presidential election to incumbent François Mitterrand.

Chambers of commerce have juridical functions unknown in most of the rest of the world. The chamber in Bordeaux, for example, runs the airport as well as much else—and was founded in the 1700s. The city's mayor, Jacques Chaban-Delmas, is probably the leading example of a politician who has retained his local power base while strutting the national and even international scene. He has been mayor since 1947—and held such posts as those of prime minister and president of the National Assembly.

The chambers wield real power and influence. Some of this rubs off on the hyphenated chambers, representing business in other countries. Those listed under Useful Numbers are rich storehouses of information. Some, such as the Franco-British Chamber, also offer meeting rooms and secretarial and other services. Many of the chambers of commerce also publish magazines or newsletters and directories of members categorized by industry or profession. All the major banks regularly publish economic and other studies of France, usually in English as well as French.

French accounting principles and practices differ from those used in the United States and the United Kingdom and by multinational corporations. Many of the larger companies, however, are now publishing annual reports in English that conform to generally accepted Anglo-American accounting standards.

France has a reputation as a difficult country in which to invest as a foreigner, but that's mainly because occasional controversies hit the headlines. In general, the authorities welcome foreign investment, as witnessed by the very large number of foreign firms operating happily and profitably in everything from the manufacture of automotive components, through information technology, to the real estate business. What the authorities do *not* welcome is a foreign takeover of a flagship French company—but even that has happened in paper making and machine tools. European Community regulations and laws make it increasingly difficult for the French or any other government to bar a merger or acquisition by a company from an EC country, although in practice many big French concerns have put together defensive, so-called "hard core," and, above all, tricolor groupings of major shareholders.

Once a byword for bureaucratic delays in matters corporate, France has lightened the paperwork burden. For example, forming a company was until recently a long, arduous, and costly process; now it can be done in a few days. A foreign company trying to locate in France once had to make the rounds of overlapping and mutually antagonistic ministries; today, the investor can deal with DATAR, the official industrial development agency, which in turn will deal with the ministries. And no ministry is any longer empowered to make agreement to an investment conditional upon its being in a particular place. Investment restrictions in and around the capital have been largely lifted.

▷ Spotlight ◁

French and Anglo-Saxon attitudes toward a deal differ greatly. Barry Stobbs explains why. He first set foot in France in 1948, runs a management consulting firm, Marketbase, and has watched both sides make mistakes. He advises: "The Anglo-Saxon deal is input-dominated: the objective is to give up as little as possible, to put as little as possible into the kitty before the other fellow signs. It follows that the happier *you* are with the deal, the more likely it is that the other fellow will become unhappy with it as time goes by, hence the legal emphasis on contractual escape clauses.

"The French deal, on the other hand, is output-dominated in the sense that it is based not on compromise, but on each side's continuing to pursue its own objectives while benefiting from the fact that many of these are shared by the partner. The French deal tends to be loose, optimistic. It very often does not envisage failure at all, and the only negative note may be the naming of a mutually acceptable referee to take care of disputes."

Stobbs concludes that many poten-tially promising deals founder before they're signed because neither side is sufficiently aware of differences in cul-ture and philosophy—even though they both agree on the value of the deal itself and are even enthusiastic about it.

A guide that is good on the regions and conference facilities is *France.* Address: 14 Rue La Fayette, 58204 Cosne-sur-Loire. Tel.: 8626-6060 (dial 16 prefix from Paris).

Social tips. People not fluent in French should avoid the *tu* (familiar) form of address. It's acceptable when you're speaking to very young chil-dren or domestic pets, but is an insult when addressed to civil servants and, above all, the police: they regard it as a condescension at best, an in-sult at worst. Safe bet is to use the formal *vous* at all times.

The *baisemain,* or kissing of the hand, is still practiced in some circles. However, never perform this apparently innocent act with an unmarried woman—or outdoors. If you're invited to somebody's home for a meal, arrive with flowers if you know the hostess. If you don't know her, send flowers the next day.

Conversational hint: Rising executives like to show off the extent of their travels. Best to pretend that you don't know half the places they claim to know—which is often twice the number they do.

▷ Useful Phone Numbers

Emergencies		Local Information	
Ambulance	4567-5050	Airports	
American Hospital	4747-5300	Le Bourget	4862-1212
Anti-poisons	4205-6329	Orly	4884-3210
Fire	18	Charles de Gaulle-Roissy	4862-2280
Police	17	City airline terminals	
		Invalides	4555-0772
		Maillot	4299-2005

Train schedules—all
terminals   4582-5050

Business Information

Ministries

Defense	4555-9520
Economy, finance	4260-3300
Foreign affairs	4753-5353
Foreign trade	4555-5071
Industry	4555-6363

Financial

Banque de France	4292-4292
Stockbrokers Association (Agents de Change)	4261-8590
DATAR (industrial development agency)	4783-6120
Treasury	4297-2000
Customs information	4260-3590

Chambers of Commerce

American	4723-8096
Belgium-Luxembourg	4562-4487
Franco-American (U.S.)	4256-0500
Franco-Arab	4553-2012
Franco-Asian	4526-6701
Franco-British	4562-3456
Franco-Canadian	4359-3238
Franco-German	4575-6256
Franco-Indian	4306-8897
Franco-Israeli	4225-4013
Franco-Netherlands	4563-5430
Franco-Portuguese	4266-3479
Franco-Soviet	4225-9710
Franco-Spanish	4742-4574
Italian	4225-3980
Japanese	4563-2742
Parisian	4561-9900

Swedish	4261-4232
Swiss	4296-1417
European Community	4501-5885
International (ICC)	4561-9900

Consulates/Embassies

Algeria	4225-7070
Argentina	4553-1469
Australia	4059-3300
Austria	4555-9566
Belgium	4380-6100
Bolivia	4224-9344
Brazil	4225-9250
Bulgaria	4551-8590
Canada	4723-0101
Central African Republic	4224-4256
Chad	4553-3675
Chile	4551-4668
China (People's Republic)	4723-3677
Colombia	4265-4608
Costa Rica	4525-5223
Czechoslovakia	4734-2910
Cyprus	4720-8628
Denmark	4723-5420
Egypt	4720-9770
El Salvador	4720-4202
Ethiopia	4783-8395
Finland	4705-3545
Gabon	4224-7960
Germany (East)	4500-0010
Germany (West)	4299-7800
Ghana	4500-0950
Greece	4723-7228
Guatemala	4227-7863

Hungary	4500-4159	Poland	4551-8222
Iceland	4522-8154	Portugal	4727-3529
India	4520-3930	Qatar	4550-2297
Indonesia	4503-0760	Romania	4705-4954
Iran	4720-4440	Rwanda	4227-3631
Iraq	4501-5100	Saudi Arabia	4766-0206
Ireland	4500-2087	Senegal	4705-3945
Israel	4256-4747	Singapore	4500-3361
Italy	4544-3890	Somalia	4500-7651
Japan	4766-0222	Soviet Union	4504-0550
Jordan	4624-2379	Spain	4723-3661
Kenya	4553-3500	Sri Lanka	4266-3501
Korea (South)	4753-0101	Sudan	4720-0786
Kuwait	4723-5425	Sweden	4555-9215
Lebanon	4500-2225	Switzerland	4550-3446
Liberia	4763-5855	Syria	4550-2490
Libya	4553-4070	Tanzania	4622-6139
Luxembourg	4555-1337	Thailand	4704-3222
Madagascar	4504-6211	Tunisia	4555-9598
Malaysia	4553-1185	Turkey	4524-5224
Mali	4548-5843	Uganda	4727-4680
Malta	4562-6816	United Arab Emirates	4553-9404
Mauritius	4227-3019	United Kingdom	4266-9142
Mexico	4553-7643	United States	4296-1202
Morocco	4520-6935	Uruguay	4500-9150
Netherlands	4306-6188	Vietnam	4326-8193
New Zealand	4500-2411	Yugoslavia	4504-0505
Niger	4504-8060	Zaire	4225-5750
Nigeria	4704-6865	Zambia	4723-4352
Norway	4723-7278		
Oman	4723-0163		
Pakistan	4262-2332		
Panama	4783-2332		
Peru	4704-3453		
Philippines	4704-6550		

Airlines

Aer Lingus (Ireland)	4742-1250
Aeroflot Soviet Airlines	4225-4381

Aerolineas Argentinas	4253-3116	Cathay Pacific Airways	4227-7005
Aeromexico	4742-4050	Compagnie Air Littoral/CAL	4884-4884
Air Afrique	4561-9620		
Air Algerie	4260-3062	Continental Airlines	4225-3181
Air Canada	4742-2121	Corse Air	4260-3074
Air Europe	4256-2205	Crossair (Switzerland)	4720-1432
Air France	4535-6161	Cubana Airlines	4742-9121
Air Gabon	4359-2063	Cyprus Airways	4501-9338
Air India	4266-1372	Czechoslovak	
Air Inter (France)	4539-2525	Airlines/CSA	4742-3845
Air Lanka	4297-4344	Delta Air Lines	4335-4080
Air Madagascar	4260-3051	Egyptair	4266-0886
Air Mali	4562-9620	El Al Israel Airlines	4742-4129
Air Malta	4549-0650	Europe Aero	
Air Mauritius	4742-7519	Service (France)	4686-8728
Air UK	4535-6161	Finnair	4742-3333
Air Zaire	4703-9487	Garuda Indonesian	
Alia Royal		Airways	4562-3866
Jordanian	4261-5745	Gulf Air	4723-7070
Alitalia	4256-6500	Iberia (Spain)	4723-0023
American		Iran Air	4225-9906
Airlines	4289-0522	Iraqi Airways	4562-6225
Austrian		Japan Air Lines/JAL	4225-8505
Airlines	4266-3466	Jersey European	
Avianca (Colombia)	4260-3522	Airways	4296-0244
Balkan-Bulgarian		Kenya Airways	4261-8293
Airlines	4742-6666	KLM Royal Dutch	
Biman Bangladesh	4289-1147	Airlines	4266-5719
British Airways	4778-1414	Korean Air	4261-5174
British Caledonian		Kuwait Air Ways	4260-3060
Airways	4778-1414	LAM (Mozambique)	4266-4646
British Midland	4742-1444	Libyan Arab	
Brymon Airways		Airlines	4562-3300
(England)	4535-6161	London City	
CAAC (China)	4500-1994	Airways	4266-4646
Cameroon Airlines	4742-7817	LOT Polish Airlines	4742-0560

Lufthansa German Airlines	4265-3735	South African Airways	4261-5787
Luxair	4535-6161	Swissair	4581-1101
Malaysian Airline System	4742-2600	Syrian Arab Airlines	4742-1106
Malev Hungarian Airlines	4261-5790	TAAG (Angola)	4296-8299
		TAP Air Portugal	4296-1609
Middle East Airlines	4266-9393	Tarom (Romania)	4535-6161
Olympic Airways	4265-9242	Thai Airways	4720-6450
Pakistan International Airlines	4562-9241	Transport Arien Transregional (France)	4687-3553
Pan Am World Airways	4266-4545	Tunis Air	4265-9334
		Turk Hava Yollari	4742-6085
Philippine Airlines	4227-0693	TWA	4720-6211
Royal Air Maroc	4266-1030	UTA (France)	4266-4646
Sabena Belgian World Airlines	4742-4747	Varig (Brazil)	4720-0333
		Viasa (Venezuela)	4742-2007
SAS Scandinavian Airlines	4742-0614	Yemenia	4256-0600
Saudi Arabian Airlines	4723-7272	Yugoslav Airlines/ JAT	4268-0606
Singapore Airlines	4261-5309		

▷ Shopping

Napoleon scornfully described England as a nation of shopkeepers. What would he say about Paris today if he returned from the grave? Certainly, it's a city of shopkeepers, from the humblest neighborhood *mercerie* selling buttons, thread, and other useful little items ("notions store" is the closest American equivalent, "haberdashery" the British one) to very chic boutiques and *les grands magasins,* the huge department stores. If you can't buy something in Paris, it probably doesn't exist.

The question remains: *What* to buy? What can you find here that you can't elsewhere—or can find elsewhere only at far lower prices? We're going to start by answering with two negatives.

First, try not to buy anything imported. You're in France, which makes a huge variety of goods, so there's little point in buying imports. Also note that value-added tax (VAT), essentially a very complicated form of sales tax, is calculated on the retail price—and on any customs duties. The tax can add as much as a third to the retail price—but you won't know, because it isn't stated separately.

Second, do not complain that Paris prices are exorbitant. Whether you find them high or low depends mainly upon where you live, what that country's tax regime is, and the present rate at which its currency exchanges for French francs. In recent years, for example, the Japanese have flooded Paris stores, astonished by the cheapness of everything; but Americans, thanks to the dollar's up-and-down weakness, have muttered that Paris is outrageously expensive.

▷ Spotlight ◁

Tax-free shopping. Many stores offer tax-free shopping. Note, though, that for people living within the European Community, the minimum purchase qualifying for tax-free treatment is FF 2400; and for those outside, FF 1200. Among leading duty-free stores: E*iffel Shopping*, 9 Avenue de Suffren, 7me; *For You*, 380 Rue St-Honoré, 1er; *Liza*, 194 Rue de Rivoli, 1er; M*ichel Swiss*, 16 Rue de la Paix; *Paris Opéra*, 16 Avenue de l'Opéra, 2me; M*itsukoshi France*, 49 Avenue de l'Opéra, 2me.

The most prudent course, the one that will keep blood pressure and credit-card companies at bay and the family happy, is to shop shrewdly. So here's our very selective list.

Street and other markets offer an astonishing range of goods. Along the left and right banks of the Seine, particularly the sections facing Notre Dame Cathedral, are stalls that sell books, old magazines and newspapers, prints, and other memorabilia. Where to look: the *quais de Louvre, de la Messagerie, Grands Augustins, de Conti,* and *de Malaquais.* Prices are usually marked, but you can bargain.

At 2 Place du Palais-Royal, 1er, is *Le Louvre des Antiquaires* (tel.: 4297-2900). Once a department store, this cavernous building has been nicely rebuilt to house some 250 antiques dealers. Also worth an hour or so of browsing is the *Village Suisse* market, 78 Avenue de Suffren, 7me. There are some fine, old-fashioned shopping arcades and passageways. Among the best: *Galerie Vero-Dodat,* 19 Rue Jean-Jacques Rousseau, 1er; *Passage Choiseul,* Rue St. Augustins, 2me; and *Galerie Vivienne,* 4 Rue des Petits-Champs, 2me.

Starting at 10:00 a.m. every Thursday, Saturday, and Sunday, dealers in postage stamps and postcards gather under the trees along the avenues *Gabriel* and *Matignon,* 8me, just off the Avenue des Champs-Elysées at the Rond-Point (when you go from the Arc de Triomphe toward the Place de la Concorde, the Rond-Point is roughly two-thirds of the way down). In bad weather, dealers gather in nearby cafés, particularly those on or around the Rue Jean Mermoz. At number 11 in that street is the antique dealers' trade association, the *Syndicat National des Antiquaires*. Tel.: 4225-4433.

Paris flea markets are famous—but many have priced themselves out of the bargain basement. That is notably true of the largest of them all, at *Porte de St. Ouen-Porte de Clignancourt*, 18me. You will find some wonderful things there, but the prices tend to be in wonderland. A better bet is to watch out for sales at *Salle Drouot*, 9 Rue Drouot, 9me. The city's largest and best auction rooms, Drouot, offer everything from the schlocky to the superb. No credit cards or checks drawn on nonFrench banks, so take cash or travelers checks. Another way is to open an account with a dealer who will bid for you up to an agreed price. Tel.: 4246-1711.

Fashion. From the old to the new...Paris *is* fashion. The big shows are in January and July for *haute couture* and in March and October for ready-to-wear. Fashion and perfume—most for women, but some for men:

Balmain, 44 Rue François 1er, 8me; *Cardin,* 27 Avenue de Marigny, 8me; *Carven,* 6 Rond-Point des Champs-Elysées, 8me; *Chanel,* 31 Rue Cambon, 1er; *Courreges,* 40 Rue François 1er, 8me; *Dior,* 30 Avenue Montaigne, 8me; *Feraud,* 88 Rue du Faubourg St-Honoré, 8me; *Givenchy,* 3 Avenue George V, 8me; *Gres,* 1 Rue de la Paix, 2me; *Guerlain,* 68 Avenue des Champs-Elysées, 8me; *Hanae Mori,* 17 Avenue Montaigne, 8me; *Hermes,* 34 Rue du Faubourg St-Honoré, 8me; *Jean Patou,* 7 Rue Saint-Florentin, 8me; *Kenzo,* 3 Place des Victoires, 2me; Lacroix, 73 rue du faubourg Saint-Honoré, 8me; *Lanvin,* 23 Rue du Faubourg St-Honoré, 8me; *Nina Ricci,* 39 Avenue Montaigne, 8me; *Paco Rabanne,* 7 Rue du Cherche-Midi, 6me; Saint Laurent, 6 and 12 place Saint-Sulpice, 7me; *Per Spook,* 18 Avenue George V, 8me; *Scherrer,* 51 Avenue Montaigne, 8me; *Serge Lepage,* 15 Rue Duphot, 1er; *Ted Lapidus,* 23 Rue du Faubourg St-Honoré, 8me; Torrente, 9 Rue du Faubourg St-Honoré, 8me; *Ungaro,* 2 Avenue Montaigne, 8me.

Les grands magasins—department stores—are vast bazaars; so vast, indeed, that each would take a full week to explore. Even then, one would have missed something, for the stock changes rapidly. In the list below we've shown adjacent Métro stations rather than addresses, because *les grands magasins* tend to occupy whole city blocks, and even straddle two or more: *Bazar de l'Hôtel de Ville* (Hotel de Ville), *Bon Marché* (Sevres-Babylone), *Galeries Lafayette* (Chausée d'Antin), *Printemps* (Havre-Caumartin), *Samaritaine* (Pont-Neuf), *Trois Quartiers* (Madeleine).

Food. Every neighborhood is rich in food stores. The most fashionable of the lot is *Fauchon,* 28 Place de la Madeleine, 8me: the best of France—

and some other countries. You can gain weight just by gazing at this stupendous selection of *haute cuisine* and fine wines and liqueurs, all displayed with artistic flair. Of the many open-air food markets, the best is in the *Place d'Aligre,* 12me—one of the last remaining touches of the Paris of Edith Piaf.

▷ After Hours

We've never quite understood the city's reputation for naughtiness—what one might call the "ooh-la-la!" factor. At one time, a century or so ago perhaps, when a glimpse of stocking was something shocking, Paris was more free-and-easy than, say, London or Boston.

Or was Paris more open about the sensual side of life? Recent biographies of eminent Victorian gentlemen on both sides of the Atlantic suggest that they found little difficulty in discovering dalliance both fleeting and permanent, but kissed and didn't tell. Their French contemporaries, in contrast, both dallied and told in their respective circles, and a cabinet minister or industrialist without a mistress or two was almost an oddity.

Beyond a doubt, Paris today is no naughtier than any other big European city—and a good deal less naughty than some. To be sure, there is entertainment to suit all tastes, and some of it is raw. On the other hand, those epitomes of "ooh-la-la!", the Moulin Rouge, the Folies Bergère and the Crazy Horse Saloon, have long been places to which only the most puritanical could object. You can see on television programs a good deal raunchier, and far less tasteful and elegant. All the big houses spend fortunes on mounting new shows. The Moulin Rouge, for example, spent $9 million on *Formidable,* celebrating its centenary.

Contemporary Parisians express ennui about the night scene, and the Beautiful People pictured in the glossy magazines do look bored. Paris Society with a capital *S,* what was known as *Tout Paris,* has virtually disappeared except as a list of people to invite to film premieres. One Parisian even admits, "There's more fun and frolic in London."

Paris does have a red-light district, *Pigalle,* and there are sex shops and exotic theaters in Les Halles and the Rue St. Denis area. However, the AIDS scare has put a bit of a damper on the business of ladies of the evening. Safer to look than touch these days.

Music Halls/Cabarets

Crazy Horse Saloon, 12 Avenue George V, 8me. Tel.: 4723-3232. The city's most artistic—and erotic—striptease. Le Crazy is nearly always packed, largely by French businessmen entertaining foreign clients.

Folies-Bergère, 32 Rue Richer, 9me. Tel.: 4246-7711. Large, luxurious shows; audiences are a mingling of married couples celebrating something, tourists, and business executives.

Lido, 116 Avenue des Champs-Elysées, 8me. Tel.: 4563-1161. The Bluebell Girls, all more than 6 feet tall and most of them English, strut their disciplined stuff here in a luxurious but rather cramped hall.

Moulin Rouge, Place Blanche, 8me. Tel.: 4606-0019. The great pre-World War II music hall star Mistinguett said of the world of illusion, "It is women. It is plumes and it is people. It is nothing and it is everything. In short, it is life itself." It is the Moulin Rouge.

Paradis Latin, 28 Rue du Cardinal-Lemoine, 5me. Tel.: 4325-2828. You'll learn nothing of the language of the Romans here, but much about female anatomy, precision dancing, and how to mount a spectacular show.

Clubs/Discos

Baiser Sale, 58 Rue des Lombards, 1er. Tel.: 4233-3771. Live Brazilian rock in the heart of the new clubland.

Balajo, 9 Rue de Lappe, 11me. Tel.: 4700-0787. Tango hall. If you've got to mention the Falklands, remember to call them *Las Malvinas*. Once a street of cutthroats, now fashionable.

Castel's, 15 Rue Princess, 16me. Tel.: 4326-9022. Less snobbish than it was, but difficult to enter without an impressive business card.

La Locomotive, 90 Boulevard de Clichy, 18me. Tel.: 4257-3737. New and hot—on three levels. Next to Moulin Rouge.

Le Montana, 28 Rue St.-Benoit, 6me. Tel.: 4548-9308. Long bar at street level, downstairs *cave*. Heart of one clubland.

Les Bains, 7 Rue du Bourg l'Abbé, 3me. Tel.: 4887-0180. Stars and models; dress smartly.

New Morning, 7–9 Rue des Petites-Ecuries, 10me. Tel.: 4523-5141. Venerable, but still excellent. Jazz, Brazilian, and African music.

Olivia Valere, 40 Rue du Colisée, 8me. Tel.: 4225-1168. Lots of chic girls—and quite a lot of CEOs.

Palace, 8 Rue du Faubourg Montmartre, 9me. Tel.: 4246-1087. First huge disco to mix the social classes, and still going strong. Special corner for gentlemen who don't fancy ladies.

Regine's Club, 49 Rue Ponthieu, 8me. Tel.: 4359-2160. For the super-rich (the Rothschilds helped to launch Regine). Officially members-only, but the rules may be relaxed for people with bulging billfolds.

Bars/Piano Bars/Watering-holes.

Alexandre, 53 Avenue George V, 8me. Tel.: 4720-1782. Comfortable hangout for movie and press people—and some undercover U.S. agents. Piano.

Ascot, 66 Rue Pierre Charron, 8me. Tel.: 4359-2815. Elegant decor, impeccable service; frequented by the horseracing set—and by personable young ladies anxious that gentlemen not be lonely. Piano.

Calavados, 40 Avenue Pierre-1er-de-Serbie, 8me. Tel.: 4720-3139. The incomparable Joe Turner has been playing piano for as long as anyone can remember. Late-night haunt of jet-setters.

Closerie des Lilas, 171 Boulevard du Montparnasse, 6me. Tel.: 4326-7050. Hemingway's old joint. Much changed, but still chic, particularly the summer terrace.

Conway's, 73 Rue Saint-Denis, 1er. Tel.: 4508-0707. New York-style bar, Miss Conway's gift to France.

Deux Magots, 6 Place Saint Germain-des-Prés, 6me. Tel.: 4548-5525. People watching other people watching other people watching other people. . .

Harry's, 5 Rue Daunou, 2me. Tel.: 4261-7114. City's most famous American bar, where the Bloody Mary was invented.

Kitty O'Shea's, 10 Rue des Capucines, 2me. Tel.: 4015-0808. Combines the French love of the Irish, whiskey, and women.

Pont Royal, 7 Rue Montalembert, 7me. Tel.: 4544-3827. Famous literary bar; watch for French imitators of Tom Wolfe.

Rosebud, 11 bis, Rue Delambre, 14me. Tel.: 4335-3854. An "in" singles bar that is a last touch of the old Montparnasse neighborhood.

Ritz Hotel, Rue Cambon, 1er (you can also enter from the Place de Vendome and walk through the hotel corridor, lined with showcases). Tel.: 4260-3830. As famous as Harry's; a quiet haven in the afternoon. A new, chic night bar.

▷ Sights and Sounds

Paris is filled with memorable sights, from the Eiffel Tower to the small, green Wallace fountains in the neighborhood squares; from Sacré Coeur church on the hill of Montmartre to Notre Dame Cathedral on the Île-de-la-Cité; from the Arc de Triomphe to modest statues in quiet squares celebrating the lives of people half-forgotten. The Wallace fountains, incidentally, are named for a British benefactor of neighborhood life. The Statue of Liberty in New York harbor, a gift from France to the United States, is commemorated by a miniature version on a tiny island near the Eiffel Tower—and a full-size replica of the statue's torch can be seen at the place de l'Alma. Our list of recommended sights and sounds rests upon two main criteria. First, each is worth seeing for its own sake. Second, each tells part of France's story. Please note that all art galleries and museums are closed on Tuesdays, except the Musée d'Orsay, which closes on Mondays.

Assemblée Nationale (parliament), Palais Bourbon, 35 Quai d'Orsay, 7me. Tel.: 4063-6000. Guided tours (see local "what's on" guides). Newly cleaned exterior; magnificent site looking across the bridge to the Place de la Concorde.

African and Oceanic Arts Museum *(Musée National des Arts Africains et Océaniens),* 293 Avenue Daumesnil, 12me. Tel.: 4343-1454. The three main sections are devoted to the arts of black Africa, North Africa, and the Pacific Islands.

Arab Institute *(Institut du Monde Arabe),* 23 Quai Saint-Bernard, 5me. Tel.: 4634-2525 (museum closed Mondays). France and the Arab League countries financed this striking, glass-walled building. Art shows, library, conferences; excellent restaurant.

Eiffel Tower *(La Tour Eiffel).* Not the world's tallest structure by a long way, but one of the most famous. Newly refurbished, its ancient elevators replaced, and the ironwork lacery lit at night by Philips (a Dutch company), the grand old lady is looking fine.

Invalides, 7me. Under a huge cupola is the tomb of Napoleon, upon which one A. Hitler gazed briefly (he didn't learn from history: like the emperor, Hitler made the mistake of attacking Russia in winter). In this huge complex of buildings are the *memento mori* of France's glorious military past: armor, uniforms, weapons, battle honors.

Louvre, Rue de Rivoli, 1er. Tel.: 4260-3926. Arguably the world's finest and most comprehensive collection of paintings, but for a long time dimmed by lack of space and questionable display policies. Prodded by President François Mitterrand, the finance ministry has surrendered this former palace. Many people intensely dislike the glass pyramid in the courtyard, designed by Chinese-American architect I.M. Pei; others think it a work of genius.

Musée d'Orsay, 62 Rue de Lille, 7me. Tel.: 4049-4814. A splendid survival of railroad barons' profligate use of investors' money; once a train station, now a museum and gallery focusing on the period 1848-1914. So powerful is the architecture that it dominates the art, or so say some critics. See for yourself. (Closed Mondays.)

Opéra, Place de l'Opéra. The opera itself has moved to a new building at Bastille that resembles an airport terminal, but the ballet will remain. So will the ceilings by Chagall and the subterranean lake featured in *Phantom of the Opera.* Guided tours; a must. Tel.: 4742-5750.

Pompidou Center, Rue Rambuteau, 4me. Tel.: 4277-1233. Externally an oil refinery in central Paris, complete with pipes; internally rather grubby, but with many eye- (and mind-) catching exhibitions. One of the city's most popular tourist attractions. Even so, we consider it an eyesore, symbolizing the architectural profession's blatant and arrogant disregard of scale, style, and consonance (the main architect was British, by the way).

Science City *(Cité des Sciences et de l'Industrie),* Parc de la Villette, 19me. Tel.: 4624-1313. Here France trumpets (with the help of an electronic synthesizer, no doubt) its achievements in space, oceanography, and the like. The nearby Geode cinema claims to have the world's largest screen.

▷ *Spotlight* ◁

Special-interest museums. Paris has many special-interest museums, evidence of the city's diversity of culture and taste. Among them:

Affiche et Publicité, 18 Rue de Paradis, 10me. Tel.: 4246-1309. A huge collection of poster art; shows how much imagination and work went into adver-

PARIStising such things as bicycles and soap.

tising such things as bicycles and soap.
Arts Decoratifs, 107 Rue de Rivoli,
1er. Tel.: 4260-3214. The decorative
arts, often given second billing in "serious" galleries, are here the stars of a
very large and varied collection.
Bibliothèque Nationale, 58 Rue Riche-
lieu, 2me. Tel.: 4703-8126. A magnet
for bibliophiles and bibliomaniacs.
Carnavalet, 23 Rue de Signe, 3me.

Tel.: 4272-2113. The city's history told
through artifacts, paintings, documents, and much else.
Musée Hôtel Sale, 5 Rue de Thorigny,
3me. Tel.: 4271-2521. Picasso, adopted
son of France, is here celebrated with
works that exemplify his entire career.
Musée Rodin, 77 Rue de Varenne,
7me. Tel.: 4705-0134. Works of one of
Europe's finest, most subtle sculptors.

▷ Out of Town

Palaces

The Château de Versailles is always worth another visit: who has yet ex-
plored its riches fully? Furthermore, restoration continues, and with it the
return of furniture and furnishings that strengthen reminders of *la gloire*
that was created by Louis XIV and XVI and their courts. Versailles is
only 22 kilometers (14 miles) from central Paris. If driving, take Autoroute A13 west of the city. By train, depart from the Gare Montparnasse
or the Invalides. Journey time is about 20 minutes. Versailles is a smallish
(population: 95,000) town with some good restaurants. Recommended:
Trois Marchés, 3 Rue Colbert. Elegant, eighteenth-century building. Tel.:
3950-1321.

Fontainebleau. There's another fine palace at Fontainebleau, 65 kilometers (40 miles) south of Paris. Take the A6 autoroute or a train from Gare
de Lyon. An ancient forest almost surrounds the town. Look also for the
Musée Napoleonien d'Art et d'Histoire Militaire, with its large collection
of weaponry. Two good restaurants: *Aigle Noir,* 27 Place Napoleon (tel.:
6422-3265) and *François 1er,* 3 Rue Royale (tel.: 6422-2468).

▷ Spotlight ◁

In Search of art. Combine a visit to
Fontainebleau with a tour of the
haunts, houses, and graves of the
nineteenth-century painters of the Barbizon and Impressionist schools who
revolutionized art. *Barbizon* is on the
forest fringes. If driving, take the A6
from Paris and watch for the N37 exit

on your left. The town is associated
with the lives and work of Corot, Mil-
let, and Rousseau. *Moret,* on the far
side of the forest, has rich associations
with Sisley, Monet, and Pissarro. To
reach it from Barbizon, drive through
the forest on the southbound N6.

Coastal Resorts

Further afield are the Normandy coastal resorts of Cabourg and Deauville. To drive to either, or both, take the A13 autoroute and watch for the exit signs.

Cabourg, 225 kilometers (140 miles) from Paris, is a small, nostalgically elegant little town (population: 3,250) with a casino, a fine beach, and an original street plan: it's based on a spider's web. Marcel Proust set some episodes in his *A la Recherche du Temps Perdu (Remembrance of Things Past)* in Cabourg. The *Pullman Grand Hôtel,* Promenade Marcel-Proust, is the quintessence of that vanished world (tel.: 3191-0179).

Deauville, 19 kilometers (12 miles) along the coast, is another custom-built nineteenth-century vacation town. Small like Cabourg (only 4,800 people live there), Deauville is *Paris-sur-Mer*—the Paris, that is, of the fashionable *arrondissements.* As well as a newly refurbished casino (now with slot machines), the town has a golf course, a racetrack, a polo ground, a yacht marina, and a long boardwalk. The two top hotels are the *Normandy* and the *Royal,* facing the beach. The Normandy (tel.: 3188-0921) has a deceptively rustic exterior: it's actually very chic. The Royal's architecture is more formal (tel.: 3188-1641). Across the river is the popular resort town of *Trouville,* which in July and August is bustling with tourists enjoying the long, sandy beach. There's also a casino.

For golf in Normandy and throughout France, contact the French Golf Federation in Paris. Tel.: 4502-1355.

▷ Spotlight ◁

History. All of Normandy is redolent with history. William the Conqueror set sail from these shores to conquer King Harold of England in 1066; that exploit is illustrated in the quite remarkable tapestry at Bayeux, still vivid and fascinating after more than a millennium. The Allied forces landed on the Normandy beaches in June 1944; their exploits are commemorated in museums at Arromanches and Caen. You can also visit the beaches them-selves. All are about an hour's drive west of Cabourg-Deauville. Our choice of hotel in Bayeux is the *Lion d'Or,* 71 Rue Saint-Jean (tel.: 3192-0690), an old coaching inn with comfortable rooms and the best kitchen in town. A few minutes' drive out of town, on highway D158, is the eighteenth-century *Relais Château d'Audrieu,* set in spacious parkland. Luxurious rooms, excellent restaurant. Tel.: 3180-2152.

ROME

Modern Times in the Eternal City

Population: 2.83 million (1981). Administrative, political, and cultural capital of the Italian Republic (population: 52.7 million). *Location*: central Italy on the Tiber River, 26 kilometers (16 miles) from its mouth on the Mediterranean. Site also of the Vatican city-state (at .44 of a square kilometer, or about 108 acres, the world's smallest), center of the Roman Catholic Church. *Economy*: fashion; the media, including publishing and television and film production; service industries and tourism. Italy is a member of the European Community (EC) and the Organization for Economic Cooperation and Development (OECD) and is a signatory to the General Agreement on Tariffs and Trade (GATT).

▷ Background Briefing

All roads no longer lead to the Eternal City set on the seven hills—Milan has far more economic clout. Rome is still the cultural leader, however, an architectural treasure largely owned by the Vatican, the city's chief landlord, and the Italian state. World-weary Romans will tell you in one breath that their city is being ruined by too much traffic, too much pollution, too many tourists—too much of everything; and in the next breath that Rome is the world's most beautiful city. There's some truth in both views.

Beauty aside, though, Rome has in some ways become a provincial backwater, relegated to that role by history and geography. At the height of the Roman Empire's power in the 100s A.D., the city had a population of about a million; that shrank to a mere 30,000 in the Middle Ages. Even by 1870, when Rome became capital of the new Kingdom of Italy, only

200,000 people were living there. The city's growth to nearly 3 million to-day has come mainly in the past half-century, particularly during the time of the Italian "economic miracle," called *il sorpasso,* of the 1950s and 1960s, when Italy changed rapidly from an agricultural to an industrial-ized country.

The miracle didn't happen everywhere in Italy, however. Chiefly, it af-fected the north, leaving the south largely untouched, with an invisible boundary between the two. Rome sits astride that divide, its life combin-ing aspects of the vigorous, fast-paced north with the slower, more tradi-tional south. The mixture is fascinating—and can be infuriating. The Romans drive like bats out of hell when they have half a chance—and then end up in a bad-tempered traffic jam.

The bureaucracy is tortuous, policy obviously being that it never puts off until tomorrow what it can put off until next week—or next month. However, while you wait endlessly in City Hall for a document, you can comfort yourself with the thought that Michelangelo designed the build-ing. And if it takes you 45 minutes to change travelers checks, you can pass the time by taking pleasure in the bank's beautiful baroque façade. Rome is for the patient—the very patient. But as most foreign residents will tell you, the countless frustrations of daily life are a price worth pay-ing for Rome's unique charm and inexhaustible interest.

▷ Arriving

By Air

Leonardo da Vinci Airport has separate terminals for international and national flights. Situated 30 kilometers (18 miles) from the city, it is one of Europe's busiest—and, thank heavens, it's working much better than it did a few years back, when it was plagued by strikes and was regarded as a near disaster by foreign airlines. These days you can even find luggage trolleys. There is one—yes, just one—reasonably efficient though small and expensive snack bar. There still isn't a visible clock. That may be a leftover from the days when an Alitalia executive knelt before Leonardo's statue and intoned, "What have they done in your name?" Perhaps out of respect for the great man, most people know the airport as Fiumicino, taken from the name of the nearby seaport.

When leaving by air, remember that checkin lines tend to be long un-less you are traveling first or business class. Even if you are, allow at least two hours.

A direct rail link scheduled to open for the 1990 World Cup football (soccer) championships should speed the journey to the city. At present the choice is between a bus, often offering only standing room, and a taxi. The bus takes about 40 minutes, the taxi a little less. Both at the airport and at the city airline terminal, avoid unmetered taxis. Most drivers are sharks.

By Rail

Termini Station is the worst possible introduction to Rome. Set in the sleaziest part of town, it's a camp for vagrants and other urban lowlife. The station is dirty, porters are rare, and lines for tickets stretch like lines for bread during a famine. Buses from the Termini are hunting grounds for pickpockets. If you are going to travel by train, remember that an express is a *rapido*—whereas an *expresso* stops for the slightest excuse, or none at all.

▷ Money

The basic (and only, for all practical purposes) unit of currency is the lira. International code: ITL. Lire banknotes come in denominations of 1,000, 2,000, 5,000, 10,000, 50,000, and 100,000. It's easy to confuse the larger denominations, and short-changing is a local sport. There has been some talk in recent years of revaluing the lira by knocking off a couple of zeros, bringing it more closely in line with other European currencies. However, the government has been slow to take any real action on such a plan. For Americans, it's rather a kick to stuff your wallet with such high-denomination bills—until you realize that even a drink or an ice cream bar from a street vendor costs 1,000 lire!

The commonest coins are 50, 100, 200, and 500 lire. However, there's often a shortage of small change, and copper *gettone* for phone kiosks are often passed around in place of 200-lire coins.

In other cities, we've advised readers to change money at banks whenever possible. In Rome, by contrast, you have to balance the better rate of exchange you'll get at a bank against the extra time you'll spend there rather than at the hotel cashier's counter.

▷ Language

Most Romans speak only Italian, apart from a smattering of English and French. The police are an exception. So are business executives and staff at the top hotels. A pocket phrasebook helps immensely when you're on your own in public.

▷ **Communications**

Country code: 39. City code: 6 (not needed within the city). Quality of service is appalling. In theory, you can dial both local and international calls direct from most hotels—but theory isn't practice. Ministerial and other numbers sound the busy signal for much of the day; when a number does ring, the operator may take 10 or more minutes to answer. Even some of the international-class hotels employ "deaf operators." The postal service is practically worthless, and corporations often use private mail carriers instead.

▷ **Getting To Know the City**

The roads leading to Rome are as straight as they were in the days of the chariots, but the city itself can be confusing at first because of the north-to-south meandering of the Tiber River. The Vatican and Saint Peter's, as well as the ancient and romantic quarter of *Trastevere* ("across the Tiber"), are on the west bank. Political and business Rome, the commercial and shopping areas, and the major hotels are on the east bank. However, one twist in the Tiber means that part of historic Rome on the east bank, the area around the Piazza Navona, juts like a peninsula toward the Vatican.

The best way to fix the city's topography in your mind is to divide the main, eastern part of the city into east and west of the Via del Corso, the main artery that runs from the Via del Popola in the north down to the Piazza Venezia. Here stands the massive and ugly Vittorio Emanuele monument that marks the unification of Italy. Nearby are the Capitoline Hill, the Colosseum, and the ruins of the Forum. This is where Rome began.

Another way to understand the city's topography is to view it from the Janiculum ridge above Trastevere. From this vantage, you can take in the honey-brown mass of Roman roofs and pick out the monuments and church domes. There are other great views, notably from the gardens of the Villa Medici, up behind the Spanish Steps. Close by is the celebrated Via Veneto; like New York's Fifth Avenue and the Champs-Elysées in Paris, its name is a synonym for luxury and elegance. See for yourself.

▷ **Moving Around**

Rome traffic is fierce and very often gridlocked. There are four rush hours, because most shops and offices close for lunch and many people go home to eat. Being on time for an appointment means that you are up to half an hour late. One solution for the business visitor who wants to get around fast is to hire a guide. If the guide has a car, he or she will know the short cuts and the complicated parking rules. Ask the hotel concierge to recommend a guide, and be sure to negotiate a price in advance. Don't rent a car unless you know the city well.

In theory, much of the center is closed to nonresidents' cars—but still the jams persist. However, the heart of Rome is small enough for any point to be reached on foot within 15 minutes.

There are only two subway lines, useful because they connect the main railroad station with downtown Piazza di Spagna and Piazza del Popolo and serve the Vatican neighborhood as well as the satellite city of EUR *(Esposizione Universale Roma),* seat of several ministries and state companies, notably Alitalia and ENI.

Rome has about 5,000 buses, but half the fleet is usually being repaired. One ticket takes you anywhere in the city—but a ticket may be hard to find. You have to buy one before boarding the bus, and newsstands and *tabacchi* (cigarette stores) often have none. The big cafés at the Termini station are usually a better bet. However, hardly anyone uses the ticket canceling machines on the buses, so if you don't have a ticket, well...

The 5,500 taxis are not nearly enough for a city of Rome's size and are scarce at peak periods and at shift changeover times (7:30 a.m. and 2:30 and 10:00 p.m.). The Romans don't wait in line for anything, so stand up for your rights if you're first at a taxi stand.

▷ Spotlight ◁

Security. Sophia Loren once played a thief working the buses. A razor blade concealed in her mouth, she cut the straps of handbags. A local TV station staged a pickpocket championship for nimble-fingered youngsters. A good laugh—unless your pocket is picked. It could happen. The Termini railroad station is notorious. Among high-risk bus routes: the 64 to Saint Peter's and the 46, 81, and 492, all serving tourist areas. Buy a money belt before going to Rome, and avoid the Piazza Navone and Villa Borghese areas after dark: there are muggings.

▷ Hotels

Hotels in the five- and four-star categories emphasize personal service. What is more flattering than to have three waiters at the Hassler-Villa Medici deliver your breakfast to your room? One pushes the trolley, another sets the table, and the third opens the shutters and almost breaks into song as he describes the weather. At the Excelsior, guests get the royal treatment, and at the Grand, they are fawned upon as though they were the heads of central banks. Rome is noisy, so when reserving, specify a room at the back—though the best hotels have discovered double glazing.

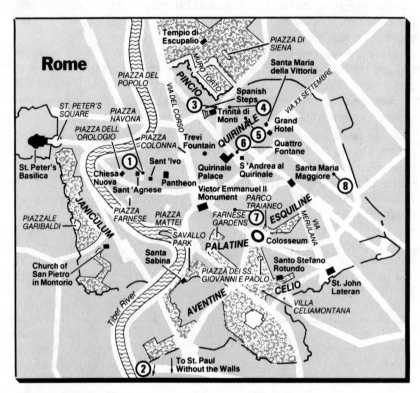

1. Hotel Raphael
2. EUR/Hotel Sheraton
3. Hotel Hassler
4. Hotel de la Ville
5. Hotels Ambasciatori
     Eden
     Excelsior
6. Hotel Bernini
7. Hotel Forum
8. Main Station

Deluxe

Ambasciatori Palace, Via Veneto 70. Tel.: 47493. Telex: 610241. Fax: 6799303. Rooms/suites: 164. A modern (by Roman standards) palace opposite the American Embassy. Direct-dial phones, good restaurants, separate grill bar and piano lounge. Sauna; conference and reception facilities. A Preferred Hotel recommended for business executives.

Bernini Bristol, Piazza Barberini 23. Tel.: 463051. Telex: 610554. Fax: 4750266. Rooms/suites: 127. Close to the most fashionable shopping area. Marbled public rooms; bedrooms in traditional and modern styles (specify your preference when reserving). Excellent business and meeting center with direct-dial phones.

Cavalieri Hilton, Via Cadlolo 101, Monte Mario. Tel.: 3151. Telex: 610296. Fax: 3151 xtn 2221. Rooms/suites: 398. Slightly out of town, but with a regular shuttle bus except on Sundays. Spectacular views, quiet location. Highly efficient, with 24-hour telex, secretarial, and courier services. Several restaurants; health club, tennis, pool, disco.

Eden, Via Ludovisi 49. Tel.: 474-3551. Telex: 610567. Fax: 474-2401. Rooms/suites: 110. Noted for its service, the Eden has long been a favorite with visiting business travelers, particularly Americans, who mingle with their Roman counterparts in the Penthouse roof bar, with its superb view of the city.

Excelsior, Via Veneto 125. Tel.: 4708. Telex: 610232. Fax: 4756205. Rooms/suites: 383. Next door to the U.S. Embassy. White outside and plush inside, the Excelsior is closely associated with the myths and realities of the *dolce vita* (sweet life). King Farouk of Egypt, the Shah of Iran, Elizabeth Taylor, and Richard Burton helped to give the hotel its exotic reputation. Today's realities are that the service and restaurants are fine.

Grand, Via Orlando 3. Tel.: 4709. Telex: 610210. Fax: 474-7307. Rooms/ suites: 171. Near the main railroad station and a short walk from the Piazza di Spagna. Spacious in the old, grand manner—and the Aga Khan's Ciga chain means to keep it that way. Notably good grill and restaurant; impeccable service for the international bankers who stay at the Grand and the cardinals who give receptions there.

Hassler-Villa Medici, Piazza Trinita dei Monti. Tel.: 678-2651. Telex: 610208. Fax: 679-9278. Rooms/suites: 103. The best site in Rome, at the top of the Spanish Steps, with breathtaking views of St. Peter's from the top-floor restaurant; lunch in summer in the garden. Rome at its most elegant.

Lord Byron, Via de Notaris 5. Tel.: 360-9541. Telex: 611217. Fax: 360-9541. Rooms/suites: 50. Intimate, very smart, and very quiet; close to the Villa Borghese and the exclusive Parioli residential district. *Le Jardin* restaurant specializes in private business lunches and dinners.

Sheraton Roma, Viale del Pattinaggio, EUR. Tel.: 5453. Telex: 614223. Fax: 542-0689. Rooms/suites: 643. Presidential suites: 2. In the EUR suburb, site of some ministries and headquarters of state-owned companies. Close to the airport; in-house Alitalia checkin. Bus shuttles and subway connection to the city. Very much a business hotel, with modern rooms, good restaurant, and sports facilities.

Four Stars

De La Ville, Via Sistina 67. Tel.: 6733. Telex: 620836. Fax: 678-4213. Next to the Hassler and therefore in the same excellent location. Business center and a lovely garden. La Saletta and American piano bars and Patio restaurant.

D'Inghilterra, Via Bocca di Leone 14. Tel. (and Fax): 672161. Telex: 614552. Rooms/suites: 105. Authors Henry James and Ernest Hemingway (at different times, of course) regarded this as their private club; today's movie stars take the same view. Try for one of the fifth-floor rooms: they have terraces. Elegant private rooms for business meals; first-class secretarial and interpreting services.

Forum, Via Tor dei Conti 25. Tel.: 679-2446. Telex: 622549. Fax: 679-9337. Rooms/suites: 80. A Renaissance palace converted into a palatial hotel with dining on a terrace that overlooks the Forum; friendly staff.

Holiday Inn, Viale Castello della Magliana 65, EUR. Tel.: 68581. Telex: 613302. Fax: 685-7005. Rooms/suites: 324. About 10 kilometers (6.25 miles) from the city, convenient to the airport.

Holiday Inn, Via Aurelia Antica 415. Tel.: 5872. Telex: 625434. Fax: 623-7190. Rooms/suites: 334. About 6 kilometers (3.75 miles) from the city center.

Raphael, Largo Febo 2. Tel.: 650881. Telex: 622396. Fax: 687-8993. Rooms/suites: 83. The place to go for political gossip: it's near Piazza Navona and the Senate. Bettino Craxi, a former premier, has lived in a Raphael penthouse for 20 years. Recently refurbished—the hotel, that is, not him.

▷ Restaurants

People who know Italian dishes only as they are served in other countries will have a pleasant surprise in Rome. To be sure, pasta is an essential part of lunch and dinner, but it comes in so many forms that its versatility is amazing. It often is "merely" an entrée, with the main course consisting of meat or poultry. Italian cuisine is remarkably varied and certainly the most sophisticated in Europe apart from that of France. Because this is a guide for business travelers, we've listed restaurants suitable for entertaining.

The Roman business executive likes to eat well, even conspiciously well, with little regard for expense. Lunch starts around 1:00 p.m. and dinner around 9:00 p.m. The Roman is particularly anxious to have a good lunch, because breakfast was probably nothing but a cup of coffee and a pastry.

▷ Spotlight ◁

A *dining alternative.* When you have time to spare, are sated with sophisticated food, and are feeling adventurous, wander the streets to find one of the many little *trattorie*. At most you can eat (and drink) magnificently at surprisingly low cost. Your hotel concierge will be delighted to recommend a *trattoria*—but be sure to insist that you want the real thing, not a tarted-up tourist trap. Take your phrasebook, because many authentic *trattorie* are family-owned by friendly people who speak little, if any, English.

Alberto Ciarla, Piazza San Cosimato 40. Tel.: 581-8668. Many connoisseurs rate this as the best restaurant in southern Italy, not just Rome. Specialties are fish and the choicest game and meats. Situated in the old quarter of Trastevere, across the Tiber; outdoor eating in season. Very expensive.

Al Moro, Vicolo delle Bollette 13. Tel.: 678-3495. A Roman classic, just a stone's throw from Trevi Fountain. Great food, but there are too many people and too much noise for really serious business talks.

Bacaro, Via degli Spagnoli 27. Tel.: 686-4110. Near the Pantheon, Bacaro specializes in fish, much of it cooked *nouvelle cuisine*-style and in a superior selection of Italian wines.

Charles, Roof Garden dll'Hotel Eden, Via Ludovisi 49. Tel.: 4743351. A favorite with politicians and top businesspeople. Excellence of the food and service is rivaled by that of the ambience. Very expensive.

Dal Bolognese, Piazza del Popolo 1. Tel.: 361-1426. Wonderful view from the terrace of one of the world's handsomest squares while you savor one of Italy's greatest regional cuisines, that of Bologna. Good, thoughtful service.

Elefante Bianco, Via Aurora 19. Tel.: 483718. A natural for expense-account meals, with luxurious food and surroundings. Not quite great because its formula lacks imaginative touches.

El Toulà, Via della Lupa 29. Tel.: 687-3750. Exceptionally fine cuisine, with waiters who read customers' minds. The English-style bar is cozy and intimate.

Il Drappe, Vicolo del Malpasse 10. Tel.: 687-7365. Sardinian regional cuisine from a trio of enthusiasts who treat their island's superb produce with the respect and inventiveness it merits.

La Rosetta, Via della Rosetta 9. Tel.: 656-1002. Probably the city's top fish restaurant; the seafood and raw fish starters are famous. Is very expensive.

Pianeta Terra, Via Arco del Monte 94. Tel.: 656-9893. The temple of *nouvelle cuisine* Italian from a genial husband-and-wife team. Elegant bar for pre-meal lubrication. Very expensive.

Quinzi e Gabrielli, Via della Coppelle 5. Tel.: 659389. A great, elegant, and very popular fish restaurant with a superb wine list. Reserve well in advance—and check your credit-card limit.

Relais de Jardin, Hotel Lord Byron, Via Giuseppe de Notaris 5. Tel.: 360-9541. Creative cuisine of the highest order. The Relais is in the rich Parioli district, out of the city center, but is well worth the journey.

Sabatini, Piazza Santa Maria. Tel.: 582-2026. Another good fish restaurant. Delightful outdoor dining during the summer.

▷ Tipping

In theory, tips are included. In practice, most servitors expect something on top. Federico Fellini, the renowned Italian movie director, suggests that you tip the chambermaid 20,000 lire when you arrive at a hotel—assuring yourself of star treatment. The front desk should be tipped upon arrival—Fellini suggests 10,000 lire—and when you leave; another 10,000 is the minimum. Among Fellini's other suggestions are 1,000 lire for the bellhop who carries your bags and 500 lire for the person who finds you a cab. Leave an extra 5 percent on a restaurant check—and always tip at that Roman institution, the café. Pay first at the cash desk and then tip the server, even if you have merely sipped a cup of coffee while standing at the bar. The minimum: 100 lire.

▷ Doing Business

In the past 40 years or so, Italy has had more than 50 governments, an apparent instability that alarms many people who don't know the country. Governments come, governments go—but little changes. The Roman view is that "there's nothing more stable than Italian instability." For most of the post-World War II period, the conservative Christian Democrats have dominated government. The exception was a recent four-year period under the premiership of socialist leader Bettino Craxi, but he was far from extreme.

▷ *Spotlight* ◁

When in Rome... Millions of Italians show their independence and their contempt for government in a very practical way—by cheating on their taxes. Annual fraud is estimated at 50,000-billion lire—about $38 billion. That's about half the budget deficit. Salaried workers cannot play this popular sport with the zest of self-employed people, since they're subject to withholding taxes. This an-

gers them greatly, and up to half a million at a time have demonstrated for fair taxes. Certainly there's something odd going on. According to figures for 1984–85, the latest published, the average salaried worker earned 20 million lire—but doctors' incomes were lower, along with those of lawyers (15 million lire), retired staff (10 million), butchers (8 million), and jewelers (7 million).

Because governments rise and fall with a regularity close to that of the tides, the bureaucracy is powerful. Politicians may propose, but civil servants dispose: that's an ineluctable fact of political and economic life. The bureaucracy is a burden on business, but one that executives tend to lighten by ignoring or bypassing it; they have little choice if they want to get anything done. Many government officials and employees of state-owned businesses ("enterprises" would be too laudatory a word) have second jobs, often run from the nearest coffeeshop. The working day in most ministries starts at 10:00 a.m. and ends at 2:00 p.m. Only the most senior officials return to their offices at 5:30 p.m. or so.

Breakfast meetings are almost unheard of. A working lunch is acceptable, but dinner is a social event, and your invitation should include spouses. Romans tend to eat late: it's often drinks at 9:00 p.m. for 9:30 p.m. dinner. Strict punctuality is not necessary. If you're invited for cocktails, never, but *never,* arrive on time, particularly at a rich Roman's house: you are likely to find your host in a dressing-gown.

▷ *Spotlight* ◁

Flowery language. If you want to say it with flowers, particularly to thank your hostess, what better advice than that of the great Italian screen lover Marcello Mastroianni? He recommends *Pietro Ranocchiari*, corner of Via Veneto and Via Ludovisi. Sophia Loren also orders there. *Maurizio* *Campi*, Via Po 104, is favored by movie director Federico Fellini. From *Pina Stigliano*, corner of Via Condotti and the Via Maria dei Fiori, flowers depart for the vases of the exiled Iranian royals, Soraya and Farah, and such current princesses as Caroline of Monaco.

Business Roman-style is not all obstacles. People can be affable, charming, and genuinely helpful. Promises, though, should be treated with a large grain of salt—or even a box of it. A promise is usually meant when it's made but soon forgotten. In serious negotiations, try to write down key points and terms of agreement at each stage.

More than in northern Europe, or even northern Italy, success often hinges on knowing the right person—or at least being introduced by one right person to another. Try always to go to the top. If you cannot do that through your own contacts, you can hire one of the many respectable consultancies that open doors—for a price.

Few executives below vice-presidential level have a secretary, so if your contact's phone rings and rings, the chances are that the person really is out. Your best bet may be to send a telex or fax asking the executive to call you.

The city earns more than 65,000 billion lire in an average year—about $50 billion. Of this, services account for more than half, with a hefty slice coming from the 2.3 million Italians and 2.5 million foreigners who visit the city each year for business or pleasure, or both. Industry represents about a fifth of total economic activity, with construction until recently the most important single industry; but strict curbs on new building in the city center as well as rent controls have made real estate financially less attractive than it was.

The Bank of Italy still controls capital flows, but for foreigners—and for Italians living outside the country—the regulations are virtually non-existent. Italy has agreed to free all capital flows by 1992, with the dismantling of remaining rules starting in 1990.

▷ Useful Phone Numbers

Emergencies

All-night pharmacy	1921	Doctor	475-6741
Ambulance	5100	Highway emergencies	116

Hospitals

   Policlinico Umberti I
      (anti-poison)   490663

   Salvator Mundi (private,
      English-speaking)   586041

   Sant' Eugenio,
      EUR (burns)   5904

   San Spirito   650901

Police   113

   Police hot line   212121

Local Information

Airport   60121

   Internal flights   5456

Buses   4695

Radio taxis 3570/3875/4994/8433

Tourist office   461851

   Tourist assistance   463748

Trains   4775

   International
      departures   575-4941

Government

Finance ministry   59971

Foreign affairs   36911

Foreign trade   5993

Telecommunications   54601

Business Contacts

Rome chamber of
   commerce   6794941

Italian chambers of
   commerce abroad   3215660

Federations

Aerospace (AIA)   460247

Building   84881

Chemicals   6794954

Construction materials 864314

Electrical energy   864602

Food   59031

Leather   5810854

Phamaceuticals   311073

Quarrying   860959

Rubber   6792598

Textiles   4744457

Embassies

Albania   838-0725

Algeria   804141

Argentina   474-2551

Australia   832721

Austria   -868241

Bangladesh   878541

Belgium   360-9441

Brazil   650841

Bulgaria   360954

Cameroon   678-3546

Canada   855-3412

Chile   474-2258

China (People's
   Republic)   844-8186

Colombia   679-9586

Czechoslovakia 327-8741

Denmark   360-0441

Egypt   853334

Ethiopia   803057

Finland   858329

France   656-5541

Germany (East) 839-0045

Germany (West) 860341

Ghana   839-1200

Greece   859630

India	464642	United Arab Emirates	839-1126
Indonesia	475-9251	United Kingdom	475-5441
Iran	328-4294	United States	46741
Iraq	345-5241	Yugoslavia	360-0796
Ireland	678-2541		
Israel	874541		

Airlines

Japan	475-7151	Aer Lingus (Ireland)	475-9940
Jordan	857396	Aerolineas Argentinas	472821
Korea (South)	805292	Aeromexico	463960
Kuwait	874419	Air Afrique	480041
Libya	830951	Air Algerie	484866
Luxembourg	578-0456	Air France	475-9441
Malaysia	855764	Air India	473941
Mexico	851187	Air Malta	475-1392
Morocco	844-8653	Air New Zealand	460761
Netherlands	873141	Alia Royal Jordanian	460809
New Zealand	851225	Alisarda (Sardinia)	474-5057
Nigeria	653-1048	Alitalia	46881
Norway	575-5833	American Airlines	475054
Pakistan	327-6775	Austrian Airlines	475-9262
Philippines	803530	British Airways	47171
Poland	360-9455	Canadian Pacific Air Lines	475-8041
Portugal	873801	Continental Airlines	483978
Romania	804529	Cyprus Airways	47171
Saudi Arabia	866-8161	Czechoslovak Airlines/CSA	462990
South Africa	867837	Egyptair	474-2641
Soviet Union	474-3989	El Al Israel Airlines	479831
Spain	687-8264	Ethiopian Airlines	475-9374
Sri Lanka	805362	Finnair	474-5187
Sweden	860441	Garuda Indonesian Airways	475-5813
Switzerland	803641	Iberia (Spain)	875770
Syria	679-7791	Interflug (East Germany)	474-3629
Tanzania	361-0901	Iran Air	474-1141
Thailand	832-0729		
Tunisia	839-0748		
Turkey	474-1435		

Iraqi Airways	475-4129	Sabena Belgian World Airlines	475-0796
Japan Air Lines/JAL	475-1441		
KLM Royal Dutch Airlines	479921	SAS Scandinavian Airlines	479851
Kuwait Air Ways	462309	Saudi Arabian Airlines	460475
Libyan Arab Airlines	474-5102		
LOT Polish Airlines	462880	Singapore Airlines	475-8943
Lufthansa German Airlines	466-0210	South African Airways	474-2141
Malev Hungarian Airlines	485542	Swissair	84701
Nigeria Airways	474105	Syrian Arab Airlines	475-9902
Olympic Airways	474-2201	TAP Air Portugal	494-0811
Pakistan International Airlines	464-6623	Tarom (Romania)	460267
		Thai Airways	463527
Pan Am World Airways	4773	Tunis Air	493831
		TWA	47241
Philippine Airlines	483903	Varig (Brazil)	46771
Qantas Airways (Australia)	486451	Yugoslav Airlines/ JAT	475-1112
Royal Air Maroc	474-3032	Zambia Airways	475-6340

▷ Shopping

If one agrees that Italians are the most elegant of Europeans, then Rome as well as Milan is the place for shopping. Whereas Milan is home to the most renowned couturiers, Rome is special for leather items (coats, shoes, and gloves); silk articles, such as ties; and luxury woolen clothes— Italian purchases are among the most numerous in Europe. Chilly winters south of the city and the lack of central heating are partly responsible, but the real reason is the Italian sense of style.

The leading shops are nearly all in a triangle with its point at the *Piazza del Popolo* and its base along the *Via del Tritone.* Here are clusters of streets packed with boutiques of all kinds. Antique shops and art galleries are concentrated in and around the *Via Margutta,* off the artists' row that is the *Via del Babuino,* both close by the Spanish Steps. Opposite the steps spread the *Via Condotti, Via Frattina,* and others lined with "names" such as Bulgari (jewels), Ferragamo (shoes) and Gucci—besieged here on the Via Condotti, as elsewhere, by Japanese visitors. Prices are high in this "golden triangle," and it's no coincidence that Italian kidnappers "pick up" prominent jewelers. Shops are often closed at lunchtime, with exceptions in the tourist zones. They shut also Monday mornings and Saturday afternoons in July and August. Some choices by category:

Clothes

Giorgio Armani, Via del Babuino 102. Clothes for both sexes, although one is more favored than the other. Specialty: cashmere.

Camomilla, Piazza di Spagna 85b. Crazy clothes for the young and therefore good presents. (Same at nearby *Krizia,* Piazza di Spagna 77, specialist in limited edition T-shirts).

Eddy Monetti, Via Borgognona. Very much part of the luxury triangle. More cashmere.

Tusseda, Via Frattini 25. Noted for silks, including underwear.

Valentino (men: Via Condotti/Via Mario De Fiori; women: Via Bocca di Leone 15). By now, only a few Martians are strangers to the name.

Missoni (men: 78 Piazza di Spagna; women: 96 Via del Babuino). Famous for colorful, high-fashion sweaters, jackets, and other knitwear.

Leather/Shoes

Beltrami, Via Condotti 19. One of the most famous of the skin shops. Stars buy their crocodile shoes there.

Campanile e Spatarella, Via Condotti 58. A classical line in clothes and shoes for men and women.

Ferragamo, Via Condotti 73 (No 63 for men). Shoes, of course, at this famous house, but also scarves.

Gucci, Via Condotti 8. Has a guard to keep order. Leather goods and accessories—even a dog leash. Fashion and sportswear.

Miscellaneous

Jewels: *Bulgari,* King of the Italian jewellers, is the monarch also of the Via Condotti at No 10. The house now has branches worldwide, but the motto remains "exclusiveness"—no perfumes, no franchising, and, above all, no airport duty-free. *Massoni,* Largo Goldoni 48. Transparent watches in gold, steel, and plastic. Limited editions.

Perfumes: *Depaola,* Via della Groce. One of the top shops of its kind in Rome.

Silk ties: *Roxy,* Via Veneto 108 and Via del Corso 527. The airport duty-free shops also sell nice ones.

Stationery: *Pineider,* 63 Via Due Macelli; 7a Via della Scrofa. Luxury engraved stationery, visiting cards, invitations, plus a large selection of fine colored papers and inks. *Papirus,* Via Capo le Case 55a. Superb writing paper, notebooks—and boxes. *Franco Maria Ricci,* Via Borgognona, creator of the luxurious art magazine *FMR,* has the most chic post cards.

Violet stockings: *Gammarelli,* Via Santa Chiara 34. Suppliers to the Vatican, but lay shoppers welcome. Also has high-quality, red cotton socks for cardinals.

Street and flea markets: *Porta Portese* in the Southern sector of Trastevere. The city's oldest; Sunday mornings. *The old book market,* Piazza Fontanella Borghese (near the palace). Tuesday mornings. Prints as well as books.

▷ After Hours

Rome's legendary *dolce vita* (sweet life)—nightclubbing, dawn dips in the Roman fountains or down at the beach—was closely linked with the post-war "golden era" of the Cinecitta film studios. Fun began to evaporate in the 1970s with the decline of Cinecitta as a cinema mecca and the advent of Red Brigade terrorism. Cinecitta prospers anew with TV series and soap operas, but the stars of the video world are pale imitations of the flamboyant carousers of old with their accompanying packs of *paparazzi.* Still, traffic jams persist at 1:00 a.m., so *something's* happening.

Contemporary action is concentrated within the so-called "Bermuda Triangle," located between Piazza del Pantheon, Piazza Navona, and Piazza Campo Marzio. Here are famous bars such as *Hemingway* (Piazza delle Coppelle 10), *Le Cornacchie* (Piazza Rondanini 58) and *Le Coppelle* (Piazza delle Coppelle 68). Rome's *Harry's Bar* is at 150 Via Veneto and is the home of the best cocktails.

Clubs and discos are often victims of rapidly changing fashion. Some of the more durable:

Acropolis, Via Luciani 52. Tel.: 870504. Disco and cocktail bar in Parioli. Young crowd, high decibels.

Alibi, Via di Monte Testaccio 44. Tel.: 5743448. Gay, but no discrimination against straights. Best music in town, if very loud.

Bella Blu, Via Luciani 21. Smart, private jazz club which is a favorite with cinema and sports stars.

Hysteria, Via Giovanelli 3. Tel.: 864587. Attracts TV and show business people. Soul and dance music.

Jackie-O, Via Boncompagni 11. Tel.: 461401. Near U.S. Embassy and Via Veneto. Founded after the decline of the *dolce vita,* this disco tries with its opulent decor and fake Oscars to recapture the lost era.

La Makumba, Via degli Olimpionici 19. Tel.: 3964392. Excellent Afro-Latino music which attracts a multiracial crowd—and starlets.

Notorious, Via San Nicola da Tolentino 22. Tel.: 4746888. Best-looking young women in town, but the clientele tends not to let go in case hair is mussed. Restaurant.

Olimpo, Piazza Rondanini 36. Tel.: 6547314. Snob and jet-set. Black music.

Open Gate, Via San Nicola da Tolentino 4. Tel.: 4750464. Yuppies and would-be yuppies constitute the clientele. Music good.

Veleno, Via Sardegna 27. Tel.: 493583. Once described by a Frenchman as "Hollywood-gigolo." Fun.

Vicolo delle Stelle, Via Beccaria 22. Tel.: 3611240. The really trendy take in *Le Stelle* after Notorious on the same night. Fashionable to arrive around 4:00 a.m.

▷ Sights and Sounds

The 1980s saw restorers from the *Istituto Centrale del Restauro* erecting scaffolding and plastic shrouds in their campaign to prevent historic arches and columns from disintegrating under the attack of modern pollution. The battle now spreads into the 1990s.

Radical, if temporary, solutions were launched—such as the Athens-style banning on alternative days of cars with odd- and even-numbered automobile license plates. In addition, more areas are completely banned or have limited traffic. However, credits for restoration, notably for the Arch of Constantine and Trajan's Column, were sometimes voted down by politicians arguing that the money should be spent on improving the Romans' civic sense. The major, positive step was the partial renovation of the Colosseum, Rome's most famous monument. Perhaps superstitious politicians had recalled the saying that Rome will live as long as the Colosseum lasts. A selection of what Rome has to offer:

Apollodoro, Piazza Mignanelli 17. Paintings and modern design in this stunning, new, contemporary art gallery.

Castel Sant' Angelo. On the Vatican side of the Tiber. Built by Hadrian as a tomb but changed later to a fortress and papal home. Museum and gallery. Fine view from the terrace.

Colosseum, Piazza del Colosseo. Open from 9:00 a.m. to just before sunset. Inaugurated in 80 A.D., it was the scene of Roman games. Partly renovated. Model of the original can be seen. Nearby is the *Arch of Constantine.*

Forum. The former center of Ancient Rome—and of the then-known world. Close by are the Capitoline and Palatine hills, in Julius Caesar territory.

Fountains. The most famous is the *Trevi Fountain,* with its cascades on the Piazza di Trevi. Probably the most beautiful is the smaller *Tartaruga Fountain,* Piazza Mattei, with its four boys and bronze dolphins and tortoises.

Opera. *Teatro dell'Opera,* Via del Viminale (tel.: 461755). Season runs from November to May. Often hit by strikes. *Baths of Caracalla,* Via delle Terme di Caracalla. The former baths of Ancient Rome are the venue for the open-air summer season.

Pantheon, Piazza della Rotonda. The great dome, wider than St. Peter's, is a Roman landmark. Rebuilt by Hadrian after serving ancient gods, it later became a church where the painter Raphael rests, along with Italy's first king, Victor Emmanuel II.

Piazza Navona. This beautiful square, with Bernini's Fountain of the Four Rivers, is a baroque marvel best seen in the pink light of early morning. A colorful point of congregation and encounter in the evening.

Quirinale Palace, Via del Quirinale. The official residence of the Italian president. Limited opening.

Spanish Steps and Piazza di Spagna. The center of the artists' quarter. Much loved by the English poets Byron, Keats, and Shelley. A sea of azaleas in May.

Villa Borghese. The great Roman park with puppet shows, concerts, galleries, a lake—and one of the best views of Rome.

Villa Medicis. France's very exclusive artistic academy.

Vatican. Once on St. Peter's Square, you are in the Vatican, a sovereign state established by treaty with Italy in 1929. Popes, however, have been residing in the palace with its chambers, chapels, and galleries since 1377. Head of state is Pope John Paul II, the 264th pope of the Roman Catholic Church, the first non-Italian pontiff for 456 years and the first-ever Pole. For private or semiprivate audiences, see or write to the *Prefettura Casa Pontificia* (the Papal Prefecture), Città del Vaticano, 00120. The limited, ring-kissing audiences are arranged only in advance by local churches throughout the world or the Pope's diplomatic corps headed by *nuncios* (ambassadors). The Pope holds mass audiences indoors in the winter on Wednesday mornings (tickets available from the Prefettura) and outdoors in the summer. At noon on Sundays, he appears at a third-floor window to address the crowd in St. Peter's Square.

Behind its high walls, the Vatican is home to some 1,000 residents. Activities include the official *L'Osservatore Romano* newspaper, Vatican radio, many administrative offices, banks, a small railway station, a supermarket and department store, a gas station, a printing works, a pharmacy, and various institutes. The Vatican also has its own stamps and post office, with mail service better than Italy's.

Security is in the hands of both a police force and the colorful Swiss guards. However, not even the Vatican is sacred to pickpockets. Wear a money belt or at least transfer your wallet to a front pocket, gentlemen—that makes it harder to lift. Ladies, keep a snug hold on your purse if you must carry one. Thieves love to try to "blend in" with a group, so be wary of extraneous hangers-on.

St. Peter's Basilica and the Vatican museums are open to all. Tour guides are available. Allow 15,000 lire or more for a tour of the Sistine Chapel and the gardens. Michelangelo's masterpiece underwent a painstaking and delicate restoration in the mid-1980s, with excruciating care taken not to damage the original work. The result has produced a magnificent resurgence of color and contrast that makes the artistry even more impressive. Catholic or not, you really must see it.

The Pope retires at the height of summer to the official summer residence at *Castel Gandolfo,* outside Rome. The faithful are also received there.

▷ Out of Town

Ostia. Italian filmmakers show the capital as mortifyingly empty at weekends. The Romans leave in droves for *Ostia,* the city's favorite resort on the Mediterranean, only 35 minutes by metro from the Termini station or 30 to 60 minutes by car. Our advice is not to join them unless you enjoy cheek-by-jowl beaches, bathing in suspect waters, and packed trattorias. *Ostia Antica* is certainly worth seeing, but wait until the population returns to normal so that you can appreciate what is left of Ancient Rome's former port—and imagine more.

Tivoli. A few miles east of Rome. Tivoli was the ancient Tibur. The Emperor Hadrian indulged in a folly, Hadrian's Villa, where he reconstructed much of what he had seen on his travels, notably in Greece and the Middle East. There are sufficient remains to recapture his world.

There's also the *Villa d'Este,* a later folly of a cardinal, with its famous fountains. Pleasant restaurants with terraces in the town. Trains from the Termini station or buses. Hired cars cost from 40,000 lire daily.

STOCKHOLM
Where "Social Capitalism" Reigns

Population: 650,000 (1980). Greater metropolitan area: 1.4 million. Administrative, political, and commercial capital of the Kingdom of Sweden (population: 8.4 million). *Location*: southeast Sweden, between Lake Mälaren and the Baltic Sea. *Economy*: banking and financial services, chemicals, food processing, metalworking, paper, printing and publishing, shipping, textiles. Sweden is a member of the European Free Trade Association (EFTA) and the Organization of Economic Cooperation and Development (OECD) and a signatory to the General Agreement on Tariffs and Trade (GATT).

▷ Background Briefing

Stockholm was founded in the 1200s, grew as a trade center, and became the capital of Sweden in 1523. The city expanded and prospered through the years and has enjoyed a long tradition of sensible city planning that has helped it handle urban problems of congestion and decay. Sweden remained neutral during World War I and World War II, allowing it to escape the kind of damage experienced by other European cities.

Sweden today is a series of paradoxes. Although neutral, it is a major producer of arms and maintains sizable military forces—which many times have depth-charged foreign submarines lurking in territorial waters. Governed by the left-wing Social Democrats for most of the past half-century, Sweden is also the home of major multinational corporations, including Volvo, Electrolux, Asea-Brown Boveri, Saab-Scania, LSKF, and L.M. Ericsson.

Personal income taxes are among the highest in the world, yet more than 60 people or families have fortunes ranging from a mere $12 million to a princely $1 billion. Rumor has it that the Soviet Union's President

Mikhail Gorbachev is looking at Sweden as a possible model for his country's future. After all, it has achieved the seemingly improbable: a high standard of living, low unemployment, class unity, maintenance of the entrepreneurial spirit, and a social security system that is widely admired. It's either capitalism, socialist-style; or socialism, capitalist-style.

Under Sweden's placid surface, strong whirlpools twist. Many Swedes worry about their country's image abroad—the *Sverigebild,* or picture of Sweden. Those worries started with a big financial scandal, at the center of which were the Egyptian-born head of a pharmaceuticals company and some leading Swedish banks and businesses; continued with the assassination of Prime Minister Olof Palme; and were reinforced by revelations that Swedish armamentmakers had secretly sold weapons to Middle East and other out-of-bounds countries and allegedly bribed Indian officials. A top spy's escape from prison didn't help Swedish self-confidence, either. As one prominent business executive told an audience recently, "I doubt that many of you are proud to admit you are Swedish when you go abroad these days." That was probably a heat-of-the-moment remark, and exaggerated the problem. Sweden remains essentially a stable, prosperous country with much of which it can be proud—even if some recent events have blemished its good name. Neither are the paradoxes new. After all, the Nobel Prizes, including the one for peace, were established by Alfred Nobel, inventor of dynamite.

▷ Arriving

Arlanda International Airport is far from the city. A taxi ride takes about 40 minutes to the center, and the bus not much longer. As the bus costs only a tenth as much, it's best to take the bus, get off at the central railroad station, and catch a taxi to your hotel.

▷ Money

Currency: the krona. International code: SEK. Banknotes come in denominations of 10, 50, 100, 500, and 1,000 krona. Coins are 1 and 5 krona and 10 and 50 öre (100 öre = 1 krona). Banks are open Monday through Friday from 9:30 a.m. to 3:00 p.m. Hotel exchange rates are poor.

▷ Language

Swedish. English is spoken widely and usually fluently; many people also speak German. Street signs and even newspapers are easy for many foreigners to puzzle out, particularly if they have a smattering of German: the two languages are closely related.

▷ Communications

Good. Country code: 46. City code: 8. Most hotels offer international direct dialing, telex, and telefax. The phone company can arrange conference calls. Check with your hotel or call 90140.

▷ Getting To Know the City

Stockholm has more the air of a large country town than of a small capital city. Many cities come alive at night, as people spill out on the streets to eat and drink. Not Stockholm. People rush home to eat, watch television, or read. With few exceptions, the city's streets are dead by early evening. One reason for this is the climate. The long, bitter winters with their few hours of daylight keep the Swedes tucked away in their centrally heated homes and offices. Come the summer, with its long and usually sunny days, and they tend to flee to the countryside or the archipelago, leaving the city to tourists.

Stockholm's tranquility is part of its charm. Perched on a cluster of islands where the waters of Lake Mälaren run into the Baltic Sea, Stockholm is beautiful: azure skies and dazzling reflections in the summer, sheets of ice linking the islands into one white blanket in the winter.

The street layout is mainly rectangular, which makes for some monotony of pattern, but the skyline is dominated by church spires rather than skyscrapers, though few Swedes today are strongly religious. The neighborhood around *Sergels Torg* is an ugly mass of shopping malls and offices; by contrast, the old financial district around *Kungsträdgården* is graced with elegant buildings, such as the headquarters of Skandinaviska Enskilda Banken. A little further south lies *Gamla Stan* (Old Town), once a slum but now transformed into a smart residential area with cobbled streets, trendy shops, and houses dating from the 1400s and 1500s.

Stockholm is clean, tidy, and well-ordered. Street violence is not a serious problem. The air and water are unpolluted: even today you can fish for salmon in the very center of the city. Do not expect architectural grandeur, except here and there. Stockholm is a comfortable city, with many interesting buildings, but it does not pretend to be an imperial or world capital. Do not be misled, though, by the modesty of top executives' offices and the scarcity of chauffeur-driven limos. Sweden is an egalitarian society, and the rich don't flaunt what they have—in Sweden. Away from home, some of them could even trump Donald Trump's aces.

▷ Moving Around

Radio-call taxis are a boon and a blessing, particularly on a cold, wet night. But do they have to deafen the passenger with radio chit-chat? No. In Stockholm (and some other Swedish cities), the discreet click-whine of a high-speed thermal printer has replaced the raucous demands of radio dispatchers. The dispatcher feeds the would-be passenger's address into a computer, which searches automatically for a taxi in the zone. A driver who accepts the order presses a button, and the printout gives the passenger's name, address, and phone number. Volvo and Ericsson developed the system; Digital Equipment of the United States provided the system software.

Best to reserve a cab in advance if you want one during rush hour; your hotel will do this for you. If you find yourself at a cab rank, just pick up the phone, which will connect you free and automatically with the central reservation system. You can also hail a passing cab: the sign *Ledig* indicates it is available. Tip 10 to 15 percent on top of the metered fare.

▷ Spotlight ◁

The Key to Stockholm card (*Stockholmskortet*) provides unlimited travel on the subway, suburban trains, and buses (except to the airport). The same card also entitles the holder to free admission to 50 museums, sightseeing trips by boat or bus, and free parking on meters throughout the city. Cards are valid for up to four days. Buy a card at the Tourist Center at Sweden House and other outlets as indicated by your hotel concierge.

▷ Hotels

Standards are high, service is seldom less than competent, and breakfast is a meal to be remembered. Swedes like to start the day on a full stomach. A recent survey shows that they have taken to business breakfasts, starting as early as 7:00 a.m. Many of the hotels listed have waterfront views (W is the symbol) or are in the charming *Gamla Stan,* or Old Town (OT). All offer nonsmoking rooms guaranteed not to reek with a previous guest's fumes. Always reserve well ahead. Stockholm is a busy congress city and, particularly in the spring and summer, rooms are scarce.

Amarenten, 31 Kungsholmsgatan. Tel.: 541060. Telex: 17498. Fax: 526248. Rooms/suites: 415. A lively place with a Japanese-style recreation area and an executive tower with a roof garden and luxurious rooms and suites.

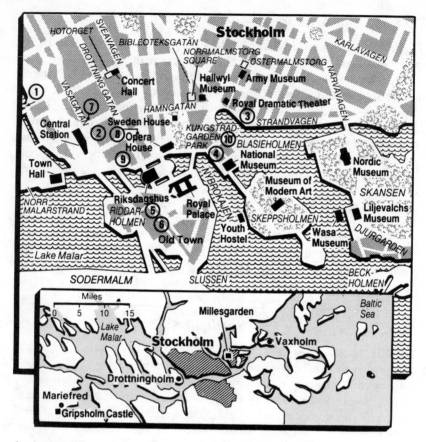

1. **Amarenten**
2. **Continental**
3. **Diplomat**
4. **Grand**
5. **Lady Hamilton**

6. **Lord Nelson**
7. **Royal Viking**
8. **Sergel Plaza**
9. **Sheraton**
10. **Strand**

Clas på Hörnet, 20 Surbrunnsgatan. Tel.: 165130. Telex: 14619. Fax: 335310. Only 10 rooms in an elegant town house 200 years old with excellent restaurant.

Continental, Vasagatan. Tel.: 244020. Telex: 10100. Fax: 113695. Rooms: 250. Convivial bar and two restaurants, favored by middle-ranking executives. Close to Central Station and business section.

Diplomat, 7 Strandvägen. *W.* Tel.: 663-5800. Telex: 17119. Fax: 733-6634. Rooms/suites: 132. Cozy and charming, with a wonderful, watery view from the bar.

Grand, 8 Blasieholmshamnen. *W.* Tel.: 221020. Telex: 19500. Fax: 218688. Rooms/suites: 352. Friendly bar, terrace cafe, French restaurant, *thé dansant* on Sundays. Built and run on the grand scale; faces the Royal Palace across the water. Superb banqueting for up to 1,000 people.

Lady Hamilton, 5 Storkyrkobrinken. *OT.* Tel.: 234680. Telex: 10434. Rooms/suites: 35. Turned into a hotel in 1980 from a house built in 1470; lots of charm and antiques.

Lord Nelson, 22 Västerlånggatan. *OT.* Tel.: 232390. Telex: 10434. Rooms: 31. Twinned with Lady Hamilton, naturally; nautical atmosphere, including cabin-size rooms.

Reisen, 12 Skeppsbron. *OT.* Tel.: 223260. Telex: 17494. Fax: 201559. Rooms: 125. Quiet, pleasant, small: a home-away-from-home. Some rooms have their own saunas.

Royal Viking, 1 Vasagatan. Tel.: 141000. Telex: 13900. Fax: 108180. Rooms/suites: 390. Modern, right in the city's heart. Relaxation center, winter garden with atrium 36 meters (120 feet) high; panoramic view from the skybar. Owned by SAS Scandinavian Airlines, which means you can check your bags at the hotel and then pick them up at your destination.

Scandic Crown, Guldgränd 8. Tel.: 702-2500. Telex: 11019. Fax: 428358. Rooms: 250/Suites: 14. Spacious, central, views over the city. A fine addition to the top category of the capital's hotels.

Sergel Plaza, 9 Brunkbergstorg. Tel.: 226600. Telex: 16700. Fax: 21507. Rooms/suites: 407. Also in the city center, next to the building in which the Stockholm disarmament talks took place. Trees and waterfalls in the hotel's glass-roofed lobby.

Sheraton, 6 Tegelbacken. *W.* Tel.: 142600. Telex: 17750. Fax: 217026. Rooms/suites: 475. Superb views of the busy harbor; very comfortable rooms; good bar and restaurants. *Le Bistro* is open until 2:30 a.m.

Strand, 9 Nybrokafen. *W.* Tel.: 222900. Telex: 10504. Fax: 204436. Rooms/suites: 134. Built for the 1912 Olympic Games, a favorite with former Finnish president Urho Kekkonen and with people who know a good hotel when they try one. Winter garden with a ceiling seven stories high. Owned by SAS Scandinavian Airlines, so there's an airline checkin desk.

▷ Restaurants

There's only one kind of restaurant: expensive. That's mainly because of high taxes on all forms of alcohol. But some establishments offer better value for (much) money than others, and they're on this list. Swedish cuisine emphasizes fish and game, which can be excellent. Although they're costly, wines are usually good. As one of the world's largest single buyers, the state monopoly gets favored treatment from vineyards and shippers. Search not for take-out sandwich bars if you want a quick, light snack; there are very few. Instead, try one of the following:

Glada Laxen, Gallerian shopping mall, 23 Regeringsgatan. Wide variety of salmon dishes.

Grand Hotel bar, Grand Hotel, 8 Blasieholmshamnen. Tel.: 211020. Excellent sandwiches and light snacks, both hot and cold; carafe wines; Pripps export beer on tap.

Ortagarden on Ostermalmstorg, 31 Nybrogatan. Help yourself to as much as you want of fresh vegetarian salads and dishes from the hot-food bar.

▷ Spotlight ◁

Drinking. Few peoples talk more about the perils of alcohol than the Swedes—and few drink less, if official consumption figures are to be believed. Trouble is, most concentrate their drinking into the weekend—which means that many have hangovers on Monday. One doctor specializing in the treatment of alcoholics says, "The Swedes do not have an alcohol problem as much as they have a problematic relation to alcohol. When they drink, they do so chiefly to get drunk."

For the visitor, the practical results of all this are that the hotel minibar contains only nonalcoholic drinks, and in the whole country there are only 300 liquor stores, all state-owned. They are open from 9:30 a.m. until

6:00 p.m. Monday through Friday—
and closed all weekend. Avoid the Friday rush. The state, while condemning

alcohol, obtains about 7 percent of its
total revenues from it.

Aurora, 11 Munkbron. Tel.: 219359. A 300-year-old house in the *Gamla Stan* (Old Town) where one eats in small, pleasant rooms in the vaults. Food and service are outstandingly good.

Caesar, 4 Fredrikshovsgatan. Tel.: 660-1599. Cellar, with menu chalked on the board; attracts politicians and artists.

Café Tranan, 14 Karlbergsvagen. Tel.: 343139. French bistro atmosphere; popular with young people.

Erik's, 17 Österlånggatan, and Strandvägskajen (berth 17). Tel.: 238500 and 660-6060. Two locations: the first is in the *Gamla Stan* (Old Town), the second in a ship. Quiet, unfussy; some of the best fish and seafood in town.

Kajplats, 9 N. Malarstrand. Tel.: 524545. Resembles a prefabricated construction site office from the outside. Don't be put off. Good view over the waterfront, and the fish dishes are reasonably priced.

Operakällaren, Opera House. Tel.: 111125. Where the rich—and they need to be—socialites wine and dine. Remarkable elegance, service, food, and wines. Reservations essential.

▷ Spotlight ◁

Fjaderholmarna, an island with a restaurant of the same name, is a half-
hour boat ride from Stockholm. The
restaurant is open for three weeks
over Christmas and from May to Sep-

tember. Sybaritic food, idyllic setting.
Boats leave from quays outside the
Grand and Strand Hotels. Tel.: 718-
3355.

▷ Tipping

Bars and restaurants usually include the tip with the check, but it's good manners to leave some small change. Tip cabdrivers 10 to 15 percent on top of the metered fare.

▷ Doing Business

Sweden has long been an important player in world trade. Its exports of goods are some 29 percent of its gross domestic product: aerospace, agricultural and automotive equipment; chemicals and pharmaceuticals; electrical and electronics equipment; food and fiber; forest products; telecommunications—the list goes on and on (by comparison, Japan's figure is just under 11 percent). And that isn't the end by a long way of this small nation's large involvement with and reliance on the rest of the world.

Swedish companies are increasingly important overseas investors. They're forced to be: Sweden doesn't offer a big enough market for such automotive manufacturers as Saab and Volvo or, indeed, for most of the major corporations. But the European Community's plans for 1992 hang like a thundercloud over Sweden and the other Nordic nations that aren't members. The essay "Europe: Realities, Rumors, Myths" at the front of this book explores these concerns.

So Swedish companies are getting into the European Community while the getting is good—by merger, by acquisition, and by joint venture. Business leaders fear that when the community's 12 members have demolished their internal barriers, they will strengthen external ones, and Sweden will be left on the outside looking in.

Swedish business is looking eagerly for links that will open up new markets and find new trading partners, and for ways to use its undoubted financial and industrial muscle to grow to global scale. At the same time, most Swedish companies are "niche" players: they find a market gap, fill it, and concentrate on doing what they know best.

The best-known name in Swedish banking and industry is Wallenberg. This family runs a powerful network of influence—influence rather than dominance. Among enterprises within its financial and managerial orbit are Asea-Brown Boveri, result of a recent merger between Swedish and Swiss electromechanical engineering companies (Switzerland, too, fears that 1992 may leave it on the outside looking in at Europe); Saab-Scania, the aerospace and automotive company; Electrolux, one of the world's largest makers of "white goods"—domestic appliances; and L.M. Ericsson, which makes telecommunications equipment. At the center of the web is the Skandinaviska Enskilda Banken. A rival empire is clustered around Volvo, the diversified automotive manufacturer headed by Pehr Gyllenhammar, one of the few Swedish business executives to have made it to the world stage. Up and coming and chipping away at Wallenberg supremacy are such newcomers as Rune Andersson, head of Trelleborg, a fast-growing conglomerate, and takeover artists Anders Wall and Eric Penser.

At first glance, the concentration of industrial and financial influence in a few hands seems an odd contrast with the socialism of a party that has ruled with only one or two breaks since the 1930s. After a second look, it really doesn't. The Social Democrats are pragmatists. Their strategy has been to allow business to do what it does excellently, which is to produce the wealth. But—and the price is high—it has taxed personal incomes steeply, so that the ordinary citizen is protected from womb to tomb.

Furthermore, the informal alliance of government, business, and the labor unions created the famous consensus, with banker-industrialist Marcus Wallenberg its most famous moderator and symbol. But he died in 1982; since then, labor-management relations have soured slightly. Though Wallenberg has gone and Sweden and the world have changed, some of the old consensual spirit remains.

So what is it like to do business in Sweden today? The consensus, the concept of "social partners," springs from a well deep in the Swedish psyche. The Swedes do not like adversarial politics or business relationships. Yes, an executive will bargain hard—but almost always politely. Because the Swedish business and banking community is tiny by larger countries' standards, nobody can afford to be a shyster—or cannot afford to be one for very long.

The visiting business executive will find that these are the unwritten but somewhat inflexible rules:

- *Be punctual.* Stockholm is a compact town; there's seldom cause to be late. If you have to be, phone and explain.

- *Be prepared.* Swedish business hasn't become as big and successful as it is by being vague, so be specific.

- *Be flexible.* Theirs is a small nation. Many Swedes deeply resent visitors from a larger and more powerful one whose attitude is "take it or leave it."

Business hours run from 8:00 a.m. to 4:00 or 5:00 p.m. Dress is often informal, shirt-sleeved (even in the winter; offices are heated well).

Don't press hospitality on somebody you don't know. If after a first meeting you've established a good personal relationship, suggest a lunch or dinner. There are two things to remember. First, your guest almost certainly will not drink at lunchtime—or at most will drink a weak beer or glass of wine. Second, remember that the best restaurants are very expensive—so don't invite to one a junior or middle-ranking executive. Such a person will be flattered, but embarrassed because the expenses budget may not allow return hospitality at a similar restaurant. Remember, too, that alcoholic beverages are not an allowable business expense for Swedish taxpayers, so go easy on the drinks when you're invited.

▷ **Spotlight** ◁

To sauna or not to sauna —that, sooner or later, is the question the visitor must ask himself or herself. This idiosyncratic form of therapeutic torture requires one to sit or lie naked on wooden slats in a wooden hut heated to—well, too highly. Real enthusiasts beat each other with birch twigs and every now and then pour water over the stones that provide the heat. After all that is over, the victim is supposed to plunge into water, the colder the better. The Finns, who claim to have invented the sauna, are the real fanatics, but the Swedes run them a close second; and fortunate is the business traveler who spends any time in Stockholm without being asked to join a sauna party (contrary to rumor, this is virtually always a unisex gathering).

Of course, there are those who like saunas, but how do you decline gracefully if you don't? The easiest way is to plead that your doctor has advised against any shock to the system—and a sauna is a shock unless you're a veteran user.

▷ **Useful Phone Numbers**

Emergencies

General number	90000
Hospitals	
Danderyd	555000
Karolinska	729-2000
Nacka	718-6000
Sophiahemmet	796-0700

Business and Economic Information

Foreign Ministry trade division	763-1000
Industry Ministry	763-1000
Stockholm Chamber of Commerce	231200

Tourist Information

Stockholm Information Service	789-2000

Consulates and Embassies

Algeria	211070
Angola	242890
Argentina	202685
Australia	244660
Austria	233490
Bangladesh	109555
Bolivia	112440
Brazil	663-1285
Canada	237920
Chile	662-0444
China (People's Republic)	217539
Colombia	218490
Denmark	231860
Ecuador	103043
Finland	240270
France	663-0270
Germany (East)	235030

▷ *Spotlight* ◁

Sweden House, at 27 Hamngatan, corner of Kungstradgarden, is a rich repository of English-language brochures and books about Sweden. Tourist information is on the ground floor; economic and social upstairs.

Much of it is free. A half-hour's browsing will provide you with more than you thought you wanted to know about Sweden—and then you'll probably go back for more.

Germany (West)	663-1380	Turkey	230840
Greece	660-8860	United Kingdom	667-0140
Guatemala	535369	United States	783-5300
India	107008	Uruguay	660-3196
Indonesia	663-5470	Venezuela	110996
Iran	767-0470		
Iraq	796-7975	**Airlines**	
Ireland	661-8005	Alitalia	245845
Israel	663-0435	Arlanda Air Taxis	733-5577
Italy	245805	Austrian Airlines	142850
Japan	663-0490	Avianca (Colombia)	144055
Jordan	505075	British Airways	791-7800
Korea (South)	160480	Canadian Pacific	
Malaysia	145990	Air Lines	213066
Netherlands	247180	Delta Air Lines	796-9400
Norway	667-0620	Finnair	244330
Pakistan	663-5905	Garuda Indonesian	
Panama	511787	Airways	218811
Peru	110041	Iberia (Spain)	202420
Poland	114132	Icelandair	249930
Saudi Arabia	238800	Japan Air Lines/JAL	233430
Singapore	663-7488	KLM Royal Dutch	
Spain	661-6005	Airlines	231350
Switzerland	231550	Korean Air	100962
Thailand	667-8090	LOT Polish Airlines	243490
Tunisia	236470	Lufthansa German	
		Airlines	230505

Malaysian Airline System	791-0030	SAS Scandinavian Airlines	240000
Pan Am World Airways	231920	Swissair	143040
		Thai Airways	145100
Qantas Airways (Australia)	231635	Turk Hava Yollari	218534
		TWA	232245
Sabena Belgian World Airlines	230980	United Airlines	(020) 795402
		Varig (Brazil)	140910

▷ Shopping

Stockholm sets lures for visitors with a wide range of luxury goods, chief among them being furs, crystal, and traditional crafts honed to high sophistication. Look for the duty-free signs in many shop windows: these mean that you can claim back at the airport local sales taxes, *provided* you haven't opened your sealed package before preparing to leave the country.

Swedish glassware design reflects, in both senses of the word, the snow and ice that cover most of the country for many months of the year: hauntingly and eerily beautiful. Look for products of the *Orrefors* and *Kosta Boda* companies. There's a good selection of their work at the *NK (Nordiska Kompaniet)* department store on Hamngatan. NK is crammed from basement to roof with quality goods, many at reasonable prices.

At the *Hemslöjd,* or craft shops, you will find handmade wooden products such as fruit bowls, chairs, and carvings, as well as silverwork and carved reindeer bone objects. Two leading stores are *Svensk Hemslöjd,* at 44 Sveavägen, and *Stockholms Lans Hemslöjdsforening,* at 18 Drottninggatan.

The *Kungsträdgården,* a pleasant place where people play chess on giant boards when the weather is good, is lined with restaurants and a few commercial art galleries. Well worth a look.

Arlanda Airport duty-free shops are good. If you haven't had time to browse and shop in the city, and your luggage is bulging already, you can always buy smoked or marinated salmon or reindeer steaks at the airport.

▷ After Hours

Scandinavian exports of sexy movies—and sexy blondes—have left much of the world with the belief that Stockholm is a swinging city. It isn't. Like most seaports, it has some lowlife, but "high" life is another matter, tame by the standards of many other cities. To be sure, there is a topless bar, but it is reputed to be dangerously expensive, with one customer complaining in the local press that he had paid the equivalent of $460 for a few drinks. Less financially lethal if tamer are these discos:

Melody on Birger, 27 Jarlsgatan.

Daily News, Kungsträdgården.

▷ Sights and Sounds

Royalty. Stockholm is a royal city, and though the monarchy is less visible than that of the United Kingdom, it's still there. Among the royal sights and sounds are the smartly uniformed guardsmen outside the palace. That huge building—it's actually larger than London's Buckingham Palace—was built between 1690 and 1734. Some parts are open to the public; and do not be surprised if you meet members of the royal family, for they pride themselves on informality.

Opera plays a prominent part in Stockholm's cultural life, and the opera house is a splendid building. Check with your hotel concierge for performances and availability of seats. If you're keen on serious music, buy recordings of works by Karl Atterberg and Lars-Erik Larsson, modern composers who deserve to be known better outside Sweden than they are.

Museums. The city has no fewer than 32 museums. Sweden House publishes a detailed list, and it covers subjects ranging from the army, through dance, to wines and spirits—the latter with the emphasis on Swedish antialcohol legislation from the Middle Ages onward. *Skol!*

▷ Out of Town

The Stockholm archipelago is a collection of 30,000 rocky skerries and lush islands that fan out from the city into the Baltic Sea. Most are unspoiled, and many are bird sanctuaries. For a quick sampling, take the boat to *Fjaderholmarna* (we've already listed the excellent restaurant); in summer, the last boat often leaves as late as midnight. Hourlong boat trips take you around the main adjacent islands. Boats leave from the quay alongside the *Stadshuset* (town hall). Opened in 1923, that building also is worth a visit for its own sake. Topped with three golden crowns, the Stadshuset is the setting for the annual Nobel Prizes banquet.

A leisurely all-day trip takes one along the beautiful Stromma Canal to *Sandhamn,* where there are a marina, a collection of traditional Swedish houses, and a sandy beach. Topless sunbathing is available for those who like that kind of thing, either as observers or participants.

Summer fun: a hot-air balloon trip that gives a really superb view of the city, the archipelago, and the countryside. Contacts: *Casbar Anderson.* Tel.: 393957. *Scandinavian Balloons.* Tel.: 343410/303002.

VIENNA
Waltz in a Minor Key

Population: 1.5 million. Capital of the Austrian Republic (population: 7.56 million). Location: northeastern Austria, on the Danube River. Economy: banking and financial services, brewing, construction materials, electrical equipment, food processing, machine tools, motor vehicles, textiles, tourism. Vienna is also host to many international organizations. Austria is a member of the European Free Trade Association (EFTA) and the Organization for Economic Cooperation and Development (OECD) and a signatory to the General Agreement on Tariffs and Trade (GATT).

▷ Background Briefing

Austria had a bad time and a bad press in the second half of the 1980s. What did President Kurt Waldheim do during World War II? And did most Austrians reject or welcome the *Anschluss,* the forced union between their country and Nazi Germany in 1938? The linked debates generated much heat but rather less light. They did, however, bring into sharp focus the country's past and present loyalties and a dilemma that has faced Austria ever since the Habsburg empire collapsed after World War I: What is the country's role in the world?

When looking at Vienna's present or future, one must always remember its past. At the turn of the century, some two million people lived there, and it was the world's fourth largest city. Since then, it has lost at least half a million inhabitants. Vienna was also the capital of an empire that dated from the 1200s and at its height covered most of central Europe. The imperial grandeur remains only in the architectural sense;

power long ago evaporated. After World War II, the victorious Allies occupied Austria—and the Russians then were not the bringers of *glasnost* and *perestroika* that they are today. The Viennese experienced the full, grim force of a marauding Red Army out for the spoils of victory. Not until 1955 was Austria allowed to become an independent state, and then only on the condition it remain neutral. That it is to this day.

▷ **Spotlight** ◁

The Third Man, a film written by Graham Greene and directed by Sir Carol Reed, isn't history in the academic sense. What it does, brilliantly, is give the viewer an unforgettable picture of Vienna when it was divided into American, British, French, and Russian sectors. The foreign armies have gone; the haunting music of the zither, some of the cobbled streets, and the smoky, cozy cafés remain. And some of the spies. Vienna is a pleasant place to hand over documents.

The Viennese are nothing if not resilient. Over the centuries, after all, what is now Austria has been invaded by the Romans, the Huns, the Slovenes, the Turks, the Germans, and a great many other peoples. Austria's former role as a battlefield is the result of its geographical position, which gives it borders with no fewer than six countries. Three of them today are nominally communist. One joke has it that "Vienna is where East thinks it's West—and vice versa." A paradox is that this once imperial but still cosmopolitan city today has a provincial air, from the secretaries in their traditional, tight-waisted *dirndl* skirts to people settling into their midafternoon coffee with cream and rich pastries as though cholesterol had never been discovered. Note, too, the common use of *"Gruss Gott"* ("God's greetings")—a distinctly old-fashioned usage.

This provincial air is misleading, though. Vienna's banking and business executives are internationalists to a man (there are few female executives in the upper ranks). They trade with anyone who offers a good deal—and they're particularly skilled at negotiating with Eastern Europe.

▷ **Arriving**

By Air

Schwechat Airport has just had a $120-million facelift that has speeded passengers' way through customs and immigration—and speeded their baggage. A shuttle bus leaves at 20-minute intervals for the city terminal, next to the Hilton Hotel—but only until mid-evening. The bus ride takes about 20 minutes. Taxis are faster but, of course, much more expensive.

By Rail

Vienna is accessible by rail from other cities in Austria and throughout Europe. Some express trains run into the city. If you have the time for a train ride, the gorgeous Austrian scenery is worth it. Your travel agent can help you map out an appropriate itinerary. The largest railway stations in Vienna are the Westbahnhof and the Sudbahnhof.

▷ Money

The basic unit of currency is the Austrian schilling. International code: ATS. Banknotes come in denominations of 20, 50, 500, and 1,000 schillings. Coins are minted in amounts of 1, 5, 10, 20, 25, 100, 500, and 1,000 schillings and 2, 5, 10, and 50 groschen (100 groschen = 1 schilling). Money can be changed at banks, *bureaux de change,* the airport, and some railway stations. Most banks are open from 8:00 a.m. to 3:00 p.m. Monday through Friday, some until 5:30 p.m. on Thursdays.

Central Bank policy is to maintain a stable rate of exchange between the Austrian schilling and the West German Deutsche mark—West Germany is Austria's largest trading partner. So expect, roughly, West German prices.

▷ Language

German. However—and it's a big however—many Germans need a glossary and a keen ear to understand Viennese dialect. English is gaining ground as the business language of this cultural and geographical crossroads between Western and Eastern Europe. The city's name in German is *Wien.*

▷ Communications

Excellent. Country code: 43. City code: 222 (not needed when calling within the Vienna area). Note that some phone numbers have only four digits while others up to eight.

▷ Getting To Know the City

The heart of Vienna is within the *Ringstrasse,* an inner ring road lined with former palaces, many of them now hotels, such as the SAS Palais. Most of the city's political, economic, and cultural life flows around the Ringstrasse. At one end are the Stock Exchange, the University, the Burg Theater, the *Rathaus* (city hall), and *Landtmann,* one of the great coffeehouses. In the middle is the *Opera,* a city within the city, with its great performances and disputes of operatic intensity over their merits. Within the Opera neighborhood, the most important names to note are *Karntnerstrasse* and *Stephansplatz,* both around the cathedral, and the *Graben,* with its cafés and bookstores. Most of this neighborhood is now one huge pedestrian zone, wonderful for quiet explorations of the many architectural splendors but an obstacle if one has an urgent appointment on the other side.

If one does have time, though, walking to and from appointments in the business-banking-governmental areas is rewarding (except on bitter winter days). Buildings left over from the imperial past make much of Vienna a museum-like city.

Outside Vienna proper, on the banks of the Danube, is United Nations City, a huge and confusing complex of buildings in which many thousands of people work in specialized agencies known by initials or acronyms, the meaning of which only experts understand: Unis, Unpa, CSDHA, ITLB, and Matcom are examples. Among the more interesting agencies:

International Atomic Energy Agency (staff: 1900). Committed to peaceful uses of nuclear technology; sets safety standards, in some countries monitors their observance. *UNIDO* (staff: 1400). Encourages industrial growth in developing countries. *UNRWA* is the relief organization for Palestinian refugees chased out of Beirut. *UNFDAC* is the United Nations fund for discouraging drug abuse—supported, strangely, by voluntary contributions. *DND* is the secretariat to the UN Commission on Narcotic Drugs.

▷ *Spotlight* ◁

The Danube. One of the world's most durably famous compositions is Johann Strauss's *Blue Danube* waltz. But is the Danube blue? It may have been once, but today it is a brownish river busy with both pleasurecraft and barges plying to and from industrial centers—indeed, it is the waterway equivalent of a major highway or railroad track. Through its tributaries and connecting canals, the Danube links landlocked Austria with the North Sea, the English Channel, and the Mediterranean Sea. Above all, it establishes a link with Budapest.

▷ Moving Around

There is a new, very clean *U-bahn* subway system, and everyone—from government ministers to the women who clean their offices—uses the old-fashioned streetcars along the Ring. You can buy strips of tickets at *Tabak Trafik* (cigar stores). The Viennese don't like using taxis, which are expensive. A quaint and fun way to get around if you're not in a huge hurry is by *fiaker*, a horse-drawn carriage. Fiaker stands dot the inner city.

▷ Hotels

Vienna may soon have too many four- and five-star rooms. That's bad news for owners, good for business travelers. The 4,000 additional rooms being built or planned will take the total to 21,000—too many, really, for a city of Vienna's size. Except, that is, at peak times—and they're not when the first-time visitor might think. From the end of December until the end of March, no fewer than 400 balls are held in Vienna, with the Opera Ball the big one. April through June can also be difficult. Opec also meets in Vienna.

Bristol, 2 Karntner Ring. Tel.: 515160. Telex: 112474. Fax: 5011-0410. Rooms/suites: 152. Bristol Executive Club: 30 rooms plus club room. Sauna, chauffeured limousine service. Almost a century old, the Bristol has blended modern touches with traditional elegance. Exceptionally good bar and restaurant.

City Club, 2 Parkallee, Vosendorf. Tel.: 693535. Telex: 134855. Fax: 693317. Rooms/suites: 471. Unique—a hotel, a conference center, and a leisure complex with a tropical pool, all under one glass pyramid. Some 20 minutes from the city, but you are going to the tropics, aren't you? Managed by France's Club Mediterranée.

Hilton, 1 Am Stadtpark. Tel.: 452652. Telex: 136799. Fax: 756-5220. Rooms/suites: 615. Penthouse suites (executive floor): 8. Designed mainly for the business traveler, with translation, telecommunications, and courier services; meeting rooms; five restaurants; a health club; and jogging in the adjacent Stadtpark. Rooms have color TV with round-the-clock news service.

Imperial, 16 Karntner Ring. Tel.: 501100. Telex: 112630. Fax: 5011-0410. Rooms/suites: 162. The grandest place in town: the Duke of Wurttemberg's old house, transformed into a hotel in 1873 and since then the official residence for visiting heads of state and government. Public rooms are palatial, and the restaurants are majestic.

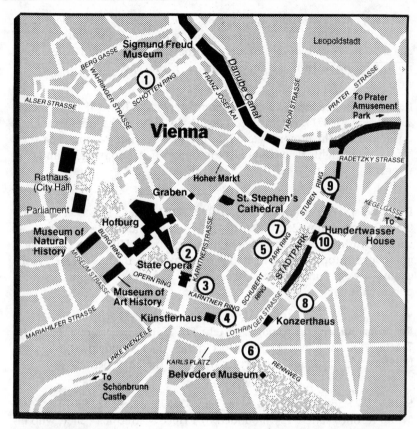

1. **Hotel Plaza Wien**
2. **Hotel Sacher**
3. **Hotel Bristol**
4. **Hotel Imperial**
5. **Hotel SAS Palais**
6. **Hotel Palais Schwarzenberg**

7. **Hotel Marriott**
8. **Hotel Inter-Continental**
9. **Vienna Chamber of Commerce**
10. **Hotel Hilton**

Inter-Continental, 28 Johannesgasse. Tel.: 711220. Telex: 131235. Fax: 713-4489. Rooms/suites: 498. Sixth floor entirely nonsmoking. Climate-controlled—important, because Viennese winters can be very cold, and summers very hot. Services include saunas, gymnasium, tennis courts, and ice skating.

K+K Palais, 11 Rudolfsplatz. Tel.: 631353. Telex: 134049. Fax: 5331-35370. Rooms/suites: 66. Modern hotel in a historic building that was once the home of a mistress of Emperor Franz-Joseph I.

►473

Marriott, 12a Parkring. Tel.: 515180. Telex: 112249. Fax: 51518-6736. Rooms: 304. Suites: 38. Some nonsmoking rooms. A good international chain at its best: two restaurants, two bars, Garten Café (coffeeshop), pool, whirlpool, fitness club, and sauna. Even typewriters.

Palais Schwarzenberg, 9 Schwarzenbergplatz. Tel.: 784515. Telex: 136124. Fax: 784714. Rooms: 38. Though downtown, the hotel feels like a ducal home in the provinces and bills itself as "a unique baroque palace." That's about right. Beautiful halls for dinners, receptions, balls, and conferences.

Plaza Wien, Am Schottenring 11. Tel.: 31390. Telex: 135859. Fax: 3139-0160. Rooms/suites: 252. There are presidential and royal suites and a security floor indicating that this brand new, luxury Hilton on the Ring is going for the top of the market. Three restaurants. Business center. Hotel claims lowest commissions for currency exchange and international phone calls.

Romischer Kaiser, 16 Annagasse. Tel.: 512-7751. Telex: 113696. Fax: 512-775113. Rooms/suites: 27. Comfort rather than grandeur—though the building is a baroque-style former palace in the city's heart.

Sacher, 4 Philharmonikerstrasse. Tel.: 525575. Telex: 122520. Fax: 514-57810. Rooms/suites: 124. Founded by Prince Metternich's chef, who invented the famous chocolate *sachertorte,* which can be eaten in the hotel or bought at the takeaway. The Sacher is right behind the Opera. Red plush everywhere. The Red and Blue bars are meeting places for Viennese society. One American ambassador loved the place so much that she ran off with the owner.

SAS Palais, 32 Weihburggasse. Tel.: 515170. Telex: 136127. Fax: 512-2216. Rooms/suites: 165. A successful melding of palatial, nineteenth-century architecture and (late) twentieth-century attention to the business traveler's needs: trouser press and three-hour laundry service are instances, along with a business center, health club, and SAS Scandinavian Airlines checkin (with baggage) at the front desk.

Scandic Crown, 269 Handelskai. Tel.: 21777. Telex: 133318. Fax: 21777/199. Rooms: 367. This topclass Swedish hotel is the only one of its category on the Danube. Close to UNO-city. All rooms are the size of normal suites.

▷ Restaurants

One of Vienna's legacies of empire is a cuisine that runs all the way from Bohemian (in the geographical sense) to Italian. *Powidlatscherkerln* (plum jam pastries) originated in old Bohemia, now part of Czechoslovakia; goulash and other spicy dishes came from Hungary; and the famous *Wiener Schnitzel* was invented in Milan.

Vienna has at least four categories of dining establishments:

- Elegant restaurants for local and visiting people with deep pockets or expense accounts;
- *Beisln,* simple and relatively inexpensive taverns to be found all over town;
- Coffeehouses, where people go to eat, talk, think, read the papers, and play chess or billiards;
- *Heurige* (new-wine) taverns on the edge of the city.

Citydwellers would almost certainly add two more categories: pastry shops, a Viennese institution, and *Wurstlstand,* or sausage stalls. Always good, and now chic, these are seen as a barrier against U.S. fast-food chains.

▷ Spotlight ◁

Austrian wine is good—but is it safe to drink? In the 1980s some *dummkopf* (stupid-head) had the brilliant idea of "improving" the stuff by adding antifreeze. A British maker of antifreeze promptly launched an advertising campaign that announced, tongue-in-cheek, that its product was guaranteed to contain no wine. The scandal hit the industry hard.

The truth is rather less sensational than the rumors. Only a fraction of production was contaminated. So is it safe to drink Austrian wine? The answer is a resounding "yes." Little is exported, except to West Germany, so a visit to Vienna is a chance to taste something exotic. The best whites can be excellent: the reds tend to be light (thin would be a bolder description), but are very drinkable.

Restaurants

Drei Husaren, 4 Weihburggasse. Tel.: 513-1778. Many generations of leading Viennese families have eaten here, making this one of the oldest and most distinguished restaurants.

Korso bei der Oper, Hotel Bristol. Tel.: 51516/51546. A hotel restaurant in the grand style that leans toward French *nouvelle cuisine.* Immaculate service. And it *is* just by the Opera.

Le Siecle, SAS Palais. Tel.: 515170. Traditional French cuisine and Austrian and Scandinavian specialties, including Norwegian salmon flown in fresh daily (SAS is an airline, after all). Rising in the gourmet ratings—and deservedly so.

Mattes, 8 Schonlaterngasse. Tel.: 526275. Reservations essential—this is a small place. French-style cuisine, strong on seafood; good wine list.

Rotisserie Prinz Eugen, Hilton Hotel. Tel.: 752-6520. The decor is kitsch, but the food is tops. Piano.

Steiereck, 8 Rasumofskygasse. Tel.: 733168. Regional and modern Austrian dishes, excellent wines and service. Government ministers and leading bankers and business executives are to be seen here.

Coffeehouses

Braunerhof, 2 Stalburggasse. Tel.: 523893.

Diglas, 10 Wollzeile. Tel.: 512-8401.

Frauenhuber, 6 Himmelpfortgasse. Tel.: 524323.

Hawelka, 6 Dorotheergasse. Tel.: 512-8230.

Korb, 9 Brandstatte. Tel.: 637215.

Landtmann, 4 Dr. Karl Lueger Ring. Tel.: 630621.

Mozart, 2 Albertinaplatz. Tel.: 512-2707.

▷ Tipping

A 15 percent service charge is usually added to the restaurant check, but it's customary to round this off to about 20 percent. Tip cabbies about 10 percent of the metered fare.

▷ Doing Business

Austrian heavy industry was long dominated by state-owned companies. Then three things happened: the steelmaker Voest-Alpine lost huge sums; voters showed disenchantment with Austria's rather mild form of socialism; and market economics ceased to be a term of contempt. The epoch of big, state-subsidized companies drew to a close and the era of privatization opened.

But the subsidy habit dies hard, so foreigners find that the national and city governments are more than receptive to the idea of offering financial help to new ventures that promise to mop up some of the surplus labor. Big outsiders can negotiate deals as good as or better than those offered anywhere in western Europe: 30 percent of the costs is just for openers. A good, helpful source: *Vienna Business Promotion Fund,* 2 Ebendorfer-strasse. Tel.: 4350, Extension 463. WWFF (the Fund's German initials) finds business partners, sites, and money. For export advice on many subjects, including legal help, try *Vienna Service Office.* Tel.: 2361, Extension 4234.

Another functioning symbol of the country's determination to do business is the *Austria Center,* a modern complex of 14 conference and exhibition halls next to UN City. Physical facilities are good, and security is tight, but the rest of the staff still have much to learn about handling international expositions and meetings. Tel.: 236-9347.

Though Vienna no longer dominates East-West trade, some 500 large and small trading houses remain. Two stand out: *Bank Winter,* founded by the king of switch traders, Simon Moskovics, who arrived from Poland after the war "with just a few gold coins;" and the firm recently founded by the elegant horseman Philipp Schoeller, who sold the family bank to start a specialized trading house. They represent two different styles, Moskovics with his 13 telephones putting together multifaceted East-West deals, Schoeller finding time to move back and forth from his country home and riding stables.

The Viennese virtually invented the modern version of what is variously called barter, switch trading, or countertrade. But what is this arcane business? Essentially, it's a series of deals that allows a country without hard cash to import goods by paying for them with other goods, which the vendor of the imports almost certainly doesn't want. Enter the middleman, who needs a computerlike brain and steel nerves. This intermediary takes the risk, juggles oranges, wine, and other commodities, and somehow gives all the parties what they want eventually: the importer the goods and all the other intermediaries the cash. How many links in the chain? As many as necessary to give the switch dealer what he or she wants: money. These days, barter is big again and even U.S. multinationals have departments trading machinery for fruit or liquor. (The French take olives as partial payment for jet fighters.)

▷ *Spotlight* ◁

Simon Moskovics is the emperor emeritus of switch trading, and though he may not have invented it, he certainly turned it into a fine art.

Moskovics became rich and famous by using his gift of *gewisst wo* and *gewisst wer* (Yiddish for "knowing where" and "knowing who"). He recalls with relish how he learned his first lesson in commodity switching: "When I studied at the rabbinical college at Cracow (in Poland), Italy had just invaded Abyssinia (Ethiopia). Hungary sided with Italy, Poland with Abyssinia. Therefore, Italy imposed sanctions on Poland and stopped shipping oranges. The Poles wanted oranges, and Poland and Hungary were on friendly terms. Thus, the Hungarians ordered more oranges and shipped them to the Poles, and the Poles paid the price in Polish goods to Hungary." And that was a *simple* deal . . .

Vienna could teach Geneva and Zurich a thing or two about bank secrecy. A foreigner can open a schilling account without giving a name or a foreign currency account in a name known to only one bank official.

How does all this square with the decidedly left-wing tilt of politics until recently? It doesn't, of course, except in the Austrian sense, for this is a nation of pragmatists. A national discussion among government, business, and labor is known as "social partnership." The idea—a good one—is to identify and discuss issues before they become problems.

▷ *Spotlight* ◁

Titles. Most Austrians dearly love high-sounding titles, and one thing the Habsburgs did was bestow a great many of them. But a law forbids the use of aristocratic titles, even the relatively humble *von*. Forget it; nobody is going to arrest you for giving a prince his due. Address him as Prinz, a count as Graf, and so on—and any member of the professional classes as Herr Doktor. Even if he isn't a doctor of anything, he'll be charmed by your assumption that he is.

Much business is still done in the leading coffeehouses, among them *Landtmann, Mozart,* and *Hawelka.* The Viennese passion for coffee seems to date from the Turkish invasion and occupation, which didn't end until 1683.

Austria has looked at the implications for it of the European Community Single Market that is supposed to bloom with the snowdrops on January 1, 1993. It has decided to go for membership. Like all members of "the other Europe"—the countries that aren't members of the EC—Austria is anxious that as trade and other barriers fall within the community, a wall will not rise around it. Unlike EFTA, of which Austria is a member, the EC is a political as well as an economic grouping, and permanent neutrality was a key component in Austria's peace treaty with the Soviet Union. But the Kremlin now has changed its position on Austrian membership of the EC. Meanwhile, Austria is seeking strategic business and banking alliances that will strengthen its trade within the European Community.

▷ Useful Phone Numbers

Emergencies

Ambulance	144
Car breakdown	120 or 123
Doctor	141
Pharmacy service	1550
Police	133

Local Information

Airport: flights	7770 or 6800
Chamber of commerce	51450
Danube boats	266536
Trains	1717
Tourist office	431608

Government Ministries

Economic Affairs	75000
Finance	514330
Public Economy/ Transport	757-6310

Chambers of Commerce

American	315751
Germany (West)	554565
Honduras	533-2057
Hong Kong	533-9326
Italian Trade Institute	515214
Jetro (Japan)	421578
Korea (South)	963073
Latin American Institute	933315
Netherlands	505-5708
Switzerland	512-5959

Embassies

Albania	369-1229
Algeria	368-8530
Argentina	533-8463
Australia	512-8580
Belgium	567579
Brazil	512-0631
Canada	5333691
Chile	512-92080
China (People's Republic)	753149
Czechoslovakia	822629
Denmark	512-7904
Egypt	361134
Finland	247251
France	654-7470
Greece	655791
Germany (East)	823654
Germany (West)	736511
Hungary	533-2631
India	658666
Indonesia	342533

Iran	722650	Austrian Airlines	683-5110
Iraq	738195	Balkan-Bulgarian	
Ireland	754246	Airlines	587-5418
Israel	311506	British Airways	657691
Italy	725121	Czechoslovak	
Japan	659771	Airlines/CSA	512-3805
Luxembourg	362186	Egyptair	587-4532
Mexico	535-1776	El Al Israel Airlines	524561
Netherlands	248587	Finnair	587-5548
New Zealand	526636	Iberia (Spain)	567636
Nigeria	726685	Interflug (East	
Norway	756692	Germany)	533-1861
Pakistan	367381	Kuwait Air Ways	586-1410
Philippines	368448	LOT Polish Airlines	639810
Poland	827444	Lufthansa German	
Portugal	567536	Airlines	58836
Saudi Arabia	362316	Malev Hungarian	
Soviet Union	731-1215	Airlines	587-3475
Sweden	334-5450	Olympic Airways	587-7623
Switzerland	784-4521	Pan Am World	
Turkey	655559	Airways	526646
United Kingdom	731575	Qantas Airways	
United States	315511	(Australia)	587-7771
		Sabena Belgian	
		World Airlines	587-3506

Airlines

		SAS Scandinavian	
Aer Lingus		Airlines	513-1105
(Ireland)	318494	Singapore Airlines	513-4656
Aeroflot Soviet		South African	
Airlines	512-1501	Airways	587-1585
Aerolineas		Swissair	658996
Argentinas	587-1678	Tarom (Romania)	345306
Air Algerie	567552	Thai Airways	650-9773
Air Canada	567474	Turk Hava Yollari	563768
Air France	526652	TWA	650-9721
Air India	587-21470	Varig (Brazil)	587-9588
Alitalia	651707	Yugoslav Airlines/JAT	512-2229

▷ Shopping

High prices are reduced by a tax-free shopping scheme that gives 10 to 20 percent off. Many stores participate. Ask for form U-34 at the refund window at the airport. Winters are sharp, so the unprepared visitor may well look for a thick, warm woolen coat. Specialized stores: *Trachten Just,* 2 Lugeck, and *Tostmann,* 3 Schottengasse. Other local specialties:

Antiques and jewels: *Dorotheum* auction house, 17 Dorotheergasse. A fascinating place; ask your hotel concierge to check times.

Chocolates: *Lehmann,* 12 Graben, and *Sluka,* 8 Rathausplatz.

Women's fashions: *Peter Hermann,* 22-15 Margaratenstrasse. In the city of Freud, it's appropriate that top designer Hermann is a psychiatrist.

Books: *British Bookshop,* 8 Weihburggasse and 3 Blumenstockgasse. Volumes about the city, and virtually anything else.

For a gift typical of Vienna, browse the many stores that sell *petit point,* the tiny embroidery for evening bags and cushions.

▷ After Hours

Vienna has some old-fashioned strip clubs on or near the *Opernring* and *Kärtnerstrasse.* The monthly *Halo Wien* tourist guide lists them, as well as the local Eros Center. A quiet word with your urbane seen-it-all Vienna concierge is probably advisable.

"In" Vienna nightlife is limited to the fashionable, late-night cafés near the St. Ruprecht church—*Salzamt,* Ruprechtsplatz 1, and *Ma Pitom,* Seitenstettengasse 5. Later, the Beautiful People go to *Tanzlokal,* Annagasse 3a (superb young women and soul music) or *U4,* Schönbrunnerstrasse 222, Vienna's biggest disco. A somewhat wilder ambience.

▷ Sights and Sounds

Buildings of imperial splendor bespeak the power and pretensions of Vienna before World War I and the Versailles Treaty toppled the Habsburgs. Among the most impressive structures (check opening times with your hotel concierge or the tourist office):

Architecture and History

Schoenbrunn Palace, Schoenbrunner Schloss-strasse. The palace was built to rival Versailles, and does, with some 1,400 rooms and landscaped gardens of extraordinary elegance and beauty. Empress Maria Theresa, who ruled from 1740 to 1780, lived here.

Belevedere Palace, 6a Rennweg and 27 Prinz Eugenstrasse. Prince Eugen of Savoy ordered up this magnificent pair of chateaux, with baroque gardens between the two buildings. One of them houses the *Oesterreichische Galerie*, with works by Klimt and Schiele. The Imperial Apartments are in the Hofburg on Michaelerplatz: see how the emperors lived.

St. Stephen's Cathedral, Stephansplatz, is one of Europe's most celebrated examples of medieval church architecture, with a bell tower soaring 127 meters (406 feet) above the city center. Magnificent views.

Danube Tower, Donaupark, is the tallest building in Austria at 252 meters (806 feet). At the 170-meter (544-foot) level are the look-out and a revolving restaurant. On a clear day, you can see as far as the Alps and the Carpathian hills of Czechoslovakia.

For perspectives of a very different kind:

Art History Museum, Maria-Theresien-platz. Entire suites of rooms filled with works by Dürer, Titian, the Breughels, Rembrandt, and Rubens.

Sigmund Freud Haus, 19 Berggasse, is where he spent much of his life before fleeing to London when the Nazis seized power.

Entertainment

Orson Welles and Joseph Cotten had their famous conversation on the big wheel in the *Prater Fairground* in the movie *The Third Man*. The wheel is still there, in better repair now, and the fairground is where Viennese of all classes and ages go for some innocent fun. The rather simple restaurants are worth trying.

Far from simple are the intricate balletic movements of the horses at the *Spanish Riding School* at the Hofburg. One of the world's most famous equestrian centers, founded in the 1500s, the school features the beautiful, nimble, and highly intelligent Lipizzan horses. Frequent performances; tickets from the Hofburg and travel agents (your hotel concierge will help).

Music

The sound of music is loud and persistent in Vienna—everything from symphony concerts, grand opera, and string quartets to light opera and performances of works by the Strauss family. The annual festival, usually held in May and June, offers concerts by the Vienna Philharmonic, the Vienna String Quartet, and visiting orchestras, and is staged at the *Musikvereinsaal,* the *Hofburg,* and various halls. Festival tickets are available from *Gesellschaft des Musikfreunde,* Karlsplatz 6, Wien 1010. Tel.: 658190. Telex: 111062.

At the same time, there is a full program at the *State Opera House,* with virtually a different production each night over a five-week period. Simultaneously, light opera is staged nightly at the *Volksoper,* entrancing the Viennese and visitors with works by Strauss, Lehar, and Offenbach. Even *My Fair Lady* and *Cats* are staged. State Opera and light opera tickets are available from *Osterreichischer Bundestheaterverband,* Goethestrasse 1, Wien 1010. Tel.: 514440. Telex: 113775.

The world-famous *Vienna Boys' Choir* sings from January through June and from the middle of September through December, the regular days and times being Sundays at 9:15 a.m. at the Burgkapelle in the Imperial Palace and on religious holidays. Standing room is free; for seats write to the *Hofmusikkapelle,* Hofburg, Wien 1010. A few tickets are available for Fridays at 5:00 p.m.—a maximum of two per applicant.

▷ Out of Town

Vienna is again the gateway to the East after years of arduous travel restrictions imposed by Czechoslovakia and Hungary and their Soviet mentors. Prague is about five hours away by car and Budapest about three hours. Bratislava, the Slovene capital, is just up the road, no more than two hours.

Prague and Budapest are ancient and exciting cities where most hearts beat to a western rhythm after more than 40 years of communism. The Czech authorities may not like *glasnost* and *perestroika,* but they've arrived and are probably irreversible.

You will still need visas, though. Those for Czechoslovakia can be obtained from main travel agents in Vienna—but expect a wait of two or three days. Visas for Hungary are delivered usually within 48 hours, and there's an "express" visa for which the authorities charge extra.

A scenic way of visiting Budapest is to take the Danube hydrofoil, a voyage of four to five hours. If you don't fancy driving or the hydrofoil, there's a three-hour train ride to Budapest. Some Viennese businessmen now commute. Railroads serve many other Eastern European cities. By air, there's no beating Austrian Airlines, which has unparalleled knowledge of the area, as well as the most frequent flights.

ZURICH
Where Not All Is Gnomish

Population: 370,000 (estimated). Capital of Swiss *canton* (state) of Zurich (population: 1.23 million). *Location*: at foot of Alps on Limmat river at northwest end of Lake Zurich in Switzerland. *Economy*: banking and financial services, electrical and mechanical engineering, machine tools, printing and publishing, tourism, transportation equipment. Switzerland is a member of the European Free Trade Association (EFTA) and the Organization for Economic Cooperation and Development (OECD) and is a signatory to the General Agreement on Tariffs and Trade (GATT).

▷ Background Briefing

During a sterling crisis in the 1960s, Britain's foreign secretary, George Brown, denounced Zurich currency dealers as "gnomes." (That was rich, coming from him: he stood knee-high to a grasshopper.) The label stuck, much to the annoyance of Zurich bankers, many of whom are notably tall. George Brown's epithet, however, does epitomize the suspicions that some people harbor about this city of banks—all 350 of them.

What goes on in these Temples of Mammon? Why should a smallish city in a small country wield financial power on a world scale? And for whose benefit do the banks wield it? The Zurich bankers answer that their activities benefit everyone from shareholders and employees to the international financial and economic system itself—not to mention Switzerland. Or drug traffickers, for the slime of narco-dollars has washed ashore in this beautiful lakeside city and transformed one green space into a "needle park."

The banks' answer certainly would not have appeased the late George Brown, who blamed the "gnomes" for speculating against and weakening the British pound. The bankers' view was also contested vigorously in a 1978 book, *Switzerland Exposed,* by a Social Democrat member of the Swiss parliament, Professor Jean Ziegler—a book that still rankles. He saw Zurich (and Geneva) as one of the command posts of a worldwide imperialist system: "The Swiss banking barons...have managed to identify their strategy of pillage and receiving stolen goods with the national interest of the Swiss state and people." The "stolen goods" were, presumably, illicit deposits. Ziegler concluded that the Swiss banking system was "monstrously hypertrophied."

The political and moral issues are important, and consensus is probably impossible. The pragmatic question is *why* Swiss banks are so successful. Their legendary secrecy cannot be more than a tiny part of the explanation. More likely, the banks have grown to their current size and influence mostly because managers are very good at their job—which, essentially, is to nurture money with skilled, reverent care. A look of horror crosses the countenance of a Zurich banker at the sight of a crumpled note.

We've dwelt on the banks because they are pervasive, because they're the one thing most strangers know about Zurich. There's much more to the city than banks, however. A third of the country's top industrial groups (food, aluminum, machinery, arms, diesel motors) have their headquarters in the Zurich-Winterthur area (Baden with Asea Brown Boveri is only a few kilometers away). Neither is the city about business only. The chief landmark is not a bank or corporate headquarters building, but rather the magnificent, twin-towered twelfth-century Grossmunster Cathedral, bastion of Huldreich Zwingli (1484–1531), the Swiss religious reformer, and refuge at various times for persecuted Protestants from various parts of Europe. A tolerant city which at different times has welcomed Einstein, Lenin, and James Joyce (the last-named is buried there).

▷ Arriving

By Air

Kloten Airport returns some of the pleasure to air travel. Clean, efficient, attractive, and well-designed, Kloten is only 11 kilometers (7 miles) from the city center—less than half an hour by train, bus, or taxi.

Swissair has made checkin and baggage handling high priorities. It is developing worldwide a hotel-to-final destination baggage system and introducing self-service ticket machines, which are described in the *Arriving* section of the Geneva entry.

By Rail

Zurich is a busy railroad center, with frequent, rapid trains to other parts of Switzerland and to the rest of Europe. The *Hauptbahnhof* (central station) is an impressive structure—efficient, and with helpful staff.

▷ Money

The standard unit of currency is the Swiss franc. International code: SFR. Banknote denominations include 10, 20, 50, 100, 500, and 1,000 francs. Coins come in denominations of 10, 20, and 50 centimes (100 centimes = 1 franc) as well as 1, 2, and 5 francs. Banks offer the best exchange rates.

▷ Language

German—of a kind. The local dialect, the Zurich version of Swiss German, is impenetrable to anyone who speaks only *Hochdeutsch* (High German), the formal and standardized form. But all educated people are able to switch from dialect to High German in an *Augenblick* (blink), and virtually all speak English and French as well. Don't be confused because the French names of some Swiss companies and banks have vanished in Zurich. Credit Suisse, for example, is *Schweizerische Kreditanstalt* in German. Italian is also spoken—Italy is just a mountain range away to the south.

▷ Communications

Country code: 41. City code: 1. The city couldn't have become one of the world's leading banking and foreign exchange centers without an excellent telecommunications system. Everyone benefits.

▷ Getting To Know the City

The "spine" of central Zurich is the *Bahnhofstrasse*—literally, "Railway Station Street"—which runs from the station to the shore of Lake Zurich. This broad thoroughfare is lined by banks, but also by some of the best department stores and boutiques, much-frequented by ladies decked in furs in the winter or in summer in those simple little dresses that only the very rich can afford. At any time of the year, a glitter of jewels is *de*

▶487

rigueur. Going toward the lake along this chic commercial artery, you will find the main banking district to your right. To the left is another busy, slightly nondescript commercial area and, beyond it, the Limmat river. On the far side of the river is the old town, a maze of narrow streets.

When you reach the lake, you will see a wonderful panorama on a clear day. Ahead is the lake itself, narrow here, but broadening rapidly. To the left and to the right start the foothills of mountains; on a clear day, you can see their peaks aspiring to the sky.

▷ Moving Around

Zurich's buses and blue streetcars (the latter marked "VBZ") are frequent, clean, fast, and comfortable—except in rush hours. But after studying a street map, you'll find that you can keep many of your appointments by walking; business and banking Zurich is compact. Taxis are not so plentiful. Car rental is available from major American and European companies.

An ancient, but solid, funicular car runs from near the station to an observation terrace as well as to the Federal Institute of Technology and Cantonal Hospital.

▷ Hotels

Zurich is both a business and a vacation center. Its 112 hotels range from two of the world's finest, aimed at central bankers and corporate chieftains, to establishments meant for less senior business executives and for tourists. All are clean and comfortable.

Atlantis Sheraton, 234 Doltschiweg. Tel.: 463-0000. Telex: 813338. Fax: 4630388. Rooms/suites: 161. Situated at the bottom of the Uetliberg Forest and recreation area, the hotel has one foot in the country—yet it's only 10 minutes by shuttle bus from the city center. Good restaurants, fine health club, parking space galore. The friendliest of Zurich's top hotels. Atlantis Sheraton Guesthouse: 63 rooms.

Baur au Lac, 1 Talstrasse. Tel.: 221-1650. Telex: 813567. Fax: 211-8139. Rooms: 141. Suites: 16. Set in a private park on the lake, the Baur au Lac is often listed as one of the world's best hotels. It's at the top end of the Bahnhofstrasse, has a spectacular view of the lake, and is close to the major banks. The rustle of serious money.

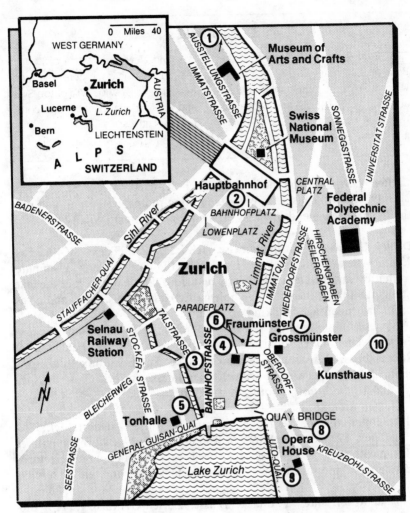

1. Hotel Zurich
2. Hotel Schweizerhof
3. Hotel Savoy Bauer en Ville
4. Hotel Carlton Elite
5. Hotel Baur au Lac

6. Hotel Zum Storchen
7. City Hall
8. Neue Zurcher Zeitung
9. Hotel Eden au Lac
10. Hotel Dolder

▷ **Spotlight** ◁

Club Baur au Lac. Adjacent to the Baur au Lac hotel is the Villa Rosa, which houses the influential Club Baur au Lac. With its discreet elegance, punctilious service, and hushed tones, it is reminiscent of good clubs in London and New York. Much of Zurich's real business is done here. The membership list is a *Who's Who* of top Swiss and international banking and corporate executives.

Carlton Elite, 41 Bahnhofstrasse. Tel.: 211-6560. Telex: 812781. Fax: 2113019. Rooms/beds: 117. With its meeting rooms, restaurant, and pub, the Carlton is a blend of Swiss efficiency and (rarer) joviality.

Dolder Grand, 65 Kurhausstrasse. Tel.: 251-6231. Telex: 816416. Fax: 2518829. Rooms/suites: 194. High above the city, but only 15 minutes from it by car, the Dolder is quietly luxurious. Some rooms face the lake, others the forest; there's a nine-hole golf course, tennis, pool, and a vast park that encourages walking or jogging.

Eden au Lac, 45 Utoquai. Tel.: 479404. Telex: 816339. Fax: 479409. Rooms/beds: 75. A small jewel on the lake. The Eden mixes old world charm (plus a roof garden) with the very latest comfort. Close by is the *Neue Zurcher Zeitung,* another institution.

Hilton International, 10 Hohenbuhlstrasse, Kloten Airport. Tel.: 810-3131. Telex: 825428. Fax: 8109366. Rooms/suites: 294. A well-appointed Hilton with the business executive's needs very much in mind: secretarial service, good message-taking, round-the-clock telex and telefax service.

Ramada Renaissance, 1 Talackerstrasse, Zurich-Glattbrugg. Tel.: 810-800. Rooms: 196. Suites: 8. Brand new and packed with business, social, and health facilities. Adjacent Renaissance Club accommodation: security controlled and VIP attention.

Savoy Bauer en Ville, Paradeplatz. Tel.: 211-5360. Telex: 812845. Fax: 2211467. Rooms/beds: 146. Sophisticated and stylish—the Swiss even call it stately. (It is next to two of the Big Three banks.) Extreme attention to detail including local, French, and Italian cuisine.

Schweizerhof, 7 Bahnhofplatz. Tel.: 211-8640. Telex: 813754. Fax: 2113505. Rooms/suites: 150. Banquets/meetings. Opposite the railroad station, but newly soundproofed; close to main business districts. Generously large desks in rooms.

Storchen, 2 Weinplatz. Tel.: 211-5510. Telex: 813354. Fax: 2116451. Rooms/suites/beds: 110. Highly recommended by people in the know as a reasonably priced, *gemutlich* (cozy) hostelry. Nicely located in the old town, just across from the Grossmunster Cathedral and close to the Fraumunster Church, with its Chagall windows.

Zürich, Neumühlequai 42. Tel.: 363-6363. Telex: 56809. Fax: 3636015. Rooms: 211. Suites: 10. The hotel overlooks a park and the city. The rooms are ultra-modern. Two restaurants, pool, and health club. Excellent conference facilities.

Airport Hotels

Movenpick, Glattbrugg. Tel.: 810-1111. Telex: 57979. Fax: 8104038. Rooms: 333. Comfortable airport hotel with business center and recommendable restaurant.

Novotel, 21 Talackerstrasse, Glattbrugg. Tel.: 810-3111. Telex: 828770. Fax: 8108185. Rooms: 256. Five minutes from the airport and near the exhibition center. Thoughtful touch for the business traveler: large work desks in rooms.

▷ *Spotlight* ◁

Winterthur. This industrial town (population: 87,000) is 20 kilometers (12 miles) northeast of Zurich. Recommended hotel: *Krone*, 49 Marktgasse. Tel.: (052) 232521. The hotel has been perfecting hospitality since 1448—and has gotten it right at last. Quiet, comfortable rooms. In a pedestrians-only area, but there's access for guests' cars. Winterthur also is home to the outstanding Oscar Reinhart collection of paintings.

▷ Restaurants

The Atlantis Sheraton, the Baur au Lac, and the Dolder Grand are among listed hotels that offer excellent dining and wining that match or even surpass the standards found in other major European cities. Elsewhere, food tends to be hearty rather than refined, reflecting more German influence than French—though there are exceptions. A selection:

Agnes Amberg, 5 Hottingerstrasse. Tel.: 251-2626. *Haute cuisine* and Swiss specialties. Very chic, very in. Agnes Amberg is described by some connoisseurs as the *grande dame* of Swiss cuisine.

Au Premier, Hauptbahnhof. Tel.: 211-1510. As in France, people in Switzerland often go to the railroad station restaurant for a meal—even if they're not traveling. Au Premier explains why.

Bierhalle Kropf, 16 Im Gassen. Tel.: 221-1805. Large, hearty meals, including liver dumplings. Original decor, with 1900s baroque ceiling.

Chez Max, 53 Seestrasse, Zollikon. Tel.: 391-8872. Out of town (10 kilometers or 6 miles), but worth the trip: elegant, stylish, luxurious. Prices to match culinary art of the highest order.

Kindli Swiss Chalet, 1 Pfalzgasse. Tel.: 211-4182. Many Swiss specialties, including evening folklore shows.

Kronenhalle, 4 Ramistrasse. Tel.: 251-6669. Zurich tradition at its best: excellent food under valuable paintings: noted for wines.

Mère Catherine, 8 Rudenplatz. Tel.: 692250. Rustic bistro well-known for its fish.

Petermann's Kunststuben, 160 Seestrasse, Kusnacht. Tel.: 910-0715. A beautiful restaurant, always aglow with flowers, particularly irises (*Patron* Horst Petermann's wife is Iris). About 13 kilometers (8 miles) from Zurich, but don't be deterred.

Waldhaus Dolder, 20 Kurhausstrasse. Tel.: 251-9360. Neighbor of the other Dolder; can be reached by funicular. Grillroom and terrace with lake and mountain views.

Witschi's Restaurant, 55 Zurcherstrasse, Tel.: 750-4460. One food critic says that *Patron-chef de cuisine* Heinz Witschi brings to the culinary arts "a quasi-scientific knowledge" of the ingredients. Perhaps. The results are superb: the sauces enhance rather than obscure.

▷ *Spotlight* ◁

Guilds. Back in 1336, one Rudolph Brun, although a knight, sided with unhappy skilled workers rather than his fellow nobles or the merchants. Thanks largely to him, 13 guilds came into being and by the 1500s virtually controlled the city. Since then, their political and economic power has declined—but membership has a social cachet. Some guild restaurants are open to the public. Among them:

Zur Ruden, 42 Limmatquai. Tel.: 479550. Late Gothic barrel-vaulted ceiling in oak.

Zur Wag, 8 Munsterhof. Tel.: 211-
0730. Famous for its veal dishes.
Zur Zimmerleuten, 40 Limmatquai.

Tel.: 340834. More veal plus a view of
the river.

▷ Tipping

Tips are included in bar and restaurant checks and on the taxi meter, but
it's polite to leave small change. Hotel concierges expect a tip for extra
service: $5 is the minimum. Leave at least $20 when you depart.

▷ Doing Business

Back to the banks. They have excellent research departments and put out
numerous publications on the macroeconomy, on industry sectors, on
market trends, and on country prospects. Commercial banking is dominated by the Big Three: *Union Bank of Switzerland,* 45 Bahnhofstrasse
(tel.: 234-1111); *Credit Suisse,* 8 Paradeplatz (tel.: 215-1111); and *Swiss
Bank Corporation,* 6 Paradeplatz (tel.: 223-1111). SBC is, in fact, headquartered in Basel, but its Zurich operation is large and enjoys much
autonomy.

The banks are behind the world's biggest gold trading center in Zurich,
heavily used by the Moscow comrade bankers to raise foreign exchange.
The banks also are behind the 600 to 700 billion Swiss francs' worth of securities traded annually on the stock exchange, which is in the world's top
half-dozen (and twice the size of Geneva's exchange). A quarter of the
population is employed by the banks and insurance companies. A rough
distinction is that Zurich and its banks are turned towards the United
States, West Germany, and Britain, whereas Geneva looks more to the
French-speaking world and the Arab world. Zurich is proud of its cultural scene, but pride of place across from the Hauptbahnhof is given to a
statue of Alfred Escher, founder of the Swiss Credit Bank.

Private banking is led by *Bank Julius Bar* and *Bank Vontobel.* Neither
is private in the classic sense, since each has brought in outside capital in
recent years; but the families remain in control. The private banks claim
that they can offer private investors more personal service than the commercial ones—custom-tailored, so to speak.

▷ *Spotlight* ◁

How profitable are Swiss banks? Outsiders will never know: there is considerable difference between the banks'
real and declared profits. Many admit

to having lost money in the October 1987 stock market crash, but how much is another mystery. Whatever the figure, the Big Three retained their high Dun and Bradstreet, Moodys, and Standard and Poor ratings—and the number of banking members of this club has been falling rapidly.

A visitor from almost any industrialized country will find a branch of his hometown bank in Zurich—or a representative office, at least. The most recent invasion: Japanese.

The banks are the first port of call for the traveler prospecting business possibilities in Switzerland. In the Zurich area alone, these prospects are multiple. The city has become a center for the fashion and jewelry industries; and Winterthur, 20 kilometers (12 miles) northeast, is both an important manufacturing center and a headquarters town for major corporations.

The city and canton of Zurich welcome foreign investment—but, as their counterparts do elsewhere in Switzerland, they insist that the proposed operation be of high quality. It's not easy, either, to obtain cantonal residence and work permits for foreign employees unless they are vital to the operation and Swiss residents with comparable qualifications are not available. They often are not; Switzerland has one of the lowest unemployment rates in the world.

If the old saying that the early bird catches the worm isn't a translation from Swiss German, it should be. Business meetings start as early as 7:30 a.m.

▷ Useful Phone Numbers

Emergencies

Ambulance	144
Car breakdown	140
Hospitals (Universitatsspital)	255-1111
Pharmacy (all-night)	251-5151
Police	117
Non-urgent	216-7111

Local Information

Airport	812-7111
Exchange rates	160

Exhibitions	188
Road conditions	163
Stock market news	166
Tourist Office	211-4000
Weather	162/348342

Chambers of Commerce

Austria	251-8313
Belgium-Luxembourg	361-6412
Britain	553131
China-Switzerland	211-2909
Czechoslovakia	462-1385

Finland	202-3630	Italy	201-5000
France	252-2894	Japan	250-2206
Germany (West)	221-3702	Luxembourg	471355
Hong Kong	251-0185	Netherlands	251-8818
India	365-8365	Spain	363-0644
Iran	211-4202	Sweden	471770
Israel	477480	Turkey	363-0644
Italy	202-8383	United Kingdom	471520
ICE Institute	201-6820	United States	552566
Netherlands	211-0990		
South Africa	554405		

Airlines

Soviet Union	241-3170
Spain	241-0080
Sweden	471770
Taiwan	363-4242
United States	211-2454
Yugoslavia	211-8021

Aer Lingus (Ireland)	211-2850
Aeroflot Soviet Airlines	221-4633
Air France	211-0594
Air India	211-1757
Alitalia	302-3333
Austrian Airlines	211-5890

Banks

British Airways	211-4090
Credit Suisse	215-1111
Iberia (Spain)	211-1445
Swiss Bank Corporation	223-1111
Japan Air Lines/JAL	211-1557
Union Bank of Switzerland	234-1111
KLM Royal Dutch Airlines	211-0161
Lufthansa German Airlines	211-4133

Consulates

Olympic Airways	211-3737
Austria	252-7200
Sabena Belgian World Airlines	211-2171
Belgium	362-5577
Brazil	251-8836
SAS Scandinavian Airlines	810-4080
Denmark	201-6670
Finland	211-3692
South African Airways	211-5130
France 251-8544 251-8343 (visa)	
Swissair	251-3434
German (West)	251-6936
TAP Air Portugal	211-2733
Greece	252-7200
TWA	361-4111
Israel	252-2700
Varig (Brazil)	221-0011

▷ Shopping

The high density of fur coats on the *Bahnhofstrasse* and streets nearby attests to the quality of goods in the shops: Vicuna-wool coats, cashmere sweaters, crocodile-skin briefcases with gold fittings, *haute couture* clothes for women (and men), super-slim watches with pale gold cases that are guaranteed to be chronometers (time is money). . . The list is endless, and the consumption is conspicuous. The Bahnhofstrasse today is reserved for pedestrians, but nearby wait the chauffeured Rolls-Royces, Bentleys, Mercedes-Benzes, Jaguars, and mere Cadillacs.

Shopping hours. Monday through Friday from 8:00 a.m. to 12 noon and 1:30 to 6:30 p.m. Saturday from 8:00 a.m. to 12 noon and 1:30 to 4:00 p.m. Many city-center shops don't close for lunch and stay open until 9:00 p.m. on Thursdays.

The *crème-de-la-crème:*

Chronometrie Beyer, 31 Bahnhofstrasse. Probably the largest selection of watches under one roof in all of Switzerland.

Grieder Les Boutiques, 30 Bahnhofstrasse. Famous for silks.

Gübelin, 36 Bahnhofstrasse. Jewelry designed in the firm's own atelier and made in its workshops.

Leder Locher, 91 Bahnhofstrasse. Tel.: 211-7082. Leather and travel goods; the firm was founded in 1822.

Low Boutique, 78 Bahnhofstrasse. Women's clothing and accessories.

Schweizer Heimatwerk, Rudolf Brun-brucke. Linen, wood carvings, embroidery, dolls, music boxes.

▷ After Hours

Much of the night life is boisterous, particularly on beer-swilling Saturday nights. In a city where the streets are paved with banknotes, there are many of those dimly lit clubs where the price of champagne becomes obscured. Some of the better places:

Blackout, Kloten Airport. Disco dancing, laser light show right by the runways.

Diagonale, 1 Talstrasse. The upmarket nightclub of the Hotel Baur au Lac.